Science, TECHNOLOGY, and Society

Through text, visuals, and a time line, this feature focuses on a technological advance and its short and long term impact on society.

Geography: Impact on History

The five geographic themes are explored through pivotal developments in United States history.

Social Studies Skill

Social Studies Skills provide learning and practice in the context of historical and geographical topics.

DIAGRAPHICS

Through diagrams, maps, statistical information, and annotated visuals, complex concepts are clearly and accurately depicted.

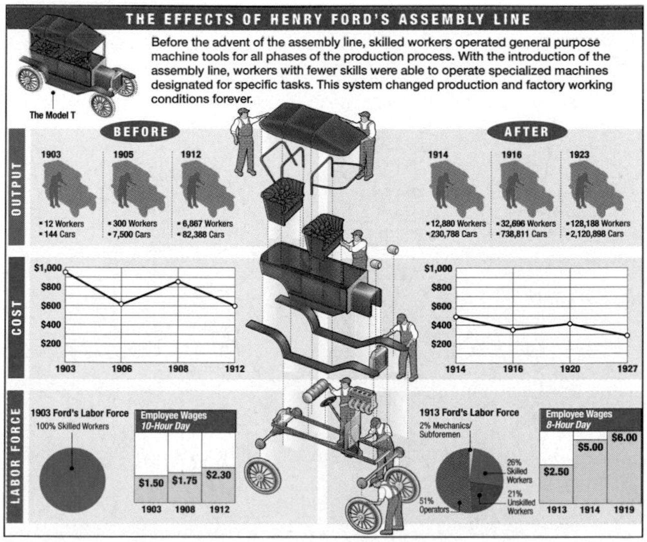

DIAGRAPHICS (continued)

MAPS

THE GREAT WHITE FLEET, 1907–1909

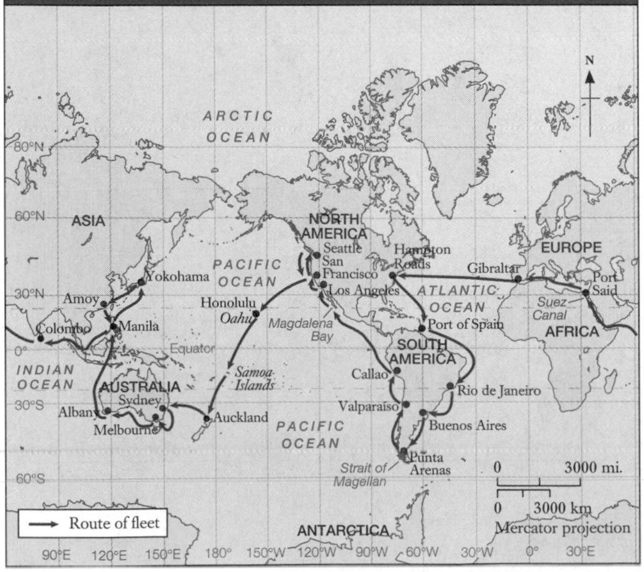

SECTION 1

The Five Themes of Geography

1542: EXPLORER PUBLISHES SENSATIONAL TRAVEL JOURNAL

© SUPERSTOCK

A Land of Great Variety
Newcomers to the Americas saw animals and plants that they had never seen before.

IT WAS A GRIPPING STORY OF SURVIVAL THAT ALVAR NÚÑEZ CABEZA DE VACA HAD TO TELL. This Spanish noble had been a member of an expedition sent to claim new lands in America for the Spanish king. The explorers experienced terrible misfortunes, including shipwreck and disease. In presenting his journal to King Charles V, Cabeza de Vaca admitted that the expedition had failed to achieve its goals. He was convinced, however, that his journal was a worthwhile offering to the king.

The value of his report, Cabeza de Vaca wrote, was its information about the new lands, including descriptions of native peoples, the environment, the kinds of food people ate, and the location of places and the distances between them.

In describing these discoveries to the king, Cabeza de Vaca was writing about **geography,** the study of people, places, and environments. Geography looks at space on the earth and how specific spaces are alike or different. It is a rich subject filled with intriguing, even astonishing information. To help organize such a huge body of information, today's geographers cluster their subject matter around five themes: location, place, movement, human/environment interaction, and region.

AS YOU READ

Vocabulary

- geography
- location
- place
- movement
- human/environment interaction
- region

Think About . . .

- what geography is and what it reveals about people, places, and environments.
- how the five themes of geography help organize geographical information.

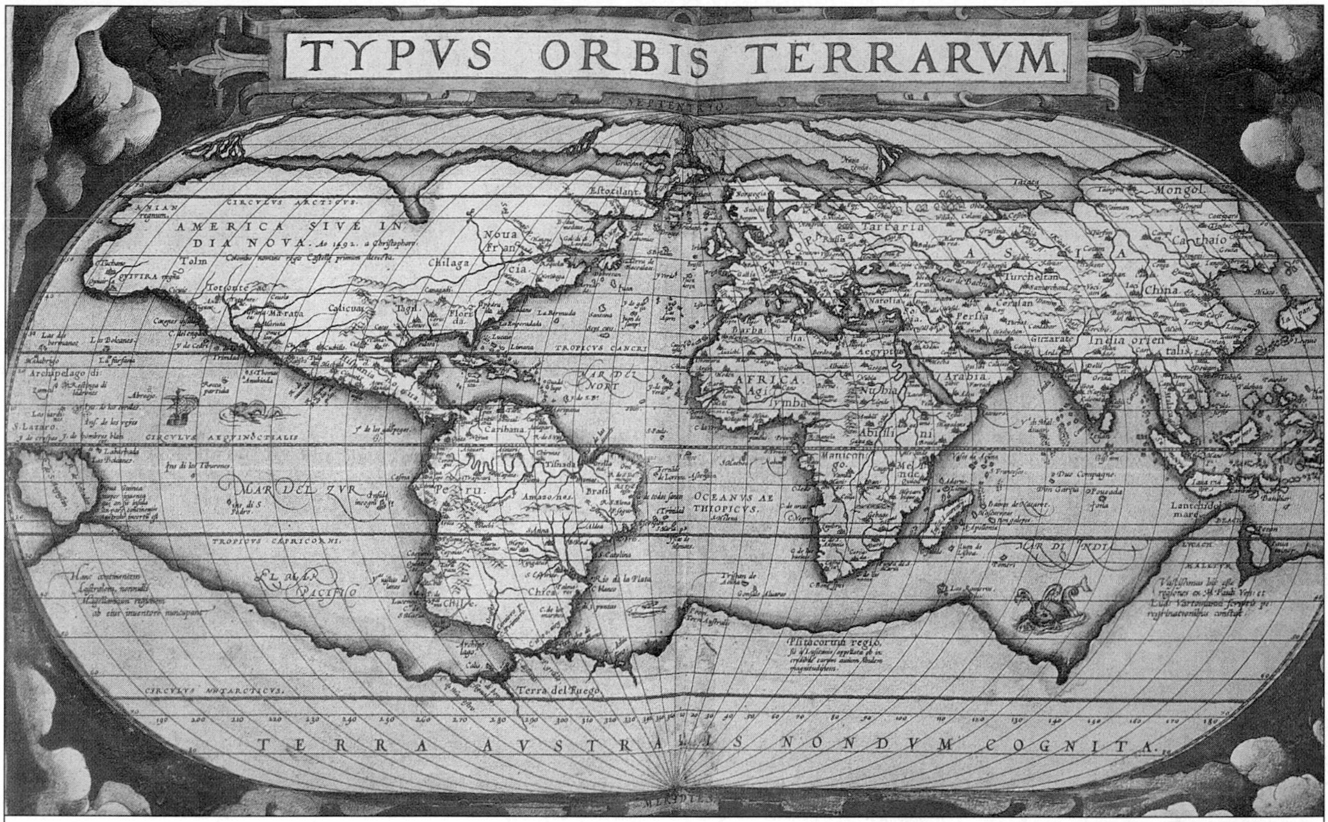

A World Map From 1570 This map shows many misunderstandings about the size and shape of North America, South America, Australia, and Antarctica. *Which parts of this map look like maps of today?*

Location

Finding Places Anywhere on Earth

The theme of **location** focuses on a specific place and considers the question of its position on the earth's surface. People may talk about the location of a place just out of curiosity, or they may actually want to travel to a place.

Absolute Location

In 25 B.C. a young man named Strabo had the chance to visit Alexandria, then the Roman capital of Egypt and a cosmopolitan meeting place for travelers. In a library built by Egyptian royalty, Strabo found an enormous collection of scholarly writings. He pored over those works, especially those related to geography and mapmaking, and evaluated what he read. He eventually published his conclusions in an 18-volume book on world geography. Two of Strabo's central conclusions were that the earth had the shape of a sphere, and that the best map of the earth would employ a grid of intersecting lines, a plan that is still in use today.

One set of grid lines consists of the lines of latitude, which circle the earth parallel to each other and to the Equator, an imaginary line around the center of the earth. The Equator is measured at 0°, and the poles are measured at 90° N (north) or S (south). The other set of lines comprises longitude lines, which run from pole to pole and measure distance east or west of a starting line called the Prime Meridian. During most of the history of mapmaking, individual mapmakers chose where to locate the Prime Meridian—usually placing it where they lived. Finally, in 1884, the United States held the First International Meridian Conference. The delegates decided to locate the Prime Meridian at an observatory in Greenwich, England. The other meridians are measured east or west of the Prime Meridian up to 180°. This grid system enables people to give the exact, or absolute, location for any place on the earth.

Relative Location

In everyday life people usually think of a place's location in relation to other known places, a concept called relative location. Even before there was a written language, people showed each other relative location by using simple maps such as those drawn in sand or made with sticks and stones. They also spoke of relative location, saying, for example, that Europe is north of Africa. Today following oral or written directions that are based on relative location continues to be a common way for people to get to their destinations.

FACTORS INFLUENCING VEGETATION

Climatic factors—such as the amount and intensity of sunlight, annual temperature patterns, and the annual rate of precipitation—limit the kinds of plants that grow naturally in a region. The type of soil and the local landforms also affect a region's vegetation.

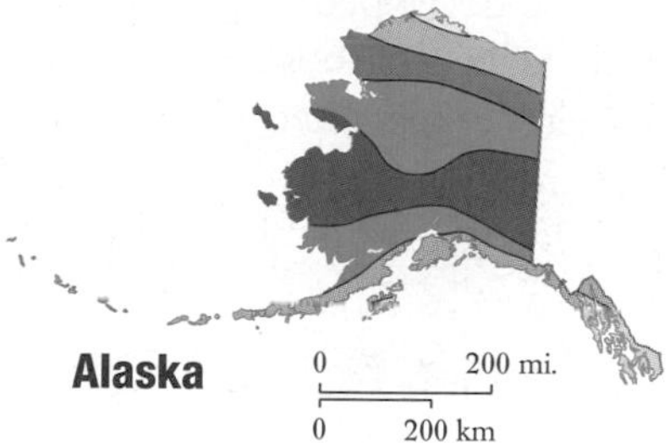

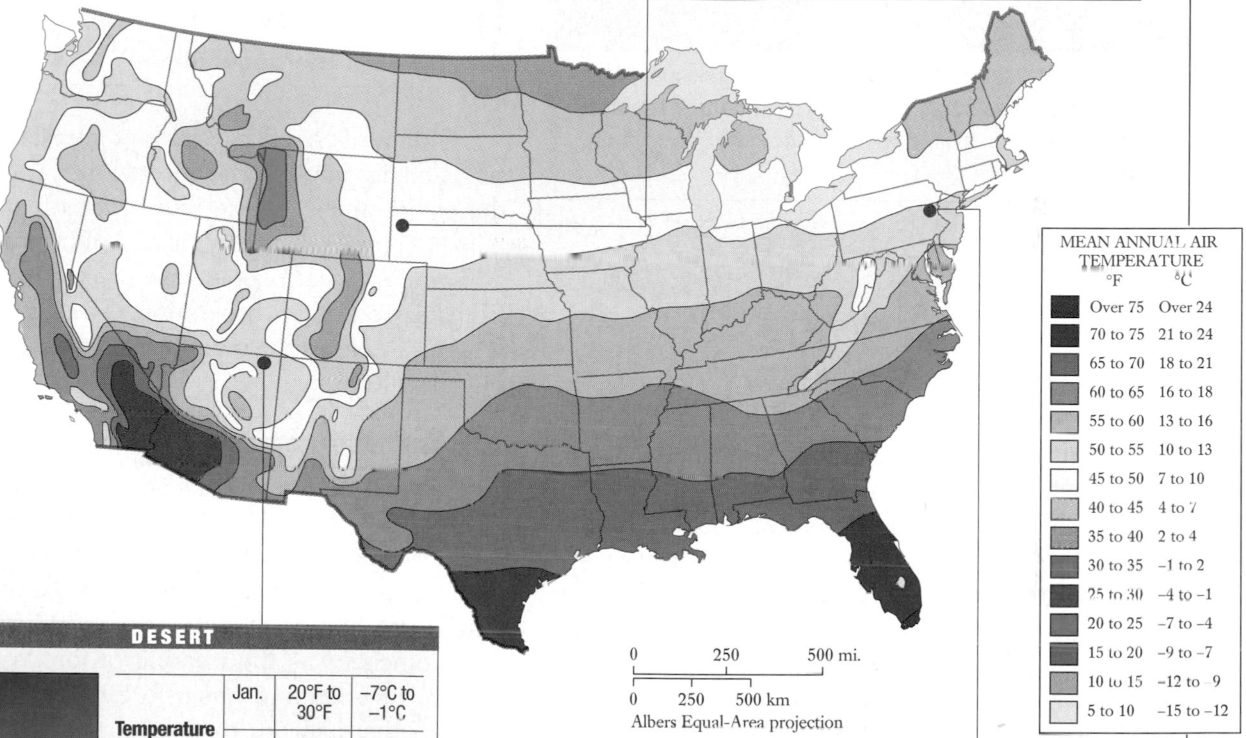

GRASSLAND

© DAVID MUENCH

Agate Fossil Beds, Nebraska

Temperature	Jan.	10°F to 20°F	–12°C to –7°C
	July	80°F to 90°F	27°C to 32°C
Annual Precipitation		Less than 20 in.	Less than 51 cm

Grasses feed animals and people throughout the year. In the winter, cattle and other grazing animals eat dried or fermented grass products. People eat foods made from wheat, oats, corn, and rice.

DESERT

© ROB BOUDREAU/TONY STONE IMAGES

Monument Valley, Arizona

Temperature	Jan.	20°F to 30°F	–7°C to –1°C
	July	74°F to 82°F	23°C to 28°C
Annual Precipitation		8 in. to 12 in.	20 cm to 30 cm

Adaptations enable desert plants to survive in a dry climate. Mesquite tree roots can grow to depths of about 260 feet (79 m). Many cacti expand to store rainwater and then shrink as they use water during dry periods.

FOREST

© MICHAEL GADOMSKI/PHOTO RESEARCHERS

Delaware Water Gap, Pennsylvania

Temperature	Jan.	24°F to 28°F	–4°C to –2°C
	July	72°F to 74°F	22°C to 23°C
Annual Precipitation		44 in. to 48 in.	112 cm to 122 cm

Every autumn the flat green leaves of this forest change color. The cooler, shorter days cause the breakdown of the green pigment chlorophyll. Other pigments in the leaf now become visible as the yellow, orange, and red colors of fall foliage.

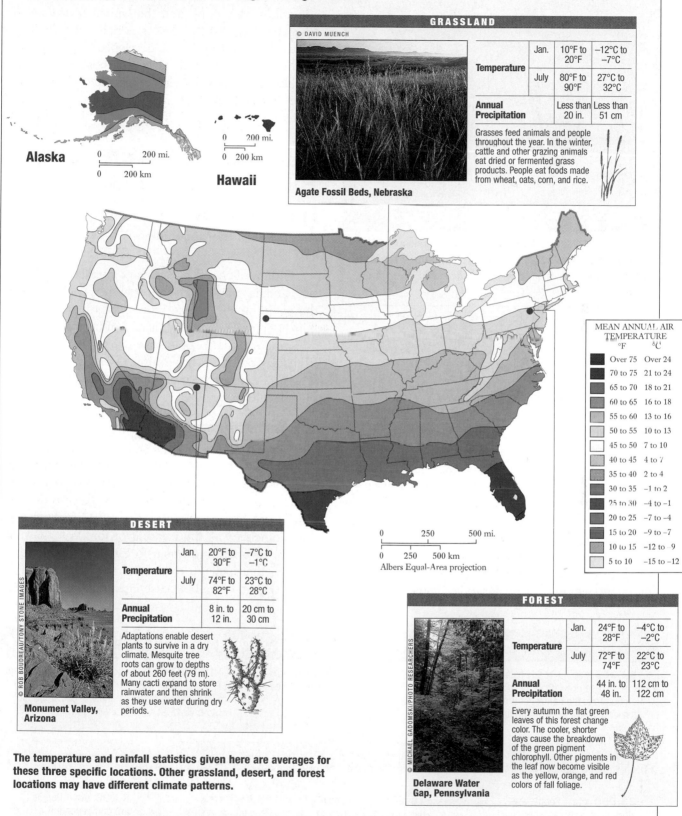

The temperature and rainfall statistics given here are averages for these three specific locations. Other grassland, desert, and forest locations may have different climate patterns.

Climate and vegetation are interrelated. *How important is a region's vegetation to the people who live there?*

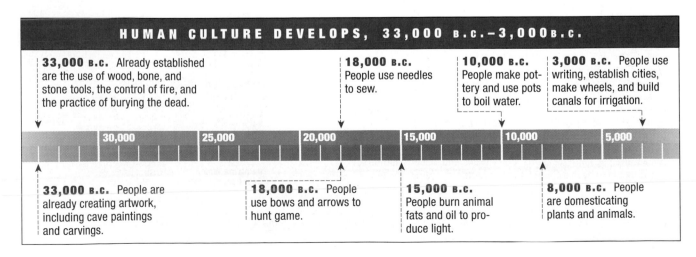

© TONY STONE WORLDWIDE

Facilitating Movement Modern highways include many features to improve safety, such as controlled traffic patterns at intersections. *How might a well-planned network of highways influence people's lives?*

Movement

People Come to the Two Continents

Fifty thousand years ago, North and South America were filled with a fascinating array of animals, but there were no people there at all. Anthropologists infer that the first human ancestors appeared in Africa a few million years ago. Their descendants migrated into Europe and Asia slightly less than 1 million years ago.

That migration took place during the most recent Ice Age, which ended about 10,000 years ago. Much of the earth's water was locked up in glaciers, and the ocean level was lower than it is today. Sometime toward the end of that Ice Age, while the ocean floor between Alaska and Asia was exposed and could serve as a "land bridge," the first humans migrated into North America from Asia.

From that moment until the present, a series of migrations have populated the United States and the other countries of the Americas. A rich understanding of United States history can be developed, in part, by tracing the reasons for and the effects of those migrations. A consideration of the goods, information, and ideas that have flowed into and out of the United States over the centuries can further enhance one's knowledge of history.

Human/Environment Interaction

An Inevitable Interdependence

Groups of people have always interacted with their surroundings in ways that affected the people as well as the environment. These interactions have produced human culture—the combination of institutions, ideas, and products that people have created and passed on from generation to generation. The time line below describes some of the milestones in the development of human culture.

The Early Centuries

The earliest Americans adapted to the variety of environments they discovered on the new continents. Some of their ways of life, for example, hunting and gathering, had a minimal impact on the surroundings. The single human activity that most changed early environments was the clearing of forests for farming and for fuel. Cutting down forests begins a series of changes that includes the loss of topsoil, the silting of rivers, and an overall increase in an area's temperature.

HUMAN CULTURE DEVELOPS, 33,000 B.C.–3,000 B.C.

33,000 B.C. Already established are the use of wood, bone, and stone tools, the control of fire, and the practice of burying the dead.

33,000 B.C. People are already creating artwork, including cave paintings and carvings.

18,000 B.C. People use needles to sew.

18,000 B.C. People use bows and arrows to hunt game.

15,000 B.C. People burn animal fats and oil to produce light.

10,000 B.C. People make pottery and use pots to boil water.

8,000 B.C. People are domesticating plants and animals.

3,000 B.C. People use writing, establish cities, make wheels, and build canals for irrigation.

30,000 | 25,000 | 20,000 | 15,000 | 10,000 | 5,000

After burning the branches and leaves, they hoed the rich ash into the ground as a fertilizer.

The Mississippians passed on another influence, too. With their clusters of domed wigwams, occasionally surrounded by a palisade, the villages of many Eastern Woodland groups resembled the villages most Mississippians had called home. No Eastern Woodland village ever competed in size or sophistication with Cahokia. Still, excavation of one Huron town in the Great Lakes region revealed that it had housed about 5,000 people in more than 100 large structures. Its size exceeded that of the average European village of the 1500s.

The Iroquois Alliance

Eventually, the Iroquois became the most populous and powerful of all the groups that lived along the eastern seaboard. The group controlled territory from the Adirondack Mountains to the Great Lakes and from Pennsylvania to northern New York.

The power of the Iroquois derived from a long-standing alliance of 5 Native American groups—the Mohawk, Oneida, Onondaga, Cayuga, and Seneca. Europeans later called the Iroquois alliance the League of the Iroquois. The Iroquois themselves called their alliance *Ganonsyoni,* or The Lodge Extended Lengthwise, after the lodges, or longhouses, that as many as 20 families shared.

In an Iroquois longhouse, a woman and her female relatives ruled. The women owned the house and all its belongings. Women also controlled the fields where they planted their crops. When a son married, he left his mother's longhouse to move in with his wife's family. Iroquois women held power in the outside world as well. They chose the chiefs, or sachems, and could also depose them. Though only men could speak in the community councils, women exerted behind-the-scenes influence—determining, for example, the fate of captive warriors from enemies.

At one time, the 5 groups that formed the Iroquois League had themselves been enemies. By the late 1400s the constant feuding that had rendered the Iroquois people powerless in the face of their mutual enemy, the powerful Algonquian people, spurred them to form the league for mutual protection.

In Iroquois legend the league began when a Mohawk sachem named Hiawatha had a vision. In Hiawatha's vision a spirit named Dekanawidah dictated how the five groups should affiliate with one another. According to the legend, Dekanawidah spoke these words:

> We bind ourselves together by taking hold of each other's hands so firmly and forming a circle so strong that if a tree should fall upon it, it could not shake nor break it, so that our people and

EASTERN NATIVE AMERICAN GROUPS, 1500s

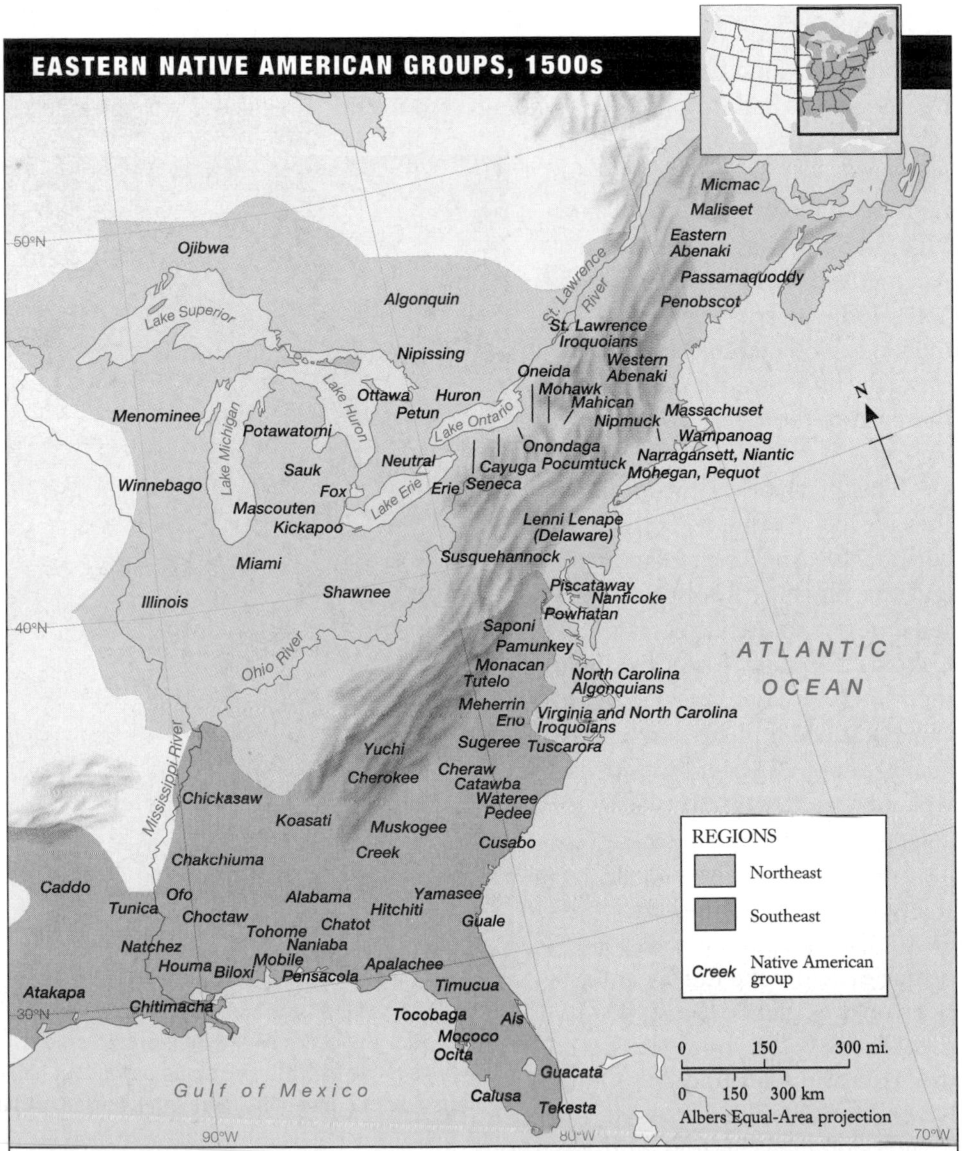

Native American groups in eastern North America supported themselves to varying degrees with agriculture. *In what areas are most groups of Native Americans concentrated?*

THE IROQUOIS LONGHOUSE

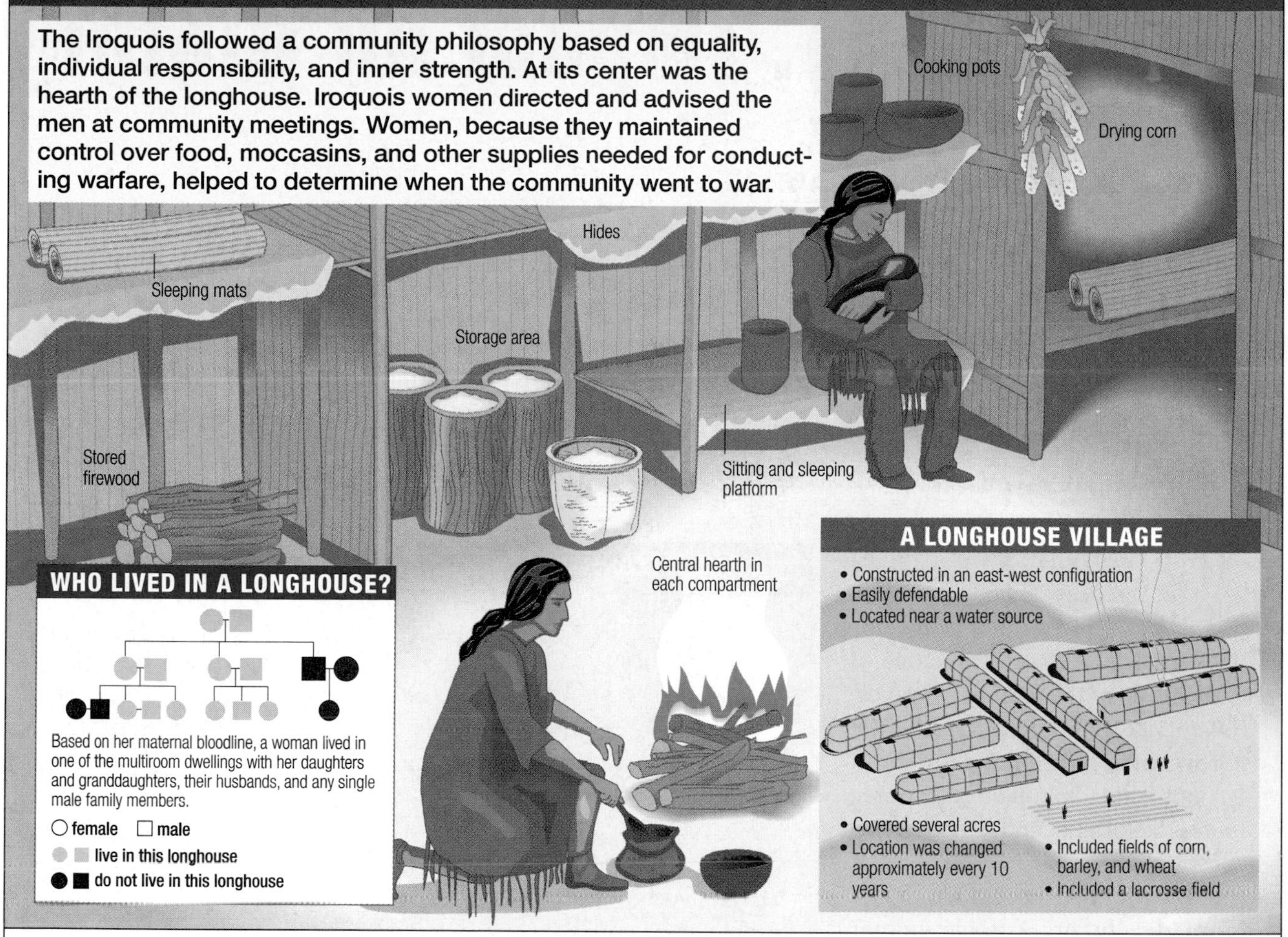

The Iroquois followed a community philosophy based on equality, individual responsibility, and inner strength. At its center was the hearth of the longhouse. Iroquois women directed and advised the men at community meetings. Women, because they maintained control over food, moccasins, and other supplies needed for conducting warfare, helped to determine when the community went to war.
Cooking pots
Drying corn
Hides
Sleeping mats
Storage area
Stored firewood
Sitting and sleeping platform
Central hearth in each compartment
A LONGHOUSE VILLAGE
• Constructed in an east-west configuration
• Easily defendable
• Located near a water source
• Covered several acres
• Location was changed approximately every 10 years
• Included fields of corn, barley, and wheat
• Included a lacrosse field
WHO LIVED IN A LONGHOUSE?
Based on her maternal bloodline, a woman lived in one of the multiroom dwellings with her daughters and granddaughters, their husbands, and any single male family members.
female
male
live in this longhouse
do not live in this longhouse

In the world of the Iroquois, nothing expressed the idea of community more than the longhouse. *How did women affect the group's decision to go to war?*

grandchildren shall remain in the circle in security, peace, and happiness.

—quoted in Gary Nash's *Red, White, and Black: The Peoples of Early America,* 1982

European Attitudes

The Europeans who colonized the eastern seaboard wrongly considered the Native Americans to be ignorant savages. Nevertheless, they praised the organization of the Iroquois League. Benjamin Franklin wrote, "It would be a very strange Thing, if six Nations of ignorant Savages should be capable of forming a Scheme for such a Union . . . and yet that a like Union should be impracticable for ten or a Dozen English Colonies, to whom it is more necessary." For the European colonists, the Iroquois League offered a model for achieving unity among disparate states. For the Native Americans, the Iroquois League proved a powerful tool that enabled them to deal shrewdly with the European newcomers.

Section Review

Vocabulary

1. Define: nomadic, sedentary, egalitarian.

Checking Facts

2. Why did people first cross the land bridge into North America?
3. What spurred the Iroquois to form an alliance?

Critical Thinking

Evaluating Information

4. Explain why you agree or disagree with this statement about the Anasazi: "Their greatest creativity flowered in architecture."

Linking Across Time

5. Compare the influence of women in Iroquois society to that of women in modern American society. Do women today have as much power?

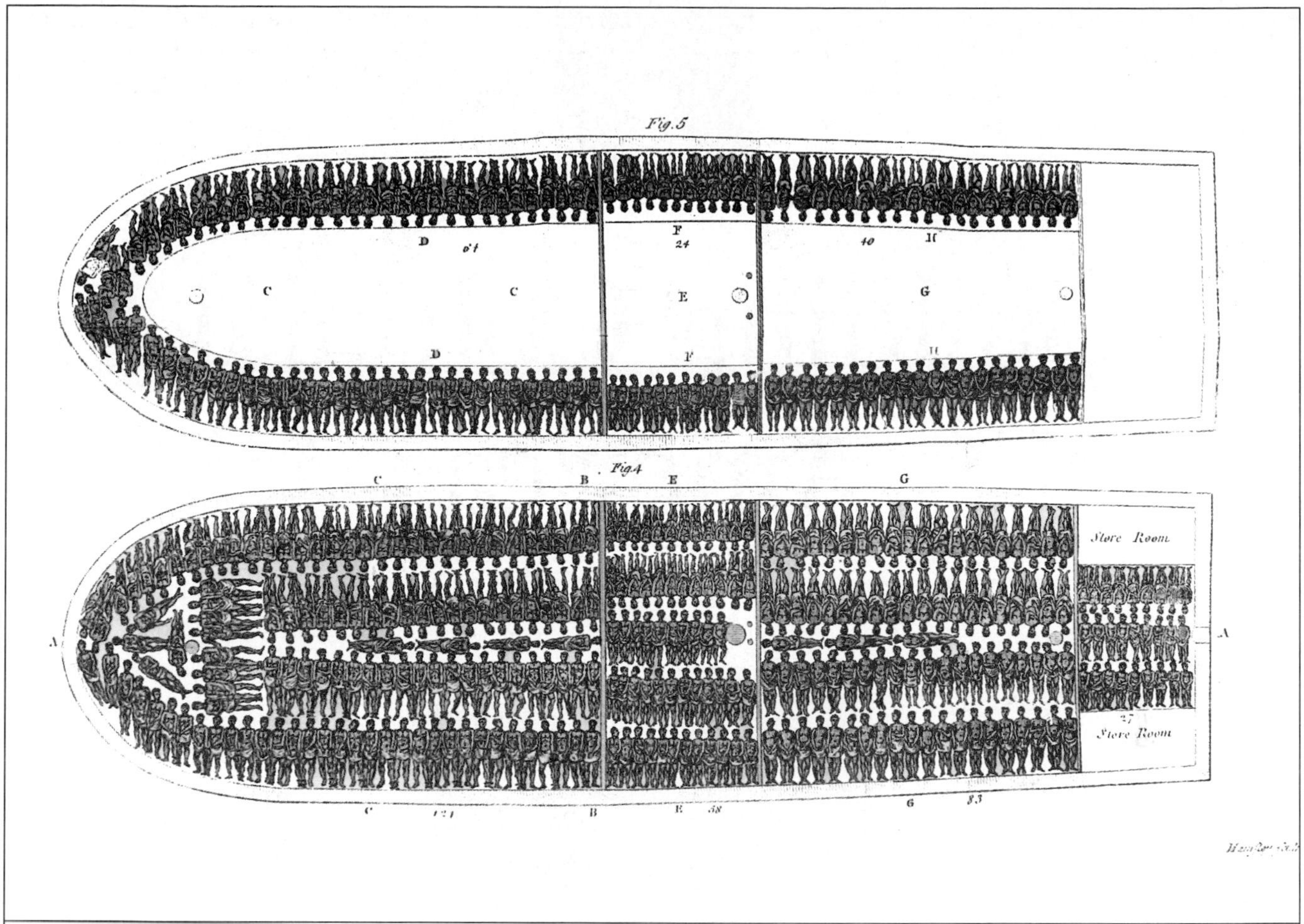

THE LIBRARY COMPANY OF PHILADELPHIA

The Middle Passage **Illustrations such as this one, which appeared in the early 1700s, showed slave traders how to pack their holds as efficiently as possible.** *How many Africans died on slave ships during their journey to the Americas?*

jumped into the sea, immediately another quite dejected fellow . . . also followed; and I believe many more would very soon have done the same if they had not been prevented by the ship's crew.

—Autobiography of Olaudah Equiano

At least 10 million enslaved Africans made the same journey, unwillingly transported to the Americas in the largest forced migration the world has ever seen. By the mid-1700s, enslaved Africans represented about 40 percent of the population in America's Southern Colonies. In South Carolina after 1710, enslaved Africans outnumbered white colonists.

This massive migration not only enriched the European nations who traded in human flesh, it profoundly changed the character of the Americas. During the 300 years between Columbus's journey and the American Revolution, 6 out of 7 persons who crossed the Atlantic came to the Americas against their will. These Africans soon learned European ways. With their complex religious and musical heritage as well as their agricultural knowledge, they also began to Africanize America's European culture.

Section Review

Vocabulary

1. Define: western passage, conquistador, indigenous.

Checking Facts

2. What did Columbus mistakenly believe he had found on his voyages?
3. What was the most common cause of death among Native Americans after contact with Europeans?

Critical Thinking

Predicting Consequences

4. How would the early history of the Americas have been different if there had been no slave trade?

Linking Across Time

5. The quadrant and the caravel helped Portugal gain an early lead in the race to find new ocean routes. Name a recent invention that helps people explore.

SECTION 3

Building Colonial America

SPRING 1630: PURITANS ESTABLISH MASSACHUSETTS BAY COLONY

© NORTH WIND PICTURE ARCHIVES

Arrival of the Puritans
This etching depicts Winthrop's fleet of ships arriving in New England.

IN THE SPRING OF 1630 THE SHIP *ARBELLA* HEADED A FLEET OF 11 SHIPS SAILING FOR MASSACHUSETTS. Along with cows, horses, goats, pigs, and chickens, the ships carried 1,000 Puritans. In England these Puritans had failed to purify the Protestant Church of England of rituals they deplored as traces of Catholicism. The Puritans hoped Massachusetts would provide a more hospitable home for their strict religious practices.

Aboard the *Arbella,* John Winthrop, newly elected governor of the Massachusetts Bay Colony, summoned his fellow Puritans for a sermon. Although in England the Puritans had spurned church and state authority, Winthrop urged them to submerge their individuality in favor of a community that would adhere strictly to Christian ideals. Only if the Puritans could "rejoyce together, mourne together, labour and suffer together," Winthrop preached, could their settlement serve as an example to others:

> . . . for wee must Consider that wee shall be as a Citty upon a Hill, the eies [eyes] of all people are uppon us; so that if wee shall deale falsely with our god in this worke . . . wee shall be made a story and a by-word through the world, wee shall open the mouthes of enemies to speake evill of the wayes of god. . . .
>
> —John Winthrop, "A Model of Christian Charity," 1630

As You Read

Vocabulary
- mission
- presidio
- selectman
- pacifism
- indentured servant

Think About . . .
- where Spanish, French, and English settlers established claims in the Americas.
- how the European settlers adapted to the land and made their livings.
- the differences in the resources and economies of the New England, Middle, and Southern Colonies.

Turning Point

were called to recant. Reverend Wheelwright refused and was banished from the colony, along with some of his supporters. Many other supporters were stripped of their citizenship.

The court called Anne Hutchinson to trial. Governor Winthrop sat as both judge and chief prosecutor. Anne Hutchinson addressed the court alone, without the benefit of a jury, lawyer, or witnesses.

The Opinions

The quotations on the previous page show divided opinions about Anne Hutchinson. Many in Boston were inspired by her, but they realized it was dangerous to speak against those in power. William Coddington, one of Boston's most successful business leaders, rallied to Hutchinson's defense.

Hutchinson spoke calmly, clearly, and eloquently in her own defense during the two-day trial. Although the governor and the ministers had little evidence against Hutchinson, they spoke strongly. Their strident judgments rang throughout the trial.

The Outcome

The verdict—banishment—surprised neither Hutchinson's supporters nor her detractors. Because winter was near, the court voted to allow Hutchinson to remain in the area under house arrest until spring.

The Bay Colony leaders still felt threatened by Hutchinson, who refused to alter her views. In March, they held a church trial. At the end of the trial, Hutchinson recanted her views in one breath and insulted the ministers in the next. They responded by excommunicating her.

The banishment was carried out a few days later. Hutchinson left with her family for the settlement of Aquidneck in present-day Portsmouth, Rhode Island. This region had become a haven for religious dissenters, including Roger Williams, who had been banished from the Bay Colony in 1635. Harassment by the Bay Colony continued. Ministers came to try to convince Hutchinson to reform; the colony also threatened to take over the Hutchinsons' land.

With the death of her husband in the summer of 1642, Anne Hutchinson decided to try to escape ever-present threats of the Bay Colony. The family eventually moved to the shores of Long Island, near Pelham Bay. Anne Hutchinson was killed there during a Native American attack in 1643.

© FORREST FRAZIER/COURTESY OF THE DEDHAM HISTORICAL SOCIETY, DEDHAM, MA

Most Puritan households contained only one chair, which was usually reserved for the man of the house. Anne Hutchinson sat in a chair when she held her meetings, thus violating this convention. One Hutchinson critic, Reverend Thomas Weld, sarcastically remarked that "the custom was for her scholars to propound questions and she (gravely sitting in the chair) did make answers thereunto."

Sir Henry Vane (left), a supporter of Hutchinson's, was governor of the colony from 1636–1637. When John Winthrop (right) succeeded Vane, he used the power of the governor's office against her.

COURTESY, AMERICAN ANTIQUARIAN SOCIETY

COURTESY, AMERICAN ANTIQUARIAN SOCIETY

The Significance

The religious controversy Anne Hutchinson sparked ravaged the Bay Colony. More than two dozen families left. Some followed Reverend Wheelwright to the settlement he founded at Exeter, now in New Hampshire. Most settled with the Hutchinsons in Aquidneck. As John Winthrop later noted, the colony's finest citizens were among the ranks of those who followed Hutchinson.

Winthrop himself eventually became disheartened about Hutchinson's banishment. In 1649 he refused to sign an order banishing another religious dissenter, saying, "No, of that work I have done too much already."

In the years between Hutchinson's banishment and Winthrop's expression of remorse, the Massachusetts Bay Colony slowly and subtly began a transformation. The power of traditional government authority, which had been intimately tied to the church, was curtailed. For instance, the personal power of the colony's main leaders was limited in 1641 when a written code of law was drawn up. The colony's laws were no longer based on the leaders' interpretations of the Bible but on the body of English common law.

The establishment of a two-house legislature in 1644 further cut into the power of the Bay Colony's traditional leadership. In 1646 business leaders who gained power in the lower house of the legislature, pushed to suspend laws that discriminated against people who held unpopular religious views. With these acts, the intertwining of the church and the state gradually began to be disentangled. This separation of church and state became an important principle in the Massachusetts colonial government and a cornerstone of the United States Constitution.

RESPONDING TO THE CASE

1. In what ways was Anne Hutchinson a threat to the Massachusetts Bay Colony?

2. What do you think would have happened in Boston if Hutchinson's supporter Henry Vane had been reelected governor in 1637 and for several subsequent years?

3. Before Hutchinson was called to trial, the leaders of the colony had warned her to tone down her teachings. Do you think Hutchinson could have championed her views better if she had heeded their warnings, thereby avoiding banishment? Do you think she would have gained more influence if she had remained a citizen of Boston? Explain.

4. Many Puritans left England for New England so that they would be able to worship according to their own consciences. As you read in the chapter, however, they tolerated no dissent from their own religious views once they had their own colony. Based on what you know of this contradictory attitude, are you surprised, or do you think it was inevitable that religious toleration would become an issue for Puritans in America? Explain your views either way.

PORTFOLIO PROJECT

Using what you have learned about Anne Hutchinson, write a speech she might have given to the people who came with her to Aquidneck, thanking them for their support. In the speech, look to the future and describe the dreams you have for the settlement.

SECTION 4

Conflict and Growth in the Colonies

1744: VIRGINIANS OFFER EDUCATION TO NATIVE AMERICANS

BENJAMIN FRANKLIN WAS BORN IN BOSTON IN 1706, THE FIFTEENTH CHILD AND YOUNGEST SON OF A POOR CANDLE MAKER. Fleeing a hateful apprenticeship to his older brother, Franklin crafted a successful life as a printer in the bustling port of Philadelphia. In his pamphlet "Information to Those Who Would Remove to America," Franklin contrasted the world views held by white colonists and Native Americans, saying, "The learning on which we value ourselves, they regard as frivolous and useless." Franklin illustrated his point with the following story.

In 1744 the commissioners of Virginia had invited the chiefs of 6 Native American nations to send 6 of their sons to college in Williamsburg, Virginia. The chiefs declined with thanks and this explanation:

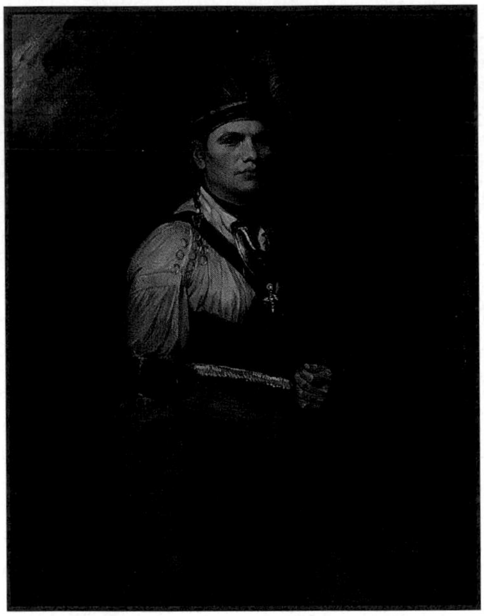

NATIONAL GALLERY OF CANADA/THE BRIDGEMAN ART LIBRARY

A Mohawk Leader
Joseph Brant, who once served as a missionary among his people, translated part of the New Testament into Mohawk.

> Several of our young people were formerly brought up at the colleges of the Northern Provinces; they were instructed in all your sciences; but when they came back to us, they were bad runners, ignorant of every means of living in the woods, unable to bear either cold or hunger; knew neither how to build a cabin, take a deer, or kill an enemy; spoke our language imperfectly; were therefore neither fit for hunters, warriors, or counsellors; they

AS YOU READ

Vocabulary
- kachina
- legislature
- revivalism

Think About . . .
- why Native Americans rebelled against the colonists.
- how England became the dominant power in the colonies.
- how conditions in the colonies after the Seven Years' War fostered new ideas that foreshadowed independence.

were totally good for nothing. . . . if the Gentlemen of Virginia will send us a dozen of their sons, we will take great care of their education, instruct them in all we know, and make *men* of them.

—Zall, P.M., *Ben Franklin Laughing: Anecdotes from Original Sources by and about Benjamin Franklin,* 1980

In the 1600s and 1700s, conflicts erupted between colonists and Native Americans over such differences in values, but more importantly, over the colonists' persistent encroachment onto Native American territories.

Native American Wars

Colonists Conflict With Native Americans

In the Spanish Southwest, Native Americans succeeded for a time in ridding themselves of a hateful colonial presence. On the Eastern seaboard, however, coastal peoples soon succumbed to the English colonists' superior strength. The more powerful interior peoples would hold onto their own power only as long as France and England vied for supremacy on the continent.

Popé's Rebellion

In the 1600s Spain built missions in New Mexico. Nearby, Spanish soldiers occupied forts called presidios. With the aid of guns and horses, a few Spaniards subdued numerous Native Americans, converted them to Christianity, and forced them to toil for the Spaniards.

To destroy the Native American religion that competed with Christianity, the Spanish priests banned Native American dances, imprisoned and beat Taos Pueblo holy men, and burned sacred **kachina** dolls. In 1676 Spanish priests in New Mexico proudly reported the destruction of 1,600 Native American priestly masks.

Four years later, a Native American religious leader named Popé united Taos Pueblo people who spoke seven different languages into a formidable fighting force. Popé and his fighters leveled all but two Spanish villages in New Mexico and drove the hated priests back to Mexico, where they remained for more than a decade.

Victories such as Popé's did not occur in the East, where Native Americans came into conflict with American colonists who coveted their land. On the East Coast, two major defeats finally overpowered the Native American societies of the Atlantic seaboard.

King Philip's War

Massasoit, the Wampanoag chief, had befriended the earliest English colonists in Massachusetts, even bestowing the English names of Alexander and Philip on his sons, Wamsutta and Metacom. Eventually, Metacom (Philip) became chief. He detested the colonists, who had greedily overrun Wampanoag hunting and fishing lands. Unwilling to lose any more land or to be pushed westward, Metacom enlisted the aid of other seaboard peoples to fight the English. From 1675 to 1676, about 600 colonists and 3,000 Native Americans lost their lives in the bloody war.

COURTESY, AMERICAN ANTIQUARIAN SOCIETY

King Philip Almost 100 years after King Philip's War, Paul Revere created this engraved portrait of him. *How many Native Americans died in the war?*

Bacon's Rebellion

While New England colonists were fighting King Philip's War, settlers in Virginia were complaining that Virginia's royal governor, Sir William Berkeley, had reserved too much frontier land for Native Americans. Though his conciliatory policies pleased Native Americans and wealthy plantation owners, Berkeley's rulings infuriated new settlers and former indentured servants who coveted Native American lands.

In 1676 a planter named Nathaniel Bacon rallied troops of angry Virginians. First they declared war on all Native Americans, including those who were friendly, and then they battled the governor and his troops.

EUROPEAN LAND CLAIMS, 1763

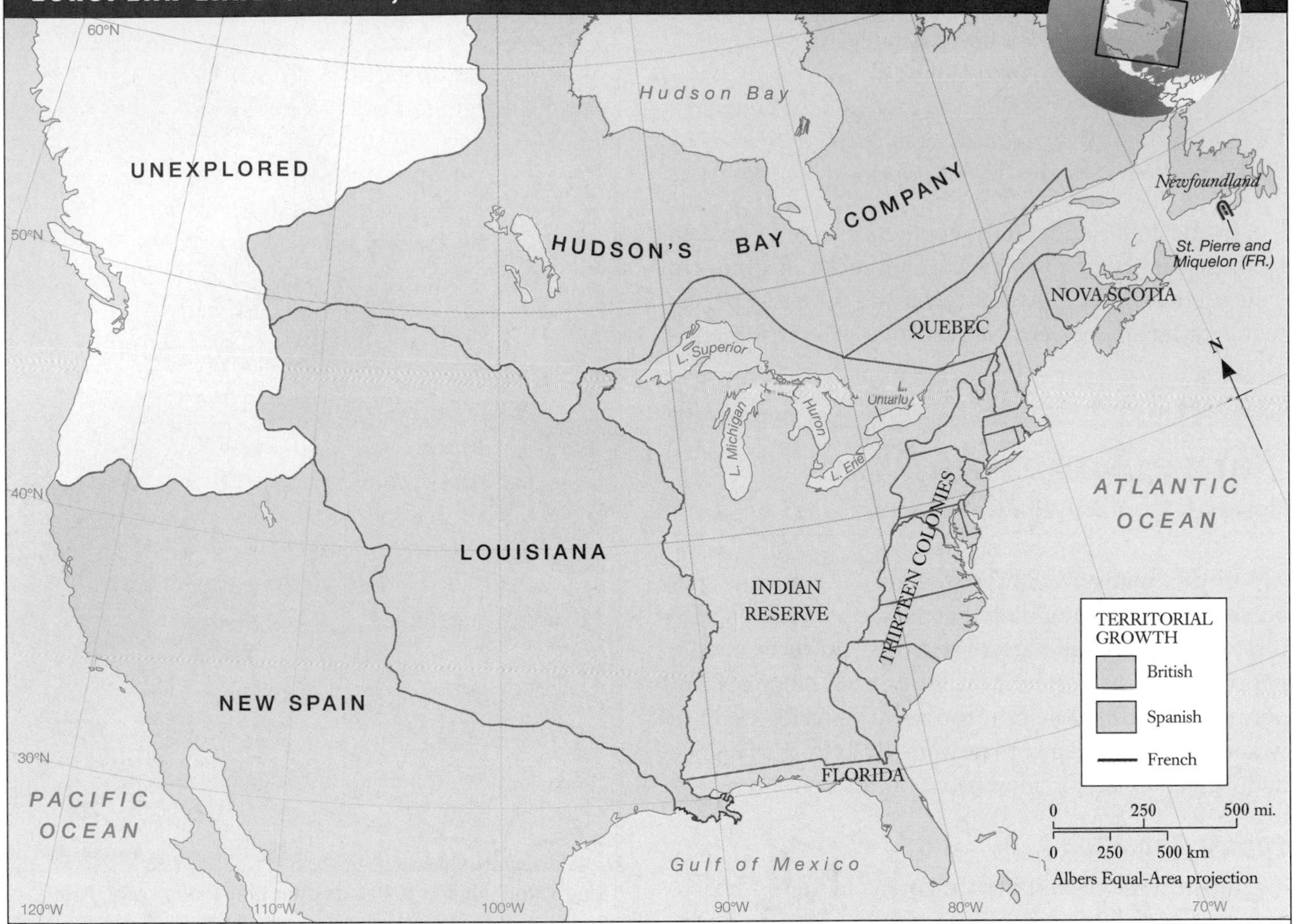

The Seven Years' War clearly established Britain as the dominant power in eastern North America. *What territories did France lose to Britain as a result of the war?*

Hundreds of settlers and Native Americans died in what became known as Bacon's Rebellion. Bacon was killed, but his followers later gained seats in the Virginia **legislature,** or lawmaking body, where they immediately voted to legalize Native American slavery. When English investigators arrived in 1677, they condemned the "inconsiderate sort of men who so rashly and causelessly cry up a war and seem to wish and aim at an utter extirpation [elimination] of the Indians."

France and Britain Struggle for Control

Britain Emerges Victorious

The Iroquois, Cherokee, Creek, and Choctaw of North America's interior wielded far greater power than did the smaller coastal peoples who submitted to the colonists in the 1600s. At first the interior Native Americans shrewdly protected their interests and maintained power by refusing to side with either France or England. As the growing white population of the English colonies pushed up against French-held territory, long-standing religious and commercial hostilities between the European rivals expanded into a deadly territorial struggle.

In 4 wars between 1689 and 1763, Protestant England sought to expel its Catholic French rival from the Americas. Foiled by weather, disease, and the hardship of transporting supplies, France and England each soon discovered that their best chance for success lay in recruiting colonial soldiers and in paying Native American allies to fight for them.

The fourth war, called the Seven Years' War in Europe and the French and Indian War in the colonies, proved climactic. By 1759, after the tide of victory turned indisputably toward Britain, the powerful Iroquois calculated that their interests would be best served by supporting the eventual victors. By the end of the Seven Years' War in 1763, France had lost Canada and all territory east of the Mississippi River except New Orleans; Britain held sway in the eastern part of North America; and thirteen separate colonies congratulated themselves on uniting against a common enemy. The Native Americans of North America's interior, however, had forever lost the power they had previously enjoyed from playing off one colonial power against another.

A People Emerges

New Ideas Foreshadow Independence

The Seven Years' War extracted a high price from the colonies. During the course of the long war, most working-class Boston men fought, and many died. In 1764 census takers in Boston counted 3,612 women but only 2,941 men. In addition the peace that put an end to the bloodshed precipitated an economic depression as 40,000 British troops suddenly departed.

Despite its heavy costs, the Seven Years' War left the colonists heady with victory and seeking westward expansion. Territory that had been newly wrested from French control grew even more attractive to colonists who wished to escape the crowded Eastern seaboard.

The Population Explosion

The population of the colonies had increased at an extraordinary rate between 1680 and 1770, rising more than tenfold from 150,000 to 1,700,000. A mere one-fourth of this increase stemmed from the willing immigration of indentured servants from Germany and Ireland, and the forced immigration of Africans. Fully three-quarters of the population explosion stemmed from a high birthrate accompanied by a low death rate. For European colonists and their descendants, North America's pure drinking water, healthful climate, and spacious territory made life both longer and healthier. Enslaved Africans who formed families also began to have children by the 1720s, producing as many children as whites and soon outnumbering enslaved persons who had been born in Africa.

THE BETTMANN ARCHIVE

George Whitefield **Drawn by his riveting style as a performer, more than 20,000 people attended Whitefield's farewell sermon in Boston.** *What did revivalism emphasize?*

Africans had brought to North America not only the agricultural know-how that enriched Southern farmers, but also the medical expertise that saved many white colonists from smallpox, a dreaded killer. The Boston minister Cotton Mather learned from a "Guramantee" servant—probably a West African man shipped from the Gold Coast fort at Kormantin—about a method of inoculation common in West Africa. In this method, "juice of small-pox" inserted into a cut produced a weakened form of illness, thereby conferring lifelong immunity. In July 1721 Mather wrote in his diary, "I have instructed our Physicians in the new Method used by the Africans . . . to prevent and abate the Dangers of the Small-Pox, and infallibly to save the Lives of those that have it wisely managed upon them." After inoculation took hold in colonial cities, smallpox virtually disappeared as a major killer.

A Great Awakening

At the same time that the population in the colonies was skyrocketing, many Americans came under the sway of **revivalism**—a movement that emphasized individual religious experience instead of church doctrine. A series of Christian revivals called the Great Awakening swept different regions between 1720 and 1760, arousing a widespread hunger for spiritual renewal. The timing and character of the Great Awakening differed from region to region. Still, regardless of region, revivalism posed a serious challenge to accepted sources of authority and introduced patterns of activity that helped fuel the revolutionary movement of the next generation. George Whitefield, a tiny 24-year-old Anglican priest with a magnificent voice, began by exciting audiences in his native Britain. In 1739 and 1740 Whitefield ignited the American Great Awakening on the first of 7 open-air preaching tours along the Atlantic Coast.

Awakeners like Whitefield preached that established congregations were dead because "dead men preach to them." The Awakeners shocked established clergy by encouraging individuals to participate by "lay exhorting." A lay exhorter could be any converted person—man or woman, young or old, African or white—who wished to preach "the Lord's truth."

Enslaved Africans were especially drawn to the revivalists of the 1740s and 1750s. Unlike professional Protestant clergy, whose sermons were typically dry and uninvolving, the revivalists preached personal rebirth in a freewheeling participatory style that gave Christianity mass appeal. Not surprisingly Africans' conversion experiences prompted many new African Christians to question the basis for their enslavement. On May 25, 1774, a group of Africans in Massachusetts addressed the following appeal to Thomas Gage, the royal governor: "There is a great number of us sincear . . . members of the Church of Christ(;) how can the master and the slave be said to fulfil that command Live in love. . . ."

All Americans, not just enslaved Africans, began to question received authority as a result of the Great Awakening. The ideas spread during this period encouraged people to create new churches and to take responsibility in other matters of importance, such as communal betterment and self-government.

NATIONAL PORTRAIT GALLERY, SMITHSONIAN INSTITUTION/ART RESOURCE, NY

Ben Franklin **Franklin's many accomplishments included founding the first city hospital and the University of Pennsylvania.** *What virtues did Franklin promote?*

Benjamin Franklin, Yankee Paragon

Though he shunned formal religion, the genial Benjamin Franklin offered George Whitefield accommodations on the preacher's 1745 visit to Philadelphia. Even if Franklin did not worship at any particular church, he nevertheless lived the maxim that "a good example is the best sermon." The sermon the self-educated Franklin preached promoted the Puritan virtues of thrift, hard work, education, and community responsibility. In his *Poor Richard's Almanack,* a collection of weather predictions and other useful information, Franklin coined many popular sayings giving practical advice about such subjects as working hard and saving time. Two of these familiar sayings are "A stitch in time saves nine" and "Lost time is never found again." After the Bible, Franklin's annual almanac was the most popular book in the colonies.

Over a career that spanned decades, Franklin became the most famous colonial American. In the second half of the 1700s, thanks to his experiments with electricity and his lightning rod, Franklin's name had traversed the Atlantic and was a household word in France. There the wealthy and famous man who had begun life as a poor boy seemed the embodiment of a freshly minted American spirit.

Colonial Self-Government

The American spirit Franklin celebrated expressed itself in the way the colonies governed themselves. Though each colony's government differed slightly, all the governments shared an important inheritance from the British system of government: an elected legislature. In most colonies, these legislatures consisted of two chambers that approximated the English House of Lords and House of Commons. As in the House of Lords, members of the council were wealthy appointees of the royal governor. As in the House of Commons, members of the assembly were elected by white male property holders.

The legislatures provided a check on the power of the appointed royal or proprietary governors, many of whom proved to be corrupt at worst or mediocre at best. In the 1700s, the colonies' legislatures won the right to initiate bills, to settle contested elections, and to determine taxes.

Following the Seven Years' War, a French diplomat looked at the colonies' smoothly functioning governments and made an uncanny prediction. The diplomat warned an unbelieving Britain that the colonies no longer needed its protection: "You will call on them to contribute towards supporting the burden which they have helped to bring on you; they will answer you by shaking off all dependence."

SECTION REVIEW

Vocabulary

1. Define: kachina, legislature, revivalism.

Checking Facts

2. What prompted King Philip's War?
3. How did England emerge victorious over France in the struggle for territory in North America?

Critical Thinking

Recognizing Ideologies

4. How did the practice of enslavement conflict with the practice of revivalism?

Linking Across Time

5. How do the struggles between colonial powers for North American territory compare with wars fought over world territory today?

Critical Thinking Skill

MAKING GENERALIZATIONS

Learning the Skill

Any item of information is like an isolated piece of a jigsaw puzzle. You need to look for patterns in information and put those facts together into a larger picture.

Making a generalization is making a general statement about a pattern you find in information you study. This skill helps you clarify your understanding of a situation so you can make decisions and act on your understanding.

Making Generalizations

To make a generalization, follow these steps:

a. Pull together the facts that are relevant to the topic.

b. Figure out categories or ways of grouping the information.

c. Look for patterns and relationships within the categories or groups.

d. Make a general statement based on the information.

Recall that in the last paragraph of the text on page 50, the French diplomat said:

You will call on them to contribute towards supporting the burden which they have helped to bring on you; they will answer you by shaking off all dependence.

This statement may have been based on facts such as the following:

a. Each of the thirteen colonies had an elected legislature to make laws.

b. The colonial governments were maturing and becoming more confident.

c. The legislatures had provided a check on the power of the appointed royal governors.

d. The legislatures won the right to initiate bills and to determine taxes.

You can see that each of these facts relates to the category of government. A pattern you can observe is that the colonists were working together and governing themselves successfully. The French diplomat could make the generalization that the colonial governments were able to function independently. Based on this generalization, the diplomat made his statement to England.

Debating Ideas The colonists discussed news and public events in town meetings and in informal gatherings. *State a generalization that a colonist of the time might have made about government.*

Practicing the Skill

Use the facts below to answer the questions.

Around A.D. 900, the Anasazi built 400 miles (643.6 km) of road to Chaco Canyon and lived in huge apartment complexes housing more than 1,000 people.

Between A.D. 900 and 1100 the Moundbuilders built a gigantic mound. It faces the site of a city that once housed as many as 35,000 people.

1. What facts fit in the category of time?

2. What facts fit in the category of people?

3. What patterns do you see in each category?

4. What common patterns do you see in the histories of the Anasazi and the Moundbuilders?

5. What generalization can you make about the earliest Americans?

Applying the Skill

Read a newspaper or magazine article that contains many facts. Make a list of categories and write down any patterns that you notice. Make a generalization based on those facts.

Additional Practice

For additional practice, see Reinforcing Skills on page 53.

Chapter 2 Review

Reviewing Key Terms

Choose the vocabulary term that best completes each sentence below. Write your answers on a separate sheet of paper.

conquistador **egalitarian**
indigenous **pacifism**
indentured servant **revivalism**

1. A wealthy colonist might hire an _________ to work on his plantation for several years in exchange for passage to America.

2. The Anasazi functioned as equals and had no leaders because theirs was an _________ society.

3. Hernando Cortés was a Spanish _________ who conquered the Aztec.

4. As a Quaker, William Penn believed in tolerance of differences among people and in _________, or opposition to the use of force.

5. The Great Awakening, which swept colonial America between the 1720s and 1760s, was based on the movement called _________.

Recalling Facts

1. What did the contents of the burial mounds reveal about the Native American Moundbuilders?

2. What were "the three sisters," and how did they support each other?

3. What five Native American nations combined to form the Iroquois League?

4. What was Columbus trying to find when he first sailed west from Europe?

5. What were the 2 major inventions that helped advance Portuguese navigation in the second half of the 1400s?

6. Why did the enslavement of Africans occur soon after the Europeans explored and began colonizing in the Americas?

7. Why did the Puritans leave their homes in England and come to Massachusetts?

8. What physical and social factors drew people to settle in the Middle Colonies, especially in the colony of Pennsylvania?

9. How were Native Americans instrumental in helping to establish Great Britain, rather than France, as the dominant power in North America?

10. What conditions in the thirteen colonies after the Seven Years' War fostered a growing spirit of independence?

Critical Thinking

1. Drawing Conclusions The Iroquois alliance was organized with the major purpose of ending the battles between Native American nations. A council of 49 chiefs, delegated by the 5 participating nations, governed the alliance and had the power to make decisions for all the Iroquois villages. Under this political structure, the people in the Iroquois alliance were more united and stronger than before. What does the success of this ruling body, organized before Columbus arrived in North America, indicate about those who organized it?

2. Identifying Assumptions What erroneous assumptions did the Europeans who colonized the Eastern seaboard of North America make about the Native Americans who were living there when the Europeans arrived?

3. Recognizing Ideologies Using missions such as the one in the photograph below as their bases, Spanish priests tried to convert the indigenous peoples of the Southwest to Roman Catholicism. How did their treatment of the Native Americans conflict with the ideology of Christianity that they espoused?

4. Making Comparisons Life in the colonies was different depending upon whether a colonist lived in the New England Colonies, the Middle Colonies, or the Southern Colonies. Make a chart that compares the advantages and disadvantages of life in each of these colonial regions. Include social life as well as issues of work and religion.

5. Demonstrating Reasoned Judgment The Puritans followed the European theory that land that was not settled was available to be claimed by them as "civilized" people. In this way, they justified claiming lands where Native Americans "roamed" but had not settled. Do you think this distinction was just? Why or why not?

Portfolio Project

Imagine that you could ask Benjamin Franklin five questions about what life was like in colonial America after the Seven Years' War. Write these questions, and use them to do more research about this historic period. Put the results of your research into your portfolio.

POPULATION GROWTH IN THE COLONIES

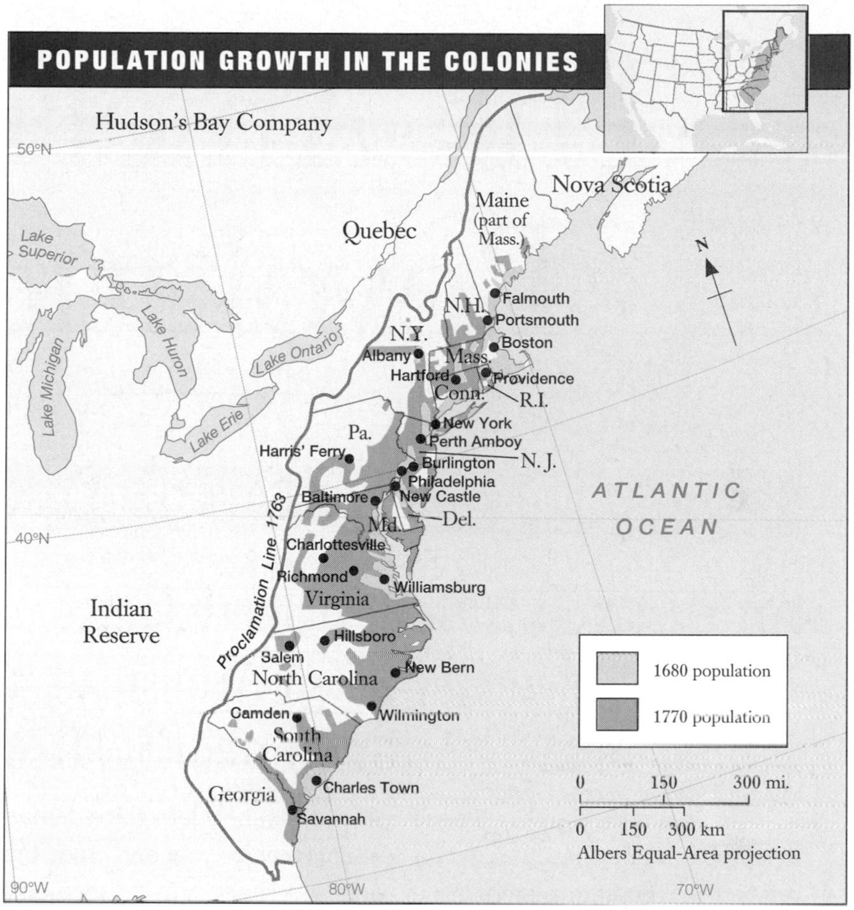

Cooperative Learning

Working in small groups, research factors (other than epidemics) that contributed to the decline in the population of Native Americans and factors that contributed to the increase in the population of Africans in North America by 1750. Present your findings to the rest of the class.

Reinforcing Skills

Making Generalizations Write a letter to a friend from the point of view of a Puritan colonist, expressing generalizations you believe a member of that religious group would make about other religions in North America.

Geography and History

Study the map on this page to answer the following questions:

1. Which colonies had no significant population in 1680?

2. Which colonies experienced the most growth from 1680 to 1770?

3. Locate the Proclamation Line established in 1763 after the Seven Years' War. Colonial governors were ordered to reserve all lands west of this line for Native Americans. Which colonies had people living closest to that line in 1770?

4. Which colonies—Northern, Middle, or Southern—were more likely to expand westward over the Proclamation Line first? Why?

HISTORY JOURNAL

Write specific facts that you have learned about how the Spanish, French, and English treated indigenous peoples in North America.

CHAPTER 3

The American Revolution

OCTOBER 19, 1781: BRITISH SURRENDER AT YORKTOWN

An enslaved African named James gained permission from his owner, William Armistead, to join the Continental Army stationed nearby. It was March 1781.

The general commanding these American troops was Marie Joseph Lafayette, a young French aristocrat, who had volunteered to serve with the American army. That spring Lafayette sent many spies to the nearby British camp, but no one was as important as James. The secret information James gathered helped Lafayette and the Americans corner the British at Yorktown, Virginia. In October 1781 the British surrendered there, ending the fight for independence. At the end of the war, however, Lafayette went home a hero, and James went home an enslaved person.

Yet, with Lafayette's help, James was to be given his freedom. The Frenchman wrote a letter describing James's "essential services" during the war and urged that James be released by his owner in recognition of the value of those services. In 1786 the Virginia legislature finally freed James in thanks for his military efforts during the American Revolution.

James Armistead's story was exceptional, but the lives of many Americans—African and white, male and female, famous and unknown—changed during the Revolutionary era. Americans tasted new freedoms as they faced new challenges after the Revolutionary War. People of all backgrounds struggled together to forge their new nation. ■

HISTORY JOURNAL

Before reading the chapter, write about your understanding of the Revolutionary War and how you think the war may have changed people's lives.

VIRGINIA HISTORICAL SOCIETY

JAMES ARMISTEAD BEGAN CALLING HIMSELF "JAMES LAFAYETTE," IN HONOR OF THE MAN WHO HELPED FREE HIM.

SECTION 1

Toward Revolution

AUGUST 14, 1765: BOSTON CROWD PROTESTS NEW TAX

Tax Protest
Mobs of colonists vented their anger on stamp officers, who were appointed by the British to see that taxes were collected.

THE SOUND OF SCUFFLING FEET AND SHOUTING VOICES SHATTERED THE QUIET SUMMER EVENING. Hundreds of people, led by a poor, 28-year-old shoemaker named Ebenezer MacIntosh, stormed up the street. Men walking at the head of the crowd carried an effigy—a rag-stuffed dummy.

The effigy represented Andrew Oliver, a wealthy Boston merchant. Oliver had recently been made stamp officer for Massachusetts to help collect from the colonies a British tax authorized by the Stamp Act. Many Bostonians hated the tax; MacIntosh was leading a group to protest it.

The crowd carried the effigy through the streets of Boston. Then, after burning Oliver's effigy on a nearby hill, they attacked Oliver's luxurious house.

Oliver heard the crash of glass, the splintering of wood, and hoarse shouts. When the noise died down, Oliver found his "garden torn in pieces, his house broken open, his furniture destroyed." Standing before MacIntosh and his mob, Oliver "came to a sudden resolution to resign his office" as stamp agent. The common people had scored a victory.

On that hot August night, Ebenezer MacIntosh, the poor Boston shoemaker, found himself at the forefront of a movement that strained the bonds between Great Britain and its thirteen colonies. Yet MacIntosh did not always oppose the British. Only a few years before, he had proudly fought for Britain's colonies in the French and Indian War (also known as the Seven Years' War). As recently as 1763, he had joined with other colonists in celebrating Britain's victory over France in that war. In the intervening years, Britain's treatment of her subjects ignited the ire of MacIntosh and many other colonists.

AS YOU READ

Vocabulary
- external tax
- internal tax
- treason

Think About . . .
- what life was like in the thirteen English colonies in the 1760s.
- the changing relationship between Great Britain and the colonies in America at the dawn of the Revolutionary era.
- the origins of the Revolution.

Paying for Security

Parliament Taxes the Colonies

Britain's leaders celebrated the end of the war in Europe and North America as heartily as did the colonists. The British victory ended more than 70 years of fighting with France in North America. As a result of a treaty signed in February 1763, King George III took possession of all French territory east of the Mississippi River, including lands in Canada. Yet the decades of fighting had left the British government struggling with a large national debt. British politicians also faced the expense of paying for an army in North America to secure the new borders and defend the enlarged territory.

The Proclamation of 1763

After the British victory, settlers began moving into the newly acquired lands west of the Appalachians. New settlers claimed the Native American hunting grounds that the French had protected. In May 1763, Native American resentment erupted in a bloody uprising led by Pontiac, an Ottawa chief. Within a few months, Native Americans captured or destroyed British forts on the frontier and killed many settlers.

EASTERN NORTH AMERICA, 1763

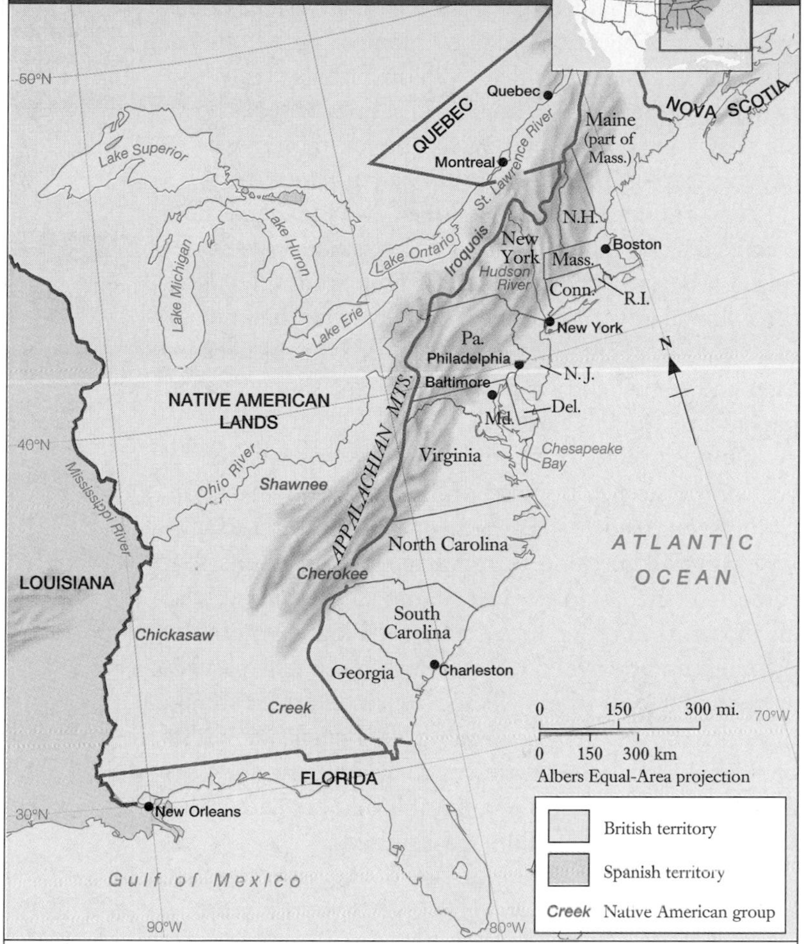

This 1763 map of North America reflects many national interests. *Who would settlers come in conflict with as they moved westward and claimed lands between the Appalachian Mountains and the Mississippi River?*

To prevent another war, which Britain could not afford, King George III issued the Proclamation of 1763. The document proclaimed that all lands west of the Appalachians were reserved for Native Americans and closed to colonial settlement. For the British, the proclamation preserved peace with the Native Americans and prevented colonists from moving westward, farther from Britain's control.

Some colonists, however, felt that Britain had slammed shut a door of opportunity. They deeply resented being forbidden to settle on lands they had helped win from France. The colonists' resentment grew when Parliament demanded that they help pay for the army that Britain maintained to defend the frontier.

The Sugar Act

Beginning in 1764 Parliament tried to collect a series of taxes from the colonies to ease the war debt and strengthen the British Empire. The colonists' reaction was strong; it was most violent in Boston. The Sugar Act hurt Boston especially, because that city depended heavily on shipping and trade. Payment of all duties, or taxes, on molasses and sugar imported to North America from places outside the British Empire would now be strictly enforced. The act also placed new or higher duties on other foreign imports such as textiles, coffee, and wine.

These new duties caused the price of goods in the colonies to skyrocket, hurting businesses and customers alike. Just as important, the act also restricted smugglers by toughening the enforcement of customs laws. Smuggling formed a sizable part of colonial trade, in part because customs duties were high. The act had the overall effect of widening the division between Britain and the colonies. Americans resented having no representatives in Parliament to determine how the British rulers would spend their tax money.

Boston merchants protested the Sugar Act with orderly petitions. "If these taxes are laid upon us, in any shape," one petition read, "without our having a legal representation where they are laid, are we not reduced . . . to the miserable status of tributary slaves?" Yet these petitions had little impact on Parliament, and the Sugar Act remained law.

The Stamp Act

In 1765 Parliament passed a tax on all official documents and publications in the colonies. To be official, marriage licenses, mortgages, diplomas, bills of sale, and newspapers had to bear an official stamp, or seal, showing that a duty had been paid. The tax money was to pay for keeping British troops in North America.

The Stamp Act affected almost everyone, and most colonists hated it. Landowners and business owners despised it because the tax money raised went directly to the colonial governor. Colonists themselves had no say in how it was spent. Poorer people hated the tax because they had to pay extra for everyday items such as newspapers and playing cards.

Opposition to the stamp tax focused not just on the cost of the stamps but also on the method of taxation. Colonists agreed that Parliament had the right to levy an **external tax,** one to regulate trade in goods that came into the colonies. The Stamp Act, however, was an **internal tax,** one levied on goods made within the colonies, and designed only to raise revenue. Colonists argued that only their elected representatives should have the right to levy internal taxes. Because colonists could not elect representatives to Parliament, they believed that the right to levy an internal tax should belong to their elected colonial assemblies.

Protests over the Stamp Act united the colonists. Daniel Dulany, an attorney from Maryland, wrote a pamphlet rejecting Britain's right to impose internal taxes on Americans. John Dickinson of Pennsylvania published a pamphlet that denied the authority of Parliament to tax the colonists in any form. It was James Otis, a Massachusetts lawyer, who gave the colonists their rallying cry with his statement, "Taxation without representation is tyranny!"

Tea Protests **Here colonists have tarred and feathered a tax collector and are forcing him to drink scalding hot tea.** *How did the Stamp Act unite both wealthy colonists and common people in protest against Britain?*

The Coming of the Revolution

Tensions Explode in the Colonies

The taxation crisis of the 1760s heated the debate between Britain and its colonies. Colonists argued that Parliament violated their cherished right as British subjects to consent to all taxes levied on them. Feelings of resentment grew. People had been asking, Who has the power to tax us? Now the question became, Who has the power to govern? A movement toward self-government began to take shape. Protests against British authority intensified and, in some cases, became violent.

Sons of Liberty

Men like Samuel Adams of Boston felt that speeches and petitions against unjust British laws were not enough. A genial yet cagey politician, Samuel Adams came from a respected family and had attended Harvard College. He ran his own business, but after 20 years he was deep in debt. By the 1760s Adams was very involved in local politics and sought support for his ideas from the people of Boston.

Throughout 1765 Adams and leaders in other colonies formed a network of local groups called the Sons of Liberty to organize opposition to the Stamp Act. Often led by men of high position, these groups did not hesitate to resort to violence. They destroyed the homes of British officials and forced stamp agents to resign. To enforce a boycott of British goods, the Sons of Liberty threatened merchants. Anyone who imported or sold British goods risked being smeared with hot tar and covered with feathers.

In October 1765 delegates from nine colonies met in New York City and drafted a petition demanding repeal of the Stamp Act. This protest was effective, but the economic impact of the boycott was much stronger. The combination forced Parliament to repeal the Stamp Act in 1766. In its place Parliament passed the Declaratory Act. This law flatly declared Parliament's right to make laws concerning the colonists without their consent.

The Boston Massacre

Conflict over taxation prompted Britain to send troops to Boston to enforce laws and maintain order. The presence of British soldiers only raised tensions. Clashes between citizens and soldiers became common in Boston. On the evening of March 5, 1770, the tensions exploded into violence in an event that came to be called the Boston Massacre.

Accounts of the incident vary, but most agree that it began when a mob of townspeople taunted a British sentry on duty. Other British soldiers, led by Captain Thomas Preston, came to the sentry's aid. Tempers flared. The crowd threw snowballs and rocks at the soldiers. In the confusion, shots rang out. Some reports say that one soldier's musket went off by mistake, and then other soldiers began to fire. Others say an unidentified person commanded the soldiers to fire. Three colonists, including Crispus Attucks, a sailor of African and Native American ancestry, lay dead. Two more colonists later died from their wounds. Captain Preston was put on trial and acquitted. Two of his men were convicted of manslaughter and were branded on the hand.

A period of uneasy calm followed the Boston Massacre. Samuel Adams continued to use the incident to stir up anti-British feelings, but no violent protests resulted.

New trouble began in 1773. Parliament passed the Tea Act to save the East India Company, a British trading company, from bankruptcy. According to this law, only the East India Company could sell tea to the colonies. Though the tea would sell for a lower price than Americans were used to paying, they would still have to pay the import tax on it. Most of all, colonists resented the East India Company's monopoly on selling tea. To protest the tea tax, Boston's Sons of Liberty disguised themselves as Mohawks and went to the pier one night. There they tossed 342 chests of tea into the harbor.

As punishment for the so-called Boston Tea Party, Parliament closed Boston Harbor to all shipping until the tea was paid for. General Thomas George Gage, commander of British troops in North America, took over as governor of the colony to restore order to the rebellious city.

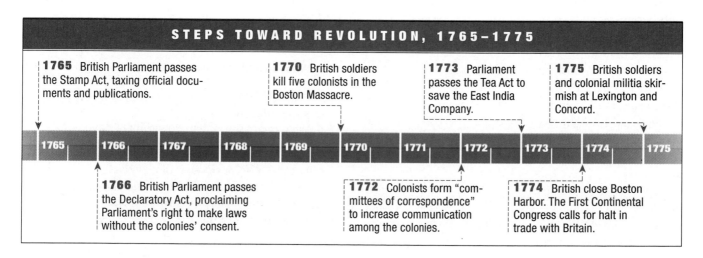

COURTESY, AMERICAN ANTIQUARIAN SOCIETY

Violence Erupts **This engraving is called *The Bloody Massacre Perpetrated in King Street.*** *Why would the colonists want to refer to the Boston shootings as a massacre?*

Committees of Correspondence

While Bostonians fought for their rights, people in other colonies also struggled against British control. Their struggle took different forms as tensions mounted. As early as the Stamp Act crisis in 1765, Virginia's assembly opposed Parliament with decrees worded so strongly that some colonists called them **treason,** or a betrayal of Britain. In 1768 merchants up and down the coast boycotted British goods to protest the Townshend Acts of 1767. Five years later, patriots from New

STEPS TOWARD REVOLUTION, 1765–1775

1765 British Parliament passes the Stamp Act, taxing official documents and publications.

1766 British Parliament passes the Declaratory Act, proclaiming Parliament's right to make laws without the colonies' consent.

1770 British soldiers kill five colonists in the Boston Massacre.

1772 Colonists form "committees of correspondence" to increase communication among the colonies.

1773 Parliament passes the Tea Act to save the East India Company.

1774 British close Boston Harbor. The First Continental Congress calls for halt in trade with Britain.

1775 British soldiers and colonial militia skirmish at Lexington and Concord.

1765 | 1766 | 1767 | 1768 | 1769 | 1770 | 1771 | 1772 | 1773 | 1774 | 1775

Hampshire to Virginia dumped or boycotted tea to protest the Tea Act. The Boston Tea Party was only the best known of these protests.

Most colonists, however, viewed the crisis with Britain as a local matter. A Philadelphia lawyer, a New England fisher, and a Carolina planter might all oppose a tax on tea, but they felt little in common with each other beyond that. Many colonists thought that Bostonians had brought trouble on themselves and felt no obligation to solve or share their problems.

A group in Boston tried to change that attitude in 1772 by forming what it called a "committee of correspondence." The committee would "state the rights of the colonists . . . and communicate and publish the same to the several towns and to the world." Within a year dozens of towns in Massachusetts and assemblies from nearly every colony had created similar letter-writing committees.

The letters carried along the muddy roads leading from colony to colony did much to bring North and South, town and country, closer together in the struggle for self-government. Farmers had been slow to join the protests against Britain, but now they too argued against unfair taxes. Many farmers organized against the British as city people had done earlier.

News in 1774 that the British had closed Boston Harbor circulated through the committees of correspondence and outraged Americans everywhere. This news especially distressed merchants and planters, for if Britain closed the main ports of their colonies, they would be ruined. So when Bostonians called for a meeting to discuss the crisis, twelve of the thirteen colonies sent representatives.

Continental Congress

Fifty-six men from twelve colonies traveled to Philadelphia late in the summer of 1774 for the First Continental Congress. Most of them had served in colonial assemblies, but few knew any of the other representatives. John Adams of Massachusetts wrote, "We have numberless prejudices to remove here." Nobody knew what to expect of this unprecedented—and perhaps treasonous—meeting.

The First Continental Congress called for a halt in trade with Great Britain and resolved to meet again in the spring of 1775. In the process of discussing the crisis that had brought them together, the delegates had succeeded in removing some of their prejudices against one another and helped make Boston's crisis an American crisis.

By 1775 the machinery of the British Empire—governors, councils, courts—had broken down. In its place grew a ramshackle system of local committees and congresses of men who ignored British authority.

© BONNIE MCGRATH/RAINBOW

Old North Bridge At this site in Concord, Massachusetts, militia skirmished with British soldiers sent to destroy rebel supply stores. *Why was the exchange of gunfire at Lexington later referred to as "the shot heard round the world"?*

General Gage, the governor of Massachusetts, received orders from London to arrest just such a group of men. On an April night in 1775, 700 British soldiers marched toward Concord, about 15 miles from Boston. At the town of Lexington, 70 American militia stood waiting. After a brief skirmish at dawn, the British left 8 Americans dead on the village green and marched on to Concord.

At Concord, fighting again broke out. As the British began the return march to Boston, colonists hid behind rocks, trees, and fences all along the road and picked off scores of British troops. By the time the British forces reached Boston, they had suffered 273 casualties, and 88 Americans had fallen. The struggle to defend the colonists' rights had become a war.

Section Review

Vocabulary

1. Define: external tax, internal tax, treason.

Checking Facts

2. What were the purposes of the Proclamation of 1763 from the British point of view?
3. What were the consequences of the Sugar Act?

Critical Thinking

Making Inferences

4. What might the British government have done to prevent revolution?

Linking Across Time

5. Under what conditions might the people of a country feel justified in revolting against their government today?

The Declaration *of* Independence

In Congress, July 4, 1776. The unanimous Declaration of the thirteen united States of America,

The printed text of the document shows the spelling and punctuation of the parchment original. To aid in comprehension, selected words and their definitions appear in the side margin, along with other explanatory notes.

Preamble

When in the Course of human events, it becomes necessary for one people to dissolve the political bands which have connected them with another, and to assume among the powers of the earth, the separate and equal station to which the Laws of Nature and Nature's God entitle them, a decent respect to the opinions of mankind requires that they should declare the causes which impel them to the separation.—

impel *force*

Declaration of Natural Rights

We hold these truths to be self-evident, that all men are created equal, that they are endowed by their Creator with certain unalienable Rights, that among these are Life, Liberty, and the pursuit of Happiness.

endowed *provided*

That to secure these rights, Governments are instituted among Men, deriving their just powers from the consent of the governed,—

People create governments to ensure that their natural rights are protected.

That whenever any Form of Government becomes destructive of these ends, it is the Right of the People to alter or to abolish it, and to institute new Government, laying its foundation on such principles and organizing its powers in such form, as to them shall seem most likely to effect their Safety and Happiness. Prudence, indeed, will dictate that Governments long established should not be changed for light and transient causes; and accordingly all experience hath shewn, that mankind are more disposed to suffer, while evils are sufferable, than to right themselves by abolishing the forms to which they are accustomed. But when a long train of abuses and usurpations, pursuing invariably the same Object evinces a design to reduce them under absolute Despotism, it is their right, it is their duty, to throw off such Government, and to provide new Guards for their future security.—

If a government does not serve its purpose, the people have a right to abolish it. Then the people have the right and duty to create a new government that will safeguard their security.

Despotism *unlimited power*

List of Grievances

Such has been the patient sufferance of these Colonies; and such is now the necessity which constrains them to alter their former Systems of Government. The history of the present King of Great Britain is a history of repeated injuries and usurpations, all having in direct object the establishment of an absolute Tyranny over these States. To prove this, let Facts be submitted to a candid world.—

usurpations *unjust uses of power*

He has refused his Assent to Laws, the most wholesome and necessary for the public good.—

Each paragraph lists alleged injustices of George III.

He has forbidden his Governors to pass Laws of immediate and pressing importance, unless suspended in their operation till his Assent should be obtained; and when so suspended, he has utterly neglected to attend to them.—

relinquish *give up*
inestimable *priceless*

He has refused to pass other Laws for the accommodation of large districts of people, unless those people would relinquish the right of Representation in the Legislature, a right inestimable to them and formidable to tyrants only.—

He has called together legislative bodies at places unusual, uncomfortable, and distant from the depository of their public Records, for the sole purpose of fatiguing them into compliance with his measures.—

He has dissolved Representative Houses repeatedly, for opposing with manly firmness his invasions on the rights of the people.—

Annihilation *destruction*

convulsions *violent disturbances*

He has refused for a long time, after such dissolutions, to cause others to be elected; whereby the Legislative powers, incapable of Annihilation, have returned to the People at large for their exercise; the State remaining in the meantime exposed to all the dangers of invasion from without, and convulsions within.—

Naturalization of Foreigners *process by which foreign-born persons become citizens*

He has endeavoured to prevent the population of these States; for that purpose obstructing the Laws for Naturalization of Foreigners; refusing to pass others to encourage their migrations hither, and raising the conditions of new Appropriations of Lands.—

He has obstructed the Administration of Justice, by refusing his Assent to Laws for establishing Judiciary powers.—

tenure *term*

He has made Judges dependent on his Will alone, for the tenure of their offices, and the amount and payment of their salaries.—

Refers to the British troops sent to the colonies after the French and Indian War.

He has erected a multitude of New Offices, and sent hither swarms of Officers to harass our people, and eat out their substance.—

He has kept among us, in times of peace, Standing Armies without the Consent of our legislatures.—

He has affected to render the Military independent of and superior to the Civil power.—

Refers to the 1766 Declaratory Act.

He has combined with others to subject us to a jurisdiction foreign to our constitution, and unacknowledged by our laws; giving his Assent to their Acts of pretended Legislation:—

quartering *lodging*

For quartering large bodies of troops among us:—

For protecting them, by a mock Trial, from punishment for any Murders which they should commit on the Inhabitants of these States:—

For cutting off our Trade with all parts of the world:—

For imposing Taxes on us without our Consent:—

For depriving us in many cases, of the benefits of Trial by Jury:—

For transporting us beyond Seas to be tried for pretended offences:—

Refers to the 1774 Quebec Act.

render *make*

For abolishing the free System of English Laws in a neighbouring Province, establishing therein an Arbitrary government, and enlarging its Boundaries so as to render it at once an example and fit instrument for introducing the same absolute rule into these Colonies:—

For taking away our Charters, abolishing our most valuable Laws, and altering fundamentally the Forms of our Governments:—

For suspending our own Legislatures, and declaring themselves invested with power to legislate for us in all cases whatsoever.—

abdicated *given up*

He has abdicated Government here, by declaring us out of his Protection and waging War against us.—

He has plundered our seas, ravaged our Coasts, burnt our towns, and destroyed the Lives of our people.—

perfidy *violation of trust*

He is at this time transporting large Armies of foreign Mercenaries to compleat the works of death, desolation and tyranny, already begun with circumstances of Cruelty & perfidy scarcely paralleled in the most barbarous ages, and totally unworthy the Head of a civilized nation.—

He has constrained our fellow Citizens taken Captive on the high Seas to bear Arms against their Country, to become the executioners of their friends and Brethren, or to fall themselves by their Hands.—

He has excited domestic insurrections amongst us, and has endeavoured to bring on the inhabitants of our frontiers, the merciless Indian Savages, whose known rule of warfare, is an undistinguished destruction of all ages, sexes and conditions.

insurrections *rebellions*

In every stage of these Oppressions We have Petitioned for Redress in the most humble terms: Our repeated Petitions have been answered only by repeated injury. A Prince, whose character is thus marked by every act which may define a Tyrant, is unfit to be the ruler of a free people.

Petitioned for Redress *asked formally for a correction of wrongs*

Nor have We been wanting in attentions to our British brethren. We have warned them from time to time of attempts by their legislature to extend an unwarrantable jurisdiction over us. We have reminded them of the circumstances of our emigration and settlement here. We have appealed to their native justice and magnanimity, and we have conjured them by the ties of our common kindred to disavow these usurpations, which would inevitably interrupt our connections and correspondence. They too have been deaf to the voice of justice and of consanguinity. We must, therefore, acquiesce in the necessity, which denounces our Separation, and hold them, as we hold the rest of mankind, Enemies in War, in Peace Friends.—

unwarrantable jurisdiction *unjustified authority*

consanguinity *originating from the same ancestor*

Resolution of Independence by the United States

We, therefore, the Representatives of the united States of America, in General Congress, Assembled, appealing to the Supreme Judge of the world for the rectitude of our intentions, do, in the Name, and by Authority of the good People of these Colonies, solemnly publish and declare, That these United Colonies are, and of Right ought to be Free and Independent States; that they are Absolved from all Allegiance to the British Crown, and that all political connection between them and the State of Great Britain, is and ought to be totally dissolved; and that as Free and Independent States, they have full Power to levy War, conclude Peace, contract Alliances, establish Commerce, and to do all other Acts and Things which Independent States may of right do.—

rectitude *rightness*

And for the support of this Declaration, with a firm reliance on the protection of divine Providence, we mutually pledge to each other our Lives, our Fortunes and our sacred Honour.

The signers, as representatives of the American people, declared the colonies independent from Great Britain. Most members signed the document on August 2, 1776.

John Hancock
President from Massachusetts

GEORGIA
Button Gwinnett
Lyman Hall
George Walton

NORTH CAROLINA
William Hooper
Joseph Hewes
John Penn

SOUTH CAROLINA
Edward Rutledge
Thomas Heyward, Jr.
Thomas Lynch, Jr.
Arthur Middleton

MARYLAND
Samuel Chase
William Paca
Thomas Stone
Charles Carroll of Carrollton

VIRGINIA
George Wythe
Richard Henry Lee
Thomas Jefferson
Benjamin Harrison
Thomas Nelson, Jr.
Francis Lightfoot Lee
Carter Braxton

PENNSYLVANIA
Robert Morris
Benjamin Rush
Benjamin Franklin
John Morton
George Clymer
James Smith
George Taylor
James Wilson
George Ross

DELAWARE
Caesar Rodney
George Read
Thomas McKean

NEW YORK
William Floyd
Philip Livingston
Francis Lewis
Lewis Morris

NEW JERSEY
Richard Stockton
John Witherspoon
Francis Hopkinson
John Hart
Abraham Clark

NEW HAMPSHIRE
Josiah Bartlett
William Whipple
Matthew Thornton

MASSACHUSETTS
Samuel Adams
John Adams
Robert Treat Paine
Elbridge Gerry

RHODE ISLAND
Stephen Hopkins
William Ellery

CONNECTICUT
Samuel Huntington
William Williams
Oliver Wolcott
Roger Sherman

SPORTS: Sons of Liberty restrict extravagance of public sport as war with British approaches.

One Day in History

Wednesday, April 19, 1775

MARKET BASKET

Here is where money will go:

Ferry prices for taking cargo across the Susquehanna River at Wright's Ferry in Continental currency

A six-horse wagon $90
A horse and rider $12

THE BETTMANN ARCHIVES

Prices at the Ellery Tavern in Gloucester, Massachusetts: s.=shilling; d.=pence

Lodging for two .... 6d.
Bread and cheese .... 7d.
One dinner .... 9d.
One mug cider .... 1.5d.
Breakfast .... 9.5d.
15 lbs. (6.81 kg) tobacco .... 7s. 6d.

PRINT COLLECTION MIRIAM AND IRA D. WALLACH DIVISION OF ART, PRINTS AND PHOTOGRAPHS THE NEW YORK PUBLIC LIBRARY

British Assault on Minutemen British troops led by Lieutenant Francis Smith vastly outnumbered the armed minutemen they fired upon in Lexington.

The Shot Heard Around the World

Patriot minutemen and British redcoats clash at Lexington and Concord

LEXINGTON, MA—Fighting broke out today in Lexington and Concord between British troops and volunteer minutemen. An unconfirmed number of deaths and casualties occurred.

Boston patriots learned last night of a plan for a British attack on the colonial arms depot at Concord. Paul Revere and William Dawes rode to warn the people of Lexington and Concord that the British were on the march.

In Lexington about 70 armed minutemen confronted some 700 British troops. Although no one knows who fired the first shot, 8 patriots lay dead when the smoke cleared. One group of redcoats then clashed with minutemen at the North Bridge in Concord, causing more casualties. The British then retreated to Boston, beset by residents who fired at them from behind stone walls and trees. It appears that a war for our freedom has begun.

NATION: The Continental Congress creates its own postal system and names Benjamin Franklin postmaster general.

Daniel Boone Cuts New Road

FORT BOONE, KY—With about 30 woodchoppers, Daniel Boone completed the Wilderness Road, which is 250 miles (402.25 km) long and runs through the Allegheny Mountains from North Carolina to Otter Creek near the Kentucky River. Settlers from Virginia and North Carolina plan to follow this road to found a fourteenth colony.

Daniel Boone

Treaty With Cherokee

KENTUCKY—By the terms of a treaty with the Cherokee, the Transylvania Land Company acquired all land south of the Ohio River, north of the Cumberland River, and west of the Appalachians in exchange for goods worth $10.

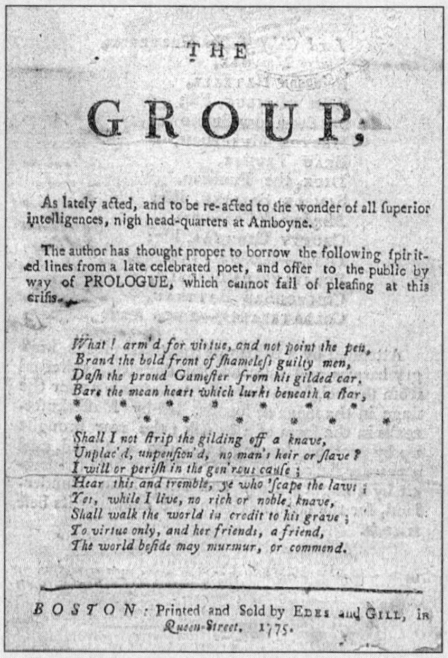
THE

GROUP,

As lately acted, and to be re-acted to the wonder of all superior intelligences, nigh head-quarters at Amboyne.

The author has thought proper to borrow the following spirited lines from a late celebrated poet, and offer to the public by way of PROLOGUE, which cannot fail of pleasing at this crisis.

What! arm'd for virtue, and not point the pen,
Brand the bold front of shameless guilty men,
Dash the proud Gamester from his gilded car,
Bare the mean heart which lurks beneath a star,
* * * * * * * *
Shall I not strip the gilding off a knave,
Unplac'd, unpension'd, no man's heir or slave?
I will or perish in the gen'rous cause;
Hear this and tremble, ye who 'scape the laws;
Yet, while I live, no rich or noble knave,
Shall walk the world in credit to his grave;
To virtue only, and her friends, a friend,
The world beside may murmur, or commend.

BOSTON: Printed and Sold by EDES and GILL, in Queen-Street. 1775.

***The Group,* a play about Puritan leaders written by Mercy Warren, draws enthusiastic audiences.**

An ASTRONOMICAL DIARY: Or, ALMANACK For the Year of Christian Æra, 1775. By NATHANAEL LOW.

The VIRTUOUS PATRIOT at the Hour of Death.

Nathaniel Law's *Astronomical Diary,* or *Almanack,* is published for 1775.

IN PRINT

Women's Rights Written by Thomas Paine, the first article to expound women's rights in North America appears in *Pennsylvania Magazine.*

MUSIC

- **Popular song:** "Yankee Doodle"
- **First pianoforte:** John Behrent of Philadelphia makes North America's first pianoforte.

To the CURIOUS.

To be seen at Major Leavenworth's Stable, opposite Mr. Lothrop's, State-Stree[t]

Two CAMELS,

Male and Female, lately imported from

ARABIA.

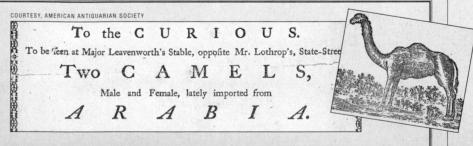

Price of Admittance for a Gentleman or Lady 9 pence

SECTION 2

War for Independence

MAY 1775: SECOND CONTINENTAL CONGRESS MEETS

BETTMANN ARCHIVES

A Rallying Cry for Independence
Paine's *Common Sense* was the most widely circulated pamphlet in America in 1776.

ON MAY 10, 1775, THREE WEEKS AFTER THE BRITISH SPILLED COLONISTS' BLOOD AT THE BATTLES OF LEXINGTON AND CONCORD, THE DELEGATES OF THE SECOND CONTINENTAL CONGRESS ASSEMBLED IN PHILADELPHIA. They faced the challenge of leading thirteen colonies against the greatest empire and strongest army on earth. The Congress attempted to deal with that awesome task in two ways. First, the delegates called for the formation of a Continental Army of 20,000 men. Second, the delegates attempted to resolve the crisis with Britain. They sent King George III a petition blaming Parliament for the current problems and asking for the King's help in solving them. In December 1775, King George rejected the petition, declared the colonies in rebellion, and sent about 20,000 more British soldiers to America.

One month later, in January 1776, colonists began reading a pamphlet that helped motivate and prepare them for independence. *Common Sense* appeared first in Philadelphia where its author, Thomas Paine, lived. Paine grew up in England and for a time worked as a tax collector. After meeting Benjamin Franklin, then the most famous American alive, Paine decided to move to Philadelphia in 1774 and soon became involved in the colonists' fight for independence.

Unlike other revolutionary writers, Paine wrote in the direct, colorful language of America's farmers and city workers. Paine called King George "the Royal Brute of Britain," and asserted that "a government of our own is our own national right." In 3 months, people purchased about 120,000 copies of *Common Sense*. Paine's arguments persuaded many Americans to join the cause.

AS YOU READ

Vocabulary
- revolution
- suffrage

Think About . . .
- how the Second Continental Congress prepared for war with Britain.
- how the strategies used by George Washington helped win the war.
- the ways that the Revolutionary War affected the lives of the colonists on the battlefield and at home.

Declaring Independence

Planning the Revolution

Compare the number of British and American victories between 1775 and 1781. *Prior to 1777 in what region of the country did most battles occur?*

Congress felt this popular push for independence. When it met in Philadelphia in June 1776, the Congress formed a committee to draft a declaration of the colonies' independence. The committee called on 33-year-old Thomas Jefferson, a lawyer from Virginia, to write it. He reluctantly agreed.

The tall, redheaded Jefferson owned a large plantation, and in the leisure hours of a planter's life, he pursued a variety of interests: law, architecture, music, science, and politics. The document this cultured lawyer created consisted of 3 parts. The first part contained a statement of what the Congress believed a government should do. "All men are created equal," Jefferson wrote, ". . . they are endowed by their Creator with certain unalienable Rights; . . . among these are Life, Liberty, and the pursuit of Happiness." Jefferson stated that governments existed to "secure these rights." The second part contained 27 "reasons for separation" from Britain, and the third part consisted of a declaration of independence from Britain.

Congress discussed the declaration for several days before voting unanimously for independence on July 2, 1776. On July 4 the delegates adopted the Declaration of Independence. Congress now turned to the business of steering the new nation, the United States of America, through a **revolution,** a violent struggle to overthrow a government.

Winning the War

Congress had made its most important decision about the war a year earlier when it called for a commander for the Continental Army. John Adams worried that the war would remain New England's war unless a Southerner took command. A Southern commander, reasoned Adams, would bring the whole nation—North, Middle, and South—into the war together.

Adams had in mind for the job a Virginian named George Washington. Washington had fought in the French and Indian War, where he had been an able soldier and leader. Delegates to the Congress approved of the aloof 43-year-old Virginian as the commander of their army. Washington had the qualities they admired in themselves and others: rank, wealth, and integrity.

Washington also had the discipline needed to turn a mass of poorly equipped, poorly trained men into an army that could survive the predicted long years of fighting. During the six years of the war, Washington's army received little support from the Congress or the states, which bickered throughout. Still, Washington managed to maintain order through defeat, freezing winters, and starvation.

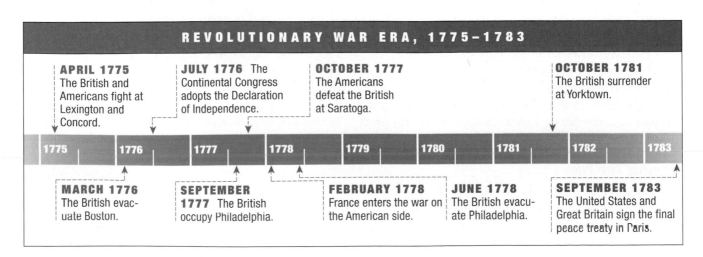

Portrait of a General This oil painting, *George Washington at the Battle of Princeton,* was done by Charles Willson Peale. *Why did the British finally surrender in 1781?*

In the first years of the war, the British aimed to divide the rebellious colonies, cutting New England off from the rest of the nation. Only a surprise American victory at Saratoga, New York, in 1777 foiled their plan. The victory boosted the Americans' spirits and persuaded the French to enter the war to fight against their British rivals. After Saratoga, the British focused their energies in the South, where they hoped the region's many Loyalists, those who supported the British, might help them.

Washington learned valuable lessons during the first years of the war. The Americans, he knew, must avoid major battles with the better-trained British troops. They had to learn to use surprise tactics and familiar terrain to their advantage. If the Americans could not defeat the British in open combat, at least they could drag the war on until the British no longer cared to fight. This strategy paid off when Washington, supported by French troops and the French navy, trapped a large British force at Chesapeake Bay in Yorktown, Virginia, in 1781. The British surrendered at Yorktown; it became clear that after six years and no conclusive victories, the British no longer cared to fight, nor could they afford to.

The war finally ended in 1783, when Congress sent John Adams, Benjamin Franklin, and John Jay to negotiate a peace treaty with Britain. In the treaty, the British promised to remove their troops from America "with all convenient speed," to recognize officially the independence of the United States of America, and to agree that the Mississippi River was the nation's western border.

Surviving the War

Victory Through Sacrifice

More than 250,000 American soldiers fought for 6 years to break the back of British rule. During that time 1 out of every 10 Americans who fought died; the British captured and occupied most major cities, including Boston, New York, and Philadelphia; and many American lives were reshaped by the American Revolution.

When America mobilized for war in 1775 and 1776, all levels of society became involved. Elite politicians

REVOLUTIONARY WAR ERA, 1775–1783

APRIL 1775 The British and Americans fight at Lexington and Concord.

MARCH 1776 The British evacuate Boston.

JULY 1776 The Continental Congress adopts the Declaration of Independence.

SEPTEMBER 1777 The British occupy Philadelphia.

OCTOBER 1777 The Americans defeat the British at Saratoga.

FEBRUARY 1778 France enters the war on the American side.

JUNE 1778 The British evacuate Philadelphia.

OCTOBER 1781 The British surrender at Yorktown.

SEPTEMBER 1783 The United States and Great Britain sign the final peace treaty in Paris.

1775 1776 1777 1778 1779 1780 1781 1782 1783

designed state and national governments. Men with military experience volunteered for army positions. Some merchants loaned money to the army and to the Congress; others made fortunes from wartime government contracts. Farmers tried to provide food for armies.

On the Battlefield

These many groups contributed to the war effort, but the poorest Americans did most of the actual fighting. Young city laborers, farm boys, indentured servants, and sometimes enslaved persons all fought bravely. A lack of money, food, and supplies made the usual wartime experiences—boredom, disease, bloodshed—worse for the soldiers in the Continental Army. In 1778 one young American gave this nightmarish description of a soldier's life: "Poor food, hard lodging, cold weather, fatigue, nasty clothes, nasty cookery."

Only the horror of battle relieved boredom. Ranks of soldiers standing in open fields fired their muskets once, reloaded, and fired again. Orderly troop movements soon broke down into hand-to-hand combat; soldiers inflicted many wounds with bayonets and knives. Mud, smoke, blood, curses, and cannon shot flew about the battlefield. Medical treatment barely existed on or off the battlefield, and most wounds were fatal.

African Americans also stood and fell on the battlefields of the Revolutionary War. One enslaved laborer named Jehu Grant escaped from his master and joined the colonists when he "saw liberty poles and people all engaged for the purpose of freedom." Yet only about 5,000 of the 500,000 African Americans living in the colonies served in the Continental Army during the war. Many more sided with the British, who promised them freedom if they fought. As many as 20,000 enslaved persons in the Carolinas and Georgia joined the British.

Many Native Americans also sided with the British. The British represented a last hope for keeping land-hungry Americans out of Native American territories. During the war, colonists fought Native Americans in bloody battles, creating long-lasting bitter feelings.

SUPPLYING THE CONTINENTAL ARMY

When George Washington was appointed commander of the army, there was no existing army and there were no resources to support one. Due to economic conditions in the colonies during the Revolutionary War, Washington faced the continual challenge of obtaining and paying for his soldiers' basic needs.

Economic conditions in the colonies…

Trade Stops
- No more manufactured goods from England
- No more salt to preserve meat and fish from British West Indies
- No export markets for colonists' crops and raw materials

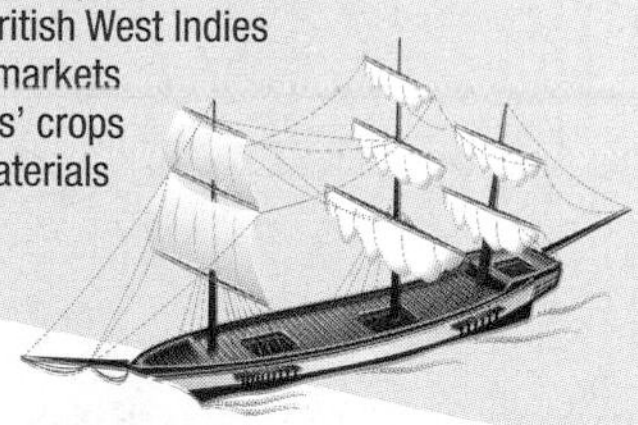

Industry Lags
- Formerly imported goods had to be made in colonies
- New sawmills, salt works, and granaries strained to meet citizen and army needs

No Stable Currency
- No uniform money system—at least 15 different types of money in circulation
- No funds to pay for war
- Congress issues Continental dollar of little or no value

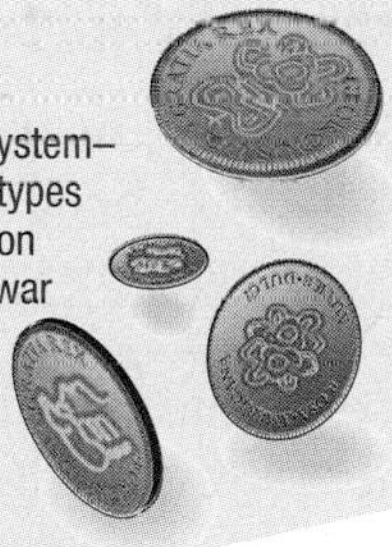

January 22, 1777
'In a word, I believe I may with truth add, that I do not think that any officer since the creation ever had such a variety of difficulties and perplexities to encounter as I have.'
—excerpt from one of Washington's letters to his stepson

Left the army in need of:

Flour and Salt
- No exports of agricultural goods, so supplies were low
- Many farmers were away fighting in war
- Farmers did not want to accept Continental dollars
- With no imports, salt supplies were low
- Price of salt rose from $1 to $36 per bushel

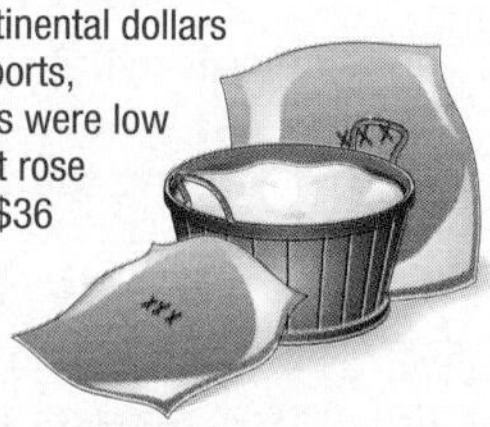

Shoes and Cloth
- Had to be made in colonies
- Merchants hoarded supplies and overcharged for them
- Soldiers brought clothes and shoes from home

Guns
- New armories could not supply army needs
- Soldiers brought their own and took British guns after battles
- France eventually sold guns to colonies

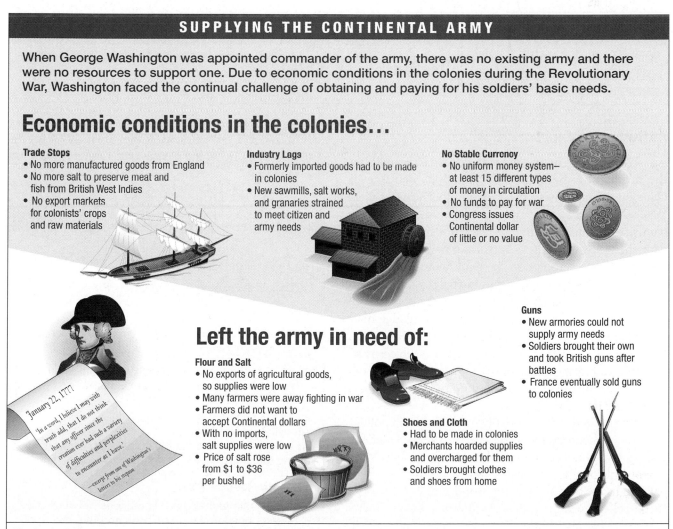

The lack of supplies left many soldiers in the Continental Army in tattered clothing, and some had to resort to eating their horses' food. *What were the three major economic problems in the colonies that caused these conditions?*

LOS ANGELES COUNTY MUSEUM OF ART, (DETAIL) BICENTENNIAL GIFT OF MR. AND MRS. J.M. SCHAAF, MR. AND MRS. WILLIAM D. WITHERSPOON, MR. AND MRS. CHARLES C. SHOEMAKER, MR. AND MRS. JULIAN GANZ, JR.

Home Front Tactics Artist Emanuel Leutze portrayed the plight of many American colonists during the Revolutionary War in this 1852 painting, *Mrs. Schuyler Burning Her Wheat Fields on the Approach of the British.* *In what other ways did the Revolutionary War change the lives of women?*

At Home

After the war, many soldiers returned to homes that the deaths of fathers, brothers, and sons had forever changed. Families were changed in other ways as well. Wives had managed farms and businesses while husbands served in the army. Other women had traveled with the army, working as cooks and nurses. These experiences gave satisfaction to many women who had never owned property nor had **suffrage,** the right to vote. Women began to express their thoughts more freely on such subjects as politics. As Philadelphia's Anne Emlen wrote to her husband in 1777, "How shall I impose a silence upon myself when the subject is so very interesting, so much engrossing conversation—and what every member of the community is more or less concerned in?"

Women actively and openly participating in politics was a new phenomenon. In less than 20 years American society had changed in unpredictable and lasting ways. A group of colonies had challenged their governing country, fought the best army in the world, and won the right to be self-governing states. As the war ended, many Americans openly wondered how their experiment in self-government would eventually turn out. "The answer to the question," said Thomas Paine, "can America be happy under a government of her own, is short and simple—as happy as she pleases; she hath a blank sheet to write upon."

Section Review

Vocabulary

1. Define: revolution, suffrage.

Checking Facts

2. What did the Second Continental Congress do to prepare for war with Britain?
3. What battle tactics did George Washington employ with success against the British?

Critical Thinking

Identifying Alternatives

4. What alternatives did the colonists have to fighting the British in the Revolutionary War?

Linking Across Time

5. Explain similarities and differences between the effects of war on the colonists and the effects of war on people today.

Study and Writing Skill

INTERPRETING A PRIMARY SOURCE

Learning the Skill

A primary source is direct evidence of an event, idea, or development. It is obtained firsthand, such as oral or written accounts from actual participants. Examples of such primary sources are official documents, speeches, diaries, autobiographies, and letters. A primary source may also consist of physical objects, such as tools or weapons, or visual evidence such as paintings, photographs, maps, or videotapes.

In contrast with a primary source, a secondary source is a written, oral, or visual account created after an event, usually produced using information from primary sources. Textbooks and biographies are examples of secondary sources.

Interpreting primary sources is a skill you can practice. One primary source to examine is the Declaration of Independence on pages 61–63. As you continue to read *American Odyssey,* you will encounter other primary source documents and speeches. Primary sources help to present a reliable and accurate picture of history. The ability to interpret a primary source allows you to make your own judgment about a historical event, one not based on secondhand interpretations.

I long to hear that you have declared independence. And by the way, in the new code of laws that I suppose you will make, I wish you would remember the ladies and be more generous and favorable to them than your ancestors. Do not put such unlimited power in the hands of husbands. Remember, all men would be tyrants if they could. If particular care and attention is not paid to the ladies, we are determined to stir up a rebellion and will not regard ourselves as bound by any laws in which we have had no voice or representation.

A Wife's Request This excerpt is from a letter Abigail Adams wrote to her husband when the Second Continental Congress was considering the Declaration of Independence. *What do her words suggest about her character?*

Interpreting a Primary Source

To interpret a primary source, use the following steps:

a. Examine the origins of the document or material to determine if it is a primary source.

b. Read the document and summarize the main ideas in your own words.

c. Read through it again, this time looking for details that support the main ideas.

d. Give an interpretation of the material in your own words.

To round out your interpretation, try putting the document or material within the context of what you know about history. It may be necessary to look at the person or people who created the source, to examine why it was created, or to explore the motive behind it. Sometimes, just looking at the title can give you insights.

Practicing the Skill

Read the passage from the Declaration of Independence and answer the questions that follow.

We hold these truths to be self-evident: that all men are created equal, that they are endowed by their Creator with certain unalienable rights; that among these are life, liberty, and the pursuit of happiness.

1. How do you know that the Declaration of Independence is a primary source?

2. What is the main idea of the passage?

3. What are the details?

4. What do you know about the writers of the Declaration of Independence?

5. Explain what you think this passage means.

Applying the Skill

Read the passage from the letter above, and give your interpretation of it as a primary source.

Additional Practice

For additional practice, see Reinforcing Skills on page 77.

SECTION 3

Creating a New America

MAY 10, 1776: CONGRESS RECOMMENDS FORMING STATE GOVERNMENTS

ON APRIL 22, 1776, JOHN ADAMS WROTE TO HIS FRIEND, JAMES WARREN, ABOUT THE REVOLUTION THAT HAD JUST BEGUN. Adams wrote that South Carolina had already adopted a constitution:

> The news from South Carolina has aroused and animated all the continent. It has spread a visible joy, and if North Carolina and Virginia should follow the example, it will spread through the rest of the colonies like electric fire.
>
> —John Adams, from a letter to James Warren

NATIONAL PORTRAIT GALLERY, SMITHSONIAN INSTITUTION/ART RESOURCE, NY

A Leader of the Revolutionary Era
John Adams served as the second President of the United States from 1797 to 1801.

At Adams's urging, the Congress officially recommended that each colony "adopt such a government as shall, in the opinion of the representatives of the people, best conduce to the happiness and safety of their constituents in particular, and America in general."

For the colonies, forming new governments was anything but a luxury. In colony after colony, royal colonial governments had collapsed at the onset of the war. After dissolving the colonial assemblies that had so boldly challenged royal authority, the British governors had escaped as best they could. Wartime responsibilities dictated the need for governmental authority to muster troops, collect money, and protect the public safety. Now the colonies hastily embarked on the daunting task of creating their own governments.

The idea that ordinary citizens could plan their own governments, draft written constitutions, and vote their approval of self-government represented something new in history, and Americans knew it. Crafting individual state constitutions also provided a rehearsal for the process of creating the national constitution during the decade that followed.

AS YOU READ

Vocabulary

- constitution
- abolition
- status quo
- coverture

Think About . . .

- how the state constitutions differed from colonial charters under British rule.
- the differences between the state constitutions of Virginia, Massachusetts, and Pennsylvania.
- how the lives of women and enslaved African Americans changed in the Revolutionary War era.

State Constitutions

A Variety of Democratic Documents

The British system on which colonists based their ideas of government did not reside in a **constitution,** one written document of a plan of government, but rather in a miscellaneous collection of laws and court cases that had developed over centuries. In contrast, American colonial leaders planned that state constitutions, and eventually the national constitution, would be documents written clearly, concisely, and specifically so that anyone who read a copy could understand the law.

Thomas Jefferson realized that the colonies could win the war for independence but lose the Revolution if they failed at these experiments in self-government: "In truth," he said, "self-government is the whole object of the present controversy." During the tumultuous war for independence, each state drafted a constitution that established self-government.

Virtually every state limited voting and government service to white male property holders. Still, most of the new constitutions established state governments that were more democratic than the colonial regimes they replaced. In place of governors appointed by a king, state executives now had to face elections. Furthermore, elected governors would wield less power than had their appointed predecessors, giving greater power to popularly elected assemblies. These assemblies in turn grew larger as farmers and artisans clamored to be represented.

Connecticut and Rhode Island merely adopted their colonial charters, carefully deleting all references to the British Crown. The other 11 states, awed by the opportunity before them, began afresh. In 1776 alone, 8 states crafted new constitutions. By 1780, all 13 states had adopted written constitutions.

Virginia's Conservative Constitution

In several states, conservatives drew up plans for governments that closely resembled the colonial regimes they replaced. For example, the Virginia constitution of 1776, drafted by Thomas Jefferson, preserved intact almost all of the institutions of the colonial era, including slavery. Though Jefferson had inserted a section in the constitution's first draft proposing **abolition,** an end to the practice of slavery, his attempt failed to win approval. Virginia's governor, now elected annually by the legislature and denied the power of the veto, held a somewhat weaker position than before the Revolution. On the other hand, Virginia's new House of Delegates looked nearly identical to its old House of Burgesses. The continuation of prewar property qualifications for voters as well as for officeholders ensured that wealthy landowners would still represent Virginians. Members of many of the same families who had served before the war continued to hold elected office after the war.

If its constitution maintained the **status quo,** or existing conditions, Virginia's Bill of Rights established a bold new tradition. This document, written by George Mason, enumerated rights, such as a jury trial and freedom of the press, that free citizens could expect from their representative governments. The Virginia Bill of Rights prompted other states to include similar documents in their constitutions. It also provided a model for the Bill of Rights that eventually crowned the national Constitution of 1787.

A Radical Document for Pennsylvania

Compared to the conservative Virginians, the liberals who wrote constitutions in other states sought to redistribute power more equitably. Vermont, Georgia, and Pennsylvania—a state that bordered Virginia—crafted the most liberal documents of all.

Pennsylvania, for example, cast off the British model of a balanced government consisting of two legislative houses and an executive, the governor. In the vacuum created by the departure of colonial leaders, the radical politicians who wrote Pennsylvania's constitution established a single legislative house. Its members would be elected each year and its debates would be open to the public. Going even further, the document also abolished the requirement that persons holding public

CULVER PICTURES

The Artisan Spirit Many hardworking blacksmiths and other artisans looked forward to better representation in state government after the Revolution. *How could they participate?*

office be property owners and opened the vote to any white male adult who paid taxes. The preamble that began the constitution clearly predicted the end of African slavery with its suggestion that government should "provide for future improvements, without partiality for or prejudice against any particular class, sect, or denomination of men whatever."

Even in liberal Pennsylvania, however, the long list of residents denied the vote included servants, dependent sons, the poor, Native Americans, and women. In only one state, for a brief period, did women get the vote. New Jersey's 1776 constitution granted suffrage to "all free inhabitants" who met property and residency requirements. Property-owning New Jersey women took advantage of their voting rights until their state reversed that ruling in 1807.

Constitutional Convention in Massachusetts

Like Virginia's conservative constitution and unlike Pennsylvania's liberal one, the Massachusetts document divided political power between a governor and two legislative houses. One house, the assembly, would represent the common people. Because the other house, the senate, would look after propertied interests, its members were required to own three times as much property as assemblymen. Constitutional architect John Adams defended this balance of power, saying, "power must be opposed to power, force to force . . . interest to interest . . . and passion to passion."

COURTESY MASSACHUSETTS HISTORICAL SOCIETY

Abigail Adams During the war her letters provided her husband with information about the British in Boston. *What else did her letters to her husband reveal?*

However conservative its constitution, Massachusetts took a radical new path to writing the document. Opposed to letting the existing legislature write the constitution, as most states had done, a Concord town meeting in October 1776 resolved that "a Constitution alterable by the Supreme Legislation is no security at all." To prevent the abuses that might follow if the legislature drafted the constitution by which it would rule, Concord suggested the novel idea of electing a special convention to do the job and requiring voters to approve the constitution. In 1780 the eligible voters of Massachusetts voted their approval of the document.

The preamble to Massachusetts's constitution read, "All men are born free and equal." Enslaved African men and women as well as white women began to wonder for how long these lofty words would exclude them.

Focus on Reforms

Expanding the Ideas of Liberty

The Revolutionary era fostered a climate of unprecedented political interest; the number of voters casting ballots doubled. A profusion of pamphlets and broadsides offered ordinary citizens instant access to Revolutionary affairs as well as exhortations about domestic matters. In his pamphlet *Common Sense,* Thomas Paine said, "We have it in our power to begin the world over again. The birthday of a new world is at hand." With a sense of unprecedented hopefulness, Americans began to write on the "blank sheet" Thomas Paine had set forth.

Republican Women

White women in Revolutionary America claimed few personal or political rights. For example, under an article of British law called **coverture,** any property a woman inherited passed into her husband's control when she married. Not until the 1900s would most American women regain the vote they so fleetingly enjoyed in New Jersey between 1776 and 1807.

Despite their inferior status compared to that of white men, white women aided the Revolution as nurses, innkeepers, suppliers of food and clothing, fund-raisers, farmers, and even as spies. Nevertheless, only the mediation of their fathers, husbands, brothers, or sons allowed those women who longed to do so to participate in the political ferment of the time.

Abigail Adams's letters to her husband John reveal a keen interest in women's rights. She marveled at the persistence of women's patriotism despite their forced exclusion from the political process: "Deprived of a voice in Legislation, obliged to submit to those Laws which are imposed upon us, is it not sufficient to make us indifferent to the publick Welfare? Yet all History and every age exhibit Instances of patriotic virtue in the female Sex; which considering our situation equals the most Heroick." After assisting at the polls in 1780, she consoled herself that her participation counted for something: "If I cannot be a voter upon this occasion, I will be a writer of votes. I can do some thing in that way."

Like Abigail Adams, Esther De Berdt Reed felt keenly that women should contribute to the Revolution. In a broadside published in 1780, she wrote, "If opinion and manners did not forbid us to march to glory on the same paths as the Men, we should at least equal, and sometimes surpass them in our love for the public good." Reed helped organize the women of Philadelphia to collect funds for Washington's troops. The women refused George Washington's suggestion that their $300,000 contribution be deposited into the Bank of the United States to be united "with the gentlemen." Instead, they used their money to buy linen shirts so the soldier recipients would recognize that women had sent the gifts.

COURTESY, THE HENRY FRANCIS DU PONT WINTERTHUR MUSEUM

Dr. Benjamin Rush This influential physician was a member of the Continental Congress and signed the Declaration of Independence. *What did he do to fight slavery?*

During the Revolution, the idea took hold that mothers could play a crucial role in educating their sons toward a lifetime of civic participation. This notion of the "Republican mother" expanded the limited domain in which women had lived and gave a rationale for increasing their participation in political life. Many Republican mothers also began to insist on a better education for themselves and their daughters.

Trying to End Slavery

While white Americans waged a revolution to gain liberty from the tyranny of Britain, some enslaved Africans viewed fighting on the British side as their own best chance to grasp liberty from the tyranny of slavery. In Virginia, Lord Dunmore's 1775 proclamation offering freedom to Virginia's enslaved persons and servants "able and willing to bear arms" attracted more than 500 eager African Americans. The first volunteers formed a regiment of African American soldiers wearing chest sashes that proclaimed, "Liberty to Slaves!" As many as 20 percent of African Americans may have crossed behind British lines to struggle for their own freedom. Only a few thousand African Americans fought on the American side during the Revolution because the Americans did not promise them release from slavery.

If the Revolution did not end slavery, it did deal the institution a powerful blow. For one thing, the importation of enslaved persons almost stopped during the war. Though importation resumed briefly afterwards, 11 of the 13 states had outlawed it by 1790.

In addition, the Revolution brought the very institution of slavery under increased attack. In the South, the legislatures of Virginia and Maryland made it easier for slaveholders to free enslaved persons. A rapid increase in the population of freed African Americans fed expanding free African American communities in cities such as Richmond and Baltimore.

In the North, where enslaved persons made up a much smaller percentage of the population, the Revolution prompted states either to abolish slavery outright or to weaken it. In 1773, Dr. Benjamin Rush, the physician and Pennsylvania leader who helped found America's first antislavery society, said, "The plant of liberty is of so tender a Nature, that it cannot thrive long in the neighborhood of slavery." In 1779 Pennsylvania legislated that all children born to enslaved women should be freed at age 21 if female and age 28 if male. Even such cautious steps demonstrated the North's understanding that human slavery could never be reconciled with the ideals of the Revolution.

Section Review

Vocabulary

1. Define: constitution, abolition, status quo, coverture.

Checking Facts

2. How did the American colonial leaders plan that state constitutions would differ from British colonial charters?
3. In what ways were state governments more democratic than British colonial regimes?

Critical Thinking

Making Comparisons

4. What were the major differences between the state constitutions of Virginia, Massachusetts, and Pennsylvania?

Linking Across Time

5. Describe at least two negative conditions relating to women and African Americans during the Revolutionary era that do not exist today.

Chapter 3 Review

Reviewing Key Terms

Choose the vocabulary word that best completes the sentences below. Write your answers on a separate sheet of paper.

internal tax	**revolution**
preamble	**external tax**
treason	**constitution**

1. Any goods that came into the colonies could be subject to an _________ .

2. Many colonists believed strongly in the idea of a _________ or written plan of government.

3. The Continental Congress heeded the push for independence and began the _________.

4. Colonists meeting to defy the British government could be considered to be committing _________.

5. To raise revenue, Parliament levied an _________ on goods made within the colonies.

Recalling Facts

1. Identify 2 major taxation acts imposed upon the colonies in the 1760s. How did these acts move some colonists to look more favorably upon the idea of self-government?

2. What were committees of correspondence? How did colonists use them to gain sympathy for the revolutionary cause?

3. What action was taken by the First Continental Congress?

4. Who was Thomas Paine and what did he write? How did his publications influence colonial attitudes toward seeking independence?

5. What was the purpose of the Declaration of Independence? Who wrote it?

6. What was the British strategy at the beginning of the war? How did that plan change in 1777?

7. In which region of the colonies were most of the early battles of the Revolution fought? Why might war have broken out there first?

8. Why did each colony create its own constitution? Which people were allowed to vote and participate in government service?

9. Which colony initiated the idea that the Constitution should be ratified by voters? Why was this voter ratification an important development?

10. In what colony were women allowed to vote between 1776 and

LIBRARY OF CONGRESS

1807? What requirements did these women have to meet to be eligible to vote?

Critical Thinking

1. Making Comparisons Compare external taxes and internal taxes. Were the colonists justified in protesting that Parliament had no right to levy internal taxes on them? Explain.

2. Making Generalizations Why do you think that the poorest Americans did most of the actual fighting in the Revolutionary War?

3. Drawing Conclusions The illustration on page 76 shows Nancy Hart defending her home against the Tories. How did the war encourage women to speak out and to assume new roles?

4. Making Inferences How did the ideals of freedom and independence that many colonists held during the Revolution help to change people's attitudes about slavery?

Portfolio Project

What do you think a good citizen is? Is it someone who follows the law? Or might it be someone who breaks the law in order to stand up for an ideal? Do you think that people like the Sons of Liberty acted as good citizens? Are there groups like the Sons of Liberty today? Do you think they are good citizens? Write a persuasive paper explaining your views.

Cooperative Learning

Work with a group of classmates to determine the positive and negative effects of the Revolutionary War. Who benefited from the war? Whose lives remained the same? Who experienced negative consequences? Consider European American men and women, African Americans, and Native Americans. Discuss these issues and make a list of positive and negative consequences for each group. Share your group lists with your classmates.

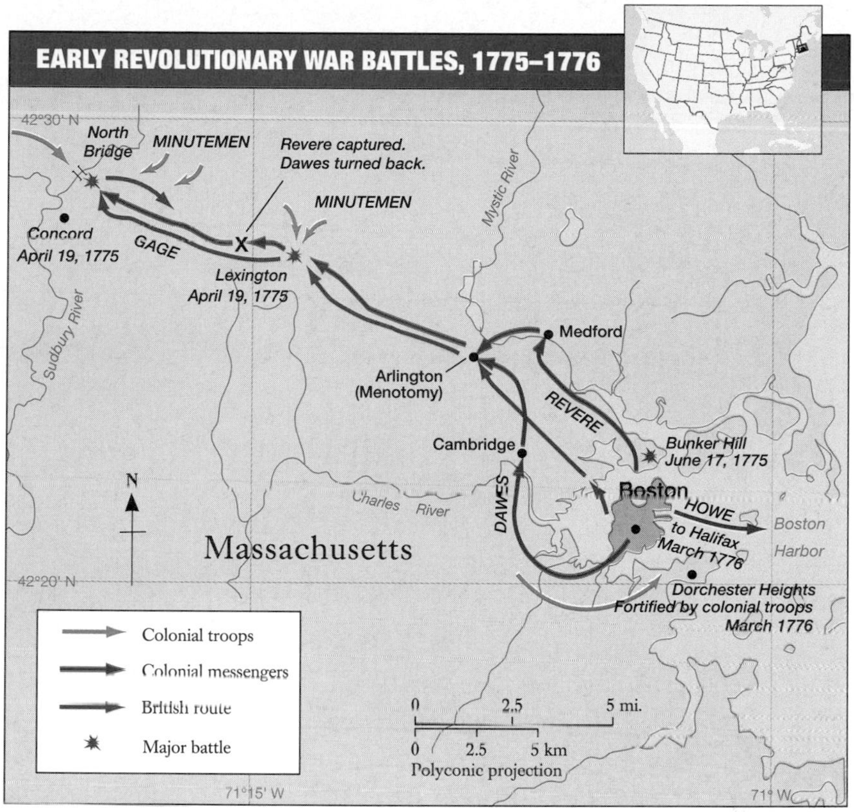

Reinforcing Skills

Interpreting a Primary Source
Read the quotation by Anne Emlen on page 70. How do you know that this is a primary source? In your own words, explain what Anne Emlen means in her statement.

Geography and History

Study the map on this page to answer the following questions:

1. How many major battles did the colonists and the British fight between April 1775 and the time when the British evacuated Boston?

2. Approximately how many miles did the British soldiers march from Lexington to Concord on April 19, 1775?

3. Describe the route taken by William Dawes when he rode to warn the colonists that the British were on the march.

4. What town marks the western limit of British troop movements on April 19, 1775?

5. For how many months after the start of the war were the British able to keep possession of the city of Boston?

HISTORY JOURNAL

Look back at your journal response to page 54. Write what you learned about how the Revolutionary War changed people's lives. Do you think the changes were positive or negative?

CHAPTER 4

A New Nation

JULY 4, 1826: THE PASSING OF JEFFERSON AND ADAMS

It was the fiftieth anniversary of the signing of the Declaration of Independence. Thomas Jefferson, the nation's third President and principal author of the Declaration, lay gravely ill at Monticello, his home in Virginia.

Jefferson said to his grandson, "I am like an old watch, with a pinion worn out here, and a wheel there, until it can go no longer." He passed away shortly after noon.

John Adams died later that same day in Massachusetts, on his lips the words, "Thomas Jefferson survives!" He did not know that his old friend and rival was already gone.

Adams's words reflected his hope that at least one Founder would remain to watch over the young nation. While their relationship was strained at times by tensions in the country that pitted Democratic-Republicans against Federalists, Jefferson and Adams were bound together by the experiences they shared in the heady days of the Revolution.

Jefferson spent his vice presidency and two terms as President working to return the country to the Republican ideals of the Declaration of Independence and the Revolutionary era. He believed his predecessors, especially John Adams, had gone too far in strengthening the powers of the federal government. "I am not for transferring all the powers of the States to the general government, and all those of that government to the Executive branch," Jefferson wrote in a letter shortly before his election to the presidency. "I am for a government rigorously frugal and simple. . . ."

Confident in the strength of the American character, Jefferson never lost sight of his belief that the people's experiment in self-government was destined to set an example for the world. ■

HISTORY JOURNAL

What do you think is the meaning of Liberty feeding the American eagle in the painting at the right? Write your ideas in your journal.

HENRY FORD MUSEUM & GREENFIELD VILLAGE

"Liberty" feeding the American eagle,
circa 1800–1810

SECTION 1

From Federation to Constitution

JUNE 17, 1788: VIRGINIANS DEBATE PROPOSED CONSTITUTION

NATIONAL PORTRAIT GALLERY, SMITHSONIAN INSTITUTION/ART RESOURCE, NY

Anti-Federalist
Patrick Henry led the opposition to the Constitution at Virginia's ratifying convention in 1788.

THE WINDOWS OF THE STATEHOUSE IN RICHMOND, VIRGINIA, STOOD OPEN ON THE HOT SUMMER AFTERNOON. Impassioned voices boomed from the building's main hall. There, 168 Virginia representatives heard arguments for and against a plan for a new government of the United States.

Patrick Henry stood before his fellow Virginians; they knew him as a former governor of their state and as a great public speaker. Henry explained his opposition to the proposed Constitution. It stripped powers away from the states, he said. It increased the powers of federal government, and it had been written by men with no authority to do so. He twisted the first words of the document into an attack on those men. "What right had they to say *We, the People?*" he asked. "Who authorized them to speak the language of *We, the People,* instead of *We, the States?*"

One of the men who helped design the new plan was at the convention. Edmund Randolph was as well known as Patrick Henry; he, too, had served as governor of the state and came from an old Virginia family. Randolph asked Virginia to accept the Constitution and unite the nation. Raising his right arm, Randolph exclaimed, "I will assent to the lopping of this limb before I assent to the dissolution of the Union."

The men debated the merits and faults of the Constitution through the rest of that warm June of 1788.

AS YOU READ

Vocabulary
- ratify
- hard money
- checks and balances
- representation

Think About . . .
- the successes and failures of government under the Articles of Confederation.
- the difficulties in creating the Constitution.
- how the Constitution increased the power of the federal government and lessened the power of the state legislatures.

Patrick Henry and his supporters argued for the rights of the states. Randolph and others urged unity under a strong federal government that the new Constitution offered. The differences between the 2 men summed up tensions that pulled at the fabric of life in the United States in the 1780s.

A Firm League of Friendship

The Articles of Confederation

Hopes for unity under a strong central government stemmed from experiences with the Articles of Confederation, an earlier attempt at a federal constitution. A federal constitution had become necessary because state governments, established in the late 1770s, issued their own money, taxed their own citizens, and competed with other states in trade and for land beyond the Appalachians. By the 1780s states acted more like 13 small independent nations—each with its own government, economy, and interests—than like parts of a larger nation.

The Plan of the Articles

Around the same time that the former colonies were creating their state governments, the Second Continental Congress appointed a committee to draw up a plan for a national government. Congress, preparing for war, wanted its powers to be officially defined and recognized. Other Americans, too, realized that the states could not do everything on their own.

The Articles of Confederation created a national government in the form of a one-house legislature, similar to the Continental Congress. Each state, regardless of its size, had one vote in the Confederation Congress. This body was given only those powers that individual states could not fulfill alone: declaring war, conducting foreign policy, and establishing a postal system were examples. The Articles denied Congress the power to collect taxes, even for the support of an army or to enforce its own laws and treaties. One rule firmly established the power of the states over Congress: only a unanimous vote of the states could change the Articles of Confederation. Many Americans believed that this new system avoided the evils of a strong government—such as Britain's government—but allowed the states to work together for their common good and protection.

Ratification Difficulties

While all the newly formed states wanted a national government, it took almost four years to **ratify,** or officially accept, the Articles of Confederation (which could only be adopted if every state consented). The primary stumbling block to ratification was the question of control of the land between the Appalachian Mountains and the Mississippi River. Larger states such as Virginia claimed these Western lands in their colonial charters and were reluctant to give up control. Small states feared that control of this territory would make large states too powerful. Moreover, if the national government took control of the Western lands, their resources could benefit all the states in the union instead of just a few. States with no claims to Western lands pointed out that it was only fair that these lands be common property because they were being "wrested from the common enemy [the British] by the blood and treasure of the thirteen states." Small states hoped to see the Western lands opened for settlement and farming, so their poorer residents might make a new start.

Eventually most smaller states agreed to ratify the Articles despite their misgivings about control of Western lands. Maryland, however, refused to ratify until New York transferred its Western land claims to Congress in 1780, and Virginia followed suit in 1781. With all states' Western land claims ceded, or formally surrendered, Maryland announced its ratification of the Articles on March 1, 1781.

NATIONAL MUSEUM OF AMERICAN ART, WASHINGTON, DC/ART RESOURCE, NY

Unspoiled Lands The land that became the state of Tennessee (seen here in a later painting) was ceded by North Carolina in 1790. *Why did small states want the federal government to control Western lands?*

The 13 states would now be joined in a "firm league of friendship."

When the states worked together, the Confederation Congress succeeded in passing laws of lasting value. The Northwest Ordinance of 1787, for example, established rules for organizing the lush region west of the Appalachian Mountains. It reached a compromise on slavery, allowing it in territory south of the Ohio River and prohibiting the importation of slaves north of the river. The ordinance also provided rules for electing assemblies in the Western territories and for admitting territories "on an equal footing with the original states."

Although effective in passing the Northwest Ordinance, Congress faced a variety of difficult problems after the war that states refused to help solve. The worst of these problems involved paying off war debts and stabilizing the American economy.

In Debt

Congress had borrowed nearly $60 million from American investors and European governments during the war. After the war Congress lacked cash to pay its old debts. Because Congress was not allowed to tax the states, the only way it could pay its debts was to print massive amounts of paper money.

Continental paper currency was nothing more than a promise that Congress would pay the holder of the bill in **hard money**—gold or silver—at some time in the future. By the end of the war, the United States had a severe shortage of hard money. The more paper money Congress printed, therefore, the less it was worth. By the mid-1780s, Continental currency was worth only one-fortieth of its face value. Since Congress had no hard money to back up the millions of dollars printed during the war, people's confidence in paper money fell. Many merchants refused to accept Continental currency, and few Americans had any hard money to spend.

Desperately in need of a new way to raise taxes, leaders in Congress tried unsuccessfully to convince the states that it should have the power to tax imports. Meanwhile, the money problems began to have dire effects on the lives of common Americans.

NATIONAL PORTRAIT GALLERY, SMITHSONIAN INSTITUTION/ART RESOURCE, NY

In the Backcountry **The Massachusetts Supreme Court sentenced Shays to death for his part in the uprising, then pardoned him in 1788. He is shown here with Jacob Shattuck, another leader in the farmers' rebellion.** *What conditions in the country led to Shays's Rebellion?*

Shays's Rebellion

One of those Americans was Daniel Shays. Shays served as a captain in the Continental Army during the Revolution. When the war was over, he returned to his small farm in western Massachusetts. In the best of times, Shays had little extra money. After the war, he had none. In a time before banks, Shays and other farmers sometimes borrowed money from wealthy neighbors to buy food and supplies, or bought goods on credit from a store in town. When the wealthy neighbor or store owner asked the farmers to pay their debts—in hard money, of course—many could not pay.

For people who could not pay their debts, there were two alternatives. If they had property, a local court seized it and sold it to pay off the debt. If they had no property, they were sent to debtors' prison. In 1786 Shays and other farmers begged the Massachusetts legislature for extra time to pay their debts. The legislature ignored the requests, and the county courts continued to seize farms.

Daniel Shays recalled the early days of the crisis with Britain when legal attempts to solve disputes with government failed. He knew what to do in the face of an arrogant legislature. In August and September 1786, disgruntled farmers marched on courthouses in Northampton and Worcester. Muskets in hand, they closed the courthouses and prevented the courts from seizing any more farms or imprisoning any more farmers.

After those successes, Shays's group gathered near Springfield, where the state's supreme court was in session and where the state arsenal also happened to be located. When wealthy New Englanders learned that angry farmers were massing near the arsenal, they feared open rebellion and attacks on their property. They called the farmers traitors and provided the money that induced 4,400 militia from eastern Massachusetts to march against the gathering farmers.

In January 1787, Shays and 1,200 farmers marched on the arsenal. When Shays's men advanced, the militia opened fire. Four farmers died and the rest scattered. The revolt broke up soon afterward.

While Shays and the other farmers believed they were patriotic, other Americans were horrified. Men of wealth and power saw the rebellion as proof of social dis-

DEPOSITED BY THE CITY OF BOSTON, COURTESY, MUSEUM OF FINE ARTS, BOSTON

© NORTH WIND PICTURE ARCHIVES

THE THOMAS GILCREASE INSTITUTE OF AMERICAN HISTORY AND ART, TULSA, OKLAHOMA

Constitutional Convention at the Pennsylvania Statehouse James Madison (right) was among the most influential figures at the convention, where delegates shaped the new government and wrote the Constitution. Samuel Adams (above) refused to attend as a protest against the formation of a stronger federal government. *Why was the Confederation congress so anxious to replace the Articles of Confederation?*

order. Congress sent a veteran of Washington's army, General Henry Knox, to investigate. Knox reported that the farmers' uprising had "alarmed men of principle and property." He declared, "What is to afford our security against the violence of lawless men? Our government must be braced, changed, or altered to secure our lives and property."

A More Perfect Union

Reinventing Government

By 1787 the flaws in the Articles of Confederation were obvious to many Americans, including most members of the Confederation congress. A group of these men worried that the nation was headed for disaster unless the Articles were altered. They called on the states to send delegates to a convention where they might correct "such defects as may be discovered to exist" in the present government.

Meeting in Philadelphia

The group that gathered in Philadelphia in May 1787 contained some of the most distinguished men in America. Adoring crowds mobbed stern, proper George Washington, a delegate from Virginia. Americans still hailed him as the hero of the American Revolution. Another Virginia delegate, the short and frail James Madison, had spent much of the previous year reading about governments in past history to prepare for the convention. Benjamin Franklin was the elder statesman of the convention. At age 81, Franklin tired easily and had other Pennsylvania delegates read his speeches for him, but he enjoyed hosting the state delegates in his home city.

The other 52 delegates had experience drafting state constitutions and serving in state governments or the Confederation congress. The delegates' average age was 45, just past the prime of life in the 1700s. Many of them had attended college. All were white, male, and wealthy.

By May 25, delegates from 7 states had arrived and the meeting began. Delegates from 3 more states arrived late; delegates from Rhode Island never showed up.

Sworn to secrecy, and meeting behind closed doors, the delegates began their work at green felt-covered tables in the Pennsylvania statehouse. The delegates quickly agreed that the Articles were beyond repair. The Virginia delegation, headed by Edmund Randolph, proposed an entirely new system of government, based on James Madison's studies. This new government would be larger and more powerful than the Confederation congress.

That plan was the basis for discussion among the delegates throughout the long, hot summer of 1787. Working in a closed hall, the delegates suffered through sweltering heat. Six days a week, from May to September, they proposed and debated idea after idea. Angry delegates threatened to walk out of the convention and some did. Slowly, a plan for a new government emerged.

Reshaping the Government

Unlike the Confederation congress, the new government was to consist of three equal but separate branches: an executive branch, a legislative branch, and a judicial branch, or system of federal courts. The job of the executive branch, headed by a President, was to enforce federal laws. The responsibility of the legislative branch, or Congress, as it was to be called, was to make laws. The judicial branch would rule on cases of federal laws. The responsibilities of these branches would overlap and interlock, creating **checks and balances** that would prevent one branch from being too powerful.

Two major differences between the Confederation government and the new one are notable. First, under the new Constitution, the President held far-reaching powers. The President was commander in chief of the army, he could veto acts of Congress, appoint judges, and put down rebellions. One delegate said that these powers might not have been so great "had not many of the members cast their eyes towards General Washington as president." A second major difference was that the new Constitution curbed the power of state legislatures. States were now prohibited from issuing paper money and from allowing debts and taxes to be paid in produce, such as tobacco and wheat, instead of with hard money. States were also forbidden from "impairing the obligation of contracts"—meaning interfering with the settlement of contracts, which included debts owed by farmers.

YALE UNIVERSITY ART GALLERY, GIFT OF ROGER SHERMAN WHITE, B.A. 1899, LL.B. 1902

Federalist Leader Roger Sherman of Connecticut was a major architect of the Great Compromise. *How did the delegates decide to compromise on slavery?*

The greatest difficulty the convention faced centered on Congress. The delegates agreed early that Congress should consist of two houses, but the question of **representation,** or how many votes each state should have, nearly broke up the convention. Delegates from small states insisted that each state have an equal vote in Congress. Those from larger states felt that was unfair: representation in Congress should be decided by population.

Learning to Compromise

After seven weeks of deadlock on this issue, the two sides agreed to what historians call the Great Compromise. Both small and large states got part of what they wanted, but neither group got all they had hoped for. In the upper house, or Senate, each state would have two votes, regardless of its size. Representation in the lower house, called the House of Representatives, would be based on each state's population.

Another conflict erupted over the way to figure the number of representatives a state could have. Southern delegates insisted that enslaved African Americans be counted in a state's population. Northern delegates objected to this proposal: some believed slavery was wrong; others realized that counting enslaved

THE THREE BRANCHES OF THE UNITED STATES GOVERNMENT

The United States Constitution separates and distributes the powers of the federal government among its three branches: the executive branch, the legislative branch, and the judicial branch.

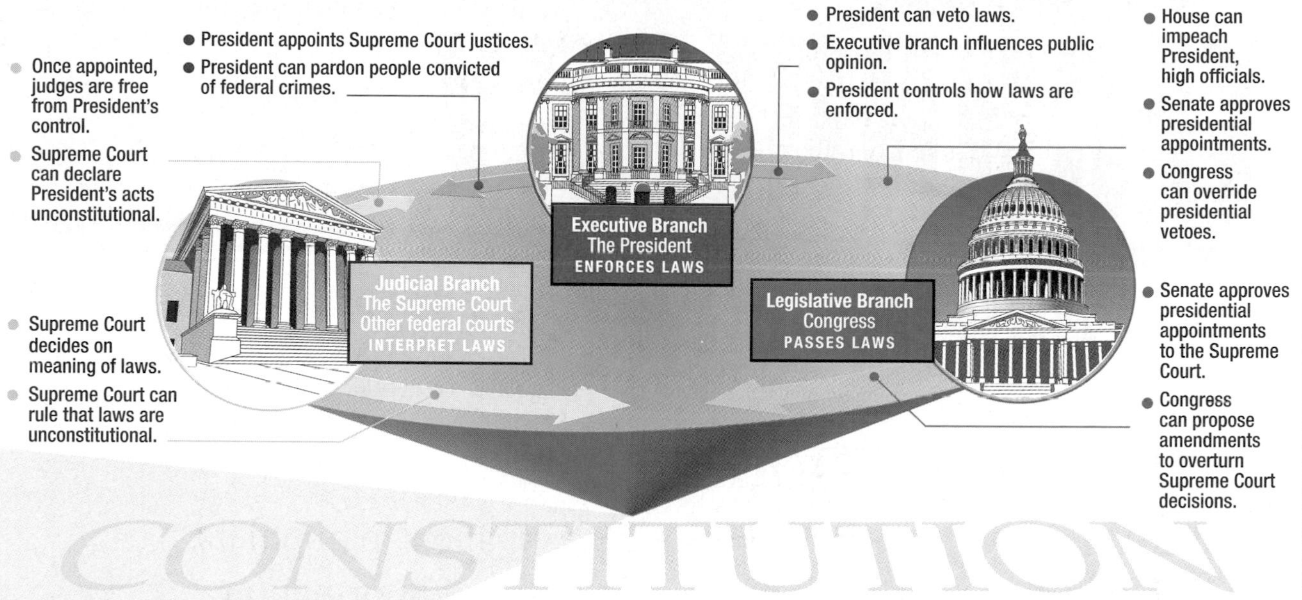

Once appointed, judges are free from President's control.
Supreme Court can declare President's acts unconstitutional.
Supreme Court decides on meaning of laws.
Supreme Court can rule that laws are unconstitutional.
President appoints Supreme Court justices.
President can pardon people convicted of federal crimes.
President can veto laws.
Executive branch influences public opinion.
President controls how laws are enforced.
House can impeach President, high officials.
Senate approves presidential appointments.
Congress can override presidential vetoes.
Senate approves presidential appointments to the Supreme Court.
Congress can propose amendments to overturn Supreme Court decisions.
Executive Branch
The President
ENFORCES LAWS
Judicial Branch
The Supreme Court
Other federal courts
INTERPRET LAWS
Legislative Branch
Congress
PASSES LAWS
CONSTITUTION

The Constitution prevents any one group from having total power by making the three branches of government depend on one another for their authority. *Using the graphic above, name two examples of the overlapping responsibilities of the branches.*

persons would increase the power of Southern states in Congress. To complicate matters, some Northern delegates threatened to outlaw the slave trade.

The 2 sides finally agreed to a compromise over slavery. Representation in the House of Representatives would be based on all of the free inhabitants of a state, plus three-fifths of all enslaved persons, even though they could not vote. The same formula would be used to figure the taxes each state owed to the federal government. The group also agreed that Congress could pass no laws abolishing the slave trade before 1808.

The delegates also decided late in their meetings that the Constitution should be ratified in specially elected conventions of the people, rather than by the state legislatures. Delegates feared that state governments would never approve their new plan, which strengthened the national government. In addition, they agreed that only 9 of the 13 states had to ratify the Constitution before the new government went into effect.

When the delegates saw the final document, many felt disappointed. Many had compromised on issues of great importance to their states. "I confess there are several parts of this constitution which I do not at present approve," said Benjamin Franklin. He also said, however, that the new plan was better than their current government and encouraged the remaining delegates to sign it. All but 3 of them did so on September 17, 1787. (See pages 91–109 to read the Constitution.)

The next day, Major William Jackson, secretary of the convention, left Philadelphia by stagecoach, carrying a copy of the Constitution to the Confederation congress in New York. He also carried a letter from the convention explaining "the necessity of a different organization."

SECTION REVIEW

Vocabulary

1. Define: ratify, hard money, checks and balances, representation.

Checking Facts

2. Why did smaller states want larger states to give up Western land claims?
3. What was the Great Compromise, and how did it satisfy all 13 states?

Critical Thinking

Analyzing Information

4. Why did the delegates at the Constitutional Convention decide to compromise with each other?

Linking Across Time

5. Give an example of a part of the Constitution that might be different if the Constitution were being written today. Explain your answer.

Science, TECHNOLOGY, and Society

Communication Media

The colonial printer-publisher issued newspapers, pamphlets, and broadsides, or posters, that communicated information and opinions concerning the debate over British rule.

(DETAIL) PHOTO COURTESY PEABODY ESSEX MUSEUM, SALEM, MASS., ORIGINAL IN THE COLLECTION OF THE MARBLEHEAD HISTORICAL SOCIETY, MARBLEHEAD, MA

KEEPING IN TOUCH

Before the availability of printing presses in the Americas, colonists used letters and journals, such as the one at left, to keep records and disseminate information. These handwritten accounts had the obvious disadvantage of not being reproducible without great effort.

FILE PHOTO BY DOUG MINDELL

300 YEARS OF COMMUNICATION MEDIA

Pre-1650	1650	1700	1750

FIRST COLONIAL PRINTING PRESS is set up by Stephen Daye of Massachusetts in 1639.

The ***BOSTON NEWS-LETTER,*** the first successful newspaper in the colonies, is first published in 1704.

BALTIMORE PRINTER Mary Katherine Goddard prints and distributes the Declaration of Independence in 1777.

FREEDOM PRESS

Boston printer Isaiah Thomas learned his trade on this printing press in 1755, when he was 6 years old. At the start of the Revolution, Thomas removed his press to a town outside Boston to keep it out of British hands. There he printed the first accounts of the skirmishes at Lexington and Concord with the headline, "Americans!—Liberty or Death!—Join or Die!"

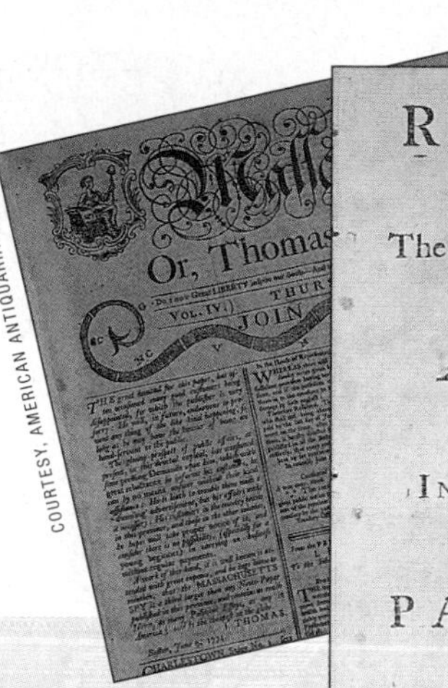

COURTESY, AMERICAN ANTIQUARIAN SOCIETY

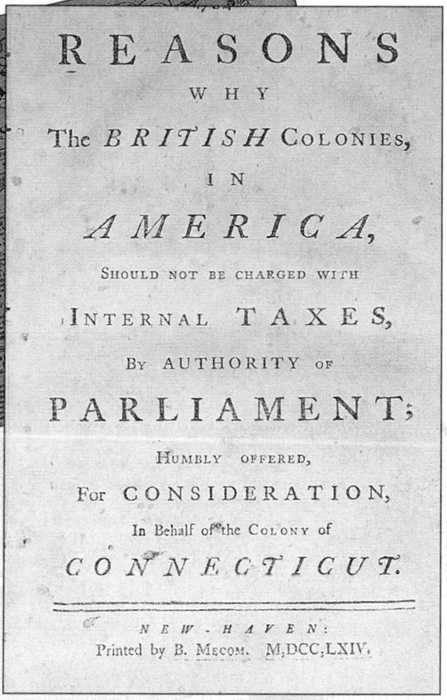

REASONS
WHY
The *BRITISH* COLONIES,
IN
AMERICA,
SHOULD NOT BE CHARGED WITH
INTERNAL TAXES,
BY AUTHORITY OF
PARLIAMENT;
HUMBLY OFFERED,
For CONSIDERATION,
In Behalf of the COLONY of
CONNECTICUT.

NEW-HAVEN:
Printed by B. MECOM. M,DCC,LXIV.

COURTESY, AMERICAN ANTIQUARIAN SOCIETY

COLONIAL WILLIAMSBURG

COURTESY, AMERICAN ANTIQUARIAN SOCIETY

COLONIAL WILLIAMSBURG

PAPERS AND PAMPHLETS

The growth of small presses and improvements in the postal service made it much easier to find out what was going on. Connecticut Governor Thomas Fitch published a pamphlet (above, right) in 1740 that stated clearly and concisely his colony's objections to taxes. Between 1763 and 1775, the number of newspapers in the colonies doubled. The *Massachusetts Spy* (above, left) was founded in 1770.

INTERNET NEWS

PORTFOLIO PROJECT

Comparisons have been made between colonial newspapers and today's electronic bulletin boards on the Internet. Do some research and write a brief report on how these media are alike and different.

1800	1850	1900	1950–1990s

THE TELEPHONE is invented by Alexander Graham Bell in 1876.

FIRST COMMERCIAL RADIO STATION, KDKA in Pittsburgh, goes on the air in 1920.

THE COMPUTER AGE begins when the first automatic digital computer is created in 1942.

THE INTERNET is born in 1969 out of a computer network built to study how the government could maintain communications in the event of nuclear war.

SECTION 2

Debate and Ratification

SEPTEMBER 17, 1787: CONSTITUTIONAL CONVENTION ADJOURNS

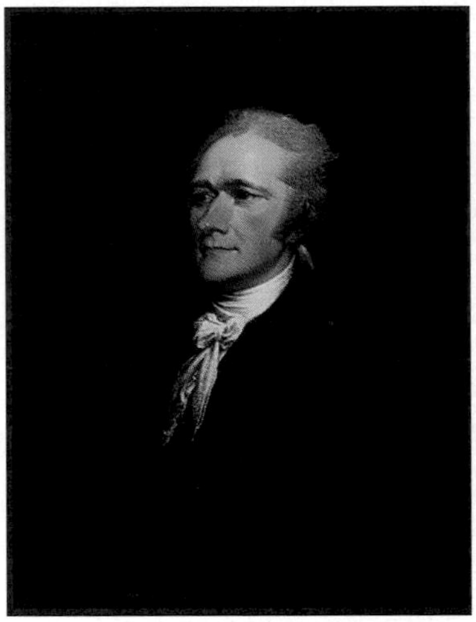
NATIONAL PORTRAIT GALLERY, SMITHSONIAN INSTITUTION/ART RESOURCE, NY

A Staunch Federalist
Alexander Hamilton was a major author of *The Federalist*, a series of 85 essays defending the Constitution.

As soon as the convention in Philadelphia ended, delegates rushed home to begin the campaign for ratification. That was a novel idea in itself. Never before had the nation's people at large been asked to ratify the laws under which they would live. The process of deciding for or against ratification produced perhaps the biggest, most informed political debate in American history.

News of the new Constitution spread rapidly through the states. Newspapers published the document and strongly worded arguments began to fill their pages. Those who favored the proposed Constitution called themselves Federalists. The Anti-Federalists opposed the new plan of government.

The idea of a strong national government frightened some Americans. Many Anti-Federalists were small farmers who had learned to be self-sufficient and had found most of their contact with government unpleasant. The Anti-Federalist leaders, however, came from all classes and all regions. State politicians who dreaded losing power to the federal government were among the most active supporters of the Anti-Federalists.

The debate over the Constitution in newspapers, letters, and public discussions revealed divisions that remained in American society. One poor Anti-Federalist farmer mistrusted the people of "wealth and talent" who had framed the Constitution:

> These lawyers, and men of learning, and moneyed men, that talk so finely, and gloss over matters so smoothly, to make us, poor illiterate people swallow down the pill, expect to get into Congress themselves; they expect to be managers of this Constitution, and get all the power and all the money into their own hands, and then they will swallow up all us little folks, like the great Leviathan, Mr. President; yes, just like the whale swallowed up Jonah.
>
> —Amos Singletary, *Massachusetts Gazette,* January 25, 1788

As You Read

Vocabulary
- majority
- amendment

Think About . . .
- why opinions were divided about the proposed new Constitution.
- how the views of the Federalists differed from those of the Anti-Federalists.
- how the addition of the Bill of Rights enhanced the Constitution.

Toward Ratification

The Debate Over Basic Rights

NORTH WIND PICTURE ARCHIVES

The People Celebrate In this print New Yorkers are shown celebrating the ratification of the Constitution in 1788. *Why was New York a key state in the campaign for ratification?*

Many of the Anti-Federalists feared that a strong central government would not preserve the essential rights of the people. Even Britain guaranteed certain rights to its citizens, they argued. Why was there no bill of basic American rights?

The leading Federalists, including George Washington, Benjamin Franklin, and James Madison, did not believe a bill of rights was necessary. All basic rights, they argued, were protected by the Constitution or by state constitutions.

The Federalists found support in the area where America's elite had always dominated, the Atlantic Coast. Wealthy landowners in these areas wanted the protection a strong central government could provide. Merchants with overseas connections and artisans in large coastal cities also supported the proposed Constitution. These men had been hard hit by the inability of the Confederation congress to control the nation's economy; they saw a strong government that would pass import taxes on foreign goods as their best chance to succeed in business.

As the ratifying conventions began to convene, the Federalists knew they had clear **majorities,** or more than 50 percent of the votes, in some states. The vote was much closer in others, including large states such as Massachusetts, Virginia, and New York. If any one of those states did not ratify, the Federalists risked total failure.

The Ratification Debate

Anti-Federalist Objections to the Constitution

- The Articles of Confederation were basically a good plan for government that could be amended.
- The Constitution made national government too strong.
- Strong national government threatened the rights of the common people.
- The Constitution favored wealthy men and preserved their power.
- The Constitution lacked a bill of rights.

Federalist Defense of the Constitution

- The Articles of Confederation were weak and ineffective.
- National government needed to be strong in order to function.
- Strong national government was needed to quell rebellions by Native Americans and small farmers.
- National government would protect the rights of the people.
- Men of experience and talent should govern the nation.
- Constitutional and state governments protected individual freedoms without a bill of rights.

Both the Anti-Federalists and the Federalists held strong views regarding ratification of the new Constitution. *According to the Federalists, what safeguards would a strong national government provide for citizens?*

FROM INDEPENDENCE TO THE CONSTITUTION, 1776–1791

- **JULY 1776** Colonists sign Declaration of Independence.
- **MARCH 1781** The Articles of Confederation are ratified.
- **SEPTEMBER 1783** The Treaty of Paris ends the Revolutionary War.
- **FEBRUARY 1787** Massachusetts militia quell Shays's Rebellion, which had started in 1786.
- **MAY 1787** Writing of the Constitution begins.
- **JUNE 1788** Ratification of Constitution by the ninth state (N.H.) makes it official.
- **APRIL 1789** George Washington is elected first President.
- **DECEMBER 1791** The Bill of Rights is ratified.

1776 | 1778 | 1780 | 1782 | 1784 | 1786 | 1788 | 1790 | 1792

The People Vote

The first state conventions were held in December 1787 and January 1788. Delaware, New Jersey, Georgia, and Connecticut all ratified the Constitution.

The first real test occurred in Massachusetts. Opponents of the Constitution, including Samuel Adams, held a clear majority when the convention met in January 1788. The state's urban craftspeople—still the source of Samuel Adams's political power—sided with the Federalists, however, and persuaded Adams to vote for ratification. The Massachusetts convention agreed to the Constitution, but only if a bill of rights was added.

In June 1788, New Hampshire became the ninth state to ratify the Constitution. The Federalists had reached the minimum number required to make the new government legal. Virginia and New York, however, still had not yet ratified. Without these 2 large states the new government could hardly succeed.

George Washington and James Madison worked hard for ratification in Virginia, but Patrick Henry and other Anti-Federalists worked just as hard against it. Finally, at the urging of Thomas Jefferson, Madison compromised and agreed to add a bill of rights.

The contest was even closer in New York. Only a last-minute promise to add a bill of rights won ratification in New York. Once New York joined the other states, the Federalists' victory was made more secure.

Adding the Bill of Rights

Five states had ratified the Constitution with the understanding that Congress would add a bill of rights. Many Federalist leaders who had made this promise served in the new Congress. James Madison represented Virginia in the Congress, and in September 1789, he recommended that 12 **amendments,** or written changes, be added to the Constitution.

Over the next 2 years, state legislatures ratified 10 of these 12 amendments. The Constitution now officially protected rights such as freedom of speech, religion, press, and assembly. In December 1791, these 10 amendments, known as the Bill of Rights, were added to the Constitution.

The Preamble of the United States Constitution states that the Constitution is designed to "promote the general welfare, and secure the blessings of liberty" of "the people of the United States." It did not, however, address the rights of many Americans. The Constitution protected slavery, ignored women, and did not acknowledge Native Americans' rights. It left to future generations problems that it could neither foresee nor solve.

Yet through the process of ratification and with the addition of the Bill of Rights, the Constitution was shaped by more people than the flawed Articles of Confederation. As they headed into the 1790s, the American people watched—with hopes and fears—to see how this latest experiment would turn out.

SECTION REVIEW

Vocabulary

1. Define: majority, amendment.

Checking Facts

2. Why did Anti-Federalists oppose the new Constitution?
3. Why did the Federalists favor the Constitution?

Critical Thinking

Identifying Assumptions

4. What assumptions were many poorer Anti-Federalists making about the Federalists as a group?

Linking Across Time

5. Give an example of an addition to the Bill of Rights that might be made if it were being written today for the first time. Explain your answer.

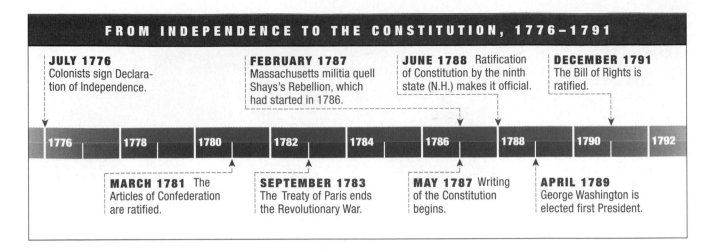

The Constitution *of the* United States

For easier study of the Constitution, those passages that have been set aside or changed by the adoption of the amendments are printed in blue.

Preamble

We, the people of the United States, in Order to form a more perfect Union, establish Justice, insure domestic Tranquility, provide for the common defence, promote the general Welfare, and secure the Blessings of Liberty to ourselves and our Posterity, do ordain and establish this Constitution for the United States of America.

Article I

SECTION 1

All legislative Powers herein granted shall be vested in a Congress of the United States, which shall consist of a Senate and House of Representatives.

SECTION 2

1. The House of Representatives shall be composed of Members chosen every second Year by the People of the several States, and the Electors in each State shall have the Qualifications requisite for Electors of the most numerous Branch of the State Legislature.

2. No Person shall be a Representative who shall not have attained to the Age of twenty-five Years, and been seven Years a Citizen of the United States, and who shall not, when elected, be an Inhabitant of that State in which he shall be chosen.

3. Representatives and direct Taxes shall be apportioned among the several states which may be included within this Union, according to their respective Numbers, which shall be determined by adding to the whole Number of free Persons, including those bound to Service for a Term of Years, and excluding Indians not taxed, three-fifths of all other Persons. The actual Enumeration shall be made within three Years after the first Meeting of the Congress of the United States, and within every subsequent Term of ten Years, in such Manner as they shall by Law direct. The Number of Representatives shall not exceed one for every thirty Thousand, but each state shall have at Least one Representative; and until such enumeration shall be made, the State of New Hampshire shall be entitled to chuse three; Massachusetts eight, Rhode Island and Providence Plantations one, Connecticut five, New York six, New Jersey four, Pennsylvania eight, Delaware one, Maryland six, Virginia ten; North Carolina five, South Carolina five, and Georgia three.

Preamble

The Preamble introduces the Constitution and sets forth the general purposes for which the government was established. The preamble also declares that the power of the government comes from the people.

The printed text of the document shows the spelling and punctuation of the parchment original.

Article I. The Legislative Branch

Section 1. Congress

The power to make laws is given to a Congress made up of two chambers to represent different interests: the Senate to represent the states; the House to be more responsive to the people's will.

Section 2. House of Representatives

1. Elections and Term of Office

"Electors" means voters. Every two years the voters choose new Congress members to serve in the House of Representatives. The Constitution states that each state may specify who can vote. But the 15th, 19th, 24th, and 26th Amendments have established guidelines that all states must follow regarding the right to vote.

2. Qualifications

Representatives must be 25 years old, citizens of the United States for 7 years, and residents of the state they represent.

3. Division of Representatives Among the States

The number of representatives from each state is based on the size of the state's population. Each state is divided into congressional districts, with each district required to be equal in population. Each state is entitled to at least one representative. The number of representatives in the House was set at 435 in 1929. Since then, there has been a reapportionment of seats based on population shifts rather than on addition of seats.

Only three-fifths of a state's slave population was to be counted in determining the number of representatives elected by the state. Native Americans were not counted at all.

The "enumeration" referred to is the census, the population count taken every 10 years since 1790.

4. Vacancies

Vacancies in the House are filled through special elections called by the state's governor.

5. Officers

The speaker is the leader of the majority party in the House and is responsible for choosing the heads of various House committees. "Impeachment" means indictment, or bringing charges against an official.

Section 3. The Senate

1. Number of Members, Terms of Office, and Voting Procedure

Originally, senators were chosen by the state legislators of their own states. The 17th Amendment changed this, so that senators are now elected directly by the people. There are 100 senators, 2 from each state.

2. Staggered Elections; Vacancies

One-third of the Senate is elected every two years. The terms of the first Senate's membership was staggered: one group served two years, one four, and one six. All senators now serve a six-year term.

The 17th Amendment changed the method of filling vacancies in the Senate.

3. Qualifications

Qualifications for the Senate are more restrictive than those for the House. Senators must be at least 30 years old and they must have been citizens of the United States for at least 9 years. The Framers of the Constitution made the Senate a more elite body in order to produce a further check on the powers of the House of Representatives.

4. President of the Senate

The Vice President's only duty listed in the Constitution is to preside over the Senate. The only real power the Vice President has is to cast the deciding vote when there is a tie. However, modern Presidents have given their Vice Presidents new responsibilities.

5. Other Officers

The Senate selects its other officers, including a presiding officer (president pro tempore) who serves when the Vice President is absent or has become President of the United States.

6. Trial of Impeachments

When trying a case of impeachment brought by the House, the Senate convenes as a court. The Chief Justice of the Supreme Court acts as the presiding judge, and the Senate acts as the jury. A two-thirds vote of the members present is necessary to convict officials under impeachment charges.

7. Penalty for Conviction

If the Senate convicts an official, it may only remove the official from office and prevent that person from holding another federal position. However, the convicted official may still be tried for the same offense in a regular court of law.

4. When vacancies happen in the Representation from any State, the Executive Authority thereof shall issue Writs of Election to fill such Vacancies.

5. The House of Representatives shall chuse their Speaker and other Officers; and shall have the sole Power of Impeachment.

SECTION 3

1. The Senate of the United States shall be composed of two Senators from each State, chosen by the Legislature thereof; for six Years; and each Senator shall have one Vote.

2. Immediately after they shall be assembled in Consequence of the first Election, they shall be divided as equally as may be into three Classes. The Seats of the Senators of the first Class shall be vacated at the Expiration of the second Year, of the second Class at the Expiration of the fourth Year, and of the third Class at the Expiration of the sixth Year, so that one-third may be chosen every second Year; and if Vacancies happen by Resignations, or otherwise, during the Recess of the Legislature of any State, the Executive thereof may make temporary Appointments until the next Meeting of the Legislature, which shall then fill such Vacancies.

3. No person shall be a Senator who shall not have attained the Age of thirty Years, and been nine Years a Citizen of the United States, and who shall not, when elected, be an Inhabitant of that State in which he shall be chosen.

4. The Vice President of the United States shall be President of the Senate, but shall have no vote, unless they be equally divided.

5. The Senate shall chuse their Officers, and also a President pro tempore, in the absence of the Vice-President or when he shall exercise the Office of the President of the United States.

6. The Senate shall have the sole Power to try all impeachments. When sitting for that purpose they shall be on Oath or Affirmation. When the President of the United States is tried, the Chief Justice shall preside: And no person shall be convicted without the Concurrence of two-thirds of the Members present.

7. Judgment in Cases of Impeachment shall not extend further than to removal from Office, and disqualification to hold and enjoy any Office of Honor, Trust or Profit under the United States: but the Party convicted shall nevertheless be liable and subject to Indictment, Trial, Judgment and Punishment, according to Law.

SECTION 4

1. The Times, Places, and Manner of holding Elections for Senators and Representatives, shall be prescribed in each state by the Legislature thereof; but the Congress may at any time by Law make or alter such Regulations, except as to the Places of Chusing Senators.

2. The Congress shall assemble at least once in every Year, and such Meeting shall be on the first Monday in December, unless they shall by Law appoint a different Day.

SECTION 5

1. Each House shall be the Judge of the Elections, Returns and Qualifications of its own Members, and a Majority of each shall constitute a Quorum to do Business; but a smaller Number may adjourn from day to day, and may be authorized to compel the Attendance of absent Members, in such Manner, and under such Penalties as each House may provide.

2. Each House may determine the Rules of its Proceedings, punish its Members for disorderly Behaviour, and, with the Concurrence of two-thirds, expel a Member.

3. Each House shall keep a Journal of its Proceedings, and from time to time publish the same, excepting such Parts as may in their Judgment require Secrecy; and the Yeas and Nays of the Members of either House on any question shall, at the desire of one-fifth of those Present, be entered on the Journal.

4. Neither House during the Session of Congress, shall, without the Consent of the other, adjourn for more than three days, nor to any other Place than that in which the two Houses shall be sitting.

SECTION 6

1. The Senators and Representatives shall receive a Compensation for their Services, to be ascertained by Law, and paid out of the Treasury of the United States. They shall in all Cases, except Treason, Felony and Breach of the Peace be privileged from Arrest during their attendance at the Session of their respective Houses, and in going to and returning from the same; and for any Speech or Debate in either House, they shall not be questioned in any other place.

2. No Senator or Representative shall, during the Time for which he was elected, be appointed to any civil Office under the Authority of the United States, which shall have been created, or the Emoluments whereof shall have been encreased, during such time; and no Person holding any Office under the United States, shall be a Member of either House during his continuance in Office.

Section 4. Elections and Meetings

1. Holding Elections

In 1842 Congress required members of the House to be elected from districts in states having more than one Representative rather than at large. In 1845 it set the first Tuesday after the first Monday in November as the day for selecting presidential electors.

2. Meetings

The 20th Amendment, ratified in 1933, has changed the date of the opening of the regular session of Congress to January 3.

Section 5. Organization and Rules of Procedure

1. Organization

Until 1969 Congress acted as the sole judge of qualifications of its own members. In that year, the Supreme Court ruled that Congress could not legally exclude victorious candidates who met all the requirements listed in Article I.

A "quorum" is the minimum number of members that must be present for the House or Senate to conduct sessions. For a regular House session, a quorum consists of the majority of the House, or 218 of the 435 members.

2. Rules

Each house sets its own rules, can punish its members for disorderly behavior, and can expel a member by a two-thirds vote.

3. Journals

In addition to the journals, a complete official record of everything said on the floor, as well as the roll call votes on all bills or issues, is available in the *Congressional Record,* published daily by the Government Printing Office.

4. Adjournment

Neither house may adjourn for more than three days or move to another location without the approval of the other house.

Section 6. Privileges and Restrictions

1. Pay and Privileges

To strengthen the federal government, the Founders set congressional salaries to be paid by the United States Treasury rather than by members' respective states. Originally, members were paid $6 per day. Salaries for Senators and Representatives are $129,500.

The "immunity" privilege means members cannot be sued or be prosecuted for anything they say in Congress. They cannot be arrested while Congress is in session, except for treason, major crimes, or breaking the peace.

2. Restrictions

"Emoluments" means salaries. The purpose of this clause is to prevent members of Congress from passing laws that would benefit them personally. It also prevents the President from promising them jobs in other branches of the federal government.

SECTION 7

1. All Bills for raising Revenue shall originate in the House of Representatives; but the Senate may propose or concur with Amendments as on other bills.

2. Every Bill which shall have passed the House of Representatives and the Senate, shall, before it become a Law, be presented to the President of the United States; If he approve he shall sign it, but if not he shall return it, with his Objections, to that House in which it shall have originated, who shall enter the Objections at large on their Journal, and proceed to reconsider it. If after such Reconsideration two-thirds of that House shall agree to pass the bill, it shall be sent, together with the objections, to the other House, by which it shall likewise be reconsidered, and if approved by two thirds of that House, it shall become a Law. But in all such Cases the Votes of both Houses shall be determined by Yeas and Nays, and the Names of the Persons voting for and against the Bill shall be entered on the Journal of each House respectively. If any Bill shall not be returned by the President within ten Days (Sundays excepted) after it shall have been presented to him, the Same shall be a Law, in like Manner as if he had signed it, unless the Congress by their Adjournment prevent its Return, in which Case it shall not be a Law.

3. Every Order, Resolution, or Vote to which the Concurrence of the Senate and House of Representatives may be necessary (except on a question of Adjournment) shall be presented to the President of the United States; and before the Same shall take Effect, shall be approved by him, or, being disapproved by him, shall be repassed by two-thirds of the Senate and House of Representatives, according to the Rules and Limitations prescribed in the case of a Bill.

SECTION 8

The Congress shall have the Power

1. To lay and collect Taxes, Duties, Imposts and Excises, to pay the Debts and provide for the common Defence and general Welfare of the United States; but all Duties, Imposts and Excises shall be uniform throughout the United States;

2. To borrow money on the credit of the United States;

3. To regulate Commerce with foreign Nations, and among the several States, and with the Indian Tribes;

4. To establish an uniform Rule of Naturalization, and uniform Laws on the subject of Bankruptcies throughout the United States;

5. To coin Money, regulate the Value thereof, and of foreign Coin, and fix the Standard of Weights and Measures;

6. To provide for the Punishment of counterfeiting the Securities and current Coin of the United States;

7. To establish Post Offices and post Roads;

Section 7. Passing Laws

1. Revenue Bills

"Revenue" is income raised by the government. The chief source of government revenue is taxes. All tax laws must originate in the House of Representatives. This insures that the branch of Congress which is elected by the people every two years has the major role in determining taxes. This clause does not prevent the Senate from amending tax bills.

2. How Bills Become Laws

A bill may become a law only by passing both houses of Congress and by being signed by the President. If the President disapproves, or vetoes, the bill, it is returned to the house where it originated, along with a written statement of the President's objections. If two-thirds of each house approves the bill after the President has vetoed it, it becomes law. In voting to override a President's veto, the votes of all members of Congress must be recorded in the journals or official records. If the President does not sign or veto a bill within 10 days (excluding Sundays), it becomes law. However, if Congress has adjourned during this 10-day period, the bill does not become law. This is known as a "pocket veto."

3. Presidential Approval or Veto

The Framers included this paragraph to prevent Congress from passing joint resolutions instead of bills to avoid the possibility of a presidential veto. A bill is a draft of a proposed law, whereas a resolution is the legislature's formal expression of opinion or intent on a matter.

Section 8. Powers Granted to Congress

1. Revenue

This clause gives Congress the power to raise and spend revenue. Taxes must be levied at the same rate throughout the nation.

2. Borrowing

The federal government borrows money by issuing bonds.

3. Commerce

The exact meaning of "commerce" has caused controversy. The trend has been to expand its meaning and, consequently, the extent of Congress's powers.

4. Naturalization and Bankruptcy

"Naturalization" refers to the procedure by which a citizen of a foreign nation becomes a citizen of the United States.

5. Currency

Control over money is an exclusive federal power; the states are forbidden to issue currency.

6. Counterfeiting

"Counterfeiting" means illegally imitating or forging.

7. Post Office

In 1970 the United States Postal Service replaced the Post Office Department.

8. To promote the Progress of Science and useful Arts, by securing for limited Times to Authors and Inventors the exclusive Right to their respective Writings and Discoveries;

9. To constitute Tribunals inferior to the Supreme Court;

10. To define and punish Piracies and Felonies committed on the high Seas, and Offenses against the Law of Nations;

11. To declare War, grant Letters of Marque and Reprisal, and make Rules concerning Captures on Land and Water;

12. To raise and support Armies, but no Appropriation of Money to that Use shall be for a longer Term than two Years;

13. To provide and maintain a Navy;

14. To make Rules for the Government and Regulation of the land and naval forces;

15. To provide for calling forth the Militia to execute the Laws of the Union, suppress Insurrections, and repel Invasions;

16. To provide for organizing, arming, and disciplining, the Militia, and for governing such Part of them as may be employed in the Service of the United States, reserving to the States respectively, the Appointment of the Officers, and the Authority of training the Militia according to the discipline prescribed by Congress;

17. To exercise exclusive Legislation in all Cases whatsoever, over such District (not exceeding ten Miles square) as may, by Cession of particular States, and the acceptance of Congress, become the Seat of Government of the United States, and to exercise like Authority over all Places purchased by the Consent of the Legislature of the State in which the Same shall be, for the Erection of Forts, Magazines, Arsenals, dock-Yards, and other needful Buildings; And

18. To make all Laws which shall be necessary and proper for carrying into Execution the foregoing Powers, and all other Powers vested by this Constitution in the Government of the United States, or in any Department or Officer thereof.

SECTION 9

1. The Migration or Importation of such Persons as any of the States now existing shall think proper to admit, shall not be prohibited by the Congress prior to the Year one thousand eight hundred and eight, but a tax or duty may be imposed on such importation, not exceeding ten dollars for each Person.

2. The privilege of the Writ of Habeas Corpus shall not be suspended, unless when in Cases of Rebellion or Invasion the public Safety may require it.

3. No Bill of Attainder or ex post facto Law shall be passed.

4. No capitation, or other direct, Tax shall be laid unless in Proportion to the Census or Enumeration herein before directed to be taken.

8. Copyrights and Patents
Under this provision, Congress has passed copyright and patent laws.

9. Courts
This provision allows Congress to establish a federal court system.

10. Piracy
Congress has the power to protect American ships on the high seas.

11. Declare War
While the Constitution gives Congress the right to declare war, the United States has sent troops into combat without a congressional declaration.

12. Army
This provision reveals the Framers' fears of a standing army.

13. Navy
This clause allows Congress to establish a navy.

14. Rules for Armed Forces
Congress may pass regulations that deal with military discipline.

15. Militia
The "militia" is now called the National Guard. It is organized by the states.

16. National Guard
Even though the National Guard is organized by the states, Congress has the authority to pass rules for governing its behavior.

17. Nation's Capital
This clause grants Congress the right to make laws for Washington, D.C.

18. Elastic Clause
This is the so-called "elastic clause" of the Constitution and one of its most important provisions. The "necessary and proper" laws must be related to one of the 17 enumerated powers.

Section 9. Powers Denied to the Federal Government.

1. Slave Trade
This paragraph contains the compromise the Framers reached regarding regulation of the slave trade in exchange for Congress's exclusive control over interstate commerce.

2. Habeas Corpus
Habeas corpus is a Latin term meaning "you may have the body." A writ of habeas corpus issued by a judge requires a law official to bring a prisoner to court and show cause for holding the prisoner. The writ may be suspended only during wartime.

3. Bills of Attainder
A "bill of attainder" is a bill that punishes a person without a jury trial. An "ex post facto" law is one that makes an act a crime after the act has been committed.

4. Direct Taxes
The 16th Amendment allowed Congress to pass an income tax.

5. Tax on Exports
Congress may not tax goods that move from one state to another.

6. Uniformity of Treatment
This prohibition prevents Congress from favoring one state or region over another in the regulation of trade.

7. Appropriation Law
This clause protects against the misuse of funds. All of the President's expenditures must be made with the permission of Congress.

8. Titles of Nobility
This clause prevents the development of a nobility in the United States.

Section 10. Powers Denied to the States
1. Limitations on Power
The states are prohibited from conducting foreign affairs, carrying on a war, or controlling interstate and foreign commerce. States are also not allowed to pass laws that the federal government is prohibited from passing, such as enacting ex post facto laws or bills of attainder. These restrictions on the states were designed, in part, to prevent an overlapping in functions and authority with the federal government that could create conflict and chaos.

2. Export and Import Taxes
This clause prevents states from levying duties on exports and imports. If states were permitted to tax imports and exports they could use their taxing power in a way that weakens or destroys Congress's power to control interstate and foreign commerce.

3. Duties, Armed Forces, War
This clause prohibits states from maintaining an army or navy and from going to war, except in cases where a state is directly attacked. It also forbids states from collecting fees from foreign vessels or from making treaties with other nations. All of these powers are reserved for the federal government.

Article II. The Executive Branch

Section 1. President and Vice President
1. Term of Office
The President is given power to enforce the laws passed by Congress. Both the President and the Vice President serve four-year terms. The 22nd Amendment limits the number of terms the President may serve to two.

5. No Tax or Duty shall be laid on Articles exported from any State.

6. No Preference shall be given by any Regulation of Commerce or Revenue to the Ports of one State over those of another: nor shall Vessels bound to, or from, one State, be obliged to enter, clear, or pay Duties in another.

7. No Money shall be drawn from the Treasury, but in Consequence of Appropriations made by Law; and a regular Statement and Account of the Receipts and Expenditures of all public Money shall be published from time to time.

8. No Title of Nobility shall be granted by the United States: And no Person holding any Office of Profit or Trust under them, shall, without the Consent of the Congress, accept of any present, Emolument, Office, or Title, of any kind whatever, from any King, Prince, or foreign State.

SECTION 10

1. No State shall enter into any Treaty, Alliance, or Confederation; grant Letters of Marque and Reprisal; coin Money; emit Bills of Credit; make any Thing but gold and silver Coin a Tender in Payment of Debts; pass any Bill of Attainder; ex post facto Law, or Law impairing the Obligation of Contracts, or grant any Title of Nobility.

2. No State shall, without the Consent of the Congress, lay any Imposts or Duties on Imports or Exports, except what may be absolutely necessary for executing its inspection Laws: and the net Produce of all Duties and Imposts, laid by any State on Imports and Exports, shall be for the Use of the Treasury of the United States; and all such Laws shall be subject to the Revision and Controul of the Congress.

3. No State shall, without the Consent of Congress, lay any duty on Tonnage, keep Troops, or Ships of War in time of Peace, enter into any Agreement or Compact with another State, or with a foreign Power, or engage in War, unless actually invaded, or in such imminent Danger as will not admit of delay.

Article II

SECTION 1

1. The executive Power shall be vested in a President of the United States of America. He shall hold his Office during the Term of four years, and together with the Vice-President chosen for the same Term, be elected, as follows:

2. Each State shall appoint, in such Manner as the Legislature thereof may direct, a Number of Electors, equal to the whole Number of Senators and Representatives to which the State may be entitled in the Congress: but no Senator or Representative, or Person holding an Office of Trust or Profit under the United States, shall be appointed an Elector.

3. The Electors shall meet in their respective States, and vote by Ballot for two Persons, of whom one at least shall not be an Inhabitant of the same State with themselves. And they shall make a List of all the Persons voted for and of the Number of Votes for each; which List they shall sign and certify, and transmit sealed to the Seat of the Government of the United States, directed to the President of the Senate. The President of the Senate shall, in the Presence of the Senate and House of Representatives, open all the Certificates, and the Votes shall then be counted. The Person having the greatest Number of Votes shall be the President, if such Number be a Majority of the whole Number of Electors appointed; and if there be more than one who have such Majority, and have an equal Number of Votes, then the House of Representatives shall immediately chuse by Ballot one of them for President; and if no Person have a Majority, then from the five highest on the List the said House shall in like Manner chuse the President. But in chusing the President, the Votes shall be taken by States, the Representation from each State having one Vote; a quorum for this Purpose shall consist of a Member or Members from two-thirds of the States, and a Majority of all the States shall be necessary to a Choice. In every Case, after the Choice of the President, the Person having the greatest Number of Votes of the Electors shall be the Vice-President. But if there should remain two or more who have equal votes, the Senate shall chuse from them by Ballot the Vice President.

4. The Congress may determine the Time of chusing the Electors, and the Day on which they shall give their Votes; which Day shall be the same throughout the United States.

5. No person except a natural born Citizen, or a Citizen of the United States, at the time of the Adoption of this Constitution, shall be eligible to the Office of President; neither shall any Person be eligible to that Office who shall not have attained to the Age of thirty-five years, and been fourteen Years a Resident within the United States.

6. In Case of the Removal of the President from Office, or of his Death, Resignation, or Inability to discharge the Powers and Duties of the said Office, the same shall devolve on the Vice-President, and the Congress may by Law provide for the Case of Removal, Death, Resignation or Inability, both of the President and Vice-President, declaring what Officer shall then act as President, and such Officer shall act accordingly, until the disability be removed, or a President shall be elected.

2. Election

The Philadelphia Convention had trouble deciding how the President was to be chosen. The system finally agreed upon was indirect election by "electors" chosen for that purpose. The President and Vice President are not directly elected. Instead, the President and Vice President are elected by presidential electors from each state who form the electoral college. Each state has the number of presidential electors equal to the total number of its senators and representatives. State legislatures determine how the electors are chosen. Originally, the state legislatures chose the electors, but today they are nominated by political parties and elected by the voters. No senator, representative, or any other federal officeholder can serve as an elector.

3. Former Method of Election

This clause describes the original method of electing the President and Vice President. According to this method, each elector voted for two candidates. The candidate with the most votes (as long as it was a majority) became President. The candidate with the second highest number of votes became Vice President. In the election of 1800, the two top candidates received the same number of votes, making it necessary for the House of Representatives to decide the election. To prevent such a situation from recurring, the 12th Amendment was added in 1804.

4. Date of Elections

Congress selects the date when the presidential electors are chosen and when they vote for President and Vice President. All electors must vote on the same day. The first Tuesday after the first Monday in November has been set as the date for presidential elections. Electors cast their votes on the Monday after the second Wednesday in December.

5. Qualifications

The President must be a citizen of the United States by birth, at least 35 years old, and a resident of the United States for 14 years. See Amendment 22.

6. Vacancies

If the President dies, resigns, is removed from office by impeachment, or is unable to carry out the duties of the office, the Vice President becomes President. (Amendment 25 deals with presidential disability.) If both the President and Vice President are unable to serve, Congress has the power to declare by law who acts as President. Congress set the line of succession in the Presidential Succession Act of 1947.

7. Salary

Originally, the President's salary was $25,000 per year. The President's current salary of $200,000 plus a $50,000 taxable expense account per year was enacted in 1969. The President also receives numerous fringe benefits including a $120,000 nontaxable allowance for travel and entertainment, and living accommodations in two residences—the White House and Camp David. However, the President cannot receive any other income from the United States government or state governments while in office.

8. Oath of Office

The oath of office is generally administered by the chief justice, but can be administered by any official authorized to administer oaths. All Presidents-elect except Washington have been sworn into office by the chief justice. Only Vice Presidents John Tyler, Calvin Coolidge, and Lyndon Johnson in succeeding to the office have been sworn in by someone else.

Section 2. Powers of the President

1. Military, Cabinet, Pardons

Mention of "the principal officer in each of the executive departments" is the only suggestion of the President's Cabinet to be found in the Constitution. The Cabinet is a purely advisory body, and its power depends on the President. Each Cabinet member is appointed by the President and must be confirmed by the Senate. This clause also makes the President, a civilian, the head of the armed services. This established the principle of civilian control of the military.

2. Treaties and Appointments

The President is the chief architect of American foreign policy. He or she is responsible for the conduct of foreign relations, or dealings with other countries. All treaties, however, require approval of two-thirds of the senators present. Most federal positions today are filled under the rules and regulations of the civil service system. Most presidential appointees serve at the pleasure of the President. Removal of an official by the President is not subject to congressional approval. But the power can be restricted by conditions set in creating the office.

3. Vacancies in Offices

The President can temporarily appoint officials to fill vacancies when the Senate is not in session.

7. The President shall, at stated Times, receive for his Services a Compensation, which shall neither be encreased nor diminished during the Period for which he shall have been elected, and he shall not receive within that Period any other Emolument from the United States, or any of them.

8. Before he enter on the execution of his office, he shall take the following Oath or Affirmation "I do solemnly swear (or affirm) that I will faithfully execute the Office of President of the United States, and will to the best of my Ability, preserve, protect and defend the Constitution of the United States."

SECTION 2

1. The President shall be Commander in Chief of the Army and Navy of the United States, and of the Militia of the several States, when called into the actual Service of the United States; he may require the Opinion, in writing, of the principal Officer in each of the executive Departments, upon any subject relating to the Duties of their respective Offices, and he shall have Power to Grant Reprieves and Pardons for Offences against the United States, except in Cases of Impeachment.

2. He shall have Power, by and with the Advice and Consent of the Senate, to make Treaties, provided two-thirds of the Senators present concur; and he shall nominate, and by and with the Advice and Consent of the Senate, shall appoint Ambassadors, other public Ministers and Consuls, Judges of the supreme Court, and all other Officers of the United States, whose Appointments are not herein otherwise provided for, and which shall be established by Law. But the Congress may by Law vest the Appointment of such inferior Officers, as they think proper, in the President alone, in the Courts of Law, or in the Heads of Departments.

3. The President shall have Power to fill up all Vacancies that may happen during the Recess of the Senate, by granting Commissions which shall expire at the End of their next Session.

SECTION 3

He shall from time to time give to Congress Information of the State of the Union, and recommend to their Consideration such Measures as he shall judge necessary and expedient; he may, on extraordinary occasions, convene both Houses, or either of them, and in Case of Disagreement between them, with respect to the Time of Adjournment, he may adjourn them to such Time as he shall think proper; he shall receive Ambassadors and other public Ministers; he shall take Care that the Laws be faithfully executed, and shall Commission all the Officers of the United States.

SECTION 4

The President, Vice-President and all civil Officers of the United States, shall be removed from Office on Impeachment for, and Conviction of, Treason, Bribery, or other high Crimes and Misdemeanors.

Article III

SECTION 1

The Judicial Power of the United States, shall be vested in one supreme Court, and in such inferior Courts as the Congress may from time to time ordain and establish. The judges, both of the supreme and inferior Courts, shall hold their Offices during good Behaviour, and shall, at stated Times, receive for their Services, a Compensation, which shall not be diminished during their Continuance in Office.

SECTION 2

1. The judicial Power shall extend to all Cases, in Law and Equity, arising under this Constitution, the Laws of the United States, and treaties made, or which shall be made, under their Authority; to all Cases affecting ambassadors, other public ministers and consuls; to all cases of admiralty and maritime Jurisdiction; to Controversies to which the United States shall be a party; to Controversies between two or more states; between a State and Citizens of another State; between Citizens of different States; between Citizens of the same State claiming Lands under Grants of different States, and between a State, or the Citizens thereof, and foreign States, Citizens or Subjects.

2. In all Cases affecting Ambassadors, other public Ministers and Consuls, and those in which a State shall be Party, the supreme Court shall have original Jurisdiction. In all the other Cases before mentioned, the supreme Court shall have appellate Jurisdiction, both as to Law and Fact, with such Exceptions, and under such Regulations as the Congress shall make.

3. The trial of all Crimes, except in Cases of Impeachment, shall be by Jury; and such Trial shall be held in the State where the said Crimes shall have been committed; but when not committed within any State, the Trial shall be at such Place or Places as the Congress may by Law have directed.

Section 3. Duties of the President

Under this provision the President delivers annual State-of-the-Union messages. On occasion, Presidents have called Congress into special session to consider particular problems.

The President's duty to receive foreign diplomats also includes the power to ask a foreign country to withdraw its diplomatic officials from this country. This is called "breaking diplomatic relations" and often carries with it the implied threat of more drastic action, even war. The President likewise has the power of deciding whether or not to recognize foreign governments.

Section 4. Impeachment

This section states the reasons for which the President and Vice President may be impeached and removed from office. (See annotations of Article I, Section 3, Clauses 6 and 7.)

Article III. The Judicial Branch

Section 1. Federal Courts

The term *judicial* refers to courts. The Constitution set up only the Supreme Court but provided for the establishment of other federal courts. There are presently nine justices on the Supreme Court. Congress has created a system of federal district courts and courts of appeals, which review certain district court cases. Judges of these courts serve during "good behavior," which means that they usually serve for life or until they choose to retire.

Section 2. Jurisdiction

1. General Jurisdiction

Use of the words *in law and equity* reflects the fact that American courts took over two kinds of traditional law from Great Britain. The basic law was the "common law," which was based on over five centuries of judicial decisions. "Equity" was a special branch of British law developed to handle cases where common law did not apply.

Federal courts deal mostly with "statute law," or laws passed by Congress, treaties, and cases involving the Constitution itself. "Admiralty and maritime jurisdiction" covers all sorts of cases involving ships and shipping on the high seas and on rivers, canals, and lakes.

2. The Supreme Court

When a court has "original jurisdiction" over certain kinds of cases, it means that the court has the authority to be the first court to hear a case. A court with "appellate jurisdiction" hears cases that have been appealed from lower courts. Most Supreme Court cases are heard on appeal from lower courts.

3. Jury Trials

Except in cases of impeachment, anyone accused of a crime has the right to a trial by jury. The trial must be held in the state where the crime was committed. Jury trial guarantees were strengthened in the 6th, 7th, 8th, and 9th Amendments.

Section 3. Treason

1. Definition

Knowing that the charge of treason often had been used by monarchs to get rid of people who opposed them, the Framers of the Constitution defined treason carefully, requiring that at least two witnesses be present to testify in court that a treasonable act was committed.

2. Punishment

Congress is given the power to determine the punishment for treason. The children of a person convicted of treason may not be punished nor may the convicted person's property be taken away from the children. Convictions for treason have been relatively rare in the nation's history.

Article IV. Relations Among the States

Section 1. Official Acts

This provision insures that each state recognizes the laws, court decisions, and records of all other states. For example, a marriage license or corporation charter issued by one state must be accepted in other states.

Section 2. Mutual Duties of States

1. Privileges

The "privileges and immunities," or rights of citizens, guarantee each state's citizens equal treatment in all states.

2. Extradition

"Extradition" means that a person convicted of a crime or a person accused of a crime must be returned to the state where the crime was committed. Thus, a person cannot flee to another state hoping to escape the law.

3. Fugitive-Slave Clause

Formerly this clause meant that slaves could not become free persons by escaping to free states.

Section 3. New States and Territories

1. New States

Congress has the power to admit new states. It also determines the basic guidelines for applying for statehood. One state, Maine, was created within the original boundaries of another state (Massachusetts) with the consent of Congress and the state.

2. Territories

Congress has power over federal land. But neither in this clause nor anywhere else in the Constitution is the federal government explicitly empowered to acquire new territory.

Section 4. Federal Protection for States

This section allows the federal government to send troops into a state to guarantee law and order. The President may send in troops even without the consent of the state government involved.

SECTION 3

1. Treason against the United States, shall consist only in levying War against them, or in adhering to their Enemies, giving them Aid and Comfort. No Person shall be convicted of Treason unless on the Testimony of two Witnesses to the same overt Act, or on Confession in open Court.

2. The Congress shall have power to declare the Punishment of Treason, but no Attainder of Treason shall work Corruption of Blood, or Forfeiture except during the Life of the Person attainted.

Article IV

SECTION 1

Full Faith and Credit shall be given in each State to the public Acts, Records, and judicial Proceedings of every other State. And the Congress may by general Laws prescribe the Manner in which such Acts, Records, and Proceedings shall be proved, and the Effect thereof.

SECTION 2

1. The Citizens of each State shall be entitled to all Privileges and Immunities of Citizens in the several States.

2. A Person charged in any State with Treason, Felony, or other Crime, who shall flee from Justice, and be found in another State, shall on demand of the executive Authority of the State from which he fled, be delivered up, to be removed to the State having Jurisdiction of the crime.

3. No Person held to Service of Labour in one State, under the Laws thereof, escaping into another, shall, in Consequence of any Law or Regulation therein, be discharged from such Service or Labour, but shall be delivered up on Claim of the Party to whom such Service or Labour may be due.

SECTION 3

1. New States may be admitted by the Congress into this Union; but no new State shall be formed or erected within the Jurisdiction of any other State; nor any State be formed by the Junction of two or more States, or parts of States, without the Consent of the Legislatures of the States concerned as well as of the Congress.

2. The Congress shall have Power to dispose of and make all needful Rules and Regulations respecting the Territory of other Property belonging to the United States; and nothing in this Constitution shall be so construed as to Prejudice any Claims of the United States, or of any particular State.

SECTION 4

The United States shall guarantee to every State in this Union a Republican Form of Government, and shall protect each of them against Invasion; and on Application of the Legislature, or of the Executive (when the Legislature cannot be convened) against domestic Violence.

Article V

The Congress, whenever two-thirds of both Houses shall deem it necessary, shall propose Amendments to this Constitution, or, on the Application of the Legislatures of two-thirds of the several States, shall call a Convention for proposing Amendments, which, in either Case, shall be valid to all Intents and Purposes, as part of this Constitution, when ratified by the Legislatures of three-fourths of the several States, or by Conventions in three-fourths thereof, as the one or the other Mode of Ratification may be proposed by the Congress; Provided that no Amendment which may be made prior to the Year One thousand eight hundred and eight shall in any Manner affect the first and fourth clauses in the Ninth Section of the first Article; and that no State, without its Consent, shall be deprived of its equal Suffrage in the Senate.

Article V. The Amending Process

There are now 27 Amendments to the Constitution. The Framers of the Constitution deliberately made it difficult to amend or change the Constitution. Two methods of proposing and ratifying amendments are provided for. A two-thirds majority is needed in Congress to propose an amendment, and at least three-fourths of the states (38 states) must accept the amendment before it can become law. No amendment has yet been proposed by a national convention called by the states, though in the 1980s a convention to propose an amendment requiring a balanced budget had been approved by 32 states.

Article VI

1. All Debts contracted and Engagements entered into, before the Adoption of this Constitution, shall be as valid against the United States under this Constitution as under the Confederation.

2. This Constitution, and the Laws of the United States which shall be made in Pursuance thereof; and all Treaties made, or which shall be made, under the Authority of the United States, shall be the supreme Law of the Land; and the Judges in every State shall be bound thereby, any Thing in the Constitution or Laws of any State to the Contrary notwithstanding.

3. The Senators and Representatives before mentioned, and the Members of the several State Legislatures, and all executive and judicial Officers, both of the United States and of the several States, shall be bound by Oath or Affirmation, to support this Constitution; but no religious Test shall ever be required as a Qualification to any Office or public Trust under the United States.

Article VI. National Supremacy

1. Public Debts and Treaties

This section promised that all debts the colonies had incurred during the Revolution and under the Articles of Confederation would be honored by the new United States government.

2. The Supreme Law

The "supremacy clause" recognized the Constitution and federal laws as supreme when in conflict with those of the states. It was largely based on this clause that Chief Justice John Marshall wrote his historic decision in *McCulloch* v. *Maryland.* The 14th Amendment reinforced the supremacy of federal law over state laws.

3. Oaths of Office

This clause also declares that no religious test shall be required as a qualification for holding public office. This principle is also asserted in the First Amendment, which forbids Congress to set up an established church or to interfere with the religious freedom of Americans.

Article VII

The Ratification of the Conventions of nine States shall be sufficient for the Establishment of this Constitution between the States so ratifying the same.

Done in Convention, by the Unanimous Consent of the States present, the Seventeenth Day of September, in the Year of our Lord one thousand seven hundred and Eighty-seven, and of the Independence of the United States of America the Twelfth. In Witness whereof We have hereunto subscribed our Names.

Article VII. Ratification of the Constitution

Unlike the Articles of Confederation, which required approval of all thirteen states for adoption, the Constitution required approval of only nine of thirteen states. Thirty-nine of the 55 delegates at the Constitutional Convention signed the Constitution. The Constitution went into effect in June 1788.

SIGNERS
George Washington,
President and Deputy from Virginia

NEW HAMPSHIRE
John Langdon
Nicholas Gilman

MASSACHUSETTS
Nathaniel Gorham
Rufus King

CONNECTICUT
William Samuel Johnson
Roger Sherman

NEW YORK
Alexander Hamilton

NEW JERSEY
William Livingston
David Brearley
William Paterson
Jonathan Dayton

PENNSYLVANIA
Benjamin Franklin
Thomas Mifflin
Robert Morris
George Clymer
Thomas FitzSimons
Jared Ingersoll
James Wilson
Gouverneur Morris

DELAWARE
George Read
Gunning Bedford, Jr.
John Dickinson
Richard Bassett
Jacob Broom

MARYLAND
James McHenry
Daniel of St. Thomas Jenifer
Daniel Carroll

VIRGINIA
John Blair
James Madison, Jr.

NORTH CAROLINA
William Blount
Richard Dobbs Spaight
Hugh Williamson

SOUTH CAROLINA
John Rutledge
Charles Cotesworth Pinckney
Charles Pinckney
Pierce Butler

GEORGIA
William Few
Abraham Baldwin

ATTEST:
William Jackson,
Secretary

Amendment 1. Freedom of Religion, Speech, Press, and Assembly (1791)
The 1st Amendment protects the civil liberties of individuals in the United States. The 1st Amendment freedoms are not absolute, however. They are limited by the rights of other individuals.

Amendment 2. Right to Bear Arms (1791)
The purpose of this amendment is to guarantee states the right to keep a militia.

Amendment 3. Quartering Troops (1791)
This amendment is based on the principle that people have a right to privacy in their own homes. It also reflects the colonists' grievances against the British government before the Revolution. Britain had angered Americans by quartering (housing) troops in private homes.

Amendment 4. Searches and Seizures (1791)
Like the 3rd Amendment, the 4th amendment reflects the colonists' desire to protect their privacy. Britain had used writs of assistance (general search warrants) to seek out smuggled goods. Americans wanted to make sure that such searches and seizures would be conducted only when a judge felt that there was "reasonable cause" to conduct them. The Supreme Court has ruled that evidence seized illegally without a search warrant may not be used in court.

Amendment I

Congress shall make no law respecting an establishment of religion, or prohibiting the free exercise thereof; or abridging the freedom of speech, or of the press; or the right of the people peaceably to assemble, and to petition the Government for a redress of grievances.

Amendment II

A well-regulated Militia, being necessary to the security of a free State, the right of the people to keep and bear Arms, shall not be infringed.

Amendment III

No soldier shall, in time of peace be quartered in any house, without the consent of the Owner, nor in time of war, but in a manner to be prescribed by law.

Amendment IV

The right of the people to be secure in their persons, houses, papers, and effects, against unreasonable searches and seizures, shall not be violated, and no Warrants shall issue, but upon probable cause, supported by Oath or affirmation, and particularly describing the place to be searched, and the persons or things to be seized.

Amendment V

No person shall be held to answer for a capital, or otherwise infamous crime, unless on a presentment or indictment of a Grand Jury, except in cases arising in the land or naval forces, or in the Militia, when in actual service in time of War or public danger; nor shall any person be subject for the same offence to be twice put in jeopardy of life or limb; nor shall be compelled in any criminal case to be a witness against himself, nor be deprived of life, liberty, or property, without due process of law; nor shall private property be taken for public use, without just compensation.

Amendment VI

In all criminal prosecutions, the accused shall enjoy the right to a speedy and public trial, by an impartial jury of the State and district wherein the crime shall have been committed, which district shall have been previously ascertained by law, and to be informed of the nature and cause of the accusation; to be confronted with the witnesses against him; to have compulsory process for obtaining witnesses in his favor, and to have the Assistance of Counsel for his defence.

Amendment VII

In suits at common law, where the value in controversy shall exceed twenty dollars, the right of trial by jury shall be preserved, and no fact tried by a jury, shall be otherwise reexamined in any Courts of the United States, than according to the rules of common law.

Amendment VIII

Excessive bail shall not be required, nor excessive fines imposed, nor cruel and unusual punishments inflicted.

Amendment IX

The enumeration in the Constitution, of certain rights, shall not be construed to deny or disparage others retained by the people.

Amendment X

The powers not delegated to the United States by the Constitution, nor prohibited by it to the States, are reserved to the States respectively, or to the people.

Amendment 5. Rights of Accused Persons (1791)

To bring a "presentment" or "indictment" means to formally charge a person with committing a crime. It is the function of a grand jury to see whether there is enough evidence to bring the accused person to trial. A person may not be tried more than once for the same crime (double jeopardy).

Members of the armed services are subject to military law. They may be tried in a court martial. In times of war or a natural disaster, civilians may also be put under martial law.

The 5th Amendment also guarantees that persons may not be forced in any criminal case to be a witness against themselves. That is, accused persons may refuse to answer questions on the ground that the answers might tend to incriminate them.

Amendment 6. Right to Speedy, Fair Trial (1791)

The requirement of a "speedy" trial insures that an accused person will not be held in jail for a lengthy period as a means of punishing the accused without a trial. A "fair" trial means that the trial must be open to the public and that a jury must hear witnesses and evidence on both sides before deciding the guilt or innocence of a person charged with a crime. This amendment also provides that legal counsel must be provided to a defendant. In 1963, the Supreme Court ruled, in *Gideon* v. *Wainwright,* that if a defendant cannot afford a lawyer, the government must provide one to defend the accused person.

Amendment 7. Civil Suits (1791)

"Common law" means the law established by previous court decisions. In civil cases where one person sues another for more than $20, a jury trial is provided for. But customarily, federal courts do not hear civil cases unless they involve a good deal more money.

Amendment 8. Bail and Punishment (1791)

"Bail" is money that an accused person provides to the court as a guarantee that he or she will be present for a trial. This amendment insures that neither bail nor punishment for a crime shall be unreasonably severe.

Amendment 9. Powers Reserved to the People (1791)

This amendment provides that the people's rights are not limited to those mentioned in the Constitution.

Amendment 10. Powers Reserved to the States (1791)

This amendment protects the states and the people from an all-powerful federal government. It provides that the states or the people retain all powers except those denied them or those specifically granted to the federal government. This "reserved powers" provision is a check on the "necessary and proper" power of the federal government provided in the "elastic clause" in Article I, Section 8, Clause 18.

Amendment 11. Suits Against States (1795)

This amendment provides that a lawsuit brought by a citizen of the United States or a foreign nation against a state must be tried in a state court, not in a federal court. This amendment was passed after the Supreme Court ruled that a federal court could try a lawsuit brought by citizens of South Carolina against a citizen of Georgia. This case, *Chisholm* v. *Georgia,* decided in 1793, was protested by many Americans, who insisted states would lose authority if they could be sued in federal courts.

Amendment 12. Election of President and Vice President (1804)

This amendment changes the procedure for electing the President and Vice President as outlined in Article II, Section 1, Clause 3.

To prevent the recurrence of the election of 1800 whereby a candidate running for Vice President (Aaron Burr) could tie a candidate running for President (Thomas Jefferson) and thus force the election into the House of Representatives, the Twelfth Amendment specifies that the electors are to cast separate ballots for each office. The votes for each office are counted and listed separately. The results are signed, sealed, and sent to the president of the senate. At a joint session of Congress, the votes are counted. The candidate who receives the most votes, providing it is a majority, is elected President. Other changes include: (1) a reduction from five to the three highest candidates receiving votes among whom the House is to choose if no candidate receives a majority of the electoral votes, and (2) provision for the Senate to choose the Vice President from the two highest candidates if neither has received a majority of the electoral votes.

The Twelfth Amendment does place one restriction on electors. It prohibits electors from voting for two candidates (President and Vice President) from their home state.

Amendment 13. Abolition of Slavery (1865)

This amendment was the final act in ending slavery in the United States. It also prohibits the binding of a person to perform a personal service due to debt. In addition to imprisonment for crime, the Supreme Court has held that the draft is not a violation of the amendment.

This amendment is the first adopted to be divided into sections. It is also the first to contain specifically a provision granting Congress power to enforce it by appropriate legislation.

Amendment XI

The Judicial power of the United States shall not be construed to extend to any suit in law or equity, commenced or prosecuted against one of the United States by Citizens of another State, or by Citizens or Subjects of any Foreign State.

Amendment XII

The Electors shall meet in their respective States and vote by ballot for President and Vice-President, one of whom, at least, shall not be an inhabitant of the same State with themselves; they shall name in their ballots the person voted for as President, and in distinct ballots the person voted for as Vice-President, and they shall make distinct lists of all persons voted for as President, and of all persons voted for as Vice-President, and of the number of votes for each, which lists they shall sign and certify, and transmit sealed to the seat of the government of the United States, directed to the President of the Senate; The President of the Senate shall, in the presence of the Senate and House of Representatives, open all the certificates and the votes shall then be counted; The person having the greatest number of votes for President, shall be the President, if such number be a majority of the whole number of Electors appointed; and if no person have such majority, then from the persons having the highest numbers not exceeding three on the list of those voted for as President, the House of Representatives shall choose immediately, by ballot, the President. But in choosing the President, the votes shall be taken by states, the representation from each state having one vote; a quorum for this purpose shall consist of a member or members from two-thirds of the states, and a majority of all the states shall be necessary to a choice. And if the House of Representatives shall not choose a President whenever the right of choice shall devolve upon them, before the fourth day of March next following, then the Vice-President shall act as President, as in the case of the death or other constitutional disability of the President. The person having the greatest number of votes as Vice-President, shall be the Vice-President, if such number be a majority of the whole number of Electors appointed, and if no person have a majority, then from the two highest numbers on the list, the Senate shall choose the Vice-President; a quorum for the purpose shall consist of two-thirds of the whole number of Senators, and a majority of the whole number shall be necessary to a choice. But no person constitutionally ineligible to the office of President shall be eligible to that of Vice-President of the United States.

Amendment XIII

SECTION 1

Neither slavery nor involuntary servitude, except as a punishment for crime whereof the party shall have been duly convicted, shall exist within the United States, or any place subject to their jurisdiction.

SECTION 2

Congress shall have power to enforce this article by appropriate legislation.

Amendment XIV

SECTION 1

All persons born or naturalized in the United States, and subject to the jurisdiction thereof, are citizens of the United States and of the State wherein they reside. No State shall make or enforce any law which shall abridge the privileges or immunities of citizens of the United States; nor shall any State deprive any person of life, liberty, or property, without due process of law, nor deny to any person within its jurisdiction the equal protection of the laws.

SECTION 2

Representatives shall be apportioned among the several States according to their respective numbers, counting the whole number of persons in each State, excluding Indians not taxed. But when the right to vote at any election for the choice of electors for President and Vice-President of the United States, Representatives in Congress, the Executive and Judicial officers of a State, or the members of the Legislature thereof, is denied to any of the male inhabitants of such State, being twenty-one years of age, and citizens of the United States, or in any way abridged, except for participation in rebellion, or other crime, the basis of representation therein shall be reduced in the proportion which the number of such male citizens shall bear to the whole number of male citizens twenty-one years of age in such State.

SECTION 3

No person shall be a Senator or Representative in Congress, or elector of President and Vice-President, or hold any office, civil or military, under the United States, or under any State, who, having previously taken an oath, as a member of Congress, or as an officer of the United States, or as a member of any State legislature, or as an executive or judicial officer of any State, to support the Constitution of the United States, shall have engaged in insurrection or rebellion against the same, or given aid or comfort to the enemies thereof. But Congress may by a vote of two-thirds of each House, remove such disability.

SECTION 4

The validity of the public debt of the United States incurred for payment of pensions and bounties for service, authorized by law, including debts in suppressing insurrections or rebellion, shall not be questioned. But neither the United States nor any State shall assume or pay any debt or obligation incurred in aid of insurrection or rebellion against the United States, or any claim for the loss or emancipation of any slave; but all such debts, obligations and claims shall be held illegal and void.

SECTION 5

The Congress shall have power to enforce, by appropriate legislation, the provisions of this article.

Amendment 14. Rights of Citizens (1868)

The clauses of this amendment were intended 1) to penalize southern states that refused to grant African Americans the vote, 2) to keep former Confederate leaders from serving in government, 3) to forbid payment of the Confederacy's debt by the federal government, and 4) to insure payment of the war debts owed the federal government.

Section 1. Citizenship Defined

By granting citizenship to all persons born in the United States, this amendment granted citizenship to former slaves. The amendment also guaranteed "due process of law." By the 1950s, Supreme Court rulings used the due process clause to protect civil liberties. The last part of Section 1 establishes the doctrine that all citizens are entitled to equal protection of the laws. In 1954 the Supreme Court ruled, in *Brown* v. *Board of Education of Topeka,* that segregation in public schools was unconstitutional because it denied equal protection.

Section 2. Representation in Congress

This section reduced the number of members a state had in the House of Representatives if it denied its citizens the right to vote. This section was not implemented, however. Later civil rights laws and the 24th Amendment guaranteed the vote to African Americans.

Section 3. Penalty for Engaging in Insurrection

The leaders of the Confederacy were barred from state or federal offices unless Congress agreed to revoke this ban. By the end of Reconstruction all but a few Confederate leaders were allowed to return to public life.

Section 4. Public Debt

The public debt incurred by the federal government during the Civil War was valid and could not be questioned by the South. However, the debts of the Confederacy were declared to be illegal. And former slave owners could not collect compensation for the loss of their slaves.

Section 5. Enforcement

Congress was empowered to pass civil rights bills to guarantee the provisions of the amendment.

Amendment 15. The Right to Vote (1870)
Section 1. Suffrage for African Americans
The 15th Amendment replaced Section 2 of the 14th Amendment in guaranteeing African Americans the right to vote, that is, the right of African Americans to vote was not to be left to the states. Yet, despite this prohibition, African Americans were denied the right to vote by many states by such means as poll taxes, literacy tests, and white primaries.

Section 2. Enforcement
Congress was given the power to enforce this amendment. During the 1950s and 1960s, it passed successively stronger laws to end racial discrimination in voting rights.

Amendment 16. Income Tax (1913)
The origins of this amendment went back to 1895, when the Supreme Court declared a federal income tax unconstitutional. To overcome this Supreme Court decision, this amendment authorized an income tax that was levied on a direct basis.

Amendment 17. Direct Election of Senators (1913)
Section 1. Method of Election
The right to elect senators was given directly to the people of each state. It replaced Article I, Section 3, Clause 1, which empowered state legislatures to elect senators. This amendment was designed not only to make the choice of senators more democratic but also to cut down on corruption and to improve state government.

Section 2. Vacancies
A state must order an election to fill a senate vacancy. A state may empower its governor to appoint a person to fill a Senate seat if a vacancy occurs until an election can be held.

Section 3. Time in Effect
This amendment was not to affect any Senate election or temporary appointment until it was in effect.

Amendment 18. Prohibition of Alcoholic Beverages (1919)
This amendment prohibited the production, sale, or transportation of alcoholic beverages in the United States. Prohibition proved to be difficult to enforce, especially in states with large urban populations. This amendment was later repealed by the 21st Amendment.

Amendment 19. Women's Suffrage (1920)
This amendment, extending the vote to all qualified women in federal and state elections, was a landmark victory for the woman suffrage movement, which had worked to achieve this goal for many years. The women's movement had earlier gained full voting rights for women in four western states in the late nineteenth century.

Amendment XV

SECTION 1

The right of citizens of the United States to vote shall not be denied or abridged by the United States or by any State on account of race, color, or previous condition of servitude.

SECTION 2

The Congress shall have power to enforce this article by appropriate legislation.

Amendment XVI

The Congress shall have power to lay and collect taxes on incomes, from whatever source derived, without apportionment among several States, and without regard to any census or enumeration.

Amendment XVII

SECTION 1

The Senate of the United States shall be composed of two Senators from each State, elected by the people thereof, for six years; and each Senator shall have one vote. The electors in each state shall have the qualifications requisite for electors of the most numerous branch of the state legislatures.

SECTION 2

When vacancies happen in the representation of any State in the Senate, the executive authority of such State shall issue writs of election to fill such vacancies: *Provided,* that the legislature of any State may empower the executive thereof to make temporary appointments until the people fill the vacancies by election as the legislature may direct.

SECTION 3

This amendment shall not be so construed as to affect the election or term of any Senator chosen before it becomes valid as part of the Constitution.

Amendment XVIII

SECTION 1

After one year from ratification of this article the manufacture, sale, or transportation of intoxicating liquors within, the importation thereof into, or the exportation thereof from the United States and all territory subject to the jurisdiction thereof for beverage purposes is hereby prohibited.

SECTION 2

The Congress and the several states shall have concurrent power to enforce this article by appropriate legislation.

SECTION 3

This article shall be inoperative unless it shall have been ratified as an amendment to the Constitution by the legislatures of the several States, as provided in the Constitution, within seven years from the date of the submission hereof to the states of the Congress.

Amendment XIX

SECTION 1

The right of citizens of the United States to vote shall not be denied or abridged by the United States or by any state on account of sex.

SECTION 2

Congress shall have power to enforce this article by appropriate legislation.

Amendment XX

SECTION 1

The terms of the President and Vice President shall end at noon on the 20th day of January, and the terms of the Senators and Representatives at noon on the 3rd day of January, of the years in which such terms would have ended if this article had not been ratified; and the terms of their successors shall then begin.

SECTION 2

The Congress shall assemble at least once in every year, and such meeting shall begin at noon on the 3rd day of January, unless they shall by law appoint a different day.

SECTION 3

If, at the time fixed for the beginning of the term of the President, the President elect shall have died, the Vice President elect shall become President. If a President shall not have been chosen before the time fixed for the beginning of his term, or if the President elect shall have failed to qualify, then the Vice President elect shall act as President until a President shall have qualified; and the Congress may by law provide for the case wherein neither a President elect nor a Vice President elect shall have qualified, declaring who shall then act as President, or the manner in which one who is to act shall be selected, and such person shall act accordingly until a President or Vice President shall have qualified.

SECTION 4

The Congress may by law provide for the case of the death of any of the persons from whom the House of Representatives may choose a President whenever the right of choice shall have devolved upon them, and for the case of the death of any of the persons from whom the Senate may choose a Vice President whenever the right of choice shall have devolved upon them.

SECTION 5

Sections 1 and 2 shall take effect on the 15th day of October following the ratification of this article.

SECTION 6

This article shall be inoperative unless it shall have been ratified as an amendment to the Constitution by the legislatures of three-fourths of the several States within seven years from the date of its submission.

Amendment XXI

SECTION 1

The eighteenth article of amendment to the Constitution of the United States is hereby repealed.

SECTION 2

The transportation or importation into any State, Territory, or possession of the United States for delivery or use therein of intoxicating liquors, in violation of the laws thereof, is hereby prohibited.

SECTION 3

This article shall be inoperative unless it shall have been ratified as an amendment to the Constitution by conventions in the several States, as provided in the Constitution, within seven years from the date of the submission hereof to the States by the Congress.

Amendment 20. "Lame-Duck" Amendment (1933)

Section 1. New Dates of Terms

This amendment had two major purposes: 1) to shorten the time between the President's and Vice President's election and inauguration, and 2) to end "lame-duck" sessions of Congress.

When the Constitution first went into effect, transportation and communication were slow and uncertain. It often took many months after the election in November for the President and Vice President to travel to Washington, D.C., and prepare for their inauguration on March 4. This amendment ended this long wait for a new administration by fixing January 20 as Inauguration Day.

Section 2. Meeting Time of Congress

"Lame-duck" sessions occurred every two years, after the November congressional election. That is, the Congress that held its session in December of an election year was not the newly elected Congress but the old Congress that had been elected two years earlier. This Congress continued to serve for several more months, usually until March of the next year. Often many of its members had failed to be reelected and were called "lame ducks." The 20th Amendment abolished this "lame-duck" session, and provided that the new Congress hold its first session soon after the November election, on January 3.

Section 3. Succession of President and Vice President

This amendment provides that if the President-elect dies before taking office, the Vice President-elect becomes President. In the cases described, Congress will decide on a temporary President.

Section 4. Filling Presidential Vacancy

If a presidential candidate dies while an election is being decided in the House, Congress may pass legislation to deal with the situation. Congress has similar power if this occurs when the Senate is deciding a vice-presidential election.

Section 5. Beginning the New Dates

Sections 1 and 2 affected the Congress elected in 1934 and President Roosevelt, elected in 1936.

Section 6. Time Limit on Ratification

The period for ratification by the states was limited to seven years.

Amendment 21. Repeal of Prohibition Amendment (1933)

This amendment nullified the 18th Amendment. It is the only amendment ever passed to overturn an earlier amendment. It remained unlawful to transport alcoholic beverages into states that forbade their use. It is the only amendment ratified by special state conventions instead of state legislatures.

Amendment 22. Limit on Presidential Terms (1951)

This amendment wrote into the Constitution a custom started by Washington, Jefferson, and Madison, whereby Presidents limited themselves to two terms in office. Although both Ulysses S. Grant and Theodore Roosevelt sought third terms, the two-term precedent was not broken until Franklin D. Roosevelt was elected to a third term in 1940 and then a fourth term in 1944. The passage of the 22nd amendment insures that no President is to be considered indispensable. It also provides that anyone who succeeds to the presidency and serves for more than two years of the term may not be elected more than one more time.

Amendment 23. Presidential Electors for the District of Columbia (1961)

This amendment granted people living in the District of Columbia the right to vote in presidential elections. The District casts three electoral votes. The people of Washington, D.C., still are without representation in Congress.

Amendment 24. Abolition of the Poll Tax (1964)

A "poll tax" was a fee that persons were required to pay in order to vote in a number of Southern states. This amendment ended poll taxes as a requirement to vote in any presidential or congressional election. In 1966 the Supreme Court voided poll taxes in state elections as well.

Amendment 25. Presidential Disability and Succession (1967)

Section 1. Replacing the President

The Vice President becomes President if the President dies, resigns, or is removed from office.

Section 2. Replacing the Vice President

The President is to appoint a new Vice President in case of a vacancy in that office, with the approval of the Congress.

The 25th Amendment is unusually precise and explicit because it was intended to solve a serious constitutional problem. Sixteen times in American history, before passage of this amendment, the office of Vice President was vacant, but fortunately in none of these cases did the President die or resign.

This amendment was used in 1973, when Vice President Spiro Agnew resigned from office after being charged with accepting bribes. President Nixon then appointed Gerald R. Ford as Vice President in accordance with the provisions of the 25th Amendment. A year later, President Richard Nixon resigned during the Watergate scandal, and Ford became President. President Ford then had to fill the Vice Presidency, which he had left vacant upon assuming the Presidency. He named Nelson A. Rockefeller as Vice President. Thus both the presidency and vice-presidency were held by men who had not been elected to their offices.

Amendment XXII

SECTION 1

No person shall be elected to the office of the President more than twice, and no person who had held the office of President, or acted as President, for more than two years of a term to which some other person was elected President shall be elected to the office of the President more than once.

But this Article shall not apply to any person holding the office of President when this Article was proposed by the Congress, and shall not prevent any person who may be holding the office of President, or acting as President, during the term within which this Article becomes operative from holding the office of President or acting as President during the remainder of such term.

SECTION 2

This article shall be inoperative unless it shall have been ratified as an amendment to the Constitution by the legislatures of three-fourths of the several States within seven years from the date of its submission to the States by the Congress.

Amendment XXIII

SECTION 1

The District constituting the seat of Government of the United States shall appoint in such manner as the Congress may direct:

A number of electors of President and Vice President equal to the whole number of Senators and Representatives in Congress to which the District would be entitled if it were a State, but in no event more than the least populous State; they shall be in addition to those appointed by the States, but they shall be considered, for the purposes of the election of President and Vice President, to be electors appointed by a State; and they shall meet in the District and perform such duties as provided by the twelfth article of amendment.

SECTION 2

The Congress shall have power to enforce this article by appropriate legislation.

Amendment XXIV

SECTION 1

The right of citizens of the United States to vote in any primary or other election for President or Vice President, for electors for President or Vice President, or for Senator or Representative in Congress, shall not be denied or abridged by the United States or any State by reason of failure to pay any poll tax or other tax.

SECTION 2

The Congress shall have power to enforce this article by appropriate legislation.

Amendment XXV

SECTION 1

In case of the removal of the President from office or his death or resignation, the Vice President shall become President.

SECTION 2

Whenever there is a vacancy in the office of the Vice President, the President shall nominate a Vice President who shall take the office upon confirmation by a majority vote of both houses of Congress.

SECTION 3

Whenever the President transmits to the President pro tempore of the Senate and the Speaker of the House of Representatives his written declaration that he is unable to discharge the powers and duties of his office, and until he transmits to them a written declaration to the contrary, such powers and duties shall be discharged by the Vice President as Acting President.

SECTION 4

Whenever the Vice President and a majority of either the principal officers of the executive departments or of such other body as Congress may by law provide, transmit to the President pro tempore of the Senate and the Speaker of the House of Representatives their written declaration that the President is unable to discharge the powers and duties of his office, the Vice President shall immediately assume the power and duties of the office of Acting President.

Thereafter, when the President transmits to the President pro tempore of the Senate and the Speaker of the House of Representatives his written declaration that no inability exists, he shall resume the powers and duties of his office unless the Vice President and a majority of either the principal officers of the executive departments or of such other body as Congress may by law provide, transmit within four days to the President pro tempore of the Senate and the Speaker of the House of Representatives their written declaration that the President is unable to discharge the powers and duties of his office. Thereupon Congress shall decide the issue, assembling within forty-eight hours for that purpose if not in session. If the Congress within twenty-one days after receipt of the latter written declaration, or, if Congress is not in session, within twenty-one days after Congress is required to assemble, determines by two-thirds vote of both houses that the President is unable to discharge the powers and duties of his office, the Vice President shall continue to discharge the same as Acting President; otherwise, the President shall resume the power and duties of his office.

Amendment XXVI

SECTION 1

The right of citizens of the United States, who are eighteen years of age or older, to vote shall not be denied or abridged by the United States or by any State on account of age.

SECTION 2

The Congress shall have power to enforce this article by appropriate legislation.

Amendment XXVII

No law, varying the compensation for the services of Senators and Representatives, shall take effect, until an election of Representatives shall have intervened.

Section 3. Replacing the President With Consent

If the President informs Congress, in writing, that he or she cannot carry out the duties of the office of President, the Vice President becomes Acting President.

Section 4. Replacing the President Without Consent

If the President is unable to carry out the duties of the office but is unable or unwilling to so notify Congress, the Cabinet and the Vice President are to inform Congress of this fact. The Vice President then becomes Acting President. The procedure by which the President may regain the office if he or she recovers is also spelled out in this amendment.

Amendment 26. Eighteen-Year-Old Vote (1971)

This amendment made 18-year-olds eligible to vote in all federal, state, and local elections. Until then, the minimum age had been 21 in most states.

Amendment 27. Restraint on Congressional Salaries (1992)

Any increase in the salaries of members of Congress will take effect in the subsequent session of Congress.

CULTURE OF THE TIME

The Colonial Period

Immigrants brought European customs with them to the colonies. Familiar clothing styles, religious beliefs, amusements, and cookery helped settlers feel at home.

COURTESY, AMERICAN ANTIQUARIAN SOCIETY

KEEPING THE FAITH

Most newcomers to the colonies practiced Christianity. **Spiritual songs and writings** helped settlers keep their faith in spite of the challenges that faced them in this new land.

LUXURY GOODS

Throughout the period, wealthier colonists bought **imported European goods,** such as this elaborately dressed doll, and the fine items of clothing shown at bottom right.

COURTESY OF THE WEKHAM MUSEUM, WENHAM, MA

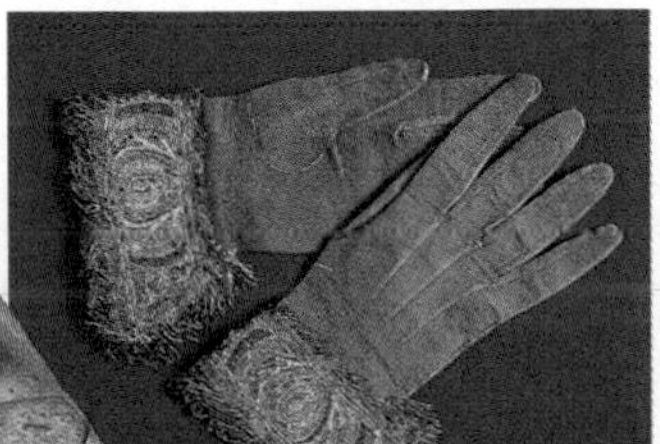
COURTESY PEABODY ESSEX MUSEUM, SALEM, MASS.

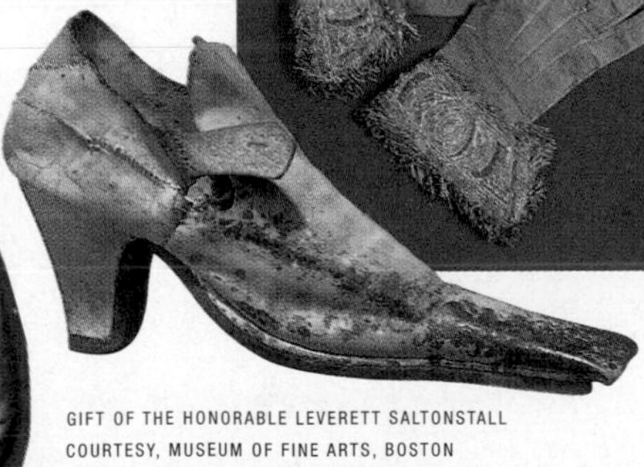
GIFT OF THE HONORABLE LEVERETT SALTONSTALL
COURTESY, MUSEUM OF FINE ARTS, BOSTON

COLONIAL CLOTHING

This colonial couple is dressed in clothing typical of the English middle class in the 1620s. Men's full baggy breeches were called **"slops."** Styles, of course, varied from region to region.

COURTESY OF PLIMOTH PLANTATION

GUILFORD COURTHOUSE NATIONAL MILITARY PARK

MAKING MUSIC

Craftspeople made instruments by hand, such as this painted **war drum.** Colonists played traditional European music and composed and played new music of their own.

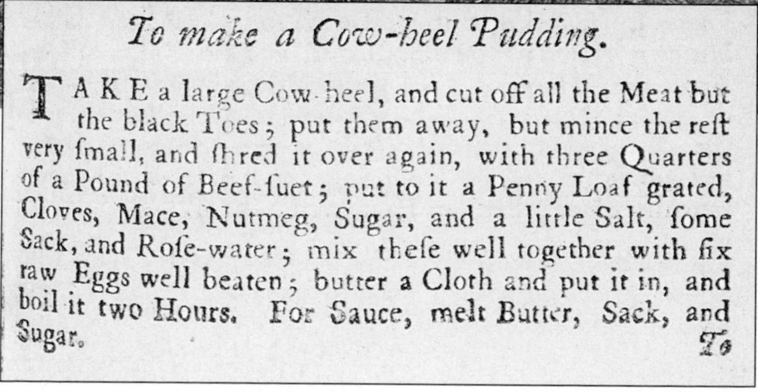

To make a Cow-heel Pudding.

TAKE a large Cow-heel, and cut off all the Meat but the black Toes; put them away, but mince the reſt very ſmall, and ſhred it over again, with three Quarters of a Pound of Beef-ſuet; put to it a Penny Loaf grated, Cloves, Mace, Nutmeg, Sugar, and a little Salt, ſome Sack, and Roſe-water; mix theſe well together with ſix raw Eggs well beaten; butter a Cloth and put it in, and boil it two Hours. For Sauce, melt Butter, Sack, and Sugar.

To

COURTESY, AMERICAN ANTIQUARIAN SOCIETY

HOME ECONOMICS

Colonial cooks adapted to scarcity when necessary. This recipe for **cow-heel pudding** shows one way colonists economized.

SECTION 3

Launching the New Government

MARCH 4, 1801: A NEW PRESIDENT IN A NEW CAPITAL

JUST BEFORE NOON ON MARCH 4, 1801, THOMAS JEFFERSON LEFT HIS BOARDINGHOUSE AND WALKED THROUGH THE DUSTY STREETS OF WASHINGTON, D.C. As he stepped up the hill toward the unfinished Capitol building, one observer noted that his clothing was "usual, that of a plain citizen, without any distinctive badge of office." Yet that day Jefferson assumed the highest office in the nation: he became the third President of the United States.

Jefferson faced a number of firsts that day. He became the first President to be sworn into office in the nation's new capital city. He also became the first Chief Executive to succeed a political opponent in office. Jefferson had served as Vice President under President John Adams, but by the time of the election the two men headed conflicting political parties: Adams led the Federalists, and Jefferson led the Democratic-Republicans.

When Jefferson won the presidential election, Americans feared that the transition from one political party to another might result in violence. Many Federalists worried that Jefferson would punish them as political enemies.

In his Inaugural Address, however, Jefferson asked all American people to "unite for the common good." "Every difference of opinion," he explained, "is not a difference of principle. We have called by different names brethren of the same principles. We are all Republicans—we are all Federalists."

NATIONAL PORTRAIT GALLERY, SMITHSONIAN INSTITUTION/ART RESOURCE

A President for the Common Man
Thomas Jefferson believed strongly in the people's right to self-government and civil liberties.

AS YOU READ

Vocabulary
- cabinet
- national debt
- speculator
- neutral
- impressed
- embargo

Think About . . .
- how federal power was used in the 1790s.
- the conflicts between the Federalist and Democratic-Republican political parties.
- the role the Marshall Court played in shaping the government.
- how the foreign policy of the United States emerged.

After Jefferson's speech, many Americans breathed a sigh of relief. Yet their fears had been real. The struggles between the two parties threatened the stability of the nation. Even more disturbing, this political conflict had arisen in such a short time.

Washington and the Government

Stabilizing Economic Conditions

Just 12 years earlier, in 1789, George Washington took the same oath after being unanimously elected President. While bonfires and parties marked the people's excitement, Washington himself had grave concerns. "I walk on untrodden ground," he said. As the first President, Washington had no examples to follow. Every move he made set a precedent. He also knew the nation faced dire problems.

Congress created several departments to help the President run the country. The heads of those departments made up the President's **cabinet,** or official advisers. Among others in his cabinet, Washington appointed fellow Virginian Thomas Jefferson as secretary of state, in charge of relations with foreign countries. He named 34-year-old Alexander Hamilton of New York as secretary of the treasury.

The brilliant and handsome Hamilton had served as Washington's assistant during the Revolution, and the two men remained close friends after the war. Both served at the Constitutional Convention, and both fought for ratification. Hamilton felt, however, that the Constitution fell short of providing the type of government the United States needed.

As head of the Treasury Department, Hamilton hoped to increase the powers of the United States government. Under his guidance, he said, the government would work closely with "the rich, the well-born, and the good" to create wealth and stability in the young nation. Starting in 1790 he proposed a series of plans that helped to make this vision a reality.

Hamilton's Plans

The **national debt,** money owed from the American Revolution, remained the country's most serious economic problem. The United States government owed about $12 million to European countries and investors and about $40 million to American citizens. In addition the state governments had war debts of nearly $21 million. Most of these debts took the form of bonds that the government had sold to investors to pay for the costs of the war. Like Continental currency, bonds were worth a fraction of their face value in 1790 because people doubted that bondholders would ever be paid. Hamilton worried that if the United States could not make good on its own bonds, it would never establish credit—or credibility—with other nations or with its own citizens.

In 1790 Hamilton proposed to Congress that the government should pay off its bonds at full value and assume the debts of all the states as well. Congress agreed that foreign debts should be paid, but a storm of controversy arose over the rest of Hamilton's plan.

Some members of Congress argued that paying off domestic bonds at full value was unfair. The people who originally bought the bonds had given up hope of ever collecting on them. Many of them—mostly farmers and others who lacked cash—had sold their bonds at a discount to **speculators,** people who bought the bonds in the hopes that their value would go up again. Under the plan, wealthy speculators, not the common people who originally bought the bonds, would benefit. Hamilton believed that wealthy people were the key to the nation's economic development.

Other members of Congress complained about paying off the states' debts. Some Southern states had already paid their debts, while most New England states had not. Hamilton's plan favored the North, where most speculators lived. Southerners did not want to pay other states' debts after they had paid off their own.

ALL PHOTOS, COURTESY OF NATIONAL NUMISMATIC COLLECTION, SMITHSONIAN INSTITUTION

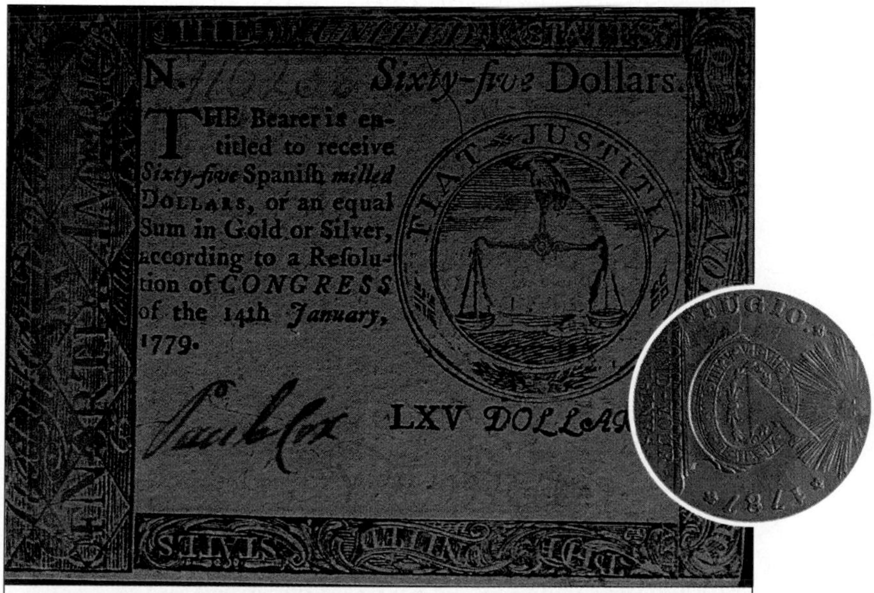

Money Problems "Not worth a Continental" became a popular saying after the war. *Why were Continental currency and bonds of little value to investors in 1790?*

GENERAL GEORGE WASHINGTON.
Reviewing the Western army at Fort Cumberland the 18th of Octob

COURTESY, THE HENRY FRANCIS DU PONT WINTERTHUR MUSEUM

Quelling the Whiskey Rebellion **In 1794 President Washington reviews federal troops at Fort Cumberland in Maryland. The Maryland militia was called in to help end the Whiskey Rebellion.** *Why were the farmers so opposed to the tax on their whiskey?*

Hamilton brushed these criticisms aside. His intentions were to favor the commercial North over the agricultural South, and he hoped to ally the government with the wealthy men who had speculated in bonds. To get Congress to pass the plan, he struck a deal with Southern leaders. According to that deal, Southerners agreed to support Hamilton's debt plan, while Hamilton and other Northerners agreed to locate the proposed "federal city" near Virginia, away from Northern influence.

Hamilton then proposed the creation of a national bank. As a major stockholder, the government would have much influence on the operations of the Bank of the United States, as it would be called, but private citizens would own most of its stock. The bank would issue money, regulate the nation's financial affairs, and loan money to American citizens.

Before signing the bank bill into law, Washington asked the members of his cabinet to give him a written opinion of the plan. Jefferson argued that the plan was illegal; the Constitution said nothing about the government having the power to create a bank. Hamilton argued that, in addition to powers spelled out, the Constitution gave the government "implied" powers to do anything "necessary and proper" to carry out its responsibilities. The Bank, he said, was necessary for the government to regulate the economy. Washington carefully considered both Jefferson's strict reading of the Constitution and Hamilton's loose interpretation. Though not entirely convinced by Hamilton's argument, Washington sided with Hamilton and signed the bill in early 1791.

Whiskey and Taxes

Later that year Hamilton proposed a tax on distilled liquor. This tax would increase revenue and test the government's ability to tax—one of its most important powers, Hamilton thought.

The liquor tax aroused strong opposition from farmers in the hills of western Pennsylvania. Most backcountry farmers made whiskey to sell in the eastern part of the state. This had always been the best way to transport processed corn, and whiskey proved to be a reliable source of extra cash. Hamilton's tax threatened to make this practice unprofitable.

For these farmers the liquor tax brought back memories of the days before the American Revolution. At first the farmers simply refused to pay. Then they began to tar and feather tax collectors. Finally, in July 1794, 500 armed men surrounded the home of a local tax collector and demanded that he resign. When the farmers discovered soldiers in the house, they opened fire. In the violence that followed, several men were wounded, and the tax collector's house was destroyed.

When the farmers ignored several orders to obey the law and pay their taxes, Washington and Hamilton reacted vigorously. In the fall of 1794, Henry Lee, accompanied by Hamilton, led a federal army to put down the rebels and demonstrate the power of the federal government. Threatened with this force, the "whiskey boys" dispersed and the Whiskey Rebellion ended. Two of the farmers were later convicted of treason, but Washington pardoned them both.

Conflicts at Home and Abroad

Party Politics and Foreign Policy

The Whiskey Rebellion confirmed Hamilton's worst fears about the common people—"that great beast," as he called them collectively. "How can you trust people who own no property?" he asked. The army had been needed, Hamilton argued, to enforce the laws of the land and put down a dangerous rebellion.

Thomas Jefferson, however, believed that "such an armament against people at their ploughs" had shown unnecessary force. The differences between Hamilton and Jefferson went beyond the Whiskey Rebellion, however. The two men had very different ideas of what the United States should be.

Hamilton envisioned a nation with bustling cities, churning factories, big banks, and a powerful government. He found backers for his plans and ideas in large Northern cities and New England—places where trade and manufacturing thrived.

The freedom of the common people thrived in Thomas Jefferson's America. "I know of no safe depository," Jefferson wrote, "of the ultimate powers of the society but the people themselves." Democracy worked best, he believed, in a society of small farmers, living in quiet, rural areas. Jefferson found support on plantations in the South, farms in the Middle Atlantic states, and farms on the Western frontier.

The people that these men attracted formed America's first political parties, groups that promoted ideas and supported candidates. As Hamilton and his Federalists continued to appeal to people with commercial interests, support for Jefferson and the Democratic-Republicans grew among common people. The parties not only differed on domestic issues; their conflicts over foreign policy nearly split the nation in the 1790s.

EDWARD S. ELLIS, YOUTH'S HISTORY OF THE U.S., NY, 1887

Citizen Reaction Angry Americans burn an effigy of John Jay upon his return from treaty negotiations in Britain. *Why were Americans so upset by the terms of the Jay Treaty?*

France and Britain

In 1789 revolution erupted in France. What began as an effort to reform a corrupt monarchy turned into a violent, bloody battle that completely upset French society. Fearing the spread of revolt against monarchy and aristocracy, other nations, including Britain, declared war on France.

Jefferson, formerly the United States minister to France, supported the French. He and other Republicans believed the French Revolution continued the struggle for liberty that America had begun. They also remembered France's support during the American Revolution and argued that the alliance between the two countries remain intact. To Federalists like Hamilton and Vice President Adams, the French Revolution showed the destructiveness of the common people. They sided with the British, admired the stability of the British government, and believed that America's economic livelihood depended on close ties with Britain.

Despite mounting pressure to enter the war on one side or the other, Washington chose to keep the United States **neutral,** or not allied with any side. Washington's decision did nothing to calm tensions in the United States or on the Atlantic Ocean. Both French and British ships seized American merchant vessels bound for Europe, and American trade suffered. The British navy **impressed,** or forced into service, American sailors (and British deserters) and forced them to serve on British ships. In addition the British had not removed all of their troops from forts in the western United States after the American Revolution. In 1794 war between the United States and either France or Britain seemed likely.

Fearing Britain's military power, Washington sent John Jay, a Federalist, to London to negotiate a treaty. When Jay returned home in 1795, however, it became clear that the new treaty was not very successful. The British agreed to remove their troops from the western United States, but not until 1796. To get this, Jay gave up American rights to ship cotton and sugar to British colonies. In addition he resolved nothing about the impressment of American sailors. The treaty seemed to please no one but those Federalists who wanted to maintain good relations with Britain at all costs. Democratic-Republicans called the Jay Treaty "the death warrant of American liberty."

The Beginnings of Party Rivalries

The political harmony of Washington's early years in office had long since disappeared, and Washington decided to leave office in 1797. In his Farewell Address, he urged the new nation to avoid conflicts with foreign nations and warned about the dangers of political parties.

In 1797 President John Adams ignored Washington's plea and sent 3 Americans to secure a treaty with France. In Paris the French foreign minister demanded a bribe of $240,000 from the Americans and hinted that if they refused to pay it France would declare war on the United States. This threat allowed Adams to sway American public opinion away from the French and the Democratic-Republicans.

The Alien and Sedition Acts

Adams called for the formation of an army to defend against the expected French invasion in 1798; he also signed the Alien Act, giving him the power to expel any aliens, or foreign-born residents of the United States, who were "dangerous to the peace and safety of the United States."

Another law signed by Adams during the crisis—the Sedition Act—was aimed directly at the Democratic-Republicans themselves. This law made it a crime for anyone to "write, print, utter, or publish . . . any false, scandalous, and malicious writing" about the President or the government. As a result, about 10 Democratic-Republican editors, printers, and politicians were jailed.

The Alien and Sedition acts proved very unpopular, and public opinion turned against the President and the Federalists. When peaceful relations with France were restored in 1800, it appeared that the Federalists had manufactured the entire crisis. As a result, Adams and his party were in chaos as the presidential election of 1800 approached. Jefferson and his party were ready to challenge them.

Tie Vote The Twelfth Amendment, establishing separate balloting for President and Vice President, was ratified in 1804 in response to a tie between Jefferson and Aaron Burr (above) in the election of 1800. *Why were the Federalists in turmoil before the election?*

The Election of 1800

In 1800 the American people witnessed a hard-fought and noisy presidential campaign. Democratic-Republicans spread rumors that President Adams would soon name himself "King of America." New England Federalists whispered that Jefferson planned to burn every Bible in the nation. The final count of votes was close, but Jefferson won.

Jefferson chose to let the nation heal rather than churn up old political conflicts. He quietly stopped enforcing the Alien and Sedition acts and allowed them to expire. He reduced military spending. He even allowed the Bank of the United States to continue to exist.

John Marshall and Judicial Power

Strengthening the Supreme Court

After losing the election, John Adams sought ways to make Federalist ideas continue in a government dominated by Democratic-Republicans. He found his solution in the judiciary.

Packing the Courts

In the winter before their terms ran out, Adams and the Federalist Congress worked together to pass the Judiciary Act of 1801. This law added 21 positions to the roster of federal judges. Adams named Federalists to these positions. Adams also named John Marshall, a strong Federalist, chief justice of the United States.

Adams signed the appointments of the new Federalist judges the night before Jefferson's inauguration, leaving several of the appointments to be delivered by the new administration. Yet Jefferson's secretary of state, James Madison, refused to do this. When a Federalist named William Marbury did not receive his expected appointment, he appealed to the Supreme Court.

John Marshall found himself in a difficult position. As a Federalist, he would have liked to order Jefferson to make Marbury a federal judge. If he did, however, Jefferson and Madison would probably ignore the order, reducing the authority of the Supreme Court. Yet Marshall could not give in.

Marshall's Solution

Marshall's solution bypassed short-term gains for the Federalists, but it had long-term national effects. In 1803 he ruled that Marbury was entitled to his appointment and that Madison had violated the law in not delivering it. Marshall ruled, however, that the Court could not require delivery of the appointment because a part of the law giving the Court that right—the Judiciary Act of 1789—was unconstitutional, or violated the Constitution. Marshall had established the right of the Supreme Court to judge an act of Congress illegal. It is "the duty of the judicial department to say what the law is," he wrote. "A law repugnant to the Constitution is void."

What began as a petty political fight ended by strengthening the Supreme Court. John Marshall served as chief justice for 34 years, and during that time he consistently supported the Federalist program of a strong federal government. In this way, Marshall remained the chief adversary of Democratic-Republican Presidents for the next 16 years and helped Federalist policy endure long after the party ceased to exist.

Foreign Policy

The War of 1812: Another War With Britain

Along with the Federalist judiciary, conflicts with European nations troubled Thomas Jefferson's presidency. France and Britain continued to victimize the United States. Navies of the 2 nations seized nearly 1,500 American merchant ships. By 1807 the British had captured as many as 10,000 American sailors. The British fired on the American frigate *Chesapeake,* killing 3 Americans and wounding 18. Across the nation, Americans called for action against the British.

The Embargo Act

Jefferson did not believe that the United States could fight a war against Britain. He also remembered the trouble that foreign conflicts had caused during the 1790s, and he hoped to avoid such conflicts now.

Still, Jefferson knew that something had to be done. He believed that the European powers needed American food and materials. So in 1807 Jefferson signed the Embargo Act. The **embargo** stopped the export of all American goods and forbade American ships from sailing for foreign ports.

Jefferson thought that by depriving European countries of American products they would stop harassing the young nation. He was wrong. The Embargo Act had almost no effect on Britain and France. Instead, it proved to be a disaster for the United States, especially in the trading centers of New England. Depression and unemployment swept the country. Americans from South Carolina to New Hampshire openly defied the law.

Jefferson left office after 2 terms in 1809, but not before he convinced Congress to repeal the Embargo Act. James Madison won the presidency easily, but opposition to timid Democratic-Republican policies against the British grew. By 1811 a new breed of politician had swept into Congress.

The War Hawks

These politicians came from the West and were the first generation of politicians to come of age after the Revolution. They earned the name "war hawks" for their calls for action against the British.

The British had heaped one insult after another on the American people, the war hawks charged. They impressed American sailors, attacked American ships, and stirred up trouble between settlers and Native Americans. To Westerners accustomed to action, the economic warfare of Jefferson and Madison seemed pathetic. "Is the rod of British power to be forever suspended over our heads?" asked war hawk Henry Clay of Kentucky.

Madison recognized the growing power of these new politicians, and in 1812 he made a deal with them. If they supported him for reelection as President, he would ask for a declaration of war. The war hawks agreed, and by the summer of 1812 the United States and Britain were locked in combat.

COURTESY U.S. NAVAL ACADEMY MUSEUM

A British Defeat at Sea **This painting shows the frigate *USS Constitution,* nicknamed "Old Ironsides," defeating the British warship *Guerrière* in the War of 1812.** *What actions by the British led to war?*

Flames in Washington This British cartoon shows President Madison fleeing the burning capital during the British attack on Washington in 1814. *Why was the War of 1812 so significant for the United States?*

American goals in the war were unclear. The war hawks had boasted of conquering Canada and Florida, but these plans were squelched when the British invaded the United States. Each side scored victories in battles around the Great Lakes, near Washington, D.C., and on the Atlantic Ocean. By the end of 1814, British leaders, more concerned with European matters, wearied of the American war and offered to make peace. The treaty, ratified in 1815, resolved few of the problems that had caused the conflict. It simply ended the fighting and restored everything to what it had been before the war.

The United States had not won the war—no one had—but the War of 1812 became an important event for the young nation. The war hawks hailed it as the "Second War for Independence." United States victories stimulated national pride and confidence. The war, which had been urged by Western politicians, also created a new Western hero: General Andrew Jackson of Tennessee, who scored a sensational victory over the British near New Orleans. The War of 1812 also marked the end of United States involvement with European conflicts for more than a century.

After the war Americans looked eastward to Europe less and looked westward across their own continent more. At last the United States put its colonial past behind it and headed toward its future as a nation of lush prairies, growing cities, and a restless, changing people.

Section Review

Vocabulary

1. Define: cabinet, national debt, speculator, neutral, impressed, embargo.

Checking Facts

2. How did Alexander Hamilton increase the powers of the federal government?

3. What were the main conflicts between the Federalists and the Democratic-Republicans?

Critical Thinking

Demonstrating Reasoned Judgment

4. How did John Marshall's actions shape the role of the Supreme Court?

Linking Across Time

5. Impressment was an act of aggression against the United States that led to war. If it occurred today, do you think war would result? Why?

Critical Thinking Skill

ANALYZING INFORMATION

Learning the Skill

The newly independent Americans had to vote to ratify the laws under which they would live. They had to analyze information in order to decide how to vote. Analyzing information involves breaking it into meaningful parts so that it can be understood. Subsequently the reader or listener is able to form an opinion about it.

The ability to analyze information is important in deciding your position on a subject that could affect your life. You need to analyze a political document to determine if you should support it. You would analyze a candidate's position statements to determine if you should vote for him or her. You would analyze an article or editorial to arrive at your own opinion of it.

Analyzing Information

To analyze information, use the following steps:

a. Identify the topic that is being discussed.

b. Examine how the information is organized. What are the main points?

c. Summarize the information in your own words, and then make a statement of your own based on your understanding and what you already know.

Read the following passage from Article II, Section 1, of the Constitution of the United States.

No person except a natural-born citizen, or a citizen of the United States, at the time of the adoption of this Constitution, shall be eligible to the office of President; neither shall any person be eligible to that office who shall not have attained to the age of thirty-five years, and been fourteen years a resident within the United States.

The first step is to determine the general topic. This passage is about the qualifications for the President of the United States. Next, identify the three main points: the President must be a citizen of the United States by birth, must be at least thirty-five years old, and must have lived here for at least fourteen years. Then give a brief summary, such as: "People who want to become President must fulfill these three requirements." Finally, make a statement of your own, such as: "These requirements restrict the presidency to people who have a reasonable amount of life experience and keep from power people who were not born in the United States or who have not lived here very long."

ARTICLE II.—Sec. 1.—The power of this government shall be divided into three distinct departments; the Legislative, the Executive, and Judicial. . . .

ARTICLE III.—Sec. 1.—The Legislative power shall be vested in two distinct branches; a Committee and a Council, each to have a negative on the other, and both to be styled the General Council of the Cherokee Nation. . . .

ARTICLE IV.—Sec. 1.—The Supreme Executive Power of this Nation shall be vested in a Principal Chief, who shall be chosen by the General Council and shall hold his office four years. . . .

ARTICLE V.—Sec. 1.—The Judicial Powers shall be vested in a Supreme Court, and such Circuit and Inferior Courts as the General Council may from time to time ordain and establish. . . .

Constitution of the Cherokee Nation In 1827 elected delegates of the Cherokee Nation met to establish their own constitution. *How do these excerpts compare with related passages in the Constitution of the United States?*

Practicing the Skill

Read the excerpts above and practice analyzing information by answering these questions.

1. What is the subject of the document?

2. What are the most important points?

3. What do you notice about the organization of the document?

4. What does it mean that the Committee and the Council "each to have a negative on the other"? How is this similar to the "checks and balances" of the United States Constitution?

5. Summarize the passage in your own words, and make a statement of your own regarding it.

Applying the Skill

Find a short, informative piece, such as a political candidate's position paper, an editorial in a newspaper, or an explanation of a new law that will soon be implemented. Analyze the information and make a statement of your own.

Additional Practice

For additional practice, see Reinforcing Skills on page 121.

Chapter 4 Review

Reviewing Key Terms

Choose the vocabulary term that best completes the sentences below. Write your answers on a separate sheet of paper.

amendments	**embargo**
cabinet	**representation**
ratify	**impressed**

1. The smaller states demanded equal _________.

2. Ten _________, known as the Bill of Rights, were added to the Constitution.

3. American sailors were forcibly _________ into the British navy.

4. The President's _________ consists of department heads who serve as official advisers.

5. The state representatives urged the voters to _________ the Constitution.

Recalling Facts

1. What were the Articles of Confederation? Why were some states reluctant to accept them?

2. What restrictions on slavery were included in the Northwest Ordinance of 1787?

3. What was the difference between hard money and paper money? Which type of money did the Confederation Congress use? Why?

4. Why did the Constitution include a system of checks and balances for the new government?

5. Who were the Federalists? What type of government did they support?

6. What reasons did the Anti-Federalists give for opposing the Constitution?

7. Why did some states demand that a bill of rights be added to the Constitution?

8. Identify at least five rights guaranteed by the Bill of Rights.

9. Which Americans' rights were not guaranteed in the Bill of Rights?

10. Why did Alexander Hamilton feel a national bank was necessary?

11. What events caused the Whiskey Rebellion? What other rebellions did it resemble?

12. Why did George Washington decide to step down as President?

13. Who was John Marshall and what effect did he have on the federal government?

14. What is an unconstitutional law? Which branch of government can declare a law to be unconstitutional?

15. Why was the War of 1812 known as the "Second War of Independence"?

Critical Thinking

1. Identifying Assumptions Were Daniel Shays and the farmers who followed him justified in going outside the law to address their grievances? Explain.

2. Making Comparisons Compare how class and geographic location affected people's support of the Constitution. Did the groups of supporters and nonsupporters divide along class lines? Explain.

3. Drawing Conclusions Under the Alien and Sedition acts, was jailing people for publicly criticizing Federalist policies a violation of the First Amendment, or was it justified by the ongoing crises? Explain.

4. Making Comparisons Compare the views of the 2 political parties on economic and foreign policies. Who would be most likely to support the Federalists? Who would support the Democratic-Republicans?

5. Making Inferences The illustration below shows the guillotine with which French revolutionaries executed King Louis XVI. What arguments might favor the overthrow of an oppressive government by force? What arguments might favor a political system where tyrants could be removed only by the force of law?

Portfolio Project

PORTFOLIO PROJECT

Prepare a chart that compares the American and French Revolutions. What were the causes of each? How long did each last? What were the results of each? In what ways were they similar? Different? When you are finished, put the chart in your portfolio.

Cooperative Learning

Working with a small group, read the Bill of Rights that was added to the Constitution (pages 91–109). Rewrite the amendments in your own words. Use modern English. Then compare the rewritings done by various groups of your classmates. How do they differ from the original amendments in the Bill of Rights?

GIRAUDON/ART RESOURCE, NY

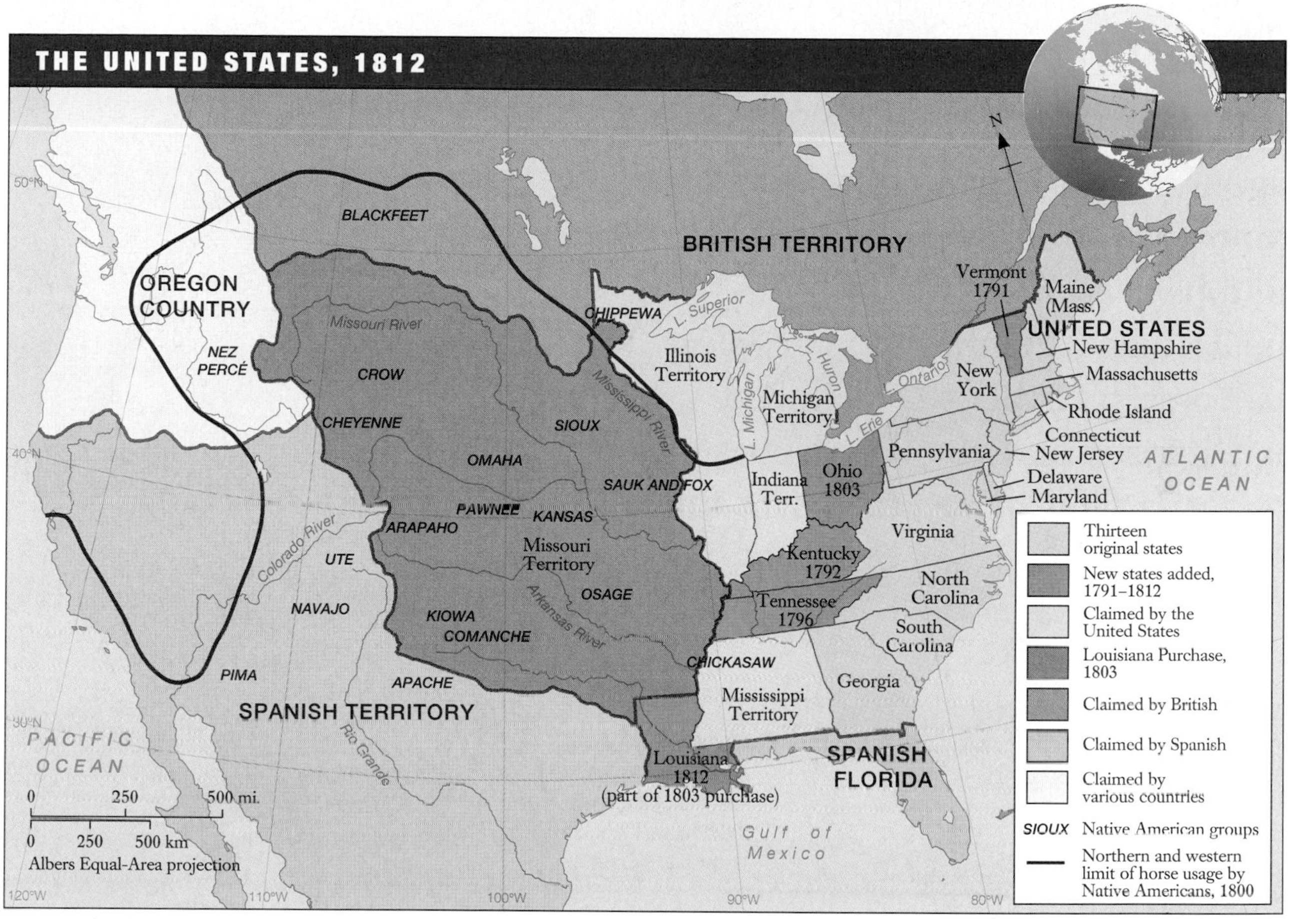

Reinforcing Skills

Analyzing Information Find a copy of the Northwest Ordinance in an encyclopedia or history book. Read the slavery clause and analyze the importance of this clause to African Americans.

Geography and History

Study the map on this page to answer the following questions:

1. Notice the five new states that were added to the original colonies. In which direction does the United States seem to be expanding the most? Why do you think this is so?

2. United States territory expanded as a result of the Louisiana Purchase. Why do you think it was advantageous to have a state (Louisiana) in that region?

3. France and the United States negotiated the Louisiana Purchase without consulting the Native Americans who lived west of the Mississippi. How might this have contributed to future conflicts between white settlers and Native Americans?

4. Why might the United States of 1812 have been a more formidable opponent for the British than the thirteen colonies of 1775?

5. Consider the order in which the first 18 states were admitted to the union. Which areas are likely to have been next to gain statehood?

HISTORY JOURNAL

Reread your response to the History Journal activity at the beginning of Chapter 4. Now that you have read the chapter, do you still agree with your interpretation of the painting *Liberty?* Revise your previous journal entry to reflect what you learned in the chapter.

Then...

Conestoga Wagon

By the mid-1700s, sturdy Conestoga wagons, called "Ships of the Inland Commerce," transported settlers and tons of their freight over the Appalachian Mountains. As people pushed even farther westward, the characteristic outline of the Conestoga was seen rolling across the plains toward Oregon and finally to California.

2 The boat-shaped wagon's high front and back kept goods from falling out on steep mountain trails.

1 Six to eight draft horses or a dozen oxen pulled the wagon. The driver rode or walked beside the animals.

NORTH WIND PICTURE ARCHIVES

Fun Facts

CRACKING THE WHIP

Wielding whips equipped with noisemaking "crackers" at the tips, drivers frequently had to snap them within inches of the ears of mules to keep the animals moving on the long treks over difficult terrain.

3 **A high, white cloth cover stretched over hoops, or wagon bows, gave passengers protection from heat, rain, and snow.**

ALL PHOTOS, COURTESY THE LANDIS VALLEY MUSEUM, PHOTOS BY CARL SOCOLOW

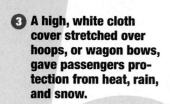

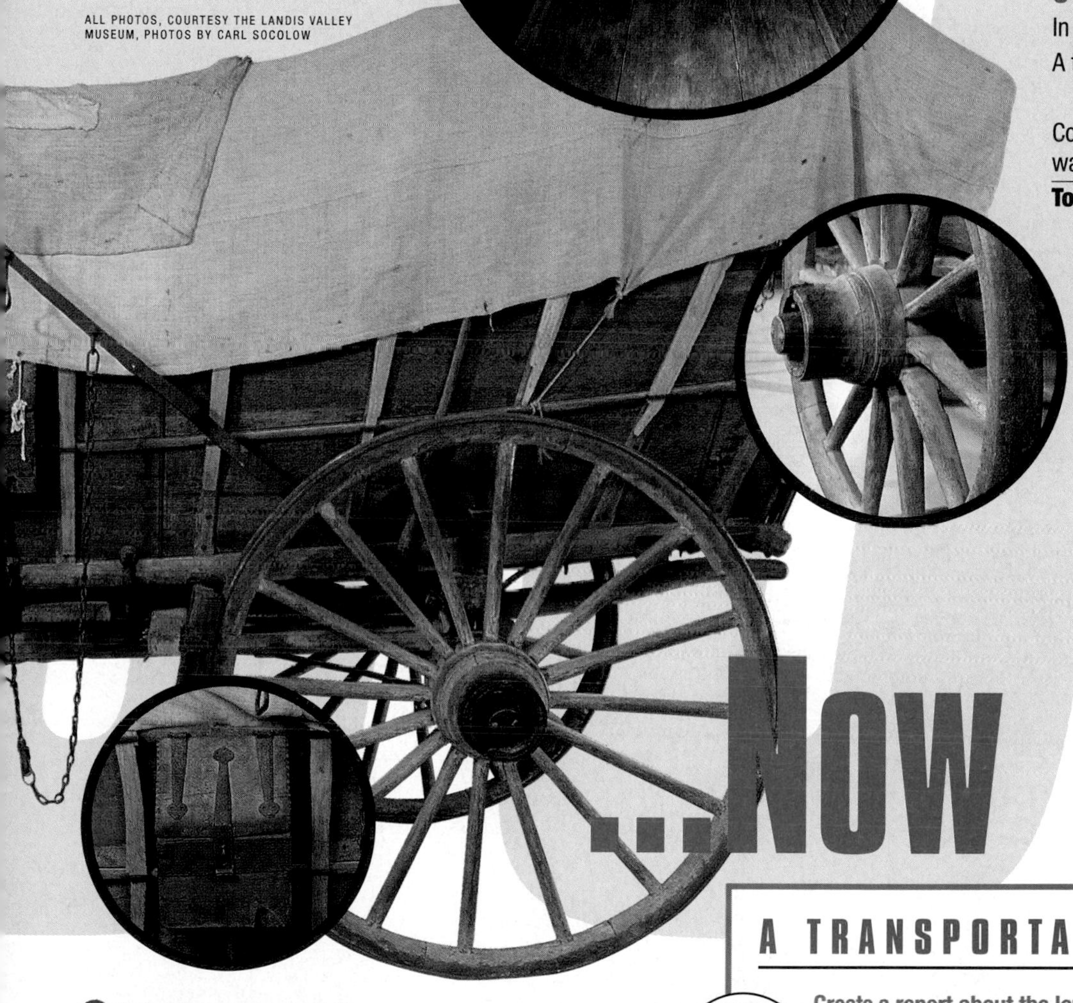

5 **Broad wheels helped keep the heavy wagon from being mired in the mud.**

4 **A toolbox attached to the side of the wagon held spare parts for needed repairs.**

Stats

WAGON NUMBERS

- Average wagon box: 21 feet long, 11 feet high, 4 feet in width and depth
- Average wagon weight: 1.5 to 2 tons (3,000 to 4,000 pounds)
- Wagon capacity: up to 6 tons (12,000 pounds) of cargo

COSTLY TRANSPORT

In the 1800s:

A team of horses:	
	Approximately $1,000
Construction of a wagon:	$250
Total:	**$1,250**

...Now

A TRANSPORTATION REPORT

PORTFOLIO PROJECT

Create a report about the length of Conestoga wagon journeys and how far they could typically travel in a day. Include a list of items that the settlers may have loaded for their trip. Then compare the modes of transportation available today, gathering statistics about how long a specific Conestoga trail would take by automobile or airplane.

THE "CONESTOGA STOGIE"

The wagons were named after the place where they were first built in the 1700s—the Conestoga Creek region of Lancaster, Pennsylvania. The word *stogie* derived from the cigars smoked by Conestoga wagon drivers.

UNIT 2

1800–1900

Rift and Reunion

COOPER-HEWITT, NATIONAL DESIGN MUSEUM, SMITHSONIAN INST./ART RESOURCE, NY

Roots

BY ALEX HALEY

Oral history, folklore, and tradition connect us to the past. In this excerpt from the autobiographical novel Roots, *author Alex Haley learns his family history from a Mandinka griot, an elder who commits events of the past to memory and retells them to new generations.*

THE KOBAL COLLECTION

Recreating Roots LeVar Burton (left) played Kunta Kinte in the 1977 televised version of the family saga of Alex Haley (right). Nightly audiences of 80 million tuned in to the 8-part show, more than half of all American viewers.

There is an expression called "the peak experience"—that which emotionally, nothing in your life ever transcends. I've had mine, that first day in the back country of black West Africa.

When we got within sight of Juffure, the children who were playing outside gave the alert, and the people came flocking from their huts. It's a village of only about seventy people. Like most back-country villages, it was still very much as it was two hundred years ago, with its circular mud houses and their conical thatched roofs. Among the people as they gathered was a small man wearing an off-white robe, a pillbox hat over an aquiline-featured black face, and about him was an aura of "somebodiness" until I knew he was the man we had come to see and hear.

As the three interpreters left our party to converge upon him, the seventy-odd other villagers gathered closely around me, in a kind of horseshoe pattern, three or four deep all around; had I stuck out my arms, my fingers would have touched the nearest ones on either side. They were all staring at me. The eyes just raked me. . . .

One of my interpreters came up quickly and whispered in my ear, "They stare at you so much because they have never here seen a black American." When I grasped the significance, I believe that hit me harder than what had already happened. They hadn't been looking at me as an individual, but I represented in their eyes a symbol of the twenty-five millions of us black people whom they had never seen, who lived beyond an ocean.

The people were clustered thickly about the old man, all of them intermittently flicking glances toward me as they talked animatedly in their Mandinka tongue. After a while, the old man turned, walked briskly through the people, past my three interpreters, and right up to me. His eyes piercing into mine, seeming to feel I should understand his Mandinka, he expressed what they had all decided they *felt* concerning those unseen millions of us who lived in those places that had been slave ships' destinations—and the translation came: "We have been told by the forefathers that there are many of us from this place who are in exile in that place called America—and in other places."

The old man sat down, facing me, as the people hurriedly gathered behind him. Then he began to recite for me the ancestral history of the Kinte clan, as it had been passed along orally down across centuries from the forefathers' time. It was not merely conversational, but more as if a scroll were being read; for the still, silent villagers, it was clearly a formal occasion. The *griot* would speak, bending forward from the waist, his body rigid, his neck cords standing out, his words seeming almost physical objects. After a sentence or two, seeming to go limp, he would lean back, listening to an interpreter's translation. Spilling from the *griot's* head came an incredibly complex Kinte clan lineage that reached back across many generations.... To date things the *griot* linked them to events, such as "—in the year of the big water"—a flood—"he slew a water buffalo." To determine the calendar date, you'd have to find out when that particular flood occurred.

HE HAD JUST ECHOED WHAT I HAD HEARD ALL THROUGH MY BOYHOOD YEARS.

Simplifying to its essence the encyclopedic saga that I was told, the griot said that the Kinte clan had begun in the country called Old Mali. Then the Kinte men traditionally were blacksmiths, "who had conquered fire," and the women mostly were potters and weavers. In time, one branch of the clan moved into the country called Mauretania; and it was from Mauretania that one son of this clan, whose name was Kairaba Kunta Kinte—a *marabout,* or holy man of the Moslem faith—journeyed down into the country called The Gambia. He went first to a village called Pakali N'Ding, stayed there for a while, then went to a village called Jiffarong, and then to the village of Juffure....

[His] youngest son, Omoro, stayed on in Juffure village until he had thirty rains—years—of age, then he took as his wife a Mandinka maiden named Binta Kebba. And by Binta Kebba, roughly between the years 1750 and 1760, Omoro Kinte begat four sons, whose names were, in the order of their birth, Kunta, Lamin, Suwadu, and Madi....

Now after he had just named those four sons, again he appended a detail, and the interpreter translated—"About the time the King's soldiers came"—another of the *griot's* time-fixing references—"the oldest of these four sons, Kunta, went away from his village to chop wood . . . and he was never seen again...." ...

I sat as if I were carved of stone. My blood seemed to have congealed. This man whose lifetime had been in this back-country African village had no way in the world to know that he had just echoed what I had heard all through my boyhood years on my grandma's front porch in Henning, Tennessee... of an African who always had insisted that his name was "Kin-tay"; who had called a guitar a "*ko,*" and a river within the state of Virginia, "Kamby Bolongo"; and who had been kidnaped into slavery while not far from his village, chopping wood, to make himself a drum.

Responding to Literature

1. **Why does the author define listening to the griot as a "peak experience"? Describe a peak experience from your own life.**
2. **The griot relates a detailed history from several centuries ago. What devices does Haley use to recall and retell this history? Compare some of the techniques used in oral history and recorded history.**

CHAPTER 5

The Expanding Nation

OCTOBER 26, 1825: ERIE CANAL OPENS

A large flatboat, the *Seneca Chief*, strung with flowers, led "a grand aquatic procession" through New York Harbor on November 4, 1825. The fleet sailed to a spot near Sandy Hook, New Jersey, where the other boats circled the *Seneca Chief*.

On deck stood DeWitt Clinton, governor of New York. He raised a small wooden keg, pulled the cork, and said: "May the God of the heavens and the earth smile on this work and render it subservient to the best interests of the human race." Then he emptied the keg, which contained water from Lake Erie, into the Atlantic Ocean.

The "Marriage of the Waters" concluded the official ceremonies marking the opening nine days earlier of the Erie Canal, the most important national waterway built in the United States. It stretched from the Hudson River to Lake Erie and connected New York City with the fertile regions to the West.

The building and subsequent success of the Erie Canal changed the way Americans traveled, conducted business, and practiced politics. This vital link between the East Coast and the Western frontier also changed the way many Americans thought about their country. The canal served as a symbol of pride and economic determination. ■

HISTORY JOURNAL

Write about some of the ways in which the United States might experience growth in the 1800s.

New York Governor DeWitt Clinton leads the ceremonies opening the Erie Canal.

CASE STUDY

Turning Point

Cherokee Expulsion

WINTER 1838

DECISION

Chief Justice: John Marshall

Case: Worcester v. Georgia

Date: 1832

The Cherokee nation, then, is a distinct community, occupying its own territory, with boundaries accurately described, in which the laws of Georgia can have no force, and which the citizens of Georgia have no right to enter, but with the assent of the Cherokees themselves. . . .

It is the opinion of this court that the judgment of the superior court . . . of Georgia, condemning Samuel A. Worcester to hard labour, . . . was pronounced by that court under . . . a law which is void . . . and ought, therefore, to be reversed and nullified.

The Case

The Cherokee and their supporters were jubilant. The case of *Worcester* v. *Georgia* was decided, and the Supreme Court of the United States had ruled in favor of Samuel Worcester, reversing the state's earlier judgment against him.

Worcester, a missionary who had lived among the Cherokee for years, had broken a Georgia state law. This law stated that non-Cherokee people living on Cherokee lands could either sign an oath of allegiance to Georgia or leave the Cherokee land. Worcester refused to do either. Instead, he chose a prison sentence of four years and appealed his case to the United States Supreme Court.

The Supreme Court ruling promised far more than just freedom for Worcester. Chief Justice John Marshall's words implied that the Cherokee would be free to control their own fate, without interference from the state of Georgia. No one could enter the Cherokee Nation without the permission of the Cherokee, and the Cherokee could invite whomever they wanted to live on their land. The United States government would protect their lands.

The victory proved to be an empty one. President Andrew Jackson is said to have remarked, "John Marshall has made his decision; let him enforce it now if he can." It was true—the decision could not be enforced. Jackson did nothing to see that the ruling was obeyed, and Worcester stayed in prison.

The Background

The Cherokee had held their land long before European settlers arrived. Through treaties with the United States government, the Cherokee became a sovereign nation within Georgia.

By the early 1800s the Cherokee were principally an agricultural people, having adopted many of the customs and ways of life of neighboring white farmers. They had their own schools, their own newspaper, their own judicial system, and their own written constitution. Chief Sequoya's invention of a Cherokee alphabet enabled many of the Cherokee to read and write in their own language as well as in English. The Cherokee farmed some of Georgia's richest land, and in 1829 gold was discovered there. Settlers, miners, and land speculators were steadily encroaching on Cherokee territory in pursuit of its riches.

By the time of *Worcester* v. *Georgia* in 1832, federal and state laws had opened the door for Cherokee removal. In 1830 Congress had passed the Indian Removal Act, allowing Jackson to pursue his goal of relocating Eastern Native Americans to lands west of the Mississippi River.

That same year Georgia lawmakers had decreed that all Cherokee lands were under state jurisdiction, erasing Cherokee claims to sovereignty. Furthermore, the Cherokee could not testify against a white person or dig for the gold discovered in their own nation. Their laws were nullified. Finally, in December of 1830, Georgia restricted the presence of white settlers on Cherokee lands, a law that led to the *Worcester* case.

In 1832, when Jackson ignored the Supreme Court's ruling, the Cherokee realized their hopes for federal protection were in vain. Jackson recognized that the Cherokee had not been treated fairly. Nevertheless, he believed that the Eastern Native Americans would have to be relocated, because a separate nation could not continue to exist within an American state. Long before *Worcester* v. *Georgia,* Jackson had warned Congress against "encroachments upon the legitimate sphere of State sovereignty." It was no surprise that Jackson chose not to enforce the Supreme Court's ruling.

The Opinions

Read the opinions of some of the people involved in the Cherokee drama. President Jackson and Governor Lumpkin of Georgia favored removal, while Massachusetts Senator Everett sided with Cherokee Principal Chief Ross in upholding the sovereignty promised in earlier treaties and outlined in the Cherokee Constitution of 1827.

Among both United States and Cherokee officials, people's views on the issue of removal differed

"My opinion remains the same, and I can see no alternative for them but that of their removal to the West or a quiet submission to the State laws."

President Andrew Jackson, 1831

LIBRARY OF CONGRESS

"Any attempt to infringe the evident right of a state to govern the entire population within its territorial limits . . . would be the usurpation of a power never granted by the states."

Wilson Lumpkin, governor of Georgia, 1832

LIBRARY OF CONGRESS

"Whoever read of such a project? Ten or fifteen thousand families, to be rooted up. . . . There is not . . . such a thing in the annals of mankind. . . ."

Edward Everett, senator from Massachusetts, 1830

MASSACHUSETTS HISTORICAL SOCIETY

"The lands solemnly guaranteed and reserved forever to the Cherokee Nation by the Treaties concluded with the United States, . . . shall forever hereafter remain unalterably the same."

Constitution of the Cherokee Nation, formed by a convention of delegates led by Principal Chief John Ross, 1827

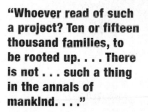

ARCHIVES AND MANUSCRIPTS DIVISION OF THE OKLAHOMA HISTORICAL SOCIETY

CASE STUDY

Turning Point

ROBERT LINDEUX, THE TRAIL OF TEARS. WOOLAROC MUSEUM, BARTLESVILLE, OK

Robert Lindeux's painting *The Trail of Tears* depicts the Cherokee on the forced march across the Appalachian Mountains from their homes in the Southeast. One soldier noted that he had seen 22 people die in a single night during the journey.

sharply. The government's removal policy would serve the interests of expansionists and miners, who wanted both rich soil and gold. On the other hand, most of the Cherokee wanted to remain on the land of their ancestors. Not only did they have a settled life on that land, they had also heard about the hardship and suffering of those who had already moved west.

The Assumptions

Quotations from the players involved reveal another basis for their opinions—underlying assumptions. For example, President Jackson professed to have "the kindest feelings" toward the Cherokee. Even so, his words and actions reveal a bias against them. On another occasion President Jackson had addressed the Cherokee, saying, "I tell you that you cannot remain where you now are. Circumstances that cannot be controlled, and which are beyond the reach of human laws, render it impossible that you can flourish in the midst of a civilized community." Notice the assumption that underlies Jackson's words in that last sentence.

Jackson based much of his argument for removal on his belief in state sovereignty. Governor Lumpkin had less sympathy for the Cherokee than Jackson and far less knowledge of them. Like Jackson, however, he based much of his argument against the Supreme Court's ruling on his belief that the powers of the state government took precedence over those of the federal government.

Everett's underlying assumptions caused him to speak passionately on behalf of the Cherokee. Unlike Jackson, Everett thought of them as "essentially a civilized people." This assumption led to his vehement expressions of indignation.

What about the Cherokee themselves? What were their assumptions? They at first assumed that the federal government would uphold the promises of previous administrations, such as those made during Thomas Jefferson's presidency. The Cherokee had worked hard, in the words of Cherokee orator John Ridge, ". . . to form a republican government, . . . cultivate the earth, and learn the mechanic arts." They made the basic assumption that the white senators would come to regard Native Americans as equals, with shared values and basic human rights.

The Outcome

For years John Ross, the principal chief of the Cherokee, was able to maintain unity among his people. He and other Cherokee leaders—such as Major Ridge and his son John Ridge—all opposed the Cherokee removal at first.

John Ridge When news of the *Worcester* v. *Georgia* decision reached John Ridge, he was exuberant. He believed that the Supreme Court, and therefore the Cherokee, would prevail over Georgia. Ridge then spoke to Jackson himself, however, and learned that the President had no intention of enforcing the decision. Jackson told him that the only hope for the Cherokee was in "abandoning their country and removing to the West."

By the mid-1830s John Ridge, his father, Major Ridge, and his cousin Elias Boudinot, the editor of the *Cherokee Phoenix,* had begun to believe that removal was inevitable. These Cherokee leaders and their supporters realized that the United States government would never protect the Cherokee lands in Georgia. They also believed the government was making the Cherokee a better offer in terms of land and assistance than ever before.

Two Factions The two factions that developed among the Cherokee were the Treaty party, which favored removal, and the National party, which continued to oppose it. John Ross and the National party viewed their opponents as traitors. They never came to accept removal. Major Ridge, knowing that many of the people he loved considered him an enemy, pleaded with them:

> I am one of the native sons of these wild woods. I have hunted the deer and turkey here more than fifty years. . . . The Georgians have shown a grasping spirit lately; they have extended their laws, to which we are unaccustomed, which harass our braves and make the children suffer and cry. . . . I know the Indians have an older title than theirs. We obtained the land from the living God above. . . . Yet they are strong and we are weak. We are few, they are many. We cannot remain here in safety and comfort. I know we love the graves of our fathers. . . . We can never forget these homes, I know, but an unbending, iron necessity tells us we must leave them.

Pressure to complete the Cherokee relocation intensified. The National party, representing about 16,000 Cherokee, adamantly resisted the move, yet the administration dealt only with the minority Treaty party. Its leaders signed a relocation treaty, ratified by Congress and the President in 1836.

Still, in 1838 after the deadline set for removal had passed, few Cherokee had moved voluntarily. Soldiers with rifles and bayonets forced more than 18,000 Cherokee from their homes and marched them approximately 1,000 miles to what is now Oklahoma. During the march nearly 4,000 Cherokee died from malnutrition, exposure to the cold, cholera, and physical hardship. Their grueling trek earned the name the Trail of Tears.

RESPONDING TO THE CASE

1. Jackson spoke of the Cherokee as hunters who had no right to "tracts of country on which they have neither dwelt nor made improvements, merely because they have seen them from the mountain or passed them in the chase." Why do you think Jackson made this statement? What was he purposely ignoring?

2. Senator Theodore Frelinghuysen, in a speech on the Indian Removal Act, asked: "Do the obligations of justice change with the color of the skin?" Which views presented on page 137 would Frelinghuysen probably agree with?

3. Before the Trail of Tears, the Ridges had decided that their people had no choice but to go west. Although at first they were opposed to relocation, what events changed their minds? Why?

4. In what respects was Major Ridge in sympathy with the Cherokee who continued to oppose removal? What were some of the values and assumptions he shared with them?

PORTFOLIO PROJECT

Imagine that you are a Cherokee leader faced with the threat of removal. Write a speech addressed to the Cherokee people urging the case of either the Treaty party or the National party. Keep the speech in your portfolio.

SECTION 2

The Economy Grows

APRIL 4, 1839: MILLWORKER DESCRIBES FACTORY LIFE

AFTER 14 HOURS ON THE JOB, MALENDA EDWARDS WALKED TO HER BOARDINGHOUSE, WEARILY CLIMBED THE STAIRS, AND SAT AT THE DESK IN HER ROOM. Her ears still ringing from the din of the mill machinery, Malenda found a piece of paper and began a letter to her cousin Sabrina. "You have been informed, I suppose," she wrote, "that I am a factory girl." She continued:

> There are many young ladies at work in the factories that have given up millinery dressmaking and school keeping for to work in the mill. But I would not advise anyone to do it, for I was so sick of it at first I wished a factory had never been thought of. But the longer I stay the better I like it.
>
> —Malenda Edwards, from a letter to Sabrina Bennet, April 4, 1839

MUSEUM OF AMERICAN TEXTILE HISTORY, NORTH ANDOVER, MA

New Line of Work
The change from farm to factory meant a complete change in lifestyle for these young women.

In 1839 Malenda Edwards had left her parents' quiet farm and moved to Nashua, New Hampshire, to work in a textile mill. She traded her days of milking cows, spinning thread, and raking hay for work in a 5-story, red-brick factory. Every day but Sunday, she started work at 5:00 A.M. and operated a power loom until 7:00 P.M., with only short breaks for meals. Most of the 250 workers in the factory were women.

Despite the long hours, Malenda was happy to work in the mill. For a 70-hour work week she earned $3.25—more than most women could make as teachers, seamstresses, or servants. In the years between 1839 and 1845, Malenda would work in the factory for part of the year, then return home to enjoy her earnings and take care of her aging parents.

AS YOU READ

Vocabulary
- textile
- wage
- turnpike
- tariff

Think About . . .
- the development of factories in the United States and their features.
- how immigration contributed to the growth of American manufacturing.
- how roads, canals, and railroads united the country.
- the connections between economics and sectional politics.

In 1845 Malenda Edwards got married, stopped working in the mills, and moved to a small town. She was just one of thousands of Americans who made the journey from farm to factory in the 1800s.

From Farms to Factories

Manufacturing Picks Up Speed

In 1800 most Americans worked on farms. Whether raising cotton in the South, planting in the meadow of a Western forest, or farming near an Eastern town, American farmers led a quiet, rural life. They prided themselves on being self-sufficient. Their farm supplied the family with food, and farm women made day-to-day necessities like soap, candles, and maple sugar.

Most other necessities could be found within a few miles of the farm. Items that could not be made at home were manufactured—by hand, one at a time—by local blacksmiths, shoemakers, and tailors in exchange for corn or wheat. In the more populous areas of the nation, small country stores provided farmers with hard-to-find goods, like gunpowder, coffee, and tea. **Textiles,** or cloth and fabric, from Europe were especially popular in American stores.

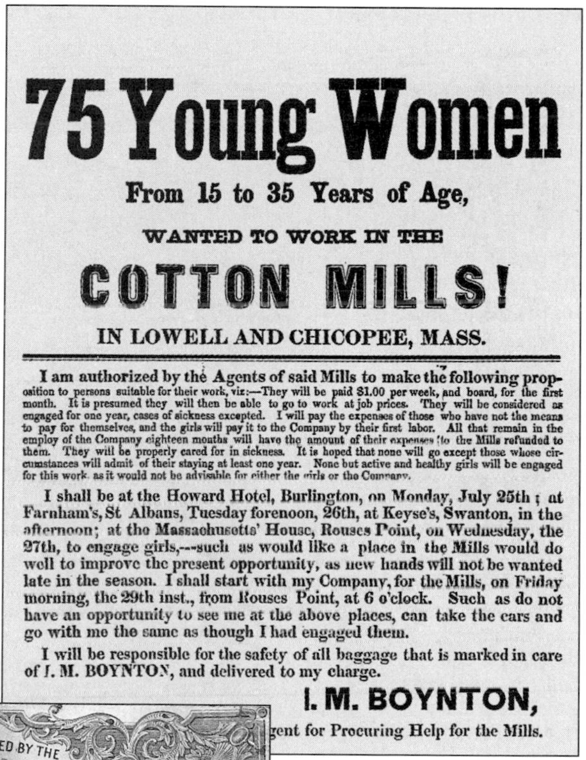
75 Young Women

From 15 to 35 Years of Age,

WANTED TO WORK IN THE

COTTON MILLS!

IN LOWELL AND CHICOPEE, MASS.

I am authorized by the Agents of said Mills to make the following proposition to persons suitable for their work, viz:—They will be paid $1.00 per week, and board, for the first month. It is presumed they will then be able to go to work at job prices. They will be considered as engaged for one year, cases of sickness excepted. I will pay the expenses of those who have not the means to pay for themselves, and the girls will pay it to the Company by their first labor. All that remain in the employ of the Company eighteen months will have the amount of their expenses to the Mills refunded to them. They will be properly cared for in sickness. It is hoped that none will go except those whose circumstances will admit of their staying at least one year. None but active and healthy girls will be engaged for this work as it would not be advisable for either the girls or the Company.

I shall be at the Howard Hotel, Burlington, on Monday, July 25th; at Farnham's, St Albans, Tuesday forenoon, 26th, at Keyse's, Swanton, in the afternoon; at the Massachusetts' House, Rouses Point, on Wednesday, the 27th, to engage girls,---such as would like a place in the Mills would do well to improve the present opportunity, as new hands will not be wanted late in the season. I shall start with my Company, for the Mills, on Friday morning, the 29th inst., from Rouses Point, at 6 o'clock. Such as do not have an opportunity to see me at the above places, can take the cars and go with me the same as though I had engaged them.

I will be responsible for the safety of all baggage that is marked in care of I. M. BOYNTON, and delivered to my charge.

I. M. BOYNTON,

[A]gent for Procuring Help for the Mills.

BAKER LIBRARY, HARVARD UNIVERSITY

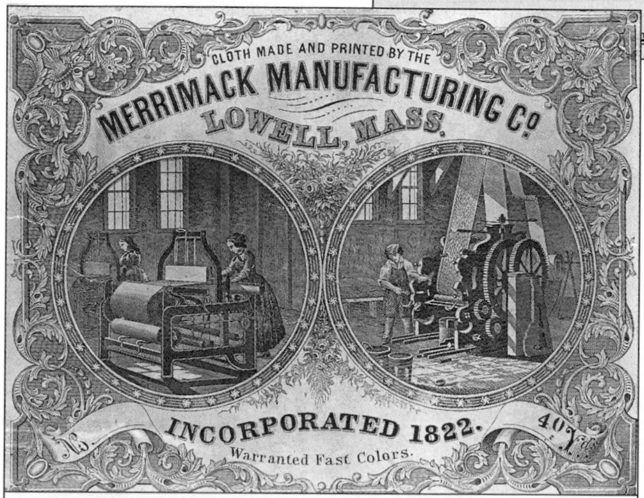

COURTESY AMERICAN ANTIQUARIAN SOCIETY

Millworkers The Merrimack label shows the weaving and printing of cloth under one roof. Mills recruited young women (poster, above) rather than young men because women were more easily spared from farmwork. *How did the Embargo Act spur the development of factories?*

By 1800 all but those farmers living on the most remote fringes of the frontier survived on a mix of homemade goods, handcrafted products of local artisans, and store-bought items imported from Europe. This way of living began to change in 1807.

A Changing Economy

Trade between the United States and Europe had increased steadily. In 1803, however, war broke out between Great Britain and France, resulting in harassment and capture of United States merchant ships. To avoid a war with Britain or France, President Jefferson signed the Embargo Act in 1807, stopping all trade between Europe and the United States. Trade remained choked until after the War of 1812. The resulting economic slowdown had several effects. First, the British wool, Irish linen, and Indian cotton that had flooded the American market no longer arrived. As a result, the home manufacture of textiles boomed. A second effect of this situation was that merchants who had traded with Europe now looked for other ways to make money.

One of those merchants, a Bostonian named Francis Cabot Lowell, recognized the demand for textiles in the United States. He had seen dozens of tiny spinning mills crop up across New England. Lowell took advantage of the postwar slowdown in trade with Britain and began a bold experiment. He started to organize an entirely new system of textile production that was bigger, more efficient, and more profitable than any in the United States.

Lowell's Experiment

In 1813 Lowell set about designing a new spinning and weaving machine. With help from employee Paul Moody, the machine was finally perfected. Lowell and his business partners built a three-story factory on the banks of the Charles River in Waltham, Massachusetts. The current of the river turned waterwheels, which were connected to gears and belts that ran the machinery in the factory.

Unlike the tiny spinning mills of New England, Lowell's plant contained all the stages of textile production under one roof: spinning, weaving, bleaching, dyeing, and printing. The fabric Lowell's factory turned out was rougher than the fine textiles of Europe, but it suited the needs of Americans who bought his cloth. Lowell's factory—larger and more ambitious than any other in the United States—launched the nation's Industrial Revolution, the change from manufacturing at home to manufacturing in factories.

New Workers

Where would Lowell find workers to operate his spinning and weaving machines? In the rural areas around Waltham, no farmer wanted to give up his property and independence to earn **wages,** or daily pay, in a textile factory. Lowell discovered, however, that the farmers' daughters were happy for an opportunity to earn money. Many parents were also happy to receive some of these earnings.

Lowell began recruiting young (mostly ages 15–29) farm women to live and work at his factory. He promised parents that their daughters would live under strict moral supervision in company dormitories, be required to attend church services, and be held to a nightly curfew. After persuading many parents to allow their daughters to move to Waltham, Lowell opened his factory in 1814.

Lowell's Waltham mill was an enormous success. It was so successful that following Lowell's death in 1817, his partners built a new, larger plant located on the Merrimack River in 1823. The town that grew up at that spot

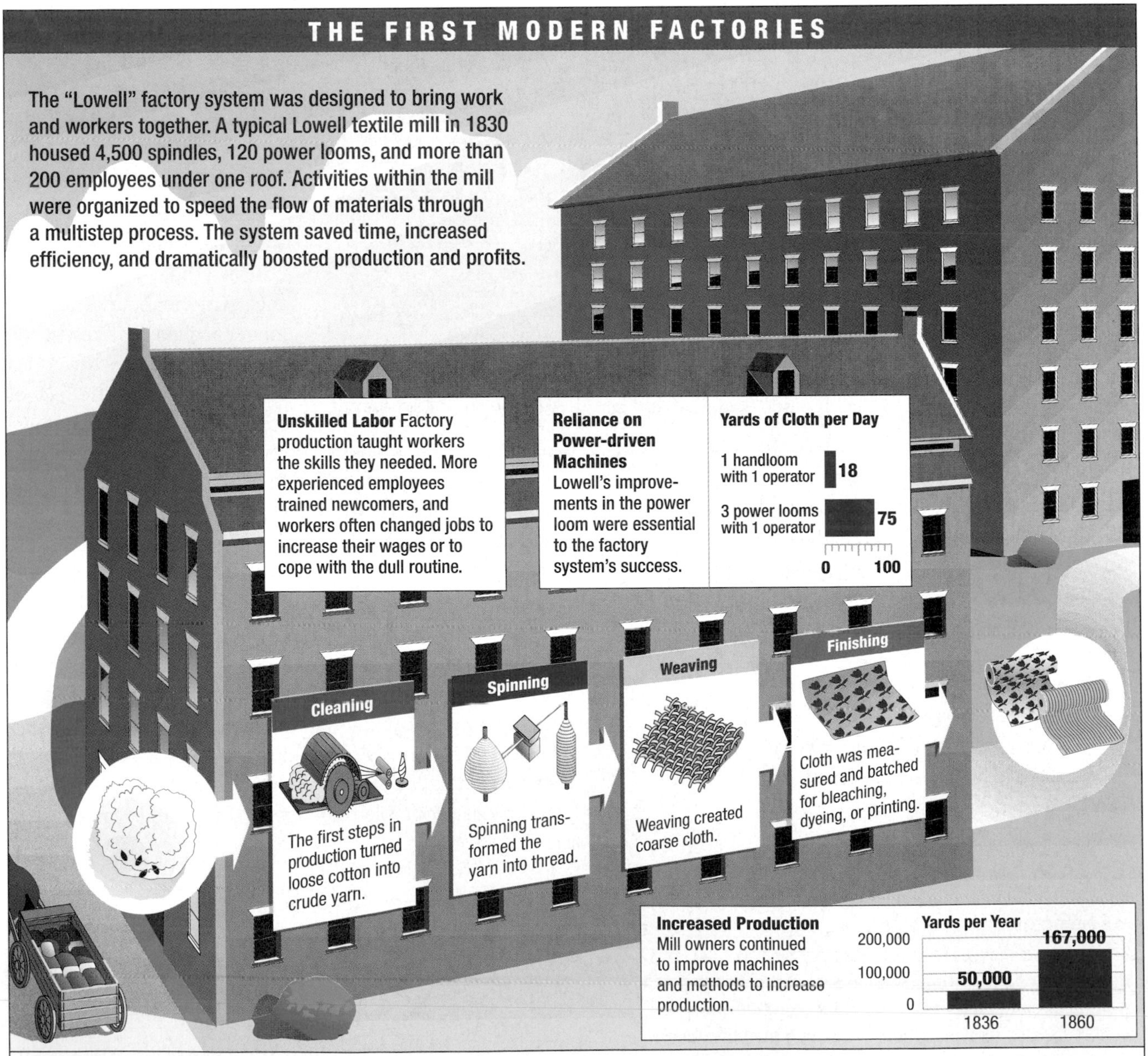

THE FIRST MODERN FACTORIES
The "Lowell" factory system was designed to bring work and workers together. A typical Lowell textile mill in 1830 housed 4,500 spindles, 120 power looms, and more than 200 employees under one roof. Activities within the mill were organized to speed the flow of materials through a multistep process. The system saved time, increased efficiency, and dramatically boosted production and profits.
Unskilled Labor Factory production taught workers the skills they needed. More experienced employees trained newcomers, and workers often changed jobs to increase their wages or to cope with the dull routine.
Reliance on Power-driven Machines Lowell's improvements in the power loom were essential to the factory system's success.
Yards of Cloth per Day
1 handloom with 1 operator 18
3 power looms with 1 operator 75
0 100
Cleaning
The first steps in production turned loose cotton into crude yarn.
Spinning
Spinning transformed the yarn into thread.
Weaving
Weaving created coarse cloth.
Finishing
Cloth was measured and batched for bleaching, dyeing, or printing.
Increased Production Mill owners continued to improve machines and methods to increase production.
Yards per Year
200,000
100,000
0
50,000
167,000
1836
1860

Technological innovation and economic opportunity combined to make the first textile mills possible. *How many more yards of cloth could an operator produce each day tending three power looms instead of one handloom?*

became known as Lowell, Massachusetts. Other textile mills that were located in Lowell also adopted the factory system. By 1840 textile mills employed 8,000 workers, almost 40 percent of Lowell's population.

Business leaders built textile mills all over New England and the mid-Atlantic states in the 1830s and 1840s. Most of the workers in these factories were women like Malenda Edwards. The rest of the labor force was made up of children from local farms and a growing number of men who sought factory work after failing at farming.

After 1840 another source of labor began arriving in the factories of the Northeast. Political turmoil and failed crops drove thousands of Germans and Irish from their European homes. Most of these immigrants arrived on American shores desperate for jobs. Many came to the textile mills of the Northeast and offered to work for lower wages than the farm women.

For factory owners this new, cheap source of labor came just in time. The success of the factory system had created intense competition between textile companies. Mill owners struggled to find ways to increase production and lower costs. Many cut wages and increased the workload of employees. Some women went out on strike to protest wage cuts. In response factory owners began to hire more and more immigrants. By 1860 European immigrants had replaced farm women as the largest group of workers in American factories. This influx of labor willing to work for low wages continued to make the factory system profitable in the United States.

A New Economy

The census of 1850 reported that in the past most "manufacturing was carried on in the shop and the household by the labor of the family." By 1850 it was done by "a system of factory labor, compensated by wages, and assisted by power." Factories producing textiles, shoes, furniture, carriages, and other goods appeared all across the Northeast. Many of these factories were built in growing cities that attracted immigrant workers.

The growth of factories meant that more Americans bought more goods in stores. After 1850 farmers did not get their shoes handmade from a cobbler two miles from home. Instead they bought factory-made shoes from a store that had ordered them from a merchant hundreds of miles away. The transportation revolution that also occurred after 1800 made more goods available to more people in more places than ever before.

The Transportation Revolution

Road, River, and Rail

By 1850 American manufactured goods and farm produce were being transported to most places where people wanted them, whether in Boston or Chicago. Moving goods and people from one place to another had not always been so simple, however.

Roads and Turnpikes

Before 1800 roads and rivers were the most important links between farms, villages, and cities. Yet travel over these roadways and waterways was impossible during some seasons and difficult during the best times. Dry seasons turned many rivers into trickling streams. Hot weather turned roads to dust and rain turned them into muddy troughs. Shipping goods from east to west was expensive: it cost more to haul a ton of goods 9 miles (14.5 km) inland from the ocean than it did to bring that same ton of goods from Europe.

An early solution to American transportation problems was the development of **turnpikes,** roads that required travelers to pay tolls. Private companies built the first turnpikes hoping to earn back the cost of the roads by charging tolls. Turnpike companies often built their roads of stone and gravel, making better traveling conditions. By 1832 the

WELLS FARGO BANK

Riding the Mail Coach Improving the transportation network helped industry and linked the people of different regions. *How might failure to improve transportation have affected the social development of the nation?*

United States had nearly 2,400 miles (3,861.6 km) of toll roads linking together most important cities.

Roads to the West were the most common projects during the turnpike era. The federal government funded construction of the most important route west, the National Road. This stone road that was 80 feet (24.3 m) wide was started in 1811 and ran westward from Cumberland, Maryland. By 1818 it stretched about 130 miles (209.2 km) to Wheeling, in present-day West Virginia. By 1852 it spanned approximately 600 miles (965.4 km), ending in Vandalia, Illinois.

Rivers and Canals

Transportation by water was much less expensive than by road. During the early 1800s, flatboats floated down the Ohio and Mississippi Rivers, carrying crops raised by Western farmers to export markets and to pioneers in other areas. Upstream travel remained slow and expensive, but rivers were a popular and cheap way to move people and goods from place to place.

The rise of steam power made the nation's rivers even more crowded. After 1810 steamboats began churning up and down the rivers, bringing trade in their wake. Between 1830 and 1860, riverboats were especially important on the Mississippi, where they helped make Western farms profitable.

Of course, rivers had limited usefulness. For one thing, most run from north to south, so travel from east to west was often difficult. "Rivers are ungovernable things," Benjamin Franklin wrote. "Canals are quiet and always manageable." Franklin neglected to note that canals were also expensive and hard to build. Nevertheless, the early 1800s witnessed the growth of a network of canals linking the nation's natural waterways.

After the War of 1812, a group of New Yorkers pushed for a canal connecting the Hudson River to Lake Erie. The Erie Canal was to be 363 miles (584.1 km) long at a time when the longest existing canal in the nation was less than 28 miles (45.1 km) long. Construction began in 1817, and over the next 8 years laborers dug by hand a canal 40 feet (12.2 m) wide and 4 feet (1.2 m) deep through the wilderness of northern New York.

Completed in 1825, the Erie Canal was a phenomenal success. Thanks to the business the canal generated, by 1830 New York City replaced Baltimore as the

THE BETTMANN ARCHIVE

Big Dig The completion of the Erie Canal and other canals, together with the rise of steam power, solved many transportation problems. *What transportation problems could not be solved by the use of waterways?*

major Eastern port leading to the interior of the nation. Freight rates to western New York fell by 90 percent after the canal opened. The benefit of this modification to the nation's geography and transportation system was clear.

The Erie Canal's success spurred the construction of canals throughout the nation between 1830 and 1850. In the East, canals connected the backcountry to the ocean. Further inland canals linked Eastern cities with the growing settlements of the Ohio River valley. In the Midwest, canals connected the Great Lakes with the Mississippi River. By 1840 Americans had constructed more than 3,300 miles (5,309.7 km) of canals. In a land of mountains, forests, and plains, however, canals did not solve every transportation problem. Soon Americans were looking for another way to travel.

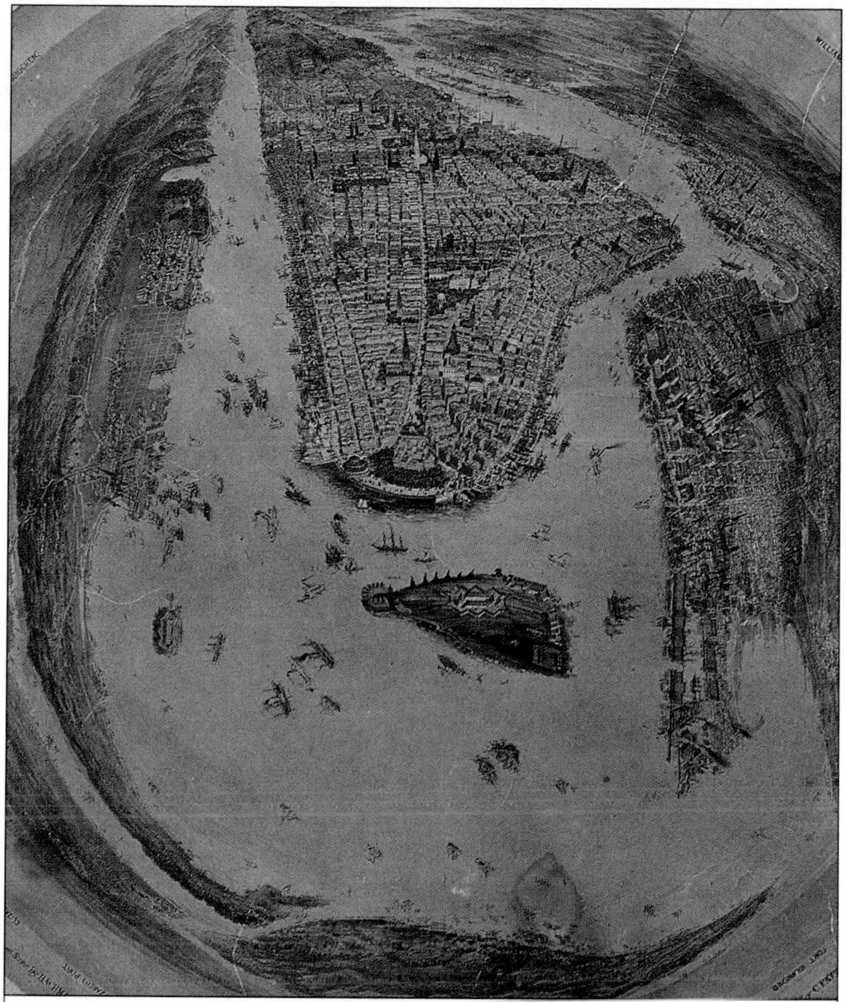

Bird's-Eye View **While transportation systems spawned new inland cities, they also built up older port cities such as New York, shown in this 1859 engraving.** *What effect did the opening of the Erie Canal have on the commerce of New York City?*

ENO COLLECTION, NEW YORK PUBLIC LIBRARY

Tracks and Steam Engines

The success of the Erie Canal took business away from Baltimore merchants who had profited from their location near the National Road. Some of them hatched a plan to restore Baltimore's importance as a seaport by building a railroad from Maryland to Ohio. In 1828 these merchants launched the Baltimore and Ohio, or B & O, Railroad.

Railroads had been invented in Britain. The idea, however, seemed tailor-made for the United States and its huge, varied landscape. Fast transportation that could cover virtually any terrain offered obvious advantages over canals. As a result, people eagerly invested large sums of money in infant railroad companies. During the 1830s more than 3,300 miles (5,309.7 km) of iron rails were built across the nation. A trip from New York to Cincinnati that had taken 2 months over roads took only 1 week by train in 1850.

WATER TRANSPORT DEVELOPMENTS, 1811–1850

1811 Robert Fulton's steamboat cruises down the Mississippi River. Previously, flatboats carried cargo along Western rivers.

1816 Capt. Shreve's steamboat, *The Washington,* travels upstream as well as down on the Ohio River.

1817 Construction on Erie Canal begins. First steamboat travels on the Great Lakes.

1825 Erie Canal is completed, connecting New York City to Great Lakes.

1833 Laborers, many of whom had worked on the Erie Canal, complete canal system in Ohio.

1840s Sharp decline in freight rates on canals and increase in allowed tonnage on lakes and rivers leads to heyday for water transport.

1848 Illinois and Michigan Canal connects the Great Lakes to the Mississippi.

1850s Private railroad companies break the transportation monopolies of state waterways. Toll rates decrease. Water and rail transport increase.

1810 · 1820 · 1830 · 1840 · 1850

By 1860 railroads carried goods and passengers at lower cost and in less time than roads, canals, or rivers. They made money for investors, merchants who shipped by rail, and people who settled in the towns and cities that sprouted along the track of the locomotive during the 1840s and 1850s. The need for railroads, like roads and canals before, came from industry and trade. The growth of railroads, in turn, created thousands of jobs and stimulated new industries, such as those for iron, steel, and railroad car manufacturing.

Politics and the Economy

National and Regional Interests Clash

"It is an extraordinary era in which we live," said Daniel Webster, a senator from Massachusetts, in 1847. "It is altogether new. The world has seen nothing like it." Revolutions in industry and transportation in the United States made this new world possible. While private investors had funded many of these developments, government also helped nurture America's economic growth in the 1800s.

PHOTO BY STEVE LASCHEVER/COURTESY OF MUSEUM OF AMERICAN POLITICAL LIFE, HARTFORD, CT

Henry Clay for President **Clay began campaigning for President in 1824 and ran in three elections. Like other candidates of the period, his likeness appeared on practical and playful items, such as this bandanna.** *What effect did Clay expect a new Bank of the United States to have on the national economy in 1816?*

One of the strongest supporters of government's role in the economy was Henry Clay. A member of Congress from Kentucky, Clay had gained prominence during the War of 1812 as a Western war hawk. At that time he opposed a strong national government and programs such as the Bank of the United States, which gave the federal government significant centralized economic power.

As America's economic power grew, however, Clay's views changed. He organized his new ideas into an economic plan called the American System.

The American System

Clay's American System was based on the idea that a stronger national government would benefit each of the different sections of the country. As part of this system Clay supported an 1816 bill to increase **tariffs,** or fees on imported goods. The tariffs were designed to protect American manufacturers—nearly all of whom were located in the East—from European competition. Clay believed that healthy Eastern industries would help the whole nation. This bill passed despite the objections of Southerners in Congress. The South, a region with little manufacturing, would gain nothing directly from the tariff. Consequently, the tariff would have the effect of higher prices for the South, because Southerners imported a great deal of foreign goods.

In 1816 Congress faced the decision of whether to charter a new Bank of the United States (the charter of the first Bank expired in 1811). Clay supported the Bank, arguing that it would stabilize the economy and encourage investments. The Bank bill passed.

Another part of Clay's American System met with less success than the first two. Clay wanted the government to supply money for improvements such as road and canal building. Other Westerners in Congress voted for these plans, which would greatly benefit the frontier regions they represented. Southerners in Congress generally favored Clay's plans because the South also stood to benefit from such improvements. Northerners, however, clashed with Clay over these improvements. For one thing, their roads and canals were already built and dug, so they would not

PHOTO BY STEVE LASCHEVER/COURTESY OF MUSEUM OF AMERICAN POLITICAL LIFE, HARTFORD, CT

Transportation Ticket This silk campaign ribbon shows the loyalty of a strong Clay contingent: the wagoneers, or cartmen. *What specific proposals did Clay put forward that could have won him the wagoneers' support?*

benefit directly from federal assistance. Also, many Northerners feared the growing power of the Westerners and did not want to help them grow stronger.

The greatest opposition to Clay's plans, however, came from the Executive Office of the President. Between 1817 and 1830, three of Clay's internal improvement bills were passed by Congress and then vetoed by three different Presidents. President James Madison, who argued that the Constitution did not give Congress the power to build roads, vetoed the first. On the same basic grounds, in 1822, President James Monroe vetoed a proposal to improve the National Road. Finally, in 1830 President Andrew Jackson vetoed the use of federal funds to improve Kentucky's Maysville Road.

Clay was disappointed that these Presidents paid so little attention to internal improvements, but the government did encourage the nation's growth in other ways. After 1816 Congress passed a series of tariffs that protected the nation's young industries. Between 1830 and 1860 New York, Pennsylvania, Ohio, and Virginia built many of their canals with state funds. Canal and railroad companies usually obtained land from federal and state governments at bargain prices. The combination of private investments and public policy reshaped American life after 1815.

A New Nation

Shortly after steamboats began to paddle down the nation's rivers, a newspaper editor exclaimed that steam power would "diminish the size of the globe." It would make Americans "one single people, one nation, one mind." In some ways, the nation did seem more unified after the transportation and industrial revolutions. After 1850 the farmer's solitary self-sufficiency no longer seemed practical. Cooperation between people with different interests and from different regions replaced it. New Englanders gave up most of their farming and devoted resources to manufacturing. Farmers from the western side of the Appalachians now produced most of the American grain. Southern planters devoted more land and slave labor to cash crops like cotton.

Regional specialization, however, could lead to conflicts. A law that helped Northern manufacturers, such as the tariff, might hurt Southern planters. Tensions between different sections of the nation and between different groups of people began to grow. The forces that changed America's economy in the 1800s also changed the politics and beliefs of its people.

Section Review

Vocabulary

1. Define: textile, wage, turnpike, tariff.

Checking Facts

2. Describe Lowell's experiment and explain its significance.
3. Explain the success of the Erie Canal and the railroads.

Critical Thinking

Predicting Consequences

4. Why might factory owners have feared labor shortages in the 1830s when they increased production and cut wages? Who helped solve the owners' labor problems?

Linking Across Time

5. In 1816 sectional interests partly determined how people reacted to a proposal such as Clay's tariff bill. How might sectional interests today influence a person's position on, for example, environmental legislation?

Geography: Impact on History

MOVEMENT

The Rise of American Cities

Changes in trade and transportation set off a burst of urban growth from 1800 to 1860. All along trade and transportation routes, older cities grew larger and new ones were born. Topography, too, played a key role in this rise of American cities because terrain usually dictated locations of trade routes.

Early American Cities

Most American cities in the thirteen colonies grew up along the Atlantic coast. The ocean linked them with Britain and other countries. Ports and coastal cities such as New York, Charleston, and Boston are still important centers of transportation and industry today.

Inland cities tended to grow up along rivers that provided easy access to the coast and water power to run industries. As American technology overcame obstacles of distance and rugged terrain, the people moved steadily westward.

Steamboats bucked the currents in inland rivers to carry cargo; mules plodded along towpaths, pulling canal boats laden with everything from beeswax to lumber. Trains, spitting sparks and belching steam, hauled freight at the amazing speed of 15 miles per hour. With these 3 modes of transportation now in full swing west of the Appalachians, the pace of trade in the interior picked up. Soon river outposts, canal communities, and railroad whistle-stops developed into cities, while settlements off the beaten track stagnated, sometimes completely disappearing from the map.

Three cities exemplify how trade, transportation, and topography directed the course of urban growth in the United States.

Riverside City

A bonanza of waterways transformed the fur-trading center of St. Louis into a sizable city. Encircled by farmland, St. Louis is situated on the Mississippi just south of where that mighty river meets the Illinois and Missouri Rivers. By midcentury steamboats chugged into St. Louis from north and south, so many that sometimes they lined up for a mile along the docks. From St. Louis, both boats and barges traveled along the Illinois to the

TRANSPORTATION ROUTES, 1800–1860

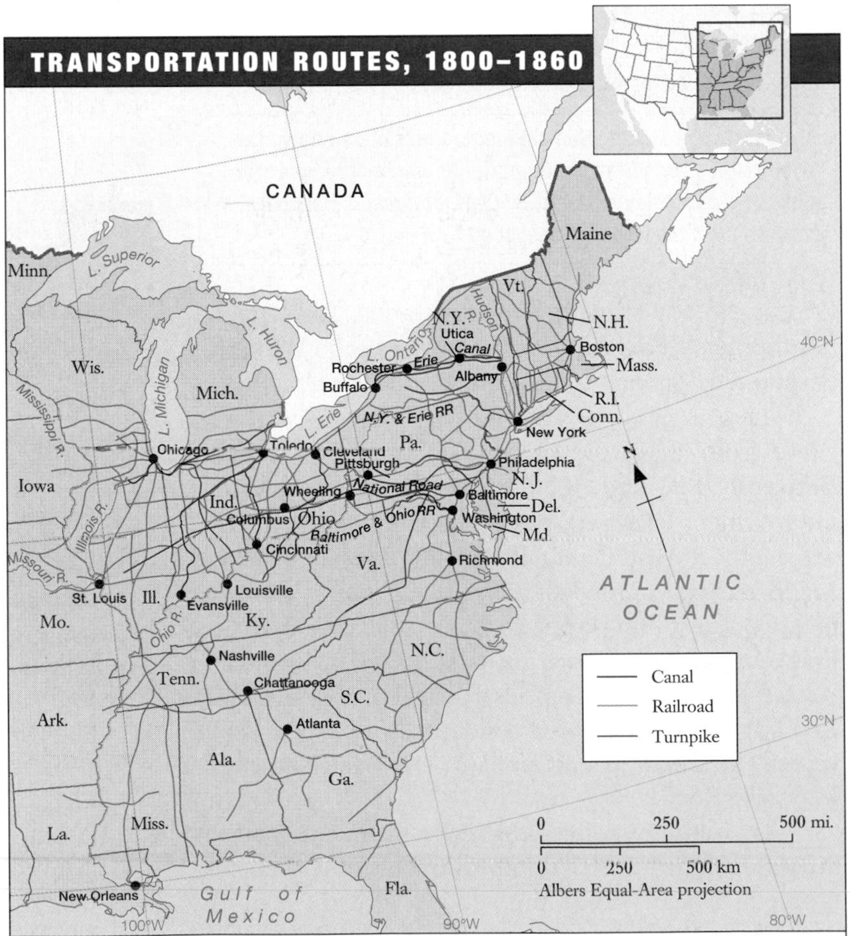

Three kinds of transportation routes linked American cities in the early 1800s.
How did geography help make Chicago a major transportation center?

NORTH WIND PICTURE ARCHIVES

A Busy Port **Between 1800 and 1860, major new cities like Chicago, St. Louis, and Buffalo developed along transportation routes. This print from the 1870s shows heavy traffic at the docks in St. Louis.** *What factors made St. Louis an ideal spot for urban growth?*

prairies, along the Missouri to the West, and down the Mississippi to New Orleans, gateway to the Gulf of Mexico. This intense activity helped boost the one-time fur-trade outpost to a city of 160,773 by 1860.

Along the Canal

In 1810, Buffalo, New York, was nothing but a settlement of 1,500 people at the east end of Lake Erie. When the Erie Canal opened in 1825, Buffalo's population grew to more than 2,400, and hundreds of new buildings were added. By 1860 the population had risen to 81,000.

The 363-mile (584-km) canal ran across New York State from Albany to Buffalo. At Albany, the Hudson River linked the canal with the coast, tying the Atlantic seaboard to the Great Lakes. Canal boats poked along at speeds of between 1 and 5 miles an hour, but rates were cheap. Shipping freight from New York City to Buffalo cost as little as $5 a ton. Transporting the same load by wagon cost $100 and took twice as long.

Although railroads soon outran canals, the Erie Canal remained in operation. Today it is part of the 524-mile (843-km) New York State Barge Canal System, and Buffalo remains a major transportation center.

The Hub of the Rails

As the railroad roared westward, Chicago changed its shape from swampy settlement to megacity. In 1840 the community numbered only about 4,500 people. Eight years later, as the first trains rumbled into town, grain, lumber, and livestock began opening up the city's growing market. Population rose to 109,260 by 1860.

Located on level land in the heart of the nation, with Lake Michigan at its front door, Chicago was perfectly placed for a rail center. Rail tycoons bypassed landlocked communities and charted their tracks to Chicago. By 1860 Chicago was the nation's top rail city, with 11 lines radiating from its hub.

Other industrial centers sprang up across Ohio and the Midwest; canal and rail networks gave them access to both raw materials and markets. Gradually these cities developed the political systems, educational facilities, and cultural institutions that were already flourishing in the older port cities.

Making the Geographic Connection

1. Identify the different kinds of transportation that linked American cities.
2. Trade and transportation often spur urban growth. What factors expand trade and transportation?
3. **Movement** In 1950 railroads carried 56 percent of American intercity freight. By 1988 they only carried 37 percent. What kinds of transportation are greatly affecting urban growth today?

SECTION 3

A Changing People

AUGUST 1801: 20,000 WORSHIP AT KENTUCKY CAMP MEETING

COURTESY OF THE NEW YORK HISTORICAL SOCIETY, NEW YORK CITY

Open-Air Sermon
Camp-meeting preachers often held enormous audiences spellbound.

THE NOISE RISING FROM THE CLEARING IN THE FOREST "WAS LIKE THE ROAR OF NIAGARA." The sound of singing, weeping, shouting, and moaning of thousands of people came from the meadow. "The vast sea of human beings," observed young James Finley, "seemed to be agitated as if by a storm." The power that stirred the people at Cane Ridge, Kentucky, on that warm August afternoon was religion.

The Cane Ridge meeting began early one Friday and continued for 6 full days. More than 20,000 people flocked from the surrounding countryside to attend. For these people camp meetings were a rare chance for contact with others and for a religious service. At night they slept in a city of canvas tents; by day they heard sermons by traveling preachers.

"I counted seven ministers all preaching at once," reported Finley. Some stood on tree stumps, others in wagons. Using vivid images of Satan and fiery hell, the preachers evoked powerful feelings among the listeners. Their sermons offered straightforward choices: sin or salvation, evil or good, wrong or right. The decision was in each person's hands.

Like many others, James Finley was powerfully affected by what he heard at Cane Ridge. "A peculiar strange sensation came over me," he said. "My heart beat tumultuously, my knees trembled, my lips quivered, and I felt as though I must fall to the ground." Finley never forgot this experience; several years later he became a preacher himself.

To many people, religion was the solution to the problems facing the United States in the early 1800s. As the nation expanded, Americans became participants in disturbing conflicts—conflicts between rich and poor, Easterner and Westerner, Northerner and Southerner, African American and white. Some people tried to escape these tensions by joining religious communities.

AS YOU READ

Vocabulary

- spoils system
- nullification
- secede
- temperance
- abolitionism

Think About . . .

- the changes in early nineteenth-century politics that brought Andrew Jackson to power.
- the connection between the Second Great Awakening and social reform.
- how participation in the abolition movement and other social movements gave women and African Americans a political voice.

Others tried to reform American society, while still others turned to politics as a way of bringing change to the nation.

A New Era in Politics

Courting the Common Man

New ideas about politics were sweeping the United States in the early 1800s. The most important of these ideas involved the question of who should be allowed to vote. Many Western states allowed all adult men to vote, regardless of how much land they owned. In the 1820s many Eastern states also eliminated property requirements for voters. During that decade, more white men than ever before gained the vote. Many of these new voters were Westerners, men who had left the East to seek wealth and opportunity on the frontier. These new voters wanted a new type of politician. They found one in Andrew Jackson.

Jackson and the Common Man

Thanks to his exploits in the War of 1812, Andrew Jackson became one of the nation's best-known heroes. Though he professed little interest in politics, friends persuaded him to run for President in 1824.

Jackson entered one of the wildest elections Americans had yet seen. After 23 years of solid control over the presidency, the Democratic-Republican party was split by factions battling along sectional lines. John Q. Adams, a Northerner and son of the second President, had the support of President James Monroe. Another veteran Democratic-Republican, Henry Clay, hoped to be elected by the Westerners he represented. A Southern candidate, William Crawford of Georgia, had won the support of many members of Congress.

Jackson was the fourth candidate. By far the least experienced politically, he nonetheless impressed people. His image as a no-nonsense frontiersman who had worked his way up the ladder of society, appealed to many voters. His political ideas were as direct as a frontier preacher's sermon: He favored a "Democracy of Numbers" over the "moneyed aristocracy."

Jackson's supporters in the West and South gave him the most electoral and popular votes in the contest, but no candidate had a clear majority. The contest—according to the Constitution's rule—was turned over to the House of Representatives. Henry Clay, who served as speaker of the House that year, threw his support to Adams. When the House vote was taken in February 1825, Adams won with the votes of 13 states to Jackson's 7 states. Jackson's supporters claimed that Clay and Adams had made a "corrupt bargain," a charge that seemed justified when Adams named Clay secretary of state.

The election of 1824 split the Democratic-Republican party once and for all. Supporters of Adams and Clay began to call themselves National Republicans. Jackson's supporters, calling themselves Democrats, began to make plans for the 1828 presidential election.

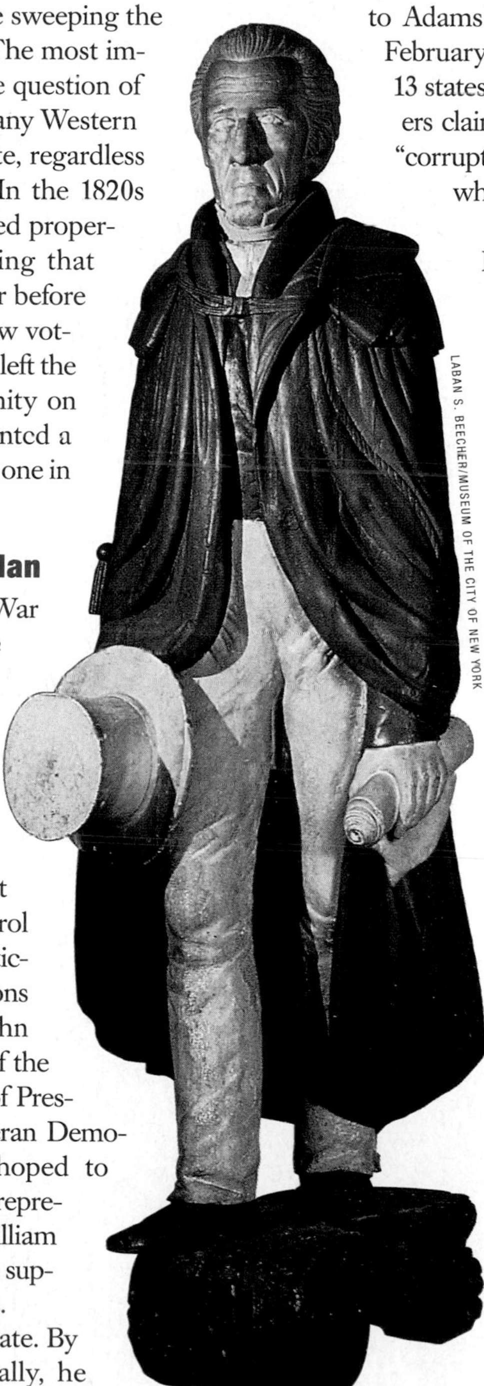

LABAN S. BEECHER/MUSEUM OF THE CITY OF NEW YORK

Andrew Jackson This figurehead representing Jackson was used on a ship in 1834. *Why do you think Jackson made enemies among traditional politicians?*

The Election of 1828

Both Adams and Jackson had observed the changing political climate, and both designed their campaigns with the "common man" in mind. The result was a mean-spirited but lively campaign that avoided most serious issues.

National Republicans called Jackson "a gambler, a cockfighter, a brawler, a drunkard, and a murderer." The Democrats attacked Adams as a "stingy, undemocratic" aristocrat. They asked Americans to choose between "John Quincy Adams, who can write, and Andrew Jackson, who can fight."

The political tide of democracy favored Jackson in 1828. Almost three times as many people voted as had in 1824, and these new voters helped deliver a resounding victory for Jackson.

After his Inaugural Address in March 1829, Jackson rode down Pennsylvania Avenue to the White House followed by thousands of his celebrating supporters. The crowd swarmed into the White House behind Jackson, grabbing the cakes, ice cream, and punch that had been set out for the inaugural reception. The people broke china, tore curtains, and knocked over furniture. Jackson had to escape the mob through a window. It was apparent to everyone in Washington that a new era in politics had begun.

"The people expect reform," Jackson said. "They shall not be disappointed." One of his first changes was to fire a number of allegedly "lazy" government workers, many of whom had supported Adams. Jackson replaced them with his own supporters.

This practice of rewarding government supporters with government jobs was known as the **spoils system.** Jackson claimed that replacing workers every so often made the government more democratic. The duties in most government jobs, he argued, were so "plain and simple" that anyone could do them. Dismantling the old bureaucracy, however, was a small matter compared with Jackson's war on the powerful Bank of the United States.

The Bank Crisis

The Bank of the United States was an important financial institution that exerted significant influence over Congress and the nation's economy. The United States owned 20 percent of the Bank's stock, and the government's money was deposited there. This money, along with private investments, was used to promote commerce and manufacturing. This had the effect of promoting the interests of Northeastern industries.

To Jackson, the Bank was undemocratic and unconstitutional. It represented the "moneyed aristocracy" that he so hated. He called the Bank a "monster" that threatened to "control the Government and change its character." Henry Clay and Daniel Webster knew how Jackson felt and planned to strengthen the Bank and embarrass the President at the same time. Clay and Webster drafted a bill rechartering the Bank, even though the Bank's original charter still had four years remaining. They reasoned that Jackson would not dare veto a bill—a rare occurrence in that era—in his reelection year. The bill passed Congress and reached the President's desk in July 1832.

Jackson saw this early bank bill as an attack. "The bank . . . is trying to kill me," he told an adviser, "but I will kill the bank." Jackson not only vetoed the Bank bill, he also made it the central issue in his campaign that fall. "When the laws," he said, "make the rich richer and the potent more powerful, the humble members of society—the farmers, mechanics, and laborers—. . . have a right to complain." Many people agreed, and in the 1832 election Jackson defeated his opponent Henry Clay.

LIBRARY OF CONGRESS

People's Reception Andrew Jackson brought to Washington the spirit of the rugged frontier or a shocking lack of refinement, according to how one viewed him. *Do you think Jackson would have been as politically successful earlier in the history of the United States? Why or why not?*

During his second term, Jackson was determined to destroy the Bank. He closed the government's accounts at the Bank and moved federal funds to state banks. In 1836 the Bank's charter expired for good.

The Tariff Controversy

As Jackson battled the Bank, another crisis split his administration and threatened to divide the nation. Tariffs had been part of the country's economic policy since 1816. Tariffs were unpopular in the South, however. When Congress passed a high tariff on some European imports in 1828, many Southerners complained loudly. One of these angry Southerners was Jackson's Vice President, John Calhoun. Calhoun wrote an essay invoking states' rights and the theory of **nullification.** A state, wrote Calhoun, had the right to nullify, or reject, any law that the state felt violated the Constitution.

Jackson supported states' rights, but as President he could not accept nullification because it threatened the federal government's power and the states' unity. Still, some Southerners tried to win Jackson's support by inviting him to a large ceremonial dinner with Calhoun in 1830. When Jackson stood to make the toast before dinner, he let the nullifiers know exactly where he stood on the matter: "Our Federal Union: It must be preserved." Jackson's toast—which plainly put the power of the federal government above the power of the states—silenced the room. A stunned Calhoun rose with his own toast to defend states' rights: "The Union," he said, "next to our liberty, most dear."

In 1832 the controversy became a crisis when Congress passed yet another high tariff. This act enraged politicians in South Carolina. During the fall of 1832 the state legislature nullified the tariff. They also threatened to **secede,** or leave the Union, if the government tried to collect tariff duties in the state. John Calhoun resigned as Vice President and took over one of South Carolina's seats in the Senate.

In December, Jackson directed warships and troops to move toward South Carolina. Then Congress passed a Force Bill permitting the President to use military force to collect the state's tariff duties.

As tensions mounted, Henry Clay designed a compromise plan to reduce all tariffs for 10 years. South Carolina accepted this peace offering and withdrew its nullification of the tariff. Clay's compromise bill resolved the crisis, but states' rights would remain a burning issue for the next 30 years as Southern and Northern politicians battled over slavery.

The Whig Party

While Jackson remained a popular figure, he made many political enemies. By 1834 opposition to Jackson had unified as the Whig party. The new party included Republicans such as Henry Clay and Federalists such as Daniel Webster, plus supporters of the Bank of the United States, manufacturers who favored tariffs, and wealthy business leaders in large cities. The Democrats maintained their support among working people, immigrants, and the small farmers of the South and West.

The Democrats retained the White House in 1836 as Jackson's chosen successor, Martin Van Buren, won the election. In 1840, however, the Whigs retaliated. They portrayed Van Buren as an aristocrat who ate from gold plates. The Whig candidate was a military hero in the Jackson mold, William Henry Harrison. By ignoring the issues and portraying him as a common, cider-drinking man, the Whigs were able to capture the White House.

In the election of 1840, the Whigs made use of the Jacksonian idea that power and success were available to everyone, not just the elite. That idea was echoed in the sermons of preachers on the Western frontier.

An Awakening Interest in Religion

Revivalism Sweeps the Land

While voters were expressing displeasure toward the "moneyed aristocracy," many Americans were finding they had little in common with the traditional colonial Christian churches: the Anglican (Episcopal), the Congregationalist, and the Presbyterian. These churches often had an air of wealth and privilege. Services tended to be formal affairs that inspired little enthusiasm. As the nation expanded, Americans began seeking new forms of religion more in keeping with the spirit of a restless, growing young nation.

Western Revival

Beginning in the 1790s, a revival in religious interest known as the Second Great Awakening swept the Western frontier. The style of these growing churces—especially Methodist and Baptist—was less formal than the better established churches of the East. Circuit riders, or traveling ministers, rode about the frontier preaching to farmers. Rallies such as the camp meeting at Cane Ridge, Kentucky, attracted people from miles around.

The sermons delivered at these meetings and churches could be frightening—damnation awaited all sinners. The message behind them remained personal, emotional, practical, and even democratic. The idea that anything—even victory over sin—was possible with hard work and prayer appealed to many Americans.

Perfecting Society

As the powerful ideas of the Second Great Awakening spread through the country, the nature of its message changed. One preacher who took this message and developed it was Charles Grandison Finney. A tall man with thinning blond hair and blazing eyes, Finney began with the idea that sin was a failure of will. Those who could avoid the temptation of sin could make themselves perfect.

Finney went on to say that not only could Christians make themselves perfect, they could—indeed, must—make the world around them perfect. No Christian could fail to see a thousand evils that needed to be corrected, reformed, and eliminated. The ideas of Finney and other preachers unleashed enormous energy in Americans. The urge to perfect the nation grew stronger during the 1830s and thereafter.

Reforming American Society

Fighting Evils From Alcohol to Slavery

The Second Great Awakening inspired different responses from different groups. Some withdrew to create their own "perfect" communities. For example, the Shakers and the Mormons, two religious groups, attempted to build their own utopia, or ideal world, away from mainstream American life.

Others set about changing the mainstream itself. They saw a host of evils in the rapidly changing society of the 1800s. Churchgoers in the populous areas of the North were among the first to organize reform groups. These groups usually saw social problems in religious terms of "evil" and "sin."

In the Promised Land These survivors of the 1847 Mormon trek across the plains and mountains to the Great Salt Lake were photographed 50 years later. *What other religious society of the time set out to build its own utopia?*

In an era when women had limited opportunities for education or jobs, reform groups offered an outlet for their energy and skills. Women filled the ranks of many reform efforts during the mid-1800s, but others considered it "unfeminine" for women to play an active role in these movements. As a result of these tensions, women's rights became one of the dominant issues during the reform era.

While women's rights concerned some, other evils were more visible and easier to attack. Alcohol, for example, was blamed for crime, insanity, and the breakdown of the family. As a result, the **temperance,** or antidrinking, movement became one of the first organized reform movements in the United States.

FRUITLANDS MUSEUM

Nine Steps to Destruction This illustration reflects the temperance movement's belief that alcohol drove people to ruin. *What other reform movements developed in the wake of the temperance movement?*

Demon Rum

Starting in the 1830s reformers targeted the evils of "demon rum." They flooded the nation with tracts and articles. One of the best-selling novels of the 1850s, *Ten Nights in a Bar Room and What I Saw There,* warned against the excesses of alcohol. Reformed alcoholics traveled to meetings in city after city, telling their stories. These efforts got results. Hard liquor sales fell by half during the 1830s alone.

Gradually the fight against drunkenness became a war on alcohol itself. More and more Americans chose to avoid all liquor and became "teetotalers." Reformers took their case to state legislatures. In 1838 Tennessee passed the first statewide regulation of liquor. Temperance reformers won another victory when Maine passed a tougher liquor law in 1851. While some citizens protested and bootleg liquor poured into the state from Canada, reformers counted the Maine law as a victory.

The success of the temperance movement inspired dozens of other reform efforts: the push for better prisons, mental health care, free public education, and aid for the blind and the deaf. Some reformers, however, perceived an evil much greater than all of these—an evil endorsed by politicians, protected by laws, and defended by an entire section of the nation. That evil was slavery.

Fighting Slavery

Slavery had troubled some Americans since before the Revolution. In 1787 the Northwest Ordinance forbade slavery in territories north of the Ohio River, and by 1804 every Northern state had provided for the end of slavery. Few white Americans, however, took an active stand on slavery between the passage of the Constitution and the 1820s.

At this time dozens of publications appeared spreading the ideas of **abolitionism,** the movement to end slavery. Most of these papers called for a gradual end to slavery, believing that the slow pace would bring liberation while it protected the businesses of Southern planters.

Other abolitionists had less patience. David Walker, a former slave living in Boston, called for an immediate end to slavery in 1829. He argued that enslaved individuals were entitled to use violence to obtain their freedom.

Two years later William Lloyd Garrison began publishing a newspaper called *The Liberator.* In his black suits and steel-rimmed glasses, Garrison looked more like a schoolmaster than a radical reformer. His pen, however, spouted fire as he called for the immediate emancipation of all enslaved persons. "I am in earnest," he wrote. "I will not retreat a single inch—AND I WILL BE HEARD!"

BROWN BROTHERS

CHICAGO HISTORICAL SOCIETY

COURTESY OF THE BOSTON PUBLIC LIBRARY, PRINT DEPARTMENT

COURTESY OF THE BOSTON PUBLIC LIBRARY, PRINT DEPARTMENT

Freedom Fighters The abolition movement brought forth many notable historical figures. From left to right: top, Frederick Douglass and Sojourner Truth, both fugitives from slavery; bottom, William Lloyd Garrison, a member of the clergy, and Lucretia C. Mott, who was also a temperance leader.
What issues divided the abolition movement?

Garrison was heard. In 1833 a group of his supporters met in Philadelphia and formed the American Anti-Slavery Society. The goals of the society were to end slavery in the United States by stirring up public sentiment and flooding the nation with abolitionist literature. The society grew throughout the 1830s. With success, however, came controversy. Southerners worried about the effect of Garrison's message on their enslaved laborers and mounted vicious verbal attacks on him. Northerners blasted his views on the Constitution, which he called a "compromise with tyranny" and "an agreement with hell" because it allowed slavery.

Tensions Within the Movement

White leaders of the abolitionist movement discovered that African Americans, especially those who had escaped from bondage, made the most convincing arguments against slavery. Soon, fugitives became the star attractions at meetings of the American Anti-Slavery Society. One of the best speakers was Frederick Douglass, a brilliant man who had made a dramatic escape from slavery in 1838 at age 21. Douglass was a spellbinding speaker. "I appear before this immense assembly," he addressed one crowd, "as a thief and robber. I stole this head, these limbs, this body from my master, and ran off with them."

Sojourner Truth, a tall, deep-voiced woman, had also become free after serving several masters for 30 years. In the 1840s she attracted large crowds throughout the North and West with her abolitionist speeches.

For all their talent, African American abolitionists found that white opponents of slavery were generally unwilling to accept them into their organizations. In addition, abolitionists often disagreed over how to attack slavery. Some abolitionists advocated the use of violence and urged enslaved persons to revolt. They felt that the speeches and tracts of the American Anti-Slavery Society were useless against a problem like slavery. Others, like Frederick Douglass, believed that change could only come from within the political system.

Women also chafed at their role as second-class citizens within the movement. Recognizing the important contributions of women, Garrison supported women's rights and encouraged their role in the movement. Other male leaders, however, refused to accept women as equals.

In 1840 all these tensions within the American Anti-Slavery Society splintered it. The split in the society, however, was not the end of abolitionism. In the 1840s and 1850s abolitionism was one of the issues—along with western expansion and the nation's changing economic identity—that widened the split between Northern and Southern states.

Section Review

Vocabulary

1. Define: spoils system, nullification, secede, temperance, abolitionism.

Checking Facts

2. How was William Henry Harrison's appeal to voters similar to Jackson's?
3. How did the Second Great Awakening relate to reform movements of the time?

Critical Thinking

Making Comparisons

4. Abolitionists differed among themselves in their strategies for ending slavery. Compare their opinions.

Linking Across Time

5. How is name-calling used in modern election campaigns? Is it ever effective? Explain your answer.

Social Studies Skill

MAKING TELESCOPING TIME LINES

Learning the Skill

A telescoping time line highlights a relatively short period of time, showing selected events within a larger time span. The activities of abolitionist William Lloyd Garrison can be represented with a part of the time line that telescopes—or extends—from one point along the historically broader part of the time line. The two sections of the time line work together to show a historical movement and a critical point in that movement.

Placing Events on a Telescoping Time Line

To decide where an event belongs, do the following:

a. First examine the subject and dates of the broad part of the time line. The upper time line section on this page shows the growth of slavery and abolitionism in the United States, 1619–1840.

b. Next examine the highlighted part of the time line. Here the lower time line section shows one abolitionist leader's activities beginning in 1828 and continuing to 1840.

c. Choose an occurrence from the general time span and determine where it belongs. For example, the Missouri Compromise occurred before 1826 and relates to abolitionism but not to Garrison. Therefore it belongs on the upper section of the time line.

Practicing the Skill

Study the telescoping time line below and answer the following questions.

1. When did Garrison edit Boston's *National Philanthropist* and Vermont's *Journal of the Times*?

2. Where would you place the start of the abolitionist newspaper the *Liberator* in 1831? Why?

3. Where would you place an entry for abolition of slavery in New York State in 1827? Why?

4. How might the 1688 entry on the upper part of the time line relate to Garrison's activities?

5. Name another time span that could extend or telescope from the broader time line section.

Applying the Skill

Try making a telescoping time line for United States expansion from 1776 through 1850. Choose a focus and a smaller time span to highlight.

Additional Practice

For additional practice, see Reinforcing Skills on page 161.

Abolitionism and William Lloyd Garrison: A Telescoping Time Line, 1619–1840

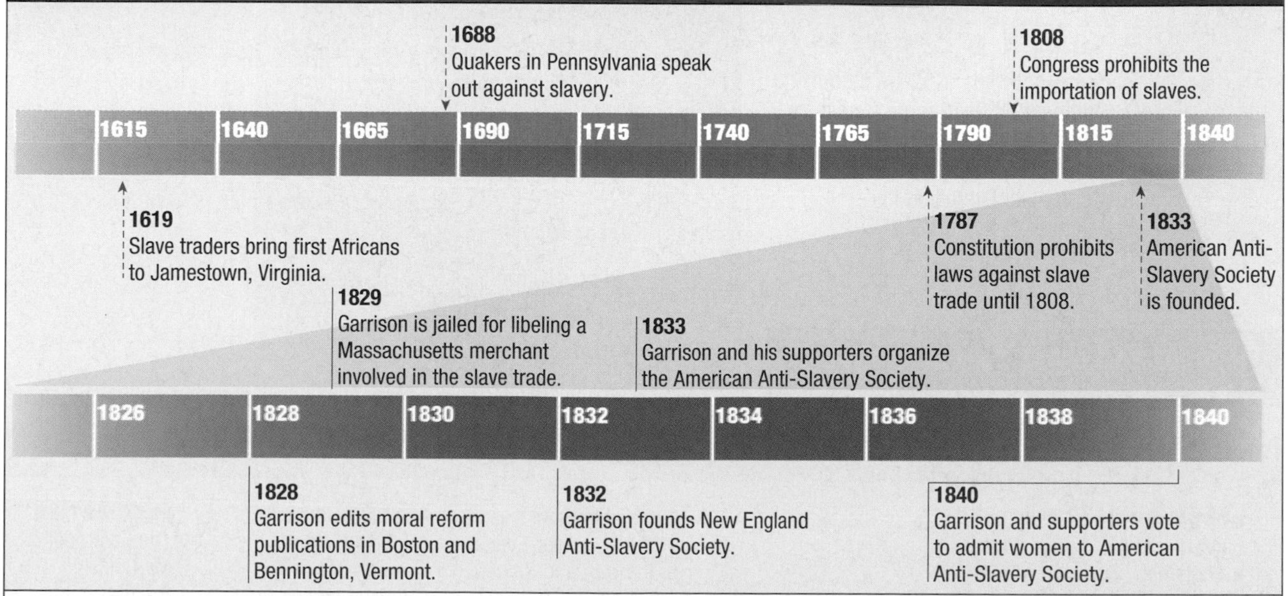

1688
Quakers in Pennsylvania speak out against slavery.
1808
Congress prohibits the importation of slaves.
1615
1640
1665
1690
1715
1740
1765
1790
1815
1840
1619
Slave traders bring first Africans to Jamestown, Virginia.
1787
Constitution prohibits laws against slave trade until 1808.
1833
American Anti-Slavery Society is founded.
1829
Garrison is jailed for libeling a Massachusetts merchant involved in the slave trade.
1833
Garrison and his supporters organize the American Anti-Slavery Society.
1826
1828
1830
1832
1834
1836
1838
1840
1828
Garrison edits moral reform publications in Boston and Bennington, Vermont.
1832
Garrison founds New England Anti-Slavery Society.
1840
Garrison and supporters vote to admit women to American Anti-Slavery Society.

Newspaper editor and public speaker William Lloyd Garrison stirred the fires of abolitionism prior to the Civil War. His accomplishments are highlighted in the telescoping time line above. *Why might Garrison's work have come at a critical time?*

Science, TECHNOLOGY, and Society

The Steam Engine

By the mid-1800s the steam engine had wrought enormous changes in American society, especially in transportation. Steam engines were not only turning the wheels of steamboats and locomotives, but were powering manufacturing, mining, and agricultural machinery as well.

© MICHAEL FREEMAN

NATIONAL MUSEUM OF AMERICAN HISTORY, DIVISION OF ENGINEERING AND INDUSTRY, SMITHSONIAN INSTITUTE

TOWER OF POWER
A 40-foot-high (12.2-m) steam engine, built by George Corliss, supplied power to all 8,000 machines on display at the 1876 Centennial Exhibition in Philadelphia.

HISTORY OF STEAM POWER

1760s | 1780s | 1800 | 1820s

STEAM ENGINE Building on earlier work, James Watt, a Scotsman, develops a true steam engine in 1769. He also devises a measure of output—*horsepower.*

HIGH-PRESSURE STEAM Oliver Evans in the U.S. and Richard Trevithick in England pioneer the high-pressure engine in 1801.

STEAMBOAT Robert Fulton's steamboat on the Hudson begins practical steam-powered travel in 1807.

LOCOMOTIVE The Liverpool & Manchester Line is the first public railroad to use steam power, 1830s.

NATIONAL MUSEUM OF AMERICAN ART, SMITHSONIAN INSTITUTION/ART RESOURCE, NY

GETTING UP STEAM

Steamboats, the floating palaces of their day, plied the Mississippi River from New Orleans to St. Paul. Steamboat captains and the public loved racing, despite its danger. In 1870 in a contest celebrated in story and song, the *Robert E. Lee* beat the *Natchez* in a race from New Orleans to St. Louis.

THE "IRON HORSE"

After the heyday of the steamboat, the steam locomotive took center stage. It sparked the railroad building boom that reached its climax with the completion of the transcontinental railroad in 1869.

RUNNING ON STEAM

PORTFOLIO PROJECT

Research and report on a machine mentioned on these pages—perhaps the steam locomotive or the steamboat—or another steam-driven machine such as the Stanley steamer car. Illustrate your report if you wish. Keep the report in your portfolio.

CULVER PICTURES

FULL SPEED AHEAD

The locomotive engineer was king, but no one worked harder than his understudy, the fireman, to keep the train "highballing"—going at top speed. In the early years the boiler was fueled by wood, but later by coal.

1840s | **1860s** | **1880s** | **1900s**

ON THE WATER The paddle wheeler dominates river transportation, but the young business is reaching its peak by the 1840s.

ON THE LAND By the 1860s the locomotive has transformed land transportation. Steam drives the Industrial Revolution in factories and mines, and on farms.

STEAM TURBINE In 1879 Irishman Charles Parsons invents a steam turbine to generate electricity to power ocean liners. Steam turbines are still used.

STEAM TAKES A BACKSEAT The steam engine gives way to electricity and to the internal combustion engine, though many uses for steam remain. Researchers are now developing steam-driven microchips; possible applications include microsurgery.

Chapter 5 Review

Reviewing Key Terms

Choose the vocabulary term that best completes each sentence below. Write your answers on a separate sheet of paper.

frontier	**turnpike**
tariffs	**spoils system**
nullification	**temperance**

1. Before they could travel on a _________, travelers were required to pay a toll.

2. One provision of Henry Clay's American System aimed to protect American manufacturers by increasing the _________ on imported goods.

3. When Andrew Jackson was elected President, he rewarded his supporters with government jobs, a practice that became known as the _________.

4. Large numbers of new settlers began to take over Native American lands as they continued to push the _________ westward.

5. During the 1830s reformers in the _________ movement attacked the evils of alcohol, which they were able to get prohibited in several states.

Recalling Facts

1. How did the United States acquire the territory that the Lewis and Clark team explored? Identify three purposes of the Lewis and Clark expedition.

2. General Anthony Wayne defeated the Ohio confederation at the Battle of Fallen Timbers and then concluded the Treaty of Greenville. In what way did these events contradict the Northwest Ordinance?

3. Who were the brothers Tecumseh and Tenskwatawa? What was their message to the Shawnee about relations between Native Americans and white settlers?

4. Who was Sequoyah, and what was his contribution to Native American literacy? What was the *Cherokee Phoenix?*

5. Why were the early textile mills of New England built along rivers? What group made up the principal labor force of these mills?

6. What were some bodies of water linked by the canals that were built in the early 1800s? What advantages did the railroads have that allowed them to take business away from the canals?

7. Describe the features of Henry Clay's American System. What parts of it were most successful? What part was less successful?

8. What changes in voting requirements made possible the era of the "common man"? In what ways did President Andrew Jackson represent this new era?

9. How was the question of women's rights related to the reform movement?

10. Describe the abolitionist work of Sojourner Truth and Frederick Douglass.

Critical Thinking

1. Analyzing Information How did the Cherokee attempt to adapt to the ways of the white settlers? What was the consequence of their adaptations?

2. Making Comparisons Compare the life of a young woman employed in a Lowell mill with the life of a young woman employed on the family farm.

3. Determining Cause and Effect After 1850 the system of canals, which had only recently been completed, ceased to be heavily used. What caused the rapid decline of the canals?

4. Identifying Central Issues What were the differences of opinion among abolitionists that caused the antislavery movement to break into factions?

5. Making Inferences The picture below shows a campaign ribbon used in William Henry Harrison's 1840 presidential campaign. How are campaign paraphernalia such as this used to gain voter support?

COURTESY OF MUSEUM OF AMERICAN POLITICAL LIFE, HARTFORD, CT/PHOTO BY STEVE LASCHEVER

CHAPTER 5 REVIEW

Portfolio Project

Choose one of the Native American peoples mentioned in the chapter—Mandan, Shoshone, Shawnee, Miami, Wyandot, or Cherokee—and research their history. Find out about their original way of life, their customs, and the regions they inhabited. Find out where and how they live today. Write a report and keep it in your portfolio.

Cooperative Learning

With a small group, construct a time line for the 1800s showing significant events in the history of industrial development. Beneath it, construct another time line showing the important developments in the history of women's rights. Is there a relationship between the developments in both? Add other time lines for the antislavery movement, the addition of new states to the Union, and the growth of the railroads. Draw your own conclusions about the period from studying these parallel developments. Do they appear to show that progress always occurs steadily?

Reinforcing Skills

Making Telescoping Time Lines

Use the years 1790 to 1840 for a standard time line showing major events discussed in the chapter. Your telescoping time line can focus on events during the presidencies of John Quincy Adams and Andrew Jackson, especially those related to political change and to the development of national political parties.

Geography and History

Study the map on this page to answer the following questions:

1. What does the yellow area on the map indicate?

2. How did the United States acquire the territory that became the state of New York?

3. When did the Indiana Territory become a part of the United States?

4. The Spanish government was distressed to learn that France had sold the Louisiana Territory to the United States. What inference can you make from the map about why the Spanish government might have been worried?

5. What was the northern boundary of the Louisiana Purchase? What geographical feature marked the eastern boundary? To what body of water did the southern boundary extend?

HISTORY JOURNAL

Write briefly in your journal about what you learned in this chapter. Include an account of what you understand to be the connection between the westward expansion of the frontier and developments in transportation.

CHAPTER 6

Civil War and Reconstruction

MAY 1856: POTTAWATOMIE, KANSAS

Proslavery and antislavery forces were fighting for control of Kansas by 1855. Proslavery residents of Missouri had poured into Kansas by the hundreds to elect proslavery leaders to office.

The legislature that they elected then passed harsh laws to prohibit even the free expression of opinions against slavery. By the fall of 1855, however, more Kansas residents opposed slavery than supported it. These antislavery forces, determined to defy the proslavery laws, armed themselves, called for new elections, and then drafted a new state constitution.

In response, in the spring of 1856, a group of proslavery Missourians lugged five cannons to the outskirts of Lawrence, Kansas, the antislavery stronghold. The invaders ransacked and burned homes and businesses and killed several men. Outraged by this action, militant antislavery leader John Brown, with his four sons and two other men, kidnapped and brutally executed five proslavery settlers in Pottawatomie, Kansas.

In subsequent raids by the proslavery and antislavery forces, about 200 people were killed before federal troops could stop the violence. The confict in "Bleeding Kansas" foreshadowed the turmoil that later would engulf the nation. ■

HISTORY JOURNAL

Write in your journal about your reaction to the story of Pottawatomie and the picture on the opposite page. What kind of man do you think John Brown was?

THE STATE HOUSE, TOPEKA, KANSAS/PHOTO COURTESY OF PHOTO ONE

In John Steuart Curry's mural, John Brown calls down the storm of civil war.

SECTION 1

Slavery and Politics

MARCH 6, 1857: SUPREME COURT RULES ON *DRED SCOTT* CASE

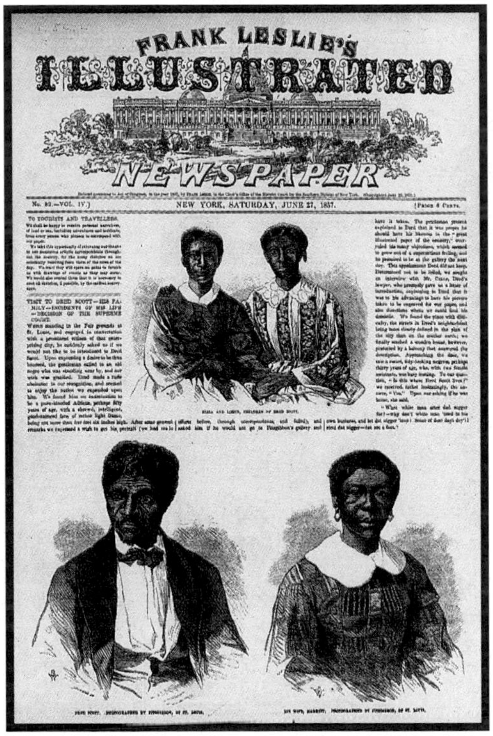
FRANK LESLIE'S ILLUSTRATED NEWSPAPER

No. 82.—VOL. IV.] NEW YORK, SATURDAY, JUNE 27, 1857. [PRICE 6 CENTS.

Landmark Case
The Supreme Court handed Dred and Harriet Scott a grim decision. The Scotts' daughters, Eliza and Lizzie, are shown above them.

Dred Scott and his wife, Harriet Scott, anxiously awaited the Supreme Court decision. The Scotts were legally enslaved, but they were hoping the Supreme Court would set them free because they had resided with a former master in Illinois and in the Wisconsin Territory, where the Missouri Compromise prohibited slavery. The year was 1857, however, and people who were enslaved did not have any legal rights in the United States. Furthermore, the Scotts were again living in Missouri, a slave state.

At last Chief Justice Roger Taney read the majority opinion of the Court and crushed the Scotts' hopes for freedom. Enslaved African Americans were considered legal property, and no state could deprive citizens of their property without due process of law, Taney said. In addition the Court ruled the Missouri Compromise unconstitutional, declaring that Congress could not prohibit slavery in American territories.

Several weeks later the Scotts were again sold. Their new owner freed them, and they slipped quietly into obscurity. The decision from their lawsuit, however, did not travel quietly. The Court's ruling angered Northerners because it meant that new American territories could now become slave states. The ruling threatened to upset the balance of power between free and slave states, fueling a heated debate that in 1861 would erupt into a bloody war.

As You Read

Vocabulary

- sectionalism
- gospel tradition
- fugitive

Think About . . .

- methods of coping with bondage and various forms of resistance to slavery.
- the contrast between the Northern and the Southern political agendas.
- the North's and the South's efforts at compromise and their effects.

The Roots of Conflict

Diverging Interests of North and South

THE BETTMANN ARCHIVE

King Cotton A steamship in New Orleans carries a load of cotton bales. Most cotton bales weigh about 500 pounds or 227 kilograms. *How did increased cotton production affect the economies of the North and the South differently?*

In the late 1700s, many farmers in the upper South—Maryland, Virginia, and North Carolina—shifted from tobacco to grain crops because these crops required less labor. The result was that a once-booming slave trade declined in this region. In 1793, however, a single event abruptly stopped any possible downward trend in the enslaved labor trade. In that year Eli Whitney introduced the cotton gin, a machine that greatly reduced the amount of time and work required to remove the seeds from cotton.

Suddenly, large quantities of cotton could be profitably grown with the aid of the enslaved labor force. Almost overnight, vast numbers of landowners throughout the South converted their fields to cotton production and thousands of would-be cotton farmers poured into the South from other regions. These new cotton planters figured they could increase their profit margins if they used enslaved laborers to pick and clean their cotton.

With the profitability of cotton production ensured by Whitney's invention, slavery quickly gained a new economic foothold. It was a foothold white Southerners were determined to protect.

By the mid-1800s, the Northern economy relied mostly on manufacturing and an ever-increasing immigrant workforce. Therefore, the Northern economy did not rely on enslaved laborers. Northern workers feared that if slavery were to extend northward, their own jobs

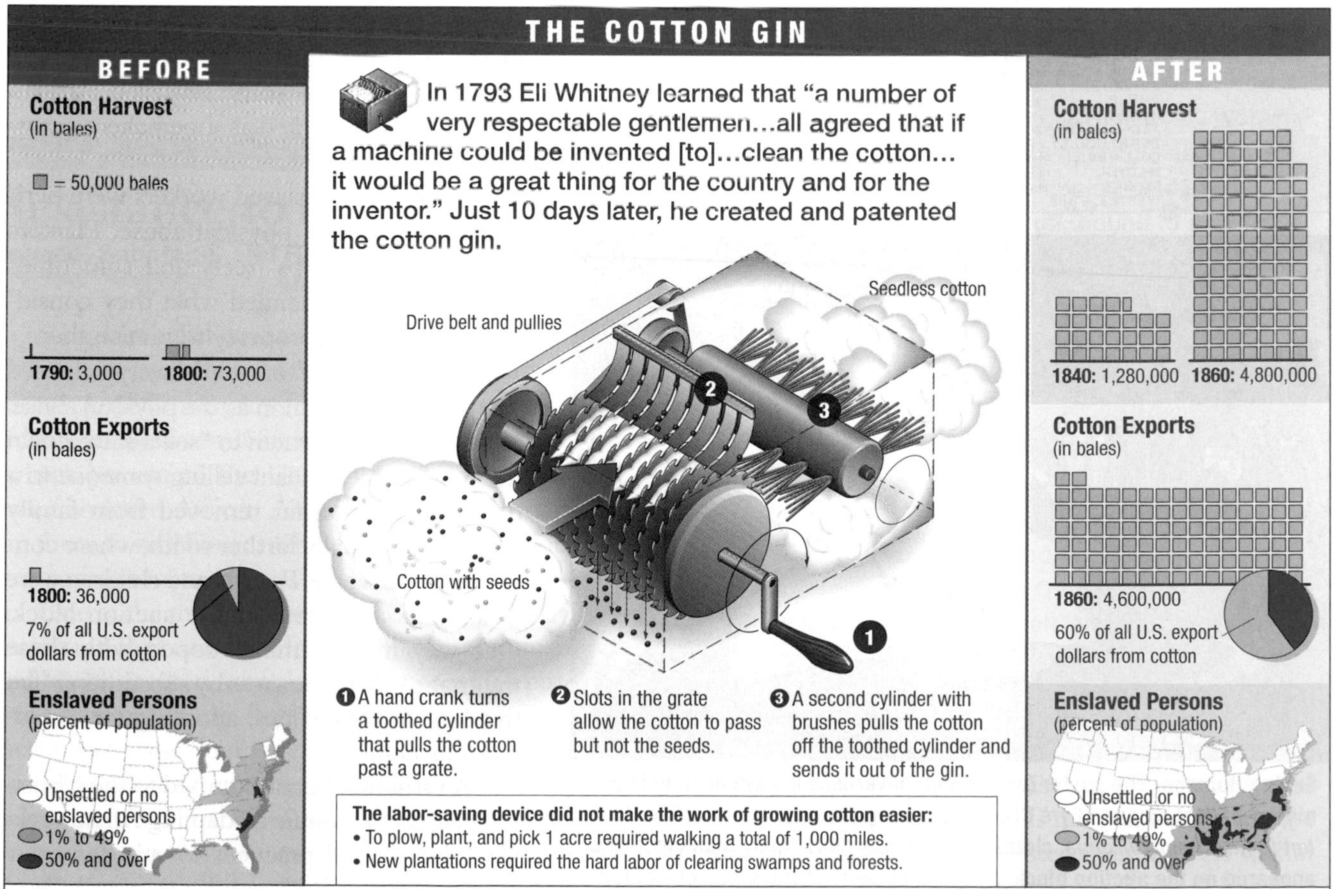
THE COTTON GIN
BEFORE
Cotton Harvest
(in bales)
= 50,000 bales
1790: 3,000
1800: 73,000
Cotton Exports
(in bales)
1800: 36,000
7% of all U.S. export dollars from cotton
Enslaved Persons
(percent of population)
Unsettled or no enslaved persons
1% to 49%
50% and over
In 1793 Eli Whitney learned that "a number of very respectable gentlemen...all agreed that if a machine could be invented [to]...clean the cotton... it would be a great thing for the country and for the inventor." Just 10 days later, he created and patented the cotton gin.
Drive belt and pullies
Seedless cotton
Cotton with seeds
1 A hand crank turns a toothed cylinder that pulls the cotton past a grate.
2 Slots in the grate allow the cotton to pass but not the seeds.
3 A second cylinder with brushes pulls the cotton off the toothed cylinder and sends it out of the gin.
The labor-saving device did not make the work of growing cotton easier:
• To plow, plant, and pick 1 acre required walking a total of 1,000 miles.
• New plantations required the hard labor of clearing swamps and forests.
AFTER
Cotton Harvest
(in bales)
1840: 1,280,000
1860: 4,800,000
Cotton Exports
(in bales)
1860: 4,600,000
60% of all U.S. export dollars from cotton
Enslaved Persons
(percent of population)
Unsettled or no enslaved persons
1% to 49%
50% and over

After the invention of the cotton gin, Southern growers reaped large profits using enslaved labor to plant, harvest, and transport cotton. *Approximately how closely did the increase in cotton production match the increase in enslaved labor?*

Plantation owners feared open defiance from individuals but were even more afraid of a collective rebellion. A number of early slave revolts—such as Gabriel's Revolt in Richmond in 1800 and the Denmark Vesey Conspiracy in Charleston in 1822—aroused concern. This concern turned into panic in 1831 when, on August 22, an enslaved preacher named Nat Turner led 75 armed followers in a rebellion. During the 2 days before they were subdued, these rebels killed between 55 and 60 whites.

The hysteria that spread throughout the South after the Turner revolt prompted slaveholders to take elaborate precautions to protect themselves. They created a complicated system of permits for slave travel and patrols to enforce the system. Believing that literacy would lead to empowerment and revolt, masters tried to prevent enslaved workers from learning to read and write. Additionally, Southern legislatures passed laws that made it difficult for masters to free captive African Americans. They wanted to prevent the freed population from increasing because free African Americans could organize revolts much more easily than an enslaved group. While these tactics seemed to halt slave rebellion in the South, Northern opposition to the spread of slavery grew.

Conflict and Compromise

The Slavery Debate Gathers Fire

The majority of Northern politicians did not oppose slavery as a labor force or as a way of life. For purely political reasons, they opposed the extension of slavery into the new territories gained by the Louisiana Purchase. If these territories became slave states, the South would have greater representation in the Senate than the North. Greater representation would give Southern politicians a better chance of fulfilling their political agenda.

To protect slavery and their way of life, white Southerners insisted that the federal government keep out of all matters that the Constitution had not clearly defined. In addition, Southerners wanted tariff laws that encouraged Southern development.

As mentioned in Chapter 2, white Southerners opposed high tariff laws, which raised prices on many articles from overseas. Because the South bought large quantities of manufactured goods from Great Britain, which in turn bought the South's cotton for British cotton mills, the high tariffs threatened the South's prosperity. The Southerners argued that Congress did not have the right to make laws that caused one section of the country to suffer unfairly. They were determined to maintain the political balance.

The Missouri Compromise

Until 1818 there had been an equal number of slave and free states, and likewise an equal number of senators representing the interests of North and South. Then, in 1818 when Missouri petitioned to enter the Union as a slave state, this delicate balance of power was threatened. Northern legislators amended Missouri's petition by stipulating that Missouri could become a state only if it outlawed slavery. Southern politicians were outraged.

Lawmakers eventually resolved this conflict with a series of legislative compromises. The northern part of Massachusetts, which had petitioned for statehood soon after Missouri, would be admitted as the separate free state of Maine. Missouri would be admitted to the Union as a slave state. In addition, the region south of the 36°30′ latitude line in the Louisiana territory would be open to slavery, whereas all the land north of it, except Missouri, would be free. These agreements were collectively known as the Missouri Compromise.

SLAVE REVOLTS, 1600s–1831
1600s Rebellions frequently occur aboard ship during passage to the United States.
1700s Twice in New York enslaved and indentured servants join forces to attempt revolt. Harsh retaliation follows.
1800 Gabriel of Virginia answers "divine calling" to attack Richmond, but his plans fall short.
1600
1625
1650
1675
1700
1725
1750
1775
1800
1825
1850
1804 In the Caribbean Haiti gains independence from France when slaves revolt and claim the island.
1822 In South Carolina Denmark Vesey plans revolution based on Haiti's model, but he is betrayed.
1831 Nat Turner leads a revolt in which 60 whites are killed. Panic and retaliation follow.

White Southerners were unhappy with the compromise because it made more land available for settlement as free territory than as slave territory. Southerners were also concerned because the majority of immigrants pouring into the country were seeking jobs in Northern urban

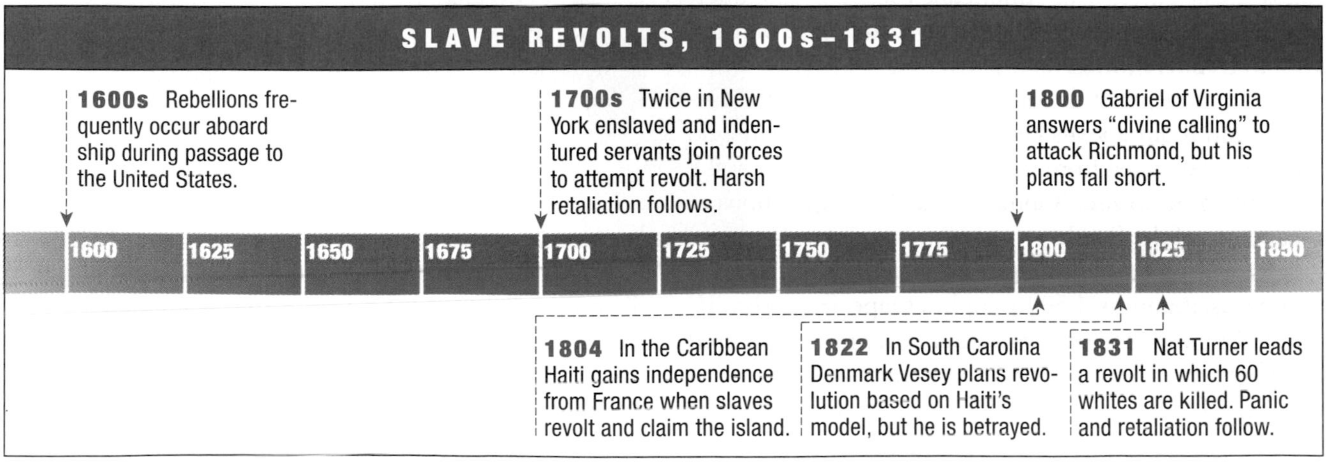

centers. This trend meant that the North's population would soon far exceed the South's. The North would then be entitled to far more seats in the House of Representatives and would be able to advance the goals of its free labor agenda. The North already had more seats, and this had helped them push the Missouri Compromise through.

NORTH WIND PICTURE ARCHIVES

A Treaty for Half of Mexico **This nineteenth-century engraving shows General Zachary Taylor at Buena Vista, where he defeated General Santa Anna in 1847. Following Buena Vista it took five major battles to win the war.** *What modern states are in the lands Mexico surrendered to the United States at the end of the war?*

War With Mexico

In 1836 when Texas declared its independence from Mexico, white Southerners hoped to acquire Texas as a new slave state. Northerners feared that the admission of Texas to the Union would not only increase the South's power in Congress but would also embroil the United States in a war with Mexico. Nevertheless by 1845 enough politicians were caught up in the fervor of westward expansion—believing that it was the destiny of the nation to reach from shore to shore—that white Southern politicians were able to prevail in getting Texas admitted to the Union as the twenty-eighth state. Mexico was outraged at this action. After a border skirmish between American troops and Mexican troops, the United States declared war on Mexico in May 1846.

On February 2, 1848, after almost two years of fighting, the nations ended the war by signing the Treaty of Guadalupe Hidalgo. This treaty gave the United States vast new regions that today include California, Arizona, New Mexico, Utah, Nevada, and parts of Colorado and Wyoming. The fear that these territories would organize into states intensified the sectional conflict between the North and the South. Many Northerners opposed the extension of slavery even into the newly acquired lands that lay south of the line established by the Missouri Compromise.

The Compromise of 1850

In 1850, 15 free states and 15 slave states made up the Union. California threatened this delicate balance of power by applying for admission to the Union as a free state. Congress once again faced the need to hammer out a legislative compromise. Senator Henry Clay of Kentucky introduced 4 compromise resolutions that became the basic proposals making up the Compromise of 1850: first, that California be admitted to the Union as a free state; second, that territorial governments in Utah and New Mexico let the people of the territories decide the slavery issue for themselves; third, that the slave trade—but not slavery—be prohibited in the District of Columbia; and fourth, that a new fugitive slave law require federal marshals to assist in recapturing **fugitives**—people who had escaped from slavery and were running from the law.

Clay's proposals touched off months of heated debate in Congress. Some of the greatest orators of the time lined up on opposite sides of the issue. John C. Calhoun of South Carolina bitterly opposed Clay's plan. Weak and near death, Calhoun sat silent while his final speech was read to the Senate. In it he warned that the Union could be saved only by giving the South equal rights in the acquired territory and by halting the agitation over slavery. Daniel Webster, who supported Clay's ideas, captivated the Senate with a sentence that has since become famous:

> I wish to speak today, not as a Massachusetts man, nor as a northern man, but as an American. . . . I speak today for the preservation of the Union. "Hear me for my cause."
>
> —Daniel Webster, March 7, 1850

Webster argued that there was no need to exclude slavery from the territories because it would not prosper there due to the soil and climate.

President Taylor opposed a compromise, but his untimely death in July 1850 brought Millard Fillmore to the presidency. With Fillmore's backing, Clay and his supporters succeeded in pushing the proposals through Congress. The package of four laws that became known as the Compromise of 1850 temporarily settled the question of slavery in the territories. The problems did not go away, however, because they were rooted in the issue of slavery itself.

The Kansas-Nebraska Act

Just four years later, in 1854, Illinois senator Stephen A. Douglas guided a highly controversial bill through Congress. This bill was the Kansas-Nebraska Act.

Douglas was serving as chairman of the Senate Committee on Territories. He wanted to see the unorganized territory west of Missouri and Iowa opened for settlement. This land lay north of the line established by the Missouri Compromise. Yet rather than letting the land become a free territory according to this legislation, Douglas proposed that the people in the territory decide for themselves whether or not they wanted slavery.

In 1854, after much negotiation, the Kansas-Nebraska Act was passed. It divided the Nebraska territory into two separate territories, Kansas and Nebraska; and it repealed the prohibition of slavery north of the Missouri Compromise line. The citizens of each territory would be able to determine by vote whether their state would be slave or free. In effect the act voided the Missouri Compromise, enabling slavery to expand northward.

Many of the antislavery politicians detested Douglas's bill as a violation of the "sacred pledge" of the Missouri Compromise: no slavery north of the 36°30′ line. These politicians broke from traditional party politics to form the Republican party in February 1854. The Republicans defended Northern sectional interests under the slogan Free soil, free labor, free speech, free men.

Kansas meanwhile became the battleground for sectional and party conflicts.

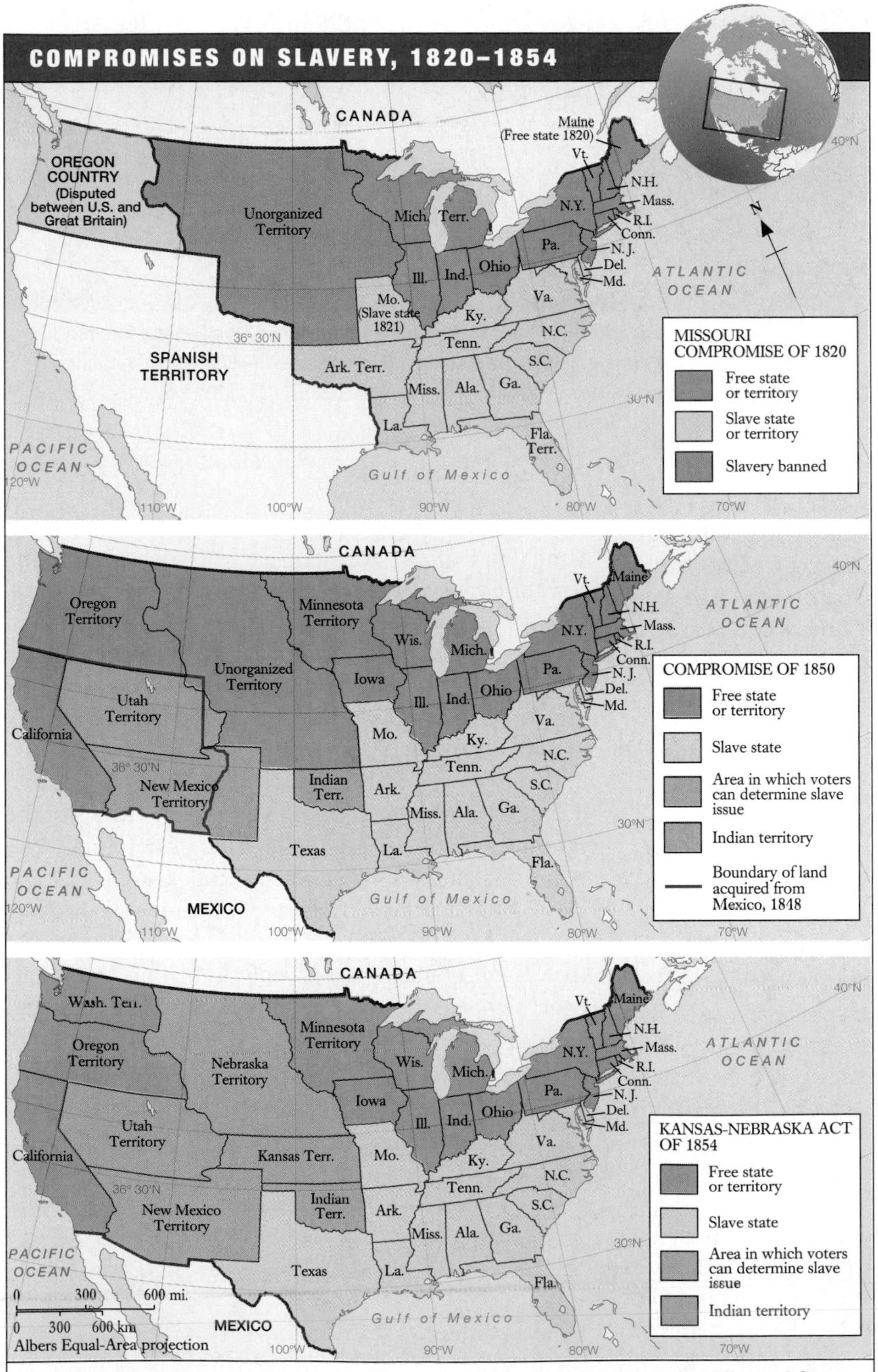

Three important stages in the slavery dispute are shown in these maps: The Missouri Compromise, the Compromise of 1850, and the Kansas-Nebraska Act. Note the status of the territories in each map. *How does the territories' slavery status change from one map to the next?*

By 1856 Kansas had turned into a cauldron of violence between antislavery and proslavery groups.

Violence Reaches Washington, D.C.

"Bleeding Kansas" became the catchword for the escalating violence over slavery—and the blood spilled all the way to Capitol Hill. In May 1856 Congressman Preston Brooks of South Carolina entered the nearly empty Senate chamber and beat Massachusetts Senator Charles Sumner with a cane. Brooks felt that Sumner's "Crime Against Kansas" speech, which verbally attacked Brooks's kinsman, had warranted this retaliation.

SOUTHERN CHIVALRY _ ARGUMENT VERSUS CLUB'S.

BOSTON ATHENAEUM

Brawl on the Senate Floor **Violence over slavery spread to Congress when a Southern congressman attacked a Northern senator.** *Who are the two men pictured in this famous cartoon and what prompted the attack?*

It was in the wake of these events that the Supreme Court handed down its decision in the *Dred Scott* case in March 1857. Naturally enough, this decision gave rise to fear among Northern politicians. The Free-Soil Republicans, worried that the extension of slavery into all the territories was forthcoming, gained more popular support, causing Southern forces to defend slavery even more stubbornly.

An unsettled nation approached the 1858 elections. In this tense atmosphere, Abraham Lincoln, a little-known one-term congressman from Springfield, Illinois, opposed Senator Stephen A. Douglas in the race for the Senate and challenged him to a series of debates. The debates gave Lincoln the opportunity to make his political views, including his defense of Northern interests, nationally known. Lincoln lost the election, but the debates catapulted him into the national spotlight.

Hostilities Intensify

Then, in October 1859 a violent clash captured the nation's attention. Abolitionist John Brown, leading an interracial band of 21 men, attacked the federal arsenal at Harpers Ferry, Virginia. Brown said he hoped to spark a slave rebellion that would end slavery and "purge this land with blood."

Although Brown and his men were captured within 36 hours, the revolt prompted intense public reaction. White Southerners initially responded hysterically, fearing an outbreak of slave insurrections. The fear calmed as they realized that Brown had not, after all, managed to incite even one slave to join him in the Harpers Ferry revolt. Northern response was initially cool. Brown's eloquence during his trial, however, swayed public opinion. Some Northerners, including many African Americans, proclaimed Brown a hero.

By the time Brown was sentenced to hang, writer Ralph Waldo Emerson predicted that Brown would "make the gallows as glorious as the cross." The editor of a Kansas newspaper supported Emerson's prediction; he wrote, "The death of no man in America has ever produced so profound a sensation. A feeling of deep and sorrowful indignation seems to possess the masses." With Northerners gripped by indignation and most white Southerners gripped by fear or anger, the nation prepared for the upcoming presidential election of 1860.

Section Review

Vocabulary

1. Define: sectionalism, gospel tradition, fugitive.

Checking Facts

2. What were the economic differences between the North and the South that led to the Civil War?
3. What were some ways that enslaved individuals coped with and fought the conditions of slavery?

Critical Thinking

Identifying Assumptions

4. Northerners strongly opposed the Fugitive Slave Law enacted as part of the Compromise of 1850. Why do you think this was so? What assumptions did the law make about the North?

Linking Across Time

5. Compare efforts of African Americans to resist slavery in the mid-1800s with civil rights protests in the 1960s.

SECTION 2

The Civil War

APRIL 2, 1865: THE FALL OF RICHMOND

Richmond in Ruins
Citizens flee the burning Confederate capital, shown in this Currier and Ives print.

ON SUNDAY, APRIL 2, 1865, CONFEDERATE PRESIDENT JEFFERSON DAVIS WAS PRAYING IN A RICHMOND, VIRGINIA, CHURCH WHEN A MESSENGER RUSHED IN. The Union army had broken through Confederate lines and was advancing on the city. In response General Lee had ordered his troops to pull out of Richmond. The city would have to be evacuated.

By midafternoon, troops, cavalry, and townspeople were clogging the roads in a frenzied attempt to escape the city. Then as the sun set, bands of devoted Confederates set fire to their own city of Richmond to destroy any remaining goods and shelter that might be of benefit to the Union soldiers.

On April 4, just 40 hours after Davis had left Richmond, President Lincoln entered the smoldering city. As Lincoln walked the streets of the fallen Confederate capital, freed slaves waved, shouted thanks and praise, and even reached out to touch him. One woman shouted, "I know I am free, for I have seen Father Abraham and felt him."

The Start of the War

"A Hornet's Nest"

In 1860 after a hard-fought campaign, Abraham Lincoln was elected President. Of the 4 candidates who had battled for the presidency, Lincoln had obtained an overwhelming majority of electoral votes—but only 40 percent of the popular vote.

Southerners, aware of Lincoln's pro-Northern political views, reacted by calling for **secession,** or formal withdrawal, from the nation. In December 1860, South Carolina became the first state to secede from the Union. The following year Mississippi, Florida, Alabama, Georgia, Louisiana, and Texas followed, declaring themselves a new nation, the Confederate States of America.

AS YOU READ

Vocabulary

- secession
- emancipation
- lynching
- scorched earth policy

Think About . . .

- what military and political consequences resulted from the decision of the Southern states to form their own government.
- the effects of the Emancipation Proclamation on African Americans in the Southern states.

THE UNION AND THE CONFEDERACY

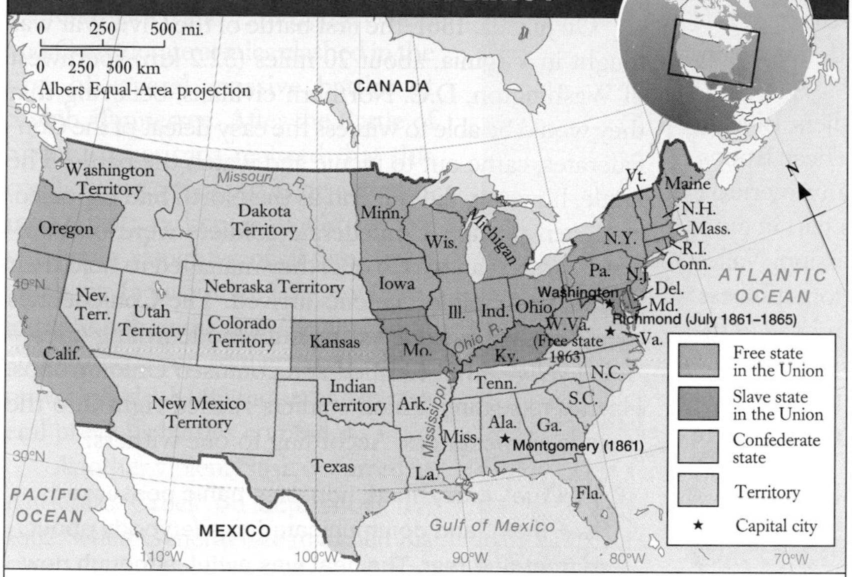

The map above shows the opposing sides in the Civil War. *Which states left the Union and decided to join the Confederacy? Which slave states remained in the Union?*

The Fall of Fort Sumter

The Confederacy's first military objective was to obtain control of Fort Sumter, a Union military installation in the harbor of Charleston, South Carolina. A prominent Southerner warned against firing on this army stronghold, "You will wantonly strike a hornet's nest. Legions now quiet will swarm out and sting us to death." Nevertheless, on April 12, 1861, the Confederate army began shelling Fort Sumter until its commander surrendered.

Proclaiming an insurrection in the South, Lincoln called for 75,000 volunteers to suppress the rebellion. In response, Virginia, Arkansas, North Carolina, and Tennessee left the Union to join the Confederacy. Headed by their newly elected president, Jefferson Davis, the Confederates prepared for a war of independence, likening their status to that of the American revolutionaries in 1776.

The Union and the Confederacy Compared

The Union could draw its fighting force from a population of 22 million that included foreign-born immigrants, free African Americans, and escaped slaves. With this size population, the North was able to raise a much larger army than the South. The 11 Confederate states had a population of only 9 million, nearly 3 million of whom the Confederacy refused to let fight because they were enslaved laborers.

What the South lacked in numbers, it made up for in military skill and experience. The Confederacy could draw from a talented pool of military minds that included many officers from West Point and veterans of the Mexican American War. It was a seasoned West Point general, Robert E. Lee of Virginia, who assumed command of the Confederate army. Also, many white Southerners were members of local militia units and were skilled marksmen.

This superior military training might have given the South a clear advantage over the North were it not for the fact that almost all resources for waging war—steel mills and iron mines, important industries, and transportation facilities—were located in the North. More than 70 percent of the nation's railroads ran through the North. Most naval facilities and ships were in the North as well. By comparison the Confederacy possessed inferior natural resources, industry, and transportation. Furthermore the South lacked the financial resources to manufacture or acquire these necessities of war.

The South tried to make up for its disadvantages by fighting a defensive war. Southerners fortified their cities and waited for the Union to invade. If the Union forces invaded, Confederate strategists reasoned that Southerners would at least be fighting on familiar terrain, amid supporters, and close to supplies.

African American Soldiers

Early in the war, Northern African Americans eagerly tried to enlist in the Union army in order to join the fight to end slavery, but they were not accepted.

PHILADELPHIA HISTORICAL SOCIETY, USA/BRIDGEMAN ART LIBRARY, LONDON

African American Troops This print, showing troops training near Philadelphia, appeared on Union recruiting posters. *How did free and fugitive African Americans give the Union an advantage?*

Nearly half the advancing Confederates were gunned down. By the time the Confederates retreated from Gettysburg, they had sustained 28,000 casualties; the Union had sustained 23,000. As wagons carried the Confederate wounded southward, a Quaker nurse wrote, "There are no words in the English language to express the suffering I witnessed today."

The Gettysburg Address

The Battle of Gettysburg cost both sides heavy casualties, but it was a crushing defeat for the South. The Confederacy would never recover from the losses it had suffered. On November 19, 1863, President Lincoln visited the battle site to dedicate a cemetery to honor the soldiers who had fallen there. In a short and eloquent address, the President stated:

> The world will little note nor long remember what we say here, but it can never forget what they [the fallen soldiers] did here. It is for us, the living, rather, to be dedicated here to the unfinished work which they who fought here have thus far so nobly advanced.
>
> It is rather for us to be here dedicated to the great task remaining before us—that from these honored dead we take increased devotion to that cause for which they gave the last full measure of devotion; that we here highly resolve that these dead shall not have died in vain; that this nation, under God, shall have a new birth of freedom; and that government of the people, by the people, and for the people, shall not perish from the earth.
>
> —Abraham Lincoln, November 19, 1863

Many people who were there that momentous day thought that Lincoln's remarks were too short and simple for such a serious occasion. The Address, however, is one of the significant developments in the history of individual rights in the United States. Here the President was telling a war-weary nation that *all Americans*—regardless of heritage—had a stake in the future of the nation. Along with that stake would eventually come equality.

Vicksburg

Yet the war was far from over in 1863. Union and Confederate forces battled to control the Mississippi River at the same time that troops fought at Gettysburg. Union troops occupied New Orleans, Baton Rouge, Natchez, and Memphis. Finally all that remained in Confederate hands was Vicksburg, located on bluffs high above the river. In mid-May 1863, Union general Ulysses S. Grant ordered a siege of the city. On July 4, the same day Lee began his retreat from Gettysburg, Confederate forces in Vicksburg surrendered. As news of the 2 strategic victories spread throughout the Union, there were, according to Carl Sandburg, "celebrations with torchlight processions, songs, jubilation, refreshments."

The War at Sea

While armies battled their way across the land, another aspect of the war took place in coastal waters and on inland rivers. At the outset of the war, Lincoln had ordered a blockade of all Southern ports. The Union navy's assorted ships patrolled the 3,500 miles (5,631.5 km) of Confederate coastline and eventually cut off Southern trade. The daring blockade runners that managed to escape capture could not carry enough goods to supply the South. The greatest blow to Confederate trade came in April 1862 when Commodore David Farragut sailed a fleet into the mouth of the Mississippi River. He steamed past the forts below New Orleans and went on to capture the South's largest city.

The Confederates almost succeeded in breaking the blockade at Chesapeake Bay. Southerners raised the frigate *Merrimack,* scuttled by Union forces when they abandoned the Norfolk navy yard, and converted it into an ironclad warship. In March 1862, the ship, renamed the *Virginia,* battled the Union's ironclad *Monitor.* Neither ship could sink the other, but the battle marked the beginning of a new era in naval warfare.

Social and Economic Battles

Controversy Over the War

The battles of 1863 turned the tide militarily for the Union, but Northerners still experienced difficulties on the home front. Social and economic difficulties plagued both sides.

Emancipation

Throughout the war, abolitionists pressured President Lincoln to free all enslaved African Americans. Abolitionists argued that Union soldiers were fighting not only to preserve the Union but also to end slavery. They also pointed out that freeing the slaves would create a new pool of recruits that could be drafted to fight for the North. Further, backers of **emancipation,** or liberation from slavery, reasoned that the Fugitive Slave Law no longer applied to Southerners, who after their secession from the Union could no longer claim to be protected by the Union's laws. By this reasoning, the North was finally rid of its obligation to return runaways, and Union troops could confiscate Southern property and slaves as spoils of war.

At first Lincoln evaded the issue of emancipation, fearing it would drive Maryland, Missouri, and

Kentucky out of the Union. On September 22, 1862, however, under extreme pressure from Republican senators to declare his position on slavery, Lincoln signed a preliminary version of the Emancipation Proclamation, which declared freedom for enslaved persons only in parts of the Confederacy not under the control of the Union army. The proclamation had no effect on enslaved African Americans in the border states that had not joined the Confederacy.

Although this proclamation freed some enslaved African Americans, it did not necessarily express Lincoln's personal views on the subject of slavery. Just a few months earlier, Lincoln had made his position known in a letter to the abolitionist Horace Greeley.

> My paramount object in this struggle is to save the Union, and is not either to save or destroy Slavery. If I could save the Union without freeing any slave, I would do it; and if I could save it by freeing all the slaves, I would do it; and if I could do it by freeing some and leaving others alone, I would also do that. What I do about Slavery and the colored race, I do because it helps to save this Union; and what I forbear, I forbear because I do not believe it would help to save the Union.
>
> —Abraham Lincoln, from a letter to Horace Greeley, 1862

CHICAGO HISTORICAL SOCIETY

Contributions to the War Effort **Mary Rice Livermore worked throughout the Civil War in support of the Union cause. She organized women's aid societies such as the group pictured. The societies raised money and sent food and clothing to Union soldiers on the battlefield.** *In what other ways did women's efforts make a difference during the Civil War?*

New Roles

As the war dragged on, Northern and Southern women had to assume many of the roles previously assigned to the men who had gone away to fight. The two armies needed food, clothing, and weapons. Women took responsibility for supplying many of these goods. In addition many women needed jobs to help support their families. So across the country, women managed their family farms, worked in factories, ran printing presses, shod horses, and also filled government positions. A handful of women even disguised themselves as men and fought in the war.

One of the many significant contributions women made to the war effort was caring for the wounded. Three thousand women served as nurses during the war. Nurses were in great demand to tend the wounded because twice as many soldiers died of infectious diseases as died of injuries sustained in combat. Doctors did not yet understand the importance of sanitation, sterile medical equipment, and a balanced diet. As a result deaths from dysentery, malaria, and typhoid were a by-product of war.

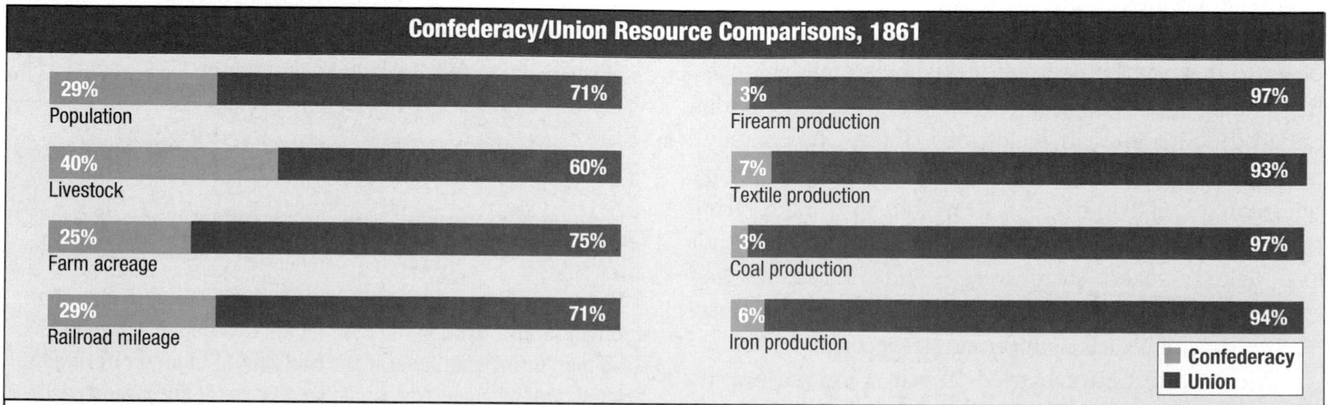

Compare the resources of the North and the South at the start of the Civil War. *In what two areas did the Union have the greatest advantage over the Confederacy? What, if any, advantages are shown for the South?*

Riots

As the bloody battles dragged on, both the North and the South experienced difficulties recruiting soldiers as well as raising money needed to keep up the fight. The Union draft law of March 1863 excused men from military service if they paid the government a $300 fee. Many Northerners who thought the law discriminated against the poor angrily took to the streets in protest.

The most violent draft riots erupted in New York City on July 13 in the wake of Union victories at Gettysburg and Vicksburg. There the draft riots had racial overtones as low-paid workers blamed African Americans for the war. Rioters set fire to an African American orphanage and began **lynching** African Americans, murdering them in ruthless mob attacks.

Resentment over the draft was also prevalent in the South. There, however, homelessness and hunger overshadowed the draft issue. Women, being the majority of those left at home to confront these issues, eventually took matters into their own hands. In 1863 riots broke out in which women looted stores, hijacked trains, and attacked Confederate supply depots to get bread and other food stored there.

The Road to Surrender

Smoldering Soil, Smoldering Resentment

Until 1864 Lincoln had been disappointed with the quality of his military commanders. Only General Ulysses S. Grant had performed close to Lincoln's expectations. In March the President appointed Grant commander of all Union forces.

One of Grant's first official actions was to order Generals William Tecumseh Sherman and Philip Henry Sheridan to pursue a **scorched earth policy** in the South. Following Grant's instructions, Sherman's and Sheridan's troops burned farmland, plantation homes, and cities in order to destroy the enemy's food, shelter, and supplies. In so doing they broke the South's will to fight. Sheridan raided the Shenandoah Valley, one of the Confederacy's main sources of food, to starve Lee's hungry troops. Sherman led 60,000 men on a "March to the Sea" from Atlanta to Savannah. On the way they burned homesteads and fields, sacked storehouses, and ripped up and twisted railroad tracks to render them useless. Consequently Savannah fell to Sherman in December 1864.

Meanwhile Grant battled Lee in Virginia, hoping eventually to take the Confederate capital of Richmond. Union and Confederate forces clashed in three major battles: in the Virginia wilderness and at Spotsylvania in May, and at Cold Harbor in early June. In three battles Grant lost almost as many Union soldiers as there were Confederates serving in Lee's army. Yet because of the Union's population advantage, Grant could replace his soldiers, while Lee could not. Grant then settled down to a long siege of Richmond.

By the fall of 1864, Lincoln called home as many Union troops as he could, hoping to generate support for his reelection. The Union victories in the South helped Lincoln win by an electoral college vote of 212 to 21 and a popular majority of more than 400,000 votes.

The War's End

Increasing desertions among Confederate troops prompted Jefferson Davis in November 1864 to allow enslaved African Americans to enlist. The Confederate Congress did not authorize the act, however, until it was too late to take effect. Still, Davis refused to surrender

BROWN BROTHERS

Victory by Siege General Ulysses S. Grant, commander of all Union forces, exuded the confidence of a capable, aggressive soldier. Grant and General Lee had fought together during the Mexican American War. *What were some of the advantages Grant held over his former compatriot? How did Grant destroy Lee's remaining resources?*

ABOLITION OF SLAVERY, 1777–1865

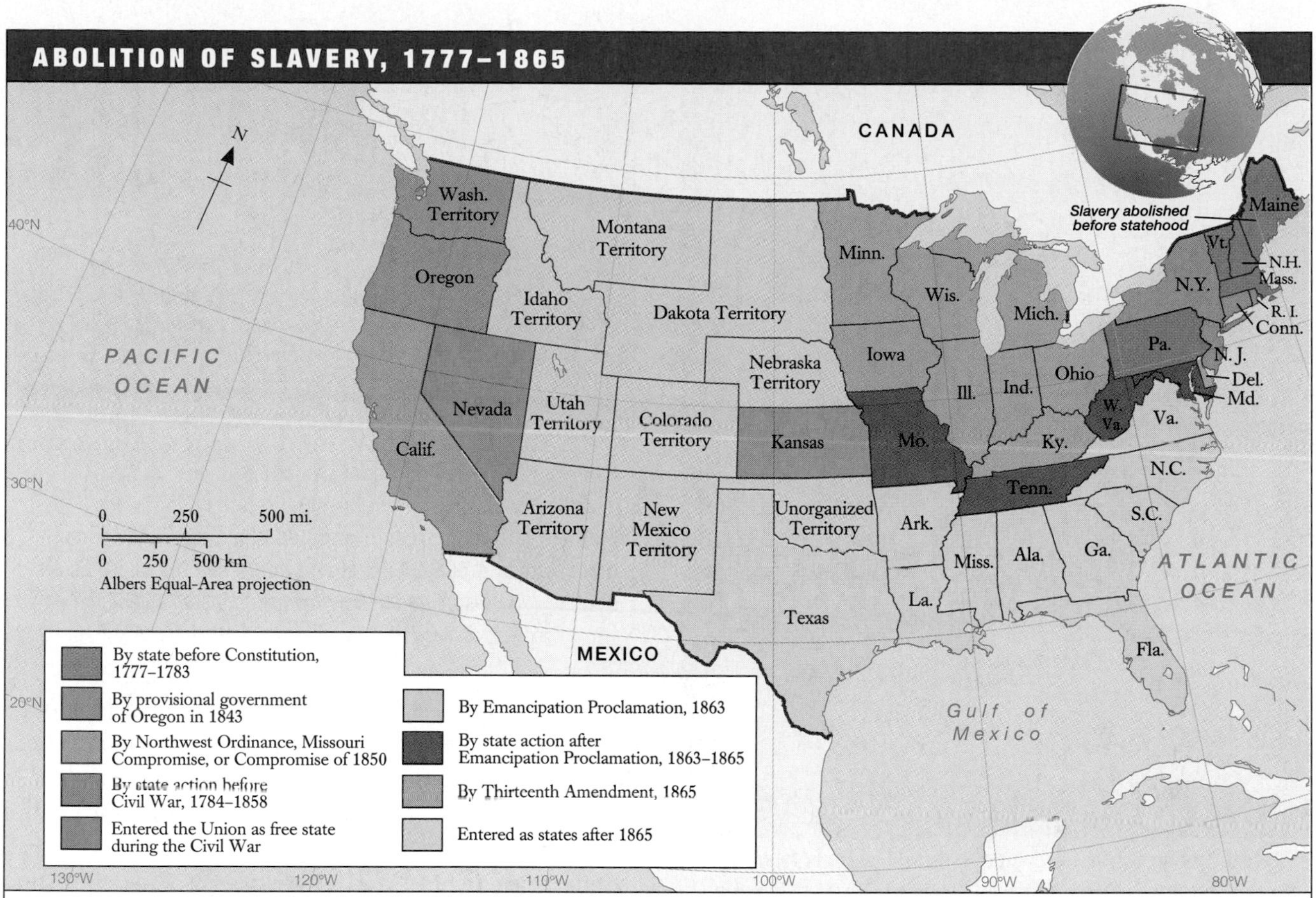

With the North victorious, the abolition of slavery was assured. The process of emancipation had been a gradual one, the result of long-fought political battles and bloodshed. *What legal action liberated enslaved people in the greatest number of states?*

unless Lincoln acknowledged the South as an independent nation.

Grant and Sheridan finally took Richmond on April 3, 1865, as the city smoldered from the fires set by retreating Confederates. Union troops pursued Lee and his exhausted army. The Confederates made feeble attempts to hold them off, but Lee's army had been reduced to about 30,000 hungry and demoralized men. On the morning of April 9, Lee led his troops into battle for the last time. Union forces had them almost surrounded and badly outnumbered. Facing an almost certain slaughter, Lee decided to surrender. That afternoon he met Grant at Appomattox Court House in Virginia. Grant's terms of surrender ensured that Confederate soldiers would not be prosecuted for treason and that artillery and cavalry soldiers would be permitted to keep their horses. Grant also arranged for 3 days' rations to be sent to the Confederate soldiers. Lee accepted.

When Union troops heard of the surrender, they began firing their guns to celebrate their victory. Grant put an end to the firing. "The war is over," he said, "the rebels are our countrymen again, and the best sign of rejoicing after the victory will be to abstain from all demonstrations."

Lee echoed these sentiments when he knew the Confederate army was defeated.

> The war being at an end, the southern states having laid down their arms, and the question at issue between them and the northern states having been decided, I believe it to be the duty of everyone to unite in the restoration of the country and the reestablishment of peace and harmony.
>
> —Robert E. Lee, April 1865

The human costs of the war were staggering. About 360,000 Union soldiers and 260,000 Confederates lay dead. Another 375,000 soldiers were wounded. Approximately 1 in 3 Confederate soldiers died in the war. These figures do not include deaths from imprisonment such as at Andersonville, a prison camp operated by Confederates in Georgia, where 13,000 out of 32,000 Union prisoners died.

Lincoln as Commander in Chief

Lincoln's main goal had been to preserve the Union. In his second Inaugural Address, he indicated that he would deal compassionately with the South after the war ended:

BROWN BROTHERS

"Peace Among Ourselves" Lincoln asked citizens to work for peace after the war. Matthew Brady's portrait of Lincoln (above) captures the peaceful spirit of the President. *How did Lincoln's agenda at the start of the war account for his post-war policy of leniency toward the South?*

ARCHIVE PHOTOS

Mourning Throngs of citizens flocked to view the President's open casket and mourn his untimely death. Parades, banners, and memorials trumpeted Lincoln's victories to those who had been disloyal and might see his death as his defeat. *What public memorials followed Lincoln's death?*

> With malice toward none; with charity for all; with firmness in the right, as God gives us to see the right, let us strive on to finish the work we are in; to bind up the nation's wounds; to care for him who shall have borne the battle, and for his widow, and his orphan. . . .
>
> —Abraham Lincoln,
> *Second Inaugural Address,* March 1865

Unfortunately Lincoln never got to carry out his plan. On April 14, 1865, five days after the South surrendered, Confederate sympathizer John Wilkes Booth shot President Lincoln at a theater in Washington, D.C. Lincoln died the next morning. The nation, and indeed the world, mourned his death.

Even those who had sharply criticized Lincoln's policies acknowledged his leadership and accomplishments. The *New Orleans Tribune* stated: "Brethren, we are mourning for a benefactor of our race." An outpouring of sympathy came from Britain and others who had supported the Confederate cause. Admirers as well as critics agreed that replacing Lincoln would be difficult.

A funeral train carried Lincoln's body on a 1,700-mile (2,735.3-km) journey from Washington, D.C., to Springfield, Illinois. Millions of people lined the route. At night, bonfires and torches lit the way. By day, bells tolled and cannons fired.

Lincoln's second Inaugural Address, read at the cemetery, reminded Americans of his plan "to do all which may achieve and cherish a just, and a lasting peace, among ourselves, and with all nations." The future, however, was in the hands of those who favored harsher measures against the former Confederates.

Section Review

Vocabulary

1. Define: secession, emancipation, lynching, scorched earth policy.

Checking Facts

2. What advantages did the North have upon entering the war? The South?
3. What were the social and economic battles fought during the Civil War?

Critical Thinking

Analyzing Information

4. From what you have learned about Lincoln, why do you think he initiated a postwar policy of leniency toward the South?

Linking Across Time

5. Lincoln's actions helped bring an end to slavery, but African Americans continued to fight for genuine freedom long after the Civil War. What specific effects of slavery do you see in United States policies and culture today?

Social Studies Skill

COMBINING INFORMATION FROM MAPS

Learning the Skill

Thematic maps aid in the communication of information by presenting place-related data in a concise way. Sometimes two or more maps can convey information that cannot be presented easily on a single map.

Finding Connections

To find and combine geographic patterns:

a. First examine the map on this page to find information about industry and agriculture in 1860.

b. Note any significant patterns. For example, a quick look reveals that New England farmers mainly raised dairy cattle and hay, which are small farm enterprises.

c. Then examine the map on the abolition of slavery on page 179, which shows, for example, that the New England states prohibited slavery before the framing of the Constitution.

d. Try to visualize relationships between the two maps. In each, there are patterns differentiating the North and the South. Combining these maps suggests a state's decisions about slavery or abolition may have related to how the people in that state made a living.

Practicing the Skill

Study the map below and the map on page 179 and answer the following questions:

1. What relationship do you see between plantation crops and the abolition of slavery?

2. Compare industry in cotton-growing states and in other states. What pattern do you notice?

3. What connection can you make between a state's economy and its stand on slavery?

4. What was produced in the West and Midwest?

5. How might the economies of the West and Midwest have affected the slavery debate nationwide?

Applying the Skill

Using two other maps, draw five conclusions about the combined information they present.

Additional Practice

For additional practice, see Reinforcing Skills on page 193.

AGRICULTURE AND INDUSTRY, 1860

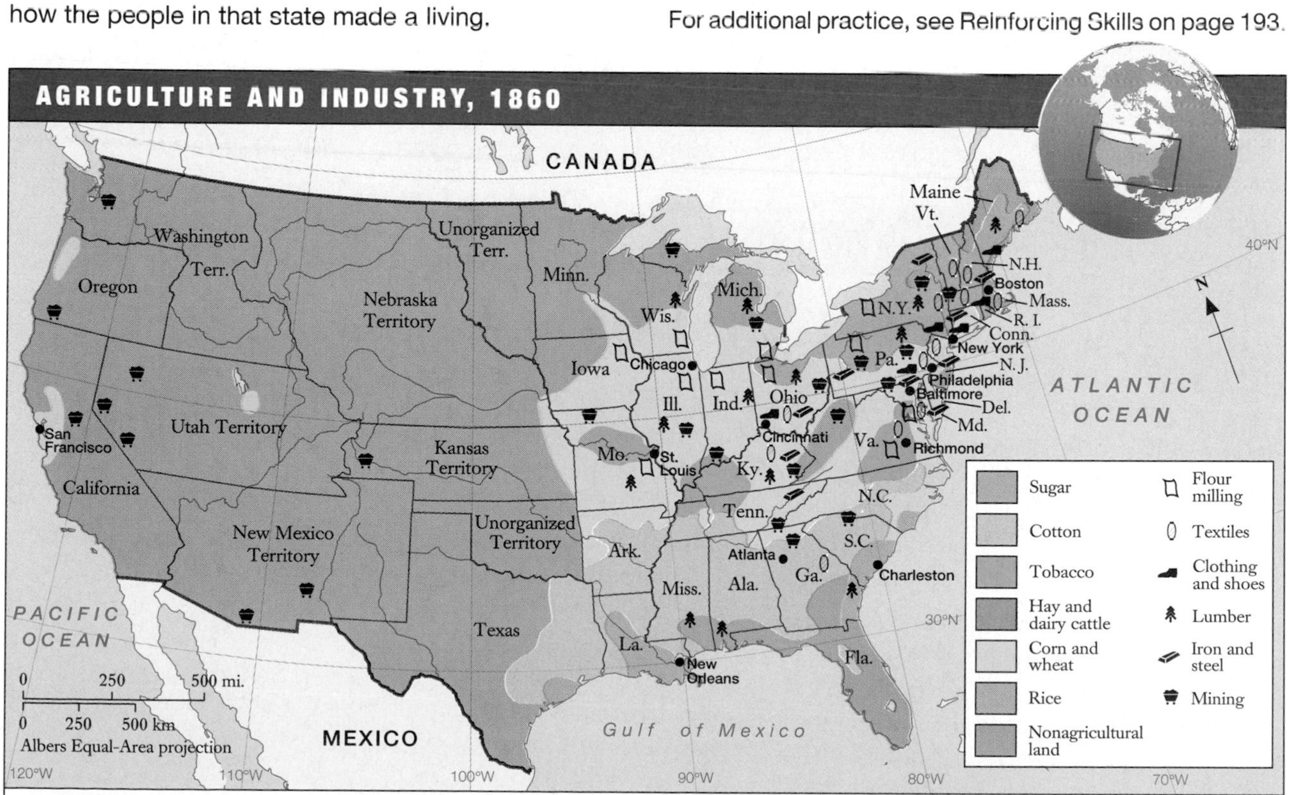

By 1860 textile and shoe factories fueled the economies of New York and New England, while plantation crops such as cotton and tobacco were the mainstay of the Southern economy. *What states depended on flour milling?*

SPORTS: "Fly rule" adopted: The baseball must be caught before it bounces to get the batter out.

One Day in History

Sunday, April 9, 1865

MARKET BASKET

Here is where a dollar will go:

Stereoscopic pictures...... $1.50/dozen
Barnum's American Museum ticket........... 15¢ child
.... 25¢ adult
Theater ticket ..... 25¢ child
.... 50¢ adult
Printing press $3,500

Collar $1.25/dozen
Coffee.......... 7 to 25¢/lb.
Pocket watch $10
Artificial leg........... $75

Daguerreotypes .... 25¢ to $1
Medical consultation fee .. $5
Harper's Weekly magazine .... 10¢
New York Times newspaper .... 3¢
Yarn.............. 2¢/spool
Stove polish....... 10¢/cake
Sarsaparilla compound $1/bottle

Dignity in Defeat Rising to this sorrowful occasion, General Lee, in full dress uniform, agrees to peace terms with General Grant and signs the articles of surrender.

Confederates Surrender

Union Victory! Peace! General Lee Surrenders

APPOMATTOX COURT HOUSE, VIRGINIA—This afternoon General Robert E. Lee surrendered the Army of Northern Virginia to General Ulysses S. Grant, ending four years of bloody civil war and ensuring the survival of the American Union. Officers and men of the Confederate army will be allowed to return to their homes, and officers will retain their side arms and private property. All former Confederate fighters will be required to swear and sign an oath of loyalty to the Union.

The details of the treaty were negotiated at the home of a man named McLean, the same man who saw the first bombshell of the war fall on his front lawn. Colonel Ely S. Parker, a Seneca man and an aide to General Grant, recorded the proceedings.

One Day in History, Sunday, April 9, 1865

NATION: Maria Mitchell, discoverer of comet, is appointed to chair at Vassar; she becomes the first woman astronomy professor in the nation.

COURTESY OF SPECIAL COLLECTIONS, VASSAR COLLEGE LIBRARIES

Editorial

APRIL 1, 1865, from the *New Orleans Tribune,* an African American daily newspaper

> *Before 1863, the planters said that it was for the sake of the negroes that they kept them in slavery; it was from a feeling of humanity that they retained in bondage a race of men whom they proclaimed unfit to lie under any other status. . . . going so far as to have them whipped and put into the stocks—as a means of promoting their advancement. . . .*
>
> *The planters defended slavery on the ground of sympathy for the negro. But it was all shame. They clung to slavery for the sake of making money. There is no disputing about it.*

THE BETTMANN ARCHIVE

Actor Edwin Booth, brother of John Wilkes Booth, appears in *Hamlet.*

COURTESY OF THE BARNUM MUSEUM, BRIDGEPORT, CT

Owner P.T. Barnum has improved his museum by hiring trapper Grizzly Adams to stock the menagerie.

MUSIC

"Battle Hymn of the Republic"
"When Johnny Comes Marching Home"
"Follow the Drinking Gourd"
"Many Thousand Gone"
"Oh, Susanna"
"Swanee River"
"My Old Kentucky Home"

AMUSEMENTS

At Barnum's American Museum:

The Great Dancing Giraffe
Punch and Judy
Bohemian Glass Blowers
Two Glass Steam Engines in Motion
Prof. Hutchins, lightning calculator
Poultry, pigeon, and rabbit show

SMITHSONIAN INSTITUTION

Free Mail Delivery

WASHINGTON, D.C.—Mail will now be delivered free in all cities with populations of 50,000 or more. Recent improvements in rail and steamship transport make this free delivery possible.

Scovill's
Sarsaparilla Compound
For the cure of Liver Complaint, Dyspepsia, Scrofula, Dropsy, Neuralgia, Boils, Tumors, and Epilepsy
It's a sure cure! $1.00/bottle

BROWN BROTHERS

SECTION 3

Reconstruction

FEBRUARY 24, 1879: BANKS OF THE MISSISSIPPI RIVER

HUNDREDS OF AFRICAN AMERICANS, WITH THEIR BELONGINGS BUNDLED ON THEIR BACKS, WAITED ON THE SHORES OF THE MISSISSIPPI RIVER FOR THE STEAMER THAT WOULD CARRY THEM ACROSS TO ST. LOUIS. From there they would head by train to Kansas, where they hoped to begin new lives. These people were called the Exodusters, so named because they left their homes to make better lives in the dusty new land, just as the Israelites had done centuries earlier in their exodus from Egypt to Canaan.

FROM HARPER'S WEEKLY, MAY 1, 1880

Exodusters
This drawing from an 1880 *Harper's Weekly* contrasts the new exodus with the old (inset), as African Americans fled the South.

During the exodus of 1879, more than 20,000 African Americans migrated to Kansas, their Canaan, or "promised land." A Louisiana preacher explained that they "were not emigrating because of inducements held out to them by parties in Kansas, but because they were terrorized, robbed, and murdered by the bulldozing desperadoes of Louisiana and Mississippi." The African Americans hoped that their journey to Kansas would take them far from the poverty and terrorism that they experienced in the South despite the many promises of the postwar government.

Presidential Reunion Plans

Attempts at Reconciliation

In 1863 before the war had ended, Lincoln made plans to reestablish state governments in the South that would be loyal to the Union after the war. According to Lincoln's plan, for a state to be recognized as legitimate, 10 percent of the men eligible to vote in 1860 had to have sworn allegiance to the Union.

Andrew Johnson, who assumed the presidency after Lincoln's assassination, had expressed harsh sentiments toward Confederate "traitors" during the war. He therefore surprised many Northerners when he began to promote policies that seemed to continue Lincoln's intentions of "malice toward none." Congress was not in session when Johnson took office, so he proceeded with

AS YOU READ

Vocabulary
- amnesty
- black codes
- sharecropping
- carpetbagger
- gerrymandering

Think About . . .
- the possible approaches the North might have taken toward restoring the economic and social fabric of the defeated South.
- how Reconstruction altered the roles of Congress and the President.
- how Reconstruction brought both gains and hardships to African Americans.

his plans for Reconstruction—the process of restoring relations with the Confederate states.

In a Reconstruction proclamation issued in May of 1865, Johnson granted **amnesty,** or pardon, to Confederates who would sign an oath of loyalty to the Union. Political and military leaders and landowners whose property was worth more than $20,000 had to apply for special pardons. Johnson granted such pardons regularly. In addition Johnson appointed provisional governors and set forth minimal requirements for reorganizing Southern state governments. By December 1865 all former Confederate states except Texas had fulfilled the requirements and had elected representatives to Congress. Johnson announced that the Union had been restored.

HISTORICAL PICTURES/STOCK MONTAGE, INC.

Federal Troops Union soldiers roamed the streets of major Southern cities, protecting the rights of the recently freed. This cartoon shows how two Southern women might have looked upon such troops. *According to Sherman, what changes were impossible to accomplish with military presence?*

When Congress reconvened in December, it refused to seat the newly elected Southern representatives. Some members of Congress criticized Johnson's leniency toward the South. They pointed out that Johnson had done nothing to prevent new Southern state governments from passing **black codes,** laws that severely restricted the rights of newly freed African Americans. In Mississippi, for example, black codes prohibited free African Americans from receiving farmland and stipulated that freed African American orphans could be assigned to forced labor. Throughout 1866 and 1867, tensions increased as the President and Congress battled over Reconstruction.

Military Occupation

In 1867 Congress passed a series of Reconstruction Acts over Johnson's veto. These acts abolished the state governments formed under Johnson's plan. They also divided the South into five military districts, each under the command of a general. Federal troops were stationed in each district to carry out the process of readmitting states to the Union. The functions of the military forces, according to the acts, were "to protect all persons in their rights of person and property, to suppress insurrection, disorder, and violence, and to punish, or cause to be punished, all disturbers of the public peace and criminals."

The provision for military occupation of the Southern states changed the tone of Reconstruction. Leadership was in the hands of Congress, and the army administered Congress's plan. Many Northerners felt that the presence of federal troops was necessary to bring about political and social changes in the South. General Sherman, however, was more astute and expressed a different view: "No matter what change we may desire in the feelings and thoughts of people South, we cannot accomplish it by force. Nor can we afford to maintain there an army large enough to hold them in subjugation [control]."

The Supreme Court's Role

In the battle between the executive and legislative branches over Reconstruction, the Supreme Court at first seemed to support President Johnson's position. In *ex parte Milligan,* the Court ruled that civilians could not be tried in military courts when civil courts were functioning. Northerners defied this decision, however, and made military tribunals part of legislation. The Court further stated that the administration of military justice in the South was "mere lawless violence." In *ex parte Garland,* a case that involved a law requiring loyalty oaths from former Confederate teachers and others who wanted to resume their jobs, the Court handed down a split decision. The majority opinion ruled that such oaths were invalid. The dissenting opinion held that such requirements were valid qualifications for officeholders and voters.

The Court soon upheld Congress's authority to reconstruct the states. In 1867 Georgia and Mississippi sought an injunction preventing President Johnson from enforcing Congress's Reconstruction Acts. The Supreme Court refused on the grounds that executive functions were not subject to judicial restraint. Johnson, who had relied on the Court's record of sympathy toward the South, began to feel increasingly isolated.

Congressional Plans

The Push to Reform the South

The Radical Republican faction of Congress had been formulating plans for Reconstruction since the early 1860s. These Republicans earned the label "radical" because they were strongly antislavery and were not willing to forgive the Confederates. Lincoln's leniency had outraged them. They wanted sweeping political change in the South, which they believed would occur only with the strong presence of Union troops. As Thaddeus Stevens, a leading Radical Republican, said, any valid unifying plan "must revolutionize the southern institutions, habits, and manner . . . or all our blood and treasure have been spent in vain."

The Radical Republicans had responded to Lincoln's terms by passing the Wade-Davis Bill in 1864. This bill would have required a majority of a state's white male citizenry to swear both past and future loyalty to the Union; only then would the federal government recognize the state's government. Considering the bill too harsh, Lincoln had vetoed it.

Johnson further outraged the Radical Republicans by promoting Lincoln's lenient policies. In 1866 Northerners fought Johnson's policies by electing a Radical Republican majority to Congress. The Radical Republicans quickly enacted legislation designed to punish the former Confederate states, to increase Republican power in the South, and to create conditions that would promote economic development and racial equality in the South.

Much of the legislation passed during Reconstruction increased the rights and freedoms of African Americans. This benefited the Republicans in two ways: it made the Republicans popular with a large new pool of voters, and it diminished white Southerners' ability to dominate the South politically and economically. In 1866 Congress passed the Civil Rights Act, which granted citizenship to African Americans and prohibited states from diminishing the rights accompanying this citizenship. In addition ratification of the Fourteenth Amendment in 1868 prevented states from denying rights and privileges to any American citizen. The Fifteenth Amendment of 1870 guaranteed that no citizen could be denied the right to vote based on race, color, or former servitude. The Enforcement Act of 1870 empowered federal authorities to prosecute anyone who violated the Fourteenth or Fifteenth Amendments.

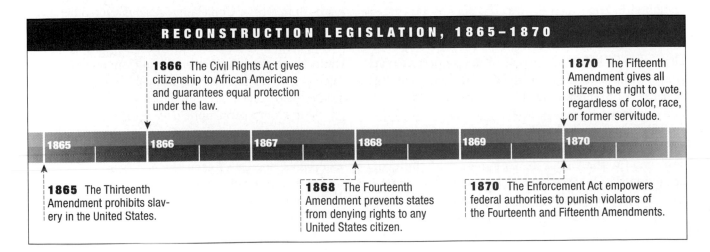

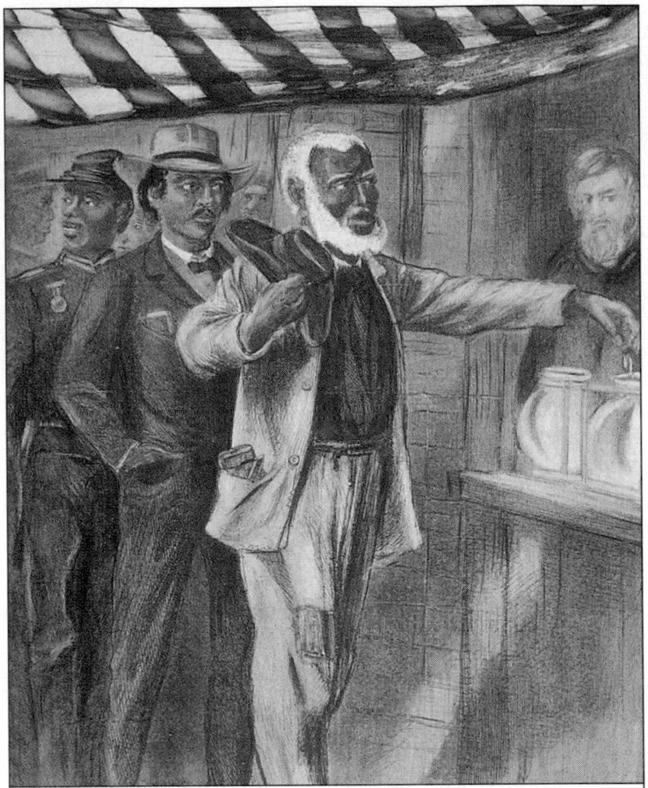

THE BETTMANN ARCHIVE

Influence at the Polls ***Harper's Weekly*** **celebrated full citizenship for African Americans with an illustration showing a soldier, a businessman, and an artisan casting their first ballots.** *What political faction promoted enfranchisement of African American citizens?*

RECONSTRUCTION LEGISLATION, 1865–1870

1865 | 1866 | 1867 | 1868 | 1869 | 1870

1865 The Thirteenth Amendment prohibits slavery in the United States.

1866 The Civil Rights Act gives citizenship to African Americans and guarantees equal protection under the law.

1868 The Fourteenth Amendment prevents states from denying rights to any United States citizen.

1870 The Fifteenth Amendment gives all citizens the right to vote, regardless of color, race, or former servitude.

1870 The Enforcement Act empowers federal authorities to punish violators of the Fourteenth and Fifteenth Amendments.

HISTORICAL PICTURES/STOCK MONTAGE, INC.

Radical Republican **Thaddeus Stevens, a Radical Republican leader in Congress, wanted African Americans to receive full rights as citizens.** *Who was the chief opponent to Stevens's proposals?*

Radical Reconstruction

New state governments were established under the Reconstruction Acts. White Southerners who protested the acts refused to vote in the elections that set up these governments. Their protest had two results: Republicans, who had little support in the South before the Civil War, won control of every new state government; and African Americans began to exert influence at the polls. One white Southerner wrote in his diary:

> Bills have passed both houses of Congress which repudiate and destroy the present civil government of the lately seceded states and substitute in their place a military government. Most of the whites are disenfranchised [deprived of the right to vote] and ineligible for office, whilst the negroes are invested with the right of voting.
>
> —Henry William Ravenel, South Carolina, February 24, 1867

When African Americans were guaranteed their right to vote, they began to exert influence at the polls in states in which they were a majority of the population: Alabama, Florida, Louisiana, Mississippi, and South Carolina. African American representatives outnumbered white representatives in the South Carolina legislature.

Radical Republicans pushed their legislation through Congress in spite of President Johnson's vetoes. In 1866 Johnson vetoed the Civil Rights Act and a bill that would have enabled the Freedmen's Bureau, an organization that assisted formerly enslaved people, to continue. Congress overrode both vetoes.

The Invisible Empire

At about the same time that Johnson was undermining African Americans' efforts to obtain equality, white supremacist organizations such as the Ku Klux Klan began terrorizing them. These organizations used intimidation and violence to prevent African Americans from voting or holding positions of power. In this environment of violence and hatred, mobs of Southern whites periodically lashed out against the newly freed citizens among them. For example, in May 1866 in Memphis, Tennessee, a crowd of white supremacists killed 46 African Americans and 2 white sympathizers.

The Impeachment Effort

Johnson's attempts to undermine congressional legislation coupled with his inability or lack of desire to control terrorist organizations further angered Radical Republicans. Their anger peaked when the President defied the Tenure of Office Act, which required Senate approval for the removal of cabinet members. Johnson failed to obtain that approval before he fired Secretary of War Edwin Stanton in 1868.

The House responded by voting to impeach the President on 11 charges of misconduct. These included charges that Johnson had violated the Tenure of Office Act. The House appointed 7 representatives to present the charges to the Senate. Johnson was defended by a

THE BETTMANN ARCHIVE

The Invisible Empire of the South **Two African American attorneys are brutalized by the Ku Klux Klan in Pulaski, Tennessee, on Christmas Eve, 1865. The Klan began as an elite club for Confederate veterans but within months was terrorizing citizens with racist attacks.** *What did the Ku Klux Klan seek to prevent?*

team of lawyers. Chief Justice Salmon P. Chase presided over the trial. Johnson did not attend.

The trial dragged on for 8 weeks. Johnson's attackers accused him of everything from alcoholism to plotting Lincoln's murder. The President's lawyers presented a purely legal defense, arguing that the Tenure of Office Act was unconstitutional and did not apply to Stanton. Conviction required a two-thirds majority of the Senate. The final tally of 35 for conviction and 19 against acquitted Johnson by 1 vote.

Limits on Freedom

Freed but Not Free

At the end of the Civil War, most African Americans expected their lives to improve radically. A formerly enslaved woman recalled the excitement she and other freed men and women had felt when they learned of the Union victory and their new freedom:

When the soldiers marched in to tell us that we were free . . . I remember one woman. She jumped on a barrel and she shouted. She jumped off and she shouted. She jumped back on again and shouted some more. She kept that up for a long time, just jumping on a barrel and back off again.

—Anna Woods, a Federal Writers' Project interview, 1930s

After the initial happiness passed, however, African Americans realized that they would have to struggle to secure their rights as a freed people. At an 1865 convention in Alabama, African Americans demanded "exactly the same rights, privileges, and immunities as are enjoyed by white men—we ask nothing more and will be content with nothing less. . . ."

The Freedmen's Bureau, an office of the War Department, was established to provide freed African Americans with food, teachers, legal aid, and other assistance. The bureau also distributed horses, mules, and land that had been confiscated during the war. With the

THE BETTMANN ARCHIVE

Elected to Office **This lithograph shows the first African Americans who served in Congress. Top row, left to right: Representatives Robert C. De Large of South Carolina, Jefferson H. Long of Georgia. Bottom row, left to right: Senator H.R. Revels of Mississippi, Representatives Benjamin Turner of Alabama, Josiah T. Walls of Florida, and Joseph H. Rainy and R. Brown Elliot, both of South Carolina.** *What important civil rights did African Americans win during the 1860s?*

MOORLAND-SPINGARD RESEARCH CENTER, HOWARD UNIVERSITY

COOK COLLECTION, VALENTINE MUSEUM

The Freedmen's Bureau Education was the bureau's primary goal. A former Union commander, O.O. Howard (left), led the organization. The children here are students at one of many Freedmen's Bureau schools in the South. *What role did the Freedmen's Bureau play in the fight for equality?*

bureau's help, about 40,000 African Americans were able to establish their own farms in Georgia and South Carolina. In the face of much opposition, African Americans obtained an education. At first, the Freedmen's Bureau and charitable organizations paid the cost of African American education. After 1871 the states began to take over the support of their own segregated schools. Many white Southerners resented African American schools, and teachers often faced intimidation or physical abuse. Progress was slow. Nevertheless, illiteracy among African Americans fell from more than 90 percent in 1860 to about 80 percent in 1870.

Voting Power

During Reconstruction African American voters exercised their political power for the first time. W.E.B. Du Bois, an important African American leader of the early 1900s, wrote: "With northern white leadership, the Negro voters . . . proved apt pupils in politics. They developed their own leadership. They gained clearer and clearer conceptions of how their political powers could be used for their own good."

African Americans were elected to office at the local, state, and national levels. Between 1869 and 1876, 2 African Americans served in the Senate and 14 served in the House of Representatives. Most of these men had been enslaved or were born of enslaved parents. Some critics claimed "they left no mark on the legislation of their time; none of them, in comparison with their white associates, attained the least distinction." Others observed: "The colored men who took seats in both Senate and House did not appear ignorant or helpless. They were as a rule studious, earnest, ambitious men, whose public conduct . . . would be honorable to any race."

Sharecropping

For many formerly enslaved African Americans, life changed little in the years after the Civil War. President Johnson returned confiscated estates to the previous Confederate owners. Freed people who had established farms on that land found themselves back on the plantations. Some worked under contract for meager wages. Others were forced into **sharecropping,** a system in which a wealthy patron would give seeds, supplies, and a small parcel of land to a farmer in exchange for a portion of the crop. If the patron required a large portion of the crop, the sharecropper might not be able to survive on what remained. If the crop failed, the sharecropper usually wound up hopelessly in debt to the patron.

"Freedom wasn't no difference I know of," complained one man. "I works for Marse John just the same." Many newly freed people did stay on the same plantations, where they worked under the same overseer. The wages or share of the crop they received hardly made up for the fact that freedom in no way meant equality.

Grant's Presidency

Corruption and Crisis

In 1868 the Republican Ulysses S. Grant won the presidency by a margin of 300,000 votes. The more than 500,000 African Americans who voted in the election certainly contributed to Grant's victory. Nevertheless, during Grant's two terms in office, from 1869 to 1877, the government began paying less and less attention to the problems of prejudice, discrimination, and racial harassment.

Government Scandal

Scandal and corruption plagued Grant's administration. A congressional investigation in the mid-1870s found that whiskey distillers and tax officials were stealing excise taxes from the government, and it linked a member of Grant's staff to the scandal. In addition, Grant's secretary of war, William W. Belknap, was accused of accepting bribes. Even Grant wrongly accepted personal gifts.

At the time successful politicians commonly rewarded their supporters by appointing them to government positions. These appointed individuals often lacked the skills and experience necessary to do their jobs. Quite often they were also greedy and dishonest. This was true of a number of the personal friends, relatives, and fellow army officers Grant appointed.

Such was also the case in the newly created Republican state governments in the South. Although these governments did implement legislation that helped to ease the South's social and economic difficulties, many of the Northerners involved in local Southern administrations were inexperienced and even corrupt. White Southerners called these Northern transplants **carpetbaggers,** mocking them for having arrived in the South with only the possessions they had been able to stuff inside their luggage. Most white Southerners believed the carpetbaggers wanted only to turn a profit or rise to power at the expense of the South. In addition, African Americans newly elected to political positions were often blamed for government wastefulness and dishonesty.

Democratic Success

As one after another of the carpetbag governments came under attack, Democrats began to regain control of Southern legislatures. They also used some underhanded tactics to neutralize the issues of equality that had begun to affect the election process.

One such technique, called **gerrymandering,** involved redividing voting districts to decrease African American representation in a particular area. Another tactic was to institute a poll tax, which the Democrats managed to do in several states. In these states voting became a privilege that required payment of a fee. Poll taxes excluded poor citizens of both races from the voting process. By 1875, aided by these strategies, Democrats had gained control of the House of Representatives for the first time since before the Civil War. By 1877 they had completely reestablished control over Southern state governments.

The Panic of 1873

Grant's administration faced economic as well as political problems. A financial crisis during his second term in office left the country in economic difficulty. The crisis was touched off in 1873 when financier Jay Cooke suddenly closed his Philadelphia bank. The bank closing prompted a panic during which 5,000 businesses closed, and thousands of people lost their jobs.

As the panic spread, concern for economic reform quickly replaced concern for social reform. In the North the demands of unemployed workers for economic relief supplanted demands for racial equality. By 1874 one-quarter of the population of New York City was out of work. In Chicago 20,000 unemployed people protested in the streets, demanding that government officials solve the problems of the economy.

In the South the sharecropping system cheated many African American farmers out of owning land or reaping profits from their labors. Meanwhile white farmers suffered devastating losses during these hard times and often accused African Americans of causing their economic troubles.

African Americans living in Northern states also faced economic and social problems. Although they had gained access to public education and transportation, they were usually trapped in low-paying, unskilled jobs; lived in poor housing; and had little voice in shaping government policies. Unlike the large freed population in the South, Northern African Americans comprised only 2 percent of the population. In both the North and the South, these newly enfranchised citizens had to struggle to claim the political and social rights that Reconstruction promised.

In the midst of the economic and social upheaval of Reconstruction, however, the United States celebrated its centennial in 1876. Ten million people paid 50 cents each to visit the Grand Exposition in Philadelphia. Displays of the nation's art, fashion, produce, appliances, and industrial development greeted the visitors. Many Americans were ready to push the problems of the Civil War into the past and forge on optimistically into the nation's second century.

The End of Reconstruction

Prejudice and Exodus

In the wake of social and economic crises, government scandals, and outbreaks of violence, the Radical Republicans lost their political power. So, too, the Radical Republican program of Reconstruction came to an end. No longer supported by the majority of voters, Republicans attempted to regain their foothold in the South by backing a moderate candidate for President—Rutherford B. Hayes, who appealed to both the North and South.

Hayes ran against Democratic candidate Samuel Tilden in what was possibly the closest presidential election battle in American history. A dispute arose over the election returns from four states. Three of these states were Southern states still under Reconstruction rule. The Democrats insisted that the majority of the people in these states favored Tilden but had been prevented from registering their votes. To settle the dispute, Congress appointed a special electoral commission.

To get Hayes elected, Republicans made many concessions to the Democrats, among which was the agreement to withdraw the Union troops that had been stationed in the South since the end of the war. These votes assured, Hayes won the election by one electoral vote. Shortly thereafter, the last Union troops withdrew from the South.

NATIONAL MUSEUM OF AMERICAN ART, WASHINGTON DC/ART RESOURCE, NY

Losing Ground By the turn of the century, conditions for African Americans in the South were in many ways indistinguishable from slavery, much like the scene in R.N. Brooke's painting, *Dog Swap*. *How were the civil rights gains during Reconstruction dismantled after 1870?*

Prejudice Persists

Without the presence of the Union army to combat terrorism, the rights of Southern African Americans were gravely jeopardized. Even before Hayes's election, the Supreme Court's 1876 ruling in *United States* v. *Cruikshank* overturned the Enforcement Act of 1870. The Court ruled that a state could not legally discriminate against African Americans, but nonstate institutions and individuals could. Specifically, the Court had overturned the convictions of three whites for their participation in a bloody massacre of African Americans on the grounds that the three individuals did not specify that their actions were racially motivated.

In subsequent administrations, the Supreme Court's support of African American rights diminished still further. For example, in 1883, during Chester A. Arthur's presidency, the Supreme Court nullified the Civil Rights Act of 1875.

Reconstruction Appraised

Although the period of Reconstruction had ended and Republicans and Democrats had temporarily united, African Americans felt as if their needs had been forgotten. Most of the legal decisions that had advanced African American rights during Reconstruction had been overturned. Furthermore the Radical Republican governments had failed to correct the problem of unequal land distribution in the South, a measure that might have provided the economic leverage that African Americans needed to protect their rights.

Discontented and afraid for their lives, African Americans left the South by the thousands. Many moved to Northern urban centers, such as Chicago and New York City. Some moved to Kansas, a state in which there was an abundance of fertile land open to homesteaders and a strong Republican government that promised unbiased treatment under the law. There, many began to enjoy a decent existence.

Section Review

Vocabulary

1. Define: amnesty, black codes, sharecropping, carpetbagger, gerrymandering.

Checking Facts

2. What legislation passed during Reconstruction aided African Americans?
3. How did Congress react to Johnson's vetoes of Radical Republican bills in 1866?

Critical Thinking

Determining Cause and Effect

4. Why did many Northern politicians stop concentrating on securing rights for African Americans after Grant's election?

Linking Across Time

5. Did Reconstruction mend the rift between North and South? Why or why not? What examples of sectionalism exist today within the two regions?

Chapter 6 Review

Reviewing Key Terms

Match each sentence below to the vocabulary term it defines or describes. Write your answers on a separate sheet of paper.

sectionalism	**black codes**
gospel tradition	**scorched earth policy**
emancipation	**gerrymandering**

1. Enslaved African Americans developed a unique musical form by combining African religious practices and beliefs with Christian practices and beliefs.

2. After the war President Johnson permitted Southern state governments to pass laws restricting the rights of newly freed African Americans.

3. In the years leading up to the war, the North and the South had developed entirely different political agendas based on their own regional economic interests.

4. Southern whites sometimes regained control of their state legislatures by the technique of redividing voting districts to dilute African American representation.

5. When General Grant became commander of the Union forces, he ordered his generals to burn and destroy the South's crops, homes, and supplies.

Recalling Facts

1. Why was the *Dred Scott* decision significant?

2. Explain how Eli Whitney's cotton gin contributed to increasing sectionalism. Discuss economic and political factors.

3. How did *(a)* the Missouri Compromise, *(b)* the Compromise of 1850, and *(c)* the Kansas-Nebraska Act reflect sectional interests?

4. What led to the secession of 11 Southern states?

5. Why were both Northerners and Southerners at first confident of victory in the Civil War?

6. Explain the significance of the battles in 1863 at Gettysburg and Vicksburg.

7. What was the Emancipation Proclamation? Did it achieve all of the goals of the abolitionists? Explain.

8. What motivated the Radical Republicans to pass civil rights legislation on behalf of African Americans?

9. Despite laws passed during Reconstruction, African Americans in the South lost many of their civil rights until the 1950s and 1960s. Explain.

10. Did the Civil War and Reconstruction end sectionalism? Why or why not?

Critical Thinking

1. Recognizing Bias White Southerners tended to support policies that enlarged the powers of the states, while Northerners supported limiting the powers of the states in certain important ways. What caused this difference in outlook?

2. Making Inferences Explain what Jerry Loguen meant when he said, "Human rights are mutual and reciprocal." How has this idea been applied to other areas, for example, women's rights?

3. Making Comparisons Make a chart showing the strengths and weaknesses of the Union and the Confederacy at the outbreak of the Civil War. What proved to be the determining factors in the war?

4. Drawing Conclusions Playing marches like "The Battle Hymn of the Republic" and "Dixie," drummers as young as 10 and 12 years old—like those in the photo at left—

SMITHSONIAN INSTITUTION

marched alongside Union and Confederate troops. Why was this music important to soldiers?

5. Determining Cause and Effect President Lincoln believed that the South should be treated with compassion after the Civil War. Did Reconstruction fulfill this objective? Explain.

Portfolio Project

Civil war has torn apart many countries in the 1900s. Choose one country, such as China, Spain, Yugoslavia, or Mexico, and investigate its civil war period. Identify the causes and effects of its civil war. In what ways was the war similar to the American Civil War? In what ways was it different? Write a report and include it in your portfolio.

Cooperative Learning

The Civil War has inspired numerous books, plays, movies, and TV dramas. For example, Margaret Mitchell's novel *Gone With the Wind,* Stephen Crane's novel *The Red Badge of Courage,* and the 1989 movie *Glory* look at the war from different perspectives. With a group of your classmates, prepare a review of different works on the Civil War. Include answers to the following questions: How historically accurate is the work in question? What evidence is there of character stereotyping? Has stereotyping changed over the years?

Reinforcing Skills

Combining Information From Maps Compare the map of transportation routes on page 148 with the map of Civil War battles on page 175. What inference can you make about why Union victories in Tennessee and battles in New Orleans caused major hardships for the South?

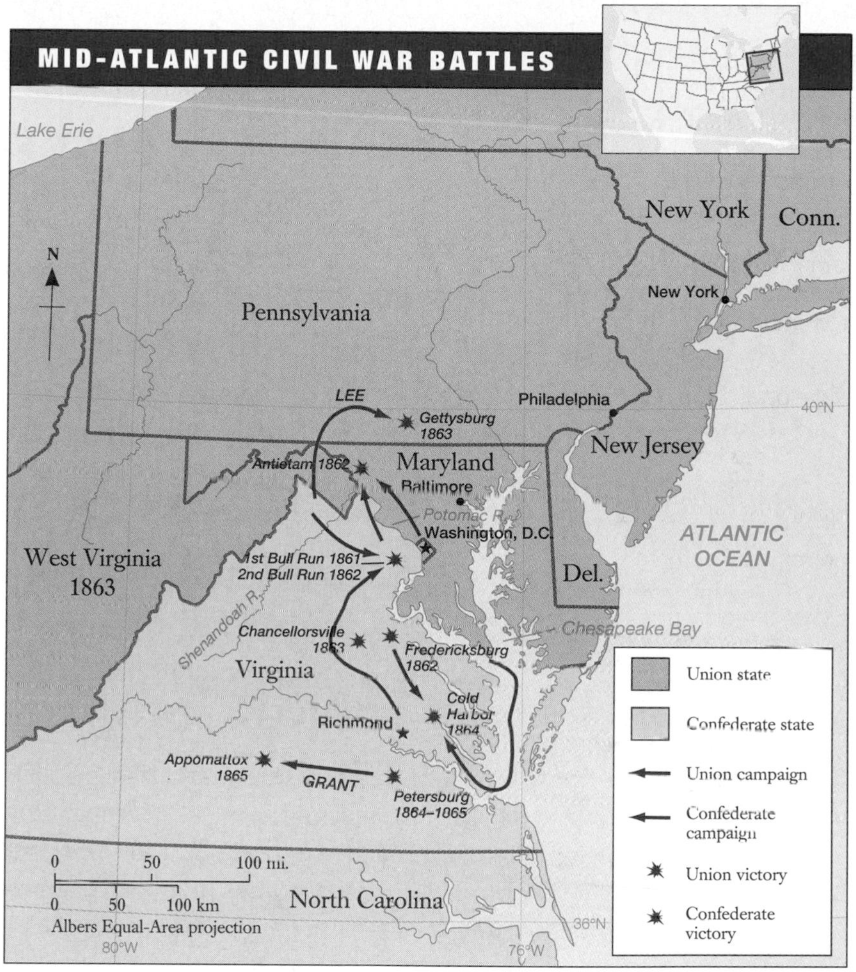

Geography and History

Study the map on this page to answer the following questions:

1. In which mid-Atlantic state did the most battles take place? Which side won most of these battles?

2. Which of the battles shown on the map were victories for the Confederacy?

3. Which battles took place in Union states?

4. In which battles did the Confederate campaign appear to threaten Washington, D.C.?

5. What Confederate general was in command at Gettysburg?

HISTORY JOURNAL

Write a brief account of what you have learned in this chapter. Include a consideration of the ways in which the institution of slavery was related to the Civil War.

CHAPTER 7

New Frontiers

MAY 24, 1883: FANFARE MARKS BROOKLYN BRIDGE OPENING

Church bells rang out all over the city. Guns boomed from forts in New York harbor. After 14 years of construction, marred by worker injuries and deaths, New York City celebrated the opening of the Brooklyn Bridge.

President Chester A. Arthur and New York Governor Grover Cleveland joined thousands of New Yorkers in the opening ceremony. The steel bridge stretched over the East River, ready to open the way from the island of Manhattan to the borough of Brooklyn.

At the time it was opened, the bridge was the longest suspension bridge in the world. Costing nearly $15 million, the bridge was suspended by 4 cables. Each cable contained more than 5,000 small wires and could hold nearly 3,000 tons. More than 100,000 people would travel over it each day.

The Brooklyn Bridge reflected the tide of industrial progress sweeping the nation in the years following the Civil War. Factories and cities grew, while advancements in technology and communications transformed the way Americans lived. As the nation continued to push its boundaries outward, the United States emerged as one of the great powers of the 1900s. ■

HISTORY JOURNAL

Write in your journal about your reaction to the story and photograph of the Brooklyn Bridge. What makes a great bridge an appropriate symbol of industrial progress?

ARCHIVE PHOTOS

Strollers enjoy the broad promenade above the roadway of the soaring Brooklyn Bridge.

SECTION 1

Moving West

APRIL 22, 1889: THOUSANDS GRAB LAND IN OKLAHOMA

THE CLOCK STRUCK NOON AND GUNSHOTS RANG OUT, BEGINNING ONE OF THE MOST REMARKABLE LAND GRABS IN AMERICAN HISTORY. Yancey Cravat, the hero in Edna Ferber's novel, *Cimarron,* describes the scene on April 22, 1889, when the federal government effectively gave away the almost 2 million acres (0.8 million ha) of land it had purchased from evicted Creek and Seminole.

ARCHIVES AND MANUSCRIPTS DIVISION OF THE OKLAHOMA HISTORICAL SOCIETY

Staking Claims
The rush into Oklahoma's Cherokee Outlet goes by in a blur of speed. Thousands of Americans claimed free land in the new territories. Claims often sparked violent disputes that took years to settle.

> There we were, the girl on my left, the old plainsman on my right. Eleven forty-five. Along the border were the soldiers, their guns in one hand, their watches in the other. . . . Twelve o'clock. There went up a roar that drowned the crack of the soldiers' musketry as they fired in the air as the signal of noon and the start of the Run. You could see the puffs of smoke from their guns but you couldn't hear a sound. The thousands surged over the Line. It was like running water going over a broken dam. The rush had started, and it was devil take the hindmost. We swept across the prairie in a cloud of black and red dust that covered our faces and hands in a minute. . . .
>
> —Edna Ferber, *Cimarron,* 1930

More than 50,000 men, women, and children participated in the rush. Although the land was free, the settlers would have to **homestead,** or settle on the land, for a number of years before they could own it. Some found their stakes too dry to farm, and disease-causing conditions drove others out; but a year later, the Oklahoma Territory boasted a population of about 259,000 people.

The success of the Oklahoma rush led the government to open more land in the West. The following year

AS YOU READ

Vocabulary

- homestead
- transcontinental railroad
- government boarding school

Think About . . .

- what influenced the development of American cowhand culture.
- what geographical, political, and technological factors led to settlement of the Plains and the West.
- how the transcontinental railroad was built.
- how federal policies adversely affected Native Americans.

federal authorities authorized settlement on millions of acres of Sioux land in South Dakota. The government could not hold back the tide of eager settlers, and after 1900 thousands descended on the former Native American reservation.

Expanding Frontiers

Farmers, Ranchers, and Miners Go West

After the Civil War, as the nation's population boomed and Midwestern agricultural land filled up, farmers looked westward to the Great Plains. Completed in 1869, the **transcontinental railroad** spanned the continent from east to west. The railroad companies then encouraged eager farmers to buy some of their enormous land holdings. More encouragement came from the Homestead Act of 1862 that awarded 160 acres (64.8 ha) of public land free to any settler who would farm the land for at least 5 years. So enticed, many settlers, including thousands of newly arrived immigrants from European countries, poured into the lands west of the Mississippi River.

COLLECTION OF WILLIAM GLADSTONE/PICTURE RESEARCH CONSULTANTS, INC.

BUFFALO BILL HISTORICAL CENTER, CODY, WY

Cowhand Culture Cowhands, one-third of whom were African American or Hispanic American, shared the hardships of the long trail drives as well as the hours of relaxation in town. These two cowhands posed for their photograph in the 1860s. *How did the cattle industry in the United States begin?*

The Cattle Frontier

On the eastern high-grass prairie of the Great Plains, enough rain fell to cultivate grain crops. Settlers used the drier western lands for cattle grazing. Herds of longhorn and other cattle were fattened on the open range lands of Texas, Kansas, Nebraska, the Dakotas, Wyoming, and Montana. They were driven to market and sold to packers and finally were sent east to feed the growing numbers of beef-hungry city dwellers.

The profits from cattle ranching could be enormous. A Texas steer, purchased as a calf for $5–$6, could be set out to graze on public land and later sold for $60–$70. For two decades after the Civil War, the cowhand and the cattle reigned supreme on the Great Plains. By the late 1880s, however, drought and an oversupply of cattle forced beef prices down.

Cowhands

American cowhands have been idealized in popular books and movies. Their unique way of life evolved from that of the vaqueros, their Mexican counterparts. The cattle industry in the United States developed from the livestock and horses that the Spanish introduced into the Americas. Similarly, cowhand culture—the clothing, equipment, work, and entertainment of American cowhands—had a partly Spanish heritage.

Cowhands' chaps—a word based on the vaqueros' word *chaparajos*—protected their legs from thorny brush on the Plains. The words *lariat* and *rodeo* also have Spanish origins. Cowhands' outfits were functional. High-heeled boots kept their feet from slipping out of the stirrups, and broad-brimmed hats kept sun, rain, and dust from their eyes.

A cowhand's work was seasonal. Ranchers hired extra help for the roundup, when cattle were branded. During a trail drive, hired hands kept the herds together and moved them as far as 1,000 miles (1,609 km) in 3 months. The work was exhausting, and the wages were low—$40 or $50 per month. Few cowhands owned their own horses, but every cowhand owned a saddle—a prized possession. The cowhands' worth was measured by their skill at roping and riding. Cattle rancher Joseph G. McCoy said of a cowhand in 1874: "He lives hard, works hard, has but few comforts and fewer necessities. He loves danger but abhors labor of the common kind, and never tires riding."

The profession was more integrated than most walks of American life. African American, Native American, Hispanic, and Anglo cowhands, as well as those of mixed ancestry, all met and worked together. Yet discrimination existed on the frontier as elsewhere. Vaqueros earned less than Anglos and seldom became foremen or trail bosses. Some saloons discriminated against Hispanics, segregated African Americans, and excluded Chinese altogether.

Few women worked as salaried cowhands. Ranchers' wives and daughters did help with many chores, such as tending animals and sewing leather britches. A widow sometimes took over her deceased husband's ranch.

During free time in the bunkhouse, cowhands entertained themselves with card games, tall tales, practical jokes, and songs. In town, after several months on the trail, many of them let off steam by drinking, gambling, and fighting in local saloons. Cow towns, where cattle were loaded on trains for shipment to market, had a reputation for lawlessness. Yet the "Wild West" gained its name not so much for gunfights as for the cowhands' rugged life.

Mountains and Valleys

West of the Great Plains, people sought their fortune from the vast mineral and forest resources of the Rocky Mountain and Sierra Nevada regions. The timberlands of California and the Northwest yielded much of the wood necessary for thousands of miles of railroad ties, fence posts, and the building of hundreds of towns.

Gold and silver provided much of the capital for an industrializing country. The Comstock Lode, a rich vein of silver in Nevada, yielded more than $292 million between 1859 and 1882. Though Western tales celebrate the lone miner toiling with pick and shovel, huge companies did most of the mining of valuable metals. These companies, in pursuit of gold, silver, lead, copper, tin, and zinc, commanded great money and power. They could build railroad lines, bring in heavy machinery, and employ armies of miners.

In California the gold discovered under the ground proved less valuable than the ground itself. As one father told his son: "Plant your lands, these be your best gold fields." Farmland turned out to be California's most valuable asset. Eager miners, believing the California soil unsuitable for crops, willingly paid high prices for farm produce: "watermelon at from one to five dollars each, apples from Oregon at one and two dollars each, potatoes and onions at fifty cents to one dollar a pound . . . eggs at two dollars a dozen," according to one older resident. More often than not, provisioners in the West made money while miners did not. By 1862 California produced a surplus of some crops.

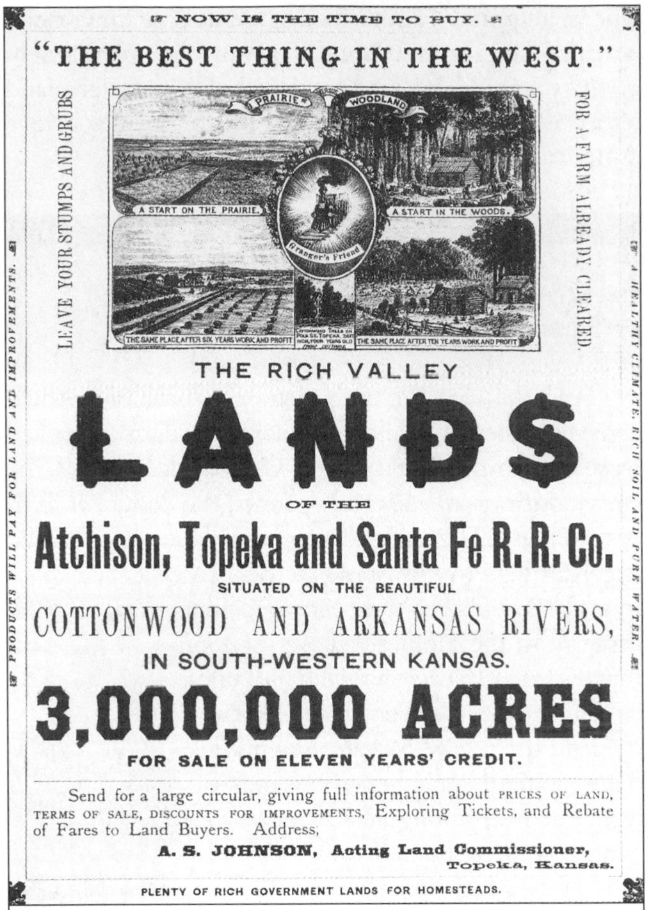

ASSOCIATION OF AMERICAN RAILROADS

Promise of the West **In this government advertisement, the new railroad service is used to attract homesteaders to stake claims.** *Why was much of the West sparsely settled before 1870?*

Like the cattle culture of the Great Plains, the agriculture of California had a partly Spanish heritage. Franciscan missionaries introduced grapes and citrus fruits to California's fertile soils in the late 1700s. With the end of the mission system in the mid-1800s, however, the vineyards and orchards fell into neglect. Enterprising settlers, once in search of gold, displaced Mexican ranchers and turned the rich California valleys into cornucopias of the Far West.

Building the Railroad

Across the Continent by Rail

California's population increased dramatically because of its gold rush and its agricultural successes. Other parts of the West remained sparsely settled, usually because they were far from transportation and markets. In the early 1860s, the federal government proposed that railroad lines should cross the entire United States.

The incredible engineering feat that provided transcontinental transportation began with the Pacific Railroad Act. Passed by Congress in 1862, the act authorized the Union Pacific Railroad to lay track westward from a point near Omaha, Nebraska, while the Central Pacific Railroad laid track eastward from Sacramento. The lines were to meet in Utah. In addition to government loans, the railroads received large land grants, 20 square miles (51.8 square km) of land for 1 mile (1.6 km) of track laid. The railroad barons made fortunes by selling this land to settlers.

Both railroads faced enormous challenges that required armies of laborers. The Central Pacific had to cross the Sierra Nevada in eastern California, while the Union Pacific had to cross the Rockies. Blasting and tunneling into rock and working through the winters, the crew suffered many injuries and deaths. In January 1865, the Central Pacific advertised for 5,000 more workers.

The quiet efficiency of Chinese laborers impressed the construction boss, and he began recruiting in China. Before the end of the year, about 7,000 Chinese laborers were at work on the line. The Union Pacific relied heavily on Irish immigrant labor, although one worker described the team as "a crowd of ex-Confederates and Federal soldiers, muleskinners, Mexicans, New York Irish, bushwackers, and ex-convicts," with a few African Americans as well.

By 1868 the work of laying track had become a race between the two railroads. The pace quickened as the lines approached each other. When the two sets of tracks met on May 10, 1869, at Promontory, Utah, special trains carrying railroad officials and their guests arrived for the completion ceremony. Leland Stanford, governor of California, drove in a gold spike, symbolically uniting the rail lines. A telegraph message informed the nation, "It is done!" By the end of the 1800s four more transcontinental rail lines crossed the United States. Passengers and freight began to crisscross the nation.

THE HARRY T. PETERS COLLECTION, MUSEUM OF THE CITY OF NEW YORK

A Dangerous Pass This photo from 1877 shows the Secrettown Trestle, 62 miles (99.8 km) from Sacramento, California. The Chinese laborers shown used picks, chisels, hammers, wheelbarrows, and one-horse carts to build the timber structures and earthen embankments that bridged these chasms in the Sierra Nevada. *When was the Pacific Railroad Act passed by Congress?*

LIBRARY OF CONGRESS

Forced Removal This photograph shows federal agents preparing to relocate a group of Apache from Arizona to Oklahoma by train in the late 1800s. Geronimo, of the Chiricahua Apache, sat third from right in front. *Why is this train bound for Oklahoma?*

The Second Great Removal

Native American Lands Taken

Not everyone benefited from the expansion of the railroads. In the summer of 1860, Lieutenant Henry Maynadier quoted one Sioux elder who warned about the expansion of the West, "We are glad to have the traders, but we don't want you soldiers and roadmakers; the country is ours and we intend to keep it."

The rapid settlement of the lands west of the Mississippi River after the Civil War led to a generation of violent conflict. Settlers fought the dozens of Native American nations that had inhabited these lands for generations.

In 1871 the federal government decreed that all Western Native American nations must agree to relocate to one of two reservation areas. The northern Plains nations were assigned to the western half of present-day South Dakota; the southern Plains nations were assigned to what is now Oklahoma. Once placed on the reservations, they would have to accept the federal government as their guardian.

Government policy, as well as military conflict with those who resisted, undermined Native American cultures. In 1871 the government ended the practice of treating each Native American nation separately. Under the new policy, Native Americans lost two rights. They could no longer negotiate treaties to protect their lands, and they could no longer vote on laws governing their fate. The Dawes Severalty Act of 1887 continued the attempt to break down Native American loyalty to their own nations. This act decreed that parcels of land be given not to nations but to individuals. Each family head was allowed 160 acres (64.8 ha). Reservation land left over was sold to white settlers.

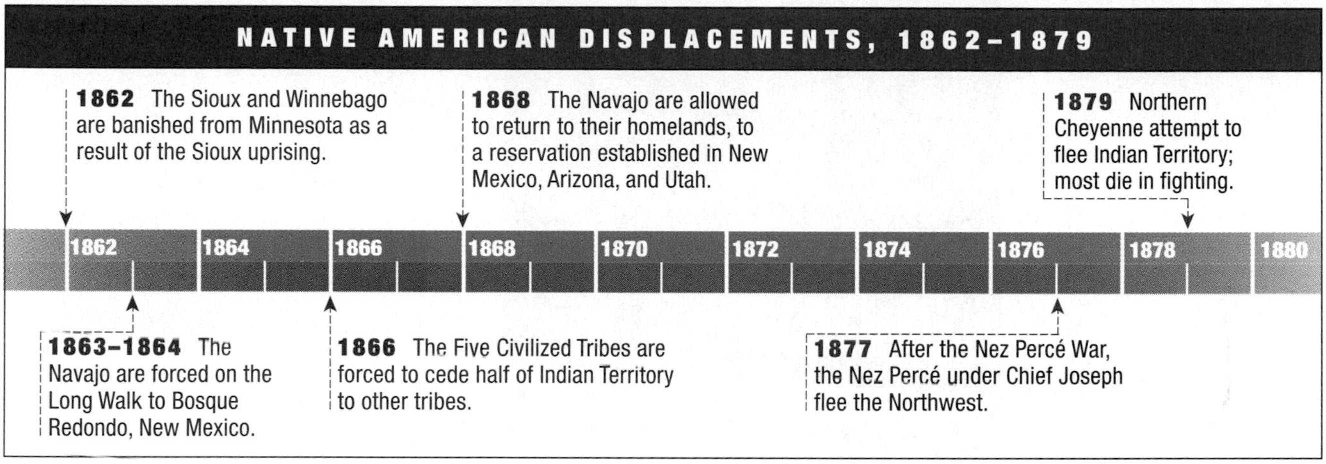

NATIVE AMERICAN DISPLACEMENTS, 1862–1879
1862 The Sioux and Winnebago are banished from Minnesota as a result of the Sioux uprising.
1868 The Navajo are allowed to return to their homelands, to a reservation established in New Mexico, Arizona, and Utah.
1879 Northern Cheyenne attempt to flee Indian Territory; most die in fighting.
1862
1864
1866
1868
1870
1872
1874
1876
1878
1880
1863–1864 The Navajo are forced on the Long Walk to Bosque Redondo, New Mexico.
1866 The Five Civilized Tribes are forced to cede half of Indian Territory to other tribes.
1877 After the Nez Percé War, the Nez Percé under Chief Joseph flee the Northwest.

Some reformers compared this act to the Emancipation Proclamation: just as enslaved people were set free, so Native Americans would gradually gain citizenship. Few reformers seemed to notice that sending Native American children to **government boarding schools,** where they were schooled in the white cultural tradition, was breaking down Native American culture.

Within 20 years after the Dawes Act, Native Americans retained control of only 20 percent of their original reservation lands. The southern Plains Native Americans in Oklahoma were severely hurt. By the time of Oklahoma statehood in 1907, most of their original acreage was in the hands of 500,000 white settlers. A newspaper editor in that year summed up the prevailing feeling among the settlers: "Sympathy and sentiment never stand in the way of the onward march of empire." The Oglala Sioux leader Red Cloud, who later represented Arapaho, Crow, and Cheyenne as well, expressed the corresponding Native American lament in 1870: "When we first had all this land we were strong; now we are all melting like snow on the hillside, while you are growing like spring grass."

S.J. MORROW COLLECTION/W.H. OVER MUSEUM

Red Cloud A chief of the Oglala Sioux, Red Cloud led the opposition to the Bozeman Trail through Native American lands in Colorado and Montana. Under his leadership, representatives were able to negotiate removal of federal troops and forts from their lands. *What was the impact of westward expansion on Red Cloud and his people?*

Section Review

Vocabulary

1. Define: homestead, transcontinental railroad, government boarding school.

Checking Facts

2. What aspects of American cowhand culture reflect its Spanish heritage?
3. Name some of the natural resources that settlers found on the Great Plains and in the Far West. How did the federal government's transportation policy contribute to the westward movement?

Critical Thinking

Recognizing Points of View

4. How did the Native Americans' view of westward expansion differ from that of the settlers?

Linking Across Time

5. Some reformers compared the Dawes Severalty Act to the Emancipation Proclamation. Just as enslaved people were set free, reformers argued, so Native Americans would gain citizenship. How would you compare the consequences of the Emancipation Proclamation and the Dawes Act? Explain.

CULTURE OF THE TIME

An Age of Ingenuity

After the Civil War, Americans yearned to shed painful memories. They channeled their creative energy into hopes for a brighter future. Inventors filed record numbers of patent applications for everything from the dentist's drill to the corn flake. They contrived new modes of travel and entertainment, and displayed their creations at exhibitions and fairs.

RON LABBE/STUDIO 3-D

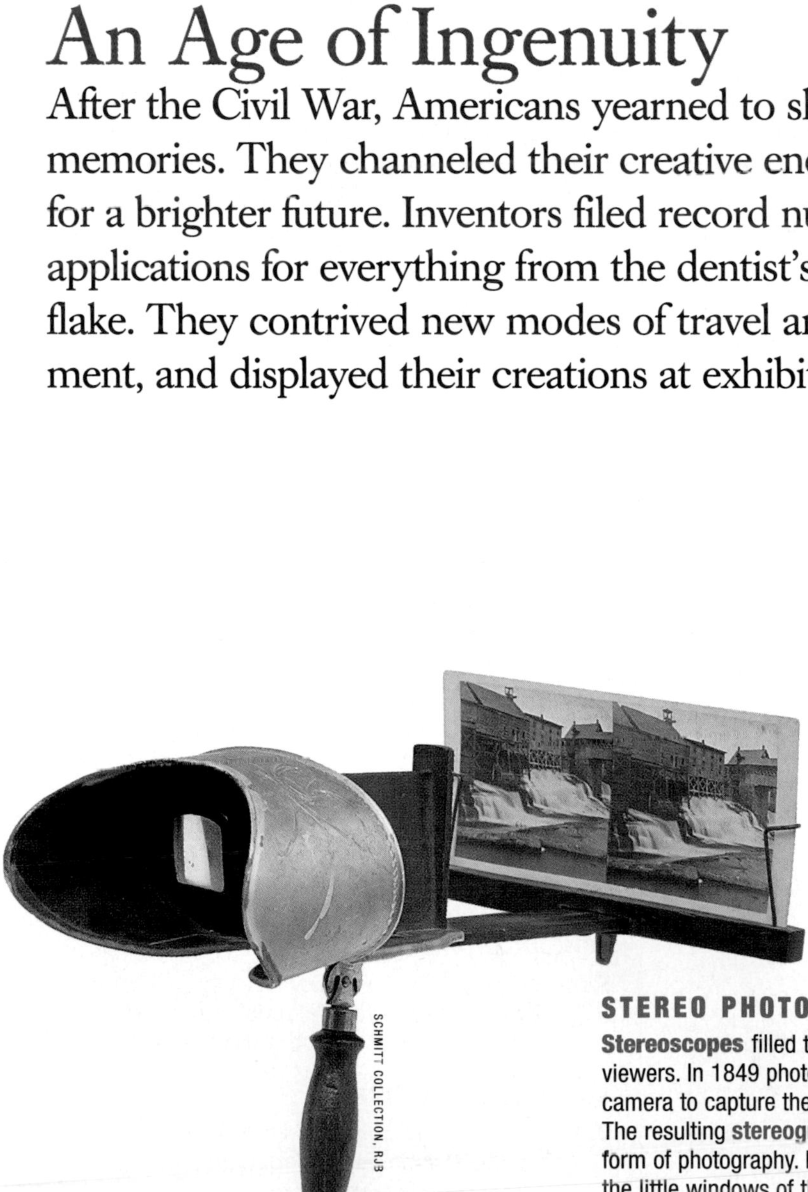

SCHMITT COLLECTION, RJB

STEREO PHOTOGRAPHY

Stereoscopes filled the imaginations and parlors of Victorian viewers. In 1849 photographers began using a double-lensed camera to capture the perspectives of the left and right eyes. The resulting **stereographs** quickly became the most popular form of photography. Printed side by side, and seen through the little windows of the stereoscope, the two views on the stereograph merged into one and popped to life in 3-D.

CURIOSITY SEEKERS

Already famous for drawing a crowd, **Phineas T. Barnum** watched 10,000 spectators flock to his first circus in 1871. Three acres of tents housed the likes of Zazel the human cannonball and Alexis the horseback-riding, hoop-jumping goat.

COURTESY OF THE BARNUM MUSEUM, BRIDGEPORT, CT

CULVER PICTURES

MECHANICAL MUSIC

Wild saloons and proper parlors alike displayed the newest musical novelty, the **player piano**. Meanwhile, employees of the **United States Patent Office** saw designs for a music-playing sewing machine and a convertible piano bed.

PATENTED

CHICAGO HISTORICAL SOCIETY

REINVENTING THE WHEEL

The 1893 World's Columbian Exposition unveiled the first **Ferris wheel**. Inventor Charles Ferris designed the ride to be the United States's answer to France's Eiffel Tower. During the Exposition the wheel carried more than 1.5 million people in its 36 trolley-sized cars.

SECTION 2

Rise of Industrialism

LATE 1800s: CARNEGIE FORGES A STEEL EMPIRE

BROWN BROTHERS

Innovator
Andrew Carnegie entered business when the use of steel was already widespread. He pioneered techniques to make steel processing more efficient and gradually took over the plants of his suppliers and distributors.

ANDREW CARNEGIE LEARNED ABOUT THE MEANING OF HARD WORK AS A YOUNG BOY. When his family fell on hard times in Scotland, he helped his mother sew shoes by threading her needles. In 1848 after the Carnegies left Scotland for the United States, 12-year-old Andrew worked with his father in a Pennsylvania cotton factory, earning $1.20 for a 72-hour week.

Little by little, Carnegie made himself a business success. At age 14 he started work in a telegraph office as a messenger and then quickly rose to the position of telegraph operator. The Pennsylvania Railroad hired Carnegie when he was 17, and his skills and hard work catapulted him in a few years to the job of assistant to the president. Through smart investments in a railroad car company and in oil wells, Carnegie made a small fortune by his early twenties and left the railroad to start his own business manufacturing iron bridges.

Carnegie was not only a shrewd investor but also a daring industrial innovator. In 1873 he began building a massive steel plant to produce railroad tracks in Pittsburgh, Pennsylvania. Carnegie introduced the revolutionary Bessemer converter and open-hearth steelmaking method, which converted iron ore into steel with much less labor than was previously required. Carnegie's mill also combined all stages of steel production—smelting, refining, and rolling—into one unified operation. As a result, the price of steel rails dropped from $107 per ton in 1870 to $32 per ton in 1890.

Innovation, ambition, and organizational skill made Carnegie hugely wealthy by the time he was 40 years old. Saying that hard work brought success, he also believed that those who acquired great

AS YOU READ

Vocabulary
- Industrialism
- national market
- merger
- horizontal integration
- vertical integration

Think About . . .
- the relationship between inventions and industrialism.
- how industrialism and the development of national markets affected business.
- the two different types of mergers.
- how industrialists applied Social Darwinism to big business.

wealth had a responsibility to return a portion of their profits to society. "The man who dies rich, dies disgraced," the self-made Scottish immigrant avowed.

By the time of his death in 1919, Carnegie had donated more than $350 million to worthy causes, including thousands of libraries, and another $30 million was disbursed through his last will and testament. His generosity was legendary throughout the world.

Industrialism Triumphant

A New World of Manufacturing

The era during which Andrew Carnegie built his steel empire witnessed a dramatic economic transformation. Between the end of the Civil War in 1865 and the end of the 1800s, the United States became an industrial giant. Manufacturing replaced agriculture as the main source of economic growth; growing **industrialism** turned the United States into a land rich with machines, factories, mines, and railroads.

BROWN BROTHERS

Growing Employment **Cotton mills, such as this one in Greensboro, North Carolina, photographed in 1895, provided jobs for many Southerners who were forced out of farming by hard times. Whole families worked in the mills.** *How were factories linked to farming?*

The Rise of Heavy Industry

Before the Civil War, manufacturing in the United States had been tied to the farming economy. Factories processed the products of the farm and forest into consumer goods—turning cotton and wool into cloth; hides into shoes and boots; and trees into ships, barrels, and furniture. After the Civil War, manufacturing branched out and concentrated increased funding and labor in heavy-industry consumer goods such as railroad tracks, steam engines, and farm tractors. Factories could now produce in huge quantities what craftspersons had painstakingly been making by hand.

Steelmaking was central to the new heavy industry. Hand in hand with steel production went the intensive development of the nation's mineral resources. Iron ore deposits in Michigan and Minnesota provided the raw substance for the steelmaking centers that sprang up in Illinois, Ohio, and Pennsylvania. Coal was equally important because it became the fuel that powered a nation of steam-run machines.

The Technology Boom

In 1876 the most ingenious American inventor since Benjamin Franklin built a long wooden shed in a little town in New Jersey where he promised to produce "a minor invention every ten days and a big thing every six months or so." Thomas Alva Edison, a brash 29-year-old at the time, was nearly as good as his word.

Edison patented more than 1,000 inventions in his Menlo Park laboratory before his death in 1931. He lit up the nation through his stunning development of an incandescent lightbulb that provided a cheap and

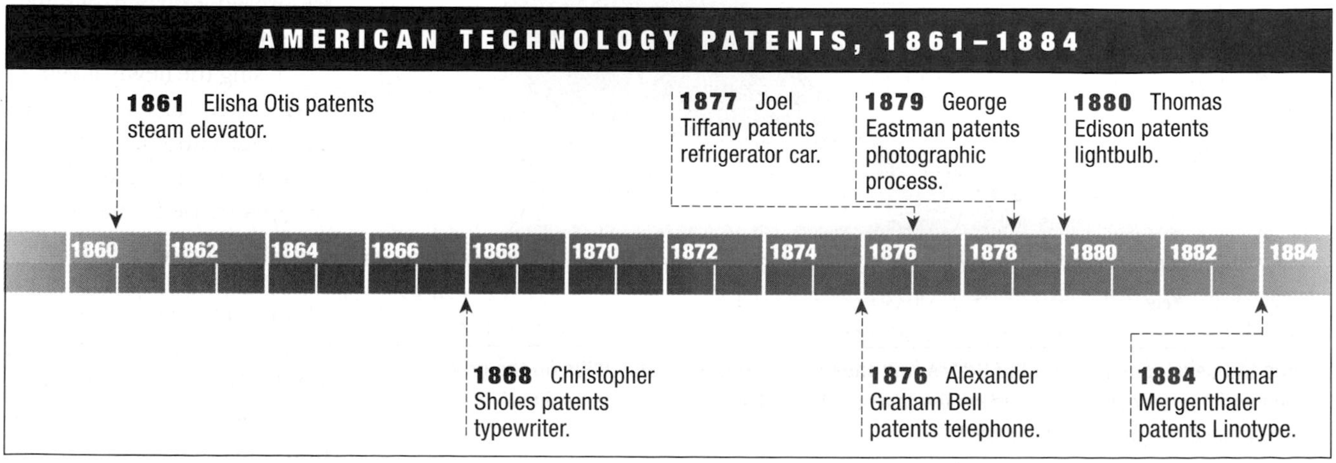
AMERICAN TECHNOLOGY PATENTS, 1861–1884
1861 Elisha Otis patents steam elevator.
1877 Joel Tiffany patents refrigerator car.
1879 George Eastman patents photographic process.
1880 Thomas Edison patents lightbulb.
1860
1862
1864
1866
1868
1870
1872
1874
1876
1878
1880
1882
1884
1868 Christopher Sholes patents typewriter.
1876 Alexander Graham Bell patents telephone.
1884 Ottmar Mergenthaler patents Linotype.

CULVER PICTURES

BROWN BROTHERS

Shopping at Home **Montgomery Ward issued mail-order catalogs to rural families across the country. People could buy thousands of items, from barn nails to sunbonnets.** *How did the mail-order business depend on railroads?*

The Growth of Big Business

Mergers Create Industrial Giants

The growth of heavy industry and the creation of vast nationwide markets brought about a fundamental change in business organization. Only large businesses gathering capital from many investors could afford to set up huge factories, install modern machinery, and employ hundreds of workers.

At the same time, the vast railroad system allowed national corporations to ship goods almost anywhere. While the typical railroad line in 1865 was only 100 miles long, by 1885 it had expanded to 1,000 miles (1,609 km) of track. Such a large enterprise, with enormous costs of construction, maintenance, and operation, demanded unprecedented amounts of capital and new methods of management.

The Managerial Revolution

In the early days of railroading, a superintendent could give his personal attention to every detail in running a 50- or 100-mile (80.45- or 160.9-km) operation. How, then, could one person oversee the operations of a business such as the Pennsylvania Railroad? By 1890 this railroad had 50,000 employees, properties spread over great distances, large amounts of capital invested, and hundreds of trains that had to be scheduled and coordinated with precision.

The answer was to separate the various functions of a business into departments and put each one under the direction of a separate manager. In a railroad, for example, one person would be in charge of people who maintained the tracks; another supervised cargo handling; another oversaw traffic. Managers reported to the central office through well-defined lines of communication.

The Merger Movement

Led by the railroads, the American industrial economy grew rapidly in the decades after the Civil War. The cutthroat competition of an uncontrolled marketplace, however, plagued businesses. Business owners feverishly overbuilt their operations in good times and cut back sharply when demand for their products slackened. In such a boom-or-bust marketplace, bankruptcy was common. In the depression of the 1870s, for example, 47,000 firms closed their doors, laying off hundreds of thousands of employees.

Some people felt that the solution to such business instability was a **merger,** or a combining of several competing firms under a single head. By merging companies in a particular industry, a junglelike market could become an orderly, predictable market. "I like a little competition now and then," exclaimed J.P. Morgan, a titan of mergers in the late 1800s, "but I like combination a lot better."

The pioneering figure in the late nineteenth-century merger movement was John D. Rockefeller. Rockefeller started out as a clerk in his boyhood town of Cleveland, Ohio. In the 1860s he founded a business that refined kerosene from petroleum and later became Standard Oil Company. Hundreds of oil refineries, mostly small and badly organized, competed fiercely in the Ohio and Pennsylvania regions.

Both wise and ruthless, Rockefeller purchased as many competing companies as possible, and by the late 1870s Standard Oil controlled almost all the oil refineries in Ohio. By 1882 Standard Oil had gobbled up most of the competition throughout the country. Rockefeller's 40 oil companies owned 90 percent of the nation's pipelines and refined 84 percent of the nation's oil. "The day of individual competition [in the oil business] is past and gone," Rockefeller pronounced.

Because he dominated the market, Rockefeller was able to demand rail shipping rates of ten cents a barrel as compared with his competitors' thirty-five cents. When Rockefeller turned the business over to his son in 1911, his fortune exceeded $1 billion.

The merger of competing companies in one area of business such as occurred to form Rockefeller's oil corporation was known as **horizontal integration.** It was often accompanied by **vertical integration** of industries, in which a firm would strive to control all aspects of production from acquisition of raw materials to final delivery of finished products. In this way a single business might gain total control over a national market, as the chart below shows. Note that when a business integrates horizontally, it merges all competing companies in one area of business. In vertical integration, one business controls all aspects of production.

In the merger movement, Swift and Armour dominated meatpacking, and the Duke family controlled tobacco. Andrew Carnegie, however, had the most success with vertical integration. Carnegie bought up coal mines and iron ore deposits for his steel mills, then bought railroads and ships to transport raw materials and send his products to market. By owning every aspect of steel production he could limit risk and guarantee profit.

When J.P. Morgan bought Carnegie's steel company in 1901, he consolidated it with several other firms to form the U.S. Steel Corporation, which controlled 60 percent of American steel production. It was the nation's first billion-dollar company. By 1913 J.P. Morgan controlled 314 directorships in 112 corporations, with an estimated collective worth of $22 billion.

The Spirit of the Gilded Age

Lavish Spending and Ruthless Competition

The wealth generated by industrial capitalism and big business led to the growth of a "nouveau riche" class with its own philosophy. Many of these self-made people proclaimed their importance with showy displays of wealth, leading humorist Mark Twain to call the late 1800s the Gilded Age.

HORIZONTAL AND VERTICAL INTEGRATION

Business mergers of the late 1800s followed two strategies: vertical—joining all areas of one business, and horizontal—joining competing businesses in one area. Although the huge companies boosted the nation's production, they exercised unfair control over industry and faced legal battles that limited their size.

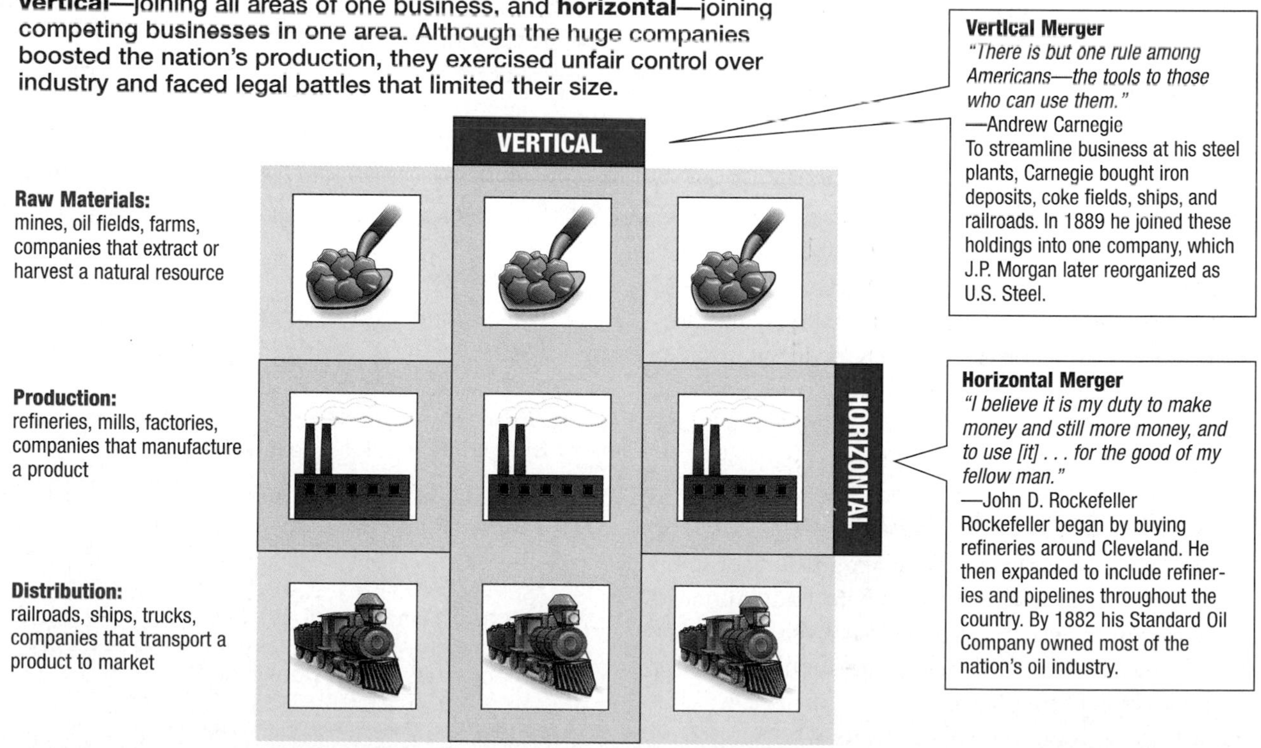

VERTICAL
Raw Materials:
mines, oil fields, farms, companies that extract or harvest a natural resource
Production:
refineries, mills, factories, companies that manufacture a product
Distribution:
railroads, ships, trucks, companies that transport a product to market
HORIZONTAL
Vertical Merger
"There is but one rule among Americans—the tools to those who can use them."
—Andrew Carnegie
To streamline business at his steel plants, Carnegie bought iron deposits, coke fields, ships, and railroads. In 1889 he joined these holdings into one company, which J.P. Morgan later reorganized as U.S. Steel.
Horizontal Merger
"I believe it is my duty to make money and still more money, and to use [it] . . . for the good of my fellow man."
—John D. Rockefeller
Rockefeller began by buying refineries around Cleveland. He then expanded to include refineries and pipelines throughout the country. By 1882 his Standard Oil Company owned most of the nation's oil industry.

The chart above illustrates horizontal and vertical business integration. When a business integrates horizontally, it merges all competing companies in one area of business. In vertical integration, one business controls all aspects of production. *What kind of business integration does U.S. Steel represent in the chart? What did it own?*

Some of these people, known as robber barons, built lavish mansions in New York City complete with solid gold bathroom fixtures. For the summer months many built castlelike estates in Newport, Rhode Island, which they dubbed their "cottages." Railroad tycoon William Vanderbilt's summer home cost $11 million. Outrageous displays of wealth were popular. At one debutante ball in Philadelphia, a young woman's parents ordered thousands of live butterflies (many of which drowned in champagne glasses) as decorations at the $75,000 party.

Social Darwinism

In the heady, expensive atmosphere of the Gilded Age, the struggle for wealth became a way of life for the most ambitious Americans. How did business leaders, bent on killing off competition in order to increase their control of the marketplace and make as much money as possible, justify their activities to a public raised on the ideology of a fair and open society? A new theory of human behavior provided an answer. It rested on the scientific theories of Charles Darwin about the origin of species and the evolution of humankind. Darwin argued that the plant and animal world had reached its present state through a long process of "natural selection" in which only the fittest had survived. Herbert Spencer, an English philosopher, loosely adapted these ideas, in a theory known as Social Darwinism, to explain the evolution of human society.

Progress, Spencer argued, occurred through competition in which the weak fell and the strong forged ahead. His strongest American supporter, William G. Sumner, put it this way: "If we do not like the survival of the fittest, we have only one possible alternative, and that is the survival of the unfittest."

American business leaders flocked to honor Spencer when he visited the United States in 1882. Here was a man whose theories justified their aggressive business practices and their attempts to eliminate weaker competitors. They heaped praise on his notion that government should never interfere with the separation of the weak from the strong because this would only hold back progress.

Concern for the Less Fortunate

Despite their seeming lack of regard for common people, many of the robber barons who had embraced Social Darwinism also supported the spirit of charity. They believed that the more fortunate should give back to society to benefit the public at large. Carnegie was but one of a host of powerful, rich patrons who supported the arts, education, and culture; funded public works; and established foundations.

These individual efforts had their limitations, however. As Jane Addams, a reformer of this time, commented concerning her native city of Chicago, "Private beneficence [charity] is totally inadequate to deal with vast numbers of the city's disinherited." Americans would have to learn new ways to cope with and solve the enormous problems created by population growth and industrialization in the United States between the Civil War and the end of the nineteenth century.

CULVER PICTURES

Newport, Rhode Island While the wealthy lounged on the steps of summer "cottages," others worked in factories and mines. *Why were the late 1800s known as an age of excess?*

Section Review

Vocabulary

1. Define: industrialism, national market, merger, horizontal integration, vertical integration.

Checking Facts

2. Name two technological advances that spurred industrial growth in the late 1800s.
3. How did the growth of railroads help to create national markets ?

Critical Thinking

Predicting Consequences

4. How might workers have reacted to the theory preached by Social Darwinists?

Linking Across Time

5. How do you think technological advances in computer science have changed the job qualifications that workers need today?

Social Studies Skill

READING STATISTICAL TABLES

Learning the Skill

Tables present statistical information by organizing it into categories. A statistical table can help you to identify patterns in employment in the United States.

Finding Information in a Table

To find the answers to statistical questions:

a. Read the title; then make sure that you understand the headings. There are three major headings: Total Labor Force, Labor Force, and Employment. Two of these heads are divided into smaller categories or heads; and of these, Manufacturing, Transport, and Service are subdivided again.

b. The lefthand column, the stub, lists another category of information, in this case, years. Find out which years the stub lists.

c. The columns of figures are the body of the table. They give data, by category, for each year.

d. Read down from one column heading and across from the corresponding year to find a measure of the labor force employed in a trade for that year.

Practicing the Skill

Study the table below, then answer the following questions:

1. In 1960 the Total Labor Force was 74,060,000. Why are there no figures in the next 2 columns?

2. What percentage worked in Trade in 1900?

3. Which category has lost the most workers?

4. By what percentage did employment in this field change?

5. Which categories gained the most workers?

Applying the Skill

Using another table, write 10 questions that can be answered from the table, and their answers.

Additional Practice

For additional practice, see Reinforcing Skills on page 225.

Labor Force and Employment, 1800–1960

Year	TOTAL LABOR FORCE (IN THOUSANDS)	LABOR FORCE (PERCENT)		EMPLOYMENT (PERCENT)											
								Manufacturing				Transport		Service	
		Free	Slave	Agriculture	Fishing	Mining	Construction	Total	Cotton Textiles	Primary Iron and Steel	Trade	Ocean Vessels	Railways	Teachers	Domestics
1800	1,900	72	28	74	0.3	1.0	–	–	0.1	0.1	–	2.0	–	0.3	2
1810	2,330	68	32	84	0.3	0.5	–	3	0.4	0.2	–	3.0	–	1.0	3
1820	3,135	70	30	79	0.4	0.4	–	–	0.4	0.2	–	2.0	–	1.0	4
1830	4,200	72	28	71	0.4	1.0	–	–	1.0	0.5	–	2.0	–	1.0	4
1840	5,660	74	26	63	0.4	1.0	5	9	1.0	0.4	6	2.0	0.1	1.0	4
1850	8,250	76	24	55	0.4	1.0	5	15	1.0	0.4	6	2.0	0.2	1.0	4
1860	11,110	79	21	53	0.3	2.0	5	14	1.0	0.4	8	1.0	1.0	1.0	5
1870	12,930	–	–	53	0.2	1.0	6	19	1.0	1.0	10	1.0	1.0	1.0	8
1880	17,390	–	–	51	0.2	2.0	5	19	1.0	1.0	11	1.0	2.0	1.0	6
1890	23,320	–	–	43	0.3	2.0	6	19	1.0	1.0	13	1.0	3.0	2.0	7
1900	29,070	–	–	40	0.2	2.0	6	20	1.0	1.0	14	0.4	4.0	1.0	6
1910	37,480	–	–	31	0.2	3.0	5	22	1.0	1.0	14	0.4	5.0	2.0	6
1920	41,610	–	–	26	0.1	3.0	3	27	1.0	1.0	14	0.5	5.0	2.0	4
1930	48,830	–	–	22	0.1	2.0	4	20	1.0	1.0	17	0.3	3.0	2.0	5
1940	56,290	–	–	17	0.1	2.0	3	20	1.0	1.0	17	0.3	2.0	2.0	4
1950	65,470	–	–	12	0.1	1.0	5	24	1.0	1.0	19	0.2	2.0	2.0	3
1960	74,060	–	–	8	0.1	1.0	5	23	0.4	1.0	19	0.2	1.0	2.0	3

The United States Bureau of the Census compiled the statistical data for this table on labor and employment. *How many different fields of employment are represented? What are they?*

SECTION 3

Populism and Protest

JULY 2, 1892: PEOPLE'S PARTY HOLDS FIRST CONVENTION

IN JULY 1892, THE DELEGATES OF A NEW POLITICAL PARTY MET IN OMAHA TO CEMENT THEIR ALLIANCE:

> We have witnessed for more than a quarter of a century the struggles of the two great political parties for power and plunder, while grievous wrongs have been inflicted upon the suffering people. . . . Assembled on the anniversary of the birthday of the nation . . . we seek to restore the government of the Republic to the hands of "the plain people."
>
> —Omaha Platform, July 1892

NORTH WIND PICTURE ARCHIVES

Stirring Words
Farmers and laborers listened to Ignatius Donnelly at the first Populist convention in 1892.

The delegates adopted the platform of the People's party, also called the Populist party, with great enthusiasm. The platform not only denounced the existing ills of society but also proposed a third-party remedy. The Populists represented a grand coalition of farmers, laborers, and reformers, which aimed to put government back into the hands of the people.

Populist leaders were as colorful and diverse as the causes they represented. Ignatius Donnelly of Minnesota, who had written the preamble to the party platform, was considered the greatest orator of Populism. Mary E. Lease, who forcefully represented farmers' interests, once advised Kansas farmers to "raise less corn and more hell." "Sockless Jerry" Simpson earned his nickname when he told a Kansas audience that he wore no silk socks like his "princely" Republican opponent. Georgia's Thomas E. Watson left the Democratic party to campaign for Populist ideals.

AS YOU READ

Vocabulary

- union
- strike
- injunction

Think About . . .

- the development of the Populist party.
- the problems facing farmers and their efforts to improve their situation.
- the development of labor unions in the late 1800s.

The Populists chose their candidates amid calls for restricted immigration and a shorter workday for industrial laborers. The party also aimed to convince the government to allow the free coinage of silver, a measure that would make silver, not just gold, legal tender. Many farmers thought this would cause inflation, thereby raising prices for farm goods, and would breathe new life into the faltering economy. The nomination for President in 1892 went to James B. Weaver, a seasoned campaigner from Iowa, who had been the candidate of the Greenback party in 1880. Second place on the ticket went to James G. Field, a former Confederate general from Virginia. As one historian observed, "Whether they knew it or not, the delegates were beginning the last phase of a long and perhaps losing struggle—the struggle to save agricultural America from the devouring jaws of industrial America."

Farmers Beleaguered

Falling Prices, Rising Debts

The rapid development of the agricultural West and the reorganization of Southern agriculture after the Civil War provided new opportunities for millions of American families. The changes also exposed these families to the financial hardships of rural life. The result was the first mass organization of farmers in American history.

Ironically the farmers' problem was rooted in their ability to produce so much. Immigrants as well as American-born farmers were tilling huge tracts of the Great Plains for the first time. Larger acreage, coupled with improved farming methods, meant bumper crops in most years. By the 1870s farmers produced more than the country—or the world—demanded. Prices dropped, as the graph shows. In addition two factors contributed to the farmers' financial problems: many farmers borrowed money to put more land under cultivation, and most of them had to pay high transportation costs to get crops to market.

Falling farm prices brought widespread rural suffering. On the Great Plains, many farmers had to borrow more money to keep afloat financially. In the South many lost their farms and became debt-ridden sharecroppers. When Eastern bankers began to foreclose on farm loans, thousands abandoned their homesteads.

Homesteaders in the late 1800s also faced nature's wrath. In 1874 a plague of grasshoppers devoured crops, clothes, and even plow handles. Droughts parched the earth in 1886. In January 1888, in the northern Plains the School Children's Storm killed more than 200 youngsters who were stranded at school or starting home.

Loneliness could be just as tormenting. One farm mother, who had not seen another woman for a year, walked across the prairie with her small children to see a woman who had come to live several miles away. The two strangers threw their arms around each other and wept.

Some families gave up and headed back East. They left behind bitter slogans: "In God we trusted, in Kansas we busted." The farmers who stayed began to seek political relief. The governor of Kansas received the following letter from a farm woman in 1894:

> I take my pen in hand to let you know we are starving. . . . My husband went away to find work and came home last night and told me that he would have to starve. He had been in 10 counties and did not get no work. . . . I haven't had nothing to eat today and it is 3 o'clock.

Farmers United

Farmers, like other beleaguered groups in society, realized that there is strength in numbers. As early as 1867 farmers banded together to form the Patrons of Husbandry, also known as the Grange. By 1875 there were about 1 million Grange members spread from New England to Texas, concentrated mainly in the South and the Great Plains. The Grangers wanted the government to

Production and Price of Wheat, 1860–1900

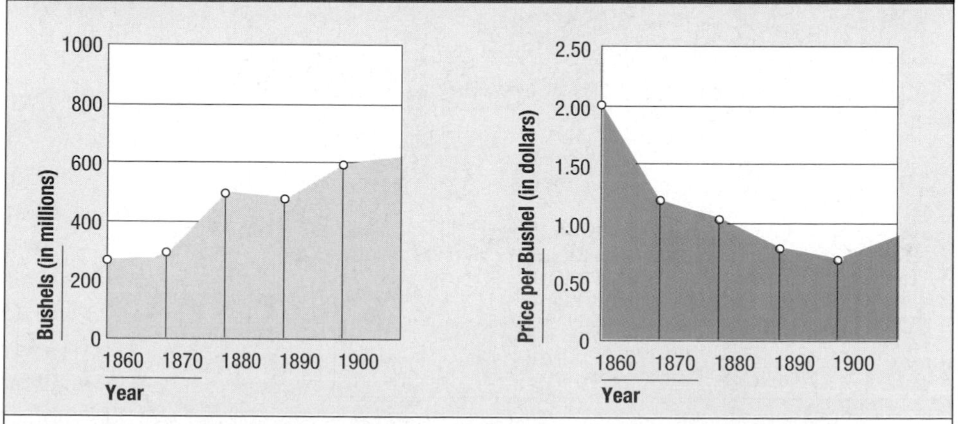

The graph on the left shows an increase in wheat production during the late 1800s. The graph on the right shows the price of wheat declining during this same period. *What conclusion can you draw from these two graphs?*

regulate railroad freight rates and to fund agricultural colleges. They also formed sales cooperatives, pooling their products and dividing profits.

In the 1880s farmers stepped up their political activism by forming groups known as Farmers' Alliances—one in the South, another on the Plains. The Alliances pooled the credit resources of their members to free themselves from the high interest rates banks charged. They formed marketing cooperatives to sell directly to large merchants and thus avoided paying extra costs to brokers. Such cooperatives could also buy bulk quantities of the supplies and machinery farmers needed.

The Populist Crusade

Despite action by the Farmers' Alliances and the Grangers, the plight of thousands of farmers worsened. By the 1890s they had become politically active as never before. The platform of the Populist party called for extensive reforms. Reformers believed that farmers and workers should be freed from the exploitative practices of banks, railroads, and merchants. Although James Weaver, the Populist candidate for President, soundly lost to Democrat Grover Cleveland in the election of 1892, his party made headway. The Populists gained 14 seats in Congress, won 2 governorships, and received the largest number of popular votes cast for any third party in the 1800s.

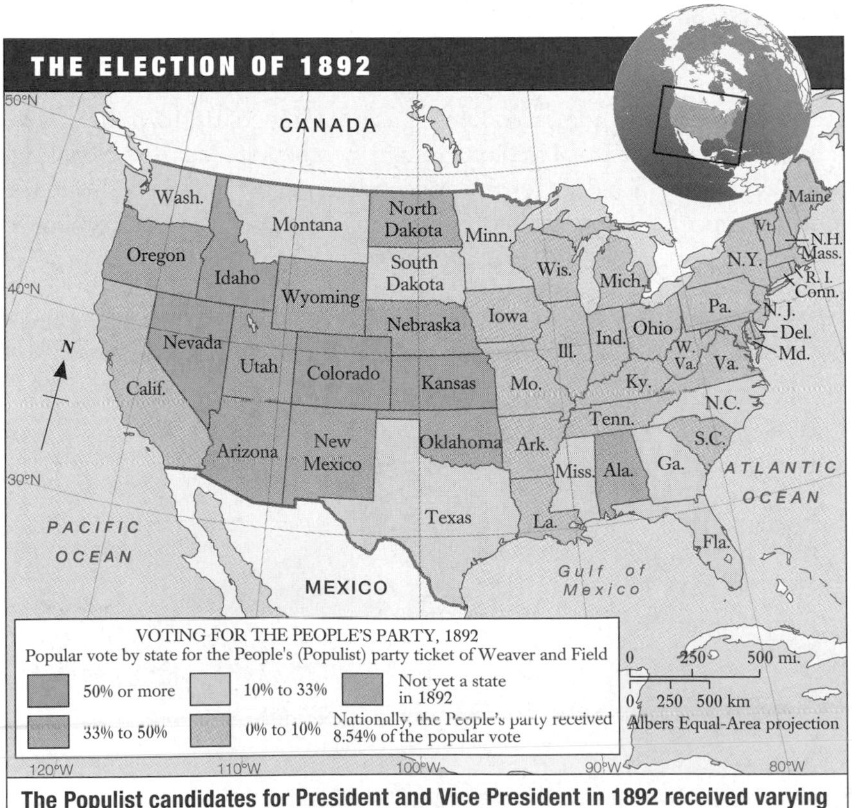

The Populist candidates for President and Vice President in 1892 received varying support from one state to the next. *In which states or regions did the Populists gain the most votes?*

Shortly after the election of 1892, the nation plunged into the deepest depression the country had yet known. In 1893 more than 2.5 million Americans, about 20 percent of the labor force, were unemployed. By the following year, the ranks of the unemployed had swollen to 4 million.

President Cleveland's seeming indifference to the economic problems caused by the depression created a popular revolt. Jacob S. Coxey, a quiet Ohio business owner, led a march of about 500 people from Ohio to Washington, D.C., to dramatize the plight of the jobless. Leaders read their grievances on the steps of the Capitol and were arrested for unlawfully trying to enter the building.

By the time of the 1896 election, the Populist party itself had declined, but some of its ideas entered the mainstream. The continuing depression forced the Democratic party into a more radical position on one key issue—unlimited coinage of silver. This stance led many Populists to support the Democratic candidate, William Jennings Bryan of Nebraska. Bryan waged a campaign in favor of "free silver," and secured endorsement by the Populist party. He traveled extensively, logging 18,000 miles (28,962 km) on the campaign trail.

The Republican nominee, William McKinley, took a more relaxed approach. McKinley had the support of big business. Standard Oil's $250,000 donation to the Republicans nearly exceeded the total amount in the Democrats' treasury. McKinley merely warned voters of the dangers of radicalism.

McKinley won by a comfortable 600,000 votes, suggesting that Americans in towns and cities heeded his warning. The discovery of gold in Alaska in 1898 increased the nation's gold reserves and eased more money into circulation, stemming the money crisis for many farmers. Populism began to decline as a political force.

The South Withholds Support

One factor limited Populism's strength in the South. By 1890 more than 1 million farmers belonged to the Southern Alliance—the Southern branch of the two Farmers' Alliances. In December the Southern Alliance met with other farmers' groups at Ocala, Florida, and drew up a list of concerns. These included cheap currency, the abolition of national banks, and the restriction of land ownership to American citizens.

Although this list resembled the Populist platform of 1892, the People's party failed to gain wide support in the South. The Southern Alliance advised its members to support major party candidates who favored agricultural interests.

The underlying reason for the failure of Populism in the South was the issue of white supremacy. The Southern Alliance feared that Populism might lead to gains for African Americans. Populist leader Thomas Watson tried to form an alliance of poor white and African American farmers. He argued that social class was more important than race. He urged citizens of both races to unite against the financial oppression that enslaved them.

Watson's career, however, mirrored the fate of Populism in the South. He was elected to Congress in 1890 but was defeated two years later as Democratic candidates who promised to exclude African Americans from political power gained support. Watson ran for President on the Populist ticket in 1904 and 1908. Embittered by his defeats, he turned against many who had supported him. He became racist, anti-Catholic, and anti-Semitic.

Labor Organizes

Unions for Skilled Workers

As early as the 1810s, skilled workers such as carpenters, printers, and tailors had formed citywide organizations to try to get better pay. Construction workers in many Eastern cities succeeded in getting a 10-hour day in 1834. As the workplace changed, however, so did the labor movement. After the Civil War, factory production replaced skilled labor. Employers often cut the cost of wages by hiring women and children. Workers, like farmers, decided to organize to maintain control over their wages and working conditions.

The first nationwide labor organizations developed during the mid-1800s. In 1867 bootmakers and shoemakers, whose wares were being undersold by machine-made products, formed the Knights of St. Crispin to try to block competition from unskilled workers. By 1870 this **union,** an organization for mutual benefit, had nearly 50,000 members. Like most early unions, however, the Knights of St. Crispin could not survive the high unemployment of the 1870s.

In 1877 a national railroad **strike,** or work stoppage, was the first of many violent confrontations between labor and the large corporations in the post–Civil War era. Clashes between railroad workers and state militias or federal troops sent in to break the strikes recurred in the 1880s. Then in 1885 successful negotiations with railroad magnate Jay Gould helped workers in all fields by convincing millions that they needed stronger unions.

THE BETTMAN ARCHIVE

Mother Jones **Mary Harris Jones became known by company bosses as "the most dangerous woman in America."** *What obstacles did Mother Jones overcome in her early life before becoming a champion for poor workers?*

The Knights of Labor

The first national labor union to remain active for more than a few years was the Knights of Labor. Tailors in Philadelphia formed it as a secret society in 1869, and it grew to national proportions in the 1880s. The Knights of Labor differed from other labor unions by accepting all gainfully employed persons, including farmers, merchants, and unskilled workers. The union proposed new laws, including one to cut the workday to eight hours and one to authorize equal pay for men and women doing the same work. Both of these were radical propositions at the time.

Women workers played a role in this growing labor movement. When Irish immigrant Mary Harris Jones lost her husband and children to yellow fever in 1867, she moved to Chicago to work as a seamstress. After losing everything else in a fire, she turned to the Knights of Labor for help. Soon she was one of its strongest campaigners. She traveled on behalf of labor for nearly 50 years—later organizing for the United Mine Workers. Beloved by her followers, she became known as "Mother Jones." The bosses, however, feared her. A West Virginia lawyer working for the mining companies called her "the most dangerous woman in America."

The American Federation of Labor

In 1886 the Knights of Labor reached its peak with more than 700,000 members. A less reform-minded group, the American Federation of Labor (AFL), soon replaced it as the leading union. Led by Samuel Gompers, a cigar maker born in England, the AFL concentrated on organizing skilled workers. It advocated using strikes to improve wages and hours.

Gompers was willing to accept the new industrial system as it was, but only if labor got greater rewards. He also advocated boycotts—organized agreements to refuse to buy specific products—as one means of peaceful protest. This tactic had only limited success.

Protests and Violence

The Labor Movement Meets Resistance

Workers in the late 1800s customarily worked 10 hours a day, 6 days a week. A strike for an 8-hour workday at the huge McCormick Harvester factory in Chicago led to violent confrontation on May 3, 1886. After police killed 4 strikers in a scuffle outside the plant, about 1,000 workers turned out for a rally at Haymarket Square.

The Haymarket Riot

Someone in the crowd threw a bomb during the Haymarket protest, killing 7 police officers and injuring 67 bystanders. The police then fired into the crowd, killing 10 and wounding 50. Uproar over the Haymarket riot continued when 8 radical strike leaders were put on trial for murder. Although no direct evidence that any of them had thrown the bomb could be found, 7 of the 8 were sentenced to death, and 4 eventually were hanged. The public outcry against labor organizers helped employers defeat the 8-hour workday reform.

CULVER PICTURES

Violent Clash Angry strikers taunt security forces sent to break up the Pennsylvania Homestead strike in this 1892 print. *Which company and which union were involved in the Homestead strike?*

The Homestead Strike

In 1892 another violent dispute took place in Homestead, Pennsylvania. The steelworkers' union called a strike when the Carnegie Steel Company reduced wages. The company hired 300 guards from the Pinkerton Detective Agency to protect its factories. Several people were killed when violence broke out between the strikers and the guards. The Homestead strike failed when most workers quit the union and returned to work.

Coeur d'Alene

Labor unrest spread to the West as well. Disputes arose between miners and mine owners over pay and conditions. Disputes also flared between nonunion miners and members of the Western Federation of Miners. Strikes plagued the Coeur d'Alene mining region of Idaho during the 1890s. Twice the strikes were broken when the governor called in federal troops.

The Pullman Strike

The depression that lasted from 1893 to 1897 brought further setbacks for labor. In 1894 Eugene V. Debs, the founder of the new American Railway Union, led a labor action against the Pullman sleeping car works near Chicago.

George Pullman saw his company town as a model industrial village where workers were paid decently and were also disciplined. "We are born in a Pullman house," said one worker, "fed from the Pullman shop, taught in the Pullman school, catechized in the Pullman church, and when we die we shall be buried in the Pullman cemetery and go to the Pullman hell."

As the depression of 1893 worsened, Pullman cut wages by one-third and fired many workers. Prices in the company stores and rents for the company houses, however, stayed the same. Angry Pullman workers joined Debs's railroad union in droves and went on strike in the spring of 1894.

Debs then led a strike of all American Railway Union members across

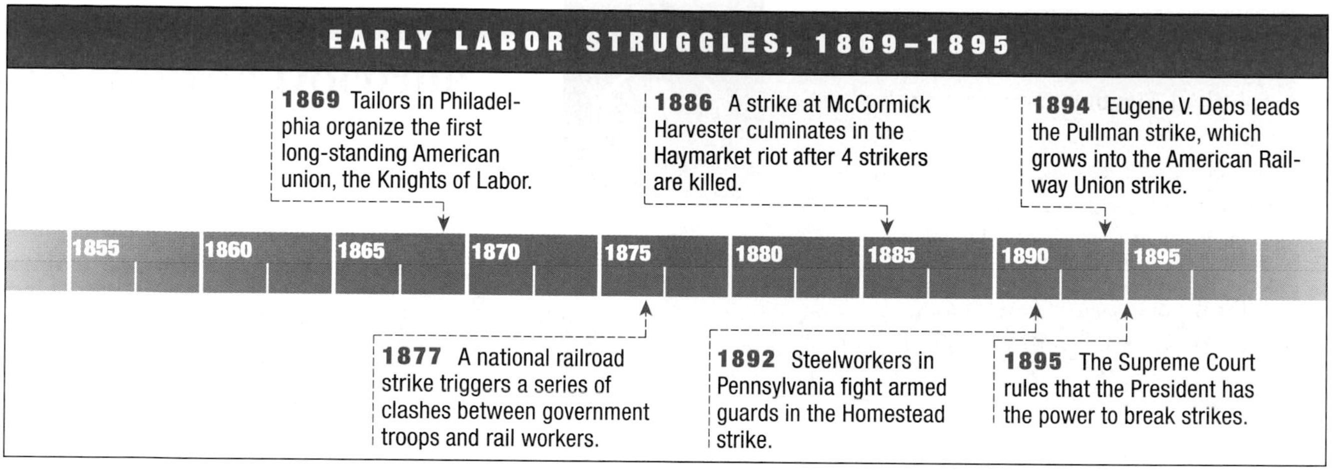

the country in sympathy with the Pullman workers. Debs promised to "use no violence" and to "stop no trains." Instead workers refused to handle trains with Pullman sleeping cars.

EARLY LABOR STRUGGLES, 1869–1895
1869 Tailors in Philadelphia organize the first long-standing American union, the Knights of Labor.
1886 A strike at McCormick Harvester culminates in the Haymarket riot after 4 strikers are killed.
1894 Eugene V. Debs leads the Pullman strike, which grows into the American Railway Union strike.
1855
1860
1865
1870
1875
1880
1885
1890
1895
1877 A national railroad strike triggers a series of clashes between government troops and rail workers.
1892 Steelworkers in Pennsylvania fight armed guards in the Homestead strike.
1895 The Supreme Court rules that the President has the power to break strikes.

Determined to break the growing union movement, 24 railroad owners persuaded President Cleveland to order United States Army troops to disperse the strikers. Violence once again centered in Chicago where strikers fought troops and railroad company guards. Strikers set boxcars on fire and brought rail traffic in the Midwest to a dead halt.

Labor did not stand united, however. Samuel Gompers refused to swing his powerful AFL behind the strike, causing it to collapse. The government arrested Debs and other union leaders and sentenced Debs to 6 months in prison. In 1895 the Supreme Court upheld the President's right to issue an **injunction,** an order to end a strike. Corporations thereby gained a powerful legal weapon that they used against unions for years.

Obstacles to Unity

Government intervention during major strikes repeatedly thwarted the nation's industrial unions. The unions, however, also tended to cripple themselves by largely excluding three important groups: women, members of minority groups, and unskilled workers. By 1900 only about 1 in every 33 American workers belonged to a union, and fewer than 100,000 of the 5.3 million working women belonged to unions.

In the South the great majority of African American workers could join only separate, segregated local unions. In the North and West white unionists feared the competition of African American workers, knowing that many bosses would pay them less.

The hostility of American-born workers toward immigrants also kept the unions weak. Suspicion often centered on German, British, or Russian immigrants, some of whom had more radical ideas about society and labor than Americans usually heard.

American-born workers strongly expressed their resentment of immigrants during the anti-Chinese movement in the West during the 1870s and 1880s. Angry mobs rampaged through Chinese areas in San Francisco, Tacoma, Seattle, and Denver in the 1870s. The Chinese Exclusion Act of 1882 reflected the widespread hostility against immigrant workers. The law halted immigration of Chinese workers and gained wide support from American labor unions.

By the turn of the century, big business had cast its shadow across most of the American economy, and in the turbulent labor struggles of the era, government took its place on the side of the employers against the workers.

Section Review

Vocabulary

1. Define: union, strike, injunction.

Checking Facts

2. How did successful growth of bumper crops ultimately hurt farmers?

3. What reforms did the Populist party advocate?

Critical Thinking

Determining Cause and Effect

4. How did attitudes toward women and minorities hurt labor unions in the late 1800s?

Linking Across Time

5. William Jennings Bryan said, "The great cities rest upon our broad and fertile prairies. Burn down your cities and leave our farms, and your cities will spring up again as if by magic. But destroy our farms, and the grass will grow in the streets of every city in the country." What did Bryan mean by this? Is this argument valid today? Why or why not?

At the same time that Spain sailed into the Caribbean, Britain and France sent troops to Mexico, pretending to collect war debts. The British soon retreated, but in 1864 the French leader Napoleon III installed Austrian Archduke Ferdinand Maximilian on the Mexican throne.

After the Union victory in the Civil War, however, American troops massed on the Mexican border, and Secretary of State Seward, citing the Monroe Doctrine, threatened war with France if its troops did not withdraw. By 1867 France complied, bringing new life to the Monroe Doctrine.

Worldwide Ambitions

Markets, Trade Routes, and Territories

Many factors contributed to the spread of expansionist fever in the United States after the Civil War. A patriotic fervor motivated many Americans. They felt that the acquisition of new lands would increase American glory and prestige throughout the world. Others saw the United States as a model country and felt a moral obligation to expand. They wanted to spread the American ideals of democracy and Protestant Christian values to people in other lands. **Missionaries,** or religious teachers, went to foreign lands to convert natives to Christianity. A new brand of American foreign policy maker supported these expansionist sentiments. These newly established foreign policy professionals wanted to make the United States a world power through trade, diplomacy, and conquest.

Amerikazin When trade with Japan began, Westerners exchanged culture as well as commodities. This 1861 woodblock print shows a family of American tourists. *What details of the figures and dress portray American style of the era?*

ARTHUR M. SACKLER GALLERY, SMITHSONIAN INSTITUTION

Perhaps the greatest motivation for expansion was the need for new economic markets. As settlers filled the Western frontier, farms and businesses produced more goods than Americans could buy. Henry Demarest Lloyd, a popular political writer at the time, wrote, "American production has outrun American consumption and we must seek markets for the surplus abroad."

Opening Closed Doors

The United States looked especially to Asia. American involvement in Asia actually began long before the Civil War. In 1844 the United States negotiated trade agreements with China and began to export cloth, iron, and fur to the Chinese in exchange for tea, silk, porcelain, and jade. Far Eastern trade became a boon to New England merchants and expanded naval production, especially after Commodore Matthew Perry "opened" Japan in 1854.

The Japanese had steadfastly refused contact with Western merchants and had closed their ports to European and American traders and missionaries for 250 years. Yet reports of Japan's great coal deposits had filtered out. Coal was an increasingly important resource for American steam-powered transportation and machinery. When Perry was sent to negotiate trade, it was important to the United States to be the first of the Western nations to access this resource. As he sailed into Tokyo's harbor under steam power, he so impressed the authorities that Japan began doing business with the United States.

By the 1880s the United States had made further inroads in the Far East by negotiating commercial treaties with Korea. The growth of these Asian markets stimulated the American economy and became a key factor in the United States's bid for world power.

Acquiring New Lands

Under the leadership of Secretary of State William Seward, foreign policy after the Civil War became more aggressive. Seward dreamed of an American empire that would include Canada, the Caribbean, Mexico, and Central America as well as Hawaii and other Pacific islands.

HAWAII STATE ARCHIVES

Hawaii for Hawaiians Queen Liliuokalani was determined to keep the United States from seizing Hawaii. *Why were the Hawaiian Islands so valuable to American interests in the Pacific?*

In 1867 Seward attempted to purchase Danish islands in the Caribbean for $7.5 million—a move that the Senate rejected. Congress also refused to approve Seward's plans for a United States naval base in the Dominican Republic.

He succeeded elsewhere, however. In 1867 the United States seized the Midway Islands in the Pacific Ocean, strategically located along the trade route to China and Japan. In the same year, Seward bought Alaska from Russia for $7.2 million.

Newspapers mocked Seward, and Alaska became known as "Seward's folly" and a worthless "polar bear garden." Seward, however, was wiser than his critics realized. Alaska paid for itself many times over with the gold that was discovered in the Yukon Valley, and its rich copper and oil resources, as well as seal and whale trade.

Moving into the Pacific

Expansionist ambitions continued in the Pacific in the last three decades of the 1800s. In 1878 the United States acquired rights to a naval station in Samoa, which was astride the trade route to Australia and New Zealand. Because Germany and England also had claims in Samoa, the three powers divided the islands in 1889.

The Hawaiian Islands were another Pacific prize. American planters and missionaries had thrived there after 1875 when the Senate allowed Hawaiian sugar to enter the United States duty-free. By 1881 the secretary of state declared the islands "essentially a part of the American system." In 1887, under strong pressure, King Kalakaua granted the United States rights to build a naval base at Pearl Harbor to protect American interests in the Pacific. Finally in 1893 American sugar planters in Hawaii staged a rebellion, determined to wrest control from Kalakaua's sister, Queen Liliuokalani. The queen had resisted American control with the slogan "Hawaii for the Hawaiians."

The United States Marines surrounded the palace, and the American minister cabled Washington: "The Hawaiian pear is now fully ripe, and this is the golden hour for the United States to pluck it." The palace coup succeeded, leaving American sugar planters and missionaries in political control of the islands. Congress moved toward official annexation, but this process would take another five years to complete.

War With Spain

Reports Become Real

The expansionist moves from the end of the Civil War through the early 1890s reached a peak in 1898 with the Spanish-American War. The war's outcome added significant new territory to the growing American overseas empire, and it demonstrated that the United States could turn its industrial muscle into formidable naval power in both of the oceans surrounding North America.

The origins of the Spanish-American War lay in the troubled island of Cuba, only 90 miles off the southern tip of Florida. The Cuban people had struggled since 1868 for independence from Spain.

Many Americans identified that struggle with their own revolution against Britain. Other Americans, beginning in the 1850s, had regarded Cuba as a natural part of the United States geographically and as an island of great economic potential because of its sugar-growing capability.

In 1895 Cuban rebels led by José Martí renewed their fight for independence, launching their first attacks from American soil. A ferocious war ensued. Spanish troops, commanded by Valeriano Weyler, forced some 300,000 Cubans into concentration camps, where tens of thousands died.

The war continued, and Americans elected William McKinley President in 1896. McKinley's campaign platform included claims to Hawaii and the Virgin Islands

Chapter 7 Review

Reviewing Key Terms

Choose the vocabulary term that best answers the questions below. Write your answers on a separate sheet of paper.

homestead	**union**
industrialism	**injunction**
merger	**expansionism**

1. If a corporation hoped to prohibit a strike or to end a strike, what kind of order might it ask a court to issue?

2. A settler who wanted to claim free land and who was willing to farm it for a number of years might do what?

3. What kind of foreign policy was the United States following when it set out to become a world power by acquiring new lands such as Puerto Rico, Hawaii, and Alaska?

4. What kind of economic and social system is marked by the development of large-scale industries concentrated in urban factories?

5. If a company's managers thought that market competition was too fierce in their industry, what solution might they choose?

Recalling Facts

1. How did cattle ranching and the work of cowhands promote the movement of settlers to the Great Plains?

2. What influence did the early railroad lines have on where people settled on the Plains and in the Far West?

3. Which groups of people benefited from the settlement of the West? Which groups did not benefit? Why not?

4. Identify three important inventions from the era of 1865 to 1900. What effect did these and other inventions have on the productivity of workers?

5. John D. Rockefeller once said, "The day of individual competition is past and gone." How did Rockefeller's own business practices illustrate his statement?

6. Explain the term *robber barons*. Why was it applied to people such as Andrew Carnegie and J.P. Morgan?

7. What were the main goals of the Populist party? Whose interests did the party represent?

8. How could labor unions have dramatically increased their size and power? What prevented them from doing so?

9. What was the Monroe Doctrine? Why was it important to the United States after the Civil War?

10. Why did the United States decide to keep control of the Philippines?

Critical Thinking

1. Predicting Consequences The 1868 Currier and Ives lithograph below captures the American march westward. Do you think the government could have kept settlers from taking Native American lands? What government measures might have been effective?

2. Making Inferences Wanamaker's, Macy's, and other department stores had marble staircases, expensive carpets, and chandeliers. Why do you think the owners spent so much money to decorate their stores? What values were they trying to appeal to in customers?

3. Making Comparisons Explain the difference between horizontal and vertical integration of industry. Why did Carnegie and other business leaders try to achieve both?

4. Making Generalizations Reread the material on the Populist party and on the labor movements. Based on this material, what generalizations can you make about farm and labor movements during the era? What evidence supports your generalizations?

5. Recognizing Bias President McKinley argued that the Filipinos were "unfit for self-government." What bias does this statement reveal? What might account for McKinley's bias?

THE HARRY T. PETERS COLLECTION, MUSEUM OF THE CITY OF NEW YORK

CHAPTER 7 REVIEW

Portfolio Project

The history of United States expansionism in the 1800s includes efforts to acquire or at least to influence Cuba, Hawaii, Alaska, Puerto Rico, and the Philippines. Choose one of these places and investigate the history of United States involvement there, carrying your research up to the present. Use your research notes to build a time line showing the major events in that involvement. Keep your time line in your portfolio.

Cooperative Learning

Form several groups to discuss the life stories of Carnegie, Rockefeller, and other robber barons. Groups should consider the following questions: Do you admire that kind of success? What is its impact on ordinary citizens? How do the robber barons compare with today's wealthy industrialists? Choose a representative to present your group's conclusions as part of a whole-class discussion.

Reinforcing Skills

Reading Statistical Tables The *Statistical Abstract of the United States* publishes annual statistics from the Bureau of the Census and other governmental agencies. Look at the latest edition in the library for information on a topic discussed in this chapter—for example, labor union membership by state, mergers of corporations, or income levels of households. Pick one table and photocopy it. What information is given in the table's title and subtitle? According to the headings, in what categories and subcategories is the information grouped? Look at the column on the left side of the table to find out how items in the table are organized. Describe any changes or patterns shown by the statistics in the table.

SECOND NATIVE AMERICAN EXPULSION

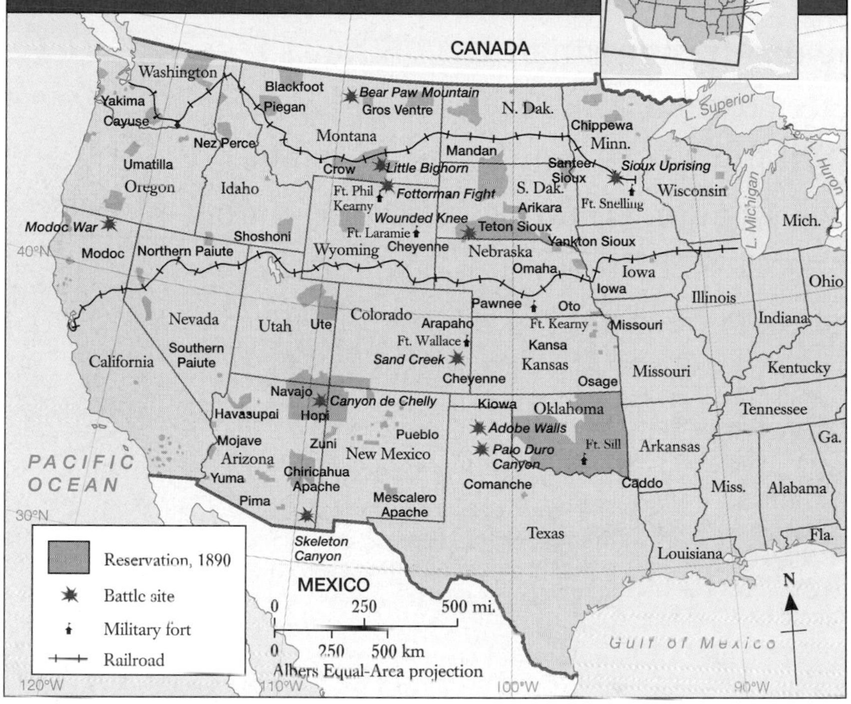

Geography and History

Study the map on this page to answer the following questions:

1. What Native American lands lay along the routes of the two transcontinental railroads shown on the map?

2. What battle took place in South Dakota? What Native American nation was involved?

3. What Native American peoples inhabited the lands that are now Arizona and New Mexico?

4. Where did the Battle of the Little Bighorn—sometimes known as Custer's Last Stand—take place? What Native American nation fought there?

5. What army fort was located near Cheyenne and Arapaho lands? What fort was near the Little Bighorn?

HISTORY JOURNAL

Write in your journal about what you have learned in this chapter. You can pull together the diverse subjects covered in the chapter by broadly interpreting "new frontiers" to include national, industrial, political, and international frontiers.

Then...

Levi's Riveted Waist Overalls

One day businessman Levi Strauss received a letter from a customer, Jacob Davis, describing a new way to make pants. Davis, a tailor, could not afford to patent the process. Instead, he persuaded Strauss to become his partner. In 1873 the two men received a joint patent for riveted clothing.

1 The word *denim* comes from the French "de Nimes," or "of Nimes," but the denim used by Strauss came from New Hampshire.

2 The pants all had button closings. The zipper was invented in 1891, but the Levi Strauss company did not use zippers in jeans until 1954.

COURTESY LEVI STRAUSS & CO. SAN FRANCISCO

FILE PHOTO BY DOUG MINDELL

Fun Facts

SELLING STRENGTH

A leather patch was added to the design in 1886 depicting two workhorses attempting unsuccessfully to pull apart a pair of Levi pants. The company never tried the stunt, but rather used the patch as a symbol of strength.

3 Copper rivets reinforced pocket corners and the base of the fly. The fly rivet, however, fell by the wayside during World War II when the government ordered conservation of precious metals.

COURTESY LEVI STRAUSS & CO. SAN FRANCISCO

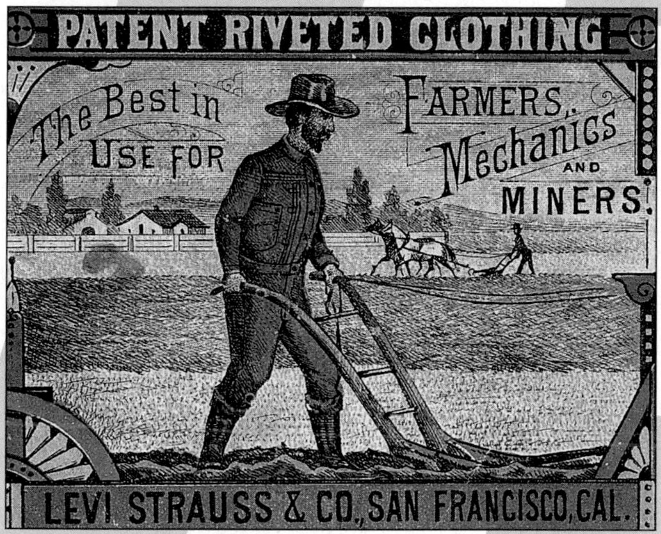

COURTESY LEVI STRAUSS & CO. SAN FRANCISCO

Stats

PROFILE

In Buttenheim, Bavaria, Hirsch Strauss taught his peddler's business to his youngest son, Levi. Upon Hirsch's death in 1847, 18-year-old Levi immigrated to New York City.

Hoping prospectors' gold would end up in his cash register, Levi took his dry goods business to San Francisco, where he brought his four nephews on board as partners.

With the success of riveted clothing, Strauss became active in San Francisco's business and cultural community, serving on boards of both utility companies and orphanages. He belonged to San Francisco's first synagogue and helped to fund a gold medal for students of its Sabbath School.

PRICE

Levi Strauss & Co. sold riveted clothing to stores. In 1879, the catalog advertised:

Riveted XXExtra Heavy blue denim pants........$17.50 /doz

4 During most of the 1800s blue dyes came from a plant called *indigo,* grown on South Carolina plantations. In the 1880s a chemical version, *indigotin,* became available.

...Now

JANE GRUSHOW/GRANT HEILMAN PHOTOGRAPHY, INC.

LEVI'S COMPARISON CHART

PORTFOLIO PROJECT

Consult the *Readers' Guide to Periodical Literature* to obtain information about Levi's clothing of today. Then draw or paste a picture of a pair of jeans in the center of a sheet of paper. Beside the left leg list the similarities between the Levi's jeans of 1873 and today's jeans. List differences beside the right leg. Include information on manufacturing, profitability, business, fashion, or culture.

WHAT'S IN A NAME?

The patented pants were called waist overalls in the Old West. The term *jeans* was not used until the 1900s, and the name "Levi's" meaning riveted denim pants did not emerge in advertising until the 1960s.

UNIT 3

1880–1920

The Roots of a Modern Nation

I. C. R. R.

Sister Carrie

BY THEODORE DREISER

In his novel Sister Carrie, *Theodore Dreiser captured the allure of rapidly expanding cities such as Chicago and New York for ambitious men and women in the late 1800s. Because he paid such careful attention to detail, Dreiser's portrait of city life at the time is as accurate as it is vivid.*

The Frenetic Movement of the City The abstract geometric shapes of Max Weber's *Rush Hour, New York* (1915) convey the hustle and bustle of the burgeoning cities of the early part of the century.

When she awoke at eight the next morning, Hanson had gone. Her sister was busy in the dining-room, which was also the sitting-room, sewing. She worked, after dressing, to arrange a little breakfast for herself, and then advised with Minnie as to which way to look. The latter had changed considerably since Carrie had seen her. She was now a thin, though rugged, woman of twenty-seven, with ideas of life coloured by her husband's, and fast hardening into narrower conceptions of pleasure and duty than had ever been hers in a thoroughly circumscribed youth. She had invited Carrie, not because she longed for her presence, but because the latter was dissatisfied at home, and could probably get work and pay her board here. She was pleased to see her in a way but reflected her husband's point of view in the matter of work. Anything was good enough so long as it paid—say, five dollars a week to begin with. A shop girl was the destiny prefigured for the newcomer. She would get in one of the great shops and do well enough until—well, until something happened. Neither of them knew exactly what. They did not figure on promotion. They did not exactly count on marriage. Things would go on, though, in a dim kind of way until the better thing would eventuate, and Carrie would be rewarded for coming and toiling in the city. It was under such auspicious circumstances that she started out this morning to look for work.

Before following her in her round of seeking, let us look at the sphere in which her future was to lie. In 1889 Chicago had the peculiar qualifications of growth which made such adventuresome pilgrimages even on the part of young girls plausible. Its many and growing commercial opportunities gave it widespread fame, which made of it a giant magnet, drawing to itself, from all quarters, the hopeful and the hopeless—those who had their fortune yet to make and those whose fortunes and affairs had reached a disastrous climax elsewhere. It was a city of over 500,000, with the ambition, the daring, the activity of a metropolis of a million. Its streets and houses were already scattered over an area of seventy-five square miles. Its population was not so much thriving upon established commerce as upon the industries which prepared for the arrival of others. The sound of the hammer engaged upon the erection of new structures was everywhere heard. Great industries were moving in. The huge railroad corporations which had long before recognised the prospects of the place had seized upon vast tracts of land for transfer and shipping purposes. Street-car lines had been extended far out into the open country in anticipation of rapid growth. The city had laid miles and miles of streets and sewers through regions where, perhaps, one solitary house stood out alone—a pioneer of the populous ways to be. There were regions open to the sweeping winds and rain, which were yet lighted throughout the night with long, blinking lines of gas lamps, fluttering in the wind. Narrow board walks extended out, passing here a house, and there a store, at far intervals, eventually ending on the open prairie.

In the central portion was the vast wholesale and shopping district, to which the uninformed seeker for work usually drifted. It was a characteristic of Chicago then, and one not generally shared by other cities, that individual firms of any pretension occupied individual buildings. The presence of ample ground made this possible. It gave an imposing appearance to most of the wholesale houses, whose offices were upon the ground floor and in plain view of the street. The large plates of window glass, now so common, were then rapidly coming into use, and gave to the ground floor offices a distinguished and prosperous look. The casual wanderer could see as he passed a polished array of office fixtures, much frosted glass, clerks hard at work, and genteel business men in "nobby" suits and clean linen lounging about or sitting in groups. Polished brass or nickel signs at the square stone entrances announced the firm and the nature of the business in rather neat and reserved terms. The entire metropolitan center possessed a high and mighty air calculated to overawe and abash the common applicant, and to make the gulf between poverty and success seem both wide and deep.

Into this important commercial region the timid Carrie went. She walked east along Van Buren Street through a region of lessening importance, until it deteriorated into a mass of shanties and coal-yards, and finally verged upon the river. She walked bravely forward, led by an honest desire to find employment and delayed at every step by the interest of the unfolding scene, and a sense of helplessness amid so much evidence of power and force which she did not understand. These vast buildings, what were they? These strange energies and huge interests, for what purposes were they there? She could have understood the meaning of a little stone-cutter's yard at Columbia City, carving little pieces of marble for individual use, but when the yards of some huge stone corporation came into view, filled with spur tracks and flat cars, transpierced by docks from the river and traversed overhead by immense trundling cranes of wood and steel, it lost all significance in her little world.

ANYTHING WAS GOOD ENOUGH SO LONG AS IT PAID—SAY, FIVE DOLLARS A WEEK TO BEGIN WITH.

Responding to Literature

1. **Would you have wanted to live in a city at the turn of the century? Why or why not?**
2. **In *Sister Carrie* the main character believes the city will provide her with new opportunities and a new life. Explain why cities would or would not represent to you such a gateway to opportunity today.**

CHAPTER

8

Progressive Reforms

JULY 7, 1903: WORKING CHILDREN MARCH TOWARD PRESIDENT'S MANSION

President Theodore Roosevelt faced a difficult decision. Should he meet with a handful of children who were marching 125 miles from Kensington, Pennsylvania, toward Oyster Bay, New York, to confront him at his home?

These marchers represented the thousands of children who worked in factories, mills, and mines. They were seeking the President's support for a law prohibiting child labor.

Though Roosevelt sympathized with the children, he feared supporting any demand voiced by their leader, radical organizer Mary Harris Jones, known as Mother Jones. President Roosevelt advocated reform, not revolution.

Finally, on July 27, after 20 days of marching, the children arrived. Through a representative, Roosevelt sent his reply: "No!" His fear outweighed his sympathy. Despite Roosevelt's refusal to meet with Jones and the children, the child labor debate did not go away.

The child labor debate was just one issue that Americans confronted between 1880 and 1920. Political corruption, labor unrest, and urban decay also plagued the United States during this period of rapid industrial and urban growth. By responding to these issues while avoiding radical upheaval, the American people fueled one of the greatest periods of reform in American history, the Progressive era. ■

HISTORY JOURNAL

Write your reaction to the working conditions for children as depicted in this photograph. What reforms would you initiate to change this situation?

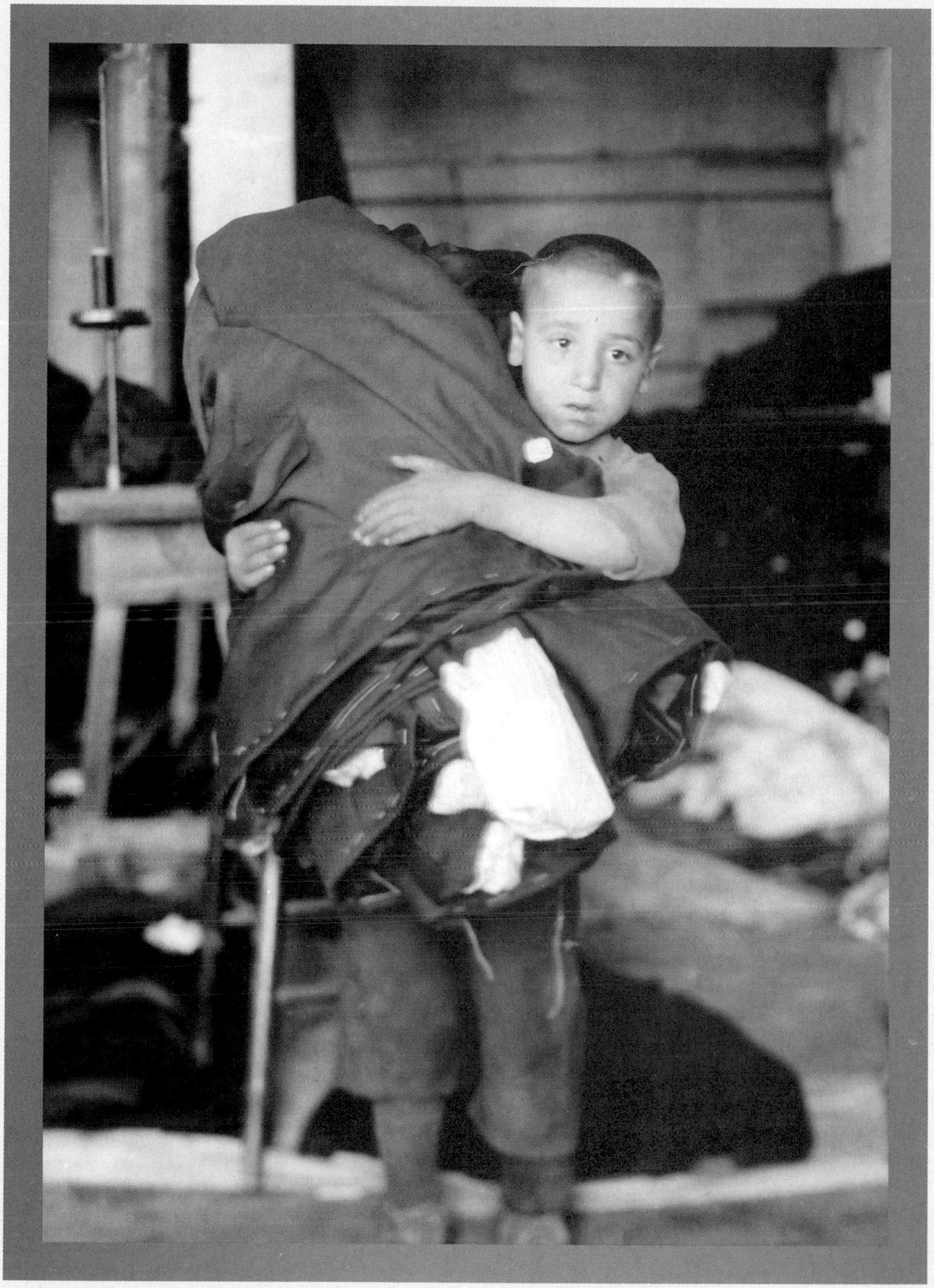

COURTESY GEORGE EASTMAN HOUSE

This young boy is carrying a bundle of work home after finishing his day in a New York City factory.

SECTION 1

Facing a New Order

1890: LIFE AND DEATH IN A NEW YORK CITY APARTMENT

PHOTOGRAPHER AND JOURNALIST JACOB RIIS HAD BREATHED ENOUGH STAGNANT AIR, SMELLED ENOUGH ROTTING FOOD, AND SEEN ENOUGH SICKLY CHILDREN TO KNOW HOW THE POOR OF NEW YORK CITY LIVED. In one of his writings he offered to take readers on a guided tour of an overcrowded apartment building:

> Be a little careful, please! The hall is dark and you might stumble over the children pitching pennies back there. Not that it would hurt them; kicks and cuffs are their daily diet. They have little else.
>
> Here where the hall turns and dives into utter darkness is a step, and another, another. A flight of stairs. You can feel your way, if you cannot see it. Close? Yes! What would you have? All the fresh air that ever enters these stairs comes from the hall-door that is forever slamming, and from the windows of dark bedrooms. . . .
>
> Here is a door. Listen! That short hacking cough, that tiny, helpless wail—what do they mean? They mean that the soiled bow of white you saw on the door downstairs will have another story to tell—oh! a sadly familiar story—before the day is at an end. The child is dying with measles. With half a chance it might have lived; but it had none. The dark bedroom killed it.
>
> —Jacob Riis, *How the Other Half Lives,* 1890

THE JASCOB A RIIS COLLECTION, MUSEUM OF THE CITY OF NEW YORK

Baxter Street Court
Jacob Riis photographed this tenement alley in New York City in 1888.

Between 1880 and 1920 people flocked to the cities from the countryside and abroad. While they often found opportunity, many also suffered from low wages, diseases, and wretched housing. How concerned citizens responded to these problems reshaped American government in the Progressive era.

AS YOU READ

Vocabulary

- tenement
- suburb
- urbanization
- immigrant
- political machine
- trust

Think About . . .

- the growth of cities in the United States.
- the impact of rapid urbanization on American life in the late 1800s.
- the experiences of immigrants in the United States.
- the reaction of middle-class people to industrialization, urbanization, and immigration.

URBAN GROWTH IN THE UNITED STATES, 1870–1920

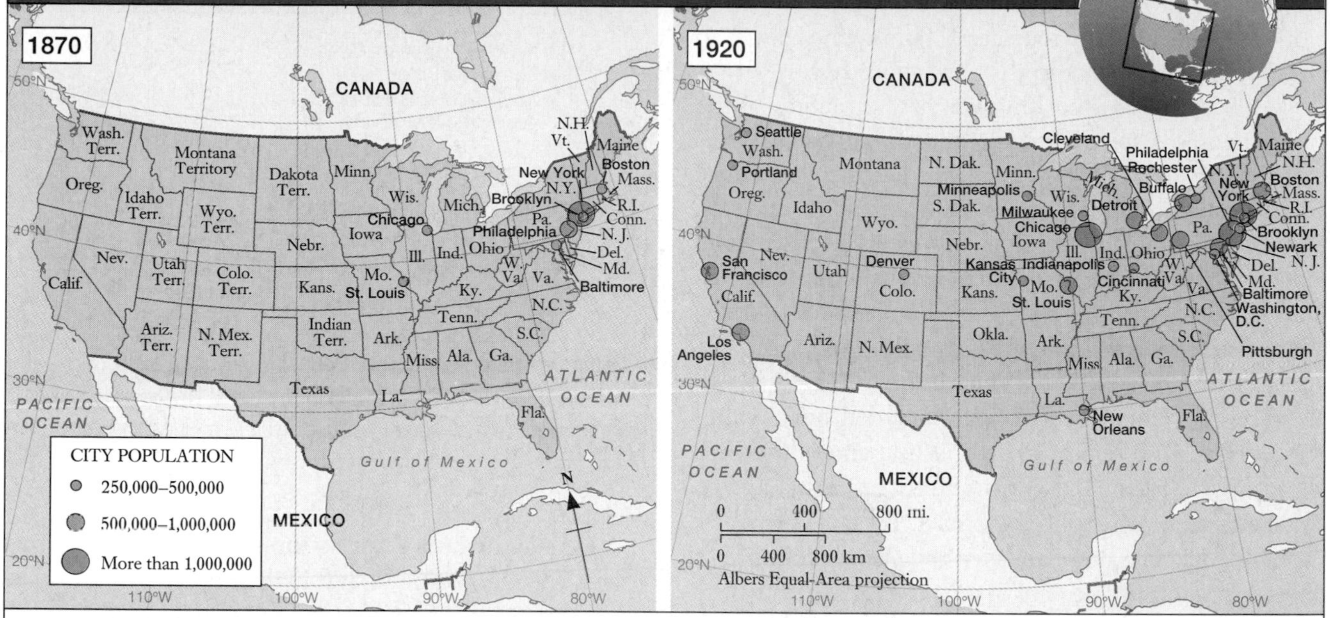

The map shows rapid urban growth near the Great Lakes, a region with large coal deposits and good transportation. *What new cities with populations of 500,000–100,000 appeared in 1920?*

Shame of the Cities

Urban Growth Brings Problems

The substandard conditions that Riis described in the New York apartment building, or **tenement**, could be found in many cities around the nation. As these cities grew, so did their problems.

Urban Growth

Cities in the United States expanded rapidly in the late 1800s. In 1860 only 20 percent of the people in the United States lived in towns or cities with populations greater than 2,500. By 1900 this percentage had doubled.

As American cities grew and became overcrowded, people who could afford to moved to **suburbs.** These communities blossomed at the edges of big cities. New forms of mass transportation developed; that enabled suburban residents to commute more easily to their jobs in the center of the city. In addition, these improvements helped everyone move around the city more efficiently. In 1873 San Francisco began construction of cable-car lines. A large cable powered by a motor at one end of the rail line moved passenger cars along. In 1888 Richmond, Virginia, pioneered the use of the trolley car, a motorized train that was powered by electricity supplied through overhead cables. In 1897 Boston opened the nation's first subway, or underground railway.

Changes in transportation were just one advancement in technology that fostered **urbanization,** the growth of cities. Before the mid-1800s water power ran machinery; therefore, factories had to be near rivers. With the application of steam power in the mid-1800s, though, factories could be established anywhere that fuel, usually coal, was available. Factory owners sought locations where they had dependable access to coal for fueling their steam-driven machinery and to minerals, sand, or other materials they needed to run their factories. They prized sites where rail lines linked with water routes, such as New York, Chicago, and St. Louis.

The opening of a factory in a city was a magnet that pulled in new residents looking for jobs. Many of these people came from rural areas where they could find no work. New machines—reapers, threshers, binding machines, combines—were rapidly replacing manual labor

Urban Growth in the United States, 1870–1920

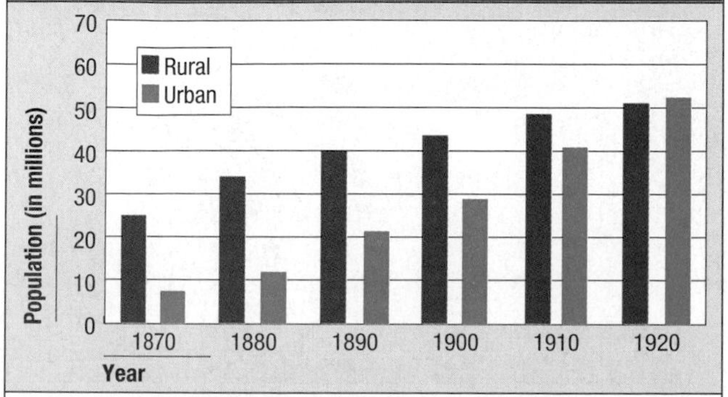

Within 50 years, urban population had quintupled. *According to the chart, by how much did the rural population change between 1870 and 1920?*

on farms. One commentator noted in 1898 that "four men with improved agricultural implements now do the work formerly done by fourteen." Those who moved to cities often found work in the expanding factories.

Although jobs were the primary attraction of the cities, people also headed to cities for other reasons. Cities offered pleasures considered luxuries in rural areas—plays, concerts, and stores with fancy clothes. City dwellers got new technology, such as electricity and indoor plumbing, long before rural residents did. (See One Day in History, pages 240–241.) Finally, cities offered anonymity. In large urban areas people could easily disappear from the scrutiny of their friends and families.

The movement to the cities included both whites and African Americans. In 1865 at the end of the Civil War, most African Americans lived on farms and in small towns throughout the South. By the late 1800s, though, African Americans were beginning to move to cities. More than 40 percent of the people in Atlanta were African Americans. In most Northern cities, the African American population was increasing but did not exceed 3 percent in any given city in 1915.

Immigration

Like rural citizens of the United States, Europeans poured into American cities in the late 1800s and early 1900s. The United States had always been a land of **immigrants,** attracting people from other countries to live there. Beginning around 1880, however, the immigrant stream became a flood. Between 1880 and 1920 about 25 million immigrants entered the United States. That was half as many people as lived in the entire country in 1880.

Changing Sources of Immigrants

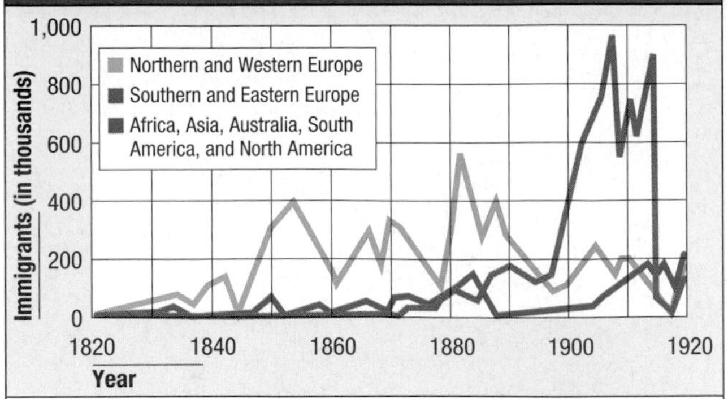

The numbers of immigrants from southern and eastern Europe increased dramatically in the early 1900s. *According to the chart, what range of years shows the greatest increase?*

Equally as important as the swelling tide of immigrants was the dramatic shift in their countries of origin, as shown on the chart on this page. Before 1890 most immigrants came from northern and western Europe—Great Britain, Ireland, Germany, and the Scandinavian countries. Many of these people spoke English, and most were Protestants. Between 1890 and 1920, though, about 80 percent of all immigrants came from southern and eastern Europe, from countries such as Italy, Greece, Poland, and Russia. They usually practiced the Roman Catholic, Eastern Orthodox, or Jewish faith. Most were poor, uneducated, and illiterate. The first sight of the United States for many of these newcomers was the Statue of Liberty and Ellis Island in New York Harbor. When Ellis Island opened in 1892, it marked the passage of processing immigrants from state to federal control.

Most immigrants arriving after 1880 settled in cities, because that was where jobs could be found. By 1920 nearly half of all urban dwellers were immigrants or the children of immigrants. The ethnic diversity of American cities impressed Danish immigrant Jacob Riis. Speaking of New York, he said, "A map of the city, colored to designate nationalities, would show more stripes than on the skin of a zebra, and more colors than any rainbow." One Polish immigrant found the large number of immigrants frustrating:

> I am polish man. I want be American citizen. . . . But my friends are polish people—I must live with them—I work in the shoeshop with polish people—I stay all the time with them—at home—in the shop—anywhere. . . . when

BROWN BROTHERS

Steerage Passengers Immigrants, such as those shown above arriving in New York in the early 1900s, often sailed on dangerously crowded ships. *Why did most immigrants to the United States settle in cities?*

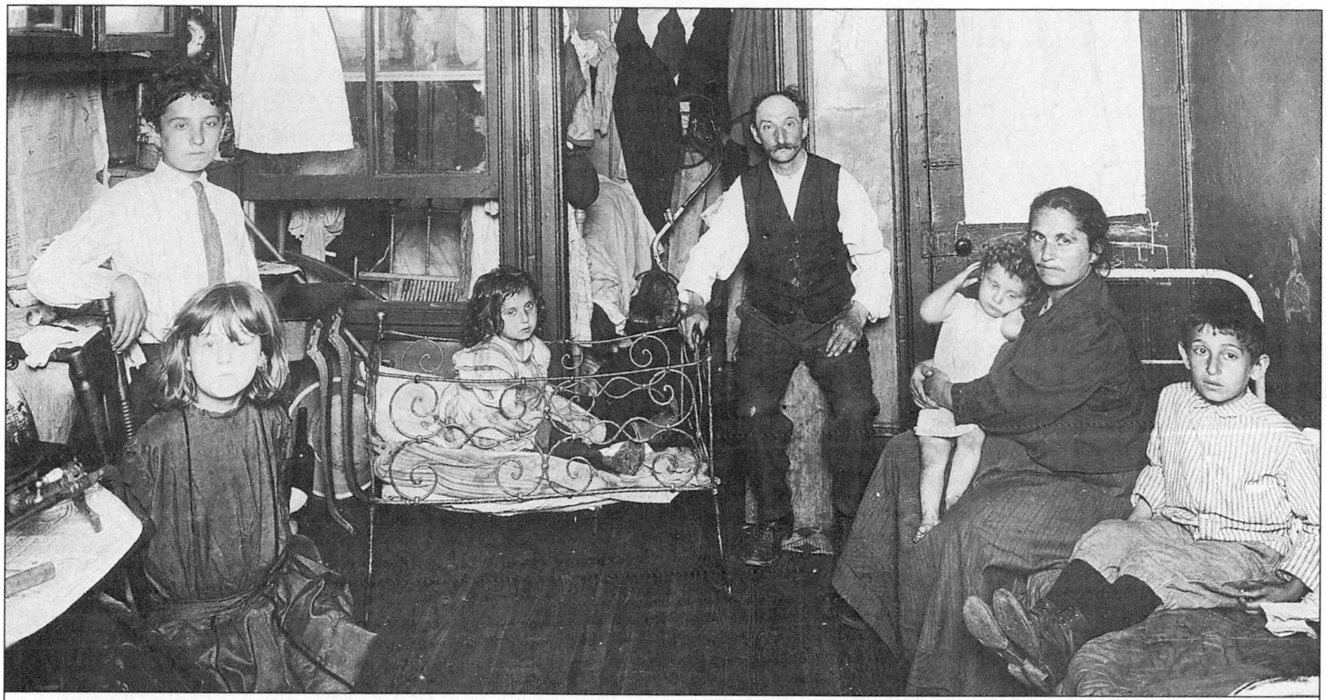

An Immigrant Apartment Jessie Tarbox Beals took this photo, "Room in a Tenement Flat," in New York City in 1910. In poor areas of New York, where political machines were strong, apartments housed an average of 1.9 people per room. *What other problems did city overcrowding create?*

> I come home—I must speak polish and in the shop also. In this way I can live in your country many years—like my friends—and never speak—write well English—and never be good American citizen.
>
> —Polish immigrant, Commission on the Problem of Immigration, 1914

Social Problems

Others found the growth of cities frustrating as well. Many Americans agreed with Congregationalist minister Josiah Strong that cities were wicked places and indeed posed threats to the very core of their civilization:

> The city has become a serious menace to our civilization. . . . Here [in the city] is heaped the social dynamite; here roughs, gamblers, thieves, robbers, lawless and desperate men of all sorts, congregate; men who are ready on any pretext to raise riots for the purpose of destruction and plunder; here gather foreigners and wage-workers; here skepticism and irreligion abound.
>
> —Josiah Strong, *Our Country,* 1885

Strong's attack on cities reflected his own dislike of immigrants. His views, however, also reflected the existence of real problems in cities. Many jobs paid so poorly that workers had to find other ways, sometimes illegal, to add to their income. Gambling, robbery, and extortion were widespread. In 1906 Chicago had an estimated 10,000 prostitutes, many of whom were under the age of 19. The city also had about 7,000 cocaine addicts. As cities grew, so did violence. The murder rate increased from 1.2 per 100,000 people in 1900 to 6.8 per 100,000 in 1920. Gang fights between rival political groups often marred election days.

Cities were not equipped to respond to their growing problems. Without enough police officers, crime was rampant. Without enough firefighters, fires quickly raged out of control. Without adequate sanitation systems, garbage and sewage piled up in the streets and polluted the drinking water. Two of the most severe urban problems were poor housing and political corruption.

Many of the people pouring into the cities could not afford their own apartments—and not enough places existed even if they could—so frequently they doubled up. Landlords divided small apartments into two or more even smaller units. Property owners converted horse stables, garages, and storage shacks into apartments. They added new buildings in the backyards of existing ones.

As buildings were carved up or constructed ever closer together, many apartments had no source of fresh air. Architects tried to combat this problem by designing dumbbell apartments. These structures were narrower in the middle than on the ends, like the letter *I.* With this design vertical spaces called air shafts could be left between buildings to allow light and air into each apartment.

The air shafts, though, became dangerous. Tenants threw garbage out of their windows into the shafts. The smell on a hot summer day could be so nauseating that tenants had to close their windows. Worse than the putrid smell were the rats, insects, and disease germs that thrived in the garbage.

Living conditions were bad for most newcomers to the city, but they were worse for African Americans. As a result of the racial prejudice of many whites, African Americans were restricted to living in only small parts of cities. As their population increased, the African American neighborhoods became even more overcrowded than the areas where immigrants lived.

Political Corruption

Politicians controlled the valuable contracts for building the new transportation lines, bridges, and firehouses that a growing city needed. Many showed more concern for filling their own pockets, however, than for solving the problems that Riis and others identified. A mayor could become wealthy overnight by accepting a bribe from a company trying to win a construction contract with the city. Businesses, then, usually added the cost of the bribe onto the contract with the city. Well-connected businesses prospered, and so did the politicians. Taxpayers paid the bill.

In order to keep the wealth flowing to themselves and their allies, politicians had to remain in office. They won the necessary votes by doing favors for people. The poor people of a city, especially immigrants and African Americans, often needed help—a job, a bag of coal, legal advice—that a wealthy politician could provide. All that the politician asked in return was a vote on Election Day. Some politicians developed and ran sophisticated organizations, known as **political machines,** to win votes. In each ward, or political district within a city, a machine representative controlled jobs, contracts, and favors. This person was the ward boss.

Controlling City Hall This lithograph by Joseph Keppler shows the power of Tammany Hall. *In what ways were political machines corrupt?*

THE BETTMANN ARCHIVE

The most famous political machine in the country controlled life in New York City and was headquartered in Tammany Hall. George Washington Plunkitt, a member of the New York State Assembly, was a minor boss in the Tammany Hall machine.

By observing Plunkitt in action and reading his diaries, a newspaper reporter pieced together a typical workday for Plunkitt. At 6:00 A.M., Plunkitt followed a fire truck to the scene of a fire and provided food, clothes, and temporary shelter for tenants who had just been burned out. "Fires," the reporter noted, "are considered great vote-getters." Later that morning, Plunkitt "paid the rent of a poor family" about to be evicted and "gave them a dollar for food." Then he found jobs for four men who had just been fired.

In the afternoon Plunkitt attended two funerals, one Italian and one Jewish. At each, he sat in the very front so everyone would see him. After dinner Plunkitt went to a church fair, where he bought tickets at every single fund-raising booth, and bought ice cream for all the children, "kissed the little ones, flattered their mothers, and took their fathers out for something down at the corner." At 9:00 P.M., he returned to his office, where he pledged to donate money to help a church buy a new bell. Later that night he attended a wedding reception and gave a "handsome wedding present to the bride." Finally, at midnight, after 18 hours of making friends and winning votes, Plunkitt went to bed.

Plunkitt's long hours paid off handsomely. His Tammany Hall associates rewarded him for his ability to deliver a large number of votes to party candidates each Election Day. For example, when the park board was planning a new park, they slipped word to Plunkitt of the location long before any plans had been made public. Then, from the unsuspecting owners, Plunkitt bought the land where the park would be established. Weeks later, when the board announced its decision to construct a new park, Plunkitt resold the land to the park board at a much higher price than he paid for it. By the time of his death, Plunkitt was a millionaire.

Industrial Disorder

Squeezing Small Businesses and Workers

Plunkitt was not the only person to prosper while others struggled just to survive. By 1910 the income of the wealthiest 2 percent of Americans accounted for almost 20 percent of the total income of all workers, double what it had accounted for in 1896.

LIBRARY OF CONGRESS

The Oil Industry This cartoon entitled *NEXT!* published in the magazine *Puck* depicts the control of Standard Oil over government and suppliers. *How did a large company also provide benefits to consumers?*

One reason for this growing concentration of wealth was the rash of business mergers and buyouts in the 1890s. Such consolidations usually resulted in the formation of **trusts,** a combination of companies dominating an industry, usually created for the purpose of reducing competition in that industry. Often a small handful of people, or even a single individual, ruled a trust.

The size of these large companies accounted for some benefits to consumers. Large firms could afford to develop and use expensive new machinery that, in turn, lowered the cost of producing goods. Companies were so large that any small cost-cutting measure could save enormous amounts of money. For example, by reducing the cost of each oil storage can by only 15 cents, Standard Oil saved more than $5 million a year. Such production efficiency could lead to cheaper retail prices. Items that were once luxuries, such as glass bottles, were now commonly available and inexpensive. "Never in human history was the creation of material wealth so easy and so marvelously abundant," pointed out one United States senator.

The senator cautioned, however, "Here are dangers it will behoove us to gravely contemplate." The new, efficient companies exacted a heavy cost in human suffering. Though wages increased slowly between 1890 and 1910, most workers lived just outside the reach of financial ruin. Everyday expenses such as rent, food, and clothes absorbed virtually all of the income of typical workers.

In between the wealthy owners and the poorly paid laborers was a growing middle class. This group consisted of managers, clerks, small-business owners, college professors, members of the clergy, lawyers, and other professionals. The middle class, which was able to afford the mass-produced goods, praised the technological triumphs that led to greater production efficiency. They felt threatened, however, by both the rich and the poor and blamed the growing problems of society on these groups:

> Nearly all problems which vex society have their sources above or below the middle-class man. From above come the problems of predatory wealth. . . . From below come the problems of poverty and of pigheaded and brutish criminality.
>
> —*California Weekly,* December 18, 1908

To many educated, honest, middle-class Americans, the traditional values that they prized were under assault. Trusts, though efficient, threatened to squeeze small businesses out of existence. Workers, plagued by crime and poverty, seemed vulnerable to revolutionary calls for radical change. Middle-class Americans and their allies responded to these threats by calling for a return to traditional values—economic opportunity, religious morality, political honesty, and social stability. This effort to reform the United States and preserve its democratic values became known as the Progressive movement.

Section Review

Vocabulary

1. Define: tenement, suburb, urbanization, immigrant, political machine, trust.

Checking Facts

2. What combination of factors attracted rural Americans as well as immigrants to cities in the United States?
3. What effect did urban and industrial growth have on life in American cities?

Critical Thinking

Determining Cause and Effect

4. How do you think the continuous flow of new workers into the cities affected the wages of all workers?

Linking Across Time

5. In what ways do the conditions in American cities of the late 1800s and early 1900s resemble those in cities today? In what ways do they differ?

SPORTS: New baseball rule allows a batter to walk to first base after receiving nine balls.

One Day in History

Thursday, January 1, 1880

MARKET BASKET

Here is where a dollar will go:

- Parasol . . . . 50¢
- Perfumed kid gloves
  - Two-button $1
  - Four-button $1.50
- Hat, trimmed $2.50

COURTESY THE OAKLAND MUSEUM HISTORY DEPARTMENT, OAKLAND, CA

- Imitation-gold pocket watch $12
- Corset $3
- Muslin shirt. $1
- Neckwear—ties, bows, scarves . . . . 25¢
- Baseball, by mail $1.50
- Dental fee: vitalized or gas . . . . 25¢
- Boys' short pantaloons . . . . 50¢
- Walking skirt with ruffle . . . . 50¢
- Black Elysian overcoat $4.50
- Waterproof cape $8.25
- Admission to
  - New York circus . . . 25¢, 50¢
  - Reserved. . . . . 25¢ extra

UPI/BETTMANN

The Edison Lamp Inventor Thomas A. Edison stands in his laboratory holding the first incandescent vacuum light tube, which uses carbonized cotton thread as a filament.

Edison's New Lamp

An invention of great promise; Menlo Park illuminated

MENLO PARK—On New Year's Eve, the little hamlet of Menlo Park, New Jersey, was illuminated by 40 streetlamps lighted with electricity. Tonight the display will be repeated. In addition to the streetlamps, there were 100 electric burners in operation in machine buildings, private buildings, and Professor Edison's laboratory. The number of lights will be increased daily until there are 800. One of the lamps now in use has been lighted, day and night, for 17 days. The others have been used for 2 weeks. The Pennsylvania Railroad Company carried passengers to and from the park at a reduced fare, and as many as 3,000 people took the opportunity to witness the illumination.

NATION: By an act of Congress, women have won the right to practice law and to argue cases before the United States Supreme Court.

CULVER PICTURES

Latimer Joins Hiram Maxim

BOSTON—After illustrating the workings of the telephone's components for Alexander Graham Bell's 1876 patent, Lewis Howard Latimer has become interested in the incandescent lightbulb invented by Thomas Edison. Latimer has agreed to join Hiram Maxim's United States Electric Lighting Company as a patent draftsman. He will work on patenting methods for manufacturing superior carbon filaments used in the new electric lamps, hoping to make the lamps last longer and cost less.

PHOTOGRAPHS AND PRINTS DIVISION, SCHOMBURG CENTER FOR RESEARCH IN BLACK CULTURE, NEW YORK PUBLIC LIBRARY, ASTOR, LENOX AND TILDEN FOUNDATIONS.

Master Draftsman Lewis Latimer earns recognition for creating technical drawings that illustrate patents.

THE PIERPONT MORGAN LIBRARY, NEW YORK, THE GILBERT AND SULLIVAN COLLECTION.

Gilbert and Sullivan's New Opera Opens The *Pirates of Penzance,* direct from London, debuted last evening at the Fifth Avenue Theatre in New York City.

MUSIC

THIS YEAR'S HIT SONGS

"Oh! Dem Golden Slippers"

"In the Evening by the Moonlight"

"A Policeman's Lot Is Not a Happy One"

BOOKS

NEW AND SOON TO BE RELEASED

Ben-Hur by Lew Wallace

Daisy Miller by Henry James

Five Little Peppers and How They Grew by Margaret Sidney

The Brothers Karamazov by Fyodor Dostoyevsky

Dance the Night Away

Use Johnson's Powdered Wax for Dancing Floors

Sprinkle lightly over the surface of the floor and the feet of the dancer will do the rest.

A steal for less than 20¢

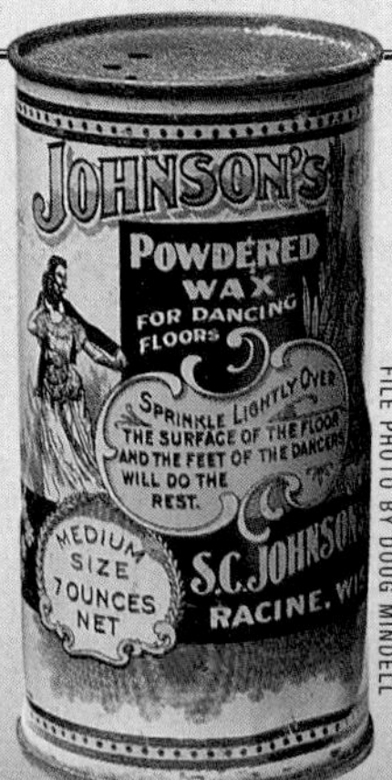

FILE PHOTO BY DOUG MINDELL

SECTION 2

A Generation of Reformers

EARLY 1890s: "SAINT JANE" OPENS NURSERY FOR THE POOR

UNIVERSITY OF ILLINOIS AT CHICAGO

Children's Advocate
Jane Addams, founder of Hull House, reads a picture book to the young children in her nursery.

WITHIN A YEAR AFTER MOVING TO CHICAGO IN 1889, YOUNG, IDEALISTIC JANE ADDAMS MET THREE CHILDREN WHOM SHE NEVER FORGOT. "One had fallen out of a third-story window, another had been burned, and the third had a curved spine due to the fact that for three years he had been tied all day long to the leg of the kitchen table." The children had each been left alone, day after day, while their parents worked. Their parents earned so little money that they could not hire anyone to watch their children.

Addams, a quiet, dignified woman from a well-to-do family in a small Illinois town, had moved to Chicago because she wanted to help the poor. She and a friend had purchased a large, but run-down, old home known as Hull House in the midst of a densely populated immigrant neighborhood. They repaired the house and made it into a community center where neighborhood residents could learn to speak English, discuss political events, and hold celebrations. In addition, because of those three injured children, Addams opened a day nursery. Working parents no longer had to leave their young children unsupervised during the day. For her work, neighbors referred to her as Saint Jane.

Addams realized that the machines that had brought such great prosperity were also the engines of great

AS YOU READ

Vocabulary
- progressive
- muckraker
- social gospel movement
- settlement house

Think About . . .
- the different types of people who became progressives.
- the aspects of American society that were criticized by the progressives.
- the different ways progressives tried to address problems associated with urbanization and industrialization.

misery. Jane Addams was just one of many Americans who, at the turn of the century, advocated reforms to confront the problems caused by industrialization and urbanization. The efforts of these reformers, the **progressives,** dominated the political landscape of the early 1900s.

Progressive Ideals

Protecting the Public Interest

During Jane Addams's youth the United States consisted mostly of small towns, small businesses, and small-scale problems. As Addams grew up, though, she watched larger cities, larger businesses, and larger problems develop. Small-town politicians never practiced corruption on the scale of George Washington Plunkitt and his Tammany Hall cronies. Rural poor people did not live in concentrations of garbage and stagnant air as did city tenement dwellers. A village blacksmith could never control a town the way a large steel company could dominate the people of a city.

Like the populists of the 1880s and 1890s, progressives feared the concentration of power in the hands of the wealthy few. While hardworking immigrants could not afford to provide for their hungry and ill children, financiers like J.P. Morgan became millionaires by manipulating ownership of the companies for which these immigrants toiled. Through campaign contributions and bribes, corporate trusts bought influence with lawmakers. Progressives wanted reforms to protect the public interest.

Unlike the populists, who usually lived in rural areas, the progressives generally lived in cities. By the 1890s cities faced crippling problems: housing shortages, political corruption, and spiraling crime rates. In the chaotic cities, progressives wanted to reestablish order and stability.

Progressives were also unlike populists in their greater faith in experts. While populists emphasized the wisdom of average people, progressives focused on the ability of knowledgeable experts to analyze and solve problems. Just as Thomas Edison had conquered technological problems in developing the lightbulb, progressives believed that trained experts could analyze and conquer crime, alcoholism, and political corruption. Many progressives praised business owners for their expertise in solving the problems of producing and distributing goods and in running a store or a factory smoothly. Though fearing the power of big businesses, progressives often respected the efficient methods they used.

Progressive Analysts

Analyzing and Publicizing Society's Problems

Progressives looked to government to solve problems. Virtually all progressives shared the hope that a well-run government could protect the public interest and restore order to society. Beyond this hope, though, progressives differed widely in their beliefs, goals, and actions.

New Intellectuals

Changes in higher education influenced many progressives. Between 1870 and 1920 college enrollment increased more than tenfold, and many schools established separate social science departments, such as economics, political science, and sociology. These departments attempted to analyze human society with the same objectivity that scientists used to study nature. Their establishment reflected a growing faith in the ability of people to analyze society and solve human problems. Many social science professors and the students they influenced became progressives. For example, Columbia University historian Charles Beard applied his knowledge of American history to reforming corrupt city governments. Not all the new intellectuals, however, worked for universities. Mary Ritter Beard, wife of Charles, wrote extensively about how scholars had ignored the contributions of women in history.

One of the influential members of the new social science fraternity was Lester Ward. Much of Ward's childhood was spent "roaming over those boundless

THE BETTMANN ARCHIVE

Lester Ward Brown University appointed Lester Ward professor of sociology in 1906 at the age of 65. *What did the new college social science departments attempt to analyze and why?*

prairies" of Illinois and Iowa in the mid-1800s "and admiring nature." After surviving three wounds as a Union army soldier in the Civil War, he got a job as a minor clerk in the United States Treasury Department. For the next 40 years, he held a variety of federal government jobs. For most of this period, he worked for the United States Geological Survey, studying rocks, plants, and animals in the lightly settled territories of the West.

In his free time, Ward taught himself Greek, Latin, French, and German, and participated in various book clubs, debating the latest ideas on science, history, and philosophy. In 1869 he began outlining his first book, *Dynamic Sociology,* which he completed in 1883. In this book and five others, Ward analyzed social concerns just as scientifically as he studied natural phenomena. He challenged the widely held belief that it was natural for the strong, such as the owners of large corporations, to prosper while the weak, the workers, suffered. What was natural, Ward argued, was for people to control and change their social environment—the laws, customs, and relationships among people—for their own benefit. "The day has come for society to take its affairs into its own hands and shape its own destinies."

LIBRARY OF CONGRESS

Exposing Unsanitary Conditions **The publication of *The Jungle* led to the passage of the first federal food-inspection laws.** *How did Sinclair prepare himself to write about exploited workers?*

Government's Job

The shaping of a society's destiny, according to Ward, was the job of the government. For example, if tenements were inadequate, then government should pass laws, spend money, or take other steps to improve housing. Ward believed that a larger role by government would improve the social environment and expand the options of individuals. "The true function of government," Ward proclaimed, "is not to fetter, but to liberate the forces of society, not to diminish but to increase their effectiveness."

In 1906 at age 65, Ward finally took his first full-time academic position. He became professor of sociology at Brown University. Social scientists such as Ward claimed that scientific study of human problems would provide better ways to run the cities. These new intellectuals often depended upon others, however, to motivate the public and to attack specific problems with specific solutions.

Angry Writers

Among those who motivated the public were many writers known as **muckrakers.** That label came from a character in a seventeenth-century book, *Pilgrim's Progress,* who spent all of his time raking up the dirt and filth, or muck, on the ground. The muckrakers combined careful research, vivid writing, and intense moral outrage. Most of these crusaders wrote long, investigative articles for popular magazines such as *McClure's, Collier's, Cosmopolitan,* and *American Magazine.* Writers attacked wealthy corporations that exploited child labor, corrupt police departments that protected prostitution rings, and prestigious churches that owned disease-ridden tenements. Ida Tarbell, a "conventional-minded lady, sweet and gracious," was one of the most famous of the muckrakers. She wrote a series of widely read articles detailing the rise of the Standard Oil Company. Tarbell exposed the ruthless methods used by its owner, John D. Rockefeller, to crush his competition—including Tarbell's father.

In addition to articles, some muckrakers, such as Upton Sinclair, wrote novels. Sinclair grew up in near-poverty in Baltimore. His father, a salesperson, suffered from alcoholism and was never very successful. By 1904 the 26-year-old Sinclair was a gentle, innocent-looking young writer. He had already completed four novels, each featuring a courageous individual who fought against social injustice. In that year a radical newspaper, *Appeal to Reason,* hired Sinclair to write a novel about the exploitation of workers in the United States.

To prepare for the contracted novel, Sinclair lived among the stockyard workers of Chicago for seven weeks. He later recalled how he sat "in their homes at night, and talked with them and then in the daytime they would lay off their work, and take me around, and show me whatever I wished to see. I studied every detail of their lives."

Based on his close observations of how workers lived, Sinclair wrote *The Jungle,* a novel about a Lithuanian immigrant who worked in the meatpacking

Preparing Meat for Consumers Complaints about unsafe meat preparation began in 1899, after United States soldiers got seriously ill from eating spoiled canned meat. *How would photos like this one of the Chicago stockyards around 1900 support the charges made by Upton Sinclair?*

industry. In focusing on one worker's life, Sinclair intended to arouse public sympathy for the common laborer. His graphic descriptions of the unsanitary conditions in the packing plant, however, sparked a reaction to the meat industry itself that completely overshadowed his intended focus. As Sinclair noted somewhat sadly, "I aimed at the public's heart, and by accident I hit it in the stomach." His book made consumers ill—and angry:

> There would come all the way back from Europe old sausage that had been rejected, and that was moldy and white—it would be dosed with borax and glycerine, and dumped into the hoppers, and made over again for home consumption. There would be meat that had tumbled out on the floor, in the dirt and sawdust, where the workers had tramped and spit uncounted billions of consumption germs. There would be meat stored in great piles in rooms; and the water from leaky roofs would drip over it, and thousands of rats would race about on it.
>
> —Upton Sinclair, *The Jungle,* 1906

Sinclair, like each of the muckrakers, had a vision of a just and orderly society. In Sinclair's society workers would receive adequate wages and consumers would purchase healthful food. The muckrakers' aim was to awaken people to the growing social, economic, and political evils and inequities in the nation.

Religious Reformers

Another group of progressives also appealed to the conscience of Americans. The **social gospel movement** included Christians who emphasized the role of the church in improving life on the earth rather than in helping individuals get into heaven.

One leader of the social gospel movement was Walter Rauschenbusch. Described by one journalist as "a tall, spare man, with a twinkle in his eyes," Rauschenbusch followed in the footsteps of six family generations and became a minister. After studying theology in Rochester, New York, and in Germany, he became pastor of the Second German Baptist Church in New York City.

Rauschenbusch's theological training did not prepare him for what he confronted in New York City. His church bordered a region aptly named Hell's Kitchen. Unemployment, alcoholism, and desperation plagued residents of this poverty-stricken neighborhood.

Rauschenbusch, as a devout Christian, turned to the Bible and his faith for a proper response to the new industrial system that made "the margin of life narrow in order to make the margin of profit wide." He concluded that the cause of many social ills was fierce competition. Owners and managers, many of whom were practicing Christians, believed they had to be ruthless or they would go out of business:

> Competitive commerce . . . makes men who are the gentlest and kindliest friends and neighbors, relentless taskmasters in their shops and stores, who will drain the strength of their men and pay their female employees wages on which no girl can live without supplementing them in some way.
>
> —Walter Rauschenbusch, *Christianity and the Social Crisis,* 1907

Rauschenbusch and other advocates of the social gospel believed that environmental conditions such as unemployment and poverty, and not an individual's personal depravity, caused the ills in society. Hence, they believed, every Christian should strive to better the economic and political conditions in the world.

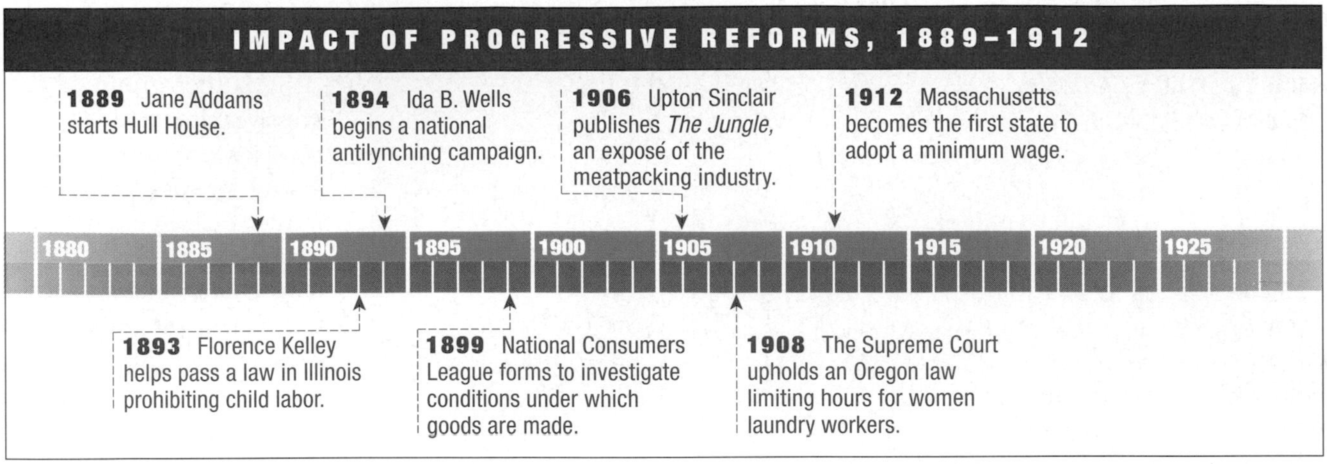
IMPACT OF PROGRESSIVE REFORMS, 1889–1912
1889 Jane Addams starts Hull House.
1894 Ida B. Wells begins a national antilynching campaign.
1906 Upton Sinclair publishes The Jungle, an exposé of the meatpacking industry.
1912 Massachusetts becomes the first state to adopt a minimum wage.
1880
1885
1890
1895
1900
1905
1910
1915
1920
1925
1893 Florence Kelley helps pass a law in Illinois prohibiting child labor.
1899 National Consumers League forms to investigate conditions under which goods are made.
1908 The Supreme Court upholds an Oregon law limiting hours for women laundry workers.

Progressive Activists

Solving Society's Problems

Most progressives who analyzed problems took action to solve them as well. Sinclair ran for Congress three times and for governor of California once. Rauschenbusch skillfully helped his parish members cope with unemployment, alcoholism, and other social ills. Sinclair and Rauschenbusch, like Ward, however, were more influential as analysts who identified and publicized problems than as activists who solved them.

Other progressives were more influential as activists who successfully won reforms on specific issues rather than as analysts. Progressives usually focused their efforts on the problems they saw firsthand or felt personally. For example, Sinclair wrote about the meatpacking workers he lived with. Rauschenbusch confronted the problems of the urban poor. Similarly, many women who were progressives emphasized the problems faced by women and children. Many African American progressives stressed issues affecting African Americans.

Concerned Women

In most families, whether urban or rural, women had more responsibility for raising the children than did men. Consequently, women were particularly outraged about the problems of children who labored in factories.

One of the leaders in the battle against child labor was Florence Kelley. Her father, a member of the United States House of Representatives, opposed slavery and supported women's right to vote. He taught Florence to read at a young age and to value education. She graduated from Cornell University in New York and attended graduate school in Switzerland.

In 1891 she went to live and work at Jane Addams's Hull House. During her seven years there, she investigated and reported on the use of child labor. "In the stores on the West Side," Kelley reported in 1895, "large numbers of young girls are employed thirteen hours a day throughout the week, and fifteen hours on Saturday."

Kelley was, in the words of a friend, "explosive, hot-tempered, determined . . . a smoking volcano that at any moment would burst into flames." What she unearthed in her investigations, though, outraged even many mild-mannered people. Kelley charged that "children are found in greatest number where the conditions of labor are most dangerous to life and health." Children working in the tobacco industry suffered from nicotine poisoning. Children in paint factories suffered

WE CONDEMN
CHILD LABOR.
Unity is Strength.
ORGANIZE.

BROWN BROTHERS

Child Labor Activists **This photograph shows one of the many child labor protest marches held in the early 1900s.** *Why are the women particularly upset about child labor?*

from breathing in toxic arsenic fumes. Children in clothing factories suffered spinal curvature from hunching over sewing machines 48 hours each week.

Kelley pressed the federal government to outlaw the use of child labor. "Why," she thundered, "are seals, bears, reindeer, fish, wild game in the national parks, buffalo, [and] migratory birds all found suitable for federal protection, but not children?"

Kelley continued her battle against child labor after she left Hull House. As general secretary of the National Consumers League (NCL), she helped organize consumer boycotts of goods manufactured by children or by workers toiling in unsanitary or dangerous conditions.

LIBRARY OF CONGRESS

NWTUL of Chicago **The National Women's Trade Union League, like the National Consumers League, united workers and middle-class reformers.** *How do its slogans reflect this?*

The National Consumers League

Most members of the NCL were, like Kelley, middle-class or upper-class women concerned about problems such as exploitation of children in factories. Many NCL members also supported the work of **settlement houses,** institutions that provided educational and social services to poor people. Hull House was the best known of the 400 settlement houses established between 1886 and 1910. In addition to their work in settlement houses, women were very active in clubs that promoted the arts, education, and community health. By the early 1920s, almost 1 million women had joined such clubs. The NCL, the settlement houses, and the women's clubs indicate that women were taking a more active role in confronting political and economic problems than they had in the past.

Some of the reforms advocated by Kelley and other women were not supported by many of the men who were progressives. For example, Walter Rauschenbusch opposed granting women the vote, even though this was a vital issue to Kelley and many female reformers.

African American Activists

For the urban African American family, racism intensified such problems as high unemployment and inadequate housing. Many white factory owners refused to hire African Americans—except as strikebreakers. In most cities African Americans could live only in well-defined areas, which quickly became overcrowded as cities grew. Furthermore, racism remained firmly entrenched in the minds of most whites, including most progressives. Many whites viewed African Americans as lazier, less intelligent, and more immoral than whites. In no other period of American history did state governments pass so many laws designed to restrict African Americans to a secondary role in society. African Americans working for reform often felt outside the Progressive movement.

The most dangerous problem for African Americans was lynching, murder by a mob without a trial, often by hanging. In 1892 about 230 people were lynched in the United States. Most of these people were African Americans, killed by groups of angry whites. Leading the antilynching movement was Ida B. Wells.

Born to enslaved parents in Holly Springs, Mississippi, in 1862, Wells remembered how much her parents emphasized education. "Our job," Wells recalled, "was to learn all we could."

When Wells was 14 her parents died in a yellow fever epidemic. Ida, the oldest of the 6 living children, refused to let her family be broken up. She lied about her age in order to get a job teaching school so that she could support her family.

In 1884 she got a better teaching job in Memphis and began writing for a local newspaper. Soon after arriving in Memphis, Wells became a controversial advocate of equality for African Americans because of an incident on a train. Upon taking a seat, she was told by the conductor that she was in a car reserved for whites and that she would have to move. Wells refused.

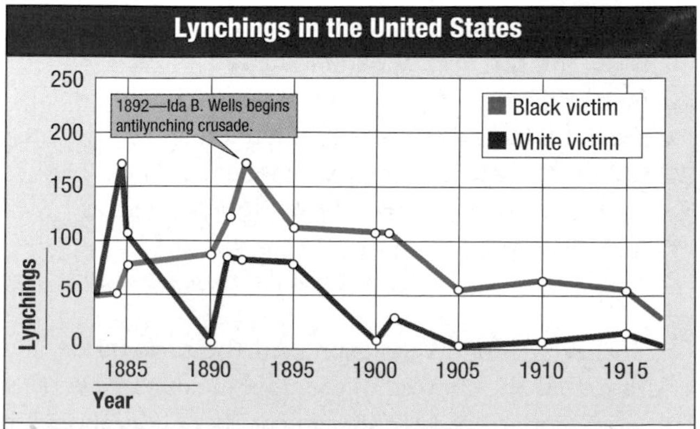

Before 1886 most lynchings were done by whites to whites. After that date the victims of lynchings, most of which occurred in the South, were usually African American. *According to the chart, when did lynchings of African Americans peak?*

UPI/BETTMANN

NEW YORK PUBLIC LIBRARY

Lynching Protest Opponents of lynching (above) appealed to national pride as one reason to end the murder of African Americans. Ida B. Wells (above right) led a national battle against lynchings. *How did Wells alert the public about the racism that motivated these mob murders?*

Though only about four and a half feet tall, Wells put up a fierce struggle:

> He tried to drag me out of the seat, but the moment he caught hold of my arm I fastened my teeth in the back of his hand. . . . He went forward and got the baggage-man and another man to help him and of course they succeeded in dragging me out. They were encouraged to do this by the attitude of the white ladies and gentlemen in the car. . . . I said I would get off the train rather than go in [to a segregated car]—which I did.
>
> —Ida B. Wells, *Crusade for Justice*

In her writing Wells expressed the same pride and courage that she showed in the train incident. Nevertheless, after writing articles criticizing the poor education that African Americans received in Memphis schools, she was fired from her teaching position. She became a full-time journalist, writing articles for several African American–owned newspapers.

The night of March 9, 1892, changed Ida Wells's life. That night a mob of angry whites lynched three African American men in Memphis. Wells wrote a scathing newspaper editorial attacking the lawless treatment of African Americans in Memphis. Moving to Chicago in 1894, Wells launched a national campaign to end lynching. From Chicago she wrote articles, gave speeches, and carried out investigations to expose the racism that motivated mob murderers. Within three years the number of lynchings went down by one-quarter.

Lynching was an extreme expression of the racism that Wells and other African Americans witnessed. Wells was not alone in fighting back, though. Racial oppression triggered the founding of the National Association for the Advancement of Colored People (NAACP) in 1909 and the National Urban League in 1910. Both organizations worked to help African Americans improve their living conditions.

As Wells and the progressives awakened the public to social ills and organized campaigns to remedy these ills, the number of people pressuring the government to respond increased. Progressives set out their agenda to reform the political structure, to modify the economic system, and to improve the moral climate of communities across the nation.

Section Review

Vocabulary

1. Define: progressive, muckraker, social gospel movement, settlement house.

Checking Facts

2. Describe some of the different methods progressives used to combat social, political, and economic injustices.
3. How did the methods of the activists differ from those of the analysts? How were they similar?

Critical Thinking

Making Comparisons

4. In your opinion, which of the methods used by the progressives was most effective in combating injustices? Explain your answer, citing as examples the actions of two of the progressives discussed.

Linking Across Time

5. Explain whether or not you think modern-day journalists consider themselves muckrakers.

Critical Thinking Skill

DETERMINING CAUSE AND EFFECT

Learning the Skill

When reading and studying historical information, it is important to determine cause-and-effect relationships in order to comprehend the significance of various events.

The skill of determining cause and effect requires considering why an event occurred. A *cause* is the action or situation that produces an event. An *effect* is the result or consequence of an action or a situation.

How to Determine Cause and Effect

Follow these steps to determine cause and effect:

a. Ask questions about why events occur.

b. Identify two or more events.

c. Look for vocabulary clues to help decide whether one event caused the other. Words or phrases such as *because*, *as a result of*, *for this reason*, *therefore*, *thus*, *as a consequence*, *as an outgrowth*, and *if . . . then* indicate cause-and-effect relationships.

d. Identify the outcomes of the events.

e. Look for relationships between the events. Check for other, more complex, connections beyond the immediate cause and effect.

For example, read the passage below:

> When Florence Kelley went to live and work at Hull House, she became an activist for outlawing child labor. Children's long working hours, detrimental health conditions, and poor factory environment were the causes of her activism. She helped organize consumer boycotts of goods manufactured by children and supported the work of settlement houses.

When studying the reform movement mentioned in the passage above, a graphic organizer such as the one below aids in understanding multiple causes and effects.

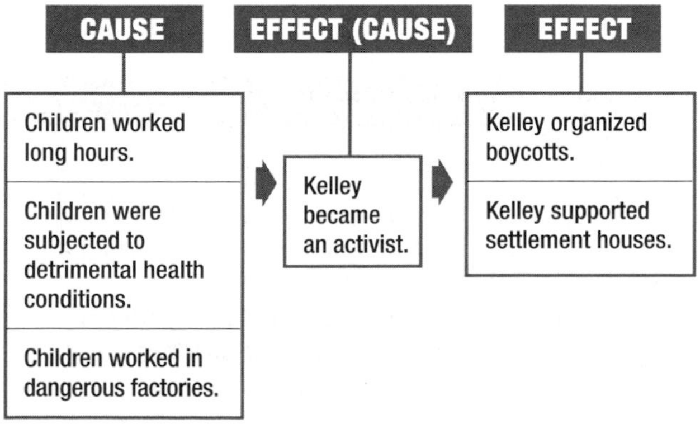

Practicing the Skill

On a separate piece of paper, make a cause-and-effect diagram for each statement below by writing the cause on the left and the effect on the right. Then connect the two parts of the statement with an arrow.

1. Not all immigrants stayed in the United States. Some became homesick and returned to the land of their birth.

2. As a result of meeting three neglected children, Jane Addams decided to open a day nursery to aid working parents.

3. If muckrakers wrote articles attacking wealthy corporations that exploited child labor, corrupt police departments that protected illegal activities, and prestigious churches that owned disease-ridden tenements, then the public would be alerted to these social ills.

4. As an outgrowth of Upton Sinclair's publication *The Jungle*, public sympathizers began to consider providing adequate wages for workers and improving sanitary conditions in the meatpacking industry.

5. Ida B. Wells launched a national campaign to end lynching by writing articles, giving speeches, and carrying out investigations to expose the racism that motivated mob murders. For this reason, the number of lynchings went down by one-quarter within three years.

Applying the Skill

Choose a contemporary reform movement—such as changing affirmative action policies, providing universal health insurance, or ensuring Social Security benefits for retirees—or select your own area of interest. Write a paragraph detailing the causes and possible effects of the reforms you might institute. Then use the information in your paragraph to construct a cause-and-effect diagram.

Additional Practice

For additional practice, see Reinforcing Skills on page 263.

STATE HISTORICAL SOCIETY OF WISCONSIN

"Fighting Bob" Robert La Follette was an eloquent spokesperson for the popular causes of his constituents. *How was La Follette able to attack the power of the political bosses?*

government, Galveston soon began to rebuild ruined buildings, to fix its destroyed streets, and to get its finances in order.

Reformers around the nation noted Galveston's quick recovery under its commissioner system. By centralizing power in the hands of a few business-oriented managers, Galveston had developed an efficient city government. Within 20 years more than 500 cities across the United States adopted a commissioner system. Another 158 cities had adopted a city-manager system in which the city council hired a professional to manage all the daily affairs of the city.

Even cities that did not adopt the commissioner system or the city-manager system learned from the example of Galveston and reduced the power of machine politicians by streamlining their government. Cutting government spending reduced the number of padded contracts that politicians could dole out to their friends. Trimming the bloated government payrolls reduced the number of jobs a politician had available to pass out as favors. These reforms made government more efficient.

In addition many cities changed their election procedures. Electing city council members at large, rather than from each ward, reduced the power of each local ward boss. Holding nonpartisan elections, in which candidates ran as individuals rather than as party representatives, reduced the power of parties. By undercutting the power of ward bosses and parties, reformers hoped that well-qualified candidates would have better chances to win elections.

Some progressives, hoping to make government more efficient, advocated reforms to undercut the machines. Others, though, supported reforms because they feared the power of immigrants and the poor. These progressives wanted to reduce the influence of immigrants and other poor people whom they blamed for causing the crime, prostitution, and disorder in the cities.

Wisconsin: Laboratory of Democracy

Many progressives believed that the solution to political corruption lay in making government more responsive to citizens. Governor Robert La Follette made Wisconsin the premier example of a state in which citizens directed and controlled their government.

La Follette was born in a two-room log cabin on a Wisconsin farm in 1855. By the time he was a student at the University of Wisconsin, he already displayed the traits that would lead him to political success. One classmate called him "the chairman of the undergraduate greeters" because of his friendly, outgoing manner. La Follette opposed with righteous indignation, however, any system by which a minority received special privileges. He felt an "overmastering sense of anger and wrong and injustice" at the gap between poor students like himself and the wealthy fraternity members.

La Follette's anger propelled him into politics. He served six years in Congress before he ran for governor. After losing two races, "Fighting Bob" finally won in 1900. Shortly after La Follette took office, one political boss swaggered into his office to cut a deal and to boast about his power over members of the legislature. "I own them," he told the newly elected governor. "They're mine!" La Follette, fiery and moralistic, refused to compromise with the boss. As he declared in his autobiography, "In legislation, *no bread* is better than *half a loaf.*"

As governor, La Follette attacked the power of the bosses through a series of reforms known as the Wisconsin Idea. He opposed the conventions at which parties nominated candidates to run for office. Because machine bosses controlled the selection of delegates, the bosses effectively controlled whom the party nominated. Reform candidates had virtually no chance of being selected to run. In 1903 La Follette pressured the legislature to pass a law requiring each party to choose its candidates through a **direct primary,** an election open to all voters within the party. As a result of that law, the power to nominate and select candidates passed from the bosses to the electorate.

In Wisconsin, as in many states, bosses also controlled the introduction and passage of bills in the legislature. Legislators felt more accountable to the bosses than to the citizens who elected them. To work around the power of the bosses, La Follette introduced three reforms, each of which had been developed in other states.

ARCHIVE PHOTOS

The Bosses of the Senate **Locate the two doorways in this 1889 political cartoon by Joseph Keppler.** *How does the difference between the doors show Keppler's view of the Senate?*

The **initiative** allowed citizens to introduce a bill into the legislature and required members to take a vote on it. The **referendum** established a procedure by which voters cast ballots for or against proposed laws. The **recall** gave citizens a chance to remove an elected official from office before the person's term ended. Wisconsin adopted all three of these proposals, thereby giving citizens power to bypass or to punish machine-controlled legislators. Other states under progressive leadership followed the example of Wisconsin and instituted similar reforms.

Attacking Corruption in the Senate

Another reform La Follette and progressives favored affected the federal government: the direct election of senators. According to the United States Constitution, each state legislature elected the two senators from that state. When a powerful political machine or large trust gained control of a state legislature, it also captured two Senate seats. Then senators repaid the machine or trust with federal contracts and jobs. By the early 1900s, muckraker Charles Edward Russell charged, the Senate had become "only a chamber of butlers for industrialists and financiers."

To counter Senate corruption, progressives called for direct election of senators by the voters of each state. In 1912 Congress proposed a direct-election amendment to the Constitution. In 1913 the states ratified the Seventeenth Amendment.

Expanding Voting Rights

Some progressives tried to increase not only the influence but also the number of citizens participating in government. After an 1848 women's rights conference in Seneca Falls, New York, women began organizing to win suffrage, the right to vote. By 1890 women had won at least partial suffrage in 19 states. In most of these states, women could vote in local or state elections, but they could not vote in presidential elections. Only Wyoming and Utah gave women full voting rights.

The suffrage movement gathered momentum in the 1890s. The National American Woman Suffrage Association grew from 13,000 members in 1893 to 75,000 members in 1910. By 1912, 9 states, all west of the Mississippi River, allowed women to vote in all elections. Suffrage advocates continued to push for a constitutional amendment to grant women full voting rights in all states. They would not achieve that goal, however, until the passage of the Nineteenth Amendment in 1920.

While women fought to win the vote, African Americans struggled to regain it. Beginning in Mississippi in 1890, state after state in the South revised its constitution and laws to prevent African Americans from voting. In Louisiana, for example, more than 130,000 African Americans voted in 1896. In 1900, after changes in the constitution and the laws, the number of African Americans registered to vote there plunged to 5,320.

Woman Suffrage Supporters **In 1916 these activists from Kentucky traveled to St. Louis to urge delegates at the Democratic National Convention to support equal rights for women.** *What other Americans were denied the right to vote?*

The drive to win voting rights for African Americans made little progress before 1915. African American progressives won little support from white progressives for their cause.

Economic Reform

Using Government to Protect Citizens

Progressives hoped that political reform would pave the way for economic reform. Once the political system was rescued from controlling private interests, citizens could use government to protect the public interest.

Regulating Big Business

Government regulation proved to be one means of taming powerful special interests. In Wisconsin La Follette established a state railroad commission. This group of experts, many from the University of Wisconsin, oversaw the operation of all railroads in Wisconsin. They held the power to revise, overturn, and thereby regulate rates charged by the railroads. Thus the commission prevented the railroads from unfairly overcharging small farmers whose livelihoods depended on the railroads for shipping their grain to market. Under regulation, factories could no longer bribe the railroads into giving them an unfair rate advantage over other factories in the state. La Follette declared that his goal "was not to 'smash' corporations, but to drive them out of politics, and then to treat them exactly the same as other people are treated."

Other states followed Wisconsin's lead, establishing commissions to regulate railroads, electric power companies, and gas companies. Some cities went beyond mere regulation, setting up and running utilities as part of city government.

Caring for Injured Workers

Owners and workers clashed repeatedly over issues such as how companies should treat injured workers. Factories, coal mines, and railroads were particularly dangerous places to work. In 1914 about 35,000 people died on the job; another 700,000 were injured. Companies often fired seriously injured workers because they could no longer do their jobs. In a fiercely competitive business climate, no company could afford the expense of caring for its injured workers unless all of its competitors did the same.

Articles by muckrakers and protests by unions slowly roused public anger at the irresponsibility of big business. In 1902 Maryland passed the first state law requiring employers to buy insurance that would compensate workers injured on the job. By 1916, the year that Congress passed the Workmen's Compensation Law, about two-thirds of the states required companies to have some type of workers' compensation program.

Limiting the Workday

In 1900 about one-fifth of all people working outside their homes were women. Most progressives believed that women were naturally weaker than men and thus

THE BETTMANN ARCHIVE

A Factory Tragedy On March 25, 1911, a fire at the Triangle Shirtwaist Factory killed 146 female workers. Because the company locked the doors from the outside to prevent workers from taking breaks, many had no chance to escape. Outrage at the deaths caused New York City to pass a strict building code. *What other laws were passed in the early 1900s to protect workers?*

more deserving of protection. Even a Tammany Hall boss, Big Tim Sullivan, worried about the ravages of work on young women: "I had seen me sister go out to work when she was only fourteen and I know we ought to help these gals by giving 'em a law which will prevent 'em from being broken down while they're still young."

In 1903 Oregon passed a law that prohibited employing women in a factory or a laundry for more than 10 hours a day. Portland laundry owner Curt Muller, fined $10 for breaking the law, challenged it. Muller, like other business owners, argued that the government had no right to interfere in a private contract between an owner and a worker. The Oregon Supreme Court disagreed with Muller and upheld the fine. Muller then appealed to the United States Supreme Court, which agreed to hear the case.

Progressives, including Florence Kelley and Josephine Goldmark of the National Consumers League, closely followed the *Muller* v. *Oregon* case. They had seen both state and federal courts strike down laws like the one passed by Oregon. If the Supreme Court upheld the Oregon law, though, similar laws in other states would also be valid.

Goldmark recruited her brother-in-law, Louis Brandeis, to defend the Oregon law. Brandeis, whose father was a Jewish immigrant from Bohemia, was a prominent Boston lawyer. Tall and wiry, with a shock of unruly hair, Brandeis earned his nickname of the "People's Lawyer" by donating his expertise to defending unions and attacking corrupt politicians.

In January 1908, Brandeis presented his brief, the statement of a client's case, to the Supreme Court. The brief included 95 pages of statistics, quotations, and other evidence collected by Goldmark showing that long hours damaged the health of women and, in effect, threatened the public interest. "The overwork of future mothers," Brandeis wrote, "thus directly attacks the welfare of the nation."

Goldmark's evidence proved persuasive. In a unanimous decision, the Supreme Court upheld the Oregon law. They agreed that a state government, to protect the public interest, had a right to regulate the work of women. After the *Muller* decision, Illinois, Virginia, Michigan, Louisiana, and other states quickly passed similar laws.

BROWN BROTHERS

A Crusading Lawyer Louis Brandeis served as an associate justice of the United States Supreme Court from 1916 to 1939. *What nickname did Brandeis earn and why?*

THE BETTMANN ARCHIVE

A High School Classroom in 1900 Students are observing an experiment and taking notes in this science class. *How many high schools existed in 1900?*

Length of School Year, 1880–1920

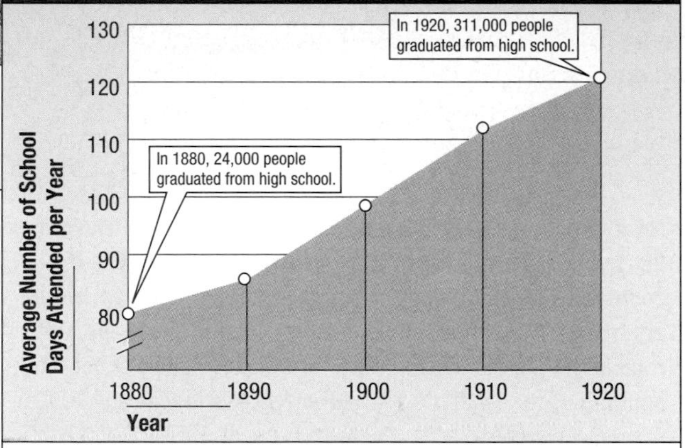

Progressives supported laws requiring attendance at school. *How many more days on average did students attend school in 1920 than in 1880?*

Brandeis's use of Goldmark's data revolutionized legal thought. Previously courts evaluated laws only on narrow legal grounds. Beginning with the *Muller* decision, courts considered the law's impact on people's lives. Brandeis and Goldmark won a major victory in the progressives' battle to carve out a new role for government as protector of the public interest.

Social and Moral Reform

Convincing Government to Support Children and Women

The progressives' desire to protect the public interest included a broad range of social reforms. Many reforms were designed to help children. For example, progressives supported establishing separate courts that would be sensitive to the needs and problems of juveniles. They also backed laws providing financial assistance to children in homes with no father present. One of the key progressive reforms for children was the expansion of public education.

Educating Children

During the late 1800s, state after state passed laws requiring young people to go to school. The number of schools jumped sharply. Before the Civil War, only a few hundred high schools existed across the nation. By 1900 there were 6,000 high schools; by 1920, there were 14,000. The expansion of public education then led to a sharp decline in illiteracy. In 1870 approximately 20 percent of the people in the United States were illiterate. By 1920 only 6 percent could not read.

In addition to growing, public education was changing. Philosopher John Dewey criticized schools for overemphasizing memorization of knowledge. Instead,

UPI/ BETTMANN

Margaret Sanger **As Mrs. Margaret Sanger (left) and her sister Mrs. Ethel Byrne leave the Court of Special Sessions in Brooklyn, New York, on January 8, 1917, they are greeted by an immigrant family.** *What kind of crusade did Sanger undertake and what law did she break in the process?*

Dewey argued, schools should relate learning to the interests, problems, and concerns of students. He believed that the "true center" of a child's education was "not science, nor literature, nor history, nor geography, but the child's own social activities." Dewey wanted schools to teach students to be good citizens. "Education," he declared, "is the fundamental method of social progress and reform." Most progressives agreed with him.

Protecting Women

Just as some progressives emphasized reforms to protect children, others focused on reforms that primarily affected women. The most controversial of these reforms was the birth control movement. A New York nurse, Margaret Sanger, had seen many women die from poorly performed abortions. In 1914 she launched a drive to inform women about ways they could prevent pregnancy. Under New York's Comstock Act of 1873, though, information describing methods of birth control was considered obscene. Almost immediately after starting her crusade, Sanger was arrested for violating the Comstock Act. Though the charges against her were dropped in 1916, Sanger faced constant opposition to her work.

Another reform that aimed to protect women was the temperance movement, the drive to restrict or prohibit the use of alcohol. Intoxicated men sometimes beat their wives and children, and the temperance movement aimed to stop such abusive behavior at the source—alcohol. The largest temperance organization was the Women's Christian Temperance Union (WCTU), founded in 1874. By 1900 it had almost 300,000 members. One-fourth of the United States population lived in areas with some restrictions on alcohol purchase or consumption.

Frances Willard led the WCTU from 1879 until her death in 1898. She encouraged the organization to attack social ills other than the abuse of alcohol. The WCTU advocated voting rights for women, lobbied for prison reform, promoted world peace, and spoke out on various health issues. Willard's slogan was, Do everything.

The WCTU under Willard was typical of many progressive organizations. While it focused on one problem that seemed to be rampant in cities, it supported several other reform causes. Although the problem it confronted was nationwide, the organization won its first victories on the city and state levels. In order to achieve a nationwide solution, the temperance movement, like other progressive reforms, would have to convince Congress and the President to take a more active role in social reform. The progressives, then, needed to develop a new role for the federal government in the United States.

Section Review

Vocabulary

1. Define: direct primary, initiative, referendum, recall.

Checking Facts

2. Explain the ruling in the case of *Muller* v. *Oregon.*
3. Describe the reforms that protected women and children.

Critical Thinking

Determining Cause and Effect

4. Why did the progressives believe that political reform was necessary before economic reform could be achieved?

Linking Across Time

5. Do big businesses have more or less influence on government today than they did around 1900? Give examples to support your viewpoint.

CASE STUDY

Turning Point

Woman Suffrage

SENECA FALLS WOMEN'S RIGHTS CONVENTION, JULY 19–20, 1848

MEMORANDUM

For: Concerned Women and Men

Subject: Women's Rights

A convention to discuss the social, civil and religious condition and rights of woman will be held in the Wesleyan Chapel of Seneca Falls, New York, on Wednesday and Thursday, 19th and 20th July current; commencing at 10 A.M. During the first day the meeting will be exclusively for women who are earnestly invited to attend. The public generally are invited to be present on the second day when Lucretia Mott of Philadelphia and other ladies and gentlemen will address the convention.

Advertisement
Seneca Court Courier
July 13, 1848

The Case

Elizabeth Cady Stanton and Lucretia Mott were amazed when about 300 people, including African American abolitionist Frederick Douglass among the 40 men, responded to their call to meet in a small chapel in Seneca Falls, New York, to discuss women's rights.

On the morning of Wednesday, July 19, organizers presented what one scholar calls "the single most important document of the nineteenth-century American woman's movement." By paraphrasing the Declaration of Independence of 1776, Mott, Stanton, Mary Ann McClintock, Jane Hunt, and Mott's sister Martha Wright produced a document they called a Declaration of Sentiments.

It stated:

> We hold these truths to be self-evident: that all men and women are created equal; that they are endowed by their Creator with certain inalienable rights; that among these are life, liberty, and the pursuit of happiness; that to secure these rights governments are instituted, deriving their just powers from the consent of the governed. Whenever any form of government becomes destructive of these ends, it is the right of those who suffer from it to refuse allegiance to it, and to insist upon the institution of a new government, laying its foundation on such principles, and organizing its powers in such form, as to them shall seem most likely to effect their safety and happiness.

Stanton had insisted on including in the declaration a resolution stating: "[I]t is the duty of the women of this country to secure to themselves their sacred right to the elective franchise"—a proposal considered unthinkable at the time. Even her husband, Henry Stanton, who was generally supportive of her views, was angry and embarrassed by her demand for entry into the white masculine domain of voting.

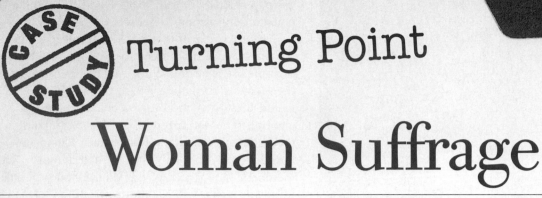

The Seneca Falls assembly unanimously adopted 11 resolutions, but Stanton's resolution on full voting rights for women—Resolution 9—met bitter resistance. Would it pass? More than that, what would happen when the convention was over?

The Background

In 1776, shortly before the drafting of the Declaration of Independence, Abigail Adams wrote to her husband, John: "If particular care and attention is not paid to the ladies, we are determined to foment a rebellion, and will not hold ourselves bound by any laws in which we have no voice or representation." Her strong words went unanswered. Only New Jersey allowed women the vote in its state constitution, and the privilege was revoked in 1806. Adams's idea was not dead, but it lay dormant for some 42 years until woman suffrage was again seriously addressed—at Seneca Falls.

Seneca Falls leader Elizabeth Cady Stanton's position as a women's rights activist took shape at the 1840 World's Anti-Slavery Convention in London, England. There she began a lifelong friendship with Quaker abolitionist Lucretia Mott. When Stanton, Mott, and all other female delegates were banned from convention debate because of their sex and only allowed to listen from behind a screen, the famous abolitionist William Lloyd Garrison joined the evicted women as a nonparticipant. He declared, "After battling so many long years for the liberties of African slaves, I can take no part in a convention that strikes down the most sacred rights of all women."

As a result of their exclusion, Stanton and Mott spent much of their time together in London discussing the plight of women. They determined to organize a convention on women's rights, but, busied by other demands, they did not pursue the idea for another eight years.

Back in the United States, Stanton later joined Ernestine Rose and Paulina Wright Davis in a huge petition drive to demolish laws that forced married women to surrender everything they owned to their husbands. That campaign helped achieve passage of the Married Women's Property Act of New York

"The family, and not the individual, has been the political unit, and the head of the family . . . has been the political representative of the rest. To give the suffrage to women would be to reject the principle that has thus far formed the basis of civilized government."

Historian Francis Parkman, "The Woman Question," *North American Review,* 1879

CULVER PICTURES

"Strange as it may seem to many, we now demand our right to vote according to the declaration of the government under which we live. . . . We have no objection to discuss the question of equality, for we feel that the weight of argument lies wholly with us, but we wish the question of equality kept distinct from the question of rights, for the proof of the one does not determine the truth of the other."

Elizabeth Cady Stanton, address delivered at Seneca Falls and Rochester, N.Y.

"All that distinguishes man as an intelligent and accountable being, is equally true of woman; and if that government only is just which governs by the free consent of the governed, there can be no reason in the world for denying to woman the exercise of the elective franchise, or a hand in making and administering the laws of the land."

Frederick Douglass, editorial, *North Star,* July 28, 1848

CULVER PICTURES

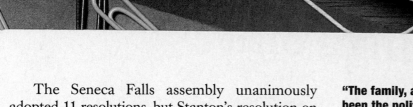

"The power of women is in her dependence, flowing from the consciousness of that weakness which God has given her for her protection, and which keeps her in those departments of life that form the character of individuals and of the nation."

Pastoral letter of the Congregational ministers of Massachusetts, 1837 in 1848, which states in part: "The real and personal property of any female who may hereafter marry, and which she shall own at the time of her marriage . . . shall not be subject to the disposal of her husband." Promotion of this act marked the first time that women had run a campaign directed specifically at furthering their own rights, and it set the stage for the Seneca Falls Convention.

U.S. POSTER COLLECTION 5084, HOOVER INSTITUTION ARCHIVES, STANFORD UNIVERSITY

Women's confidence about winning the vote increased with the victorious feeling that struck the nation at the end of World War I. This 1919 poster celebrates the passage of the Nineteenth Amendment. It was ratified by the states in 1920.

The Opinions

The opinions on the status of women excerpted on the previous page reflect the general spirit of the debate that emerged from Seneca Falls. The 1848 convention brought woman suffrage center stage. It remained a matter of fiercely divided opinion for the next 72 years.

The Outcome

The debate on suffrage divided the participants and the organizers of the Seneca Falls Convention. Stanton found support in Frederick Douglass, but many others opposed Resolution 9. Some feared that demanding suffrage at that point in time was too radical a step. Stanton's husband boycotted the convention (and even left town for the duration) because of Resolution 9. Even her dear friend Lucretia Mott told Stanton, "Thou will make us ridiculous. We must go slowly."

The convention broke temporarily and continued two weeks later in nearby Rochester, New York. There, with the influence of Stanton and Douglass, the resolution passed by a narrow margin. The demand for woman suffrage was officially added to the Declaration of Sentiments.

After the Convention As feared, the public and the press ridiculed the Seneca Falls Convention. Except for Douglass's *North Star* and Horace Greeley's *New York Tribune,* newspapers did not take the women or their meeting seriously.

The years following the convention, however, witnessed a growing number of women's meetings. These gatherings created widening public awareness of women's rights issues. For example, African American abolitionist leader Sojourner Truth attended the First National Woman's Rights Convention in Worcester, Massachusetts in 1850, and demanded the inclusion of African American women in the struggle for suffrage.

Civil War and Reconstruction When the Civil War erupted in 1861, women's rights activists put their own interests aside. Seneca Falls leaders and other women in the North worked long and hard for the Union cause. They consequently felt angry and betrayed when the Fourteenth Amendment, ratified in 1868, enfranchised African American men and omitted any reference to women. The abolitionist argument that African American male suffrage deserved precedence over women's issues resulted in a bitter rift between leaders of the woman suffrage movement and prominent abolitionists.

In the wake of the Fourteenth and Fifteenth Amendments, disagreements on how to proceed with the fight for suffrage plagued the women's rights movement. Some promoted a national amendment for woman suffrage; others promoted general reform, with suffrage in a list of demands. In 1890, however, Stanton and Susan B. Anthony merged their National Woman Suffrage Association with the rival (and more conservative) American Woman Suffrage Association, led by Lucy Stone and Julia Ward Howe. The resulting organization—the National American Woman Suffrage Association (NAWSA)—dampened the radical push for suffrage somewhat, but did restore unity to the movement.

The Twentieth Century The early years of the 1900s saw gradual advances in women's rights to education, employment, property ownership, and local election voting. Slowly the idea of women voting became slightly less terrifying or ludicrous to those in power.

Women continued to speak, march, hold meetings, and petition the government for suffrage. Finally, women's dramatic mobilization on the home front during World War I convinced many that it was wrong to withhold the vote from these citizens. One World War I era poster demanded: "We give our work, our men, our lives if need be. Will you give us the vote?"

In 1919 Congress at last voted to do just that. The states ratified the proposed amendment and it became the Nineteenth Amendment to the Constitution in 1920. That November the last surviving participant of the Seneca Falls Convention, Charlotte Woodward Pierce, voted for the President of the United States.

The Significance

The Seneca Falls Convention, though ridiculed at the time, now marks the birth of an organized women's movement for equality in the United States. The convention provided a precedent and model for women to speak publicly on their own behalf. The issues outlined in the Seneca Falls Declaration of Sentiments remained issues of concern for women well into the next century.

RESPONDING TO THE CASE

1. On passage of the 1848 Married Women's Property Act, Ernestine Rose said it was "not much . . . only for the favored few and not for the suffering many. But it was a beginning and an important step." How did the women's rights movement subsequently succeed in attracting less privileged people?

2. What impact did the Civil War years and post-war events have on the fight for woman suffrage?

3. Study the four opinions excerpted on page 259, and explain why they are said to "reflect the general spirit of the debate on woman suffrage."

4. Seneca Falls is often described as the birthplace of the woman suffrage movement. What was the turning point at that meeting?

5. Compare the original Declaration of Independence of 1776 to the adaptation for the Seneca Falls Declaration of Sentiments of 1848. Explain how language can generate enthusiasm for a cause.

PORTFOLIO PROJECT

Elizabeth Cady Stanton emerged as the leader at the Seneca Falls Convention, and she continued to be an activist for the rest of her life. Research one of the figures mentioned in this case study and write a brief biography of her or him to include in your portfolio.

Chapter 8 Review

Reviewing Key Terms

Imagine that you are a muckraker who is investigating the need for reform in your city. Use the following vocabulary words to write an article summarizing the corruption and stating your recommendations.

urbanization	**referendum**
recall	**political machine**
direct primary	**initiative**

Recalling Facts

1. Identify the major factors that contributed to the growth of cities in the late 1800s.

2. How did consumers benefit from the existence of large trusts?

3. Why did the average urban worker live on the edge of poverty?

4. How did men such as J.P. Morgan and John D. Rockefeller amass huge fortunes during this period?

5. How were the progressives different from the populists?

6. How did intellectuals such as Charles Beard, Mary Ritter Beard, and Lester Ward influence the thinking of the reformers?

7. Who were the muckrakers? How did the public react to Upton Sinclair's book *The Jungle*?

8. What were the principal features of the plan to rebuild Galveston?

9. What reforms did Robert La Follette bring about in Wisconsin?

10. How did progressive reforms benefit children?

Critical Thinking

1. Recognizing Ideologies Do you think progressives believed in democracy? In your answer clarify what you think democracy means. Then indicate whether the progressive view of democracy agrees with your view. Use examples from among the progressive reformers to support your conclusion.

2. Making Inferences The photograph on this page shows Delancey Street in New York City in 1905. What aspects of urban life are shown in this picture?

3. Drawing Conclusions List and evaluate four changes caused by the growth of cities. Explain both the benefits and the costs of each change.

4. Making Comparisons How did the women's struggle to gain the vote parallel the struggle of African Americans for equal rights? How did it differ?

5. Making Generalizations Make a list of 10 progressive individuals described in this chapter. When possible, indicate whether each came from a poor family or a prosperous one. Use this information to write a sentence describing the background of these progressives.

ARCHIVE PHOTOS

CHAPTER 8 REVIEW

MANUFACTURING EMPLOYMENT, 1899

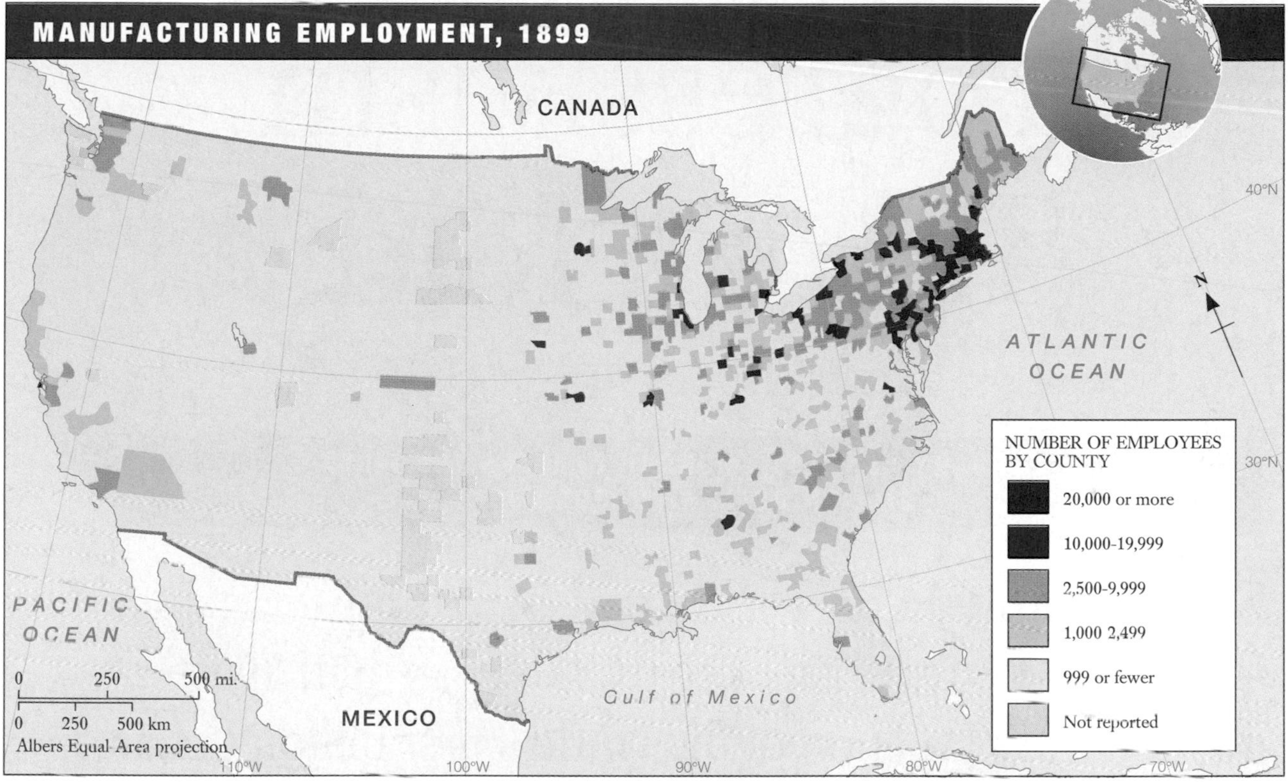

Portfolio Project

What, in your opinion, is the major problem facing the United States today? Make a list of ways in which you could enlist people to work together to solve the problem. Choose a visual or graphic format to effectively display your ideas, and share them with your classmates. Then file your written list in your portfolio.

Cooperative Learning

The progressives identified a set of problems that needed correction 100 years ago. What are the major problems facing your community today? Work with a few of your classmates to create a list for class discussion. Then, work in small groups to choose one problem and prepare to participate in a round-table discussion to explore ways of solving that problem.

Reinforcing Skills

Determining Cause and Effect

How did politicians gain power in the cities during the Progressive Era? Why did this political power often lead to corruption?

Geography and History

Study the map on this page to answer the following questions:

1. Which region of the United States had the heaviest concentration of manufacturing employment?

2. In 1890 upstart Illinois passed venerable Massachusetts to take third place in the gross value of manufactured goods. It also passed Ohio to become the leader in agricultural machinery. In what direction was the center of industry shifting?

3. The densest areas of employment were often located geographically near what power source?

4. What areas in the West led manufacturing in 1899?

5. What correlation can you make between the growth of cities and the density of manufacturing employment?

HISTORY JOURNAL

This period of history from the late 1800s through the early 1900s showed great change in response to progressive action. What changes did you feel were the most powerful? What impact do these changes have on your life today? What changes can you initiate that will affect future generations? Write your responses to these questions in your journal.

CHAPTER 9

Progressivism Takes Hold

FEBRUARY 25, 1901: MORGAN CREATES THE FIRST BILLION DOLLAR CORPORATION

For J.P. Morgan, it was a day of triumph. In just 4 months of feverish activity, Morgan had masterminded the formation of the world's first billion dollar corporation, U.S. Steel. Through buying out leading steel companies, Morgan's steel trust won control of 60 percent of the nation's steel-making capacity.

For many people, though, Morgan's triumph was a frightening one. The 168,000 steelworkers, whose 12-hour days spent in dangerous mills made the steel industry so profitable, feared they would have no bargaining power with the giant new corporation. How low would Morgan drive wages? How high would he drive steel prices?

Only one institution seemed big enough to protect average citizens from Morgan: the federal government. Since the founding of the nation, however, the federal government had done far more to nurture corporations than to challenge them. In early 1901, with President McKinley in office, people had no reason to expect much change. Little did Americans realize that the role of the federal government in American life would soon change dramatically as progressives carried out their agenda. ■

HISTORY JOURNAL

After studying this cartoon, describe your impression of J.P. Morgan. How do you think the federal government could protect "average citizens" from him?

CULVER PICTURES

THIS CARTOON SHOWS J.P. MORGAN ATTEMPTING TO FORM A TRUST WITH THE SUN AND PLANETS IN ORDER TO MONOPOLIZE THE LIGHT BUSINESS.

sadly wrote to a friend, "I do not expect to go any further in politics."

The reserved and serious McKinley, a predictable, solid Republican, provided a sharp contrast to his impulsive Vice President. To one senator, the constantly moving Roosevelt resembled "a steam engine in trousers." Wherever Roosevelt went, he became the center of attention. "When Theodore attends a wedding he wants to be the bride," noted a relative, "and when he attends a funeral he wants to be the corpse."

Not all the Republican machine bosses had approved of Roosevelt's nomination as Vice President. When Ohio Senator Mark Hanna heard of the Roosevelt nomination, he shouted at his allies, "Don't any of you realize that there's only one life between that madman and the Presidency?"

Fifteen months later, that "one life" was gone. The "madman" was President. Though Roosevelt pledged to carry out McKinley's moderate policies, the new President's dramatic style transformed the presidency.

CULVER PICTURES

Roosevelt as Conservationist **President Theodore Roosevelt and naturalist John Muir, right, survey Yosemite Valley. As a result of Muir's efforts, Yosemite became one of the nation's first national parks.** *Why did Roosevelt start the Forest Service?*

Thanks in part to his energetic speeches, Americans perceived Roosevelt as a President who could take charge. For his part, Roosevelt saw the presidency as a "bully pulpit" from which to preach the ideas he advocated. The young President captivated audiences with his toothy grin, vigorous gestures, and somewhat squeaky voice.

Throughout his government career, Roosevelt supported progressive reform in strong language while in practice he pursued a more moderate course of action. In this way, Roosevelt persuaded the public that he was a reformer at the same time he reassured the business community of his basic conservatism. For example, as governor, Roosevelt had supported progressive labor legislation but repeatedly threatened to bring out armed troops to control strikers. "We Republicans," Roosevelt had written in 1896, "hold the just balance and set our faces as resolutely against the improper corporate influence on the one hand as against demagogy and mob rule on the other."

During the late 1800s, strong Congresses and relatively weak Presidents had predominated. Roosevelt reversed that traditional division of power. The new President employed the considerable powers of his office and his own personal magnetism to bypass congressional opposition. In doing so, Roosevelt became the first modern President.

Managing Natural Resources

New Ideas About the Environment

Roosevelt put his stamp on the presidency most clearly in the area of conservation. From his boyhood explorations, Roosevelt had viewed America's minerals, animals, and rugged terrain as priceless national resources. For the good of the nation, thought Roosevelt, these treasures must be protected from greedy private developers, eager to make a quick dollar. As President, Roosevelt eagerly assumed the role of protector. He argued that the government must distinguish "between the man who skins the land and the man who develops the country. I am going to work with, and only with, the man who develops the country."

Roosevelt quickly applied that philosophy in the dry Western states, where farmers and city dwellers competed for scarce water. To increase crop yields and to protect themselves from droughts, farmers demanded more water to expand their irrigation systems. Rapidly growing cities such as Los Angeles also thirsted for this precious resource. In 1902 Roosevelt

NATIONAL PARK AND MONUMENT DESIGNATIONS, 1901–1909

- **1901** Yellowstone, Yosemite, Sequoia, General Grant (now part of Kings Canyon), and Mt. Rainier parks already exist.
- **1902** Crater Lake National Park, Oregon, is established.
- **1903** Wind Cave National Park, South Dakota, is established.
- **1904** Sully Hill National Park (now a wildlife refuge), North Dakota, is established.
- **1906** Two national parks are established—Mesa Verde in Colorado and Platt in Oklahoma (now Chickasaw National Recreation Area).
- **1906** The first four national monuments, including Devil's Tower, are established.
- **1907** Five national monuments, including Chaco Canyon, are established.
- **1908** Eight national monuments, including Grand Canyon, are established.
- **1909** Mt. Olympus National Monument is established.

supported passage of the Newlands Reclamation Act, which authorized the use of federal funds from the sale of public lands to pay for irrigation and land development projects in the dry farms and cities of the West. Under the new law, Roosevelt supported the construction of 25 irrigation or reclamation projects.

Roosevelt also backed efforts to save the nation's forests by preventing shortsighted lumbering companies from overcutting. He appointed his close friend Gifford Pinchot to head the United States Forest Service. Like Roosevelt, Pinchot was a firm believer in **resource management,** the rational scientific management of natural resources such as timber or mineral deposits.

With the President's support, Pinchot's department drew up regulations controlling lumbering on federal lands. This position satisfied neither business nor environmental interests. Business leaders, hoping to profit from unlimited cutting, criticized restrictions instituted by Pinchot as unwarranted government interference in the workings of private business. On the other hand, veteran environmental activists like John Muir of California criticized Pinchot for supporting any cutting in the few remaining unspoiled forests. They argued that forests should be kept in a completely unspoiled condition for people to enjoy.

In addition to supporting Pinchot's moderate actions in lumbering, Roosevelt took other steps to provide for the managed use of the nation's resources. He added 150 million acres to the national forests, quadrupling the amount of land they contained. Roosevelt also established 5 new national parks, created 51 federal bird reservations, and started 4 national game preserves. These solid conservation accomplishments hardly put an end to private exploitation of the country's natural treasures, but they did initiate government protection of such resources. At the very least, Roosevelt's constant championing of the causes of conservation and resource management served to place the issue on the national agenda.

Supervising Big Business

"Speak Softly and Carry a Big Stick" Does Not Apply

Other issues were already on the national agenda when Roosevelt took office. One involved the growth of large trusts—giant firms that controlled whole areas of industry by buying up all the companies with which they did business. This concentration of wealth and economic power under the control of large trusts had dramatically reshaped the American economy. Buyouts, takeovers, and mergers reached a feverish pitch between 1897 and 1903. By 1899 an elite group of 6 companies controlled about 95 percent of the railroads in the country.

Most Americans were suspicious of the trusts. By lowering prices trusts drove smaller companies out of business. They then established monopolies and were able to fix high prices without fear of competition. In 1890 Congress passed the Sherman Antitrust Act, which was designed to prohibit such monopolies, but it had proven

Mergers, 1895–1920

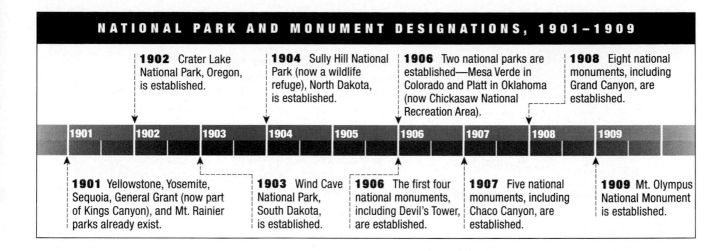

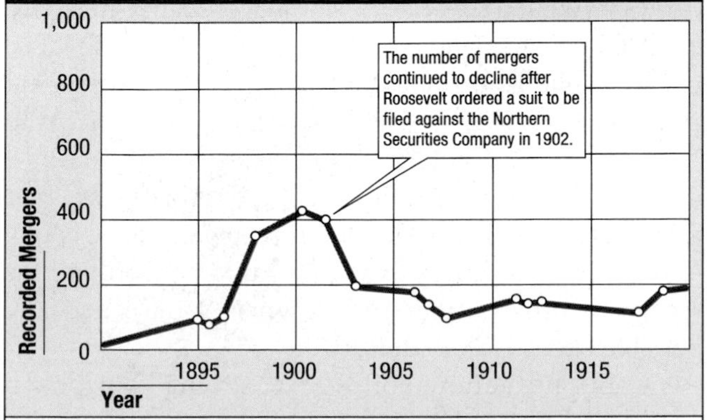
1,000
800
600
400
200
0
Recorded Mergers
1895
1900
1905
1910
1915
Year
The number of mergers continued to decline after Roosevelt ordered a suit to be filed against the Northern Securities Company in 1902.

The Progressive era resembled the 1980s in terms of the large number of recorded mergers that occurred during that time. *According to the graph above, what effect did the Sherman Antitrust Act have on mergers?*

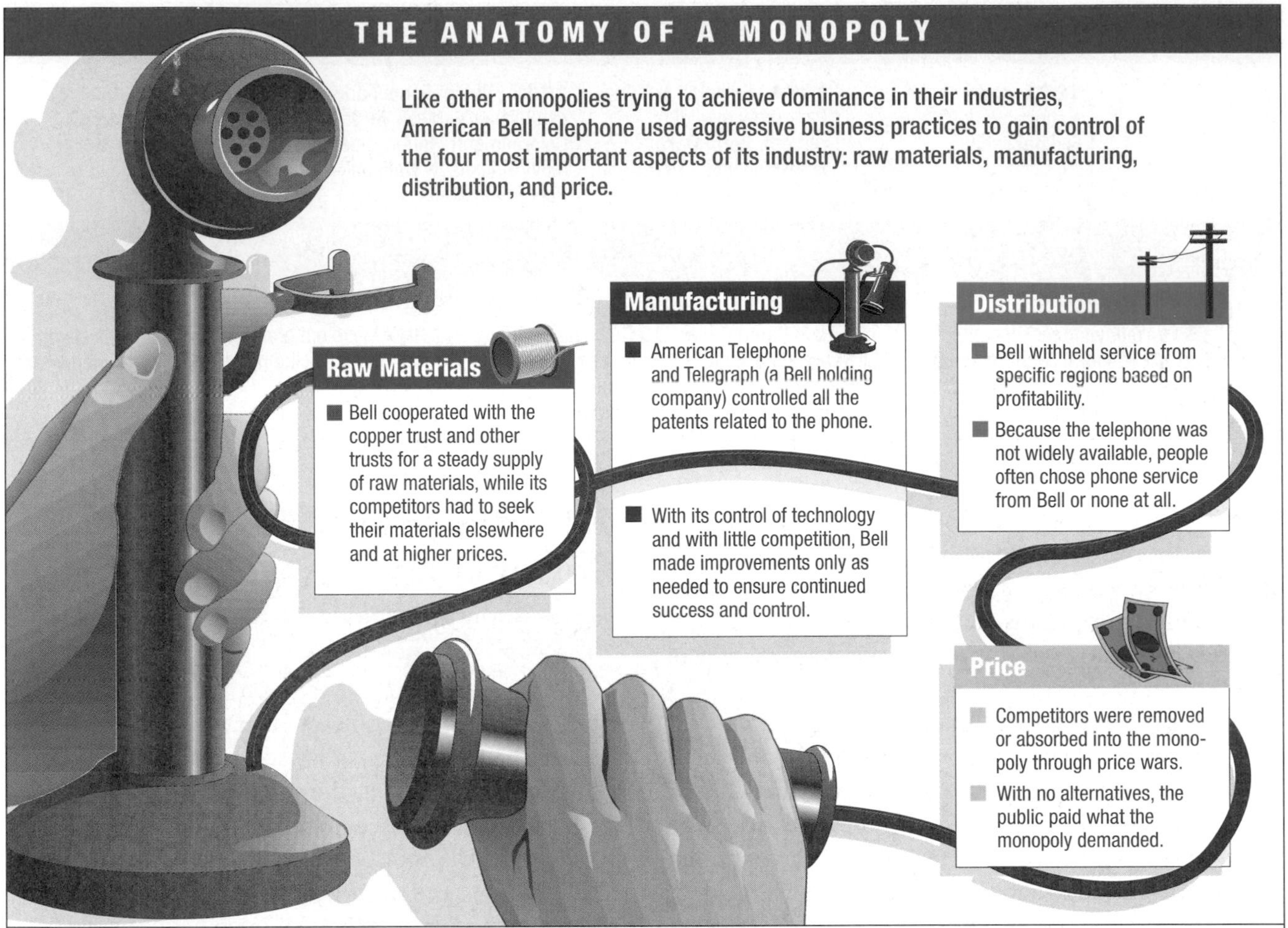

THE ANATOMY OF A MONOPOLY
Like other monopolies trying to achieve dominance in their industries, American Bell Telephone used aggressive business practices to gain control of the four most important aspects of its industry: raw materials, manufacturing, distribution, and price.
Raw Materials
Bell cooperated with the copper trust and other trusts for a steady supply of raw materials, while its competitors had to seek their materials elsewhere and at higher prices.
Manufacturing
American Telephone and Telegraph (a Bell holding company) controlled all the patents related to the phone.
With its control of technology and with little competition, Bell made improvements only as needed to ensure continued success and control.
Distribution
Bell withheld service from specific regions based on profitability.
Because the telephone was not widely available, people often chose phone service from Bell or none at all.
Price
Competitors were removed or absorbed into the monopoly through price wars.
With no alternatives, the public paid what the monopoly demanded.

American Bell Telephone was one of several large trusts and monopolies that existed at the turn of the century. Like others of his time, Alexander Graham Bell was a shrewd businessperson whose company rose to the top of a lucrative new industry. *What elements of the industry did Bell control?*

hard to enforce. Industrialists simply devised substitute methods of retaining control—for example, the **holding company.** Holding companies bought controlling interests in the stock of other companies instead of purchasing the companies outright. While the "held" companies remained separate businesses on paper, in reality the holding company controlled them.

In public Roosevelt capitalized on the widespread mistrust of the wealthy industrialists. He called them the "criminal rich," "malefactors of great wealth," and "a miracle of timid and short-sighted selfishness," yet Roosevelt avoided breaking up trusts whenever he could. "I have let up in every case," he said in describing his record of prosecuting trusts, "where I have had any possible excuse for so doing."

Cautious actions offset Roosevelt's outspoken comments. This behavior led one newspaper columnist, Finley Peter Dunne, writing in a thick Irish dialect, to summarize Roosevelt's trust policies as mixed: "On wan hand I wud stamp thim undher fut; on th' other hand not so fast."

Battling Monopolies

Roosevelt combined dramatic public relations with moderate action in 1902. J.P. Morgan, a powerful Wall Street banker, had joined with a handful of the nation's wealthiest men to finance the Northern Securities Company. This holding company combined the stock of the Union Pacific, Northern Pacific, and Burlington railroads to dominate rail service from Chicago to the Pacific Ocean. Roosevelt, deciding that the company was a monopoly in violation of the Sherman Antitrust Act, ordered his attorney general to file suit against the Northern Securities Company in 1902.

In 1904 the Supreme Court, in a 5–4 vote, sided with Roosevelt, ruling that the Northern Securities Company had indeed violated the Sherman Antitrust Act. Roosevelt declared victory, claiming it as "one of the great achievements of my administration. . . . The most powerful men in the country were held to accountability before the law."

Much of the public hailed Roosevelt as a trustbuster who challenged and defeated the most powerful financiers in the United States. The common, working people felt they had a fearless ally in the White House, one who would defend them from powerful corporations.

Despite the public praise, the Northern Securities case hardly changed the day-to-day operations of the railroads. The railroads west of Chicago continued to operate under the control of a few giant railroad firms, with little competition. None of the organizers of the trust went to jail or suffered significant financial loss for breaking the law. Instead they remained immensely powerful. Within a few months, Morgan would help Roosevelt further develop his image as a defender of the public interest.

Heating Fuel Sources, 1902

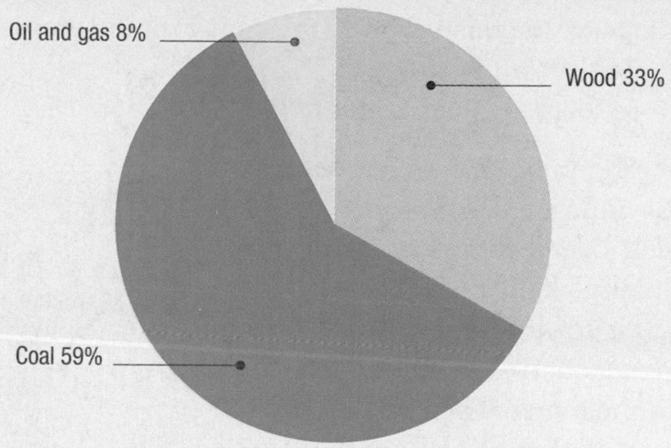

Many Americans used coal for cooking fuel as well as for heating. *How important a role did coal play as a heating resource?*

Settling Strikes

In May 1902, the United Mine Workers (UMW) called a strike of the miners who dug the anthracite, or hard coal, that fired most of the furnaces in the United States. The UMW hoped to win a 20 percent pay increase and to reduce the miners' long workday to 8 hours, while at the same time securing the mine owners' recognition of the union. For their part, the mine owners firmly opposed a union that might force them to raise wages and improve mine safety conditions. They simply refused to negotiate with the striking workers.

The strike continued through the summer and into the fall. As the reality of a cold winter approached, the shivering public demanded a settlement. President Roosevelt stepped in and urged the union and the owners to accept **arbitration,** a settlement imposed by an outside party.

Although the UMW agreed, the owners did not. They intended to destroy the union, regardless of the public interest. One of the owners, George Baer, claimed that workers did not need a union, that they should trust the selfless, conscientious owners:

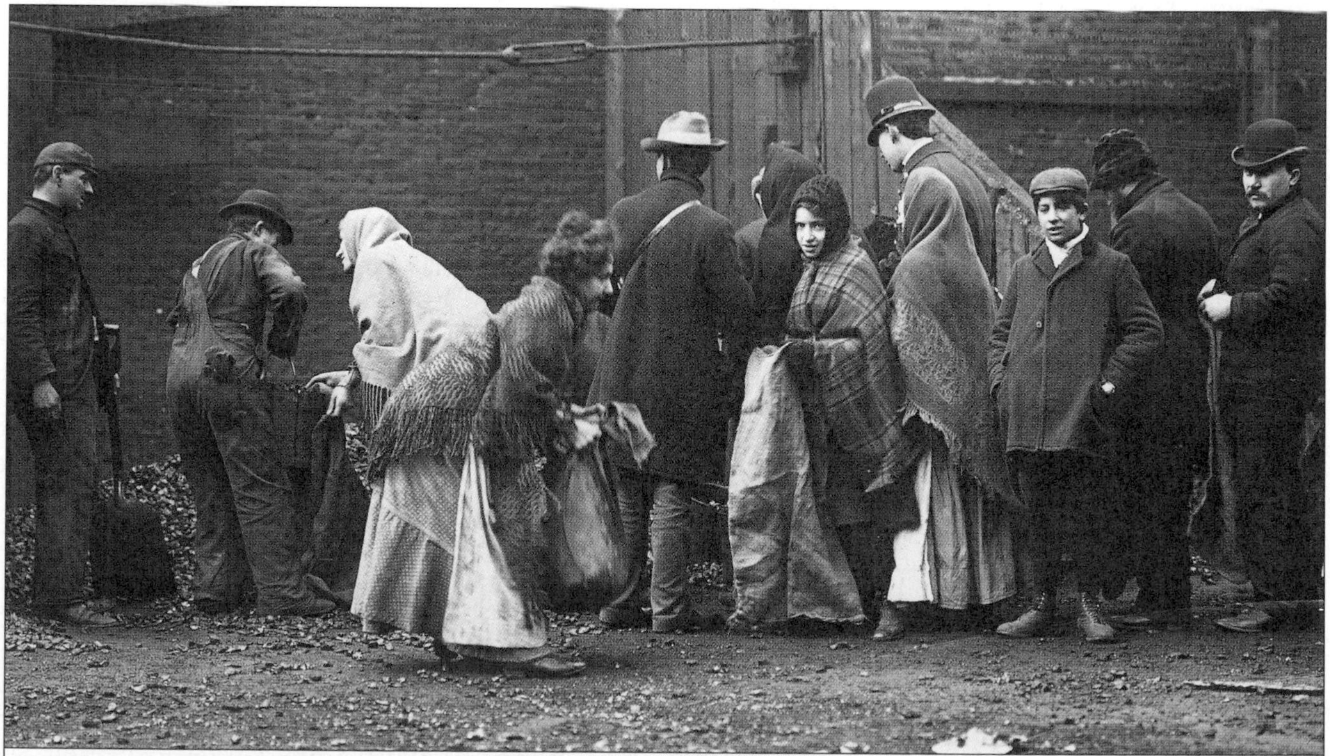

CULVER PICTURES

Coal Strike of 1902 As the coal supply dwindled during the coal strike of 1902, the lines of people fearful of facing a winter without coal grew longer. *Why did mine owners initially resist an arbitrated settlement?*

The rights and interests of the laboring man will be protected and cared for not by the labor agitators, but by the Christian men to whom God in His infinite wisdom has given the control of the property interests of the country.

—George F. Baer, *Letter to W.F. Clark*, July 17, 1902

The mine owners' stubbornness infuriated Roosevelt, who called Baer's comment "arrogant stupidity." If the owners refused to submit to arbitration, Roosevelt threatened to order federal troops into the mines. Then he sent Secretary of War Elihu Root to meet with J.P. Morgan to work out a settlement proposal. Fearing that Roosevelt would carry through on his threat and responding to the urging of the powerful Morgan, the mine owners finally accepted arbitration. The result was a compromise that gave each side part of what it had sought.

The miners won a 9-hour workday and a 10 percent pay increase, which was passed along to consumers in the form of higher coal prices. On the issue of union recognition, however, the owners won—they did not have to recognize the union.

In 1904, when Roosevelt ran for President in his own right, he coined a phrase that could have been used to describe his approach to the coal strike: "I shall see to it that every man has a square deal, no less and no more." Roosevelt saw himself standing above the battling classes, rendering to each a fair share of the spoils.

Despite the coal price hike, a relieved public felt it had been given a square deal. Americans hailed Roosevelt, whose powerful language shaped the public image of him as a fighter for their protection. Not since Abraham Lincoln had a President seemed to act so boldly on behalf of the public's interest.

THE GREAT HEALTH DRINK
Say! YOU OUGHT TO DRINK
Hires' Rootbeer

HIRES ROOT BEER: COURTESY OF THE PROCTER AND GAMBLE COMPANY

Buyer Beware Progressives were first to take action against false advertising claims by patent medicines and foods. *What legislation was passed to protect consumers?*

Protecting Consumers

Roosevelt also defended the public interest on consumer issues. He was President when Upton Sinclair published *The Jungle* in 1906, exposing the unsanitary practices of the meatpacking industry. *The Jungle* provoked a massive crusade. Roosevelt jumped to the head of the crusade and pushed the Meat Inspection Act through Congress.

The Meat Inspection Act of 1906 outlawed misleading labels and dangerous chemical preservatives. It also showed Roosevelt's willingness to compromise with the trusts. For example, Roosevelt agreed that the government, rather than the packers, should pay for the inspection. In addition, he dropped the requirement that meat be dated, which would have informed consumers about the meat's age.

★ ★ ★ Gallery of Presidents ★ ★ ★

William Howard Taft

1909–1913

"I have had the honor to be one of the advisers of my distinguished predecessor, and, as such, to hold up his hands in the reforms he has initiated. I should be untrue to myself, to my promises, and to the declarations of the party platform upon which I was elected to office, if I did not make the . . . enforcement of those reforms a most important feature of my administration."

Inaugural Address, March 4, 1909

THE BETTMANN ARCHIVE

Background

- **Born 1857; Died 1930**
- **Republican, Ohio**
- **Governor of the Philippines 1901–1904**
- **Secretary of War 1904–1908**
- **Chief Justice of the United States 1921–1930**

Achievements in Office

- **Postal Savings System (1910)**
- **Alaska given territorial government (1912)**

Though *The Jungle* focused specifically on meat, progressives worried about all of the foods and medicines that Americans consumed. Quack doctors sold concoctions of alcohol, cocaine, opium, and other drugs that claimed to heal everything from liver ailments to baldness. Many of these patent medicines, or nonprescription drugs, were worthless at best and addictive or dangerous at worst. On the same day that Congress passed the Meat Inspection Act, it also passed the Pure Food and Drug Act. This act prohibited the manufacture, sale, or shipment of impure or falsely labeled food and drugs in interstate commerce. The Food and Drug Administration (FDA) was not established until much later, in 1938. This agency broadly expanded the power of the federal government to protect consumers from fraudulent advertising claims by patent medicine dealers and from unsafe foods.

THE BETTMANN ARCHIVE

Taft's Style "There is no use trying to be William Howard Taft with Roosevelt's ways," Taft said. He was happiest as a lawyer outside politics. *What were Taft's strengths?*

Going Beyond Roosevelt

Taft Quietly Furthers Roosevelt's Work

No President before had ever served more than two terms. In keeping with that tradition, Roosevelt decided not to run for reelection in 1908. Instead Roosevelt chose his fellow Republican, William Howard Taft, an experienced diplomat and administrator, to run for President on the Republican ticket. Taft, a large, slow-moving, but extremely intelligent man, ran a mild-mannered campaign. Thanks to Roosevelt's energetic efforts on his behalf, however, Taft won the election.

In office Taft repeated the pattern he had established on the campaign trail. Instead of dashing about, making fiery speeches and remaining in the public eye, Taft remained calm, quiet, and often almost unnoticeable.

Although he had none of Roosevelt's flair, Taft carried out—and went beyond—many of his predecessor's policies. In dealing with trusts, he rejected accommodation in favor of prosecution. In only four years as President, Taft prosecuted almost twice as many trusts as did Roosevelt in his nearly eight years, including two of the most powerful, Standard Oil and the American Tobacco Company.

In other areas, Taft was at least as strong a progressive as Roosevelt. He expanded the number of acres of national forest. He supported laws requiring mine owners to improve safety. He established the Children's Bureau, a federal agency that protected the rights and interests of children.

Despite all of these achievements, Taft never received the public acclaim Roosevelt did. Taft did not view the presidency as a bully pulpit from which to lead moral crusades. Rather, he considered the presidency an administrative post, a job. He never had the eye for public relations opportunities that Roosevelt had. Nor did he have the ability to mobilize the nation with stirring speeches as Roosevelt had. By 1912 Roosevelt had become completely disillusioned with Taft; he was upset over Taft's failure to exert strong public leadership. With a new presidential election on the horizon, Roosevelt wondered if Taft was enough of a progressive activist to warrant his continued support.

Section Review

Vocabulary

1. Define: resource management, holding company, arbitration.

Checking Facts

2. What were the highlights of Roosevelt's resource management plan? How did his background influence his actions?
3. How did Roosevelt's handling of the coal strike expand presidential power?

Critical Thinking

Determining Cause and Effect

4. What effect did Roosevelt have on the attitude of the public toward the use of natural resources?

Linking Across Time

5. Compare the ideas of Theodore Roosevelt and of William Taft regarding the use of government power.

SECTION 2

Woodrow Wilson and the New Freedom

SEPTEMBER 1910: BOSSES NOMINATE WILSON FOR GOVERNOR

Thomas Woodrow Wilson
As an undergraduate, Wilson and his friends made a "compact" to become powerful and principled leaders.

"LOOK AT THAT MAN'S JAW!" EXCLAIMED A DELEGATE TO THE NEW JERSEY DEMOCRATIC CONVENTION UPON SEEING THE TALL, SHARPLY DRESSED WOODROW WILSON FOR THE FIRST TIME. That long, strong jaw of the just-nominated candidate for governor suggested an unbending moralist, one solidly in the progressive mold. Wilson, however, was not the candidate of New Jersey progressives; he was the handpicked choice of machine boss James Smith, Jr. The New Jersey machine backed Wilson, the popular president of Princeton University, because he was both electable and, as a political novice, nonthreatening to the entrenched machine. When Wilson rose to give his acceptance speech, however, he expressed views that neither the bosses nor the reformers expected from him:

> I shall enter upon the duties of the office of governor, if elected, with absolutely no pledge of any kind to prevent me from serving the people of the state with singleness of purpose.
>
> —Woodrow Wilson, Acceptance Speech, 1910

With these words, Wilson declared his independence from the machine. From a reformer in the delegation came the cry, "Thank God, at last, a leader has come!" "Go on, go on," other delegates shouted. Wilson went on to pledge his support for almost every progressive cause desired by New Jersey reformers, from direct election of senators

AS YOU READ

Vocabulary	Think About . . .	
► regulatory commission ► socialism ► capitalism	► how Woodrow Wilson's background shaped his actions as a politician. ► the similarities and differences among the presidential candidates in the 1912 election.	► examples of how Woodrow Wilson expanded the power of the presidency.

to the establishment of utility **regulatory commissions** to oversee the utilities' compliance with existing laws. At the end of his speech, the reformers, who had greeted him skeptically, applauded wildly. Some reformers ran up to the platform and tried to lift him to their shoulders, but Wilson would have none of that. His sponsors, figuring that the new politician was just playing to the crowd, assumed his backbone was not as strong as his jaw. They were wrong. Soon after election, Wilson began destroying the political machine that brought him to power.

Wilson's Rise to Power

From Professor to Progressive

Thomas Woodrow Wilson entered politics with a firm set of moral values that he had learned from his father, a Presbyterian minister, and his mother, the daughter of a Presbyterian minister. Wilson was born in Virginia in 1856 and grew up in Georgia and South Carolina. Although both of his parents were educated and avid readers, "Tommy" did not learn the alphabet until age 9 and could not read until age 11. Although he may have suffered from a learning disability, he persevered and became an excellent student. He attended law school, and eventually received a Ph.D. in political science from Johns Hopkins University in 1886. During his 16 years as a professor, he frequently won praise from students for his outstanding skills as a lecturer. In 1902 he was selected president of Princeton University, a post he held until he ran for governor.

When nominated, Wilson possessed no government experience. In dozens of articles and several books written during his academic career, however, he had expressed his political views. Wilson ridiculed Populists as "crude and ignorant" for their unquestioning trust in the wisdom of common citizens. He attacked Theodore Roosevelt and the Republicans for carrying political reforms to "radical lengths." The best model of government, he said, was the British system, which allowed for slow, orderly change under strong leadership from a well-educated elite. Because of his criticisms of most reformers and his praise for the British system, Wilson was generally branded a conservative rather than a progressive Democrat.

Once elected, however, Wilson proved that he was independent of the machine. Smith wanted to return to the seat he had once held in the United States Senate. Because the Seventeenth Amendment had not yet been ratified, the New Jersey legislature appointed the state's two senators. Smith, who had recruited Wilson to run for governor, expected Wilson's support in winning the votes of state legislators. In the Democratic primary, Smith had finished behind Thomas E. Martine. Wilson, calling machine bosses "warts upon the body politic," endorsed Martine. Without the governor's backing, an exasperated Smith and his machine lost. As one reporter put it, Wilson had "licked that gang to a frazzle."

NEWARK EVENING NEWS

Boss Smith **Wilson tried to dissuade Smith from running for senator and eventually backed Martine on principle.** *How did Wilson's first actions as governor surprise people?*

From that battle onward, Wilson supported and won one progressive reform after another in New Jersey. He revamped election laws, established utility regulatory boards, and allowed cities to change to the commissioner form of government. To the embarrassment of the New Jersey machine, in less than two years as governor, Wilson transformed the state into a model of progressive reform.

The Election of 1912

Spoilers and Third Parties

Wilson's success in New Jersey attracted national attention. The Democratic party, which had elected only 1 President since the Civil War, needed a fresh new leader. The party met in Baltimore in June 1912, to choose its presidential nominee. The leading contenders were Wilson and Champ Clark, a Missouri representative and longtime reform activist. During a solid week of feverish politicking and 45 rounds of voting, the delegates could not reach agreement on a candidate. Finally the powerful Illinois machine threw its support to Wilson, and he won the nomination. In the 1912 election, as in 1910, Wilson owed his success to machine politicians.

BROWN BROTHERS

Socialist Candidate Debs **Eugene Debs (in the train window, wearing a bow tie) takes time out from his busy whistle-stop campaign to pose with his campaign workers.** *Why did some of Debs's supporters not vote for him?*

The Republicans

The Republicans were even more divided than the Democrats. Taft retained the support of most party officials, but few progressive Republicans stood by him. Widespread Democratic successes in the 1910 congressional elections convinced many Republicans that supporting Taft would cost them the White House in 1912. Progressive Republicans turned to the only person powerful enough to challenge an incumbent President: former President Roosevelt. Fearing that Taft was not progressive enough and that other leaders like Robert La Follette were too radical, Roosevelt entered the race. At the Republican Convention, though, Taft won the nomination.

The Bull Moose Party

Instead of quietly accepting defeat, Roosevelt bolted the Republican party. Declaring himself "fit as a bull moose," he created the Progressive party, often called the Bull Moose party. Social reformers, including Jane Addams, eagerly flocked to Roosevelt. "Roosevelt bit me and I went mad," confessed Kansas journalist William Allen White. The Progressive party platform included calls for many long-standing goals of the progressives: a minimum-wage law for women; prohibition of child labor; workers' compensation laws; a federal trade commission to regulate business and industry; woman suffrage; and initiative, referendum, and recall.

THE BETTMANN ARCHIVE

Bull Moose Paraphernalia **The Progressive party was loud, colorful, and often compared to a revival meeting.** *How did the Progressive party get its nickname?*

In addition to Wilson, Taft, and Roosevelt, Eugene Debs ran for President. Debs, leader of the American Railway Union during the Pullman strike in 1894, had run in 1908 and received about 420,000 votes. Debs believed in **socialism,** an economic theory advocating collective, or social, ownership of factories, mines, and other businesses. As a response to the problems caused by private ownership of big business, socialism gained considerable support in the United States in the early 1900s. Debs rejected the moral and economic basis of **capitalism,** in which private individuals own the means of production and profit by their ownership. If trusts did not serve the public interest, Debs passionately argued, then the government should take them over and run them. His faith in people and his energy won Debs many followers. One supporter commented, "That old man with the burning eyes actually believes that there can be such a thing as the brotherhood of man. And that's not the funniest part of it. As long as he's around I believe it myself."

POLITICAL MATHEMATICS.

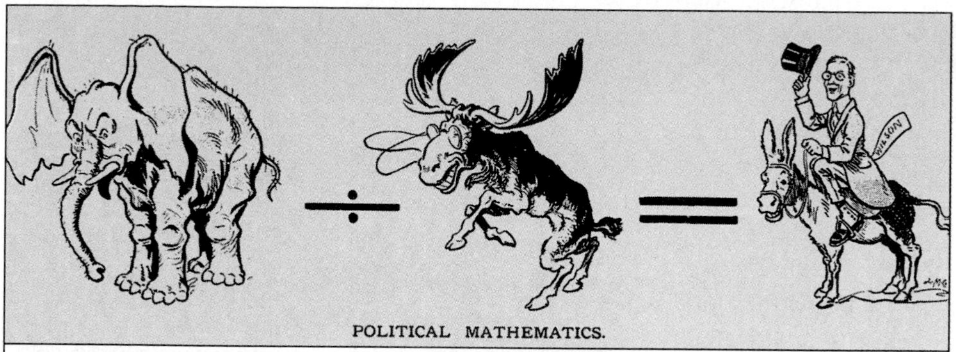

CULVER PICTURES

Party Division The cartoon above was printed on September 4, 1912. Using political and mathematical symbols, the cartoonist reduced the election to its lowest common denominator. *Which party does each animal symbolize?*

The Front-runners

Debs, despite his powerful oratory, and Taft, despite his influence as the incumbent, soon realized that they could not win. Taft recognized that many voters opposed him because they thought he lacked leadership on progressive causes. "I might as well give up," he lamented, "there are so many people in the country who don't like me." Debs attracted large crowds wherever he went, but he could not convince many of his supporters that he had a chance to win. They gave their vote instead to one of the two front-runners, Wilson or Roosevelt.

Wilson and Roosevelt agreed on many basic issues, such as the need for a stronger federal government to influence the economy, but to win votes the candidates highlighted their differences, particularly on the great question of the day—the trusts.

The Trust Issue

Roosevelt believed that trusts must be accepted and regulated. Though known as a trustbuster while President, in 1912 he maintained that breaking up the trusts was "futile madness." Big companies, Roosevelt decided, were as necessary to modern life as big factories, big stores, and big cities. He ridiculed efforts to promote competition in a trust-dominated economy as "preposterous."

Instead, government must be big enough and powerful enough to protect the public interest by controlling the excesses of big business. Just as La Follette in Wisconsin tamed the railroads by setting up a commission of experts to oversee their operation, so Roosevelt proposed establishing a federal regulatory commission to oversee trade practices of big businesses. He labeled that regulatory program the New Nationalism.

Wilson criticized Roosevelt's program as one that supported "regulated monopoly." If big businesses were destroying competition, Wilson argued, then government must break up big businesses. He urged that a strong federal government should dismantle—not regulate—the trusts so that small businesses could once again compete freely. Wilson referred to his program of restoring competition as the New Freedom. He

PRESIDENTIAL ELECTION, 1912

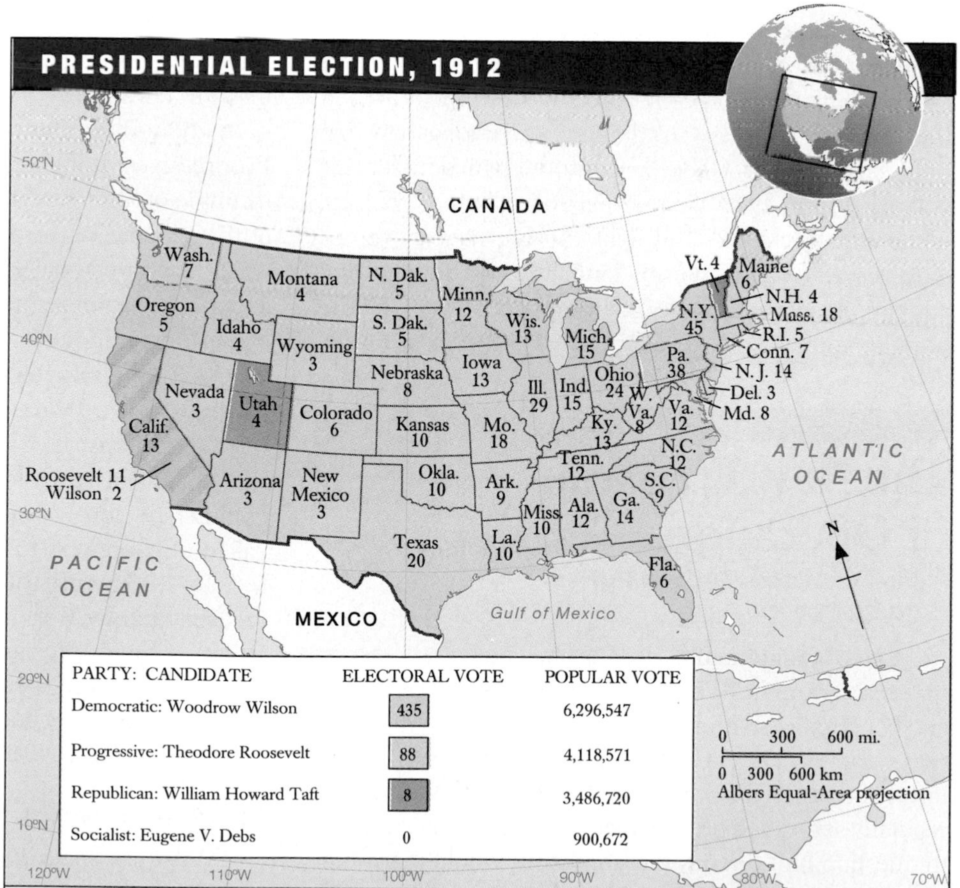

PARTY: CANDIDATE	ELECTORAL VOTE	POPULAR VOTE
Democratic: Woodrow Wilson	435	6,296,547
Progressive: Theodore Roosevelt	88	4,118,571
Republican: William Howard Taft	8	3,486,720
Socialist: Eugene V. Debs	0	900,672

In 1908 people had said that the name Taft stood for "Take advice from Teddy." By 1912, however, "Teddy" Roosevelt had abandoned the incumbent President Taft and formed a party to run against him. *Which states voted for President Taft?*

pledged to make the nation safe for aggressive young entrepreneurs once again: "What this country needs above everything else is a body of laws which will look after the men who are on the make rather than the men who are already made."

The Campaign Trail

Wilson, with a smooth, analytical speaking style honed during years of lecturing as a professor, and Roosevelt, with his energetic personality, captivated audiences wherever they spoke. Crowds of 10,000 people, straining to hear, stood and listened to hour-long speeches from each candidate. In Milwaukee on October 14, less than a month before the election, a would-be assassin shot Roosevelt as he prepared to give a speech. Slowed by his glasses case and the bulky speech still in his coat pocket, the bullet did not stop Roosevelt. "Friends," he began, "I shall have to ask you to be as quiet as possible. I do not know whether you fully understand that I have just been shot, but it takes more than that to kill a Bull Moose." He gave his speech, at times nearly fainting, before going to the hospital for treatment. Wilson, in a show of fair play, suspended his campaign until Roosevelt recovered.

The intensive campaigning and brilliant oratory, though, did not inspire the citizens. On Election Day, only 59 percent of the voters went to the polls and they seemed to follow traditional party loyalties. The only surprise was Debs, who more than doubled his vote total from 1908. Democrats united behind Wilson, while Roosevelt and Taft split the Republican voters. The result: Wilson won a landslide in the electoral college, even though he got only 42 percent of the popular vote.

The New Freedom in Operation

Wilson Increases Federal Power

Once inaugurated Wilson immediately took charge of the government. "The president is at liberty, both in law and conscience, to be as big a man as he can," Wilson had once written. "His capacity will set the limit." Two weeks into his term, Wilson became the first President to hold regularly scheduled press conferences. Allowing reporters to question him directly, Wilson knew, would make him a more powerful leader in shaping legislation. During his eight years as President, Wilson demonstrated his power as he crafted reforms affecting the tariffs, the banking system, the trusts, and the rights of workers.

STOCK MONTAGE

Wilson in Action Wilson broke a 113-year tradition by addressing Congress. *What was Wilson's view of tariffs?*

Reducing Tariffs

Five weeks after taking office, Wilson appeared before Congress—something no President had done since John Adams in 1800—to present his bill to reduce tariffs. High tariffs symbolized the special treatment government accorded big business. Adding taxes to the price of imported goods protected businesses from foreign competition. The consumers paid for this protection of big business in the form of higher prices. Progressives had long attacked high tariffs as an example of how government served the special interests at the expense of the public interest.

Wilson personally lobbied members of Congress to support the tariff reduction bill. Rarely had a President, even Roosevelt, taken such an active role in promoting specific legislation. Representatives for the trusts flooded Washington to defeat the tariff reduction bill. Wilson took the offensive. Charging that the nation's capital was so full of lobbyists for big business that "a brick couldn't be thrown without hitting one of them," he called on Congress to defend "the interests of the public." In 1913, with the attention of the voting public focused on it by Wilson's charges, Congress passed and Wilson signed into law the Underwood Tariff, which reduced the average tariff on imported goods to about 30 percent of the value of the goods, or about half the tariff rate in the 1890s.

Reforming Banks

Wilson's second major legislative initiative attempted to bolster the banking industry. The United States had not had a central bank since the 1830s, when President Andrew Jackson destroyed the Second Bank of the United States. During the economic depressions

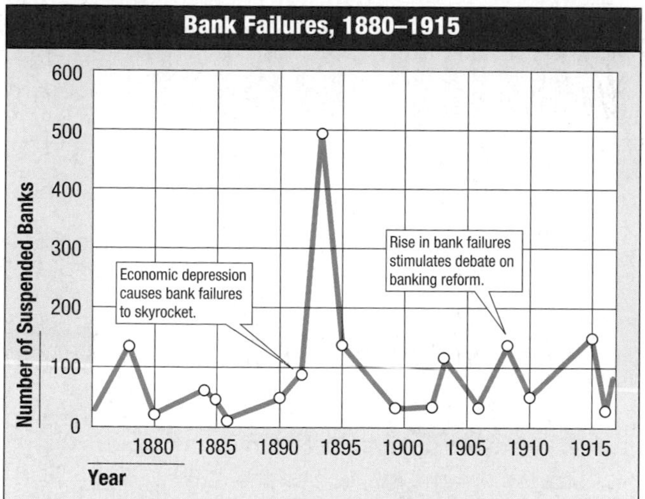

In 1907, 91 banks failed in what became known as the Panic of 1907. In 1908 the number of bank failures rose to 155.
Which year in this 35-year period saw the most bank failures?

that had hit the United States periodically over the decades that followed, hundreds of small banks collapsed in bankruptcy, wiping out the life savings of many of their depositors. To restore public confidence in the banking system, Wilson proposed establishing a Federal Reserve System. Banks would have to keep a portion of their deposits in a reserve bank, which would provide a financial cushion against unanticipated losses. If banks prepared better for economic downturns, Wilson reasoned, fewer would go broke when depressions hit. In addition, a reserve system would serve as a central bank for the entire economy, controlling interest rates and the amount of money in circulation.

Advocates of a reserve system disagreed about who should control the reserve banks. Wealthy bank presidents and industrialists argued that the big banks should control the system because they had the expertise. Many progressives favored a government regulatory agency directly controlled by the President and Congress and thereby responsive to the public. Wilson proposed a compromise system composed of 12 regional banks that a board appointed by the President would oversee. Congress approved Wilson's proposal at the end of 1913, creating the Federal Reserve System.

Regulating Trusts

When he entered the White House, Wilson vowed to break up the trusts. In 1914 Congress passed the Clayton Antitrust Act, which broadened the Sherman Antitrust Act of 1890. For example, the Clayton Act promoted competition by prohibiting interlocking directorates, which allowed companies to work together to reduce competition. The Clayton Act also made corporate officers personally responsible for violations of antitrust laws.

Wilson also backed efforts to regulate trusts. In 1914 Congress established the Federal Trade Commission (FTC), which attempted to stop unfair trading and business practices among companies. For example, the FTC could prevent companies from working together in order to keep prices high. Fair trade, Wilson hoped, would give small companies better chances to compete with larger companies.

Protecting Workers

As President, Wilson supported a variety of progressive federal labor laws. For example, in 1916, Wilson signed the first federal law regulating the use of children as workers in factories and mines. The Supreme Court struck down the law in 1918, however, claiming that whether or not children could work was a matter for the state courts.

Wilson also supported laws requiring that all companies contracting with the government provide their workers with compensation for injuries on the job. These laws greatly strengthened the role of the federal government in protecting workers.

During his presidency Wilson built upon Roosevelt's foundation. He expanded the role of the federal government and of the President. Like Roosevelt, Wilson saw himself as a crusader, using federal power to protect common citizens. In Wilson's view (and that of most progressives), however, the common citizens were white, native-born, and capitalists. Other Americans, such as African Americans, immigrants, and socialists, often suffered during the Progressive era.

Section Review

Vocabulary

1. Define: regulatory commission, socialism, capitalism.

Checking Facts

2. As governor of New Jersey, how did Wilson demonstrate his political independence? How did this independence shape his presidency?
3. How was the Clayton Antitrust Act an example of expanding presidential power?

Critical Thinking

Making Generalizations

4. Based on the actions of Roosevelt, Taft, and Wilson, what statement can you make about the value of public relations to politicians?

Linking Across Time

5. Roosevelt and Wilson's view of the presidency differed from McKinley and Taft's. Give examples to show the current President's view.

Critical Thinking Skill

MAKING COMPARISONS

Learning the Skill

When you make comparisons, you determine similarities and differences between ideas, events, or objects. Knowing how to make comparisons will help you understand historical change. Differing points of view voiced by groups and individuals can influence the course of history. For example, environmentalists may advocate the preservation of national parks as a necessary and beneficial government action; the logging industry may oppose the same preservation issue as an interference in the pursuit of their business. Comparing the positions helps in understanding the issues.

Making comparisons can help you organize information in your writing or thinking. It is also a citizenship skill that will help you choose between alternative candidates or policies.

The Process

Follow these steps to make comparisons:

a. Identify or decide what will be compared.

b. Determine a common area or areas in which comparisons can be drawn, such as positions on a certain issue, reactions to a certain event, goals of certain groups, and so on.

c. Look for similarities and differences within these areas. For example, two politicians' positions on labor rights might be very similar, very different, or similar in some respects and different in others.

d. If possible, find information that explains the similarities and differences.

Practicing the Skill

1. Using the chart below, identify the groups that share the same position on the strike.

2. Do those groups have the same reasons for their positions? Explain.

3. On what common grounds can you compare the various groups?

4. Which two groups' positions and reasons conflict the most?

5. Which point of view is probably most similar to that of the United Mine Workers?

Applying the Skill

Take an opinion poll among your classmates about a current issue in the news. Summarize the opinions and write a paragraph comparing the different results. What reasons could explain the differences or similarities?

Additional Practice

For additional practice, see Reinforcing Skills on page 291.

COMPARISON CHART

Who?	Position on the Coal Strike of 1902	Why?
United Mine Workers	Supports	They originated the strike, seeking an 8-hour workday and recognition of their union.
Mine owners	Oppose	They believe workers' demands are excessive and want to crush the union, keeping the industry free of regulation.
Coal-consuming public	Opposes	They suffer from the coal shortages and high prices that the strike engenders.
President Roosevelt	Officially neutral	He wants to halt the strike, but thinks owners are too selfish.
IWW	Supports	While not agreeing with the UMW on everything, the IWW promotes solidarity with all workers.

SECTION 3

Limits to Progressivism

NOVEMBER 1914: AFRICAN AMERICAN ACTIVIST CHALLENGES WILSON

PHOTOGRAPHS AND PRINTS DIVISION, SCHOMBURG CENTER FOR RESEARCH IN BLACK CULTURE, NEW YORK PUBLIC LIBRARY, ASTOR, LENOX AND TILDEN FOUNDATIONS.

William Monroe Trotter
In 1901 Trotter founded the *Guardian,* which reached a circulation of 2,500 within 8 months.

"Two years ago you were thought to be a second Lincoln," William Monroe Trotter angrily reminded President Wilson. Trotter, the outspoken editor of the Boston newspaper the *Guardian,* and four other African American leaders were meeting with Wilson to protest the segregation of African American and white workers in federal offices in Washington, D.C. These offices had been integrated for almost 50 years, since the end of the Civil War, and now the President had tried to change that. Wilson agreed to meet with the African American delegation, but he had little sympathy for their complaints. After nearly an hour of tense discussion, an exasperated Trotter challenged President Wilson, "Have you a New Freedom for white Americans and a new slavery for 'your Afro-American fellow citizens'? God forbid!"

Wilson resented anyone challenging his authority, particularly a defiant African American. "You have spoiled the whole cause for which you came!" barked Wilson, as he pointed to the door. The meeting was over, and the five men exited. Though unsuccessful in changing Wilson's policy, Trotter's final question did make his objective clear: he wanted progressives to address the needs of African Americans as well as white Americans.

Few white progressives thought to challenge the racism rampant in American society because they themselves had deeply negative attitudes toward all minority groups. As a result African Americans found themselves ignored by the mainstream of the Progressive movement. Two other groups—immigrants and radical workers—also found themselves battling progressives on many issues.

As You Read

Vocabulary

- accommodation
- melting pot
- nativism
- eugenics

Think About . . .

- the obstacles to and shortcomings of the Progressive movement.
- what areas of conflict existed between progressives and immigrants.
- the relationship between progressives and workers.

CULVER PICTURES

BROWN BROTHERS

Washington's Successes **Booker T. Washington (with Roosevelt, upper right) was the first African American invited to the White House for dinner. As founder and president of Tuskegee Institute (a vocational school, the print shop of which is shown above), Washington was the most admired African American leader in the beginning of the 1900s.** *What did Washington and his school promote?*

African Americans and Equality

"Jim Crow" Entrenched

For African Americans, continuing poverty and discrimination marked the Progressive era. About two-thirds of African Americans scratched out livings in the rural South. Most were sharecroppers, farmers who traded a share of their crop in return for land to plant and money to buy seeds and tools. Sharecroppers generally found that the tobacco or cotton they raised barely covered their rent and the money they had borrowed, so they were almost always in debt.

African Americans who could leave their farms joined the flood of rural people moving to cities in search of opportunity. Though most went to Southern cities, an increasing number headed north, hoping to escape racism. In Northern cities, though, African Americans found much of the same discrimination and segregation that they had experienced in the South. In addition, in the North, African Americans competed with immigrants for jobs. This competition created tension and sometimes violence between the two groups.

In both the North and the South, segregation was a matter of custom. Beginning in the 1880s, however, Southern states and cities started passing laws requiring racial segregation. Taking their name from a character in an old minstrel song, the Jim Crow laws required, for example, that trains have separate cars for African American and white passengers. They also mandated segregation in hotels, restaurants, parks, and every facility open to the public. Atlanta even required separate Bibles for African Americans and whites to swear upon when called as witnesses in court cases. In 1896, in *Plessy* v. *Ferguson,* the Supreme Court ruled that separate, segregated facilities were constitutional as long as they were equal. The only dissenter in the "separate but equal" decision was Justice John Harlan, a Southerner and former slaveholder. "Our Constitution is color-blind," protested Harlan fruitlessly.

Despite the requirements of the courts that separate facilities must be equal, they rarely if ever were. African American children received a second-class education compared to what white children received. For example, in 1900 in Adams County, Mississippi, the school system spent $22.25 per white student and only $2 per African American student.

Accommodating Racism

Leading one African American response to racism in the Progressive era was Booker T. Washington. The son of enslaved parents, Washington grew up in a log cabin with a dirt floor. He worked as a janitor to pay his way through Hampton Institute, a federally funded school in Virginia in 1868 established to educate African Americans freed from slavery. In 1881 the state of Alabama hired the mild-mannered but ambitious 25-year-old Washington to open a vocational school for African Americans in Tuskegee. Over the next 33 years, Washington molded Tuskegee Institute into a nationally prominent school where African American students could learn 38 trades and professions, including farming, forestry, plumbing, sewing, and nursing.

Washington believed that African Americans could achieve economic prosperity, independence, and the respect of whites through hard work as farmers, craft workers, and laborers. By succeeding at such jobs, African Americans would become valuable members of their communities without posing a threat to whites. Publicly Washington urged African Americans to bend to white racism by accepting without challenge Jim Crow laws, voting restrictions, and less desirable jobs. This policy, known as **accommodation,** emphasized economic success over racial equality.

Many African Americans, particularly poor farmers, agreed with Washington. Struggling to escape poverty, they believed that economic gains were more important than winning the vote, ending segregation, or directly challenging white domination.

ARCHIVE PHOTOS

William Edward Burghardt Du Bois Both Du Bois and Trotter opposed Washington's views. *What idea did Du Bois reject?*

Agitating for Equality

In spite of Washington's popularity, many African Americans opposed Washington's apparently meek acceptance of humiliating discrimination. The leading opponent of accommodation was W.E.B. Du Bois. Born in 1868 and raised in a free African American family in Massachusetts, Du Bois became the first African American to receive a Ph.D. from Harvard University. He taught history and social science at Atlanta University before helping found the National Association for the Advancement of Colored People (NAACP) in 1909. He served as that organization's director of publications for 24 years.

A proud and strong-willed man, Du Bois summoned African Americans to demand equality at once. "The way for a people to gain their reasonable rights," he pointed out, "is not by voluntarily throwing them away." Du Bois argued that the key to winning equality was not in developing vocational skills but in voting. With the vote African Americans would gain the political influence to end lynchings, to provide better schools for their children, and, in general, to challenge the white domination of society.

Reacting to African Americans

Most white people, including most progressives, ignored or actively opposed the efforts of Du Bois, Washington, and other African Americans to achieve equality. Many agreed with Theodore Roosevelt, who confided to a friend, "Now as to the Negroes! I entirely agree with you that as a race and in the mass [they] are altogether inferior to the whites."

Some progressives—usually women—did support African American reformers. Jane Addams, for example, criticized racial discrimination and helped organize the NAACP. The alliance between white female reformers and African Americans reached back to the 1830s. Many white women continued to identify with the cause for racial equality because, like themselves, African Americans were caught in a web of discrimination.

Among sympathetic whites, Washington's ideas were more acceptable than those of Du Bois because Washington did not directly challenge white social and political domination. These people might have been less supportive had they known that Washington privately supported many of the same goals as Du Bois. He quietly provided money to pay for court cases challenging Jim Crow laws, to win back voting rights for African Americans, and to support antilynching campaigns.

The activism of Washington, Du Bois, and other African Americans led to some advances in spite of the lack of support from progressives. For example, the African American illiteracy rate was cut in half between 1900 and 1910, and the number of African Americans owning land increased by 10 percent.

Immigrants and the Melting Pot

American Anxiety Comes to a Boil

Like African Americans, immigrants struggled to find their place in American society. After the flood of newcomers from eastern and southern Europe between 1890 and 1914, immigrants and their children constituted about one-third of the American population. The United States became even more of a **melting pot**—a society in which various racial, ethnic, and cultural groups were blended together—than it had been before 1890. Each immigrant went through the assimilation process of absorbing a new culture. For most the first steps in assimilating the culture of the United States, or

Americanization, were learning English and understanding the laws and system of government of the United States.

Americanizing the Newcomers

Few progressives valued the cultural diversity that immigrants brought to the United States. Most, like Theodore Roosevelt, considered the cultures of all immigrant groups inferior to the culture of the United States. Americanization, to Roosevelt, was a process of stripping away an immigrant's old habits and replacing them with new, American ones. With his usual confidence, Roosevelt had no doubt that the American melting pot could assimilate as many European immigrants as wished to come to the United States.

Not everyone shared Roosevelt's optimism about the melting pot. Among those who feared that the flood of immigrants was destroying American culture were some progressives, as well as advocates of **nativism,** a policy of favoring native-born individuals over foreign-born ones.

Many nativists were Protestants who opposed immigration because of the large number of Roman Catholics, Eastern Orthodox Christians, and Jews who arrived between 1890 and 1920. As the chart on this page shows, the Protestant domination of the United States was facing a challenge. Other nativists feared that radical immigrants, though few in number, would undermine the economic system and the government of the United States.

Opposition to immigration existed throughout society. Woodrow Wilson, while a professor at Princeton, complained that countries such as Hungary and Poland were "disburdening themselves of the more sordid and hapless elements of their population." A sign in a restaurant in California read: "John's Restaurant. Pure American. No Rats. No Greeks." Job advertisements often included a footnote, "No Irish Need Apply."

Some opponents of immigration claimed to have scientific evidence proving that some racial or ethnic groups were superior to others. In particular they asserted that the Anglo-Saxon and Nordic peoples of northern and western Europe were smarter, stronger, and more moral than the Slavs and Mediterranean peoples of southern and eastern Europe. Jews, African Americans, and Asians, they claimed, were even more inferior. Based on these mistaken beliefs, some people advocated a **eugenics** movement, an effort to improve the human race by controlling breeding. The eugenics movement successfully convinced some state legislatures to allow forced sterilization of criminals and individuals who were diagnosed as having severe mental disabilities.

Imposing Restrictions

Nativists had begun calling for sweeping restrictions on immigration in the late 1840s. At that time about 150,000 Roman Catholics from Ireland were entering the United States each year because of a disastrous famine in their homeland.

As immigration swelled after 1880, reaching more than 1 million immigrants a year by 1905, the call for restriction became a loud chorus. The federal government began limiting Chinese immigration in 1882. In 1903 Congress prohibited individuals "dangerous to the public welfare," meaning political radicals, from immigrating. In 1907 Roosevelt worked out a "gentlemen's agreement" with Japan whereby the Japanese government limited the number of Japanese allowed to leave for the United States. All of these restrictions were targeted at specific groups. Still many Americans wanted much broader restrictions that would dramatically limit immigration from southern and eastern Europe.

In 1907, in response to the concerns of nativists, Congress established a commission to study how well immigrants were assimilating into American life. In its report issued in 1911, the Dillingham Commission concluded that the new immigrants from eastern and southern Europe were not assimilating as well as the older immigrants from western and northern Europe and that they never would. Hence, the commission recommended, Congress should restrict immigration, especially from eastern and southern Europe.

Some labor unions also called for immigration restrictions, hoping that a reduction in the number of people looking for work would help push wages upward. Ironically many labor union members were themselves recent immigrants.

Under these combined pressures, Congress adopted a wide-ranging restriction on immigration in 1917. This law refused entry to immigrants over the age of 16 who

Religious Membership in the United States

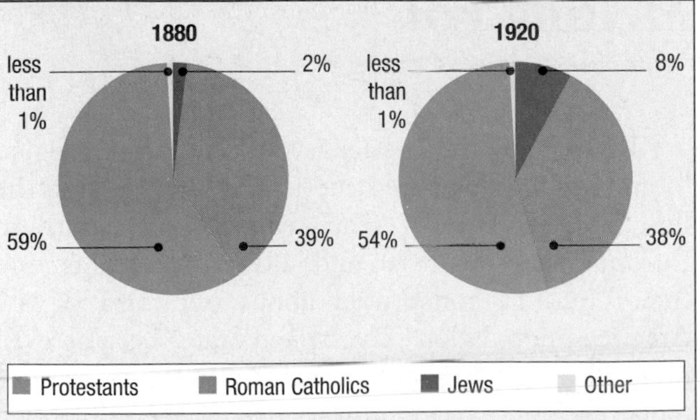

Religion has always been an important part of American life. *According to the graphs, how did the percentage of Americans who were Catholics change?*

BROWN BROTHERS

Closing the Door Behind Them Forgetting they were once immigrants themselves, many Americans demanded immigration restrictions. *What were some of the fears of those opposed to open immigration?*

could not pass a literacy test. Because schooling was limited in southern and eastern Europe, the literacy requirement affected immigration from these areas most sharply. More severe restrictions would come in the 1920s. (See Case Study, pages 404–407.)

Responding to Nativism

In a climate of restrictions and nativism, many immigrants relied upon one another for support. They formed mutual assistance societies, organizations that provided care for the sick and paid for funerals for members who died. Virtually every immigrant group had its own newspapers, its own athletic and social clubs, and its own theater groups. In many immigrant communities, churches and synagogues became centers of social as well as religious activity. There, new arrivals could meet people who spoke the same language and understood their customs.

Though old, ethnic hostilities frequently kept immigrant groups divided, they sometimes joined together for political battles, often in opposition to progressive reforms. For example, many immigrants supported the urban political machines that progressives tended to attack. Some poverty-stricken immigrant families who relied on the labor of their children to help them buy food and pay their rent opposed progressives who wanted to ban child labor. Immigrants from cultures in which drinking wine or beer was a traditional social behavior often resented progressives who advocated temperance. These conflicts over economic, social, and political issues increased tensions between immigrants and progressives.

Workers and Radicals

Progressives Uneasy as Unions Gain Strength

Progressives also had tense relationships with many labor unions and were deeply opposed to radical labor leaders and ideologies. On one hand progressives sympathized with workers in factories, mines, and mills who suffered from low wages, dangerous working conditions, and the constant threat of unemployment. Most progressives recognized that workers needed protection. On the other hand, progressives firmly supported capitalism and rejected all other economic systems. Most were horrified by socialists such as Eugene Debs, who argued that workers or the government should own the factories and operate them in the public interest.

Supporting Unions

Among progressives, the strongest advocates of unions were those who had the most contact with laboring people—the settlement house reformers. Jane Addams and others saw how unions won fairer wages, safer working conditions, and greater job stability for workers.

BROWN BROTHERS

United in Labor These picketers at a New York garment workers' strike carry signs in English, Greek, Yiddish, and Italian. *Why did some progressives dislike labor unions?*

In addition to backing unions, many progressives supported political reforms advocated by labor unions, such as limits on the length of the workday, a minimum wage for women, and an end to child labor. The largest labor organization was the American Federation of Labor (AFL), a coalition of unions that represented about 1.5 million workers by 1904. While the AFL called for these reforms, it trusted government less than did many progressives. The AFL realized that a government that could grant such reforms could also revoke them. The best protection for a worker, according to the AFL, was a strong union capable of negotiating with the owners.

AFL leaders also distrusted the government because they had frequently seen government side with owners to break strikes and crush unions. State governors or the President often sent in troops to reopen a plant shut down by striking workers. At other times courts ended strikes by declaring them illegal under the Sherman Antitrust Act, which banned all actions that restrained trade. Although this act was written to break up business monopolies, the courts used it to crack down on unions. Owners who knew that the courts or the troops would end a strike for them had almost no reason to negotiate with unions. Without that ability to strike, unions had little power.

Challenging Capitalism

Unions often included some socialists as members. While they envisioned radical changes in the long term, socialists often worked for short-term reforms that improved the lives of workers. They generally supported stronger unions that could fight for higher wages, shorter hours, and better working conditions. Socialists also called for public ownership of railroads, trolley lines, and utilities such as water and electricity. Most supported the right of women to vote.

Though the progressives shared many of the short-term goals of the socialists, the two groups analyzed problems differently and came up with different solutions. For example, when progressives saw a problem, such as the high number of workers killed on the job, they blamed insensitive owners and supported a factory safety law to solve the problem. Socialists seeing the same problem blamed the capitalist system of competition that forced owners to require workers to risk their lives so that the company could remain in business. Even if a law improved workplace safety, argued the socialists, the problems of workers would not go away until the competitive system that caused them was eliminated.

LABOR'S STRUGGLE FOR JUSTICE, 1880–1920

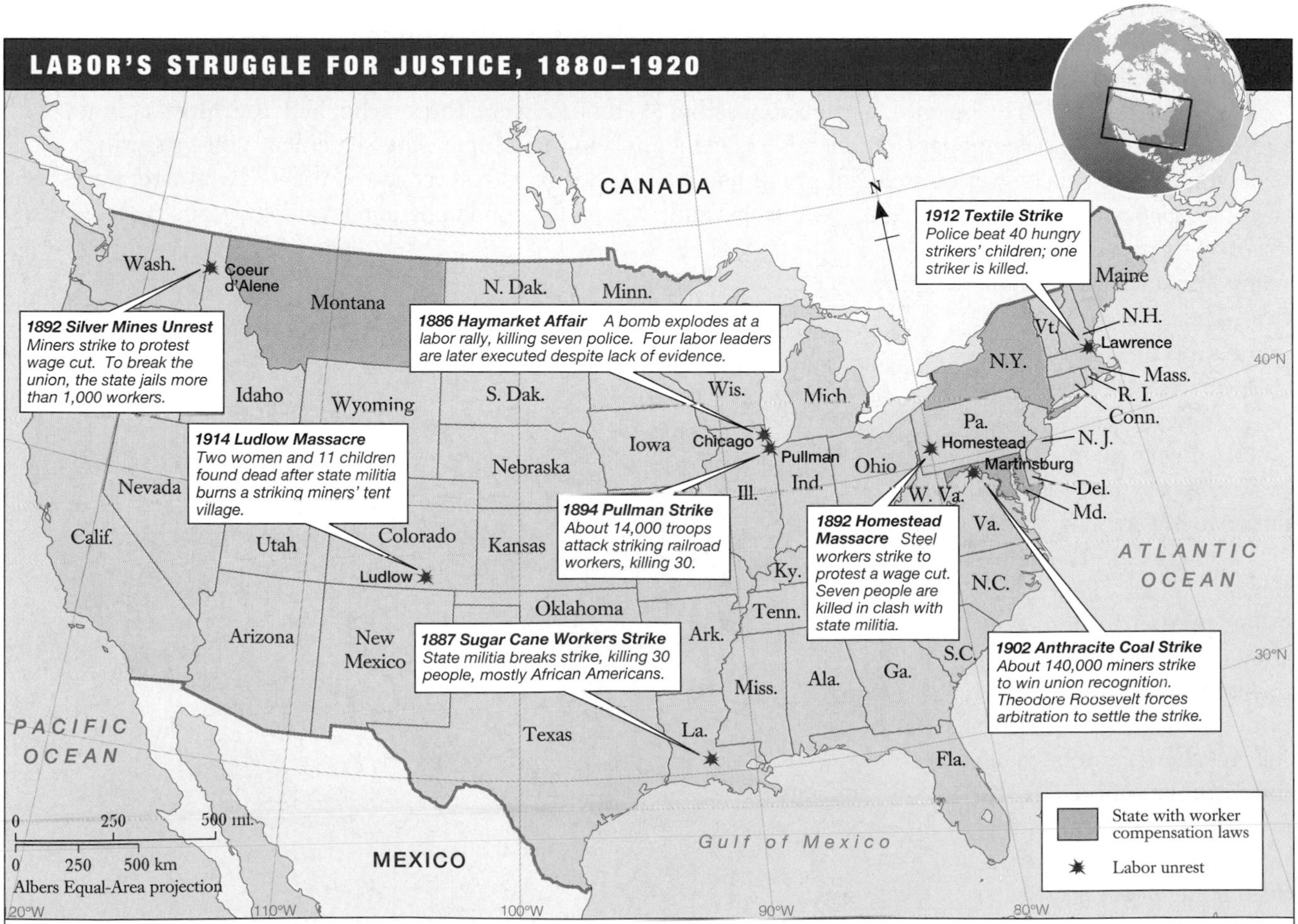
CANADA
N
1912 Textile Strike
Police beat 40 hungry strikers' children; one striker is killed.
Wash.
Coeur d'Alene
Montana
N. Dak.
Minn.
Maine
1892 Silver Mines Unrest
Miners strike to protest wage cut. To break the union, the state jails more than 1,000 workers.
1886 Haymarket Affair A bomb explodes at a labor rally, killing seven police. Four labor leaders are later executed despite lack of evidence.
Vt.
N.H.
Lawrence
N.Y.
Mass.
40°N
Idaho
Wyoming
S. Dak.
Wis.
Mich.
R. I.
Conn.
1914 Ludlow Massacre
Two women and 11 children found dead after state militia burns a striking miners' tent village.
Iowa
Chicago
Pa.
Homestead
N. J.
Nevada
Nebraska
Pullman
Ohio
Martinsburg
Ind.
Ill.
W. Va.
Del.
Md.
1894 Pullman Strike
About 14,000 troops attack striking railroad workers, killing 30.
1892 Homestead Massacre Steel workers strike to protest a wage cut. Seven people are killed in clash with state militia.
Calif.
Utah
Colorado
Kansas
Va.
ATLANTIC OCEAN
Ludlow
Ky.
N.C.
Oklahoma
Tenn.
Arizona
New Mexico
1887 Sugar Cane Workers Strike
State militia breaks strike, killing 30 people, mostly African Americans.
Ark.
S.C.
1902 Anthracite Coal Strike
About 140,000 miners strike to win union recognition. Theodore Roosevelt forces arbitration to settle the strike.
30°N
Ga.
Ala.
Miss.
PACIFIC OCEAN
Texas
La.
Fla.
0 250 500 mi.
0 250 500 km
Albers Equal-Area projection
MEXICO
Gulf of Mexico
State with worker compensation laws
Labor unrest
120°W
110°W
100°W
90°W
80°W

Across the nation, workers and their families walked the picket lines during the Progressive era. *Why was a strike an emotional and often frightening experience for the men, women, and children involved?*

Some radical labor organizations not only rejected capitalism, but they also rejected the willingness of socialists to run candidates for political office and to work with progressives. One such group was the Industrial Workers of the World (IWW), formed in Chicago in 1905. Wobblies, as IWW members were known, wanted a single union for all workers. They believed that workers should confront owners directly rather than through political battles. "Shall I tell you what direct action means?" one IWW pamphlet asked. "The worker on the job shall tell the boss when and where he shall work, how long and for what wages and under what conditions." Under the leadership of William D. ("Big Bill") Haywood, the IWW successfully organized unskilled workers that the AFL often ignored, such as miners, lumberjacks, and migrant farm laborers. In the most popular union song, sung to the tune of "Battle Hymn of the Republic," an IWW organizer and songwriter expressed the union's belief that workers needed to join together for their own protection:

IWW FILES

CULVER PICTURES

IWW Organizes Strike **Thousands of workers went on strike (sometimes called the Bread and Roses Strike) in Lawrence, Massachusetts, in 1912. One striker was killed and many others sent to prison. The union leader stated, "Bayonets cannot weave cloth."** *What did he mean?*

> When the union's inspiration through
> the workers' blood shall run,
> There can be no power greater anywhere
> beneath the sun.
> Yet what force on earth is weaker than the
> feeble strength of one?
> But the union makes us strong.
>
> Solidarity forever!
> Solidarity forever!
> Solidarity forever!
> For the union makes us strong.
>
> They have taken untold millions
> that they never toiled to earn,
> But without our brain and muscle
> not a single wheel could turn.
> We can break their haughty power,
> gain our freedom when we learn
> That the union makes us strong.
>
> —Ralph Chaplin, "Solidarity Forever," 1915

The members of the IWW, in addition to socialists, African Americans, and immigrants, often worked at cross-purposes to most progressives. Ironically these groups suffered the most from the poverty, corruption, and other social ills that motivated progressives. Despite this irony, the progressives did orchestrate an expansion of government power to meet the problems caused by urbanization and industrialization. That change in the role of government would have a significant and lasting effect on American life.

Section Review

Vocabulary

1. Define: accommodation, melting pot, nativism, eugenics.

Checking Facts

2. What led to the immigration law of 1917? How did the 1917 immigration restrictions differ from those passed in 1882 and 1907?
3. How was the Sherman Antitrust Act of 1890 used against unions?

Critical Thinking

Making Comparisons

4. How were progressives and Wobblies similar? How were they different?

Linking Across Time

5. Do you think that the United States is more or less of a melting pot today than it was in the early 1900s? Provide evidence to support your viewpoint.

CULTURE OF THE TIME

Ragtime

The ragtime years, named for the sprightly music of African American composer Scott Joplin, were an extraordinary time in the nation's history. Industrialization and innovation transformed the way Americans worked and played. Newly discovered "free time" presented the challenge of what to do with it. The invention of the camera made it possible to record many scenes of people eager to meet this new challenge.

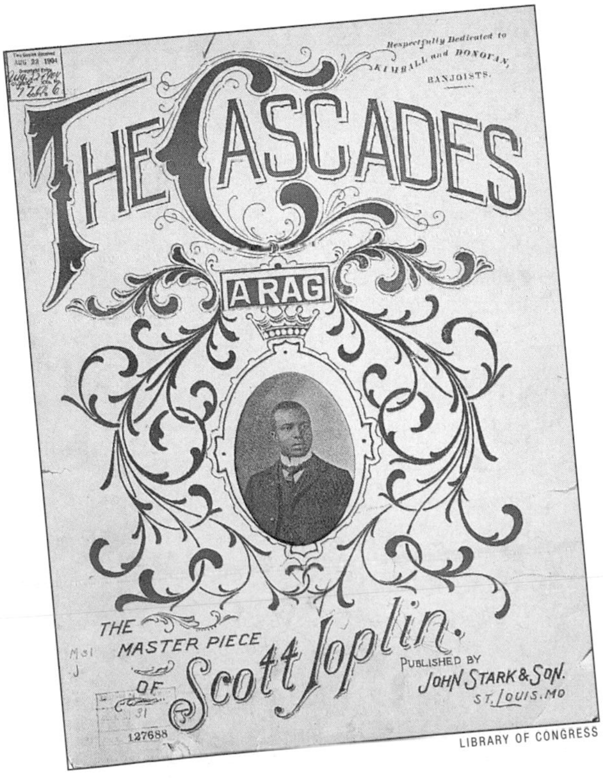

LIBRARY OF CONGRESS

THE BETTMANN ARCHIVE

WORLD TRAVELER

Ingenuity, determination, and achievement were some of the "American" virtues embodied by journalist **Nellie Bly.** Traveling around the world in 72 days (with one dress) in 1890, she outdid the record set in Jules Verne's popular novel *Around the World in 80 Days.*

POPULAR MUSIC

Sales of sheet music flourished when Scott Joplin began entertaining audiences with **ragtime piano music**—syncopated, high-stepping dance music born on the Mississippi Delta.

THE BETTMANN ARCHIVE

LIVE THEATER

The **vaudeville act,** unique to American theater, gave many actors and comedians who later became stars their start, often as children. The curtain behind the performers displayed the first commercial messages. Vaudeville, minstrel, and variety troupes toured the country, influencing community groups who then created their own shows.

CULVER PICTURES

EXCITING RIDES

Amusement parks, such as Luna Park on New York's **Coney Island,** provided a **"bully"** time for everyone. They offered exciting rides and elaborate slides for the young and daring.

THE BETTMANN ARCHIVE

SIDEWALK ENTERTAINERS

Traveling **organ grinders** in urban areas provided entertainment and amusement for city dwellers. Often they sold peanuts or popcorn and had trained animals (usually monkeys) who performed for the audience. People who lived during this time period had a chance to laugh and take a break from their tough daily routine of trying to make ends meet.

Chapter 9 Review

Reviewing Key Terms

Complete the sentences below with one of the vocabulary terms listed:

arbitration	**eugenics**
socialism	**accommodation**
capitalism	**nativism**
melting pot	**holding company**

1. _________ and _________ are two different economic systems.

2. Theodore Roosevelt helped resolve the coal miners' strike of 1902 when he imposed _________ by a third-party commission.

3. W.E.B. Du Bois opposed _________, Booker T. Washington's approach to racism.

4. One theory opposed to immigration was _________; another was the so-called science of _________.

5. A _________ can skirt antitrust laws by retaining controlling interests in companies or industries without owning them.

Recalling Facts

1. How did Theodore Roosevelt become President?

2. Give two examples of how Theodore Roosevelt expanded the power of the presidency.

3. Why was the Sherman Antitrust Act difficult to enforce?

4. Identify three progressive reforms President Taft supported.

5. Why did Eugene Debs reject capitalism?

6. How did Woodrow Wilson expand the power of the presidency?

7. How did President Wilson restore public confidence in the banking system?

8. What effect did the Supreme Court decision in *Plessy* v. *Ferguson* have on the Jim Crow laws?

9. How did the views of Booker T. Washington differ from those of W.E.B. Du Bois?

10. Briefly explain the concept of socialism. Why did it frighten the progressives?

Critical Thinking

1. Formulating Questions Assume the role of an arbitrator in the United Mine Workers strike of 1902. To settle this strike, you will need to understand the two sides' demands and recognize two opposing sets of values. Write at least three questions you would ask each side. Explain what you hope to learn from these questions.

2. Determining Cause and Effect Explain how Woodrow Wilson's family background, education, intellectualism, public speaking style, and previous leadership experience affected his actions as a politician.

3. Demonstrating Reasoned Judgment Imagine that you are a registered voter and a member of a trade union. The election of 1912 is one week away. Identify the candidates who are running for election and their platforms. Which candidate will get your vote? Give reasons to support your answer.

4. Making Comparisons Elizabeth Gurley Flynn (below) was a fiery speaker and organizer who joined the Industrial Workers of the World at age 16. Compare the main differences between the IWW's views on workers' rights and those of the progressives.

5. Recognizing Bias Reread the section entitled "Americanizing the Newcomers" on page 284. What examples of bias do you detect in the attitudes of the progressives toward the immigrants? How do their attitudes differ from those of the nativists?

BROWN BROTHERS

UNITED STATES PARKLANDS, 1909

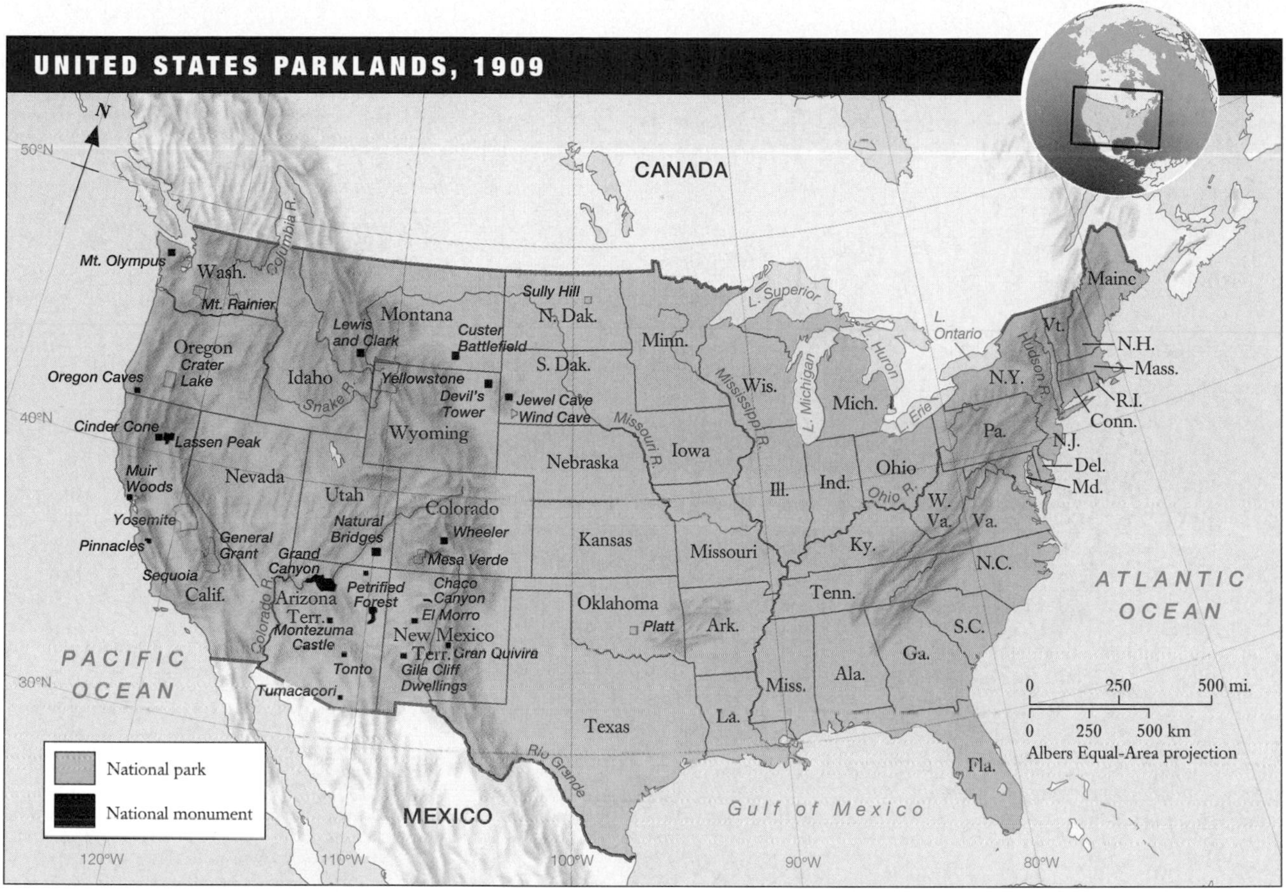

Portfolio Project

Traditionally, third parties have organized around a particular candidate, such as Theodore Roosevelt in 1912, or around an issue, such as prohibition. Identify a recent or current "third party" and research its platform. What was or is its goal? What role did or does it have in nationwide events? Write a short paper examining this party and include it in your portfolio.

Cooperative Learning

Work in 5 groups to research the 5 tariffs that were passed between 1890 and 1913. Then regroup into teams containing a representative from each of the original 5 groups. Each new group should choose its own means of presenting its findings.

Reinforcing Skills

Making Comparisons Politicians who support contrasting solutions often share similar beliefs. For example, Roosevelt, an ardent capitalist, agreed with most Socialists in blaming competition as the source of employees' overwork and inadequate pay. What other beliefs did Roosevelt and Socialists share?

Geography and History

Study the map on this page to answer the following questions:

1. Given that there were 5 national parks and no national monuments when Roosevelt took office in 1901, what does this map show about his contributions to the preservation of the country's wilderness?

2. In 1909 which part of the country contained the most national parks?

3. Which were the largest parks and monuments in 1909?

4. Were there more national parks or national monuments in 1909?

HISTORY JOURNAL

Both Roosevelt and Wilson expanded the power of the presidency in the early 1900s. Do you think they promoted a progressive agenda? Explain. In what areas did progressivism fall short of its ideals?

CHAPTER 10

Expansionism and World War I

MARCH 1901: GEORGE WASHINGTON OF THE PHILIPPINES CAPTURED

Senator George F. Hoar once called Emilio Aguinaldo the "George Washington of the Philippines" when Aguinaldo sought to liberate his country from foreign rule. When that rule was Spanish, Hoar and others had encouraged the Philippine liberation struggle.

Aguinaldo had responded in kind, shouting *"Viva los Americanos!"* This enthusiasm, however, did not last long. The United States had promised its support of Philippine independence if Aguinaldo joined the United States in its fight against Spain. After the war, that promise was not kept. President McKinley wanted to "civilize" the Filipinos before granting independence.

When the United States refused to accept Aguinaldo as the legitimate head of government, a struggle ensued. American officials no longer praised him as a founder of his country. Instead, they plotted his capture. Aguinaldo marked the United States as an enemy and led a guerrilla war to rid his country of American forces.

Aguinaldo's capture in 1901 did not end the Filipino struggle. The war lasted for another year.

How the United States became the enemy of Aguinaldo is only part of the larger story of American foreign policy under the progressives—a policy guided by an uneasy mixture of idealism and self-interest. ■

HISTORY JOURNAL

Study the illustration of this famous piece of sheet music, and write your reaction to the mood it creates. Do you think American soldiers were always welcome in foreign countries? Why or why not?

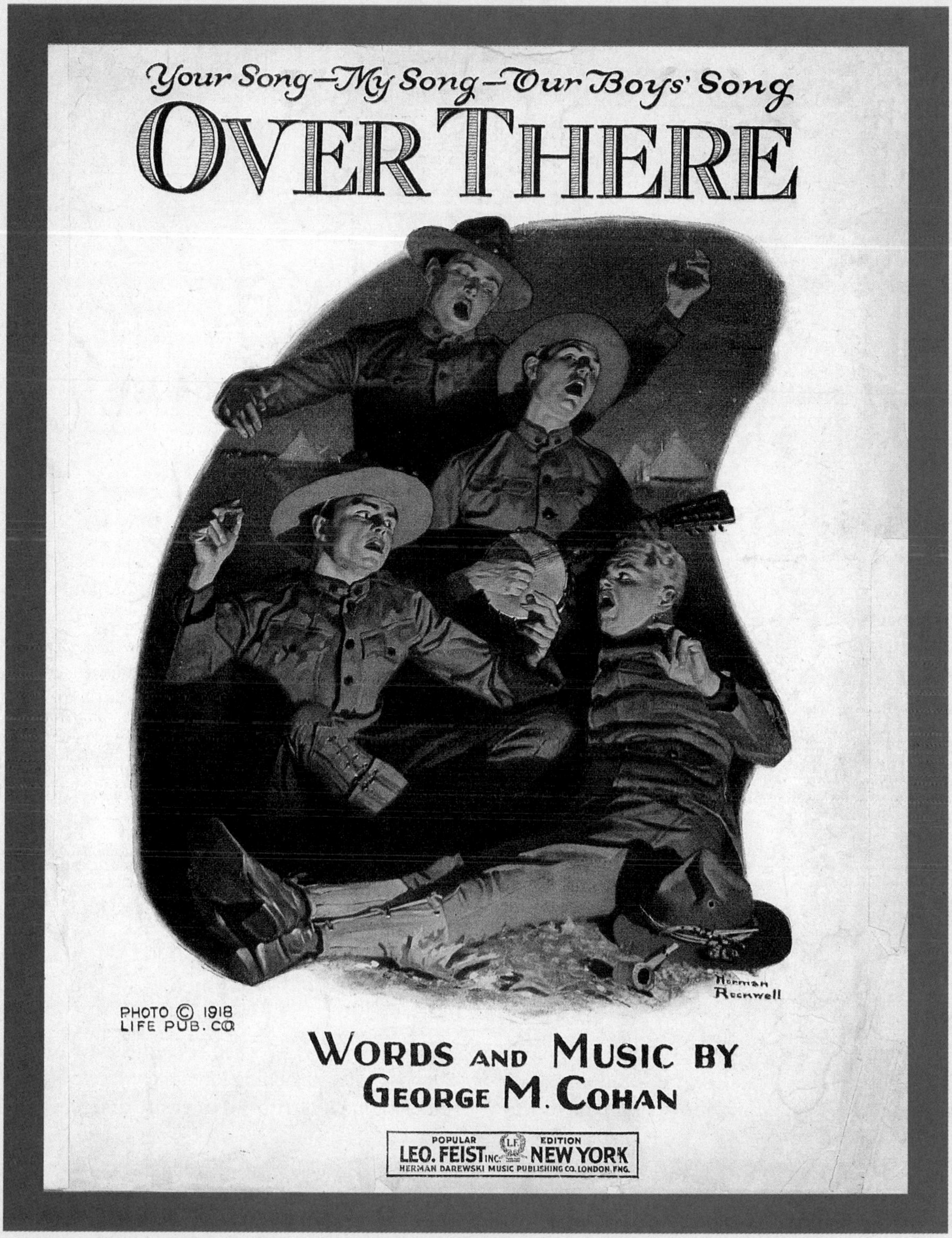

CULVER PICTURES

THIS SPIRITED PATRIOTIC SONG GLORIFIED THE ROLE OF THE UNITED STATES IN WORLD WAR I.

SECTION

1

Becoming a World Power

JANUARY 9, 1900: BEVERIDGE DEFENDS IMPERIALISM

THE BETTMANN ARCHIVE

Coasting
The original caption states, "The old horse [Monroe Doctrine] was too slow for Uncle Sam."

ALBERT J. BEVERIDGE, SENATOR FROM INDIANA, STOOD UP BEFORE THE UNITED STATES SENATE AND SPOKE WITH CANDOR. "Most future wars will be conflicts for commerce," he declared. He argued that the United States must secure new markets. As the United States acquired new markets in the countries of Asia and of Latin America, it should be willing to send troops, if needed, to protect those markets. It should even be willing to **annex,** or put under the dominion of the United States, new territories, so that only the United States could control the markets.

As Beveridge argued his ideas, he recalled that the nation's Founders were not afraid to acquire the territories of Louisiana and Florida and other continental territories farther west. "The founders of the nation were not provincial," he noted. "Theirs was the geography of the world. They were soldiers as well as landsmen, and they knew that where our ships should go our flag might follow."

A Special Destiny

Upholding Freedom Overseas

Progressives responded to the possibility of gaining foreign commercial markets and annexing new territories in vastly different ways. Some

AS YOU READ

Vocabulary

- annex
- imperialism
- corollary
- diplomacy
- territorial integrity

Think About . . .

- Roosevelt's Big Stick foreign policy and Taft's Dollar Diplomacy.
- the opinions behind the expansionist policies of Roosevelt and Taft.
- the importance of the Open Door policy for United States trade.
- the growth of United States political and economic involvement in the Caribbean, Latin America, East Asia, the Pacific, and Europe.

of them wanted to forge ahead; others did not. They all kept in mind, however, that the United States was different from the many countries of Europe. For decades the United States had a special destiny to uphold liberty and freedom. Some progressives agreed with Senator Beveridge that the people of the United States had a duty to spread the American way of life to lands recently acquired during the Spanish-American War of 1898.

To some extent the idea of exporting American capitalism and democracy to foreign lands overseas gained strength from the Progressive movement itself. The progressives had shown that Americans had the ability to organize and mobilize for social, political, economic, and even moral reform within the United States. The progressives reasoned that they could export their knowledge and products to less developed countries overseas.

Deeply ingrained racial attitudes added support to the American impulse to become involved in the affairs of other countries. Some Americans believed that the people of the Philippines, as well as the people of most of the Caribbean islands, were racially inferior and that they should succumb to the leadership of the United States.

Overseas Markets

Not only progressive ideas but also economic realities helped to spur the debate about the United States's engaging in commercial expansion around the world. Senator Beveridge touched upon the economic realities affecting industries and the workforce:

> Today we are making more than we can use. Today our industrial society is congested; there are more workers than there is work; there is more capital than there is investment. We do not need more money—we need more circulation, more employment. Therefore we must find new markets for our produce, new occupation for our capital, new work for our labor.
>
> —Albert J. Beveridge, in *The American Spirit*

Beveridge's cry for new markets struck a responsive chord in American farmers, manufacturers, and investors. As shown by the graph on this page, exports of American products rose dramatically in the early 1900s. Investors, as well as farmers and manufacturers, favored new markets.

Railroads offered a good example of an American industry that was seeking new opportunities for investment. By the turn of the century railroads already crisscrossed North America. Entrepreneurs eagerly looked overseas to lands where railroads had yet to be built. One railroad entrepreneur at the World's Fair Railway Conference spoke eloquently on his desire for commercial expansion:

Exports of the United States, 1860–1920

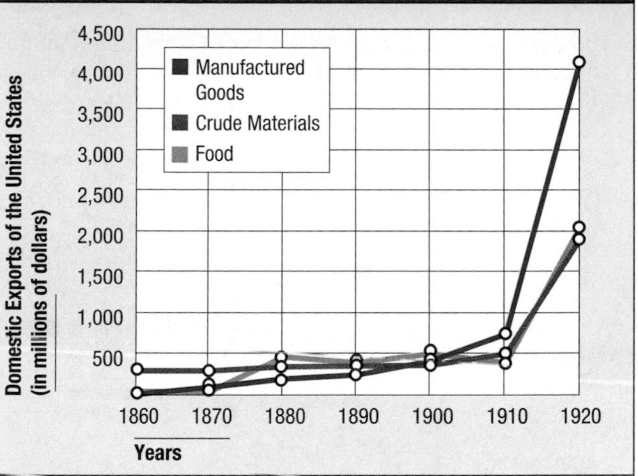

The rise of exports from the United States led to even more demands for commercial overseas markets by American farmers, manufacturers, and investors. *What types of products yielded the greatest number of export dollars in 1910?*

> We blow the whistle that's heard round the world, and all peoples stop to heed and welcome it. Its resonance is the diplomacy of peace. The locomotive bell is the true Liberty bell, proclaiming commercial freedom. Its boilers and the reservoirs are the forces of civilization. Its wheels are the wheels of progress, and its headlight is the illumination of dark countries.
>
> —Railway Conference Proceedings, in *Spreading the American Dream*

An Anti-imperialist Plea

Not all Americans favored expansion overseas. In 1902 the *Nation* magazine declared, "We made war on Spain four years ago for doing the very things of which we are now guilty ourselves." In this editorial the *Nation* pointed out that many Americans had previously opposed Spanish exploitation of local peoples, but now the government of the United States engaged in similar exploitation. Some Americans, like the author of the editorial, disapproved of **imperialism,** the policy of establishing economic, political, and military dominance over weaker nations, on humanitarian and moral grounds.

Other anti-imperialists prided themselves as Americans for being different from the Europeans, who were caught up in colonialism and militarism. They shared the sentiments of diplomat Carl Schurz, who lamented that extensive trading overseas would mean "wars and rumors of wars, and the time will be forever past when we could look down with condescending pity on the nations of the old world groaning under militarism and its burdens."

OPERATING THE LOCKS OF THE PANAMA CANAL

The three sets of locks in the Panama Canal are rectangular chambers, the largest concrete structures on earth, enabling ships to move from one water level to another by varying the amount of water in the locks. They are capable of raising and lowering vessels about 85 feet (26m), comparable to the height of a seven story building.

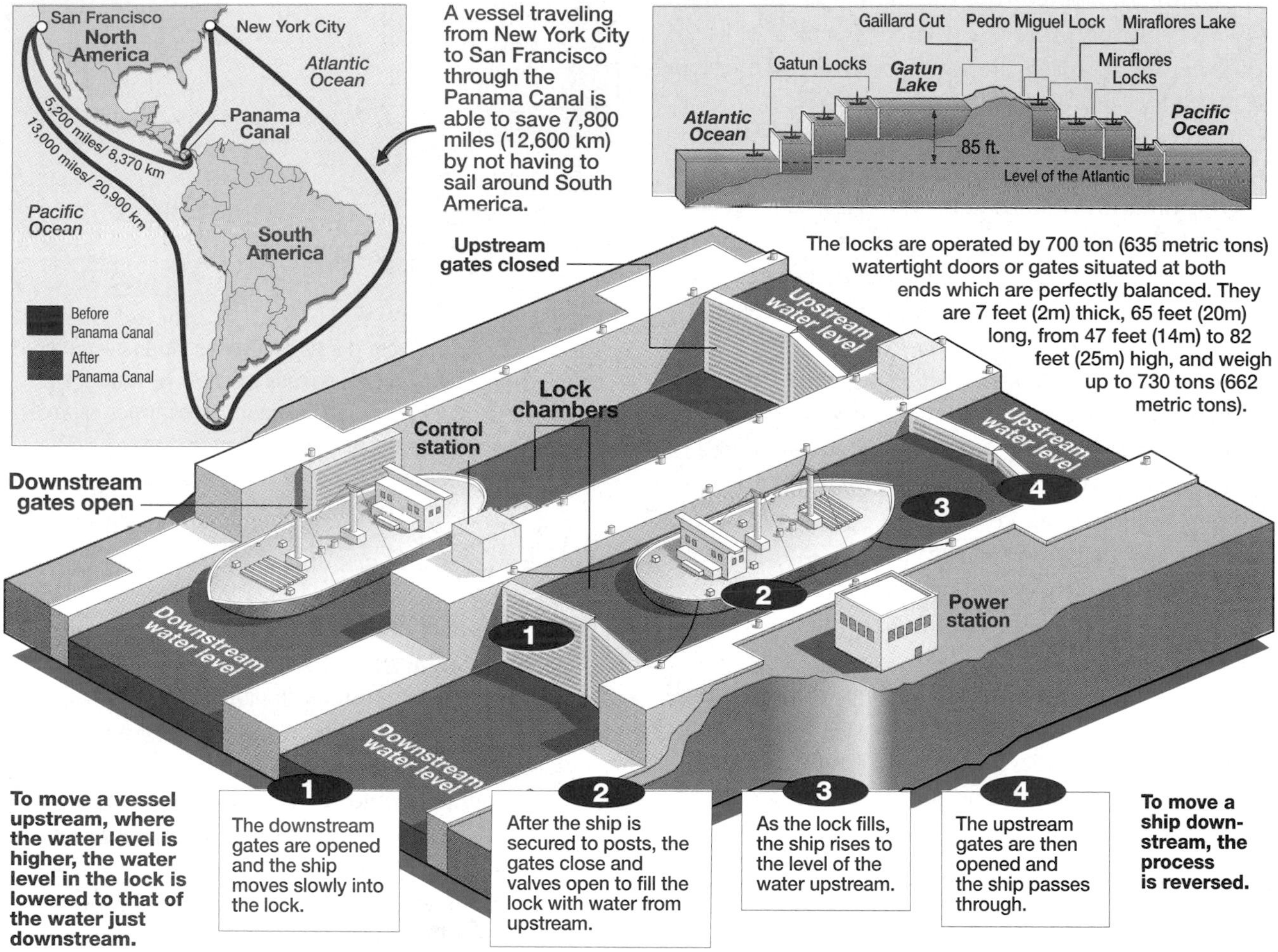
San Francisco
North America
New York City
Atlantic Ocean
Panama Canal
5,200 miles/ 8,370 km
13,000 miles/ 20,900 km
Pacific Ocean
South America
Before Panama Canal
After Panama Canal
A vessel traveling from New York City to San Francisco through the Panama Canal is able to save 7,800 miles (12,600 km) by not having to sail around South America.
Gaillard Cut
Pedro Miguel Lock
Miraflores Lake
Gatun Locks
Gatun Lake
Miraflores Locks
Atlantic Ocean
Pacific Ocean
85 ft.
Level of the Atlantic
Upstream gates closed
The locks are operated by 700 ton (635 metric tons) watertight doors or gates situated at both ends which are perfectly balanced. They are 7 feet (2m) thick, 65 feet (20m) long, from 47 feet (14m) to 82 feet (25m) high, and weigh up to 730 tons (662 metric tons).
Upstream water level
Upstream water level
Lock chambers
Control station
Downstream gates open
Power station
Downstream water level
Downstream water level
To move a vessel upstream, where the water level is higher, the water level in the lock is lowered to that of the water just downstream.
1 The downstream gates are opened and the ship moves slowly into the lock.
2 After the ship is secured to posts, the gates close and valves open to fill the lock with water from upstream.
3 As the lock fills, the ship rises to the level of the water upstream.
4 The upstream gates are then opened and the ship passes through.
To move a ship downstream, the process is reversed.

The opening of the Panama Canal reduced the average traveling time of early twentieth-century ships by 60 days. Today about 12,000 ships use its locks every year. *About how many feet can the locks raise or lower ships for passage through the canal?*

Policies in the Caribbean

Consolidating American Power

In spite of anti-imperialist arguments, the political and economic climate at the turn of the century favored commercial expansion, even if commercial expansion meant sending troops to keep order and defend markets. Such commercial and military endeavors suited the temperament of Theodore Roosevelt, who became President in 1901. "I have always been fond," Roosevelt explained, "of the West African proverb, Speak softly and carry a big stick; you will go far." Roosevelt preferred not to brag about American power, but rather to be so strong that other countries would bow to the United States. This philosophy came to be known as the Big Stick. Roosevelt's Big Stick policies in the Caribbean included the building of a canal in Panama and the extension of the Monroe Doctrine.

The Big Ditch

A canal across Central America linking the Pacific and Atlantic Oceans had been the dream of people of many different nationalities for years. The inset map above reveals the commercial and military advantages of such a canal. The reduction in travel time would save commercial fleets millions of dollars and increase the efficiency of naval fleets. The inefficiency of naval fleets during the Spanish-American War had underscored the need for a canal. When the war broke out in 1898, the battleship *Oregon* was sent from Seattle to Cuba. Because a canal did not exist at that time, the ship did not arrive until the war was nearly over.

The United States went on to negotiate the Hay-Herrán Treaty with Colombia in 1903, offering $10 million outright and $250,000 annually for a canal zone 6 miles wide in Panama, which at the time belonged to Colombia. When the Colombian legislature held out for more money, Roosevelt responded angrily and plotted to support a revolution that would make Panama an independent country —one the United States could more easily control.

When the *Nashville,* a gunboat from the United States, arrived on November 2, 1903, the Panamanians began their rebellion. On November 4, 1903, the victorious rebels read a formal declaration of independence, and 2 days later the United States recognized the Republic of Panama. The new government had little choice but to accept the United States's terms for the building of a canal. The cutting of the canal began in 1904 and was completed 10 years later. Roosevelt took pride in having skillfully secured the canal, forging ahead in spite of reservations from Congress and legal advisers. He noted, "I took the Canal and let Congress debate."

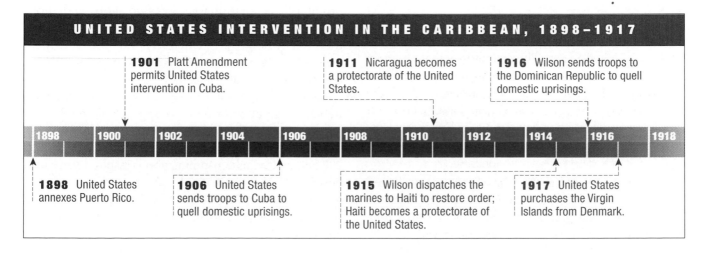

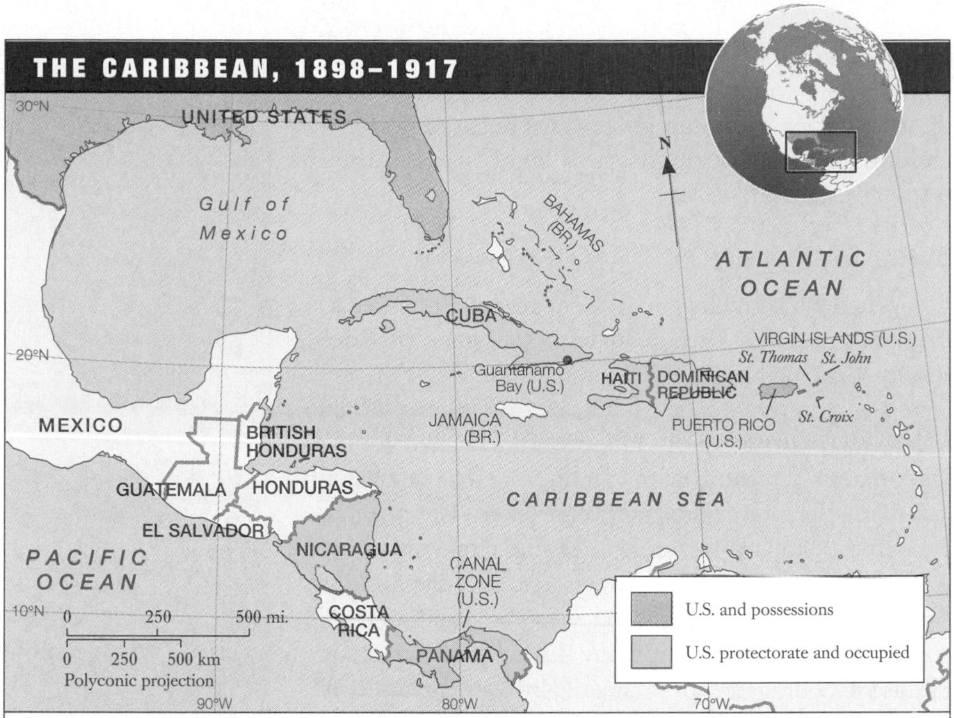

The map and the time line on this page show the pattern of United States intervention in the Caribbean from 1898 to 1917. *What islands became possessions of the United States?*

Expansion of the Monroe Doctrine

Roosevelt had supported the revolution in Panama against Colombia to secure a canal for American interests. In general, though, he did not look kindly upon revolutions or any kind of disorder in the Caribbean. Striving to keep the region stable for American investment, he put down disorders in various Caribbean countries.

In 1904 and 1905 several European powers threatened the Dominican Republic. They wanted to collect money owed by Dominican customs, but could not do so peacefully because various factions in the Dominican Republic fought for control of customs revenues. Before Germany could send troops to collect the funds owed it, American troops seized Dominican customhouses and supervised the collection of customs fees and the repayment of debts. Roosevelt justified this action by issuing a **corollary,** or proposition, extending the Monroe Doctrine. His corollary asserted that "chronic wrongdoing" or "impotence" gave the United States the right to exercise "international police powers" in the Western Hemisphere. This changed the original intention of the Monroe Doctrine, which was to ward off European colonization. The United States now committed itself to

UNITED STATES INTERVENTION IN THE CARIBBEAN, 1898–1917

1898 | 1900 | 1902 | 1904 | 1906 | 1908 | 1910 | 1912 | 1914 | 1916 | 1918

- **1898** United States annexes Puerto Rico.
- **1901** Platt Amendment permits United States intervention in Cuba.
- **1906** United States sends troops to Cuba to quell domestic uprisings.
- **1911** Nicaragua becomes a protectorate of the United States.
- **1915** Wilson dispatches the marines to Haiti to restore order; Haiti becomes a protectorate of the United States.
- **1916** Wilson sends troops to the Dominican Republic to quell domestic uprisings.
- **1917** United States purchases the Virgin Islands from Denmark.

maintaining stability in the Western Hemisphere. The commitment would cause Roosevelt, Taft, and Wilson to send troops to a number of Caribbean countries—including Cuba, Nicaragua, and Haiti—during their respective terms of office.

Dollar Diplomacy

When William Howard Taft succeeded Roosevelt as President in 1909, he agreed with the spirit of Roosevelt's Big Stick policies, but not his tactics. Taft preferred a different form of conducting international relations, or **diplomacy.** His program, called Dollar Diplomacy—a somewhat milder approach to expansion and to interference in foreign governments—was one that substituted dollars for bullets. Hoping to gain more American influence in the hemisphere, Taft encouraged American bankers to lend money to Central American countries so that they could pay debts owed to Britain. He also encouraged entrepreneurial investment in the region. Investment in Central American mines, banana and coffee plantations, and railroads increased by $72 million from 1897 to 1914. Loans and investments had the effect of further impoverishing the fragile economies of Central American countries because most of their resources had to be used to pay back money, rather than to provide goods and services to their citizens. Throughout the 1900s, the United States State Department would use its power and influence in Latin America to protect American investors from loan defaults and unfriendly governments.

Missionary Influences In 1903 United States missionary Grace Roberts taught the Bible to Chinese women at a Manchurian outpost. *In what other ways did the missionaries try to spread American values, traditions, and the American way of life to the Chinese people?*

Policies in Eastern Asia

Establishing an American Presence

At the same time the United States consolidated its power in Latin America, it also turned to Asia to look for additional markets and to spread American values. Some Americans regarded Asia as a mysterious and alluring place. Others feared the growing Asian population, especially if it meant large numbers of Asians immigrating to the United States. The stereotypes that emerged in the 1800s lingered into the 1900s and characterized Asians as heathen and exotic—"the lawless hordes," "the yellow peril." Both prejudice against and fascination with Asia influenced foreign policy during the Progressive era.

The Chinese Market

While Americans at the turn of the century feared and discriminated against Chinese immigrants in the United States, the great numbers of people in China itself attracted them. The lure of souls, more than 400 million of them, to convert to Christianity inspired missionaries. The Student Volunteer Movement for Foreign Missions sprang up on college campuses all over the United States. During the 1890s the number of American missions in China doubled to more than 500.

Missionaries not only attempted to convert Chinese people to Christianity, but also built schools and hospitals and encouraged their converts to buy American products. As missionaries became more and more involved in China, they increasingly looked toward the American government for protection and help, especially when they confronted Chinese resentment and hostility. In 1900 missionaries asked for and received American military help in putting down the Boxer Rebellion, an attempt by a group of Chinese rebels to expel foreign influence from China.

Saving 400 million souls inspired missionaries, but 400 million bodies consuming goods inspired American businesspeople. The United States was not alone in its attraction to the Chinese market. China and its promise of wealth attracted Britain, France, Germany, Russia, and Japan as well.

By the latter half of the 1800s, these powers competed for influence in a China weakened by a decaying government, the Manchu dynasty. Each power vied for a chance to expand its interests in China. The United States wanted to share in these opportunities as well. Some Americans saw the possibility of building railroads, controlling ports, and selling manufactured products. At least two factors, however, put the United States at a distinct disadvantage: its geographical location, distant from China compared with Russia or Japan; and its navy, inferior to those of Japan, Germany, and Britain.

In 1899 and 1900 Secretary of State John Hay promoted a plan that would strengthen the American position in the scramble to gain control over specific regions of China. He sent notes to Japan and the key European powers asking them to accept the **territorial integrity** of China. In other words, Hay asked them not to control a specific part of China, but to leave the door open to trade for all nations in all parts of China. Because Russia, Japan, Britain, and France were jealous of one another's influence in China, they temporarily agreed with Hay's Open Door plan. The Open Door policy became a key concept in American foreign policy during the first decades of the 1900s. The hope of getting a share of the Chinese market continued to be the driving force in American policies in Asia and played a role in the American decision to annex the Philippines.

FOREIGN EXPANSION IN EASTERN ASIA

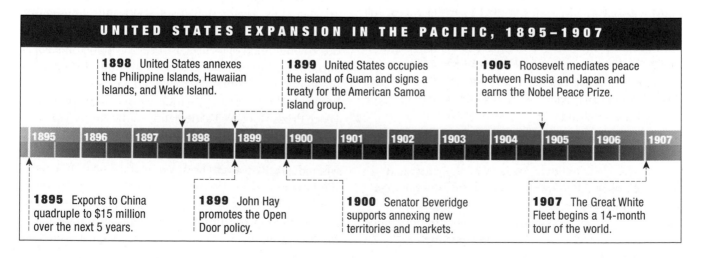

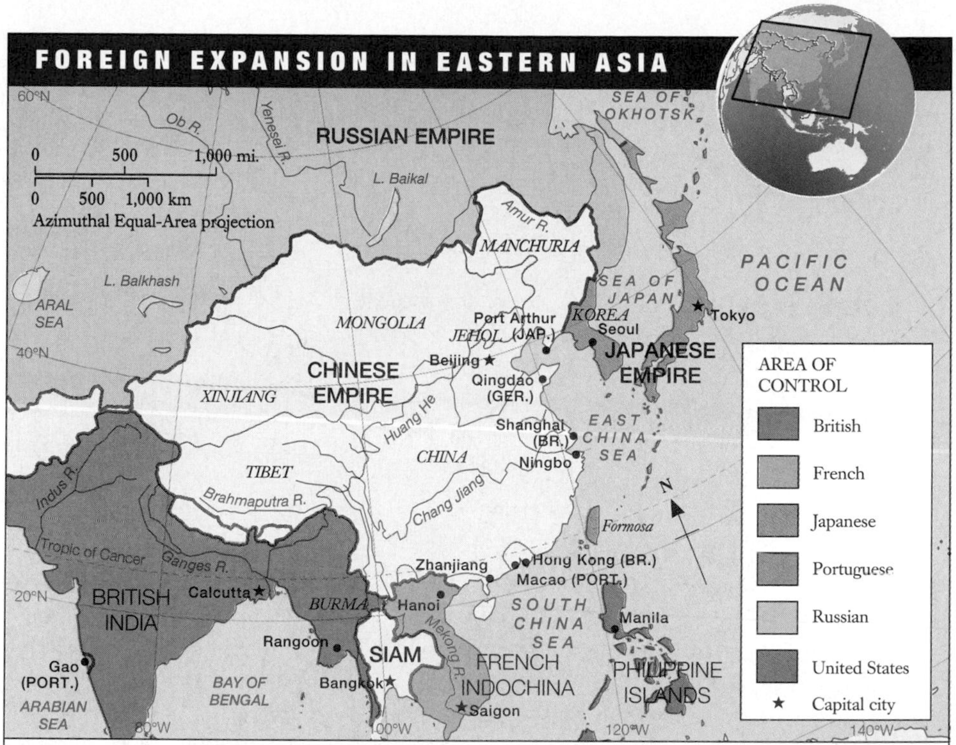

The map above shows foreign expansion in eastern Asia begining in 1842. The Philippine Islands provided a strategic location for the United States to establish commerce in eastern Asia. *How did the Open Door policy help the United States gain a foothold in eastern Asia?*

A War in the Philippines

As the United States celebrated its victory of 1898 against Spain, many wondered if the United States would allow the Philippines its independence. Before the Spanish-American War, the Filipinos had been waging a guerrilla war for independence from their colonial ruler, Spain. Filipino revolutionaries initially welcomed American forces into their country as liberators. The United States promised to support Philippine independence if the Filipino revolutionaries fought with the Americans against Spain. Moreover, the United States had drafted the Teller Amendment promising Cuba complete and unconditional freedom at the end of the war, and the Philippines expected similar treatment.

UNITED STATES EXPANSION IN THE PACIFIC, 1895–1907

1895 1896 1897 1898 1899 1900 1901 1902 1903 1904 1905 1906 1907

- **1895** Exports to China quadruple to $15 million over the next 5 years.
- **1898** United States annexes the Philippine Islands, Hawaiian Islands, and Wake Island.
- **1899** United States occupies the island of Guam and signs a treaty for the American Samoa island group.
- **1899** John Hay promotes the Open Door policy.
- **1900** Senator Beveridge supports annexing new territories and markets.
- **1905** Roosevelt mediates peace between Russia and Japan and earns the Nobel Peace Prize.
- **1907** The Great White Fleet begins a 14-month tour of the world.

THE BETTMANN ARCHIVE

The Great White Fleet **Destroyers and battleships of the United States Navy were painted a dazzling white, giving the fleet its name.** *What would be the advantage to the United States of having a port in Manila?*

To justify annexation of the Philippines, expansionists used the arguments first put forth by President McKinley, who feared "anarchy" and vowed to "educate," "uplift," and "civilize" the population. Not far behind these lofty intentions, other considerations lurked: the Philippines could provide a rich variety of natural resources, as well as a foothold in Asia—a naval stop on the way to China. McKinley decided to hoist the American flag and take control of the country.

Filipino revolutionaries, led by Emilio Aguinaldo, did not accept the American decision to annex the Philippines without a fight. They waged guerrilla war at full force in the Philippines until 1902 and at reduced levels until 1906. In total, 120,000 American troops fought in the war, 4,200 of whom died. Filipinos suffered far greater casualties: at least 15,000 rebels and 200,000 civilians died. The novelist Mark Twain depicted the supreme irony of the situation:

> There must be two Americas: one that sets the captive free, and one that takes a once-captive's new freedom away from him, and picks a quarrel with him with nothing to found it on; then kills him to get his land.
>
> —Mark Twain, "To the Person Sitting in Darkness," 1901

Balancing Russia and Japan

The port of Manila would be a stop on the way to the tempting Chinese market, and this in part explained the willingness of the United States to fight for the Philippines. As Albert Beveridge put it: "[J]ust beyond the Philippines are China's illimitable markets." This dream also shaped American policies with Japan. When Theodore Roosevelt assumed the presidency in 1901, Russia posed the greatest danger to the Open Door policy in China because it controlled the large Chinese province of Manchuria. Like Hay before him, Roosevelt attempted to change the situation through diplomacy.

In 1904 Japan launched an attack against Russia, destroying much of its fleet. Roosevelt opportunistically supported Japan because he regarded Russia as a greater enemy. In 1905 he mediated a peace agreement between the two rivals, which earned him the Nobel Peace Prize. Roosevelt's mediation of the Russo-Japanese War pleased Japan. It gained control over Korea, as well as key ports in China and the railroad in southern Manchuria. Roosevelt, however, made a point of checking Japanese power by negotiating rights for Russia in northern Manchuria and by having Japan agree to noninterference in the Philippines. His main interest was in seeing that no single power reigned supreme in Asia.

THE GREAT WHITE FLEET, 1907–1909

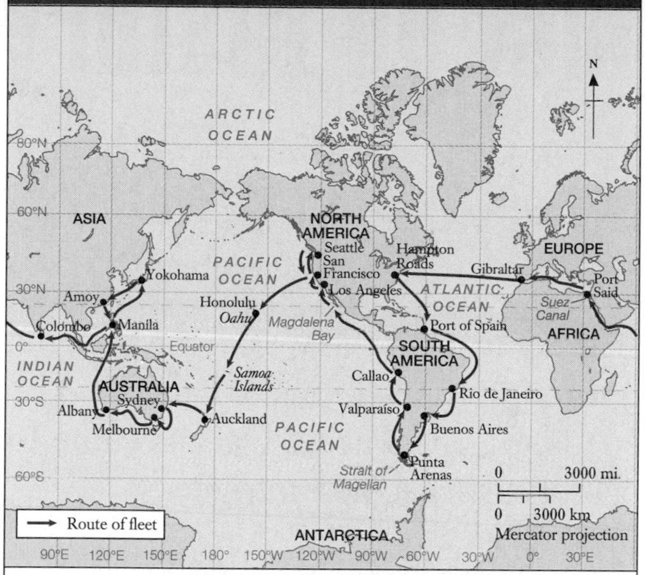

The 14-month world tour of the Great White Fleet from 1907 to 1909 covered 46,000 miles (74,014 km). *What major canal was the fleet able to use to save mileage and time?*

Racial Politics

In addition to shifting the balance of power in China, the settlement of the Russo-Japanese War also had worldwide implications for racial politics. That an Asian people, the Japanese, had humiliated a white people, the Russians, kindled new national and racial pride in both the Chinese and the Japanese.

Japan reacted by protesting the 1906 segregation of Japanese children in San Francisco schools. A respected Japanese journal urged Japan to use its navy, if necessary, to end such humiliation:

> The whole world knows that the poorly equipped army and navy of the United States are no match for our efficient army and navy. It will be an easy work to awake the United States from her dream of obstinacy when one of our great admirals appears on the other side of the Pacific.
>
> —*Mainichi Shimbun*, 1906

Roosevelt soothed Japanese humiliation with "A Gentleman's Agreement" in 1907 that ended school segregation in San Francisco—while at the same time controlling Japanese immigration to California. As the controversy raged, Roosevelt began to calculate. Perhaps the delicate balance of power was shifting. Perhaps it was time for the United States to flex its muscles for the Japanese to see. Roosevelt had been building a stronger and more modern navy, and now he resolved to send the entire American fleet of 16 battleships around the world in a show of might. The Great White Fleet made a special stop in Japan in 1908.

Entanglement With Europe

Mediating Disputes

As the United States experimented in colonial and militaristic adventures overseas, its attitude toward Europe changed. For almost all of the 1800s, the United States had shunned entanglement with Europe. The democratic institutions of the United States set it apart from the colonial and militaristic ways of Europe—or so popular opinion believed. Nevertheless, when Hay shaped his Open Door policy and when Roosevelt mediated the Russo-Japanese War, they both participated in diplomacy that affected politics in Europe. They also showed that the United States could effectively resolve conflicts of interest in other parts of the world.

In the early 1900s the United States was often called upon to mediate disputes. In 1906 Roosevelt defused a crisis between Germany and France over Morocco. In 1911 Taft arbitrated a dispute between France and Great Britain over Liberia. In part, a desire for trading privileges in Africa motivated the efforts of Roosevelt and Taft in these cases. Far more than keeping an open door for American trade, the two Presidents hoped to keep peace in Europe. By 1900 the economy of the United States depended on markets all over the world. If tensions in Europe were to explode into war, American trade might suffer disastrously.

Section Review

Vocabulary

1. Define: annex, imperialism, corollary, diplomacy, territorial integrity.

Checking Facts

2. Give examples of how American feelings of superiority shaped United States expansion in the Western Hemisphere and overseas.

3. Give examples of antiexpansionist arguments.

Critical Thinking

Making Comparisons

4. Compare the interests of missionaries with those of investors regarding American involvement in China.

Linking Across Time

5. When Roosevelt felt that Russia might dominate Asia, he favored the Japanese. When Japan became mightier, he decided to demonstrate United States strength with the Great White Fleet. How does the United States today show both friendship toward and rivalry with the Japanese?

Geography: Impact on History

LOCATION

The Panama Canal

Still considered one of the greatest engineering feats in the world, the Panama Canal cuts more than 50 miles (80.5 km) through the Isthmus of Panama. The story of how the only link between the Atlantic and Pacific Oceans came to be built on this site reads like a novel—full of suspense and intrigue.

A Race for the First Canal

When California entered the Union in 1850, the United States saw that a canal joining its 2 oceans would be a great military and commercial boon. Between 1870 and 1875, the United States Navy made official surveys of desirable locations. In 1881 a United States commission decided that a canal through Nicaragua would be the cheapest to build. It would need locks, but it would involve the least digging. Convinced that a transoceanic canal was in the best interests of the United States, the government bought a concession for a canal from Nicaragua.

About the same time, France obtained a grant to build a canal across the Isthmus of Panama. In a race with the Americans, French government officials persuaded Ferdinand de Lesseps, builder of the Suez Canal, to build it. Although he was 75, de Lesseps could not resist the offer. He formed a private company to raise money and drew up plans for a sea-level canal.

During the 6 years that de Lesseps worked on the canal, 2 out of 3 workers died of yellow fever or malaria. In 1898 de Lesseps had to admit that his plan for a sea-level canal would not work. Cutting through the continental divide was

THE ISTHMUS OF PANAMA

Panama is shaped in a long, thin curve, with a roughly east-west orientation. Ships traveling the canal from the Atlantic to the Pacific travel from northwest to southeast. *Why was Panama a good place for a transoceanic canal?*

not only extraordinarily expensive but almost impossible with the equipment he had. By then he had spent $320 million, at least 20,000 workers had died, and his company had gone bankrupt.

Panama or Nicaragua?

After the Spanish-American War, the United States renewed its interest in an American canal. Congress voted to build a canal in Nicaragua. Shortly afterward, the New Panama Canal Company (a French company that owned what was left of de Lesseps's canal in Panama) offered to sell the United States all of its canal rights and holdings for $40 million.

The United States would probably have stuck to its plan for a Nicaraguan canal, but a few days before Congress was to vote again on the canal's location, a volcano erupted in the French West Indies, killing 40,000 people. Philippe Bunau-Varilla, a representative of the French, seized the opportunity to remind Congress that potentially active volcanoes existed near the lake in Nicaragua where the approved canal was to be built. When Congress finally voted in 1902, Panama was in and Nicaragua was out as the site of the canal—by a margin of only 8 votes.

In the 1880s Nicaragua probably was the better choice for a canal; by the 1900s, Panama was a better site. The larger ships being built at that time would have had great difficulty negotiating the winding canal in Nicaragua. In hindsight, a Nicaraguan canal would have been a costly mistake because it soon would have become obsolete.

CULVER PICTURES

Miraflores Locks From the Pacific, the locks lift ships to Miraflores Lake and the next set of locks. *How long did it take to build the Panama Canal?*

Meanwhile, the intrigue continued. The Panama site depended upon the assent of Colombia, which controlled the isthmus. Colombia balked. Dissidents in Panama had long wanted to break with Colombia. Roosevelt spoke in favor of the rebels, who in turn favored an American canal. After Panama's successful revolt, it signed a treaty guaranteeing the United States the exclusive use and control of a canal zone 10 miles (16 km) wide across the isthmus, "in perpetuity."

Work Begins

In May 1904, a United States commission assumed the French property, and work began again on the Panama Canal. Colonel William C. Gorgas, an American physician who had wiped out yellow fever in Havana, Cuba, spent the first 2 years of construction clearing brush, draining swamps, and cutting out large areas of grass where mosquitoes carrying malaria and yellow fever lived. At the height of the project, more than 40,000 workers were employed. In 1914 the cost for the completed project came to more than $380 million.

The Panama Canal Today

The Panama Canal remains a crucial commercial and military waterway. Its importance diminished somewhat with the advent of supertankers and large aircraft carriers too large to go through the canal. The high speeds and low operating costs of these ships have undercut the time-saving advantage of the canal. After World War II, the canal's military importance changed, too. The United States Navy decided to maintain fleets in both the Atlantic and Pacific Oceans. Still, an average of 34 oceangoing vessels travel through the Panama Canal each day—for a total of about 12,500 ships every year.

Making the Geographic Connection

1. What was one of the main problems preventing the French from completing the canal?
2. Was the decision to locate the canal in Panama a simple one? Explain.
3. **Location** Where is Panama, and why was a canal there important to an expanding United States?

SECTION 2

Watching Europe's War

MAY 7, 1915: GERMANY SINKS *LUSITANIA*

Notice! Travellers intending to embark on the Atlantic voyage are reminded that a state of war exists between Germany and her allies and Great Britain and her allies; . . . and that travellers sailing in the war zone on ships of Great Britain or her allies do so at their own risk.

—*New York World*, May 1, 1915

"All the News That's Fit to Print."

The New York Times.

EXTRA

LUSITANIA SUNK BY A SUBMARINE, PROBABLY 1,260 DEAD; TWICE TORPEDOED OFF IRISH COAST; SINKS IN 15 MINUTES; CAPT. TURNER SAVED, FROHMAN AND VANDERBILT MISSING; WASHINGTON BELIEVES THAT A GRAVE CRISIS IS AT HAND

STOCK MONTAGE

Headlines Influence Public Opinion
After reading this news report about the sinking of the *Lusitania* and the loss of life that resulted, Americans began to unify against Germany.

The passengers who sailed from New York on the British ship *Lusitania* that day seemingly ignored the warning that appeared in the newspaper. Bound for England, they enjoyed six days of dining and dancing on the luxury liner.

Early in the afternoon of May 7, in calm waters off the coast of Ireland, a German torpedo ripped into the side of the *Lusitania*. The huge ship sank within 18 minutes, taking with it the lives of nearly 1,200 men, women, and children, including 128 Americans.

Germany defended its action on the grounds that the *Lusitania* carried a shipment of arms. It also pointed out that passengers had been warned not to sail in the war zone. Americans, however, were outraged. Some demanded a declaration of war, although most wanted to keep the United States out of the conflict. President Wilson chose to apply diplomatic pressure on Germany and try to hold it accountable for its actions. During the next few months Wilson sent increasingly severe protests to Germany. He insisted that it abandon unrestricted submarine warfare. Americans could no longer merely watch Europe's war.

As You Read

Vocabulary

- self-determination
- coup
- alliance
- neutrality
- dogfight
- emigrate

Think About . . .

- the conflict between Wilson's belief in self-determination and his interventionist actions in Mexico and the Caribbean.
- the events that caused World War I.
- the struggle of the United States to remain neutral during World War I.
- the decision of the United States to abandon neutrality and enter the war in 1917.

MUSEO NACIONAL DE HISTORIA, MEXICO

Mexican Citizens Revolt **This is just a portion of a mural found in Chapultepec Castle near Mexico City. It was created by David Alfaro Siqueiros.** *How does this mural depict the period of the Mexican Revolution?*

Wilson's Foreign Policy

Intervention in Mexico

President Wilson brought to foreign policy an element of idealism that contrasted with the pragmatism of Roosevelt and Taft. He strongly believed that all peoples of the world had a right to **self-determination,** the right to choose the form of government they live under and to control their internal affairs. Yet President Wilson intervened in the affairs of other countries more than any previous President.

Revolution in Mexico

President Wilson, like Roosevelt, upheld the principles of the corollary to the Monroe Doctrine. Wilson maintained stability in the Western Hemisphere for American investment by sending American troops to quell domestic uprisings in Haiti in 1915, in the Dominican Republic in 1916, and in Cuba in 1917. He also continued Taft's Dollar Diplomacy policies by encouraging investors to buy out British enterprises in Central America. Dealing with Mexico and Europe, however, proved problematic for Wilson.

For 30 years the powerful Porfirio Díaz ruled Mexico. The stability of his rule encouraged American, British, and German investors, so much so that they controlled 90 percent of Mexico's mines, railroads, and industry. In 1911, however, Díaz fell from power, toppled by angry peasants whose land had been taken and middle-class Mexicans who had been deprived of their civil and voting rights.

Foreign investors feared that Francisco Madero, who replaced Díaz, would confiscate their property. Foreign diplomats—including the ambassador of the United States—and businesspeople plotted with discontented elements of the Mexican army to overthrow Madero. They wanted to replace him with Victoriano Huerta.

By the time President Wilson took office on March 4, 1913, Huerta had seized power, overthrowing the government and killing Madero in a bloody **coup.** Wilson thought the violence repulsive. He refused to recognize Huerta's government, vowing not to interfere directly.

> We shall have no right at any time to intervene in Mexico to determine the way in which the Mexicans are to settle their own affairs. . . . Things may happen of which we do not approve and which could not happen in the United States, but I say very solemnly that that is no affair of ours.
>
> —Woodrow Wilson, letter, 1914

American Intervention

A few months after expressing these beliefs, Wilson changed his mind, declaring that he had to teach Mexico to elect good officials. A minor incident concerning American honor was one reason for his shift. In April 1914, Mexican officials arrested several sailors from an American naval vessel in the port of Tampico. Local Mexican officials, as well as Huerta, quickly apologized for the incident. The American admiral in charge demanded a 21-gun salute to the American flag. Huerta demanded the same salute to the Mexican flag. This infuriated Wilson, who used the Tampico incident as a pretext for sending marines to the port city of Veracruz.

Another cause for Wilson's change of mind was a rumor that a German ship bound for Veracruz carried guns for Huerta's army. In spite of Mexico's ongoing revolution, the occupation of Veracruz outraged most Mexicans. Anti-American riots broke out in Mexico and throughout Latin America. The European press condemned the American military intervention, and so did many Americans. Shocked, Wilson backed off, and agreed to allow the ABC powers—Argentina, Brazil, and Chile—to mediate.

In 1915 Venustiano Carranza followed Huerta as president of Mexico. When Wilson backed Carranza, the rebel leader Pancho Villa struck back by killing 18 American mining engineers in Mexico. Villa's band then crossed the border and killed 17 Americans in the town of Columbus, New Mexico.

Wilson sent an expedition of 15,000 troops into Mexico under the command of John J. Pershing to find and capture Villa. Though they never found Villa, both Mexican and American lives were lost in battle.

Despite this military involvement, the United States failed to control events in Mexico. By late January 1917, Wilson decided to withdraw forces from Mexico. Another, much larger, war raged in Europe.

HULTON DEUTSCH COLLECTIONS LIMITED

Archduke Franz Ferdinand of Austria The Archduke poses with his wife, Sophie, and their family. *Why were Franz Ferdinand and his wife assassinated?*

Origins of World War I

Assassination and Alliances

What set off World War I in Europe? The bullet that killed the heir to the throne of the Austro-Hungarian Empire, Archduke Franz Ferdinand, started World War I. Austria-Hungary ruled over a large part of the Balkans, a mountainous area of southeastern Europe where many ethnic groups struggled for their independence. When a Serbian who supported Balkan independence assassinated Franz Ferdinand and his wife, all of Europe held its breath.

Entangling Alliances

By June 1914, almost any troublesome event could have sparked a war in Europe. Russia vied with Austria-Hungary and the Ottoman Empire for control over the Balkans. France, Russia, Britain, and Germany wrangled with one another to control ports and colonies overseas. The new naval force of Germany challenged Britain's long-established naval supremacy. Similarly, Germany's disciplined army struck fear into the hearts of neighboring Russia and France.

To gain security, many European countries organized themselves into a number of formal **alliances,** or unions. Each country that was part of a particular alliance vowed to help the allied countries in case of war. The members of the Triple Entente—which came to be called the Allies—were Britain, France, and Russia. Opposing the Allied Powers were the Central Powers, which consisted of Germany, Austria-Hungary, and the Ottoman Empire.

Because of the alliances, leaders in Europe knew that the assassination of Archduke Franz Ferdinand might mean world war. Russia reacted first by coming to the defense of the Serbian nationalists, in hopes of gaining influence in the Balkans. Russia's move brought the countries of the Triple Entente into the dispute, but Austria-Hungary and Germany needed to protect their interests too. Soon all of Europe erupted into war.

Early Years of the War

Austria-Hungary declared war on Serbia on July 28, 1914, and Germany declared war on Russia and France in the next few days. To avoid the strong defenses on the Franco-German border, German troops stormed through neutral Belgium. As a result, Great Britain, which was committed to the **neutrality,** or impartiality, of Belgium, declared war on Germany on August 4, 1914. A year later France, Russia, and Great Britain lured Italy into World War I on their side by promising Italy territory from the Austro-Hungarian Empire after the war was over. The map of Europe on page 307

EUROPE DURING WORLD WAR I, 1914–1918

On the map above, find the countries of the Triple Entente and those that made up the Central Powers. Note their positions. Identify and locate the countries that were neutral during the war. *Where did the Central Powers gain the most territory?*

shows that battle lines, or fronts, formed in two principal places: the Eastern Front in Russia and Germany and the Western Front in Belgium and France.

By November 1914, opposing troops on the Western Front faced each other in a deadlock. French troops stopped a German advance toward Paris, but at heavy cost. For more than three years thereafter, each side held the other in check.

On the Eastern Front, the Central Powers rapidly pushed back a disorganized and unprepared Russian army. They advanced across hundreds of miles of territory and took hundreds of thousands of prisoners early in the war. Later Russian successes were less decisive. Hardship among the Russian people, coupled with plummeting confidence in the czar's leadership, threatened Russia's ability to fight at all. Talk of mutiny sped through the troops.

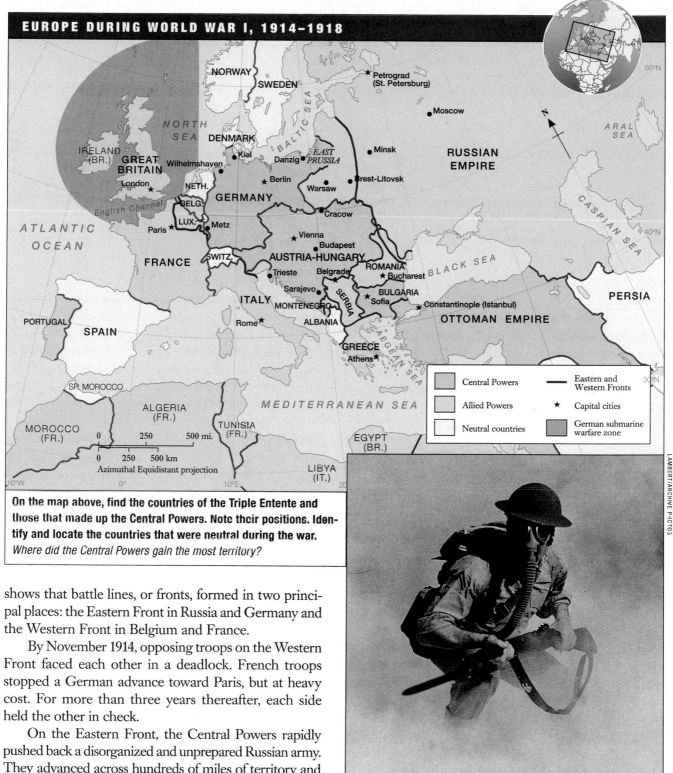

LAMBERT/ARCHIVE PHOTOS

Preparing for a Gas Attack During the war many soldiers and civilians were killed by new weapons never before used—submarines, machine guns, poisonous gases, and tanks. *How did the loss of life and property in World War I compare with losses in previous wars?*

The Fields of Death

World War I resulted in greater loss of life and property than in any previous war. In the Battle of Verdun (February to July 1916), for example, French casualties numbered about 315,000 and German casualties about 280,000. In the Battle of the Somme, Britain suffered 60,000 casualties in one day of fighting. That battle raged

MAJOR EVENTS AND BATTLES OF WORLD WAR I, 1914–1917

1914 · 1915 · 1916 · 1917 · 1918

August 1914 Germans defeat the Russians at Tannenberg, Germany.

November 1914 The Allies declare war on the Ottoman Empire.

April 1915–January 1916 A German-trained Ottoman army defeats combined British forces at the Battle of Gallipoli in Turkey.

July–August 1915 Massacres occur in Armenia. Russians lose Poland.

October–December 1916 The French regain positions around Verdun.

March–April 1917 The "February Revolution" occurs in Russia resulting in the end of czarism. Lenin returns to Russia.

July 1917 British officer T.E. Lawrence and Emir Faisal lead the Arabs to take the port of Aqaba on the Red Sea.

from July to November of 1916 and resulted in more than 1 million deaths. In the end, the Allies had advanced the front only about 7 miles. A battle at Tannenberg, in East Prussia, was so disastrous that the Russian general shot himself in despair over the defeat.

The terrible destruction of World War I resulted from a combination of old-fashioned strategies and new technology. Military commanders continued to order massive infantry offensives. The command "Over the top!" sent soldiers scrambling out of the trenches to dash across a field with fixed bayonets, hurling grenades into enemy trenches. The attackers, however, were no match for automatic machine guns that could fire hundreds of rounds in rapid succession. Defensive artillery kept each side pinned in the trenches.

Both sides developed new weapons designed to break the deadlock. In April 1915, the Germans first used poison gas in the Second Battle of Ypres. The fumes caused vomiting and suffocation. When the Allies also began using poison gas as a weapon, gas masks became a necessary part of a soldier's equipment. Flamethrowers that shot out streams of burning fuel and tanks that could roll over barbed wire and trenches added to the destruction.

The fields of battle in World War I extended to the seas and to the skies. Germany challenged Britain's sea power with its submarine blockade. The two navies squared off in a major encounter on May 31 and June 1, 1916, in the Battle of Jutland, off the west coast of Denmark. Both sides claimed victory, but Britain retained control of the seas.

Great advances in aviation came about during World War I. At first planes were used mainly to observe enemy activities. Then Germany developed a machine gun timed to fire between an airplane's propeller blades. This invention led to the use of airplanes for combat. **Dogfights,** the name given to clashes between enemy aircraft, proved deadly for pilots but had little effect on the ground war.

During 1917 France and Britain saw their hopes for victory diminish. A revolution in Russia made the situation seem even more hopeless. In March 1917 (February in old Russian calendar), an uprising in Russia resulted in the overthrow of the czar. In November, Bolshevik party leader Vladimir I. Lenin seized control of the government and began peace talks with Germany. Thus, the Russian Revolution led to the end of fighting on the Eastern Front, freeing Germany to concentrate all its forces on the Western Front. The Allies' only hope seemed to be the entry of the United States into the war.

In the Trenches

The soldiers on the Western Front spent most of their time in muddy trenches. Enemy troops were protected from one another only by dirt, barbed wire, and a stretch of land—called no-man's-land—no more than 30 yards wide in some places.

ARCHIVE PHOTOS

Life in the Trenches **British troops in a 1917 frontline trench near St. Quentin, France, rest before the next military assault.** *What stretched between the trenches of enemy troops?*

PRIVATE COLLECTION

Pacifists in World War I **Early in 1915 several feminist leaders formed the Woman's Peace party to advocate peace. After the *Lusitania* disaster, they staged a protest parade to urge the President to work for peace despite German actions.** *What was the myth of neutrality?*

When not shooting at the enemy, soldiers in trenches fought lice, rats, and the dampness and cold, as well as such diseases as dysentery, gangrene, and trench mouth. All understood the suffering they faced daily, if not the politics that created the trenches. By the end of World War I roughly 10 million soldiers and about 20 million civilians had died. Exact numbers were impossible to collect.

Many soldiers took the war as a personal challenge. Others became disillusioned. One German novelist portrayed a young German soldier crying out in protest:

> While they [government officials] continued to write and talk, we saw the wounded and dying. While they taught that duty to one's country is the greatest thing, we already knew that death-throes are stronger. . . . We loved our country as much as they; we went courageously into every action; but also we distinguished the false from true.
>
> —Erich Maria Remarque,
> *All Quiet on the Western Front,* 1929

Struggle for Neutrality

Evolving Events Lead to War

Woodrow Wilson longed to keep the United States out of World War I. In August 1914, he asked for neutrality, urging the American people not to take sides. He said, "We must be impartial in thought as well as in action." Neither side deserved America's support, thought the righteous Wilson. The American people, however, many of whom had recently **emigrated** from Europe, leaving one country to settle in another, had their favorite sides. Millions had been born in Germany, England, Austria-Hungary, Russia, Ireland, or Italy; yet, for the most part, they too preferred to distance themselves from the bloodbath overseas.

Myth of Neutrality

While Wilson publicly proclaimed neutrality of the United States, American interests leaned toward the Allies. Although United States businesses traded with both sides in the European conflict, ties with the Allies were much stronger. A representative from the House of Morgan, the mighty New York financial institution, explained:

> Those were the days when American citizens were being urged to remain neutral in action, in word, and even in thought. But our firm had never for one moment been neutral: we didn't know how to be. From the very start we did everything that we could to contribute to the cause of the Allies.
>
> —Thomas W. Lamont,
> *Manchester Guardian,* January 27, 1920

American political and business sympathy pleased the Allies. They tried to sway popular support to their side too. One of the first things Britain did when war broke out was to cut the transatlantic cable to the United States, so all news had to come through Britain. The reports that arrived vilified the Germans. Soon many ordinary Americans favored the Allies in World War I.

Bryan and the Submarines

Although public sentiment was turning toward the Allies, Secretary of State William Jennings Bryan still favored neutrality—even after German submarines attacked ships on which American citizens traveled. The

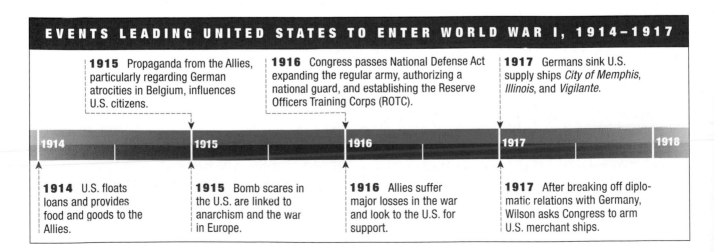

HULTON DEUTSCH COLLECTION LIMITED

A German Submarine This camouflaged German submarine, or U-boat, was typical of those that operated from 1914 to 1918. *What strategy did the Germans employ to break the British blockade of Germany?*

Germans had developed this new weapon, the submarine, and they used it to surprise enemy merchant ships in the war zone Germany monitored around the British Isles. That strategy was in response to a British blockade of Germany that had effectively begun to starve the German people. Bryan could see that both sides had military reasons for acting as they did. He encouraged Wilson to forbid Americans from traveling in the submarine zones as a way of avoiding trouble with Germany. Wilson argued, however, that free and safe travel was a right of citizens of a neutral country.

The issue reached a crisis on May 7, 1915, when German submarines attacked the *Lusitania*, a British passenger ship. More than 1,000 passengers died, including 128 Americans, as the torpedoed ship quickly sank. Germany knew that the *Lusitania* secretly carried arms and had warned ahead of time that it might be a target for attack. Nevertheless, Americans were outraged. "Damnable! Damnable! Absolutely hellish!" cried Billy Sunday, a fiery evangelist of the time. In spite of the tragedy, Wilson continued to believe that Americans should not be restricted from traveling the seas. In protest, Bryan resigned.

Reelection

The American people reelected Woodrow Wilson to the presidency in 1916 in a close race against Charles Evans Hughes. American voters responded to the Democratic campaign slogan: He kept us out of war! That slogan, however, made Wilson nervous. In spite of his neutrality efforts, he knew that the nation was edging closer to entering World War I.

The pressure on Wilson to enter the war came partly from his own moral commitment to the Allies; but it came also from American business leaders and

EVENTS LEADING UNITED STATES TO ENTER WORLD WAR I, 1914–1917

1914 U.S. floats loans and provides food and goods to the Allies.

1915 Propaganda from the Allies, particularly regarding German atrocities in Belgium, influences U.S. citizens.

1915 Bomb scares in the U.S. are linked to anarchism and the war in Europe.

1916 Congress passes National Defense Act expanding the regular army, authorizing a national guard, and establishing the Reserve Officers Training Corps (ROTC).

1916 Allies suffer major losses in the war and look to the U.S. for support.

1917 Germans sink U.S. supply ships *City of Memphis*, *Illinois*, and *Vigilante*.

1917 After breaking off diplomatic relations with Germany, Wilson asks Congress to arm U.S. merchant ships.

1914 1915 1916 1917 1918

UPI/BETTMANN NEWSPHOTOS

Campaigning for Reelection This campaign van was used by supporters of President Wilson in 1916. *Why did President Wilson want to have a say in the peace settlement after World War I?*

investors. American companies had invested deeply in an Allied victory. By 1917 American loans to the Allies totaled $2.25 billion. If Wilson helped the Allies win, the money would be paid back. Even more important, his commitment to the Allies would ensure a place for American investment in postwar Europe.

In addition to these pragmatic motives, the idealistic Wilson truly wanted to have a say in a peace settlement. He longed to make sure that after World War I, no other war would ever threaten the world again. He felt that no one would listen seriously to his ideas unless the United States had actually proved itself in battle. Ironically, Wilson's desire for a peaceful world led him closer to war.

Closer to War

Several events led the United States to finally enter the war. In January 1917, a German official named Arthur Zimmermann cabled the German ambassador in Mexico instructing him to make an offer to the Mexican government. Zimmermann proposed that Mexico ally itself with Germany. In return, Germany would make sure that after the war Mexico would receive some of the region that it lost to the United States in 1848. A British official intercepted Zimmermann's telegram and spread the news to the United States. This incident occurred shortly after Wilson withdrew from the Pancho Villa chase, so the Zimmermann note made many Americans eager to humiliate both Mexico and Germany.

Another declaration from Germany led the United States even closer to war. On January 31, 1917, Germany announced an unrestricted submarine campaign. German people were starving, and the country was desperate to end the war. Because the United States was not truly neutral, the Germans felt they had nothing to lose by an onslaught. The Germans sank one ship after another, including the American supply ship *Illinois* on March 18, 1917.

By April 1, President Wilson was brooding and pacing the floor. "Once I lead these people into war," he confided to editor Frank Cobb, "they'll forget there was ever such a thing as tolerance. To fight you must be brutal and ruthless, and the spirit of ruthless brutality will enter into the very fabric of our national life." In spite of his doubt and anguish, on April 2, 1917, the President stood before the United States Congress and asked its members to declare war on Germany.

> It is a fearful thing to lead this great peaceful people into war, into the most terrible and disastrous of all wars, civilization itself seeming to be in the balance. But the right is more precious than peace, and we shall fight for the things which we have always carried nearest our hearts,—for democracy, for the right of those who submit to authority to have a voice in their own Governments, for the rights and liberties of small nations. . . . [W]e dedicate our lives and our fortunes, everything that we are and everything that we have, . . . America is privileged to spend her blood and her might for the principles that gave her birth and happiness and the peace which she has treasured.
>
> —Woodrow Wilson,
> War Message, April 1917

Section Review

Vocabulary

1. Define: self-determination, coup, alliance, neutrality, dogfight, emigrate.

Checking Facts

2. How did Wilson continue the policies of Roosevelt and Taft?
3. What single act set off World War I? Why?

Critical Thinking

Drawing Conclusions

4. Why was the British government so eager to inform the United States of Germany's offer to Mexico? What did it hope to gain? How did this information affect Wilson's thinking on the war?

Linking Across Time

5. Wilson professed a belief in self-determination; however, he intervened in the affairs of other nations on several occasions. The United States sent troops to Grenada in 1983 and to Kuwait in 1991 to protect the interests of the United States. Do you think strong nations should have the right to intervene in the affairs of weaker nations? Why or why not?

Science, TECHNOLOGY, and Society

The Radio

With the invention of the radio, communication improved worldwide. The radio connected governments, as well as average citizens, providing information about international events and ending isolation across the globe. As a form of entertainment, the radio also impacted everyone's leisure time.

THE MARCONI COMPANY

GENERATING POWER

The use of wireless telegraphy during World War I affected the development of offensive and defensive fronts. This soldier is pedaling a stationary bike to generate the power needed to make radio contact between troops. The primary concern was communicating information between a fixed and a moving point.

IMPERIAL WAR MUSEUM

KDKA RADIO PHOTO, PITTSBURG, PA

THE "MUSIC BOX"

Frank Conrad, an engineer for Westinghouse, began broadcasting music from his garage after World War I. As interest in the broadcasts grew, Harry P. Davis, a Westinghouse vice president, launched the sale of the first commercial radio receiver in 1920 called the "music box" (above).

THE EVOLUTION OF RADIO BROADCASTING

Pre-1900s | 1900s | 1910s | 1920s

- **ELECTROMAGNETIC WAVES,** the precursor to radio, radar, and television, are demonstrated by James Maxwell in 1864.
- **ELECTROMAGNETIC WAVES** first transmit sounds in a 1900 experiment by R.A. Fessenden.
- **TRIODE VACUUM TUBE,** which allows for amplification of weak signals, is developed by Lee De Forest in 1906.
- **BROADCASTING INDUSTRY,** including hundreds of radio stations and millions of receivers, is envisioned by David Sarnoff in 1916.

WESTINGHOUSE

TRANSMITTING SIGNALS

On November 2, 1920, KDKA of Pittsburgh conducted the world's first scheduled broadcast. By the mid-1920s, KDKA personnel were testing an experimental antenna, carried aloft by a big balloon (left). This was a far cry from the first mobile radio in 1901 (below), with its cylindrical aerial that allowed telegraphic transmissions around the country and to sailing vessels. Guglielmo Marconi, standing at the extreme right, is credited with the invention of wireless telegraphy.

THE MARCONI COMPANY

ENTERTAINMENT

Singing into an early microphone, Dame Nellie Melba's clear soprano soared across European and Atlantic airwaves on June 15, 1920, from the Marconi wireless factory in Chelmsford, England. This was the first advertised program of entertainment on the radio—until then the radio had been used mostly as a news service. Civilians were prohibited from using the wireless during the war.

THE CHANGING SHAPE OF RADIO

PORTFOLIO PROJECT

How has the radio changed since its inception in 1920? What impact has this form of communication had on other sectors of life? Make a collage labeling the different forms of radio technology available today.

1930s	1940s	1950s	1960s–1990s

FM RADIO becomes available in 1929.

TRANSISTOR RADIOS become commercially available in 1952.

STEREOPHONIC RADIO BROADCASTING begins in the 1960s. Sony introduces the first personal stereo, the Walkman, in 1979. By 1982 AM radio stations begin broadcasting in stereo.

Social Studies Skill

USING REFERENCE MATERIALS

Learning the Skill

If you want to write a paper on a topic related to World War I, you will need to use a variety of reference materials for research. Familiarity with such materials sharpens your research skills and helps you decide where to look for information. Try to locate the following types of reference sources in a library's reference department:

Encyclopedias

Encyclopedia articles give an overview of a topic. Most offer suggestions for further research at the end of an article, including a bibliography, list of related articles in the encyclopedia, or additional sources of information.

Indexes of Periodicals

Periodicals from the past reflect the culture, events, and concerns of their time; current periodicals provide the most recent research on a given topic. Several indexes can help you find information in periodicals. The *Readers' Guide to Periodical Literature* is a popular set of reference books that lists magazine articles by topic.

Historical Atlases

These contain maps with information about people and events of the past, and may also have articles and time lines. National Geographic's *Historical Atlas of the United States* is one source for United States history.

Statistical Sources

For information about the United States, the *Statistical Abstract of the United States* is a good place to start. Compiled by the Bureau of the Census, it contains data on more than 30 topics. The information dates back to 1790, the year the first census was taken.

Biographical Dictionaries

These tell about the life or achievements of noteworthy people. Webster's *American Biographies* and the *Dictionary of American Biography* are good sources.

Practicing the Skill

Study the chart below, then answer the following questions.

1. For each source, make up your own research question based on material in Chapter 10.

2. Find answers to the questions you wrote in question 1 in the appropriate reference materials.

3. Write a short report about a key figure in this chapter. Tell what sources you used.

4. Where would you look to find out more about World War I battlefields?

5. Look up the Philippines in two sources, and list two facts from each source.

Applying the Skill

Check today's newspaper for a story that interests you; where would you look for more information on the subject?

Additional Practice

For additional practice, see Reinforcing Skills on page 329.

ORGANIZATIONAL PATTERNS

Source of Information	Uses	Sample Research Questions
Encyclopedias	Provide topic overviews; suggest further research	What were the main provisions of the Versailles Treaty
Periodicals	Reflect the past; supply current research on a topic	How did journalists react to the November Revolution?
Historical Atlases	Provide geographic context for historical information	Locate the Eastern and Western fronts during World War I.
Statistical Sources	Convey statistical information	What was the estimated total cost of World War I to the United States?
Biographical Dictionaries	Describe the backgounds and achievements of historical figures	Who were Emilio Aguinaldo, V.I. Lenin, and Georges Clemenceau?

SECTION 4

Reshaping the World

DECEMBER 1918: EUROPEANS CHEER WILSON

NATIONAL ARCHIVES

Celebrating Wilson and Peace
Jubilant crowds greet President Wilson and British officials on Wilson's arrival in London.

"WE WANT WILSON," THE WAR-WEARY CROWD ROARED. "Long live Dr. Wilson!" "Honor to Wilson the just!" British students with American flags smiled, tossing flowers in the President's path. Everywhere in Europe the Wilsons visited—Paris, Rome, Milan—the reception was jubilant. An Italian laborer spoke for millions when he said of Wilson:

> They say he thinks of us—the poor people; that he wants us all to have a fair chance; that he is going to do something when he gets here that will make it impossible for our government to send us to war again. If he had only come sooner! I have already lost my two sons. Do you believe he is strong enough to stop all wars?
>
> —Overheard conversation, 1918, *My Diplomatic Education*

Europeans had lost about 10 million soldiers in the war and twice as many civilians. Soldiers still suffered from wounds in crowded hospitals. French towns had been obliterated from the map. Ordinary Europeans had sacrificed, scrimping on food, often going cold and hungry. No wonder they looked for a savior—someone to end such brutality forever. They hailed Wilson hopefully because of his plan for a just and lasting peace. The President had outlined the plan in a 14-point document; his ideas came to be known simply as the Fourteen Points.

European leaders, however, regarded Wilson with skepticism. French Premier Georges Clemenceau observed, "God has given man Ten Commandments. He broke every one. President Wilson has his Fourteen Points. We shall see."

AS YOU READ

Vocabulary

- bolshevism
- irreconcilables
- reservationist

Think About . . .

- Wilson's Fourteen Points and the objections European leaders had to them.
- how events in Russia affected other nations.
- the 1919 Paris Peace Conference negotiations and resulting Treaty of Versailles.
- why the Senate rejected the Treaty of Versailles.

Wilson also unwittingly endangered his Fourteen Points with a political move at home. As the midterm congressional elections of 1918 drew near, Wilson issued an appeal urging Americans to vote Democratic. This appeal enraged Republicans, who took it as an affront to their patriotism. When voters later elected Republican majorities to Congress, Wilson lost credibility at the negotiating table with European leaders.

A Troubling Treaty

Vision and Vengeance Clash

Woodrow Wilson walked into the Paris Peace Conference at the Palace of Versailles in January 1919 with the cheers of the European crowds still ringing in his ears, but he was in a very weak bargaining position. As the conference dragged on for five long months, he would give up more and more of his Fourteen Points as well as his own good spirits and health. By April he appeared thinner, grayer, grimmer, and more nervous. His face twitched as he spoke, and he expressed greater moral rigidity than ever before. This irritated the European leaders around him. "I never knew anyone to talk more like Jesus Christ," said Clemenceau in exasperation.

An Atmosphere of Exclusion

One of the Fourteen Points promised that international negotiations and agreements would be made in the open, eliminating secret pacts. From early on, however, this principle was ignored. The press was kept away from the negotiations. The Allied Powers also pared down the number of countries actually shaping the final outcome to the "Big Four"—the United States, Great Britain, France, and Italy. Germany and Russia—two countries whose futures hinged on the outcome of the treaty—were completely shut out of negotiations.

Great Britain, Italy, and France insisted on the exclusion of a German representative. France even refused Germany the right to have observers at the proceedings. Wilson had argued for peace among equals, but now he deferred to the wishes of his three wartime allies. Before the conference concluded, France obtained concessions to occupy an industrial region of Germany for 15 years, won back its northeastern territories of Lorraine and Alsace, and established a reparations commission to assess money Germany would pay for French losses.

The exclusion of Russia at the conference stemmed from confusion and fear. In 1919 Europe seemed on the brink of revolution. Bolshevik forces had not fallen to the White Russian opposition, in spite of American and Japanese intervention. In Germany radical groups threatened to overthrow the newly established Social Democratic government. Communists gained power in Hungary. Leaders of the Western democracies at Versailles were worried about the revolutionary movements sweeping Europe.

The Big Four vacillated and disagreed. Should they include Russia to try to soften its impact, or should they use direct military action to subdue the Bolsheviks? Neither extreme won the day. Instead, they simply excluded Russia from the conference, but as a contemporary observer noted, "the black cloud" of Russia remained, "threatening to overwhelm and swallow up the world."

An Atmosphere of Self-Interest

The Fourteen Points dwindled to even fewer as the Big Four debated what to do about German and Turkish colonies in Asia and Africa. In Wilson's original plan, all colonies would have a say in their own destiny. Colonies of Allied Powers hoped this principle would include them. To victorious France and Great Britain, however, the self-determination of their colonies was completely unacceptable. Rather than losing their own colonies, they were eager to enjoy the spoils of war by absorbing the colonies of their defeated enemies.

The final compromise did little to honor Wilson's call for "impartial adjustment of all colonial claims." Allied Powers would retain their own colonies and the League of Nations would give them control over Central

THE BETTMANN ARCHIVE

Germany Impoverished Germany's huge postwar debt helped bankrupt its economy and made it fertile ground for the rise of fascism. Some poorer citizens turned to rummaging through refuse heaps in hopes of finding everyday necessities. *How was Germany treated at the Paris Peace Conference?*

NEGOTIATION OF THE TREATY OF VERSAILLES

Japanese Delegates Like the Big Four, Japan sent 5 delegates to Versailles; 22 other nations had 1 to 3 delegates each. *What did Japan request at the peace conference?*

Power colonies. These mandated colonies, however, would be ruled in the name of the League.

Italy presented another challenge to the Fourteen Points. It, too, wanted some of the spoils of war—parts of the Austro-Hungarian Empire including the ports of Fiume and Trieste. Wilson resisted Italy's expansion because his plan advocated forming Balkan states from the land of Austria-Hungary. Much of what Italy wanted would go to the newly created state of Yugoslavia (shown on the map on page 326). Soon Italians would turn to Benito Mussolini, who vowed to avenge their humiliation.

Japan, the mighty force of the Pacific, also came to Versailles to make its demands as the world shifted and realigned. Japan wanted full recognition of its rights in the Shandong Province of China, which Germany had controlled before the war. During the heat of the war, world powers had little time to protect their stake in China, leaving Japan to consolidate its interests there. Japan's demand to control the province directly opposed the self-determination provisions of the Fourteen Points.

Nonetheless, Japan devised a scheme to secure its control of Shandong. Japanese delegates asked that an article formally declaring the equality of all races be attached to the peace agreement. This request exposed the limitations of Wilson's progressive approach. Much of progressive foreign policy, especially in the Caribbean, had been based on the assumption that white people knew best. While the Fourteen Points provided for a degree of self-determination, Wilson was not ready to change the power structure of the world so radically. The Japanese proposal directly challenged not only Wilson, but all of the colonial powers at the conference who held dominion over people of color in Asia and Africa. Rather than deal with this troubling situation, the conference let Japan expand its influence in China, provided it drop its racial equality proposal. Thus, by cleverly manipulating the issue of race, Japan gained power in China. The Japanese victory enraged student radicals in China, who rioted in protest through the streets of Beijing.

By June 28, 1919, when the Treaty of Versailles was signed, a beleaguered and ill Woodrow Wilson had only one consolation left: the provision for the League of Nations had not been rejected, even though most of his original Fourteen Points had vanished. He returned to the United States driven by the idea that the League of Nations must not fail. Only an international league could deal with the injustices built into the Treaty of Versailles.

Rejection at Home

Political and Personal Obstacles

Woodrow Wilson's long stay in Europe took its toll on his health. Moreover, his rivals in Congress had united against him. Approval for the League of Nations now hinged on ratification of the Treaty of Versailles by the United States Senate.

Opposition in Congress

Opposition to the League was consolidated in two camps in Congress. One camp, the **irreconcilables,** was mostly progressive Republicans, many of whom had been in elected office since the turn of the century. They included Robert La Follette, William Borah, Hiram Johnson, and a handful of others. They called themselves irreconcilables because under no circumstances would they be reconciled to voting for the League of Nations.

Chapter 10 Review

Reviewing Key Terms

Imagine that you have kept a diary of events covering the outbreak of World War I and the United States involvement in the war. Write headlines for 10 diary entries, using each of the following terms in a headline:

alliance	**doughboys**
neutrality	**propaganda**
dogfight	**bolshevism**
mobilization	**irreconcilable**
conscription	**reservationist**

Recalling Facts

1. Why did overseas markets appeal to many Americans? Why did some oppose commercial expansion overseas?

2. What policies did Roosevelt and Taft implement in the Caribbean?

3. What is self-determination? What actions did Wilson take that were not consistent with his belief in self-determination?

4. Describe the United States's involvement in Mexico during the first 2 decades of the 1900s.

5. Why did Wilson claim neutrality before World War I?

6. Give examples of print media that historians might use to study public opinion during World War I.

7. Describe the racial bias that existed in the United States military during World War I.

8. What actions were taken to support the war on the home front during World War I?

9. How did George Creel help spread Wilson's ideas about peace?

10. Why did bolshevism frighten President Wilson and other world leaders?

Critical Thinking

1. Recognizing Bias When Roosevelt negotiated peace between Russia and Japan, he claimed neutrality. What evidence suggests that he actually favored one side? Why would it be to his advantage to pretend he was unbiased?

2. Determining Cause and Effect President Woodrow Wilson did not want to involve the United States in World War I. Instead he wished to remain neutral, supporting neither Germany nor Russia. The President wanted the people of the United States to be "impartial in thought as well as in action." On April 2, 1917, however, the President asked the members of Congress to declare war on Germany. What factors or international incidents involving the United States caused President Wilson to reverse his position?

3. Predicting Consequences Think about the convictions of Eugene Debs and Rose Pastor Stokes and the terrorization of IWW members in Oklahoma. In what ways might the abridgement of civil liberties lead to mob rule?

4. Making Generalizations The photo below depicts the devastation and ruins of the Arras Cathedral in France after a German offensive. How would people who suffered in World War I have gone about rebuilding their nations? Make a list of priorities to follow in the aftermath of a disaster of this magnitude. How did President Wilson's Fourteen Points hope to address the international efforts of postwar rebuilding?

ARCHIVE PHOTOS/POPPERFOTO

CHAPTER 10 REVIEW

Portfolio Project

PORTFOLIO PROJECT

Select a country in Europe that was involved in World War I. Research what life was like for the citizens of that country during the war. Try to locate and review primary sources to supplement textbook and other secondary source materials. Primary sources might include letters, diaries, personal memoirs, and legal documents such as wills and titles. Prepare a written report about "life during World War I." You may want to support your report with appropriate visuals—pictures from newspapers and magazines, photographs, paintings, and drawings. Share your report orally with your classmates before filing your written account in your portfolio.

Cooperative Learning

With a small group, stage the debate over the selective exclusion that occurred during the 1919 Paris Peace Conference. Use information from Section 4, as well as additional research, to represent the Big Four countries. Try to identify the reasons the Big Four finally excluded Germany and Russia from the peace negotiations.

Reinforcing Skills

Using Reference Materials

Imagine that you are a reporter who was assigned a feature story commemorating Theodore Roosevelt. Think about the various reference materials that could be sources of information about his family, his accomplishments, and his career. Refer to the Tools of Reference chart on page 320 as you list the various reference materials you could use. Explain the type of information that you expect to learn from each source.

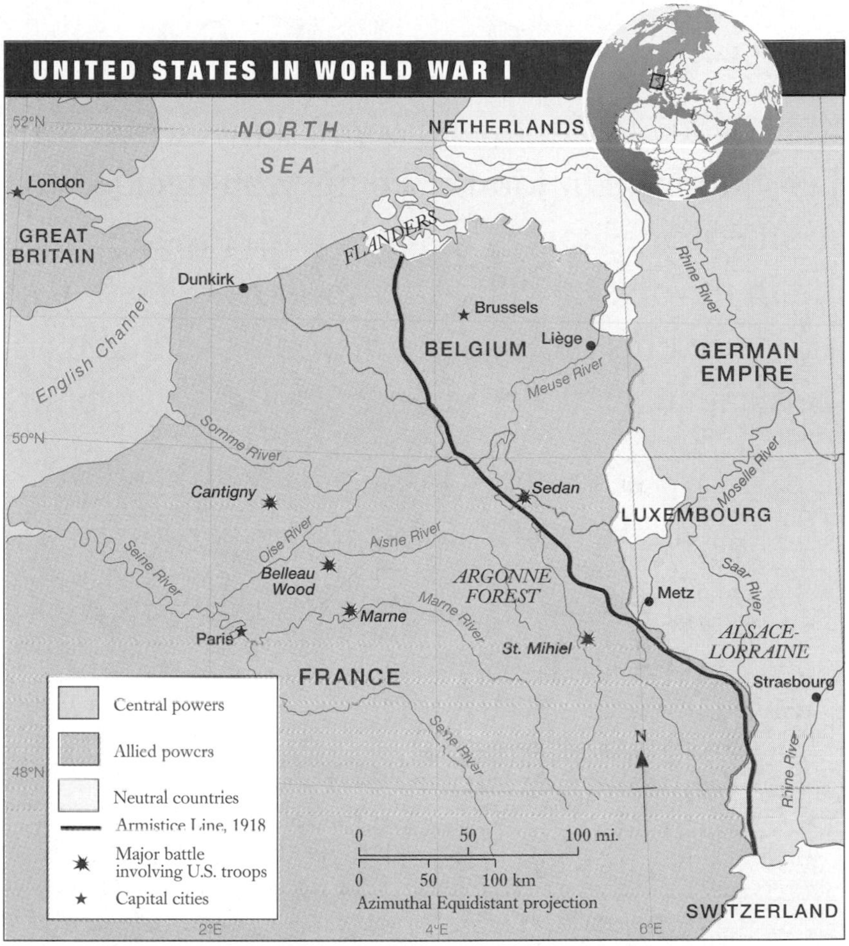

Geography and History

Study the map on this page to answer the following questions:

1. Name two important World War I battles involving United States troops. In what country did the fighting occur?

2. Which French city was an important naval landing site for British and Allied replacement troops? Why?

3. Which capital city of western Europe was most threatened by nearby warfare? How did this affect the way the war was fought?

4. Through what countries did the Armistice Line extend? Were these countries primarily Allied Powers or Central Powers?

HISTORY JOURNAL

Through the era of expansionism and World War I, the United States established itself as a world leader and entered the international political arena. How did the emergence of the United States as a world power affect the lives of returning soldiers and their families? Write your response in your journal. Compare your new entry to your original prediction in your journal response to page 292. Underline any new information that you have learned after reading this chapter.

Then...

Coca-Cola: Symbol of America

In the heyday of American cure-all medicines and soda fountains, Dr. John S. Pemberton decided to create a "medicine" tasty enough to top the lists of soda fountain flavors. In 1886, after months of taste-testing, he produced his famous "nerve tonic"—actually 99 percent sugar water—and Coca-Cola was born.

PRINTS SUPPLIED BY THE COCA COLA COMPANY

PRINTS SUPPLIED BY THE COCA COLA COMPANY

1 Pemberton's partner Frank Robinson created the product's name and its flowing script. His adjectives "delicious and refreshing" became almost synonymous with the drink. Bottles, advertising, and recipes changed, but the Coca-Cola script remained the same.

PRINTS SUPPLIED BY THE COCA COLA COMPANY

Fun Facts

FOR LOVE OF TRADITION

When the Coca-Cola Company tried altering its recipe in 1985, the popular uproar forced a reintroduction of "Coke Classic" within 3 months.

ADVERTISING AT ITS BEST

Some say that "Coca-Cola" is the second most recognized term on the earth, after "OK."

2 **Pemberton spent $150 in advertising during the first year—at a time when a streetcar sign cost a penny and 1,000 free-sample coupons could be printed for a dollar. Soon the Coca-Cola name was visible on all kinds of items, such as the 1910 baseball scorecard, below.**

PRINTS SUPPLIED BY THE COCA COLA COMPANY

DRINK
Coca-Cola
DELICIOUS
REFRESHING
Coca-Cola
5¢
THE STRENUOUS LIFE
On the street or curb or any phase of endeavor loses much of its nerve racking and physically exhausting terrors if you drink
Coca-Cola
Refreshes! Invigorates! Sustains!
5¢ Sold Everywhere 5¢

PRINTS SUPPLIED BY THE COCA COLA COMPANY

3 **At soda fountains, Coca-Cola syrup was often stored in urns like this one. It was mixed with carbonated water at soda fountains and served in a glass for 5 cents. Many soda fountains were inside drugstores, emphasizing the belief (popular since Roman times) that carbonated water had healing properties.**

Stats

PRODUCT DEVELOPMENT

	Originated	Patent Registered
Coca-Cola name	1886	1893
Coke name	1941	1945
Contoured bottle	1916	1960

ORIGINAL RECIPE

Water, sugar, lime juice, coco, citric acid, vanilla, caffeine, orange, lemon, nutmeg, cinnamon, coriander, neroli, alcohol

THE COMPETITION

- Before Pepsi Cola became a threatening competitor, Coca-Cola refused two offers to buy out the nearly bankrupt company.
- Hire's Root Beer and Dr. Pepper were already on many soda fountain menus by the time Coca-Cola arrived.
- Dr. Pemberton originally called his concoction "my temperance drink," in response to the growing temperance movement of the day.

...Now

ANALYZING ADVERTISING

PORTFOLIO PROJECT

Coca-Cola is one of the best advertised products in the country. From the start, the product name has appeared on matchbooks, blotters, clocks, calendars, lamps, serving trays, and playing cards, among other things. In what ways do you see Coca-Cola advertised today? How are today's approaches similar to and different from those of the past? What do you consider to be the most effective forms of advertisement today? Why? Compile examples and explanations for your portfolio.

PRINTS SUPPLIED BY THE COCA COLA COMPANY

EVOLUTION OF DISTRIBUTION

Bottles of ready-to-drink Coca-Cola were not widely distributed until the turn of the century when the crimped-crown bottle cap became the industry standard.

UNIT

4

The New Era of the Twenties

CHAPTER 11
Getting on With Business

CHAPTER 12
A Prospering Society

PHOTOGRAPH COURTESY NIAGARA MOHAWK POWER COMPANY

The Great Gatsby

BY F. SCOTT FITZGERALD

In this excerpt from F. Scott Fitzgerald's novel The Great Gatsby, *the narrator describes a party at a mansion on Long Island. Music, dancing, and carefree parties—with a hint of emptiness—typified the Jazz Age of the 1920s.*

There was music from my neighbor's house through the summer nights. In his blue gardens men and girls came and went like moths among the whisperings and the champagne and the stars. At high tide in the afternoon I watched his guests diving from the tower of his raft, or taking the sun on the hot sand of his beach while his two motor-boats slit the waters of the Sound, drawing aquaplanes over cataracts of foam. On weekends his Rolls-Royce became an omnibus, bearing parties to and from the city between nine in the morning and long past midnight, while his station wagon scampered like a brisk yellow bug to meet all trains. And on Mondays eight servants, including an extra gardener, toiled all day with mops and scrubbing-brushes and hammers and garden-shears, repairing the ravages of the night before.

Every Friday five crates of oranges and lemons arrived from a fruiterer in New York—every Monday these same oranges and lemons left his back door in a pyramid of pulpless halves. There was a machine in the kitchen which could extract the juice of two hundred oranges in half an hour if a little button was pressed two hundred times by a butler's thumb.

NAWROCKI STOCK PHOTO

The Spirit of '26 **Illustrator John Held, Jr., captured the jazzy verve of the 1920s in this 1926 *Life* magazine cover.**

At least once a fortnight a corps of caterers came down with several hundred feet of canvas and enough colored lights to make a Christmas tree of Gatsby's enormous garden. On buffet tables, garnished with glistening hors-d'oeuvre, spiced baked hams crowded against salads of harlequin designs and pastry pigs and turkeys bewitched to a dark gold. In the main hall a bar with a real brass rail was set up, and stocked with gins and liquors and with cordials so long forgotten that most of his female guests were too young to know one from another.

By seven o'clock the orchestra has arrived, no thin five-piece affair, but a whole pit full of oboes and trombones and saxophones and viols and cornets and piccolos, and low and high drums. The last swimmers have come in from the beach now and are dressing upstairs; the cars from New York are parked five deep in the drive, and already the halls and salons and verandas are gaudy with primary colors, and hair shorn in strange new ways, and shawls beyond the dreams of Castile. The bar is in full swing, and floating rounds of cocktails permeate the garden outside, until the air is alive with chatter and laughter, and casual innuendo and introductions forgotten on the spot, and enthusiastic meetings between women who never knew each other's names.

THERE IS A BURST OF CHATTER AS THE ERRONEOUS NEWS GOES AROUND THAT SHE IS GILDA GRAY'S UNDERSTUDY.

The lights grow brighter as the earth lurches away from the sun, and now the orchestra is playing yellow cocktail music, and the opera of voices pitches a key higher. Laughter is easier minute by minute, spilled with prodigality, tipped out at a cheerful word. The groups change more swiftly, swell with new arrivals, dissolve and form in the same breath; already there are wanderers, confident girls who weave here and there among the stouter and more stable, become for a sharp, joyous moment the center of a group, and then, excited with triumph, glide on through the sea-change of faces and voices and color under the constantly changing light.

Suddenly one of these gypsies, in trembling opal, seizes a cocktail out of the air, dumps it down for courage and, moving her hands like Frisco, dances out alone on the canvas platform. A momentary hush; the orchestra leader varies his rhythm obligingly for her, and there is a burst of chatter as the erroneous news goes around that she is Gilda Gray's understudy from the *Follies.* The party has begun.

I believe that on the first night I went to Gatsby's house I was one of the few guests who had actually been invited. People were not invited—they went there. They got into automobiles which bore them out to Long Island, and somehow they ended up at Gatsby's door. Once there they were introduced by somebody who knew Gatsby, and after that they conducted themselves according to the rules of behavior associated with amusement parks. Sometimes they came and went without having met Gatsby at all, came for the party with a simplicity of heart that was its own ticket of admission. . . .

Dressed up in white flannels I went over to his lawn a little after seven, and wandered around rather ill at ease among swirls and eddies of people I didn't know—though here and there was a face I had noticed on the commuting train. I was immediately struck by the number of young Englishmen dotted about; all well dressed, all looking a little hungry, and all talking in low, earnest voices to solid and prosperous Americans. I was sure that they were selling something: bonds or insurance or automobiles. They were at least agonizingly aware of the easy money in the vicinity and convinced that it was theirs for a few words in the right key.

As soon as I arrived I made an attempt to find my host, but the two or three people of whom I asked his whereabouts stared at me in such an amazed way, and denied so vehemently any knowledge of his movements, that I slunk off in the direction of the cocktail table—the only place in the garden where a single man could linger without looking purposeless and alone.

Responding to Literature

1. **Fitzgerald has been called the "chronicler of the Jazz Age." Based on this excerpt, how would you define the era?**
2. **What is the narrator's attitude toward the lifestyle and values of the wealthy? Explain.**

CHAPTER 11

Getting on With Business

OCTOBER 28, 1925: MISSING EPISODE OF *ANNIE* PUBLISHED

From the moment the orphan with the frizzy curls appeared in American homes on August 5, 1924, she found her way into the hearts of all.

On October 27, 1925, the *Chicago Tribune* accidentally left *Little Orphan Annie* out of the newspaper. Reader response was so strong that an apology, along with 2 *Annie* comic strips, was seen in the next day's paper.

How could a comic strip capture so much attention? In part, Annie's innocent strength seemed to reflect the self-image of the United States in the era following World War I. Annie's creator, Harold Gray, had left her without relatives or entanglements. This gave Annie the freedom to do what she wanted and go where she pleased.

Annie's foster father, Daddy Warbucks, was a weapons tycoon who showered Annie with kindness, gifts, and love. His character sent a resounding message that businesspeople could be honest and decent. In the big business era of the 1920s, millions of people seemed to agree. ■

HISTORY JOURNAL

How does the image on the opposite page illustrate the bustle of business that characterized the 1920s? Identify details from the photograph to support your response.

BROWN BROTHERS

This 1922 photo of New York City's Times Square captures the high energy that filled the country after World War I.

SECTION 1

Postwar Turmoil

AUGUST 23, 1927: SACCO AND VANZETTI EXECUTED; WORLDWIDE RIOTS

UPI/BETTMANN

Vanzetti (left) and Sacco (right)
The pair arrive for trial at the Dedham Courthouse in Massachusetts.

IN 1921 NICOLA SACCO AND BARTOLOMEO VANZETTI HAD BEEN CONVICTED OF MURDERING A PAYMASTER AND A SHOE FACTORY GUARD DURING A ROBBERY IN SOUTH BRAINTREE, MASSACHUSETTS. Many people believed that the men had been found guilty only because they were immigrants and **radicals,** advocating political and social revolution. By 1927 Sacco and Vanzetti had exhausted every legal appeal. Now they were about to be executed.

In his final defiant words to Judge Thayer, Vanzetti declared that he was innocent of the murders but unshakable in his unpopular beliefs:

> I am suffering because I am a radical and indeed I am a radical; I have suffered because I was an Italian, and indeed I am an Italian; I have suffered more for my family and for my beloved than for myself; but I am so convinced to be right that if you could execute me two times, and if I could be reborn two other times, I would live again to do what I have done already.
>
> —Bartolomeo Vanzetti, speech to Judge Thayer, 1927

The years of the trial of Sacco and Vanzetti showed the United States desperately struggling to defend itself against the dangers following World War I. Many Americans feared immigrants whose ways appeared different and threatening. For a time, many Americans also believed that the radical politics of the 1917 Russian Revolution might overtake this country. Sacco and Vanzetti seemed to represent all the fears of the United States during the turbulent postwar years.

AS YOU READ

Vocabulary

- radical
- anarchism
- prohibition

Think About . . .

- factors that led to the Red Scare.
- the causes and effects of the Great Migration.
- ways in which the Progressive movement continued during the 1920s.
- the reasons that progressivism declined during the 1920s.

Sacco and Vanzetti

A Miscarriage of Justice

Some criminal evidence linked Sacco, a shoemaker, and Vanzetti, a fish peddler, to the murders. Neither man had ever been accused of a crime before his arrest, and none of the money from the robbery was ever traced to the men.

Their trial, too, was marked by serious breaches of fairness. The judge, Webster Thayer, had repeatedly denounced Sacco and Vanzetti for their immigrant backgrounds and for their belief in a radical political theory called **anarchism.** Anarchists believe that the restraint of one person by another is evil, and they do not recognize the authority of any government.

During the six years the men stayed in jail, Judge Thayer refused repeated motions for a new trial. Finally, the Massachusetts governor appointed a special committee to review the case one more time. The committee included Abbott Lawrence Lowell, president of Harvard, and Dr. Samuel W. Stratton, president of the Massachusetts Institute of Technology.

One witness told the committee that, even before the trial, the foreman of the jury had declared, "They ought to hang anyway." The committee agreed that the judge had not behaved properly when he had referred to Sacco and Vanzetti as "dagos" and worse. The committee, however, still backed Judge Thayer's decision to execute the prisoners.

Prominent Americans, including future justice of the Supreme Court Felix Frankfurter, protested the scheduled executions. Sacco and Vanzetti, Frankfurter argued, were being punished for their "alien blood and abhorrent philosophy," rather than for murder.

Americans were not the only protesters. During the six years of appeals, the Sacco and Vanzetti case had become world famous. When Sacco and Vanzetti were executed, riots broke out from Japan to Warsaw, from Paris to Buenos Aires. Crowds menaced the United States Embassy in Rome, and workers went on strike in France, Italy, and the United States.

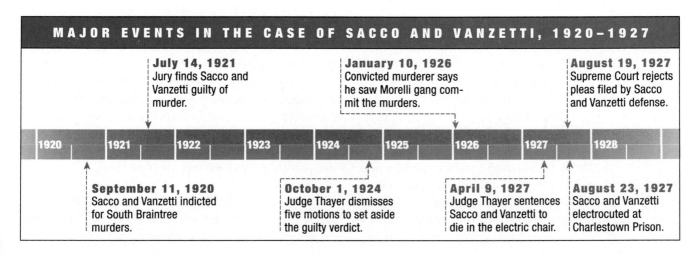

AP/WIDE WORLD PHOTOS

Sympathizers Protest **Supporters of organized labor protest the Sacco and Vanzetti guilty verdict.** *How widespread was support for Sacco and Vanzetti?*

Sacco's last words were "Long live anarchy!" Before he died, Vanzetti gave an interview to a reporter. In broken but eloquent English, he said:

> If it had not been for these thing, I might have live out my life, talking at street corners to scorning men. I might have die, unmarked, unknown, a failure. Now we are not a failure. This is our career and our triumph. Never in our full life can we hope to do such work for tolerance, for joostice [justice], for man's onderstanding [understanding] of man, as now we do by an accident.
>
> —Bartolomeo Vanzetti, *New York World,* May 13, 1927

MAJOR EVENTS IN THE CASE OF SACCO AND VANZETTI, 1920–1927

- **September 11, 1920** Sacco and Vanzetti indicted for South Braintree murders.
- **July 14, 1921** Jury finds Sacco and Vanzetti guilty of murder.
- **October 1, 1924** Judge Thayer dismisses five motions to set aside the guilty verdict.
- **January 10, 1926** Convicted murderer says he saw Morelli gang commit the murders.
- **April 9, 1927** Judge Thayer sentences Sacco and Vanzetti to die in the electric chair.
- **August 19, 1927** Supreme Court rejects pleas filed by Sacco and Vanzetti defense.
- **August 23, 1927** Sacco and Vanzetti electrocuted at Charlestown Prison.

1920 | 1921 | 1922 | 1923 | 1924 | 1925 | 1926 | 1927 | 1928

Fifty years to the day of their execution, August 23, 1977, Massachusetts governor Michael Dukakis cleared the names of Sacco and Vanzetti. Their trial, Dukakis said, had been "permeated with prejudice."

The Red Scare

Anti-Communist Panic

Judge Felix Frankfurter described the atmosphere in Boston during the Sacco and Vanzetti trial. He said that outside the courtroom "the Red hysteria was rampant; it was allowed to dominate within."

Indeed, Boston had become one of the centers for the Red Scare, a violent wave of anti-Communist panic that swept through the United States in 1919 and 1920. In November 1917, the Bolshevik Revolution had installed a Communist government in Russia. Communist uprisings in Hungary and Bavaria made it seem as though communism were spreading rapidly.

Two small Communist parties had formed in the United States in 1919. Their total membership never exceeded 70,000, just one-tenth of 1 percent of the adult population. Even so, many people began to fear that a Communist revolution like the one in Russia was brewing in this country.

During World War I, George Creel's Committee on Public Information had whipped up public hatred of Germans. After the war many Americans transferred this hatred to anyone who had been born in another country. Foreigners were especially vulnerable to attack when, like Sacco and Vanzetti, they favored radical politics.

Public officials, business leaders, and the press all contributed to the Red Scare. More than any other person, President Wilson's attorney general, A. Mitchell Palmer, directed the Red Scare.

A Climate of Fear

A progressive lawyer and politician from Pennsylvania, Palmer had no doubt that Communists were about to take over his country's government. For one thing, Palmer had spent the war serving as an alien property custodian. In this job he had collected and been shocked by reams of anti-American propaganda. As a pacifist Quaker, Palmer despised the Bolshevik theory that promoted violent revolution.

To Palmer the Bolshevik plan to take over the world seemed to become a reality on June 2, 1919, when bombs exploded in eight cities throughout the United States. One of the bombs shattered the front of Palmer's Washington, D.C., home. Although the bomb thrower was killed in the blast, evidence suggested he was an Italian immigrant and anarchist.

STOCK MONTAGE, INC.

"Put Them Out and Keep Them Out" The title of this political cartoon expressed the sentiments of those who were influenced by the Red Scare. *What was the Red Scare?*

After the bombings, Palmer asked for and got an appropriation of $500,000 from Congress to launch a campaign to "tear out the radical seeds that have entangled American ideas in their poisonous theories." Within the Justice Department's Bureau of Investigation, Palmer established the General Intelligence—or antiradical—division. Under the direction of J. Edgar Hoover, this division began to gather information about domestic radical activities.

The Palmer Raids

In November 1919, Palmer's men staged raids on the Union of Russian Workers in 12 cities. In December, 249 aliens were deported to Russia on a ship the popular press nicknamed "The Soviet Ark." Most of the deportees had never participated in any terrorist or criminal activity but merely favored nonviolent radical causes.

The following month Palmer's men arrested more than 4,000 people, many of them United States citizens, in 33 major cities during a single night of raids. Seized without warrants, many of these prisoners were denied attorneys and deprived of food, water, heat, and even bathroom facilities. In Boston one detainee leaped 5 stories to his death, 2 prisoners died of pneumonia, and another went insane. In New York guards beat many prisoners.

Some critics challenged Palmer's methods. William Allen White, newspaper editor, called Palmer's raids "un-American." He went on to argue:

And if a man desires to preach any doctrine under the shining sun, and to advocate the realization of his vision by lawful, orderly, constitutional means—let him alone. If he is Socialist, anarchist, or Mormon, and merely preaches his creed and does not preach violence, he can do no harm. For the folly of his doctrine will be its answer. The deportation business is going to make martyrs of a lot of idiots whose cause is not worth it.

—William Allen White, *Emporia* (Kansas) *Gazette,* January 8, 1920

The public, however, generally applauded Palmer's January raids. Even though most of the prisoners eventually were released because they had nothing to do with radical politics, the *Washington Post* proclaimed that this was "no time to waste on hairsplitting over infringement of liberty." Six hundred radicals were expelled from the country before the Department of Labor, in charge of aliens, halted the deportations.

By midsummer the height of the Red Scare seemed to be over. The raids and deportations had demoralized American radicals. Businesses had broken a rash of strikes. Bolshevism had failed to spread beyond Russia.

In September 1920, a bomb exploded at the corner of Broad and Wall Streets, the center of New York City's financial district, killing more than 30 people and injuring hundreds more. If the bombing had occurred the year before, Americans might have interpreted it as part of a plot to overthrow the government. Now the United States seemed to be determined not to give way to panic. One newspaper reported:

The public is merely shocked, not terrorized, much less converted to the merits of anarchism. Business and life as usual. Society, government, industry functioning precisely as if nothing had happened.

—*Cleveland Plain Dealer,* September 18, 1920

Labor Unrest

In the middle of the Red Scare, an outbreak of strikes brought the threat of revolution uncomfortably close to home. The cost of living had more than doubled from prewar levels. When their wages lagged far behind, angry workers went on strike.

Of the 3,600 strikes during 1919, the Seattle general strike, the police strike in Boston, the steel strike, and the coal strike proved the most disruptive. Each major strike further inflamed an already fearful public. During the Boston police strike, all the Boston newspapers called the strike "Bolshevistic." When labor leader Samuel Gompers asked Massachusetts governor Calvin Coolidge to help settle the strike, Coolidge wired back the refusal that launched his national political career: "There is no right to strike against the public safety by anybody, anywhere, anytime."

The 350,000 steelworkers who went on strike in September 1919 worked a 12-hour day, 7 days a week. Each time they changed between the day and the night shift, they had to work 24 hours straight, risking injury and death. Elbert Gary, the head of United States Steel, denied their simple demand—one day's rest out of the week. At first the public sympathized with the strikers. Supported by the press, however, the steel companies portrayed the strike as a radical outbreak and dangerous uprising. As public opinion began to turn against them, the strikers had little chance.

The steel owners provoked riots, broke up union meetings, and employed police and soldiers to end the strike. African Americans recruited from the impoverished South to replace the striking workers also helped break the strikes. In the end, 18 strikers were killed, and the steelworkers' union won none of its demands.

The coal strike lasted for a month in the late fall of 1919 and threatened to paralyze a country that depended on coal to heat its homes and run its factories. When the 394,000 striking miners finally obeyed a presidential order to go back to work, they went back to the same working conditions.

All the major strikes of 1919 were portrayed in the press as anti-American actions that threatened the United States government. The issues of long hours and poor working conditions got lost in the shuffle.

The Great Migration

Opportunities in the North

Between 1916 and 1920, half a million African Americans left the South for new jobs in the North. Many of these migrants were World War I veterans. These

Urban African American Population

City	1920	1930	Increase
Atlanta	62,831	90,119	43%
Birmingham	70,256	99,127	41%
Chicago	109,458	233,903	114%
Cleveland	34,815	73,339	111%
Detroit	40,838	120,066	194%
Los Angeles	15,579	38,894	150%
New York	152,467	327,706	115%
Philadelphia	134,229	219,599	64%
Washington, D.C.	110,701	132,955	20%

African American populations increased in urban areas across the United States from 1920 to 1930. *What two cities had the largest increases?*

Firefighter Recruits **Service workers such as these firefighter recruits were part of growing African American communities in the North.** *What other salaried jobs did African Americans perform in Northern communities?*

soldiers bitterly resented the discrimination they had experienced in the war. No longer satisfied to struggle on Southern farms, African Americans began to seek better opportunities in the North.

Many African Americans corresponded with a newspaper, the *Chicago Defender,* a key source of information about jobs and conditions in the North. One man wrote to the *Defender* to explain why so many African Americans were migrating north. In the South, he wrote, the wages of a grown man were 50 to 75 cents a day for all labor. "He is compelled to go where there is better wages and sociable conditions, . . . many places here in this state the only thing that the black man gets is a peck of meal and from three to four lbs. of bacon per week, and he is treated as a slave."

African Americans Find Better Pay

In the North, African Americans took jobs as meatpackers, metalworkers, and autoworkers, all for more pay than they could have made in the South. A migrant to Chicago who had found employment in the sausage department of a meatpacking plant wrote: "We get $1.50 a day and we pack so many sausages we don't have much time to play but it is a matter of a dollar with me. . . ."

Only 50 African Americans worked for the Ford Motor Company in 1916. By 1920 Ford had 2,500 African American employees. Six years later their numbers had quadrupled to 10,000.

Between 1910 and 1930, the Great Migration swelled Chicago's African American population from 44,000 to almost 234,000. Cleveland, the home of 8,500 African Americans in 1910, sheltered 68,000 by the end of the 1920s.

Northern whites, however, were no more eager than Southern whites had been to share power and opportunity with African Americans. Many Northern whites reacted violently to this Northern migration.

Racial Unrest

In 1917 race riots erupted in 26 Northern cities. Racial conflicts escalated even further after the war. Riots broke out in many cities, including the nation's capital, during the hot summer of 1919.

Southern African Americans who had migrated to Washington, D.C., during the war had been competing for jobs in an atmosphere of mounting racial tension. Newspaper reports of rumored African American violence against whites contributed to the tension.

Following one such newspaper story, 200 sailors and marines marched into the city, beating African American men and women. A group of whites also tried to break through military barriers to attack African Americans in their homes. Determined to fight back, a group of African Americans boarded a streetcar and attacked the motorman and the conductors. African Americans also exchanged gunfire with whites who drove or walked through their neighborhoods.

President Wilson had to call in federal troops to control the crowds, which finally dispersed in a driving rain. When the Washington riot ended, 4 days after it began, 4 men had been killed, 11 had suffered serious wounds, and dozens more had been injured. Three hundred people were arrested for rioting or for carrying weapons.

Few cities escaped racial violence during the early 1920s. Knoxville, Omaha, and Tulsa all experienced deadly struggles between African Americans and whites. Several radical African American groups sprang out of this ferment. Marcus Garvey's "Back to Africa" movement became the most famous.

The Garvey Movement

A black man from Jamaica, Marcus Garvey had grown up at the very bottom of Jamaican society. Black Jamaicans had no economic or political voice in this white-controlled British colony.

Educated as a journalist and filled with ambition, Garvey arrived in New York City at the age of 28. There he found an enthusiastic audience for his particular version of Booker T. Washington's African American self-help doctrine.

Where Washington advocated separate development in the United States, Garvey encouraged African Americans to return to Africa "to establish a country and a government absolutely on their own." To this end, Garvey founded the Universal Negro Improvement Association, which peaked at a membership of 250,000. With its program of African American pride and power, Garvey's "Back to Africa" movement foreshadowed the Black Muslim movement of the 1960s.

Garvey's message encouraged poor African Americans, who were his most fervent supporters. A member of the NAACP's board of directors said:

> The sweeper in the subway, the elevator boy eternally carrying fat office men and perky girls up and down a shaft, knew that when night came he might march with the African army and bear a wonderful banner to be raised some day in a distant, beautiful land.
>
> —Mary White Ovington, *Portraits in Color,* 1927

Thousands invested in Garvey's Black Star Line of ships that would take back African Americans to their "home" in Africa. The Black Star Line collapsed, however, partly because unscrupulous white business dealers sold Garvey leaky ships and faulty equipment. Arrested and charged with mail fraud, Garvey was deported as an undesirable alien.

ARCHIVE PHOTOS

A Master Showman Marcus Garvey dressed in a hat with a white plume and a fancy colorful uniform, declaring himself president of the African empire. *What did Marcus Garvey advocate?*

Whites called Garvey the "Moses of the Negroes," but some African American leaders, particularly W.E.B. Du Bois, criticized his unconventional methods and personal flamboyance. Marcus Garvey, however, gave African Americans pride and hope for the future.

Progressivism Endures

New Social Reforms Enacted

Even during this period of labor unrest and social tension, the reform impulse endured. For example, Senator George Norris of Nebraska successfully resisted efforts to turn over the government power plant at Muscle Shoals to business interests. The Women's Joint Congressional Committee lobbied for social reforms throughout the 1920s. On the state level, reformers also succeeded in instituting such programs as old-age pensions, workers' compensation, and city planning.

The postwar decade began with two important reforms whose roots were firmly planted in the Progressive Era. The Eighteenth Amendment established national Prohibition in 1919, and the Nineteenth Amendment gave women the right to vote in 1920.

Prohibition

Between 1906 and 1919, 26 states had passed laws limiting the sale of liquor. Progressives supported **prohibition,** or a ban on alcohol. They championed national Prohibition, a law that would forbid the manufacturing, transporting, and selling of liquor, arguing that an outright ban on drinking would be a great boon to society. In the House of Representatives debate on the Prohibition amendment, Congressman Richard Austin from Tennessee predicted that "a [prohibition] law which has emptied the jails in Tennessee and virtually wiped out the criminal side of the dockets of the courts will do the same in every State."

During the war, antisaloon advocates successfully linked Prohibition with patriotism. Conserving the grain that would have gone into liquor became part of the war effort. The antisaloon league also stirred up the country's anti-German hysteria, blaming German brewers for making American soldiers unfit.

By 1918, three-quarters of the population lived in "dry" states or counties. The cities, with their large immigrant populations, however, remained "wet" until the national amendment was ratified in 1919. This amendment was enforced by the Volstead Act, a law passed in 1919 declaring beverages containing one-half of 1 percent of alcohol intoxicating. When the Volstead Act took effect in January 1920, many Americans had high hopes that the new law would reduce poverty and wipe out

WOMAN SUFFRAGE BEFORE THE NINETEENTH AMENDMENT

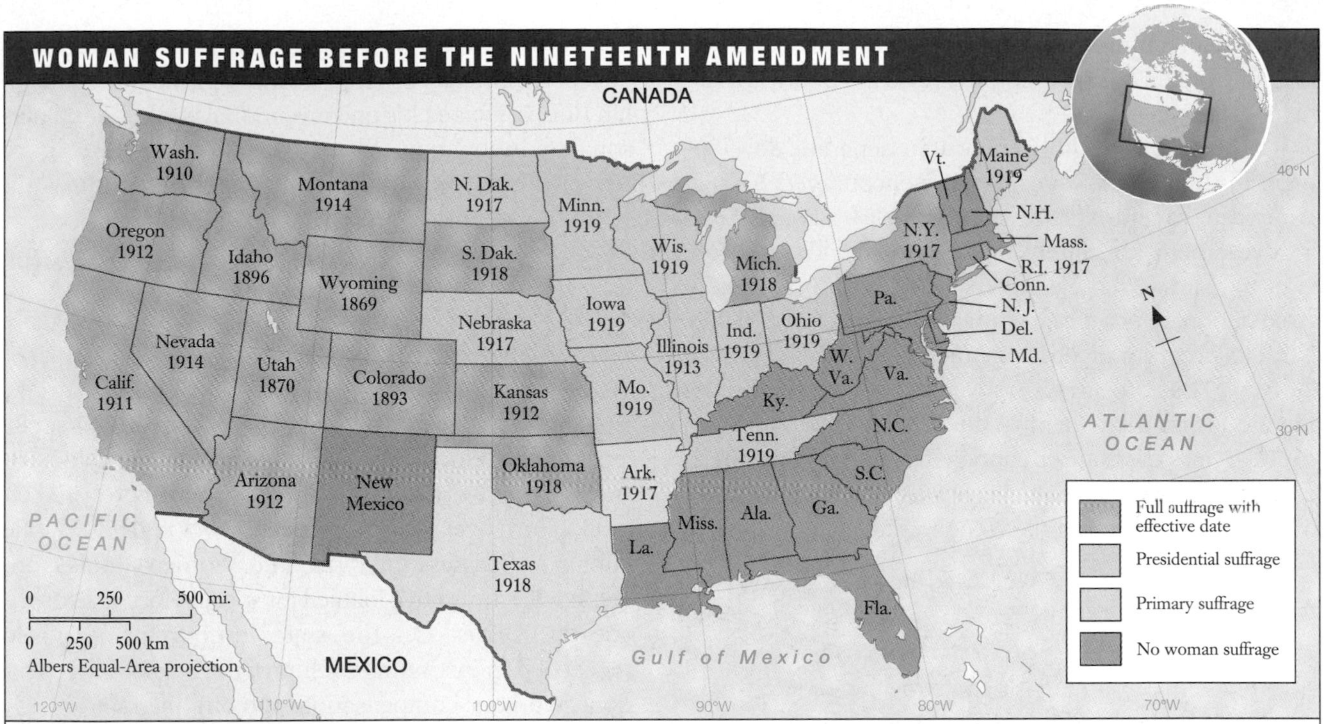

Women had voting rights in four Western states before 1900. *Which parts of the United States did not allow women to vote until after the passage of the Nineteenth Amendment?*

prostitution and crime. John Kramer, the first Prohibition Commissioner of the United States, enthusiastically proclaimed: "We shall see that it [liquor] is not manufactured. Nor sold, nor given away, nor hauled in anything on the surface of the earth or under the earth or in the air."

Suffrage

Like the fight for Prohibition, women's struggle for voting rights got its final push from the war experience. Women had begun pursuing the right to vote in 1848, but the fight died down in the decades before the Progressive Era.

Progressives supported suffrage because they believed women's votes could help pass a variety of reforms, especially those that protected women and children. A new period of activism, beginning around 1910, won rewards when several states—mostly in the West—approved suffrage.

Agnes Geelan, who later became mayor of her town and state senator from North Dakota, remembered: "We were allowed to vote in state elections . . . but there were restrictions. Women could only vote for women candidates. Men could vote for either men or women, and I didn't like that discrimination."

The campaign for national suffrage gathered steam in 1916, thanks to Carrie Chapman Catt's National American Woman Suffrage Association (NAWSA) and Alice Paul's Congressional Union, later the National Woman's party. The two groups argued intensely over tactics. The Woman's party favored radical actions, such as picketing the White House and going on hunger strikes when arrested. In a somewhat less radical way, NAWSA

WOMEN'S RIGHTS MOVEMENT, 1848–1923

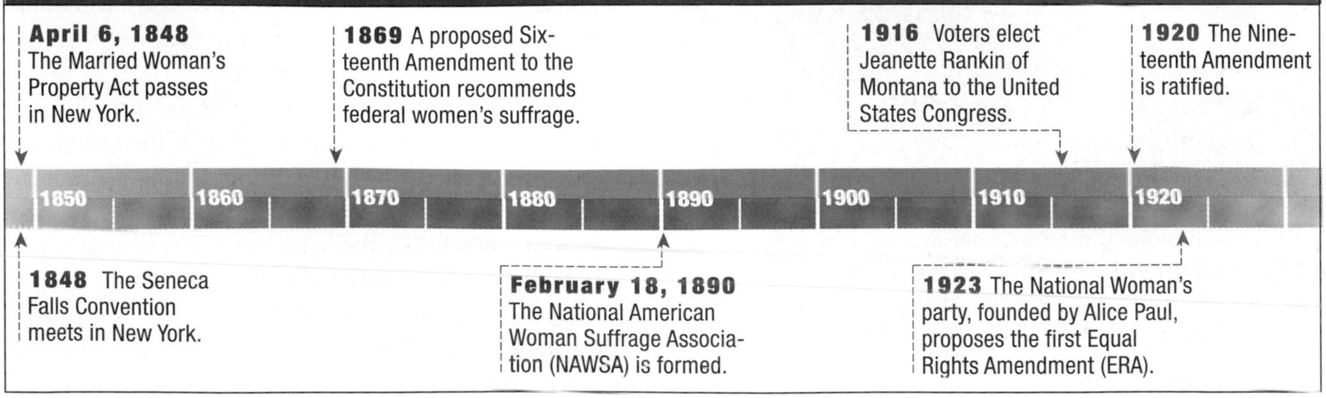

CULVER PICTURES

Carrie Chapman Catt Catt waves to supporters in New York City in 1920. *What group did Catt lead and what suffrage tactics did she support?*

publicized women's contributions to the war effort, an argument President Wilson used in urging Congress to approve suffrage. Ratification of the national suffrage amendment finally came on August 26, 1920.

The right to vote did not grant women full equality. In many states, a woman still could not serve on juries, hold office, enter business, or sign contracts without her husband's permission. Despite the years of hard work that went into gaining the right to vote, two out of three women who had the vote failed to use it in the 1920 election.

After winning the vote, women united to support one important piece of legislation, the Sheppard-Towner Maternity Act of 1921. Stimulated by high rates of maternal and infant mortality, the act provided funds for states to employ public health nurses, hold child-care conferences, and educate new mothers. The Sheppard-Towner Act was the first allocation of federal funds for welfare purposes. It had faced opposition from the American Medical Association. Other opponents argued that the bill was "inspired by foreign experiments in communism." Even so, Congress passed the Sheppard-Towner Act almost unanimously. It stayed in effect until 1929 when Congress failed to renew it.

Decline of Progressivism

Despite the passage of Sheppard-Towner, the 1920s hardly provided a friendly environment for reform. Progressive legislation that survived Congress or state legislatures frequently perished as a victim of a hostile Supreme Court.

For example, in 1916 Congress had passed a Child Labor Act, controlling the employment of children. Two years later the Court declared the act unconstitutional on the grounds that Congress could not use its commerce power to regulate labor conditions. To make it uneconomical for businesses to hire children, Congress passed a new law establishing a prohibitive tax on child-manufactured products. The Court found the new law unconstitutional as well.

Progressive legislation to benefit working women fared little better. In 1923 the Court struck down a Washington, D.C., law enacting a minimum wage for women.

Progressivism declined for other reasons besides a hostile Supreme Court. After the brutality of World War I, many reformers had lost faith in finding political solutions to social problems. The turmoil of the postwar years also helped to weaken the Progressive movement. Many progressives were middle-class property owners. Shocked by the violence of the strikes and fearful of radical political ideas, many of these progressives found their sympathies shift more firmly to the side of big business.

Section Review

Vocabulary

1. Define: radical, anarchism, prohibition.

Checking Facts

2. How did Sacco and Vanzetti symbolize the fears of many Americans in the postwar era?
3. Identify some of the reforms that continued in the 1920s as a result of the Progressive movement.

Critical Thinking

Determining Cause and Effect

4. List the factors that led many African Americans to seek better employment opportunities in the North.

Linking Across Time

5. Progressive legislation, particularly that dealing with working conditions, was often defeated by a hostile Supreme Court during this time period. Are laws to protect workers still needed today? Why or why not?

SECTION 2

The Republican Influence

NOVEMBER 2, 1920: HARDING DEFEATS COX

Campaign Buttons
Republicans held the White House through the 1920s.

RICHARD STROUT BEGAN REPORTING FOR THE *CHRISTIAN SCIENCE MONITOR* IN 1922 AND CONTINUED FOR 62 YEARS. The first three Presidents he covered—Warren Harding, Calvin Coolidge, and Herbert Hoover—could not have been more different.

Richard Strout said that Warren Gamaliel Harding, a fun-loving man who was elected in a landslide in 1920, did not have the answers. "He was furthermore aware of his inadequacies, and he was pathetic. . . . He said, 'Gentlemen, gentlemen, go easy on me. I just want to go out on the golf course today and shoot a round.'"

Calvin Coolidge, Harding's stern Vice President, succeeded to the presidency when Harding died. Coolidge then handily won the 1924 election. In an interview concerning the thirtieth United States President, Strout said:

> Calvin Coolidge only answered written questions from the press, and so, one time, we all got together and wrote down the same question. We wanted to know if he was going to run for re-election in 1928. So Coolidge looked at the first question and put it aside. Then he looked at the second and did the same thing. He went through all the slips of papers, I think there were a total of twelve, and on the last one he paused, read it to himself, and went on dryly: "I have a question about the condition of the children in Poland." We all smiled. He may have smiled too. And that concluded the press conference.
>
> —As told to Tom Tiede, *American Tapestry*, 1988

As You Read

Vocabulary
- internationalism
- disarmament

Think About . . .
- how the policies of Harding, Coolidge, and Hoover supported big business.
- how Republican foreign policy in the 1920s fostered the international expansion of big business and moved away from military and political involvement in Europe.
- the reasons for United States economic and military involvement in Latin America in the 1920s.

Herbert Hoover, the engineer who had performed brilliantly as secretary of commerce under Harding and Coolidge, easily won the presidency in 1928 after Coolidge declined to run. In the same interview, Strout said:

> Herbert Hoover was the first great man in my life. I thought he was going to be the greatest president we ever had. . . . He had each of us ask our questions, and then he would remember all of the questions and answer them one by one. It was remarkable. "As for your question, Mr. Strout, blah, blah, blah." He did it perfectly. I always thought he had a great mind, and he did.
>
> —As told to Tom Tiede, *American Tapestry,* 1988

Although their personalities were strikingly different, the three Republican Presidents pursued similar policies in the 1920s. Rejecting the social reforms of the Progressive Era, the Republican Presidents—Harding, Coolidge, and Hoover—put their faith in big business, both at home and abroad. If government allowed business to prosper, all Americans would reap the rewards.

THE BETTMAN ARCHIVE

Harding's Style **Harding (third from left) enjoys an outing in 1922 with Henry Ford and Thomas Edison.** *Who was Harding's opponent in the 1920 presidential election?*

Harding and the Teapot Dome

Scandals Strike the Administration

In 1920 Warren G. Harding trounced Democrat James M. Cox in the general election. Many observers saw this as a rejection of Woodrow Wilson's brand of **internationalism**, his policy of cooperation and involvement with other countries. As a senator, Harding had fought against joining Wilson's League of Nations. Now he promised, "We do not mean to be entangled."

Harding owed his success to Americans' exhaustion with the war years, with progressivism, and with the turbulence of 1919. Tired of reformers' attacks and President Wilson's demands for self-sacrifice, the country longed for a rest.

Return to Normalcy

Harding reassured the American people. In a campaign speech in 1920 he said, "America's present need is not heroics, but healing; not nostrums, but normalcy; not revolution, but restoration; not agitation, but adjustment; not surgery, but serenity."

★ ★ ★ Gallery of Presidents ★ ★ ★

Warren G. Harding

1921–1923

"Our supreme task is the resumption of our onward normal way. Reconstruction, readjustment, restoration—all these must follow. If it will lighten the spirit and add to the resolution with which we take up the task, let me repeat for our nation we shall give no people just cause to make war upon us. We hold no national prejudice; we entertain no spirit of revenge."

Inaugural Address, March 4, 1921

CULVER PICTURES

Background

- **Born 1865; Died 1923**
- **Republican, Ohio**
- **Elected lieutenant governor of Ohio 1903**
- **Elected to the Senate 1914**
- **Elected President 1920**

Achievements in Office

- **Washington Disarmament Conference (1921)**
- **Signing of peace treaties with Austria and Germany (1921)**

LIBRARY OF CONGRESS

Teapot Dome Affair This 1923 cartoon depicts the fall of public officials as the oil scandal was revealed. *Why did people not blame Harding when scandals during his administration came to light?*

People were not always sure exactly what the word *normalcy* meant—it was not even in the dictionary. Harding sounded presidential, however, and he most certainly looked presidential—tall, handsome, and stately.

Harding's first two years in office began well. He called a presidential conference to consider the problem of unemployment. Well aware of his own limitations, Harding named some bright and able officers to his cabinet: Secretary of State Charles Evans Hughes, Secretary of the Treasury Andrew Mellon, and Secretary of Commerce Herbert Hoover.

Harding also surrounded himself with his old friends from Ohio. People called these friends "The Poker Cabinet" or "The Ohio Gang." Alice Roosevelt Longworth described the White House atmosphere under Harding: "the air heavy with tobacco smoke, . . . cards and poker chips at hand—a general atmosphere of waistcoat unbuttoned, feet on desk, and spittoons alongside."

Some of Harding's poker buddies used their positions to line their pockets with money. The head of the Veterans Bureau was fined and sent to jail for selling off veterans hospital supplies for a personal profit. Eventually, another adviser resigned in disgrace and another narrowly avoided going to prison. Two of Harding's other advisers committed suicide rather than face public humiliation.

Teapot Dome Affair

Of the many scandalous situations that occurred during Harding's administration, the Teapot Dome Affair became the most famous. Harding's secretary of the interior, Albert Fall, leased government oil fields—one at Teapot Dome, Wyoming—to wealthy friends in exchange for hundreds of thousands of dollars in bribes. Eventually, Fall made history by being the first cabinet officer to go to prison, but the wealthy businesspeople who bribed him were never punished. A popular joke at the time quipped, "In America, everyone is assumed guilty until proved rich."

Upon hearing the news of a Senate investigation of oil leases, Harding grew depressed and distraught over his friends' betrayal. He became ill in Seattle, contracted pneumonia, and died in San Francisco on August 2, 1923, before the press began to reveal news of his administration's corruption. Americans mourned Harding, whom they had loved. Indeed the public seemed less angry at the corrupt government officials than they did at the exposers of the scandals. Senators Thomas J. Walsh and Burton K. Wheeler, who attempted to bring the crimes to light, were labeled "the Montana scandalmongers" by the *New York Tribune* and "assassins of character" by the *New York Times.* After decades of exposure, the American public had tired of muckraking and truly wanted a return to "normalcy." They got it when Harding's Vice President, Calvin Coolidge, succeeded to the presidency.

Silent Cal and Big Business

Business Prospers Under Republicans

Coolidge had a dry personality that symbolized the old-fashioned virtues of the New England in which he had been raised. The journalist William Allen White once remarked that Coolidge had the expression of one "looking down his nose to locate that evil smell which seemed forever to affront him." Alice Roosevelt Longworth said he looked as if he had been "weaned on a pickle."

Yankee Background

Born on a Vermont farm that his family had worked for five generations, Coolidge attended a one-room schoolhouse. After Harding's death, Coolidge's father, a justice of the peace, administered the presidential oath to his son by the light of a kerosene lamp. With his upright Yankee background and unquestioned reputation for complete honesty, Coolidge soon erased any damage the Harding scandals had caused the Republican administration.

Although he lacked Harding's personal warmth, Coolidge carried out Harding's programs. Both administrations rejected government programs to help ordinary citizens. When the victims of a Mississippi River flood appealed to the government for help, for example, President Coolidge replied, "The government is not an insurer of its citizens against the hazards of the elements." (See One Day in History, pages 394–395 for more on the 1927 flood.)

Policies Toward Business

Big business was another matter. The *Wall Street Journal* could justly brag that "Never before, here or anywhere else, has a government been so completely fused with business." The Harding and Coolidge administrations gave big business a boost in three ways. They appointed businesspeople to commissions that were supposed to regulate business. They selected Supreme Court justices who ruled against progressive legislation. Finally, they named conservatives to powerful cabinet positions.

Harding and Coolidge appointed to regulatory commissions people who opposed regulation. The Interstate Commerce Commission, the Federal Trade Commission, and the Bureau of Corporations soon began to overlook business's violations of antitrust laws.

Harding and Coolidge made 5 conservative appointments to the Supreme Court. From its origin in 1789 until 1925, the Supreme Court had struck down only 53 acts of Congress. During the 1920s the Supreme Court found 12 progressive laws unconstitutional, including the child labor law and the Washington, D.C., minimum wage law for women.

Cabinet positions in the Republican administrations went to wealthy business leaders who used their positions to protect big business interests. Andrew Mellon—secretary of the treasury under Harding, Coolidge, and Hoover—showed where the heart of 1920s politics lay. The third wealthiest person in the United States, Mellon immediately set out to cut government spending and reduce taxes on corporations and on people with high incomes.

Andrew Mellon's Influence

Mellon feared that if high taxes deprived a business person of too much earnings, "he will no longer exert himself and the country will be deprived of the energy on which its continued greatness depends." The multimillionaire with the straggly bow tie almost completely overturned the progressive tax policies of the Wilson years. Thanks to Mellon's efforts, a person making a million dollars a year in 1926 paid less than one-third of the taxes a millionaire had paid in 1921.

Coolidge agreed with Mellon; government should interfere with big business as little as possible. "Four-fifths of all our troubles in this life would disappear if we would only sit down and keep still," said Silent Cal. When Coolidge chose not to run in 1928, America's beloved humorist, Will Rogers, commented that Coolidge retired a hero "not only because he hadent [sic] done anything, but because he had done it better than anyone."

Herbert Hoover, The Wonder Boy

From Engineer to President

As secretary of commerce under both Harding and Coolidge, Herbert Hoover was a key architect of the Republican era. An intelligent and dedicated President, Hoover inherited the blame when the Republican prosperity later came crashing down.

★ ★ ★ **GALLERY OF PRESIDENTS** ★ ★ ★

Calvin Coolidge

1923–1929

"I favor the policy of economy, not because I wish to save money, but because I wish to save people. The men and women of this country who toil are the ones who bear the cost of the Government. Every dollar that we carelessly waste means that their life will be so much the more meager. Every dollar that we prudently save means that their life will be so much the more abundant."

Inaugural Address, March 4, 1925

AP/WIDE WORLD PHOTOS

BACKGROUND

- **Born 1872; Died 1933**
- **Republican, Massachusetts**
- **Elected governor of Massachusetts 1918**
- **Elected Vice President in 1920**
- **Assumed presidency 1923**
- **Elected President 1924**

ACHIEVEMENTS IN OFFICE

- **Kellogg-Briand Pact (1928)**
- **Improved relations with Mexico**
- **Support of American business**

Hoover, a successful mining engineer (once chief engineer for the Chinese Imperial Bureau of Mines), had brilliantly managed the United States Food Administration during World War I. As director of the Belgian Relief Committee, which provided food to starving Europeans, Hoover's name was a household word in the United States years before he became President.

Secretary of Commerce

Coolidge, who prided himself on restraint, sneered at Hoover's optimistic energy and called his secretary of commerce the "Wonder Boy." Indeed, during the 1920s, it seemed there was nothing the "Wonder Boy" could not do.

Hoover expanded the Commerce Department to control and regulate airlines, radio, and other new industries. He helped organize trade associations—groups of firms in the same line of business—to minimize price competition, which Hoover thought inefficient. Hoover also pushed the Bureau of Standards to standardize everything manufactured in the nation from nuts and bolts to tires, mattresses, and electrical fixtures.

Hoover's Achievements Herbert Hoover gained a reputation for competence during World War I. *How did Hoover's view of big business differ from his predecessors'?*

Hoover supported zoning regulations, eight-hour workdays in major industries, improved nutrition for children, and conservation of natural resources. He even pushed through the Pollution Act of 1924, the first effort to control coastline oil pollution.

Attitudes Toward Business

Hoover believed above all in volunteer effort and free enterprise. As secretary of commerce, Hoover had argued that American business was entering a new era. With the growth of trade associations, Hoover hoped businesses would show a new spirit of public service.

In 1928 many Americans agreed with Will Rogers, who said, "I always did want to see [Hoover] elected. I wanted to see how far a competent man could go in politics. It has never been tried before."

Republican Foreign Policy

Business Ties Replace Political Ties

After World War I, the United States shied away from political involvement in Europe. Nevertheless, all three Republican administrations increased the country's economic ties to Europe and the rest of the world. During the 1920s military assistance gave way to economic expansion and control. Herbert Feis, who was an influential historian of United States policy, wrote, "The soldiers and sailors had done their part, [and now] the dollar was counted on to carry on their work. It was regarded as a kind of universal balm."

In the 1920s the government encouraged United States firms to dramatically expand their international business. During this decade, American businesses came to dominate world markets in cars, tractors, electrical equipment, and farm machinery. "World peace through world trade" was how business leaders like Thomas J. Watson of International Business Machines (IBM) put it.

The Dawes Plan

Although the United States government did not direct this worldwide economic expansion, its policies fostered the international expansion of big business. The Dawes Plan showed how the United States influenced European economics without direct government intervention.

After World War I, the Allies owed $10 billion in war debts to the United States. Americans insisted on repayment, but the Allies could not pay unless they got the $33 billion Germany owed them in war reparations.

When Germany defaulted on its payments in December 1922 and January 1923, French soldiers marched into Germany's Ruhr Valley. To avert another war, the United States stepped in. The United States sent a business leader instead of an army. Charles G. Dawes, a wealthy Chicago banker, negotiated loans from

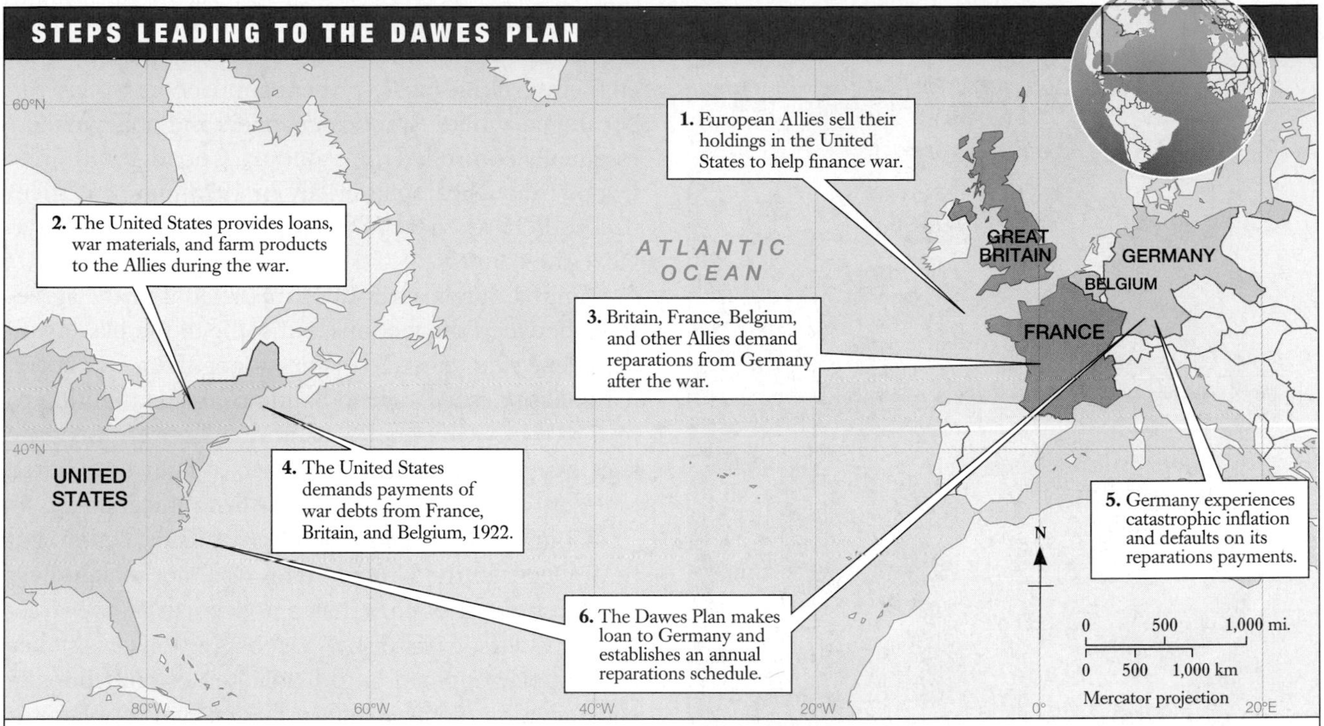
STEPS LEADING TO THE DAWES PLAN
1. European Allies sell their holdings in the United States to help finance war.
2. The United States provides loans, war materials, and farm products to the Allies during the war.
ATLANTIC OCEAN
GREAT BRITAIN
GERMANY
BELGIUM
FRANCE
3. Britain, France, Belgium, and other Allies demand reparations from Germany after the war.
UNITED STATES
4. The United States demands payments of war debts from France, Britain, and Belgium, 1922.
5. Germany experiences catastrophic inflation and defaults on its reparations payments.
6. The Dawes Plan makes loan to Germany and establishes an annual reparations schedule.
N
0 500 1,000 mi.
0 500 1,000 km
Mercator projection
60°N
40°N
80°W
60°W
40°W
20°W
0°
20°E

During World War I, the United States provided the Allies with loans and supplies. The Dawes Plan was set up to help recover the debt. *Which countries were paying war debts to the United States?*

private American banks to Germany and set up a new payment schedule.

These negotiations took shape as the Dawes Plan, a way for Germany to meet its financial obligations and avoid war. United States banks loaned Germany $2.5 billion so that Germany could make war reparations to the Allies. In turn, the Allies repaid this money to the United States government. Even though this money represented only a fraction of what the Allies and the United States were actually owed, the Dawes Plan restored payments that otherwise would not have been made. As a result, the potential for war on that score was reduced.

The most powerful nation in the world during the 1920s, the United States proved to be a reluctant giant. To stay clear of Europe's power struggles, the United States embarked on a twofold policy. The United States attempted to destroy the weapons of war through the Washington Conference. The United States also signed the Kellogg-Briand Pact to outlaw armed struggle.

The Washington Conference

In November 1921, Charles E. Hughes addressed the nine nations meeting at the Washington Naval Conference to discuss **disarmament**, the limitation or reduction of weapons. The delegates knew they were to discuss specifically the limitation of naval arms. Hughes, United States secretary of state, shocked his fellow world leaders when he asked them to destroy their battleships. Eventually, three major treaties emerged—making this the first successful disarmament conference in modern history.

After much controversy, the United States, Great Britain, Japan, France, and Italy pledged to limit the number of their largest ships and to stop constructing new ships. Great Britain and the United States got to keep 500,000 tons of ships each; Japan, 300,000 tons; and France and Italy, 167,000 tons each. The Japanese ambassador complained that the ratio of 5:5:3 sounded like "Rolls-Royce, Rolls-Royce, Ford." Japan agreed only after winning concessions that prohibited new American, British, and Japanese naval bases on the western Pacific islands.

For its part, Japan promised to respect China's sovereignty and independence. Despite this pledge, which kept the China market open to American business, the United States was concerned about Japanese power and ambitions in the Pacific.

The Kellogg-Briand Pact

The United States's second attempt to free itself from involvement in Europe, the Kellogg-Briand Pact, began as a two-nation pact initiated by France's foreign minister, Aristide Briand, to outlaw war and ensure France's security. Secretary of State Frank Kellogg, however, wanted a world treaty to outlaw war.

Fourteen nations initially signed the Kellogg-Briand Pact of 1928. Although the treaty declared war illegal, it failed to include punishments for future attackers.

César Augusto Sandino Sandino opposed the United States Marines and was a hero in his country. *Why were United States troops in Nicaragua?*

Many people scorned it as a "parchment peace," but the pact demonstrated Americans' high hopes for an end to military entanglements with Europe.

Relations with Latin America

Although the United States wanted to avoid political involvement in Europe, it chose to protect its interests in Latin America. During the 1920s, American business firms continued their long-standing expansion to the south, searching for markets and raw materials. By 1924 the United States controlled the financial policies of 14 out of 20 Latin American countries.

United States control of Latin America represented more than an extension of business-government cooperation. The United States felt it had the right and the duty to extend its civilization south of the border. Little had changed since the turn of the century.

Though the United States government had begun to reduce its military presence in Latin America after World War I, it still did not hesitate to use soldiers to protect its business interests. From 1909 to 1933, United States Marines were present almost continuously in Nicaragua, where American bankers and policymakers essentially controlled the economy. Coolidge withdrew troops from Nicaragua briefly in 1925, but sent them back in 1926 when factional fighting threatened to destabilize the country.

United States authorities mediated a peace agreement between the factions, but some of the players on the liberal side refused to sign. Among them was liberal nationalist César Augusto Sandino. At first fighting to restore the Nicaraguan constitutional government, he kept his grassroots army together to fight the United States forces until they withdrew from the country.

Congress criticized Coolidge's military action, but he argued that the United States was "not making war on Nicaragua any more than a policeman on the street is making war on passersby." Yet congressional resistance and popular opposition to Coolidge's use of troops in Nicaragua hinted at a shift in United States policy toward Latin America. By 1929 American policymakers had finally begun to recognize that United States troops in Latin America created resentment abroad and criticism at home.

Domestically and internationally the Harding, Coolidge, and Hoover administrations showed a firm commitment to promoting the country's business interests. Most Americans shared the firm belief that United States business could spread peace and prosperity to the nation and to the world at large.

SECTION REVIEW

Vocabulary

1. Define: internationalism, disarmament.

Checking Facts

2. How did the Dawes Plan show the Republicans' belief that the interests of big business and government were the same?
3. What were American businesses looking for in Latin America?

Critical Thinking

Making Comparisons

4. Briefly characterize Harding, Coolidge, and Hoover to show their differences and similarities.

Linking Across Time

5. Do you think a treaty such as the Kellogg-Briand Pact could have helped prevent World War I? Why or why not?

SECTION 3

Prosperity and American Business

1925: *THE MAN NOBODY KNOWS* IS BEST-SELLER

THE BETTMANN ARCHIVE

Best-selling Author Bruce Barton
Barton stressed the human life of Jesus with perky prose and chapter titles such as "The Sociable Man" and "His Advertisements."

BRUCE BARTON'S SUBJECT—BIG BUSINESS—AND HIS HERO—JESUS—SEEMED AN UNLIKELY COMBINATION FOR A BOOK. Surprisingly, Barton's *The Man Nobody Knows* became America's best-seller during 1925 and 1926. A one-time journalist and the founder of a large advertising agency, Barton told Americans that Jesus had been the first modern business leader. After all, he wrote, Jesus "picked up twelve men from the bottom ranks of business and forged them into an organization that conquered the world."

Barton explained that when Jesus said he must be about his father's business, he had meant more than simply religion. Barton wrote:

> Ask any ten people what Jesus meant by his "Father's business," and nine of them will answer "preaching." To interpret the words in this narrow sense is to lose the real significance of his life. It was not to preach that he came into the world; nor to teach; nor to heal. These are all departments of his Father's business, but the business itself is far larger, more inclusive. For if human life has any significance it is this—that God has set going here an experiment to which all His resources are committed. He seeks to develop perfect human beings, superior to circumstance, victorious over Fate. No single kind of human talent or effort can be spared if the experiment is to

AS YOU READ

Vocabulary

- industrial productivity
- capital
- corporation
- oligopoly
- welfare capitalism

Think About . . .

- the causes of the prosperity of the 1920s.
- what the prevailing attitudes toward big business were in the 1920s.
- changes that occurred in the structure and management of American businesses during the 1920s.
- how corporate policies of the 1920s reduced the appeal of the unions.

succeed. The race must be fed and clothed and housed and transported, as well as preached to, and taught and healed. Thus all business is his Father's business. All work is worship; all useful service prayer.

—Bruce Barton, *The Man Nobody Knows,* 1925

The Glorification of Business

Business Grows in Power and Prestige

The America that made Bruce Barton's book a best-seller changed business almost into a religion and elevated the successful businessperson to the status of a religious hero. In 1921, after touring and examining 12 of the country's biggest businesses, writer Edward Earl Purinton published an article idolizing big business. He praised the business manager of Gary, Indiana, the world's largest one-industry city, saying that successful business leaders were naturally suited to be powerful religious leaders:

He is called upon by the pastors and priests of churches of a dozen different faiths and nationalities, whose members are employees of the U.S. Steel Corporation, to address the congregations in some helpful, appropriate way. Because he is a fine business man, with power, skill and money back of him, the men of the city want to hear what he has to say. And because he is a gentleman, kind, thoughtful, and sympathetic, the women of the church listen gladly to his lay sermons.

—Edward Earl Purinton, "Big Ideas from Big Business," *The Independent,* April 16, 1921

Not only wealthy Americans revered business. After all, President Coolidge had said, "The man who builds a factory builds a temple—the man who works there worships there." As profits, salaries, dividends, and industrial wages rose during this decade, the gospel of big business became a national creed. Popular magazines printed articles praising corporate leaders, such as Walter Chrysler, *Time* magazine's Man of the Year in 1929.

A list of 59 people who "ruled" the United States appeared in newspapers in the 1920s. The list omitted all elected officials but included John D. Rockefeller, J.P. Morgan, a number of Du Ponts, and Treasury Secretary Andrew Mellon. The person who had compiled the list explained, "These men rule by virtue of their ability." Too busy to hold public office themselves, "they determine who shall hold such office."

Even universities, traditionally hostile to business matters, joined in the admiration for business leaders. In 1925 the Princeton University newspaper asked:

What class of men is it that keeps governments, businesses, families, solidly on their feet? What class of men is it that endows universities, hospitals, Foundations? . . . What class of men are the fathers of most of us—fathers who provide decently for their families, who educate their children, who believe in order and justice, who pay taxes to support jails, insane asylums and poor houses, which neither they nor theirs are likely to occupy?

—*Daily Princetonian*, January 7, 1925

Predictably, the one answer to all the questions was *business*men.

A Booming Economy

Industry on the Go

Americans thanked big business for the prosperity the country enjoyed during the 1920s. The United States had emerged from World War I in a splendid economic

BROWN BROTHERS

Increased Productivity The development of assembly lines and the use of electric generators boosted industrial productivity. *How did new technology contribute to the expanding economy?*

position. At the beginning of the war, the United States had owed other countries money. Now the United States was a creditor nation, collecting debts from war-torn Europe.

In contrast to other major powers whose farms and factories had been devastated by the war, America's productive capacity had expanded. Following a short period of social and economic unrest immediately after the war, the United States bounded into several years of record-breaking prosperity.

Between 1922 and 1928, **industrial productivity**—the amount of goods each hour of labor produced—rose by 70 percent. Corporate investors reaped the largest rewards, but many ordinary Americans also benefited. Workers earned higher wages than at any previous time in the history of the United States.

America's productivity soared as new technology and techniques introduced greater efficiency into manufacturing. Electrical motors powered 70 percent of machines in 1929, compared with only 30 percent in 1914. The assembly line that revolutionized the auto industry in 1914 soon moved into other industries as well.

When American business boomed, companies needed bigger and better offices. A growing urban population required new apartment buildings, and a spreading suburban population demanded new roads and houses. As a result, building and road construction took off during the decade.

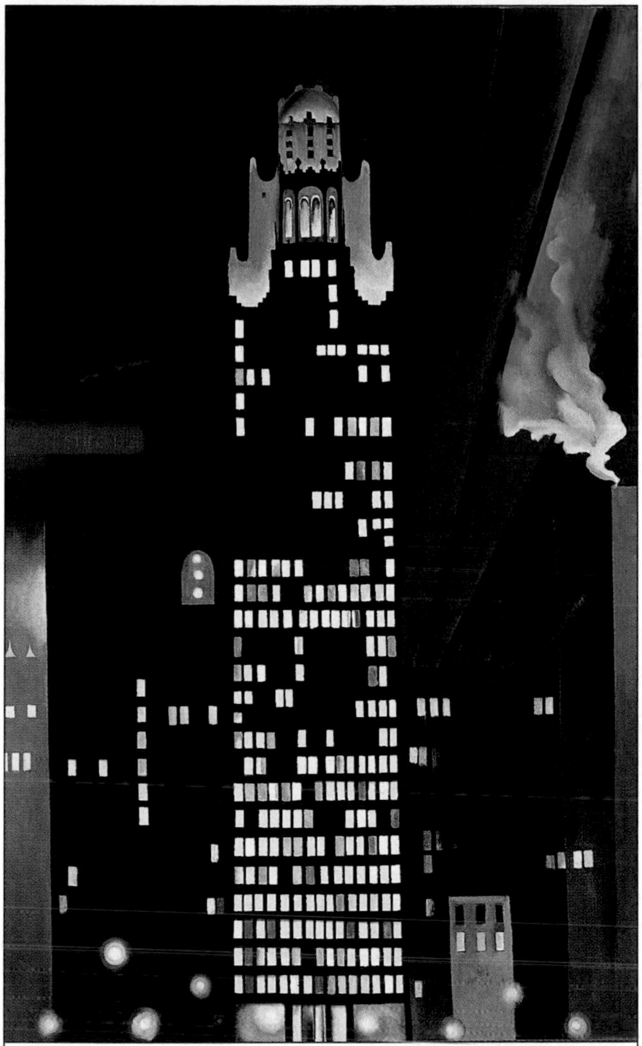

ALFRED STIEGLITZ COLLECTION, FISK UNIVERSITY, NASHVILLE

The Radiator Building, Night, New York **The skyscraper, represented here in a 1927 painting by Georgia O'Keeffe, was an architectural glorification of business.** *Where were skyscrapers built? Why?*

New Industry

New industries also sprang up, adding to the rapid growth of the decade. The manufacturing of light metals, such as aluminum; a brand-new synthetics industry; motion picture production; and radio manufacturing all provided new jobs and products for the American public.

Automobile manufacturing ranked as the most important of all the new industries. Henry Ford was one of several automobile makers, but it was his name that became a synonym for the booming new industry. In 1923 a public opinion poll declared Henry Ford would be a more popular candidate for President than President Harding. In another contest, college students voted Ford the third greatest figure of all time. Only Napoleon and Jesus got more votes.

In 1907 Ford had declared:

> I will build a motor car for the great multitude. It will be large enough for the family but small enough for the individual to run and care for. It will be constructed of the best materials, by the best men to be hired, after the simplest designs that modern engineering can devise. But it will be so low in price that no man making a good salary will be unable to own one—and enjoy with his family the blessing of hours of pleasure in God's great open spaces.
>
> —Henry Ford, quoted in *American Civilization in the First Machine Age: 1890–1940,* 1970

During 1913 and 1914, Ford introduced the moving production line, an innovation that made it possible to assemble his car in 93 minutes instead of the 14 hours it had taken a year before. By 1925 a completed auto rolled off the Ford assembly lines every 10 seconds. The auto industry's dramatic expansion in the 1920s gave birth to a host of related industries: steel, rubber, petroleum, machine tools, and road building.

The New Commercial Downtowns

As roads and automobiles remade the horizontal landscape of the United States, skyscrapers began to revolutionize the country's vertical landscape. During the war, construction had been abruptly halted. Now it seemed Americans were reaching for the sky as they made up for lost time.

In 1910 European travelers to New York City had been surprised by 20-story skyscrapers. By 1930 they found themselves in the shadows of 60-story buildings. On May 1, 1931, the new Empire State Building dwarfed even the Bank of Manhattan's 71 stories and the Chrysler Building's 77 stories. At 102 stories, topped by a slender mast, the Empire State Building had become the tallest building in the world.

If New York had its skyscrapers, the rest of the United States would have theirs, too. Houston had its Petroleum Building, Chicago its Tribune Tower, and Cleveland its Terminal Tower. Even prairie towns raised the giant buildings. Tulsa and Oklahoma City had not even existed when the first skyscraper was completed in 1885. By the end of the 1920s, these cities, too, celebrated their own new skylines.

The Corporate Revolution

New Ideas in Business Management

During the 1920s American industry produced new products and constructed soaring new monuments. In this decade the United States also witnessed the culmination of the corporate revolution that had begun in the late 1800s. Many family-run firms could no longer raise enough **capital**—an accumulation of money—to invest in research and development. Unable to purchase the new technology or to afford national advertising, small companies could not compete. American business became big business, as thousands of small firms went out of business or were absorbed into larger companies or **corporations**—businesses owned by multiple stockholders, whose personal rights and responsibilities are legally separate from the organization's.

The Urge to Merge

Between 1920 and 1928, more than 5,000 mergers joined firms together in larger and more powerful entities that could then buy out smaller companies. Thus the total number of firms dropped by hundreds. The Federal Trade Commission (FTC) had been created to protect small businesses against such takeovers. The person President Coolidge appointed to the chairmanship of the FTC, however, scorned the commission as a "publicity bureau to spread socialistic propaganda" and "an instrument of oppression and disturbance and injury instead of help to business." Under William E. Humphrey, the FTC soon began to encourage instead of to prosecute trade associations and business mergers.

Some of the most obvious examples of business mergers were seen among utility companies. Many local electric companies were absorbed into huge regional systems and utility empires. From 1919 to 1927, 3,700 local power companies turned their lights off for good. By 1930, 10 holding companies supplied 72 percent of the nation's power.

Four meatpackers, 3 major baked goods companies, and 4 tobacco producers dominated their industries during the 1920s. Such a situation, in which a few major producers influence an entire industry, is called an **oligopoly**. Oligopoly prevailed in banking,

THE NATIONAL DOLLAR STORES, LTD.

Growth of Chain Stores **Chinese American Joe Shoong founded National Dollar Stores, Inc., with one small store in 1903. It had grown into a chain of stores by the 1920s.** *How might management of a group of chain stores differ from that of a single store?*

CULVER PICTURES

Growth of Business Associations **Booker T. Washington (seated, second from left) founded The National Negro Business League. The League encouraged African American enterprises in the 1920s.** *How do you think such associations could help prevent small businesses from takeovers?*

too, as large banks swallowed smaller ones. By 1929, 1 percent of the banks controlled more than 46 percent of the country's banking resources.

A smaller and smaller number of American businesses began to wield unmatched economic power. By 1929 half of America's corporate wealth belonged to its 200 largest corporations.

As small firms went out of business, chain stores and other large companies thrived. The Great Atlantic and Pacific Tea Company (A & P) expanded from 400 stores in 1912 to 15,500 stores by 1932. A single strong leader could no longer run big businesses like the A & P. The new companies demanded a new type of leadership.

The Managerial Revolution

Everyone knew who Henry Ford was, but during the 1920s, the average American could no longer identify the chairperson of the board of directors of any other large corporation. Anonymous, replaceable managers rather than the strong personalities of the past now directed big firms.

Colleges stepped in to train the new leaders for the large corporations. Indeed, during the 1920s, almost every leading university established its own business school. In 1924 the Harvard Graduate School of Business Administration dedicated 23 elegant new buildings on a site across the Charles River from the university. The president of the First National Bank of New York had given $6 million toward the building of Harvard's business school.

During the 1927–1928 school year, Northwestern University offered more than 30 courses on business, from "Bank Practice and Policy" to "Psychology of Business Relations." New York University students could even take a course in "Restaurant, Tea Room, and Cafeteria Organization."

Smaller businesses that had grown more complicated also required a more specialized kind of managerial know-how. New college-trained business managers soon began to replace the company-trained general managers of an earlier generation.

By 1924 in Muncie, Indiana, for example, the old job of general manager of the glass factory had been divided into five new jobs: production manager, sales manager, advertising manager, personnel manager, and office manager. Companies grew by adding laborers. To supervise these larger workforces, however, they now seemed to need more layers of management.

Another plant in the same city had employed 200 workers in 1890 and supervised them with a small staff: a president, a vice president who was also general manager, a secretary, treasurer, and two foremen. By 1924 the same plant had 6 times as many workers, but now required 15 times as many foremen, as well as the addition of 2 superintendents, an auditor, and assistants to the secretary and treasurer.

Industry's Labor Policies

Suppressing Union Organization

Big corporations with specialized managerial staffs had almost complete control over the workforce during the 1920s. Immediately after the war, the Red Scare had struck a crushing blow to labor by associating unions with Communists. For the rest of the decade, corporations kept labor submissive with an effective combination of punishment and reward. The American Plan was the punishment, and welfare capitalism was the reward.

The American Plan

The American Plan was made up of a variety of activities companies used after the war to demoralize and destroy unions. Corporations called it the "American Plan" to give it the ring of patriotism. One of the plan measures, open-shop associations, allowed employers to stick together in blacklisting union members.

LIMITING LABOR UNIONS, 1917–1929

1917 *Hitchman Coal Co.* v. *Mitchell* reinforces "yellow dog contracts"; virtually decrees nonunion shop.

1921 *Duplex Printing Press Co.* v. *Deering* revokes rights to boycott, organize strikes.

1925 *Coronado Coal Co.* v. *United Mine Workers* applies Antitrust Act to labor.

1917 1918 1919 1920 1921 1922 1923 1924 1925 1926 1927 1928 1929 1930 1931

1920 5,047,800 union members

1923 3,622,000 union members

1926 3,502,000 union members

1929 3,461,000 union members

Companies also employed spies who joined unions and then informed employers about labor discontent and identified labor organizers.

As part of the American Plan, many companies offered their workers only "yellow-dog" contracts. With a yellow-dog contract as a condition of employment, an employee agreed not to become a member of a union or to organize fellow employees.

Big business, of course, tried to make it sound as though the American Plan was in the worker's best interest. Elbert H. Gary, head of U.S. Steel, wrote:

> The principle of the "open shop" is vital to the greatest industrial progress and prosperity. It is of equal benefit to employer and employee. It means that every man may engage in any line of employment that he selects and under such terms as he and the employer may agree upon; that he may arrange for the kind and character of work which he believes will bring to him the largest compensation and the most satisfactory conditions, depending upon his own merit and disposition.
>
> —Elbert H. Gary, *New York Times*, September 18, 1919

The Supreme Court favored management over labor with several key rulings. In 1915 the Court had upheld the yellow-dog contract. In 1921 it declared a union boycott illegal and drastically limited workers' rights to picket. In the 1925 *Coronado* case, the same Court that so carefully guarded the rights of big businesses ruled that unions could be sued for damages under antitrust rules.

Between 1921 and 1929, union membership dropped from about 5 million to about 3.5 million. Phil Bart, a lifelong union organizer, recalled how difficult it was to organize strikes in the auto industry in 1928:

> There were no laws to protect strikers then, and there wasn't much public sympathy either. We had to struggle against the place and time. The authorities were intolerant, and when we set up a line the police might come right in and knock hell out of us. The strikers could try to protect themselves by putting up a fight or something, but you could not go to the courts, you could not go to the government; they didn't care. . . . We never forced management to bargain, but working conditions did get better.
>
> —Phil Bart, quoted in *American Tapestry,* 1988

Welfare Capitalism

Working conditions got better partly because employers sought to reduce the appeal of independent unions. The combination of programs employers adopted in order to convince workers they did not need unions became known as **welfare capitalism**.

During the 1920s most employers improved plant conditions, hired company doctors and nurses, and provided a variety of activities from glee clubs to sports teams. For example, the Hammermill Paper Company sold its workers cheap gasoline, while Bausch and Lomb established dental and eye care clinics for its employees.

In 1922 the president of General Electric Company, Gerard Swope, had told a group of foremen in Schenectady, New York, "You are constantly being hounded to increase your output. One of the ways of getting it is to have your men cooperate with you." American business leaders heeded this message and began practicing welfare capitalism in their own companies.

During the 1920s most United States companies offered safety programs and group insurance. A few of the largest corporations instituted stock purchase opportunities and pension plans. In the 1920s U.S. Steel alone paid out more than $10 million a year in worker benefits. Even Elbert Gary, the head of U.S. Steel, had come to believe that such generosity to workers actually profited his company. In 1923 he told his stockholders, "It pays to treat men in that way."

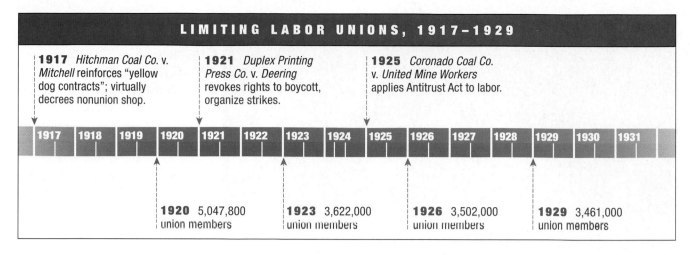

LIBRARY OF CONGRESS

Keeping the Workforce Content A company-sponsored basketball team was a benefit these employees received under welfare capitalism. *What other benefits did welfare capitalism offer, and why?*

Many companies also began programs in which workers could elect representatives to speak to management. Employers called this "industrial democracy" and boasted that it would erase the differences between workers and bosses. Edward Purinton wrote that by providing employee representation on the board of directors, "owners of a business now give the manual workers a chance to think and feel in unison with [the bosses]. All enmity is between strangers. Those who really know each other cannot fight."

Employers may have believed that the interests of worker and employer were identical and that company unions were a form of democracy. The workers knew that the company unions had no real power and called them "Kiss Me Clubs." In the absence of worker-led unions, welfare capitalism maintained the power inequalities that gave management full authority over labor. Indeed, Charles M. Schwab, the head of Bethlehem Steel Corporation, made the owners' position very clear: "I will not permit myself to be in a position of having labor dictate to management."

Welfare capitalism may not have done away with the vast inequities between employer and employed, but by the 1920s, worker-led unions were in a serious decline. By 1929 only about 1 in 12 workers belonged to a union.

While the United States was prosperous, welfare capitalism seemed to keep the workforce content. In January 1929, the head of the Chicago and Alton Railroad boasted, "In our shops since the strike of 1922, the shop employees have been very quiet. The employee is much happier. . . . He is a peaceful worker and a peaceful citizen."

As employee well-being increased efficiency and profits, welfare capitalism paid off for big business. Corporations also used welfare capitalism to restore their public image after the muckraking scandals of the Progressive Era.

During the 1920s, professional public relations experts promoted the idea of humane businesses that not only looked to the welfare of their employees but also acted in the service of society. The Western Electric Company, for example, offered to send literature teaching household management to women.

> The science of managing a home indicates the use of electrical appliances, but the company wants to teach the science whether it sells the goods or not. This is "good business" because [it is] genuine service.
>
> —Edward Earl Purinton, "Big Ideas from Big Business," *The Independent*, April 16, 1921

The idea of public service became an ideal for big business during the 1920s. Business leaders joined service groups such as the Rotary Club, whose motto became "He profits most who serves best." According to the Rotarians, "the businessman was no longer a profit-maker or even a bread-winner, he was a public servant."

SECTION REVIEW

Vocabulary

1. Define: industrial productivity, capital, corporation, oligopoly, welfare capitalism.

Checking Facts

2. List three examples that illustrate the new admiration Americans had for big business during the 1920s.

3. What two methods did corporations use to manage labor in the 1920s?

Critical Thinking

Recognizing Ideologies

4. Why would Coolidge appoint someone opposed to the activities of the FTC to be its chairperson?

Linking Across Time

5. The names "American Plan" and "open shop" cast opponents in a negative light because no one should want to support an "un-American Plan" or a "closed shop." What groups today have names that suggest nonmembers oppose something highly valued?

Science, TECHNOLOGY, and Society

The Automobile

By the 1920s Ford, General Motors, and Chrysler dominated auto manufacturing, and gasoline-burning internal combustion replaced the once wide array of power sources. Gasoline and automobile industries and related businesses drastically changed the look, pace, and values of the country.

BROWN BROTHERS

AUTOMOTIVE STATUS

Even as more people could afford automobiles, cars remained symbols of status and glamour, such as this 1929 Packard Roadster. Many independent auto makers did not survive the depression of 1920–1921, but Packard survived to become the leading luxury car of the decade. Sales of luxury cars peaked in 1928 and 1929.

PHOTOGRAPH: BENJAMIN MAGRO. COURTESY OF THE SEAL COVE AUTO MUSEUM

AUTOMOBILE DEVELOPMENTS

1920s
POST–WORLD WAR I The industry adopts wartime technology with superchargers for greater speed and shock absorbers for a better ride.

1930s
NEW FEATURES By 1930 balloon tires are widely used for a smoother ride; electric lights become standard.

1940s
POST–WORLD WAR II Wartime gas rationing ends and pleasure driving returns, with bigger, more powerful cars.

1950s
STYLE Decorative tail fins inspired by Lockheed P-38 fighter planes dominate styling.

PUBLIC SERVICES

Motorization of public services gave increased speed and efficiency to police and fire departments, the post office, even library bookmobiles. The United States Postal Service's rural free delivery (RFD) reduced rural people's isolation, and door-to-door package delivery boosted mail-order sales of companies such as Sears, Roebuck and Montgomery Ward.

THE BETTMANN ARCHIVE

PHOTO BY DECIO GRASSI

THE WORLD THAT CARS MADE

PORTFOLIO PROJECT

How have cars affected your environment? Look around your neighborhood and identify and describe features that are there only because of cars. How would it look if electricity were the primary car fuel?

ROADSIDE SIGNS

Mass auto travel prompted businesses to advertise in big, loud signs that would catch the eye of passing motorists. In the 1920s, Elizabeth Boyd Lawton led a movement to reform what she saw as a threat to outdoor beauty. She formed the Committee for the Restriction of Outdoor Advertising in 1923. One Lawton supporter lamented, "Where highways run, where the motor car goes [one sees an] eruption of filling stations, hot-dog stands, Tumble Inns, garages, vegetable booths, scarifying field and forest for rods around."

GASOLINE

Originally a little-used waste product of kerosene production, gasoline was an essential commodity by the 1920s. It was sold on city street corners and on country roads. The "pump" evolved from a hand-operated tank with a measurement container to a self-measuring, price-calculating machine.

1960s

IMPORTS American small cars first compete with imports.

1970s

OIL The Volkswagen Beetle surpasses the Model T as the best-selling car ever. After the 1973 oil crisis, government mandates high mileage standards.

1980s

NEW METHODS Computer-aided design, computer-aided engineering, and factory robots replace traditional design and manufacturing processes.

1990s

OLD IDEAS Environmental concerns and limited oil resources renew interest in electric cars and nongasoline power sources.

CULTURE OF THE TIME

The Roaring Twenties

During the 1920s—the golden age of jazz—Americans danced to the decade's joyous music at a frantic and ever accelerating pace. Inspired by jazz, Americans began to improvise leisure time activities that had no purpose other than having fun. People roared through the decade intent on enjoying every exciting moment of it, as though everyone shared an unspoken premonition that it could not last.

ARCHIVE PHOTOS

COMIC HERO

Charlie Chaplin's comic film character, "the Tramp," captured the country's imagination. His mustache, derby hat, bamboo cane, and outsize shoes were recognized around the world—and often imitated, as these young fans attest.

#203, J. WILBUR SANDISON COLLECTION, WHATCOM MUSEUM OF HISTORY AND ART, BELLINGHAM, WA

UPI/BETTMANN

DAREDEVILS IN THE AIR

A passion for flying possessed the nation, and novelty-crazed audiences were not satisfied by planes simply flying in straight lines. At almost any open field, **stunt flyers** looped, spiraled, and even played airborne tennis for thrilled spectators.

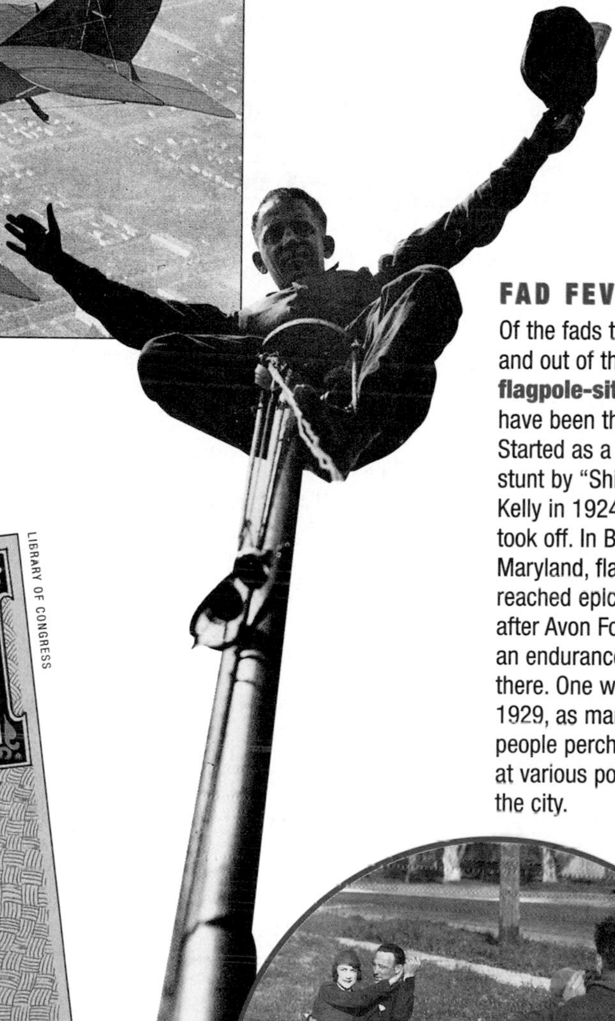

UPI/BETTMANN

FAD FEVER

Of the fads that roared in and out of the 1920s, **flagpole-sitting** may have been the oddest. Started as a publicity stunt by "Shipwreck" Kelly in 1924, the idea took off. In Baltimore, Maryland, flagpole fervor reached epic proportions after Avon Foreman set an endurance record there. One week in 1929, as many as 20 people perched on poles at various points around the city.

LIBRARY OF CONGRESS

SINGING THE BLUES

In the flourishing world of African American music, arts, and letters in the Jazz Age, singer **Bessie Smith** reigned as "Empress of the Blues." Guitarist Danny Barker said, "She could bring about mass hypnotism."

UPI/BETTMANN NEWSPHOTOS

DANCE CRAZES

The **Charleston** and the **tango** were the hot dances of the decade. The mania for dance-until-you-drop marathons branched out to other wacky dance endeavors, such as this couple's tango from Santa Monica to Los Angeles.

Chapter 11 Review

Reviewing Key Terms

On a separate sheet of paper, identify the person, people, or group from the following list who was associated with each concept in the numbered list below.

- Frederick Taylor and Henry Ford
- large employers
- César Augusto Sandino
- Woodrow Wilson
- industry-dominating businesses
- Sacco and Vanzetti

1. anarchism
2. internationalism
3. oligopoly
4. welfare capitalism
5. scientific management

Recalling Facts

1. What were some of the causes of the Red Scare? Name at least three contributing factors.

2. Why did so many African Americans migrate from the South to the North from 1916 to 1920?

3. List three factors that contributed to the decline of progressivism in the 1920s.

4. What do you think Harding meant by *normalcy*?

5. Why did Andrew Mellon believe millionaires should not pay taxes?

6. How did technology affect productivity in the 1920s?

7. Name two factors that contributed to the development of oligopolies in the 1920s.

8. List three types of welfare capitalism programs.

9. Give three reasons why Henry Ford doubled his workers' wages in 1914.

10. How did Henry Ford apply the theory of scientific management?

Critical Thinking

1. Determining Relevance In the photo below, a woman carries the American flag down New York's Fifth Avenue in a parade for woman suffrage. Women and men had been organizing, marching, and asking for the vote for women for 72 years. What factors were most important in the final push for woman suffrage, and why?

2. Synthesizing Information The Republican Presidents of the 1920s supported big business and rejected programs for the public welfare. How did the government's support of big business affect ordinary citizens both positively and negatively?

3. Determining Cause and Effect The idolization of business and business leaders created a national climate that benefited big business. What do you think might have been some negative effects of the glorification of business?

4. Making Comparisons Compare the careers of women and men in white-collar professions in the 1920s.

THE BETTMANN ARCHIVE

Portfolio Project

Research the requirements for setting up a small business in your community. Investigate areas such as government regulations, financing, and the costs of leasing space and buying equipment. The local chamber of commerce might direct you in your research. Write a report on your findings, and include your final report in your portfolio.

Cooperative Learning

Work in small groups to research and report on one of the following industries between 1919 and 1929: textiles, railroads, shipping, farming, aviation, or chemistry. As part of your research, find out whether the industry did well or had problems, and describe the causes of the success or struggle. As a group, choose a medium for presenting your findings, such as a newspaper article, skit, or collage, and share your project with the rest of the class.

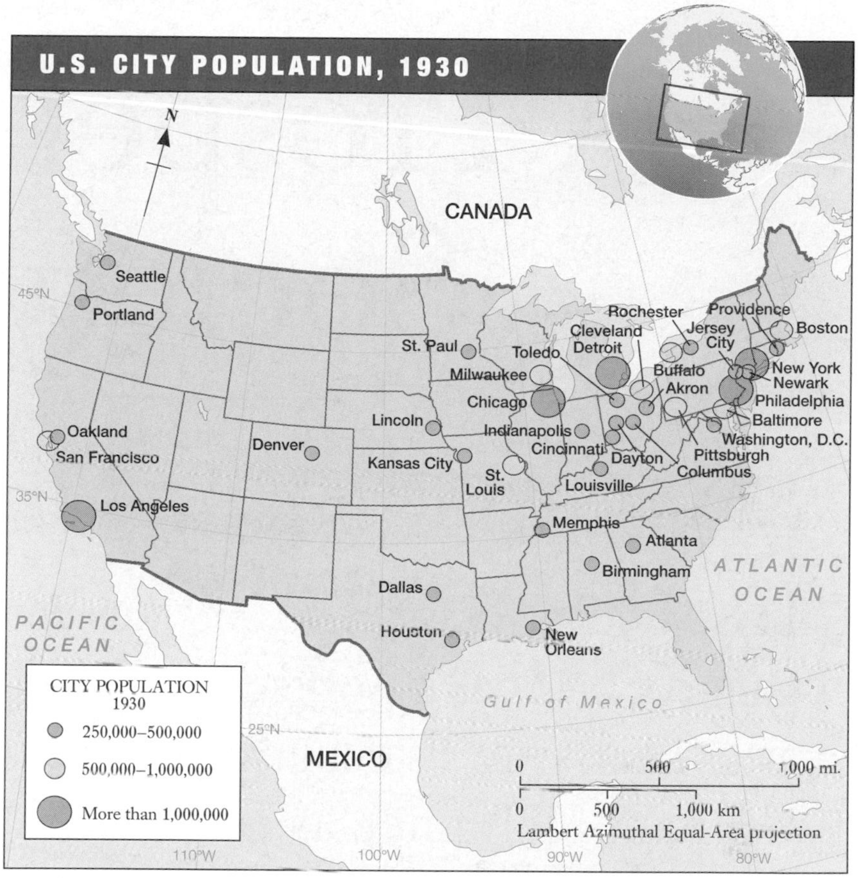

Reinforcing Skills

Identifying Text Patterns Use one of the text patterns outlined on page 369 to summarize what you have learned about one of the following subjects: the Harlem Renaissance, Prohibition, President Hoover, or business in the 1920s. Use the text clues listed in the chart on page 369 to get started.

Geography and History

Study the map on this page to answer the following questions:

1. Which cities in the United States had more than 1 million residents in 1930?

2. Which regions of the country had the densest urban population? Which had the sparsest? What might explain this population distribution?

3. How does this population map from 1930 reflect the Great Migration of African Americans from the South?

4. How does the location of the nation's five largest cities show the importance of geography in determining where large population centers are located?

5. Note that few states in the West had large population centers in 1930. How do you account for this?

HISTORY JOURNAL

The 1920s were a time of great innovation and excitement, yet also a conservative time. Can these two conditions peacefully coexist? Write a brief description identifying aspects of the 1920s where innovation dominated and those where conservatism dominated. You might consider who did well in the period and who struggled. How would you summarize the overall climate of the 1920s?

CHAPTER 12

A Prospering Society

OCTOBER 6, 1926: THE BABE SETS WORLD SERIES RECORD!

In St. Louis, Missouri, 40,000 fans witnessed the fourth game of baseball's World Series. Millions more enthusiastic fans were listening to popular radio announcer Graham McNamee as Babe Ruth came to bat.

McNamee reported, "The Babe is waving that wand of his over the plate. Bell is loosening up his arm. The Babe hits it clear into the center-field bleachers for a home run! For a home run! Did you hear what I said? Oh, what a shot! . . . Oh, boy! Wow! That is a World Series record, three home runs in one series game, and what a home run!"

No one better symbolized the period of the 1920s than home run hitter Babe Ruth. He was a contradictory man with an amazing athletic talent, a gigantic appetite for pleasure, and a casual disregard for rules.

Like its baseball hero, the United States also exhibited some basic contradictions during the 1920s. At the same time most of the country was plunging breathlessly into the new era, many Americans sought to return to a simpler past. Deep conflicts in the United States over religion and immigration added turmoil to the excitement of this decade, which was rapidly becoming full of radios, newspapers, movies, and advertising.

Babe Ruth was a perfect hero for a country undergoing vast change in a bold, hungry, and lawless era. ■

HISTORY JOURNAL

Before you read the rest of this chapter, write any other information you know about the history of baseball. Then write what societal changes you think took place in the 1920s.

NATIONAL BASEBALL LIBRARY, COOPERSTOWN, N.Y.

THE EMERGENCE OF MASS COMMUNICATION IN THE 1920S MADE SPORTS STARS LIKE BABE RUTH FAMOUS WORLDWIDE.

Geography: Impact on History

MOVEMENT

Route 66

The construction of U.S. Route 66 provided Americans with a main artery for travel that linked the Midwest with the Far West. The ensuing movement of people and goods had dramatic effects on the nation's culture and economy.

Building a Spirit of Travel

Pulitzer Prize–winning author James Agee described the American story as having five main characters: the continent, the people, the automobile, the road, and the roadside. According to Agee, these five characters met because of the restless nature of Americans:

> **The twenties made him [the American] rich and more restive still and he found the automobile not merely good but better and better. It was good because continually it satisfied and at the same time greatly sharpened his hunger for movement.**
>
> —James Agee, *Fortune,* September 1934

Cars alone could not satisfy the American hunger for movement. Only the construction of a vast network of highways would finally enable Americans to travel freely. This increased movement of people and goods contributed to the reduction of regional differences.

One famous highway, U.S. Route 66, allowed Americans to fulfill their desire to take to the road. How did the United States highway system, including roads such as Route 66, develop?

Building the Roadway

Americans enjoyed driving their cars and soon wanted better roads. People were interested in what Americans in other parts of the country were doing and how they lived.

Car owners and manufacturers were not the only ones demanding new roads. Since the early 1900s, farmers in the Midwest and the Southwest had cried out for roads on which to transport their products

THE PATH OF U.S. ROUTE 66, 1926

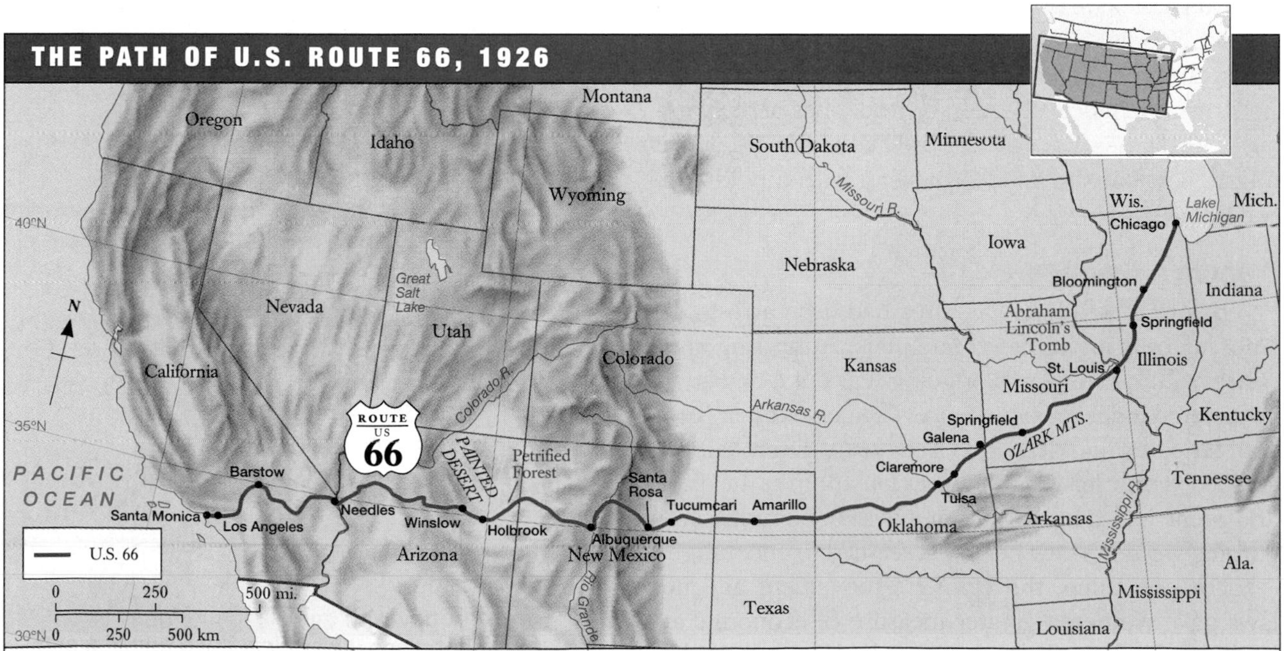

The path of U.S. Route 66 was the subject of intense negotiating as many small towns petitioned to have the road run through their community. *What other points of interest besides towns were located on Route 66?*

to market. Farmers had been dependent on trains to freight their produce at whatever rate the railroad monopoly set.

Local political-action groups pressed Congress to legislate highway building and to break the railroad's stranglehold over transportation. In 1916 the Federal Aid Road Act responded to the pleas of these groups. The Road Act provided federal aid for half of the construction costs of any rural highway intended to carry mail. The new state highway departments were to plan the routes of the new roads. A second federal provision in 1921 granted money to states that would connect their roads to the roads of other states, forming a main thoroughfare. These acts set the basis for a national highway system.

When U.S. Route 66 officially opened on November 11, 1926, it became one of the main arteries of the national highway system. This "great diagonal highway" between Chicago and Los Angeles cut through the Middle West, straddled the Great Plains, crossed the deserts of the Southwest, and reached to the very edge of the Pacific Ocean. Route 66 spanned 8 states and ran through 200 towns, covering 2,400 miles (38,616 km). In the late 1920s, Route 66 was an autotourist's vacationland.

During the Depression of the 1930s, Route 66 became famous as the road that migrants in search of jobs in California followed. John Steinbeck once wrote, "66 is the mother road, the road of flight."

BROWN BROTHERS

A Roadside Autocamp **Americans enjoyed the fresh air and fellowship found at roadside autocamps.** *What goods and services did these autotourists require?*

Building the Roadside

The car and the highways provided Americans with a new form of recreation and business in the 1920s: autocamping. Millions of Americans packed tents and headed for the countryside. Car dealers even advertised autotourism as a way to strengthen the family. They pictured the prosperous middle-class family traveling down Route 66 exploring the United States.

Much of the land Route 66 crossed had not experienced the same prosperity as the rest of the nation in the 1920s. The same technology that brought cars and highways also revolutionized farming with new machinery. When the overproduction of grains glutted the market, however, prices fell. Many farmers went bust, losing their farms as well as their jobs.

The unemployed farmers and other people who lived in rural areas throughout the western states were not quite sure what the new highways were, nor what businesses the highways could bring to their communities. When Route 66 opened, though, they soon found out.

Many unemployed farmers enthusiastically joined the retail petroleum business selling gasoline, oil, and other services to passing tourists. After these new entrepreneurs opened gas stations, they went on to build tourist courts and cafes where tourists could rest and try local foods. Billboards began advertising such roadside attractions as man-eating pythons. In those days any promise became fair in the battle to get the tourist to stop and spend money.

Making the Geographic Connection

1. What did Americans want to learn as they drove to other parts of the United States?
2. What events led to the establishment of a national highway system?
3. **Movement** As Americans traveled along roads such as Route 66, what impact did they have on the economy of local cities and towns?

SPORTS: **Princeton crew beats Yale in rowing regatta; Yale's first loss in 5 years**

One Day in History

Saturday, May 21, 1927

MARKET BASKET

Here is where a dollar will go:

Mobil oil . . . . 30¢/quart
Memorial wreath for Memorial Day. . . . . 89¢
Men's cotton broadcloth pajamas. $1.69
Gallon-size Auto Vacuum jug (keeps hot drinks hot in the car) $1.89

Wrigley's chewing gum . . . 5¢
Cotton fabric . . . . . . 39¢/yard
Silk and rayon hose. . 50¢/pair
Hatbox $2.69
6-volt battery for all small cars $5.99
2-car garage, built $350
Electric waffle iron $5
Hy-Dyve swimsuit . . . . $4–$5
Balloon-cord car tire . . . $7.98
Apartment: 5 rooms, gas, set tubs, stove $28/mo
White Mountain icebox . . . . $27.50 . . . . . . ($5 down, $1 weekly)
Kelvinator refrigerator (installment plan available) $210

Lindbergh Crosses the Atlantic

"Lone Eagle" Lands—World Sighs in Relief

PARIS—Just 33 hours and 29 minutes after he took off from New York, Captain Charles E. Lindbergh landed at Le Bourget airfield in Paris. The 25-year-old "Lone Eagle" became the first person to survive a nonstop flight across the Atlantic. "No man before me had commanded such freedom of movement over the earth," said Lindbergh. "For me the *Spirit of St. Louis* was a lens focused on the future, a forerunner of mechanisms that would conquer time and space."

The *New York Times* reported from Paris:

> *Lindbergh did it. Twenty minutes after 10 o'clock tonight suddenly and softly there slipped out of the darkness a gray-white airplane as 25,000 pairs of eyes strained toward it. At 10:24 the* Spirit of St. Louis *landed and lines of soldiers, ranks of policemen and stout steel fences went down before a mad rush as irresistible as the tides in the ocean.*

UPI/BETTMANN

"The Lone Eagle," Charles Lindbergh, becomes the first to fly across the Atlantic from New York (not Newfoundland) to Paris, and the first to do it alone.

WORLD: Yesterday Great Britain recognized Saudia Arabian independence and sovereignty in the Treaty of Jeddah.

INFORMATION OFFICE, ROYAL EMBASSY OF SAUDI ARABIA

BROWN BROTHERS

Deluge Devastates Louisiana

NEW ORLEANS—The Associated Press reports, "The restless gurgle of muddy water echoed from the northern boundary of Louisiana tonight to within 50 miles (80.5 km) of the Gulf of Mexico." About 100,000 people have taken refuge in LaFayette; more are still fleeing the water. The flood has cut a path 150 miles (241 km) long and 50 miles (80.5 km) wide across the state.

Secretary of Commerce Herbert Hoover says, "There has never been a calamity such as this flood."

The flood threatened weak points along the Atchafalaya River 140 miles (225 km) north of New Orleans. The current was tearing the embankment to pieces in McCrea, where more than 200 workers fought in the mud and rain to keep the flood off the sugar plantations of 5 parishes.

THE CARSON COLLECTION

Clara Bow, "the 'It' Girl" of the 1920s, is a huge box office draw.

MUSIC

Popular Songs of 1927:

"Ol' Man River"

"Let a Smile Be Your Umbrella"

"My Blue Heaven"

BOOKS

This Week's Best-Sellers:

Twilight Sleep by Edith Wharton

Revolt in the Desert by T.E. Lawrence

MOVIES

- ***Rough House Rosie,*** with Clara Bow
- ***Mr. Wu,*** starring Lon Chaney
- ***Slide, Kelly, Slide,*** starring William Haines, a Metro-Goldwyn Mayer picture
- Cecil B. DeMille's ***King of Kings,*** which premiered last Thursday at the grand opening of Graumann's Chinese Theater in Hollywood, California

Turning Point

supported this view. Grant claimed that heredity was the key factor in all human progress. These works seemed to "prove" that the new immigrants were inferior and an "alien menace."

World War I convinced many that the open immigration tradition had failed, since foreign ties had involved the country in a horrible war. The 1917 revolution of the Bolsheviks in Russia linked fears of communism with foreigners in American minds. Labor unrest and domestic terrorism inspired dread that the United States might collapse from internal strife.

Congress passed the first widely restrictive immigration law in 1921, with a limit of 357,000 people per year based on a national quota system. Many felt the 1921 law did not do enough. It failed to decrease southern and eastern European immigration. Representative Albert Johnson and Senators Lodge and Hiram Johnson pressed for an even stronger law. With the National Origins Act of 1924, restrictionists won the debate over immigration. This law would govern immigration until 1965.

The Opinions

Since the nation's founding, opinions have been split between open and restrictive immigration policy. Restrictionists were dominating the debate by the early 1900s, but many Americans held firm to the belief that immigration was one of the country's greatest strengths. They championed a more open policy. The quotes on the preceding page reveal the conflict in opinions on immigration and the National Origins Act.

The Outcome

The Response Many foreign governments reacted angrily to the new immigration policy. Japanese Lieutenant General Bunjiro Horinouchi stated, "We must be determined to undergo whatever hardships are necessary in avenging the insult which America has done our country." Another Japanese leader said, "If history teaches anything, an eventual collision between Japan and America on the Pacific is inevitable." Some Americans felt the act would harm all foreign relations.

Public opinion and newspaper editorials in the United States, though, reflected widespread support for the National Origins Act. The *Cleveland Plain Dealer* stated in an editorial, "Immigration is a domestic problem. The Japanese are neither as unsophisticated nor so domineering as to try to override the clearly expressed will of friendly America."

Congress soon moved to strengthen immigration restrictions even more. It created a border patrol to prevent illegal immigration—not by Mexicans or Canadians, but by Europeans trying to get around quota restrictions. It also gave immigration officers more power to arrest suspected illegal residents.

Border Patrol In 1926 these Border Patrol officers in Laredo, Texas, show off their equipment and personnel for a photo portrait by Eugene Goldbeck. They hoped to prevent Europeans from evading quotas by coming in through Mexico.

Immediate Effects The act had immediate effects on immigration. For the most part, it ended legal Chinese and Japanese immigration. The goal of encouraging more immigrants from northern and western Europe and restricting the number from other areas was achieved. The Quota Board set up by the act raised the British quota from 34,007 under the 1921 law to 65,721, while setting the Italian quota at 5,802, Poland's at 6,524, and Greece's at 307.

The National Origins Act was the main catalyst for changes in the character of United States immigration. First, total immigration fell sharply. From 1906 to 1915, 9.4 million people had immigrated to the United States. Less than 2 million immigrated to the United States from 1925 to 1948.

More notably, the national origins of immigrants changed dramatically, just as restrictionists had desired. From 1900 to 1910, northern and western Europe had sent 21.7 percent of all United States immigrants; southern and eastern Europe, 70.8 percent; Canada and Mexico, 2.6 percent; and all other countries, 4.9 percent. From 1924 to 1946, northern and western Europe sent 43.1 percent of immigrants; southern and eastern Europe, 18.9 percent; Canada and Mexico, 33 percent; and all others, 5 percent.

People scrambled to get the required visas before their country's annual quota was filled. Irma Busch from Germany recalled, "I went to Hamburg in 1924, and it was one year before I finally got my quota number. . . . At the consulate, they said to me, that if I had been born a little bit further down in Silesia, in the Polish sector, I couldn't have come here, because that would have been under a different quota. There were always more people applied from that part than there was a quota for."

Later Effects Even before and during World War II, the quotas held fast. Thousands desperate to flee the terror of fascism were shut out, including many Jews. Boats of hopeful immigrants were turned away. In 1938, as anti-Jewish violence erupted in Germany, Congress rejected a proposal to admit about 20,000 German children, most of them Jews. Congress claimed that it might draw the nation into war—and would violate the quota system. Yet in 1940 Congress admitted 15,000 English children to the United States.

As a result of the National Origins Act, the United States suffered a labor shortage, especially agricultural workers, during World War II. The United States asked Mexico to help ease the shortage. The resulting bracero program allowed Mexicans to enter the United States as short-term farmworkers. More than 4 million Mexicans served as braceros in the United States until Congress ended the program in 1964.

The Significance

For more than 40 years, the National Origins Act remained in force. Americans continued to support it, but as the early 1960s civil rights movement grew, President Kennedy and others questioned whether the act truly reflected American values. In 1965 Congress passed a new immigration law, ending the National Origins Act. The 1965 law seemed to return the United States to its former, more open status. While limiting open immigration to 200,000, it allowed in any number of relatives of United States citizens. It gave each country the same quota, 20,000, but did not end the quota system.

The main results of the National Origins Act —limits on total immigration and the use of a quota system—remained unaffected. More than 70 years after the act, its restrictive principles continue to dominate United States immigration policy.

RESPONDING TO THE CASE

1. Why did the restrictionists support a quota system for immigration? What did they hope such a system would accomplish?

2. One of the effects of the National Origins Act was that immigration from Canada and Mexico increased greatly. Would supporters of the act have welcomed these immigrants? Explain.

3. Did the National Origins Act achieve the goals of its supporters? Explain.

PORTFOLIO PROJECT

Suppose you are an opponent of the National Origins Act in the 1920s. You have the opportunity to address Congress before they decide on the bill. What would you say to them to convince them of your argument? Write a brief address you could give to the House of Representatives and the Senate explaining your views.

Then...

Old Movie Houses

The *Alabama Theatre* opening of 1927 was part of the golden age of film, when films portrayed a glittering fantasy world. To show these films, architects designed ever more opulent theaters that people nicknamed "picture palaces."

1 A local newspaper proclaimed, "Birmingham Gets a $1,500,000 Christmas Gift" when the *Alabama Theatre* opened in 1927. This movie palace has 2,500 seats spread over the three-tiered interior. Above a giant proscenium arch is an oval dome that caps the room.

BROWN BROTHERS

Fun Facts

RIGHT THIS WAY

Being an usher often required the talents of a police officer, diplomat, and valet. During a formalized training program, ushers were drilled in the proper and polite treatment of the public, including learning a variety of hand signals.